THE GREAT
MIDDLE-CLASS
REVOLUTION

Our Long March Toward
A Professionalized Society

THE GREAT MIDDLE-CLASS REVOLUTION

Our Long March Toward A Professionalized Society

Melvyn L. Fein

2005

Kennesaw State UNIVERSITY ™
Kennesaw State University Press

Kennesaw State University Press
Kennesaw State University
Bldg. 27, Ste. 220, MB# 2701
1000 Chastain Road
Kennesaw, GA 30144

Betty L. Seigel, President of the University
Lendley Black, Vice President for Academic Affairs
Laura Dabundo, Editor & Director of the Press
Shirley Parker-Cordell, Sr. Administrative Specialist
Holly S. Miller, Cover Design
Mark Anthony, Editorial & Production Assistant
Jeremiah Byars, Michelle Hinson, Margo Lakin-Lapage, and Brenda Wilson, Editorial Assistants
Back cover photo by Jim Bolt

Library of Congress Cataloging-in-Publication Data

Fein, Melvyn L.
  The great middle-class revolution : our long march toward a professionalized society / Melvyn L. Fein.
     p. cm.
  ISBN-13: 978-1-933483-04-7
  ISBN-10: 1-933483-04-0
  1. Middle class--United States. 2. Professions--United States. I. Title.
  HT690.U6F45 2006
  305.5'50973--dc22

                                        2005033585

Printed in the United States of America

10 9 8 7 6 5 4 3 2 1

To Joel Fein,

Who seems to have made it.

Preface

This book is likely to be misunderstood. With the Culture Wars in full cry, many readers are more apt to be concerned with defending their own beliefs than with reevaluating why they hold them.

Nowadays, liberalism is in crisis. Whereas conservatism suffered a profound meltdown during the Great Depression, today it is liberals who must confront the disconfirmation of many of their cherished beliefs. Sometimes, it seems as if a few are behaving like teenaged rebels, trying to prove that they will not buckle under adult hypocrisies. Yet, despite refusing to conform, they reflexively align themselves with the symbols of their sedition. Festooned with tattoos, body piercings, and spiky green hairdos, they insist they have arrived at these fashions independently. Liberals similarly take positions without acknowledging that these derive from groupthink. Like the journalists described in Myrna Blyth's <u>Spin Sisters</u>, they chatter about political issues as vacuously as if they were sitting in a high school cafeteria. Aware that the unspoken price of communal status is an acceptance of the consensus positions on abortion or affirmative action, they comply. Brent Bozell experienced a similar political conformity when he appeared on a television talk show. After its technicians inadvertently failed to turn off his earpiece, he was treated to the show's directors hooting about his conservative views while he was on the air. Much like a pack of fraternity brothers, these erstwhile professionals reveled in making sophomoric jokes about opinions they did not share. Impartially evaluating opposing views was not part of their intellectual repertoire.

The same, I fear, may be in store for the unorthodox observations that follow. Because they are different, they are apt to be dismissed by both sides of the Culture Wars. This is unfortunate, for if I am right, they offer a third path out of the ideological morass into which the Middle-Class Revolution has led us. Secular, but not collectivist, these views offer a decentralized and professionalized solution to the inevitable paradoxes of hierarchical power. A century ago, Max Weber worried that modernization would trap humankind in a bureaucratic "iron cage," but there may be another possibility. Individuals who are both well-informed and emotionally mature may be able to make personal and social decisions that redound to their individual and joint benefit. While not perfect, this is a superior alternative to the socialist Big Brotherism or laissez-faire Social Darwinism that has hitherto been prevalent.

Many sociologists have, nevertheless, virtually ignored the middle class. Trapped in a leftwing ideological ghetto, they have been distinctly unsympathetic to the middling orders. More fascinated with the upper and lower reaches of society, they concentrate on exposing the defects of social elites. It is the poor for whom they feel sympathy. Those perceived as weak are identified as their natural allies, and an effort is made to promote an egalitarian utopia deemed beneficial to them. The extent of this allegiance is revealed in how the American Sociology Association reviews professional books. <u>Contemporary Sociology</u>, the organization's flagship journal for reviews, organizes its entries under a number of headings. The first of these is "Inequalities." Though the editors might have referred to "social stratification" or "social hierarchies," they preferred an inherently tendentious classification. Inequality, of course, implies a moral judgment. It suggests that equality is the normal human condition and that anything other is abnormal. This implies Marxist assumptions, but these are not admitted. Nor is the collectivist purpose of including a subheading such as "Social Movements." Because many sociologists having been reared on the belief that capitalism is unjust, they conceive of their mission as assisting in its demise. As a result, they consider themselves "movement people," with the movement to which they are dedicated being the impending overthrow of market-based selfishness.

Since its inception, sociology has been in rebellion against modernism, which means it also has been in rebellion against middle-class influence. The discipline began as a collectivist reaction to the Industrial Revolution, and to this day most of its practitioners believe that evidence of human sociality proves their natural state is a version of socialism. (Indeed, research shows that only four percent of sociologists identify themselves as conservative.) As a consequence, they see no point in objectively studying the nature of social hierarchies or of morality. Wrenching these topics out of context, it is assumed that all that needs to be known about them is already known. The goal is instead to get down to the business of improving the human condition. Even though Marx himself put forward an historical account of the evolution of human society, they see no reason to examine this in further detail. The current circumstance of the middle class is therefore left dangling. Treated as a didactic fable, its emergence is never dissected with scientific rigor.

Both on the left and the right, the fashion has become to lament how society has developed. On the right, the primary complaint is that tradition has been violated. Its Cassandras mourn the advent of decadence and a decline in personal responsibility. On the left, the lament is about stymied progress. Here the forces of reaction are said to be selfishly preventing utopian solutions. Both sides, however, share a moralistic point of view. More concerned with making evaluative judgments than with understanding what has been happening, they ignore plainly visible trends. With even social scientists caught in this snare, they don't ask "why?" but rather "what should we do?" No wonder so little has been written about the millennia long processes that have eventuated in the emergence of a middle-class society. What follows is an attempt at a corrective. The object is to bring a colossal historic spectacle into better focus, to help us understand the social crisis entailed by the middle-class revolution and the potential of professionalization. Premised on the need to apply more "head" than "heart," it seeks to substitute mature reflection for passionate reaction. Too much of what has been written in the name of progress has been self-indulgent. Rather than exemplify genuine compassion, it has sought to comfort the purportedly afflicted. With the best of intentions, intelligent observers have allowed this to take precedence over disquieting facts. Sadly, this is self-defeating. The post-modernists notwithstanding, the truth is the truth, and unless it is assessed with an unjaundiced eye, our roadmap to the future is likely to promote many a wrong turn. Although even an accurate understanding of our social situation cannot protect us from every pitfall, it can at least make for a less bumpy ride.

Melvyn L. Fein
Kennesaw, GA

Acknowledgments

For the past twenty-five years Betty Siegel has been president of Kennesaw State University. The first female president of a Georgia state senior college, she has overseen the institution's growth from a fledgling four-year school to a regional university just about to begin offering doctorate degrees. For all this, she deserves enormous credit, but for the moment I wish to single out her role in launching the KSU Press. Determined to leave behind a first-rate academic tradition, it was she who conceived of the press and she who insisted that it be created. As one of its first authors, I therefore salute her prescience.

I must also salute the unflagging efforts of the Press's founding editor, Laura Dabundo. Presented with an enormous challenge, she has held up particularly well under the stress. As importantly, she has infused a vision and energy into this mission that bodes well for the project's future. She has also devoted her personal attention to this project. Perennially flexible and possessed of solid common sense, the following work is much improved thanks to her efforts.

Shirley Cordell, the press's secretary, and Holly Miller, its illustrator, also deserve my thanks for their cheerful cooperation.

Over all, teaching at KSU has been a fortunate experience. Living and working in the Atlanta area, at a growing university that allows for a diversity of opinion, has allowed me to pursue academic interests that might have been quashed elsewhere. I have also benefitted from interactions with colleagues, many of whom have been enormously supportive. To begin with, I must acknowledge members of my own department. Coming from an assortment of disciplines ranging from sociology through anthropology, geography, and criminal justice, they have contributed their diversity of thought and knowledge to my own education. As beneficially, their sustained collegiality has been an ongoing inspiration. In particular, but not to minimize their intellectual inputs, both our former chair Lana Wachniak and our current chair Samuel Abaidoo have offered sustained encouragement and continuous administrative indulgence (both of which I have needed). They have allowed me to do what I have done. Among the many to whom I am also grateful are Vasilis Economopoulos, Barbara Karcher, Jonathan Freedman, Judy Allen, Sutham Cheurprakobkit, Harry Trendell, Wayne Van Horne, Miriam Boeri, Michele Emerson, Ed Clack, Becky Petersen, Tino LaRosa, Mark Patterson, Garrett Smith, Donna Walls, and Cathy Farrow.

Other members of the KSU team to whom I am especially indebted are Fred Roach, Akanmu Adebayo, and Tom Scott of our History department; Kerwin Swint and Nuru Akinyemi of Political Science; Anne Hicks-Coolick of Human Services, and Dean Tim Mescon of the Coles Business College. Finally I must also acknowledge my students. Without the opportunity to teach them, I would not have been able to formulate my ideas nearly as cogently.

Contents

Greedy Conformists?

Rodney Dangerfields   1

Dominance   6

The New Middle Class   13

A Stealth Revolution   22

Social Class

Hierarchies   33

A Range of Options   38

Fundamentals   45

Sources of Power   52

Forms of Alliances   58

Middle Class Powers   65

A Way of Life

What Do You Want to Be?   77

Self Direction   84

People Skills   90

Technical Skills   96

Emotional Maturity   99

Middle Class Values and Virtues   105

Origins

Waves of Change   119

The Monetary Nexus   122

The Medieval Revival   131

The Renaissance   136

The Enlightenment   145

Industrialization

The Industrial Revolution   163
The Victorians   172
The Proud Tower   185
Reprise and Collapse   193

The Tipping Point

The Middle Class Ascendancy   209
An Occupational Survey   213
The Eisenhower Consolidation   225
The Hippie Eruption   233

The Reaction

The Reform Impulse   249
The Reforms   255
The Great Disruption   269
The Culture Wars   278

Bobos in Limbo

Bobos   295
The Liberal Hegemony   301
Contradictions of Liberalism   313
Sources of Power   323

Temples of Liberalism

Cultural Institutions   345
Progressive Education   350
Higher Education   358
Journalists   365
Entertainment   373
Lawyers and Social Workers   377
The Working Class Counterattack   380

The Family

A Bridge to the Future   391
The Post-Liberal Way of Life   396
Feminist (etc.) Lessons   406
Voluntary Intimacy   414
The Children   419

Toward a Professionalized Society

A Professionalized Humanism   433
The Division of Labor Revisited   440
Role Negotiations and Role Scripts   449
Critical Relativism   455
The Professionalized Self   462

Chapter 1

Greedy Conformists?

Little boxes on the hillside,
Little boxes made of ticky-tack. (1950s folk song)

Greed is good! Greed it right! Greed works! Greed will save
the U.S.A.! (Oliver Stone, Screenplay for <u>Wall Street</u>)

Society everywhere is in conspiracy against the manhood
of everyone of its members… The virtue in most request
is conformity. (Ralph Waldo Emerson, <u>Essays</u>, First
Series)

Rodney Dangerfields

The picture is not arresting. Little houses, boxy houses, lined
up one after another on a California hillside, each one exactly like
the one beside it. The folk song from which the image is derived
has mostly been forgotten, whereas the sentiment behind it has not.
According to the lyric, the residences all look alike, but what is worse,
the people inside are also virtually identical. Conformist clones, they
are archetypes of the tawdry emptiness that has overtaken modern
America. The song bemoans the cheapness of West Coast social
climbers, but might as well have assailed the barren life of Long Island's
Levittowners.[1] Among the earliest of the postwar suburbanites, for
many years their inexpensive, stand-alone, suburban redoubts were
the epitome of tasteless conventionality. Indistinguishable inside
and out, they were renowned for a lack of distinction.

Despite the fact that the United States has become the first
truly middle-class country in the history of the world and despite
the fact that its middle class has become socially dominant, those
who occupy this status receive little respect.[2] They have become the
<u>Rodney Dangerfields</u> of social stratification. Who, with a <u>modicum</u>
of sense, aspires to become one of their number?[3] Ordinary men

and women may wish to grow rich or famous or socially prominent; they may long for a bigger house, a fancier car, or more opulent vacations, but they do not yearn to become a part of the middling orders. Asked to which class they belong, almost 90% claim that this is already where they fit in. While they may fantasize about being elected president or making a landmark scientific discovery or building a major corporation, they do not pine for a vulgar suburban orthodoxy.[4] In their eyes, being middle class is tantamount to being mediocre. It is to be average, that is, to be like everyone else. And who would want that? Worse still, who would wish it on their children? Although the American Dream[5] is honored as the quintessence of the good life, to equate it with being average is to condemn it as routine. This would mean to abjure rising to a more stellar status, to settle for the ordinary, for being part of the common ruck. Those in the lower middle classes may secretly dream of the perquisites of the upper middle class, especially the respect accorded to doctors, lawyers, and their ilk, but otherwise, being middle class is universally spurned as trite, boring, and undistinguished. Occupation within its precincts is reserved for the other guy; the one reconciled to being second rate.

A half-century ago, just at the middle classes were emerging to preeminence, the sociologist C. Wright Mills articulated what was to become the conventional wisdom. Casting a jaundiced eye on the transformations of the modern world, he perceived what seemed to be a precipitous decline. Most people might be growing richer, but their moral standing was deteriorating. In his introduction to White Collar,[6] he writes that "the uneasiness, the malaise of our time is due to this root fact: in our politics and economy, in family life and religion—in practically every sphere of our existence—the certainties of the eighteenth and nineteenth centuries have disintegrated or been destroyed and, at the same time, no new sanctions or justifications for the new routines we live, and must live, have taken hold." Who, he inquires, is to blame for this impasse? The answer, not surprisingly, is none other than the middle classes. "Among [these] white collar people, the malaise is deep-rooted; for the absence of any order or belief has left them morally defenseless as individuals and politically impotent as a group." Alienated at work and at home, they have been transported into a Kafkaesque realm of insane rules and impotent wheel-spinning. As salaried employees, middle-class workers do not make anything. Unable to contemplate the pleasures of craftsmanship, they go "year after year through the same paper routine[s]" with their leisure time ever more dedicated to the "*ersatz* diversion" and the "synthetic excitement." No wonder they are "bored at work and restless at play, and [that] this terrible alternation wears [them] out."

But that is not all. Mills' indictment goes deeper: "In his work [the middle-class person] often clashes with customer and superior, and must almost always be the standardized loser: he must smile and be personable, standing behind the counter, or waiting in the outer office." Virtually incapable of fighting back, these "new little Machiavellians, [practice] their personable crafts for hire and the profit of others, according to rules laid down by those above them." Ultimately, "the calculating hierarchies of the department store and industrial corporation, of rationalized office and government bureau, lay out the gray ways of work and stereotype the permitted initiatives. And in all this bureaucratic usurpation of freedom and of rationality, the white collar people are the interchangeable parts of the big chains of authority that bind the society together." Evidently ineffectual ciphers, they cooperate in their own demise, either from cowardice or greed. For Mills the small-scale salesperson is the quintessence of white-collar vapidity. He/she is said to live a life dedicated to appearance, all in the service of purveying someone else's inferior products. Know-nothings by choice, such individuals do not even seek to comprehend their situation. Because genuine knowledge would interfere with the synthetic skills for which they are famed, they keep their blinders firmly in place.

The noninspirational characteristics of the middle classes are alleged to be legion. Mediocre Babbitts[7] at best, like Sinclair Lewis's fictional hero, they congratulate themselves on their successes, all the while having sold their souls for messes of flavorless pottage. Seduced by their bosses into a vacant materialism, they have become little more than the lapdogs of capitalism. Pawns of the rich, they do what they are told, a Hallelujah Chorus intent on imagining that this conformity was self-selected. In Karl Marx's[8] universe, the nineteenth-century bourgeoisie was pitted against the proletarians in a life-and-death struggle for supremacy. The middle classes were said to be marginal to this social warfare, but in occupying the front offices of the corporations, they identified with their bosses. As industrial bookkeepers and foremen, they were not in charge of what went on, but nevertheless they emulated the portly indolence of their superiors. This was why they wore the white shirts of which they were so proud. These symbolized liberation from the dirty labor of the proletarians. This was also why they saved their money to buy suburban houses loosely modeled on those of the higher-ups. Although others perceived them as little more than impoverished mimics, they remained oblivious to this state of affairs. Believing themselves intrinsic to the authority of their betters, they strutted with a bloated self-importance belied by their deeply ingrained subservience.

This lack of insight is supposedly recapitulated in the dull, plodding realities of today's middle-class existence. As Mills says, these cogs in an industrial/commercial matrix continue to prop up the institutions that enforce their obedience. In order to achieve this, however, they must impose a debilitating blindness on themselves. Insensitive to their condition, they are also oblivious to good taste and social decency. As early as the 1920s, Lewis bemoaned the vulgarity of the nouveau riche. Once it acquired more money than its parents, the glitter left its members so dazzled that they enthusiastically supported a pointless boosterism. Genuinely in awe of the inflated language they used to praise their own accomplishments, they did not realize its shallowness. This ignorance was expressed in the garishness of their purchases. Unable to distinguish quality from trash, they flaunted the mass-produced symbols of their vulgarity with all the smugness of the supercilious. Huge automobiles, cookie-cutter art, and bouffant hairdos revealed their lack of depth. What mattered to them was facade rather than substance. Flash-and-dash was sufficient to those who never peeked beneath the exterior manifestations of their ersatz Hollywood lifestyles.

Alleged to be noncreative, these middle-class nonentities are excoriated for mindlessly pushing paper and counting beans. Because a more subtle comprehension of their environment might interfere with the slavishness intrinsic to their occupations, they make certain to keep their scholarship within predictable bounds. Anti-intellectual to the core, they never ferret out root causes but instead accept conventional shibboleths. What their neighbors spout is what they believe. If they read books, they are escapist novels; if they turn on the Internet, it is for amusement or stress-free shopping. Were a neutral observer to eavesdrop on their conversations, one would hear talk dominated by sports and celebrity gossip. Barry Bond's latest home-run count or Pamela Anderson's most recent husband consume their chatter. Fine-grained conversations dedicated to genuine problem solving are, on the other hand, as rare as hen's teeth.

Nor do their dialogues sparkle with the compassion of delicately tuned intellects. Insecure and selfish, members of the middle classes inadvertently reveal themselves as phony philanthropists. Although they trumpet a concern for their less fortunate fellows, their attentions are really directed toward social climbing. Giving to charity is part of their routine, but they are actually more worried about seeming to be generous than with the outcomes of their liberality. Insincere to the marrow, they smile and mouth the socially correct words, but they care no more about the welfare of others. Broad grins go with the territory; they do not bespeak an interior kindness. More akin to Willy Loman, they are dedicated to selling themselves as much as to marketing their wares.

Television-watching bigots, rather than altruistic citizens, denizens of the middle class pass their callous self-involvement on to their children. These nonentities-in-training are also encouraged to become empty fortresses dedicated to safeguarding a purposeless existence. Appearing to be well connected, that is, to being part of the in-crowd, is the height of their aspirations. The music lessons and soccer tournaments of their youth are, in fact, aimed at getting a good job and marrying well, not at becoming insightful adults. Honed in their vacuity by being given automobiles when aged sixteen and credit cards at eighteen, they are experts in conspicuous consumption. Aspiring jocks or journeymen mallrats, they are well schooled in purchasing the material objects that substitute for inner strength. Quickly learning that new BMWs have more cachet than second-hand Chevys and that the logos of prominent designers are more highly regarded than is good taste, they eagerly display advertisements of their conformity. Eventually, they, too, become accomplished hangers-on, more infatuated with personal visibility than earned merit. For them, seeming to be important counts for more than actually being important.

Dominance

In reality, the scurrilous allegations lodged against the middle classes are green-eyed libels.[9] Their crass conformity and materialist vacuity are more a figment of their critic's imaginations than a portrait of their actual circumstances. Marx had it as wrong as do the balladeers who sing laments about ticky-tack hillsides. A drive through today's Levittown should disabuse the intellectually honest of the community's obsessive sameness. When originally built, its houses were indeed dreary in their uniformity. Erected with industrial efficiency, standardization was a means of keeping costs down and of making home-ownership available to the less affluent. But once the proprietors of these dwellings acquired the means, they raced to individualize them. Far from being conformists at heart, they made additions reflective of their diverse tastes and needs. Most even went out of their way to landscape their domains to suggest a pleasing pastoralism. Flowers, trees, and imitation waterfalls sprouted almost as quickly as did the homes themselves.

Marx vilified the few white-collar workers who populated the proprietor-owned businesses with which he was familiar. For him, they were inconsequential drones, who, in their stiffly laundered shirts, paraded an authority they did not possess and a prosperity they would never attain. Marx's universe was dominated by egotistical entrepreneurs whom he predicted would one day succeed in impoverishing almost everyone but themselves. In allowing their workers little more than subsistence wages, they would amass wealth beyond the dreams of Croesus. Conversely, their employees would struggle in torn garments and seedy tenements, nourished solely by crusts of dry bread. This image of degraded poverty has been enshrined in the concept of *exploitation*. To this day, class warriors generate cheers by invoking the alleged penury of working men and women. Supposedly imposed by the powerful, this underprivileged condition is in theory nearly universal. The trouble, of course, is that it obviously is not. Social predictions are frequently difficult to evaluate. Because they tend to be subtle, interpretations differ. Marx's prophecy, however, does not fall within this sphere; it is demonstrably wrong. The majority of people today are anything but poor. Their possessions may not measure up to those of a Bill Gates, but they too own houses, cars, and even stock portfolios. In what has become the most prosperous era ever, they are emphatically not starving. If anything, their midsections reveal an overindulgence in calories. Neither are they mere drones. Better educated and more active than previous generations, their interests are deeper and broader than those of their parents. They have become the true monarchs of the contemporary scene.

In an historical revolution that is notable for its invisibility, the middle classes appropriated the management of the modern world unto themselves.[10] Dating from not long after the Second World War, the United States experienced a unique tipping point. Before any other nation, it came to be dominated by its median elements. Although still individually deferential to those in the upper stratum, these persons collectively assumed the leadership role. The middle classes now set the social standards for all others. Their tastes and manners pervade the habits of those both above and below them. Their goals became the nation's goals; their behavioral patterns the country's patterns. In short, they became society's designated organizers. First, they calculated what needed to be done; then they implemented the most important projects. Where once the country's key judgments descended from on high, they now emerged from these intermediate sources. Ordinary people across the land took jurisdiction over their destinies and those of their contemporaries. If power can be calibrated by who gets to make essential decisions, then those who had previously been the helpmeets of the elite have now usurped their prerogatives. They have arrogated to themselves the responsibility for what happens and what does not.

The nature of this change can be discerned in what occurred within the military. There was a time when warfare was an aristocratic prerogative. In medieval Europe, kings, earls, counts, dukes, barons, and knights controlled the business of combat. From childhood, they trained in the martial arts, and when battle was in the air, they surged to the forefront. Indeed, the term "duke" is derived from a term meaning "war leader." Ordinary people, that is, the infantry, were not allowed the armor or the warhorses of their chiefs. They had to make do with farm implements and padded blouses. When battle came, they were a rabble fit only to be slaughtered by their betters. This distinction was later codified in the division between commissioned and noncommissioned officers. The former came from the nobility, albeit its lesser ranks, whereas the sergeants and corporals came from the lower stratum. While the officers were in the army for life or until they resigned their commissions, those to whom they gave orders served for specified periods after which they were required to reenlist. No matter how competent the latter were as front line fighters, they were not permitted to assume command on the battlefield. This was the privilege of the aristocrats, irrespective of training or experience. In theory, since only commissioned officers served at the pleasure of the sovereign, only they could share in his authority.

The resultant disregard for military competence extended almost into the modern era. Reverberations of it were still present during the American Civil War.[11] Many of its generals, such as Grant and Lee, were graduates of West Point, but many were not. Of these latter, more than a few were political generals who received their commissions because they could provide crucial support at the polls. One of these, Benjamin (Beast) Butler, scandalized New Orleans with his unprofessional insults to the femininity of its gentle ladies. Some, to be sure, were gifted amateurs. An obvious example would be Nathan Bedford Forrest, perhaps the South's best cavalry officer, who obtained his command by funding a company from his personal fortune. Many others merely muddled through. The point is that professionalism was not then decisive. Most people still thought bravery and social prominence were all that was necessary.

A mere half century later this was unacceptable. By World War I, the American Expeditionary Force was much better trained. It was not sent overseas until thoroughly indoctrinated in the new tactics and even then not assigned to the front lines without further preparations in France. Harry Truman could serve as a lower-level field officer, but more responsible roles went to career officers. By the time of the Second World War, former civilians were still receiving commissions but only after undergoing standardized schooling for their future commands. These ninety-day wonders were not widely respected, but they were a far cry from the Duke of Medina-Sedona who was appointed to command the Spanish Armada that Philip II sent against Elizabethan England. Medina-Sedona's credentials were limited to the circumstances of his birth, as became apparent when his fleet encountered the enemy's race-built galleons. American officers had at least to be college graduates before they were accepted for instruction.

After the middle-class tipping point, a nonhereditary professionalism became more prevalent. No longer were aristocratic pedigrees or political connections sufficient. Military competence became mandatory for those who expected to receive an appointment or a promotion. The Gulf War and the subsequent Iraq War confirmed the ascendancy of professional skill over social position. Middle-class criteria of merit had irrevocably supplanted standards of family prominence or extraneous power. Those who witnessed the crushing efficiency of the American military must be impressed with the effects of this preparation. Professionalism had become the norm up and down the line. Run of the mill soldiers spent years in training for their specialties, while their leaders devoted even more time to planning for the myriad contingencies of the battlefield. In the event of combat, officers and men alike were so well practiced that they could adjust to unexpected emergencies on the spot. Even enlisted personnel formerly consigned to unquestioning obedience could calmly organize flexible responses under withering fire.

Intimations of this coming middle-class ascendancy can be seen in Colonial America. Despite the disrespect characteristic of contemporary commentators on class, many of the nation's earliest heroes foreshadowed its coming bourgeois virtues. Perhaps the most prominent of these are Benjamin Franklin and John Adams. Although personally and temperamentally at odds, each epitomizes the individualism and integrity that has come to signify the best of middle-class achievement. Both were self-made men, and both exulted in personal accomplishment. Vain in distinct ways, they nevertheless had a great deal to be vain about. Expert in different skills, each was motivated to make his mark, and as such participated in decisions of lasting impact. They were precursors of a modern middle class that explicitly extolled the values that later facilitated a comparable professionalism.

Let us begin with Adams,[12] even though he was the younger man. He started life as the son of an ordinary New England farmer. Sent to Harvard to become a Congregationalist minister, he gravitated to the law instead. Not priggishly religious, he nevertheless inculcated enough of his puritanical Calvinist roots to fret about doing good, not merely making good. In his case, this was demonstrated by a devotion to duty that enabled him to become both a patriot and the defense attorney for a British soldier accused of murder during the Boston Massacre.[13] Ultimately, he was celebrated as the Atlas of Independency. Without his tenacity and persuasive skills, it is doubtful that the Declaration of Independence would have come to be. Thomas Jefferson is frequently accorded the credit for writing it, but it was Adams's individualism and ambition that led to its adoption. Like the middle class leaders who were to follow, he exhibited a confidence in his abilities and his right to assert them. Adams believed in merit and responsibility. Undeterred by his inauspicious origins, he assumed that he was entitled to rise as high as his talents could carry him. Beyond this, he argued that his countrymen possessed the same birthright. Though he has been long celebrated for his forthrightness and integrity, only recently have his other superior qualities been fully recognized.

Even more endearing is Franklin.[14] Remembered for the twinkle in his eye and the amusing stories on his lips, he is the friendly founder. Beginning less auspiciously than Adams as the son of a candle maker, by the age of seventeen he had run away from a Boston apprenticeship at his brother's print shop to an uncertain future in Philadelphia. Utterly self-educated, he became the colonial equivalent of a publishing magnate. His <u>Poor Richard's Almanac</u>,[15] as well as the fruits of his talents as a self-promoter and business franchiser, enabled him to accumulate the resources to retire while still in his forties. As one of the leather-apron crowd, he appreciated those who each day earned their own livings while simultaneously seeking to better themselves. Proud to be one of the middling sorts, he was to become their prophet. Throughout most of his career as a politician and an author, he penned influential paeans to hard work and ingenuity. An independent-minded do-gooder, he wanted everyone to be the same.

Among Poor Richard's middle-class aphorisms are the following: "Early to bed, early to rise, makes a man healthy, wealthy, and wise"; "Don't throw stones at your neighbors, if your windows are of glass";

"Nothing can be said to be certain except death and taxes"; "Time is money"; "A used key is always bright"; and "God helps them that help themselves." Franklin believed all this. Almost always busy, he honored initiative over conformity. Unlike Mills's hidebound losers, he led a life filled with activity and enterprise. Not for Franklin was a passive reliance on instructions from above. Continuously aboil with ingenious schemes, he became the archetypical networker. While still in his early twenties, he organized a Junta of like-minded artisans dedicated to improving their skills and to sharing opportunities. This soon became the launching pad for civic improvements such as a lending library, several volunteer firefighting companies, a hospital, and what was to become the University of Pennsylvania. Ultimately he was to participate in writing the Declaration of Independence, the Treaty of Paris, and the American Constitution. Along the way, he even had time to invent the lightening rod, investigate the properties of electricity, examine the nature of the Gulf Stream, and speculate about the meteorology of Nor'easter storms. No one could call Franklin boring or vacuous. In his day, Europe's most sophisticated philosophers and scientists considered him a peer.

Yet Franklin attributed his success to classic middle-class virtues. During his formative years, he developed what he called a "moral perfection project." First, he compiled a list of desirable qualities, and then he kept track of how well he exemplified them. Among these virtues were temperance, order, resolution, frugality, industry, sincerity, justice, and moderation. In other words, he would be sober, hard working, and honest. He later added humility as a goal, but this was never to be more than a public-relations ploy. Unlisted entirely was the virtue of tolerance, yet this was an attribute he was to exemplify until his dying day. Completely without religious bias and in his later years an abolitionist, he reveled in interdenominational observances. Above all, he took satisfaction in being what he unself-consciously described as mediocre. In America, said Franklin, "People do not enquire of a stranger, 'What is he?' but, 'What can he do?' Achievement, not nobility of birth, was, by his lights, the correct measure of merit. Thus he was able to proclaim, "The almost general mediocrity of fortune that prevails in America, obliging its people to follow some business for subsistence, those vices that usually arise from idleness are in a great measure prevented." Recently, the historian Gordon Wood[16] has observed of Franklin's contemporaries that "by absorbing the gentility of the aristocracy and the work of the working class, the middling sorts gained a powerful moral hegemony over the whole society." And as Franklin's biographer Walter Isaacson[17] further notes, no one deserves this sort of accolade more than Franklin himself, for, "he represented and helped to make [these values] integral to the new nation's character."

Paradoxically, Franklin was not able to make these virtues integral to the lives of his immediate posterity. The attractions of aristocratic privilege were to remain potent for many years to come, even within his own family. Largely thanks to Franklin's efforts, his son William was appointed the Royal Governor of New Jersey. Nevertheless, though surrounded by examples of middle-class self-sufficiency, when the American Revolution came and sides were chosen, William decided to stand with his monarch rather than his father. In the end, he lived out his final years in England, trying to ape its aristocracy, albeit without much success. His son, Temple, too would opt for the life of a dandy. Despite being set up on an American farm by his grandfather, he preferred to chase women and opulence on the Continent.

What compounds this paradox is that two centuries later even the British royal family has been infected by Franklin's middle-class virtues. So dominant have these become that the mother country's Prince Charles learned, to his chagrin, that he was expected to live according to these standards and not his ancient regal prerogatives. Thus, in his marriage to Diana, Princess of Wales he was expected to uphold a conventional fidelity. Although millions of American women fantasized about the magic of being a princess, they demanded a modernized version of the Cinderella fable. For them and their British counterparts, happily ever after means a mom and dad and two kids in a single household, even if opulent. Princess Di appeared to keep up her end of this bargain. Besides dressing well, she made regular excursions in support of solid middle-class causes. Better still, when her marriage began to crumble, she went before the television cameras tearfully to indulge in the same sort of psychobabble spoken by any betrayed housewife. Charles was less astute. When he first met Camilla Parker-Bowles on a polo field, she reminded him that her great-grandmother had been the mistress of his great-great-grandfather, Edward VII. Edward was able to engage in this sort of liaison without reproach, but his descendant could not. Charles was to be hounded by the press as an unfaithful cad. Even his private telephone conversations were tapped and publicized to demonstrate his disloyalty. Although his attachment to Camilla demonstrated a genuine love, this was trumped by his flouting of middle-class marital ideals.

Today, middle-class values and middle-class decision-making have become the norm. From top to bottom, the people Mills dismisses as compliant drones govern society. Far from being empty-headed conformists, they have been transmuted into the seat of its expertise and energy. Still, their social dominance is not always visible nor always celebrated. Human communities live by symbols, but these can be out of joint with underlying realities. This is our current situation. The sort of life that Franklin recommended and that Adams embodied has triumphed. No doubt this victory has been incomplete and is fraught with difficulties, but it is also more substantial than its critics allow. The middle-class nature of our contemporary world is not sufficiently appreciated, in large part because it has become so ordinary. People do not notice the ubiquitous background noise of their daily rounds. Nor do they treasure the constraints that personally bind them. Forced to respect middle-class sensibilities, they bridle at requirements that often feel onerous. Mills is but one of many voices chafing at the restrictions current in our present society. "No rules; just right," boasts a popular restaurant chain. "Think outside the box," goes the advertising refrain of another. People hate being imprisoned by middle-class dictates, and they say so. The theme is clear: they want this hegemony to be challenged. They long to be free to be whatever they wish. What is not investigated, however, is what are their actual options. Is there an alternative to middle-class domination? Can contemporary society function without their supremacy? Can people survive the conflicts brought on by their own uncertainties? We shall see.

The New Middle Class

"Eighty years ago, there were three quarters of a million middle class employees; by 1940, there were over twelve and a half million." Thus wrote Mills before the middle class revolution reached its crest.

In fact, he begins his chapter on the *new middle class* by observing that "in the early nineteenth century, although there are no exact figures, probably four-fifths of the occupied population were self-employed enterprisers."[18]   Most of these, of course, were farmers and independent artisans.   Part of what made the United States's labor force different from that of Europe was the freedom it enjoyed. Journeying across a broad ocean to take possession of a continent bereft of an indigenous population—thanks to the depredations of European diseases—a bold set of adventurers had either fanned out to carve homesteads from the wilderness or remained behind in coastal cities to pioneer newfangled varieties of commerce.   In both cases, they had been liberated from the oppressive traditions of aristocratic supervision.   Caucasian Americans were never serfs in America.   Some may have begun their careers as indentured servants, but they were not required to stifle their ambitions to suit the needs of hereditary ruling class—this despite the best efforts of their royal governors.   The resultant sense of autonomy not only laid the foundations for a successful political revolution, but once the Industrial Revolution took hold, it facilitated an explosion in middle-class occupations.

Mills distinguished between an old and a new middle class. The chief differences between these were a diminution of the percentage of farmers and an increase in salaried professionals, salespeople, and office workers.   By his calculations, 62% of the old middle class consisted of farmers, whereas, by 1940, this proportion was reduced to 23%. The shift had clearly been toward commercial employment. People were no longer producing for their own consumption or that of their immediate neighbors.   More likely to be market-oriented than subsistence farmers and factory workers rather than shopkeepers, their profit-making orientation had become broader.   Even within the manufacturing sphere, employment swung toward the needs of the marketplace. Thus, according to Mills, whereas, in 1870, 77% of workers were directly engaged in production, by 1940, scarcely 46% were thus engaged. The growth areas had switched into service jobs, which went from 13% to 20% of the total; into distributing jobs, which went from 7% to 23%; and into coordinating jobs, which went from 3% to 11%.   There had clearly been a reallocation of effort from making goods to getting them to the customer.

By the beginning of the new millennium, the changes were even more dramatic. An elaboration of the details of this development will await a later chapter, but for the moment it may be adequate to observe that managerial and professional employment has gone through the roof, while entrepreneurial efforts have held their own. The economists Herbert Stein and Murray Foss[19] calculate that, between 1958 and 1998, blue-collar employment declined from almost 40 % to just under 25 %. Meanwhile white-collar employment jumped from just over 40% to almost 60%. This said, rather than beginning our survey of what happened at the high end of the occupational continuum, it makes more sense to start at the opposite end of the spectrum, where jobs were lost and from whence a transformed workforce arose.

When England was establishing its North American dominions, its promoters expected their raw materials to keep the mother country's manufactories humming. Initially, this seemed the case. Even Ben Franklin assured British opinion makers that they had nothing to fear regarding cross-Atlantic competition. There was simply so much land available that the vast majority of his fellow subjects would be attracted into agriculture for the indefinite future. No one could foresee that within little more than two centuries the percentage of farmers would decline to less than 2 % of the population. Ironically, because of advances in technology, the quantity of foodstuffs was greater than ever. Indeed, so efficient has productivity become that, by 1992, the Census Bureau calculated that there were fewer than 100,000 farm enterprises, with barely more than a half-million farm workers toiling on them. Johnny had long since deserted his rural home for the more opulent accommodations of the city or, better yet, for the more comfortable habitations of the suburbs.

Similar trends have been visible in manufacturing. At the height of the Industrial Revolution, it was assumed that, as the young people left the farms, they would automatically swell the ranks of factory workers. By the 1930s, the unions were so confident of this trend that they believed these growing numbers would inexorably enhance their influence. This prophecy, too, was doomed to failure as union membership soon sank to below 15%. As might be expected, the proportion of those engaged in production fell as well. By 2001, the U.S. Department of Labor's Bureau of Labor Statistics[20] estimated that, out of almost 130 million workers, slightly more than 11 million were directly involved in production, whereas approximately 9 million were engaged in transporting the handiwork of the factory to other locations. More than this, over 13 million were engaged in sales, and another 23 million were office workers. Many years earlier, Karl Marx had derided individuals not occupied in physical production as parasites. His labor theory of value argued that wealth was created by the act of fashioning objects for material use. All other employments were subsidiary, he declared. Because capitalists and their lackeys exploited the efforts of real workers, they deserved to be relegated to the ash heap of history. As if to spite him, however, during the intervening decades, the vampires who sucked the blood of the honest proletarians multiplied disproportionately to their contributions. Although Marx had speculated that the bourgeoisie would decline in numbers as they concentrated material assets in their own hands, this has not happened. Not only was there not a revolution of the downtrodden, but the lap dogs of the affluent have proliferated into a conquering army.

Mills, in his analysis, was fascinated by increases in the clerical and sales forces, yet the upsurge in numbers of managers and professionals has been even more spectacular. Management occupations now top over seven million, and closely related business and financial occupations are approaching five million. Professional occupations are more difficult to assess and are broader in scope, but if these are taken to include computer and mathematical occupations at almost three million; architecture and engineering occupations at nearly two and a half million; life, physical, and social-science occupations at a million; community and social service occupations at a million and a half; legal occupations at almost a million; educational occupations at seven and a half million; health-care practitioners at over six million; and art and entertainment occupations at another million and a half, the total is impressive. These figures may be misleading in that they include paraprofessionals, but they still give a good idea of the range of professionalization. Moreover, they do not include some traditionally blue-collar occupations, such as that of police officer, that have also been professionalizing. Nor do they include service occupations that work in tandem with professionals, such as health-care support workers (e.g., medical assistants) or personal-care workers, such as cosmetologists and child-care workers.

Also missing from this compendium is the list of contemporary entrepreneurs. According to the 1997 census,[21] over fifteen million American companies had no employees. These were evidently enterprises of self-employed persons ranging from independent professionals to dogwalkers. Another six million plus establishments had employees and, therefore, presumably, autonomous bosses. These would range from the owners of family-held corporations to the partners in stand-alone medical offices and law firms. Some of these persons might even parallel the success of a Steve Jobs, who has successively been the moving force behind Apple Computers, Next Computers, and Pixar Animation. More than mere drones, these venture specialists focus on introducing and implementing new ideas and new products.

Now that professionals, managers, and entrepreneurs have captured the most important leadership positions of our postindustrial age, their skills, rather than the honorable sweat of traditional laborers, have proven to be the key to obtaining power. Occupational sociologists have long made a distinction between jobs that entail working with people versus those that entail working with data or with things. The modern middle classes specialize in dealing with the former two, whereas the historic proletarians were occupied with the last. As commercial activities have proliferated, an ability to deal with customers or to coordinate battalions of workers has assumed greater importance, whereas dealing with machines has declined in significance. Likewise, a competence in engineering new products or in organizing their distribution has taken precedence over physically manipulating materials in an increasingly automated environment. All of this has made a difference. The emergence of complex technologies and of mass marketing placed a premium on coping with sophisticated conceptions and unpredictable situations. Long gone is the repetitive manual toil of the chandler. Ben Franklin's father was by all accounts a hard worker, but the skills to be mastered in manipulating tallow were relatively few, even when compared with those of his son. In the elder Franklin's day, an independent productiveness could make a man a pillar of his community, including of his church. Today's assembly-line worker, albeit turning out far more candles per day, earns little respect. Compared with the decision-makers guiding his output, his contributions are regarded of lesser value.

Contemporary factory workers learn that it is not effort but the relative complexity of one's employment that produces social esteem and, therefore, influence. In contrast to their own tedious jobs, professionals are generally experts in their fields of endeavor. Trained to unprecedented levels of proficiency, they know things that others do not. It is for this reason that they receive deference. Likewise, managers must be knowledgeable about human relations. They receive more respect for their people-handling skills than for their affluence. Though sometimes disparaged, good management takes a courage and perceptiveness that is not universal. Years of experience and nowadays of college preparation contribute to an ability to organize the tasks of others. Lastly, entrepreneurs receive esteem, in part, because they wield the power of a boss; in part, from controlling the resources derived from economic success; and, in part, from the courage and knowledge implied by being able to organize a business from scratch. Evidences of successful risk-taking are their tickets to a higher status.

The increased complexity attaching to high-status occupations is manifest in the growing emphasis on formal education.[22] It has become a cliché that social success is linked to years of schooling. At present, to be illiterate is virtually to be a social outcast. Parents, teachers, and even politicians obsessively warn children that being a dropout is tantamount to being a failure. The result has been the longest schooled, if not the best educated, society in the history of the world.

Times have manifestly changed. Although New England Puritans encouraged literacy in order to promote Bible reading, even states like Massachusetts could not boast a significant high-school population until the end of the nineteenth century. Indeed, college attendance did not become commonplace until after World War II, when implementation of the GI Bill of Rights opened college to millions with working-class backgrounds. If we look back to 1869-70, that is, to just after the Civil War, barely more than fifty thousand students were studying at all of the nation's institutions of higher learning combined. By 1899-1900, this figure had risen to something over 237,000. By 1939-40, the period to which Mills refers, the total enrollment was 1,494,203. By 1999-2000, this had multiplied ten fold to 14,791,224. True, the national population also increased substantially, but the adjusted five fold gain was still dramatic. Put another way, soon more than half the country will possess college degrees, including formerly excluded women. As of now, 24% of those over 25 do so. Already about half of all recent high-school graduates receive some college education. Moreover, in 1998, a whopping 83% of Americans over the age of twenty-five were high-school graduates. This is especially impressive when one considers that the figure includes the very old, as well as immigrants from Third World countries where secondary education has been out of the question.

As might be expected, greater education is correlated with greater occupational success. Not only do college-educated individuals make more money, but they encounter a larger market for their talents. Contemporary employers frequently seek those with degrees even when the tasks at hand do not require the sort of knowledge acquired at a university. What is desired is something different; it is evidence of being self-directed. Being able to cope with the demands of a postsecondary education provides an indication of personal discipline. Thanks to this quality, those who obtain a degree are assumed to be able to master workplace uncertainties without close supervision. As a result, they are trusted to be self-starters and reliable finishers. Indeed, being self-directed and capable of managing uncertainty is the hallmark of the middle classes. The *sine qua non* of their leadership, it provides the stratum it mandates. It is, therefore, not surprising that they should endorse the delegation of authority that a superior education underwrites.

The rewards for education and occupational authority are equally evident. It is often taken for granted that wealth is equivalent to power. Those who are obscenely rich are believed to be potent to the same degree that they have been able to amass possessions. When Bill Gates can accumulate a personal fortune approaching one hundred billion dollars, some conclude that he must be a million times more dominant than an engineer earning fifty thousand per annum. But this is misleading. Undoubtedly Gates is more dominant. Undoubtedly, too, most members of the upper classes are individually more powerful than members of the middle class. But millions of times more powerful? This is absurd. Collectively, the middle classes are, in fact, more influential than the 2% to 3% of our society who belong to the upper classes. Even on a personal level, some of the former have more impact on events than do the wealthy. Arguably, the researchers who developed Post-it notes™ (not to mention the transistor) fit into this category. Their contributions influence our daily lives more profoundly than the frolics of jetsetters.

This collective clout is also reflected in the material prosperity of the middle classes. Marx predicted that most workers would be reduced to subsistence, but this too did not happen. Though on paper less well off than the privileged few in terms of their personal comfort, professionals more than hold their own. In terms of what they possess and the activities in which they can engage, they are richer than medieval princes. Whether we are talking about indoor plumbing or vacations in the Caribbean, they can do things of which Henry VIII never dreamt.

Let us consider the houses in which they live. In 1997, two thirds of all Americans owned their own homes.[23] In a nation of about 280 million, over 65 million were owners as opposed to 34 million who were renters. This compares with about half of all families that were owners in 1900. The real change, however, has been in the size of dwelling per resident. In the 1960s, the average house was 1400 square feet. By the end of the century, this had increased to 2100 square feet. Since family sizes had simultaneously declined, the number of persons per room had gone from well over one per room to less than one per every two rooms. This gave the average American almost four times as much living space as the average Russian.

But comfortable housing is not the only advantage of middle-class opulence.[24] Americans no longer walk. Nor are they confined to trolleys or subway cars. In 1997, there were a total of 776 internal-combustion vehicles per 1000 of the population. That is almost one vehicle per person, including children. As is well known, middle-class houses are now routinely built with two-car garages, and of the machines these accommodate, one is apt to be a sports utility vehicle. Once Americans fretted about gas consumption, but today their concern is with demonstrating that they can drive up Pikes

Peak if they so desire. Even teenagers are no longer satisfied with the jalopies of previous generations. These days, they believe new BMWs are their rightful legacies. Of course, this is not the only indicator of middle-class affluence. There is also the fact that almost every household has multiple television sets, with most of these hooked up to cable or satellite dishes. Increasingly, home entertainment centers boast flat screens and rear-projection monstrosities. Then, too, there are the computers, the DVDs, and the cellphones. All in all, the middle classes have invented a mobile, creature-comfort-rich, style of life that is best characterized as suburban. Both academics and public intellectuals hate the suburbs, but these are the fastest-growing sections of the country. Once they earn a sufficient income, people have been voting with their feet or more properly, with their cars. The suburbs are scorned as sprawl, but they enable people to engage in the sorts of activities that accompany affluent decision making.

Living longer, healthier, more varied lives, the new middle classes tend to be self-satisfied. They do not perceive themselves as mediocre Babbitts or, as Mills opined, in the thrall of a deep-rooted malaise due to "the absence of any order or belief [which] has left them morally defenseless as individuals and politically impotent as a group." Members of the middle class tend to feel good about themselves, their families, their friends, and their jobs. Still, they are also aware that as group they are not respected, ergo their verbal unwillingness to aspire to be that which in their daily lives they clearly value. This disconnect is exacerbated by circumstances of which they relatively unaware. Having been carried along by a vast wave of change, they do not discern how they got where they are. Although troubled by a disdain for the middle classes, Mills was on to something when he observed that "the certainties of the eighteenth and nineteenth centuries have disintegrated or been destroyed and, at the same time, no new sanctions or justifications for the new routines we live, and must live, have taken hold."

This rumination is best understood in light of William Ogburn's[25] concept of "cultural lag." Introduced in the 1920s, this insight pointed to the fact that as technological innovations accelerated, people had difficulty adjusting to the new realities. Older generations continued to prefer horses to automobiles or, more recently, desk-bound instruments to cellphones. Yet cultural lag is also applicable to personal attitudes and social institutions. Ways of behaving and methods of organizing appropriate to a blue-collar world that are no longer useful in a professionally dominated environment are nevertheless preserved.   Many people, who by occupation are undoubtedly middle class, mentally and behaviorally reproduce patterns from their lower-status childhoods. They cling to the familiar and comfortable, not because it works, but because it is what they understand.

Clearly related to this problem are the depredations of the Culture Wars.[26] People who do not understand the source of their dissatisfaction nevertheless crave solutions.   Moreover, be they liberal or conservative, they believe they recognize how things can be improved. Yet, because they are operating from a platform of ignorance, they become adamant in assertions they cannot validate. Ideologues rather than pragmatists, they maintain that their way is the only way. Each side of what has become a polarized battle is certain of its virtues and, therefore, of the merit of destroying the opposition. As self-appointed guardians of the keys of the kingdom, they insist upon being allowed to open the door.

This unrequited culture gap is a much larger problem than is generally recognized. Because the middle-class revolution has been so extensive, millions of people have been swept into positions for which they were neither emotionally nor intellectually prepared. Also significantly, society itself has been unprepared for the dislocations thrust upon it. Because no one could have perceived where events were leading, no one could groom himself or herself to accommodate them. Worse still, because none had practice in an untried future, none could predict the innovations it would demand.   Although many have engaged in prognostications, most of their guesses have been wrong; hence, attempts to implement them have often made things worse. Instead of fixing what went awry, they introduced new, and sometimes unnecessary, problems.

A Stealth Revolution

To put this in perspective, the contemporary Middle Class Revolution is embedded in a more comprehensive series of changes. If we are to recognize the gravity of what has transpired, it is necessary to appreciate that human societies have undergone several magisterial transformations. These may be respectively designated the Symbolic Revolution, the Agricultural Revolution, and the Commercial Revolution. The first of these megatransformations began when Homo sapiens moved out of Africa.[27] Some sixty thousand years ago, our ancestors were clustered in several thousand foraging bands around East Africa's Rift Valley.[28] Perilously close to extinction following the nuclear- winter-inducing eruption of Sumatra's Tuva caldera, something happened to trigger an exodus that took our species to every corner of the globe, not excluding the ferociously inhospitable Antarctica. Opinions differ on whether this was a cultural or a biological advance, but the available evidence suggests that our symbolizing abilities took a quantum leap forward.

Anthropologists' find indications of novel art objects at approximately the same time as the earliest of these migrations. People began crafting beads and almost concurrently drawing pictures on rocks. Contemporaneous evidence also suggests technological advances, such as spear throwing, which dramatically expanded hunting options. Paleontologists have even found remnants of sewed clothing and musical instruments (i.e., flutes). All of this has been interpreted as signaling a greater capacity to manipulate mental symbols, especially linguistic ones.[29] This expanded human aptitude for communicating about things and events not present in the immediate environment transfigured our ancestors' abilities to coordinate social activities.[30] People could now plan their activities with unprecedented subtlety. Whether as hunters or gatherers, they found the efficiency of their actions improved sufficiently to provide an edge over competing carnivores.[31] Unlike, let us say, lions, our forefathers could now plan ambushes of unsurpassed refinement. In any event, this Symbolic Revolution saw better-equipped and better-provisioned human beings march across Asia into Australia, Europe, and, ultimately the Americas. With their lifestyles profoundly altered, within a few short millennia, they had multiplied to several million globetrotting souls.

This advance continued until the oscillations of the Ice Age placed stress on their mounting populations, most notably in the Middle East.[32] As previously well-watered areas became desiccated, the inhabitants turned to expanding the acreage devoted to local cereal crops. By some ten to twelve thousand years ago, this strategy had evolved into protoagriculture. First embodied in a digging-stick horticulture, within a few thousand years, irrigated cultivation launched the Agricultural Revolution.[33] Instead of depending upon the bounty of untrammeled nature, farmers could manipulate plants and animals to increase the available foodstuffs. This quickly initiated a spectacular growth in population densities. More than this, it changed how humans were distributed. Where before virtually everyone was nomadic, a majority now settled down to tend their crops. Farmsteads almost immediately evolved into villages, thence into towns, and, in due course, into cities. Soon enough, village headmen developed into kings and emperors. As a result, there were not only more people, but they were consolidated into larger political entities. They also acquired greater wealth. Wandering bands can accumulate little property. Because they must physically carry whatever they possess, these objects cannot be unduly burdensome. Village dwellers, in contrast, can own houses, some of which can be impressive brick edifices. Moreover, they can supply these with furniture, hanging decorations, and extensive wardrobes. They are able, in short, to acquire extensive goods that others may come to covet and wish to appropriate for themselves.[34] This transforms clashes between foraging bands over hunting territories into piratical warfare in quest of booty. Villages raid other villages and kingships conquer other kingships. In a sense, this is the origin of history as we know it,[35] with protonations contesting with one another to see which could extend its sway over the largest and most prosperous areas.

Thomas Hobbes[36] in his pioneering social speculations imagined a state of nature in which a war of all against all was endemic. This could be said to describe the earliest political entities in that these appropriated what superior martial strength enabled them to seize. But, as Hobbes made clear, this is a tenuous way to improve one's material condition. Rather than risk the losses endemic to brigandage, people soon developed mechanisms of trade. They would now exchange the goods they produced with others who possessed objects they desired. This was safer and became widespread. Indeed, trade existed long before agricultural prosperity enhanced its attractions. Archeological digs make it plain that pre-sapien hominids engaged in long-distance transactions. Scarce, yet highly coveted, resources such as flint for tool making or seashells for necklaces have been found far from their point of origin. What the Agricultural Revolution accomplished was to swell these contacts in terms of the volumes traded, the types of materials exchanged, and the distances covered.

Finally, this trade became so extensive that it triggered a change in kind. The exact cause of this transformation is difficult to pinpoint, but the advent of money seems the likeliest cause. What transpired may be designated the Commercial Mega-Revolution. Like its predecessors, it initiated huge modifications over an extended period of time. Neither its Symbolic, nor Agricultural, antecedent achieved its ends within tens or even hundreds of years; each literally took millennia to unfold. The same is true of the Commercial upheaval. It began over six hundred years before the Common Era and continues to wreak massive alterations in how people subsist. Some trace the starting point of this progression to the invention of literacy.[37] They suggest that as agricultural production rose, it became necessary to keep track of inventories. Taxing agencies, such as the pharaoh's temples, needed to identify who had paid them what, how much was on hand, and how much of this was to be distributed where. Symbols that mutated from the spoken word to scratches in mud or dyes on parchment served the trick. Soon, it became apparent that this technology could amplify commerce by facilitating long-distance communication and by reducing misunderstandings. In the long run, without writing, the bookkeeping attendant to large-scale economic operations would not have been possible.

Nevertheless, the invention of coinage seems to have been more crucial. Before there was a standardized medium of exchange, merchants depended upon barter. They would swap an agreed upon volume of olive oil for a specified amount of grain. This was inconvenient in that it was difficult to determine commensurate value. Even more upsetting was that fact that what one person had for exchange might not be what the other desired. Money solved this problem by providing an instrument that could be exchanged at a later date for a third product from a third party. The result was an inducement to business that has not subsided in over two thousand years. Where once the possession of land and its riches, and before that of a hunting territory and its bounty, made for social power, the treasures of the marketplace became paramount. These now dominate our world and have converted our species into the masters of a planet.

Karl Marx, in what is still the dominant interpretation of social evolution,[38] attributed the shape of human societies to economic matters. In priding himself on being a hardheaded materialist, he asserted that those who controlled the means of economic production dominated succeeding civilizations. Where once aristocrats were supreme because they owned the land from which agricultural wealth was derived, capitalists replaced them by monopolizing the machinery from which industrial affluence arose. To many, this reading of events has seemed unduly mechanistic. They protest against its antihuman quality and insist that spiritual and emotional factors also be considered. Although it may sound as if in talking about agricultural and commercial revolutions, Marx's materialism is merely being updated, this would be a mistake. Economics matters, but it is not the whole story. True, how people produce and distribute goods influences lifestyles, but this does not occur in a vacuum. For starters, economics is not, as it were, the prime mover of all events. Production and distribution also have their causes. The Agricultural Revolution, for instance, might never have occurred had not climatic changes forced hungry Middle Easterners to look elsewhere for food. Nor would they have been able to find the precursors to the wheat and barley that saved them from starvation had not the aridity of their region favored the biological evolution of large-seeded grains. Second, economics has influences that redound to alter its own conditions. The way people earn livings can modify their social, political, medical, technological, and religious situations such that their economic institutions are themselves profoundly affected. It is, therefore, as essential to understand their dynamics as those of the economy. There is such an interplay among them that one who is only concerned with economics can never understand the large picture.

From the foregoing discussion, we can begin to examine the Great Middle-Class Revolution. As we shall soon see, this has been a social revolution, not merely an economic one. In recent decades, there has been increased interest in social change in general. The conditions of modern existence have transmuted so rapidly that ordinary people cannot but notice the consequences. Forced to adjust to unexpected experiences, they wonder from whence these derive and, as important, where they are headed. Will progress continue or does a new Dark Age impend? Anxieties about a nuclear winter, global warming, and the cultural wars jostle with dreams about technological wizardry, egalitarian democracy, and a Methuselah-like old age. Although futurists bombard us with their predictions, the range of divergent explanations makes it difficult to determine which is correct.

Most of the revolutions to which contemporary prophets refer are grounded in technological change, and the reason is plain. Who can deny that recent advances in manufacturing and engineering have been impressive? The plethora of automobiles, jet planes, and electronic gadgets with which we are surrounded is nothing short of magical compared with the standard equipment of our forebears. A St. Thomas Aquinas could scarcely have imagined transmitting his image via electromagnetic waves. Nor could he have fathomed earthmovers that gulp tons of rock in a single operation. That this physical power might be under the control of one man would have seemed an illusion foisted upon him by the devil. It is, therefore, fitting that we bracket the accumulation of these wonders under the rubric of the Industrial Revolution.[39] The enormous progress in our ability to manipulate the environment, beginning with James Watt's steam engine deserves to be celebrated. So do more recent developments in science, automation, and communications. Commemorating these by designating specific eras the Atomic Age, the Age of Automation, or the Information Age makes sense. Computers, in particular, have clearly inaugurated a tremendous difference. They have made it possible to manage unprecedented volumes of data and to apply them to controlling vast agglomerations of machinery—virtually without error. The problem with this emphasis, however, is that it minimizes the human element. People are portrayed as having to adjust to novel technologies, not as having undergone enormous changes in how they organize themselves. Yet the resulting social changes too have been vast.

Social scientists have not been totally oblivious to this conundrum. In consequence, many have described contemporary developments under such rubrics as modernism and postmodernism.[40] These concepts, like the more sociologically technical term Gesellschaft,[41] are related to the emergence of mass societies in which, although they are interdependent, most people are strangers to one another. They may live in massive urban agglomerations, jostle one another on crowded sidewalks and highways, and partake of the same plastic-wrapped consumer products without ever taking note of one another's existence. The difficulty is that most of us would be hard pressed to define these concepts. What exactly is modernism and how does it differ from postmodernism? Beyond the fact that these are somehow related to what presently exists, to what do they refer?

References to a Middle Class Revolution do not suffer from this difficulty. Social Class is obviously social in its orientation. It refers directly to a crucial aspect of human relationships. People are hierarchical animals. They naturally rank themselves in terms of relative power. This has been true of every society, beginning with those of our remote hunter-gatherer ancestors. It is even more the case with the mass societies with which we are familiar. Nevertheless the patterns through which social stratification are expressed have varied with time and place. Social class is not the only way that people have ranked themselves. They have also constructed caste- and estate-based civilizations. Indeed, the prominence of social class can be traced directly to the Commercial Revolution. Absent the economic dominance of market-based relationships, people could not make the distinctions between upper, middle, and lower classes that they do. Nor, of course, could they discuss a Middle-Class Revolution.

This reordering of social connections has, in turn, produced a myriad of related changes. In order for the middle classes to function in their appointed tasks, there have been modifications to other social institutions. Not just how economic transactions are conducted, but family relationships, politics, education, and morality have undergone striking transformations. Nowadays, we have grown accustomed to the resultant cultural dislocations. The media are filled with illustrations of liberals and conservatives battling each other over the proper way to reorganize a society they both bemoan as out of joint. The liberals declare a preference for progress, whereas the conservatives are alleged to be slaves to tradition. Each year the particulars of their disputes change, but their themes remain constant. Liberals generally clamor for more equality. They insist that women, minorities, and gays deserve the same rights as everyone else. This, they declare, can be achieved by increasing the role of the federal government in enforcing fairness. To this, conservatives reply by demanding more freedom. They hate government interventions, especially when these impinge on family values. Their central concern is with merit and untrammeled competition.

So vociferous have these counterclaims become that few seem concerned about their roots. People identify with one side or the other, then direct their energies toward winning, not toward understanding what is happening. A systematic exploration of a Great Middle-Class Revolution can cut through this Gordian knot. It can explain how this heated opposition evolved. More particularly, it can clarify how a cultural lag has contributed to misunderstandings and false projections. According to this view, the central problem confronting us is that those who have not fully embraced what it means to be middle class continue to cling to idealizations that have no hope of fruition. Both on the left and the right, individuals and associations harboring imperfectly internalized middle-class attitudes defend these with fantasies grounded in jejune hopes rather than careful evaluations. When members of the middle classes are characterized as greedy conformists, often by elements of their own stratum, our overall understanding of the operative machinery is distorted. Yes, some people are selfish and monotonously conventional, but others are commensurately clever, perceptive, and selfless. Crass censure of the middle classes *per se* attacks surface behaviors rather than analyzes underlying dynamics. This is a mistake the following chapters aim to correct. They will begin by taking a hard look at the nature of social class. Before achieving an accurate impression of what the middle classes have become, or are likely to develop into, it is essential to determine the parameters of what is taking place. This cannot be attained without first appreciating how people rank themselves.

Endnotes

1 Gans, H.J. 1967. *The Levittowners: Way of Life and Politics in a New Suburban Community.* New York: Alfred A. Knopf.

2 Wolfe, A. 1996. *Marginalized in the Middle.* Chicago: University of Chicago Press; Wolfe, A. 1989. *Whose Keeper?* Berkeley, CA: University of California Press.

3 Lasch, C. 1979. *The Culture of Narcissism: American Life in an Age of Diminishing Expectations.* New York: Warner Books.

4 Horowitz, I.L. (Ed.) 1971. *Power, Politics, and People: The Collected Essays of C. Wright Mills.* London: Oxford University Press.

5 Hochschild, J. 1995. *Facing Up to the American Dream.* Princeton, NJ: Princeton University Press.

6 Mills, C.W. 1951. *White Collar; The American Middle Classes.* New York: Oxford University Press; See also: Mills, C.W. 1956. *The Power Elite.* London: Oxford University Press; And Mills, C.W. 1959. *The Sociological Imagination.* New York: Oxford University Press.

7 Lewis, S. 1922. *Babbitt.* New York: Harcourt, Brace & Co.

8 Marx, K. 1967. *Das Capital,* edited by F. Engels and translated by Samuel Moore and Edward Aveling. New York: International Publishing.

9 Epstein, J. 2003. *Envy: The Seven Deadly Sins.* New York: Oxford University Press.

10 Pareto, V. 1991. *The Rise and Fall of Elites: An Application of Theoretical Sociology.* New Brunswick, NJ: Transaction Publishers.

11 Williams, T.H. 1952. *Lincoln and His Generals.* New York: Alfred A. Knopf.

12 Ellis, J.J. 1993. *Passionate Sage: The Character and Legacy of John Adams.* New York: W.W. Norton & Co.; McCullough, D. 2001. *John Adams.* New York: Simon & Schuster.

13 Adams, J. 1770. Argument in Defense of British Soldiers in the Boston Massacre.

14 Isaacson, W. 2003. *Benjamin Franklin: An American Life.* New York: Simon & Schuster.

15 Wuthnow, R. 1996. *Poor Richard's Principle: Recovering the American Dream Through the Moral Dimension of Work, Business, & Money.* Princeton, NJ: University of Princeton Press.

16 Wood, G. 1991. *The Radicalization of the American Revolution.* New York: Random House.

17 Isaacson, W. 2003. *Benjamin Franklin: An American Life.* New York: Simon & Schuster.

18 Mills, C.W. 1951. *White Collar; The American Middle Classes.* New York: Oxford University Press.

[19] Stein, H. and M. Foss. 1999. *The Illustrated Guide to the American Economy, Third Edition.* Washington, DC: AEI Press.

[20] U.S. Dept. of Labor, Bureau of Labor Statistics. 2001. *2001 National Occupational Employment and Wage Estimates.* Washington, DC: Government Printing Office.

[21] U.S. Census Bureau. 1997. *American Housing Survey for the United States: 1997.* Washington, DC: Government Printing Office.

[22] U.S. Dept. of Labor. 1991. "Research Summaries." *Monthly Labor Review, December.* Washington, DC: Government Printing Office.

[23] U.S. Census Bureau. 1997. *American Housing Survey for the United States: 1997.* Washington, DC. Government Printing Office.

[24] Moore, S. and J.L. Simon. 2000. *It's Getting Better All the Time: 100 Greatest Trend of the Last 100 Years.* Washington, DC: Cato Institute; Caplow, T., L. Hicks, and B.J. Wattenberg. 2001. *The First Measured Century: An Illustrated Guide to Trends in America*, 1900-2000. Washington, DC: AEI Press.

[25] Ogburn, W. 1922. (1966) *Social Change with Respect to Culture and Original Nature.* New York: Heubsch.

[26] Hunter, J.D. 1991. *Culture Wars: The Struggle to Define America.* New York: Basic Books.

[27] Leaky, R. 1981. *The Making of Mankind.* London: Michael Joseph Ltd.; Tattersall, I. and J. Schwartz. 2000. *Extinct Humans.* New York: Westview Press; Stanford, C.B. 1999. *The Hunting Apes: Meat Eating and the Origins of Human Behavior.* Princeton, NJ: Princeton University Press; Mason, W.A. and S.P. Mendoza. (Eds.) 1993. *Primate Social Conflict.* Albany: State University Press of New York.

[28] Klein, R.G and B. Elgar. 2002. *The Dawn of Human Culture: A Bold New Theory on What Sparked the "Big Bang" of Human Consciousness.* New York: John Wiley and Sons; Wells, S. 2002. *The Journey of Man: A Genetic Odyssey.* Princeton: Princeton University Press; Olson, S. 2000. *Mapping Human History: Discovering the Past Through Our Genes.* Boston, MA: Houghton Mifflin Co.; Cavalli-Sforza, L. and M.W. Feldman. 1981. *Cultural Transmission and Evolution.* Princeton, NJ: Princeton University Press; Cavalli-Sforza, L. and F. Cavalli-Sforza. 1993. *The Great Human Diasporas: The History of Diversity and Evolution.* Reading, MA: Perseus Books; Cavalli-Sforza, L., P. Menozzi, and A. Piazza. 1994. *The History and Geography of Human Genes.* Princeton, NJ: University of Princeton Press; Sykes, B. 2001. *The Seven Daughters of Eve: The Science That Reveals Our Genetic Ancestry.* New York: W.W. Norton and Co.

[29] Klein, R.G and B. Elgar. 2002. *The Dawn of Human Culture: A Bold New Theory on What Sparked the "Big Bang" of Human Consciousness.* New York: John Wiley and Sons; Frank, S.A. 1998. *Foundations of Social Evolution.* Princeton, NJ: University of Princeton Press.

[30] Pinker, S. 1994. *The Language Instinct: How the Mind Creates Language*. New York: William Morrow & Co.; McWhorter, J. 2001. *The Power of Babel: A Natural History of Language*. New York: HarperCollins Publishers.

[31] Harris, M. 1977. *Cannibals and Kings: The Origins of Cultures*. New York: Random House.

[32] Pfeiffer, J.E. 1977. *The Emergence of Society: A Prehistory of the Establishment*. New York: McGraw-Hill.

[33] Harris, M. 1977. *Cannibals and Kings: The Origins of Cultures*. New York: Random House.

[34] Wittfogel, K.A. 1957. *Oriental Despotism: A Comparative Study of Total Power*. New Haven: Yale University Press.

[35] Pfeiffer, J.E. 1977. *The Emergence of Society: A Prehistory of the Establishment*. New York: McGraw-Hill.

[36] Hobbes, T. 1956. *Leviathan; Part I*. Chicago, IL: Henry Regnery Co.

[37] McWhorter, J. 2001. *The Power of Babel: A Natural History of Language*. New York: HarperCollins Publishers.

[38] Sanderson, S.K. 1995. *Social Transformations: A General Theory of Historical Development*. Oxford, UK: Blackwell; Sanderson, S.K and A.S. Alderson. 2005. *World Societies: The Evolution of Human Social Life*. Boston, MA: Pearson/Allyn & Bacon.

[39] Dahrendorf, R. 1959. *Class and Class Conflict in Industrial Society*. Stanford, CA: Stanford University Press; Lipset, S.M. and R. Bendix. 1959. *Social Mobility in Industrial Society*. Berkeley, CA: University of California Press.

[40] Chirot, D. 1986. *Social Change in the Modern Era*. New York: Harcourt, Brace, Jovanovich; Ferguson, N. 2001. *The Cash Nexus: Money and Power in the Modern World, 1700 – 2000*. New York: Basic Books.

[41] Toennies, F. 1966. (1887) Community *and Society*. New York: Harper Row.

Chapter 2

Social Class

The history of all hitherto existing society is the history of class struggles. Freeman and slave, patrician and plebian, lord and serf, guild master and journeyman, in a word, oppressor and oppressed stood in constant opposition to each other, carried on an uninterrupted, now hidden, now open fight, a fight that each time ended, either in a revolutionary reconstitution of society at large, or in the common ruin of the contending classes. (Karl Marx and Friedrich Engels, <u>The Communist Manifesto</u>)

From each according to his abilities, to each according to his needs. (Karl Marx, <u>Critique of the Gotha Program</u>)

I am more and more convinced that man is a dangerous creature and that power, whether vest in many or a few, is ever grasping, and like the grave, cries "Give, give!" (Abigail Adams, Letter to John Adams)

Hierarchies

Karl Marx had a dream.[1] He imagined a world of perfect egalitarianism. The spirit of competition instilled by capitalism would be erased once communism took effect. First personal property would be abolished. As long as people vied to determine who could acquire the most wealth, they would inflict injuries to maintain their advantages. Once everything was owned in common, the motivation to obtain a bigger portion of the pie would vanish. After this, government itself would wither away. Since its primary function was to protect the property of the rich, it would lose its raison d'etre and become an anachronism. As a consequence, people would gain control over their own destinies. Choosing whether to go fishing in the morning or to amble down to the factory in the afternoon, would be at their discretion. No one would be anyone else's master; hence, not only would everyone be equal, all would be free.

The problem with this vision is that it is utterly fanciful. No human society has ever been totally without property or totally emancipated from competition. Nor has any large-scale society been able to subsist without a government. Capitalism did not cause these things; hence ridding ourselves of the marketplace cannot save us from them. To repeat a truism affirmed in Chapter 1, we human beings are hierarchical animals. We are biologically evolved to rank ourselves against one another. An accumulation of property is one of the standards used to establish relative position, but it is not the only one. Nor is property a recent, or arbitrary, invention. The rudiments of personal ownership go back to before there were modern human beings. Even monkeys hoard bananas. For that matter, monkeys also have hierarchies. They, too, make distinctions between what ethologists designate as alpha, beta, and gamma animals.

Even so, Americans have been peculiarly vulnerable to egalitarian appeals. As early as the 1830s, the young French visitor, Alexis de Tocqueville,[2] was impressed with how equal everyday relationships seemed to be. Ordinary workers, that is, those of Ben Franklin' apron-wearing class, would approach him on terms of absolute parity. As a member of his own nation's minor nobility, he was at first taken aback. At home, none of the peasants in the village for which his family was named would have dared grab his hand and shake it the way these ex-colonials did. So far as Americans were concerned, everyone was created equal, with no one inherently superior to anyone else. Some, to be sure, were wealthier, but this was deemed a temporary condition. As Tocqueville also observed, even the lowliest citizens seemed to have an eye for the main chance. They were all sure that some day one of their speculations would pay off. Their land holdings in the West would sell at an enormous profit, or the small business they were about to start would flourish on a scale comparable to Franklin's. Then, it would their turn to be honored as self-made men.

Tocqueville was ambivalent about this. Although he had come to the United States to study why its democracy, as opposed to France's, had taken root, he continued to believe that aristocratic privilege was the surest guarantee of civilization. That a barely literate backwoodsman such as Davy Crockett could get elected to Congress struck him as folly. Americans might have a greater opportunity to get ahead, but "the democratic sentiment of envy was expressed in a thousand different ways." Because they were convinced that they could succeed, undistinguished provincials resented others who got there before them. But, herein lay a paradox. Americans might deny the inequalities in their midst, overtly acting as if these did not exist, but they nevertheless pursued personal advantage with gusto. From the lowest to the highest, they admired, yet resented, the accomplishments of John Jacob Astor.[3] Who was he to grow rich on the fur trade while they were plodding along in comparative obscurity?

One of the odd contradictions that has persisted into modern times is the presence of social climbing cheek by jowl with an antipathy toward it. Marx assumed that people would one day be motivated by generosity rather than covetousness. This, however, has not been the New World experience. Many publishers have filled their coffers by purveying books that simultaneously celebrate success while ridiculing its excesses. Henry James[4] did this in his novels; Vance Packard[5] did it in his nonfictional The Status Seekers; and Paul Fussell[6] accomplished it in Class: A Guide Through the American Status System. Each of these works clucks about the absurdity of trying to be better than the next guy but in its very details reveals an obsession with the trivia of social stratification. More recently in a book the Los Angeles Times called the best of the year, Joseph Epstein[7] dissected the ins and outs of snobbery. His subject (i.e., the symbols that people flaunt in order to demonstrate their pre-eminence) was sufficiently fascinating to make the book a bestseller.

The games that people play to increase, or appear to increase, their status are legion. If Epstein is to be believed, more ingenuity is expended in the pursuit of invidious prominence than on attaining substantive achievements. Snobs, as he makes plain, are people who engage in social climbing by means of the external manifestations of success. They hold themselves a cut above others because they can distinguish a rare wine from vin ordinaire or a Bentley from a Rolls Royce. Where they live, the schools their children attend, and the clubs to which they belong take on a life-and-death significance.

God forbid they wear a sharkskin suit; someone might suspect them of being a Mafioso. Theirs is a world filled with awards, pointless philanthropies, and mind-numbing cocktail parties. It is also one permeated by superficial relationships chosen for their networking opportunities rather than their emotional depth. And yet, these people are doing what feels important. Even their phony status seems of inestimable worth. Were they to inhabit a Marxist utopia, they might take consolation in being able to do the giving to others in need on the assumption that liberality garners status points.

This mania with social standing is not exclusively human. Many social animals are hierarchical. They too spend inordinate amounts of time seeking and defending status, as opposed to food or sex. The primatologist Frans de Waal[8] has documented this propensity for a variety of species. One of these is the Rhesus monkey. De Waal begins a chapter on ranking systems among these primates by apologizing for drawing an analogy with social-class behavior, but this comparison is altogether apropos. These creatures, too, develop biologically linked orders that determine with whom they will socialize and how well they will prosper. According to de Waal, "being on top of the social ladder is not merely a pleasant, comfortable position for a wild monkey: it determines her life span and reproduction." A dominant female will get to eat better than her lesser-ranking peers, while her babies will stand a better chance of surviving into adulthood. Engaging in fights to determine who is more powerful, is not due to meanness of temper or momentary boredom. She may not consciously understand what is at stake, but evolution has provided the motivation to seek victories in such conflicts. Indeed, those she defeats are similarly motivated; hence when they lose, they are dismayed.

Thanks to Newt Gingrich, de Waal is best known for his observations of chimpanzee hierarchies. Gingrich recommended *Chimpanzee Politics*[9] as instructive about what happens among human beings; as indeed it is. Our nearest relatives were once thought of as cute circus entertainers, but this was because most people were exposed only to juvenile animals trained to give such performances. Adult chimps were not used because they are too large, too strong, and too aggressive. On their own, they can be lethal to human beings and to troop mates. As a result, it was not until the last half century that their natural behaviors became known.   Careful surveillance in the wild and in naturalistic zoo settings made it plain that they were not merely endearing; they could also be assertive and obstinate.   De Waal did his initial studies at the Netherlands' Arnhem Zoo where he quickly discovered that male animals, in particular, were preoccupied with asserting dominance.

These dominant males seemed to take joy in violent displays of power.   They would race around their enclosure with their fur standing on end to magnify their size, screaming as loudly as they could and throwing loose items in the direction of bystanders. Intimidation was the obvious aim of the exercise.   Lesser-ranking males and females were given to understand who was in charge, with fear the best way to instill this knowledge.   But isolated outbursts were insufficient.   No male, no matter how strong, could stand up against the united fury of the entire band.   What was essential to maintain control was alliances.   Two or three males in concert could defeat most challenges from below.   As a consequence, the males were continuously jockeying for position amongst themselves.   If two of them established what seemed to be a firm coalition, a third might plot to disrupt their comity.   If he succeeded, the one who was displaced would scheme on how to return the favor.   Sometimes, even the females entered these doings.   When an especially oppressive male obtained control, the females might insert themselves into the fray to remove the bully from his perch.   So serious were the shifting tides of these conflicts that death might end the reign of a hitherto unchallengeable ruler.

Among people, too, contending for dominance is more than a game.   Human struggles for hierarchical paramountcy can sometimes be deadly, as in the case of warfare.   But they are also a sport, something literally pursued for fun.   Despite their denials of ambition, even the most democratic human beings hate to lose.   They love the idea of winning so much that they invent opportunities for victory over and above those generated by contests for actual social power.   Why else do people play baseball or football?   Why else do they exult when someone on the home team hits a home run or crosses the goal line to score a touchdown?   These objectives are utterly arbitrary, but, as markers of success, they make people feel good.   Beyond this, symbolically stomping an opponent into the ground is experienced as joyful. Indeed, there is so much delight in figuratively climbing to the top of the heap that mere fans chant in excitement when their team is number one. In this respect, if none other, they feel dominant and will taunt the losers for their comparative weakness.

Women, as well as men, take pleasure in victory. In this age of feminist rhetoric, political correctness demands that cooperation be valued above competition. We are all supposed to contribute to the same team and, following Marxism, are forbidden to assume that we are better than anyone else; but this is theory. Even feminists like to win, and when they do not, as when Clarence Thomas was appointed to the Supreme Court, they hold a grudge. Like one of de Waal's chimpanzees, they conspire for the day they can depose their tormentors. Nor do women bestow their favors on men who are complaisant. Although avant-garde women boast of seeking sensitive partners, they never crow about their being losers. If anything, in their self-righteous posturing, these feminists position themselves as morally superior to their less enlightened rivals. In short, hierarchical aspirations are universal. How they are expressed may differ from person to person and society to society, but the underlying objective is similar. In contemporary America, the most noteworthy venue for these longings is social class. Such yearnings may be disparaged, yet they are enormously consequential. Paradoxically, they are also a vast improvement over conceivable alternatives. Social-class ambitions are thought of as malicious and vapid but only in comparison with more idealistic vanities. The middle classes, as silly and nasty as they occasionally are, have contributed immensely to the triumph of human comfort and achievement. Their relatively gentle dominance has paid off handsomely, not just for them, but for mankind in general.

A Range of Options

Human hierarchies take many forms.[10] Some social scientists have denied their existence because they are so variable. They say that people can organize themselves anyway they please, including in complete parity. According to this view, since all human behaviors are learned, if parents raise their children to be egalitarian, the next generation will be classless. This was the objective of the Soviets in promoting indoctrination to create the communist man.[11]

Contemporary feminists have a similar goal. They seek to instill androgynous attitudes wherein the genders are absolutely equal.[12] Despite this, human variability does not correspond to such a thoroughgoing plasticity. There is a broad range of possibilities wherein people operate, but this is far from infinite. The parameters within which specific pecking orders evolve are bounded by biological, environmental, and social imperatives. These limitations may not be obvious to those engaged in scuffling for social advantage but can be discerned by examining their scope. Moreover, it is critical to do so because what is unique about class systems, and particularly about the middle classes, cannot be appreciated without perceiving them in context. It is easy to disparage the drawbacks of their social arrangements when perceived in isolation. When measured against the shortcomings of competing schemas, however, they become attractive.

In sociology, it is rarely possible to do experiments. Societies hardly ever present themselves for objective manipulation. Frequently, the best that can be done is to analyze naturally occurring test cases. Fortunately, recorded history has been kind. Diverse civilizations have come and gone leaving sufficient residues for us to speculate about why they might have differed.[13] And they have differed often amazingly so! If we start with the smallest of communities, namely hunter-gatherer bands, we discover a way of life that has largely disappeared but that was nevertheless the one from which we evolved. Even today, people limit themselves to small numbers of close friends, very much in accord with the conditions of these earlier groups. Up until a mere ten thousand years ago, all human beings functioned as foragers. Yet, the demise of this way of life has been so complete that we are forced to speculate about preliterate social arrangements. True, there are contemporary hunter-gatherers, but they are marginalized exceptions. Thrust by more powerful civilizations into challenging environments such as the Arctic Circle or the Kalahari Desert, their relatively egalitarian dealings may be a product of having lost clashes with their more successful cousins. The Inuit and the Khoisan must of necessity travel in undersized, super-cooperative units precisely because their homelands provide few resources and many dangers. When a meager several millennia ago foraging was the norm, our forebears journeyed through more generous landscapes, the social specifics of which must per force remain unknown.

The sort of small-scale society then extant has been called Gemeinschaft.[14] Most wandering groups probably never topped one hundred and fifty before they split into rival communities. The reason was simple. Foragers need space to find sufficient provisions to keep them alive. Because any given territory will contain a limited supply of prey animals and edible plants, survival depends on population control. As Thomas Malthus[15] conjectured, this could be accomplished through famine, disease, or warfare. In any event, people got to know each other intimately. Having grown up together, faced hardships together, and overcome adversity together, these early humans formed relationships that were intensely personal. Daily engaged in face-to-face activities, they encountered ongoing opportunities to take each other's measure. This enabled them to become familiar with one another's weaknesses and to take these into account when determining rank.

Although modern collectivists like to imagine an idyllic past during which everyone was completely equal, hunting bands— especially when they survived by killing large game--- probably could not have managed this way. We know from their middens that our remote ancestors were capable of bringing down mammoths. Yet, it is impossible to imagine their doing so without tightly controlled hierarchies. Someone had to be in charge of the chase, and this person had to be obeyed. The alternative of freelancing would have entailed starvation or, more probably, a gory death. To further their joint plans, the participants probably turned to a prominent hunter for guidance and discipline.[16] Nor would discovering who was best suited for command have been difficult. Direct observation would have exposed hunting skills, personal magnetism, and comparative knowledge. Until old age slowed him down, one of the elders would likely have assumed this role. In a world without written records, a hunter with years of experience would have proven a fund of wisdom. No one else would be as familiar with the habits of the game animals, no one else as acquainted with the tricks of the chase.

Similar considerations applied to the gatherers, that is, to the women. The circumstances of their contributions differed, but they too would have valued insight and skill.[17] Almost surely, an older woman with personal charisma and years of expertise in uncovering suitable vegetation would achieve prominence. Given that gathering requires less coordination, she might have exercised a control over the group that would not have been as strict as that of her male counterpart, but she would unquestionably have been treated as possessing superior powers. She might also have benefited from distinctive skills such as those of midwife or arbiter of domestic disputes. In any event, not everyone would be considered equal. Furthermore, the attendant respect would spontaneously have translated into social control. This hegemony might not be absolute, but it would have provided material and psychological advantages.

Once the Agricultural Revolution kicked into gear, the need for hierarchy intensified, whereas the criteria for attaining prominence changed. Larger populations, more settled living conditions, and altered economic circumstances placed the emphasis on other qualities. One of the first forms of distinction that took root was that of the big man. As today can be perceived in the highlands of New Guinea,[18] village-centered horticulturalists trust their leadership to men who display unique interpersonal talents. Almost always articulate and productive, these persons gain status by being role models and social intermediaries. Their associates respect them for how they manage their gardens but, more important, for their energy and skill in settling communal disputes. Big men tend to be community-minded. They tirelessly develop schemes from which others benefit while contemporaneously reducing the tensions that arise when individuals work in close proximity. More socially astute than their fellows, they demonstrate sufficient self-control to mediate among antagonists who are less perceptive. Not surprisingly, this translates into respect and influence.

Eventually, agricultural communities grow. This makes superior status yet more problematic. With more people to know, fewer of them can be known well. This, however, coincides with greater needs for social discipline. Specifically, as prosperity increases, people acquire more property. This gives rise to covetousness and a plethora of disputes. Agriculturalists principally need ways to resolve issues over land ownership. As a result, chieftainships evolve. Big men societies depend on the spontaneous manifestation of individuals of superior talents, but larger communities require a more reliable source of leadership. This is often achieved by making the position of supreme authority elective or hereditary. The village may unite to appoint a headman, or it may develop a tradition that the child of the deceased headman (usually the eldest son) takes over. Here, the trappings are a bit less personal. The qualities of the chief also become more mystical. Less subject to direct observation, they are as likely to be projected as perceived.

This tendency is exacerbated as agricultural communities burgeon in size. Under these conditions, chieftains metamorphose into kings and eventually into emperors. Small settlements amalgamate into large towns, and the paramount leadership role becomes more remote from ordinary villagers. Especially when irrigation becomes prominent, there may develop what has been called hydraulic society. Irrigation both enlarges the volume of production and creates the need to cooperate in developing public works. The villagers must somehow arrive at an agreement on how to divide the water supply and the means of distributing the edible products of their labor. This increases the desirability of powerful leadership. Under these circumstances, a king must have the leverage to enforce his will. Understandably, this emerging disparity in authority is apt to amplify the monarch's taste for command. Eventually, his power becomes so immense that he is perceived as superhuman. Now perhaps considered a god, he demands the perquisites of a deity and receives them. Kingdoms and empires are hierarchies where the distance between the top and the bottom has enormously expanded in scope. Especially within empires, which are traditionally composed of unrelated peoples, the leader may have little in common with those who are led and may cease even considering them human. Under these conditions, supremacy tends to be coercively enforced. Not only are relationships no longer face to face, but, from the perspective of the participants, they may appear impervious to challenge. The comparative superiority of some seems a fact of nature one that may be regretted but is nevertheless deemed impossible to revise. Indeed, it may not even be regretted but be celebrated as the best of all conceivable arrangements.

If we switch our focus from the top of the pecking order to the next segment down, we come to the aristocracy. In kingships, membership in the nobility is as likely to be perceived as hereditary as the top spot. Often biologically related to the monarch, these individuals too may have powers conceived as divine. This sort of hierarchy, which is widespread in agriculturally based societies, is frequently designated an estate system. As recently as the beginning of the French Revolution,[19] France was divided into three such estates. The clergy was theoretically on top, then came the nobility, and finally the third estate, the commoners. Different societies have divided these orders in distinctive ways (e.g., the Romans were famously partitioned between the patricians and the plebeians). What these arrangements have in common is that their alignments are supposedly fixed. If a person is born into one of these estates, he will theoretically die in it. Aristocrats are always noble, even if they fall on hard times, whereas merchants are always ignoble, despite the riches they may acquire. The rationales for these distinctions differ, but they are generally interpreted as natural. Thus, a noble station will sometimes be attributed to better blood or superior breeding and at other times to Divine Right. Either way, everyone within the hierarchy is expected to accept his/her fate.

Closely related to estate systems are caste systems.[20] The difference between these is that the latter are more rigid. Usually drawing their legitimacy from religious sanctions, their paradigm is found in India. Under Hinduism, it has been believed that souls migrate from one lifetime to another, in each incarnation being reborn in line with the karma accumulated in the previous materialization. Those who were righteous might return as a Brahmin, with all the privileges due this priesthood, whereas those who were evil would return as Sudras, that is, as lower status peasants. (The intermediate castes were the warrior Kshatriyas and the merchant Vaishas.) Changing one's status was, therefore, impossible. It would be tantamount to a zebra wanting to be a horse or a horse a human being. Analogous to caste systems are slave systems. These too offer less mobility than estate societies. In the latter case, merchants sometimes cross the line to become squires, but slaves are regarded as property. They cannot rise any more than a walking stick can strike out on an independent journey. Classified by no less an authority than Aristotle as naturally inferior, they are thought not to possess the abilities to manage autonomously. Biologically closer to the beasts than human beings, they are obviously destined to be owned by their betters. Since their inadequacies are indelible, even manumission cannot remove the stains of their births.

All of this contrasts markedly with social-class systems, which are associated not with agriculture but commerce. They are the legacy of an expanding marketplace and are characterized by greater social mobility. Class systems, too, have an upper, a middle, and a lower designation, but these are neither predetermined nor permanent. Relative status within them can change, particularly when wealth changes. A person born a peasant, if he becomes a prosperous merchant, thereby elevates his standing within the community. People may remember his roots but will be dazzled by his later munificence. It is even possible for him to mount to the summit of such a society. To cite an obvious illustration, John D. Rockefeller[21] began life in obscurity yet ultimately climbed to be the equivalent of royalty. During his lifetime, he and his ilk were disparaged as robber barons. Though not literally aristocrats, they lived as opulently and with as much influence as their medieval counterparts.

Also characteristic of social class is a decentralization of power. Decision-making is less concentrated on the top, with people lower in rank having greater control over their own fates. Generally, they too get to determine local issues, such as where to live or what job to perform, frequently in an idiosyncratic fashion. Moreover, class-oriented societies are characterized by their anonymity. Because they are massive agglomerations, such societies are populated by people who do not personally know each other. Their relationships are not face-to-face; hence, even though they depend on one another for their daily sustenance, they cannot directly judge relative power. Under these conditions money becomes a surrogate for power, albeit an imperfect one.

Social class could not exist outside market-oriented communities. The requisite mobility and anonymity are not possible without the flexibility inherent in large-scale commerce. To begin with, trading property provides opportunities for an accumulation of wealth that are not available in agricultural societies. By the same token, the sorts of power that facilitate social prominence are market related. Many, such as a talent for numbers, are directly connected with what is needed to flourish in commercial ventures. Of special relevance to the Middle Class Revolution is that such capabilities become increasingly concentrated in the middle classes. To an unprecedented degree, members of this stratum monopolize the skills needed to organize a modern economy. As a result, their impact and control rise. And with control comes respect and enhanced status.

Still, the middle classes have been reluctant to assume the mantle of their success. Many among them deny their prominence and continue to think of the upper classes as in charge. The inevitable question is Why? Why they are not as proud of their preeminence as were their predecessors? The answer lies in the circumstances of its achievement. Because their positions are inherently mobile and anonymous, they are individually bedeviled by insecurities. Never quite sure of where they stand or how long they will stand there, they adopt a defensive modesty or, conversely, a defensive snobbery.[22] Either they hope to be camouflaged by being unassuming in their claims or they attempt to be intimidating by professing unsupported ones. Theirs is an ambivalence born of uncertainty. This is why contemporary Americans display a discomfort in acknowledging the reality of inequality side by side with their fascination with its manifestations. While this may seem strange, a closer examination of the nature of hierarchies should dispel the apparent contradiction. Perhaps, it might even make this protective ignorance less necessary by reducing the need for the destructive romanticism in which social class has so often been cloaked.

Fundamentals

Hierarchy is a puzzling phenomenon.[23] Instead of examining how ranking systems are created and maintained, even social scientists tend to be concerned with the way power is distributed. They want to know who ranks higher and lower rather than why. More than this, they are often intrigued with the possibility of rearranging these ranks. Themselves human and, therefore, part of the status game, they play it with enthusiasm. Usually scions of lower-status families, they have sympathized traditionally with the underdogs. As a consequence, rather than study social class per se, they become absorbed with exploring the social movements they believe will promote a more just allocation of influence. This has attracted their attention to larger social arrangements rather than to the smaller processes of which they are composed. As a result, scholars have missed the fundamental mechanisms through which status is negotiated. Nevertheless, these instruments are not particularly strange nor difficult to understand. Indeed, they will be instantly recognizable to most readers. Nor are they unique. Although they differ in detail from some other hierarchical mechanisms found within the animal kingdom, they are continuous with them. The central machinery is essentially the same distinguished among humans primarily by a greater complexity and greater dependence on the intricacies of symbolic communication.

The most important building block of hierarchies is the test of strength.[24] Individuals determine where they stand in the scheme of things in concrete clashes whereby they compare their power with specific others. They literally face off in activities designed to exhibit their relative vigor. Just as rams butt heads to settle who is physically more powerful, people engage in analogous matches. They match up, perhaps in a fistfight, to see who will win. After this combat is over, one is acknowledged the victor and the other the loser. Typically the loser breaks off the engagement by signaling deference to his now determined superior. Among sheep and other animals, this victory is rewarded by access to fertile females; among humans, the forms of compensation are more extensive. Reproductive benefits may follow, but so does access to greater resources and superior authority within group activities.

One of the major differences among humans and other animals is that our tests of strength cover a greater range of powers than do theirs. With rams, the arena is biologically determined. The battle will be horn against horn, the triumph going to the physically more potent. Among people, there are similar contests, with the laurels going to the better wrestler or the more skilled rifle shooter. Nonetheless, what counts as stronger can widely vary. Because we use tools to augment our muscle power, success can depend as much on the skillful manipulation of a weapon as on brute force. More than this, because we are social creatures, the person who prevails may be the one with better social skills. As we shall shortly see, alliances matter; hence, the person who can demonstrate superior communicative abilities may prevail over the one who has spent years working out in a gymnasium. Good talkers frequently outmaneuver the heavy-fisted in a manner that no male sheep could emulate.

The test of strength, however, is but the starting point of hierarchical supremacy. Winning one changes the conditions under which the players operate. Of crucial significance is the transformation in their reputations.[25] Owing to human cognitive abilities, the combatants will note what has occurred and modify their behaviors accordingly. To begin with, the victor obtains a reputation for being more powerful, which discourages the loser from challenging the outcome. Correspondingly, the loser is judged less powerful and, therefore, easier to defeat. These beliefs stabilize their relationship such that the victor is recognized as stronger and his position is not challenged—that is, until the circumstances appear to have changed. By the same token, bystanders will be impressed by these events. They, too, will reckon the victor stronger and the loser, weaker. This will then influence their own hierarchical standing in that it may decide whom they attempt to challenge. Clearly, they will shy away from confronting those with commanding reputations but will be undeterred by those with weaker ones. In the end, this results in a comprehensive ranking system without every participant having to engage in a test of strength with every other participant. Because power is deemed transitive, the players tend not to dispute those who appear to be stronger.

As suggested above, people also differ from other social animals to the degree that their tests are collective events. Humans derive their potency not merely from tool use but from the social methods used to exploit these implements. Experience has demonstrated that cohesive hunting parties are more effective than lone operators. The same applies within social groups. Cohesive alliances can defeat individual opponents in tests of strength irrespective of the abilities of the isolated person. In almost every case, numbers matter. This places a premium on assembling and maintaining coalitions. Individuals with an aptitude for doing so thereby acquire a reputation commensurate with the powers of their supporters. Being articulate, that is, being persuasive, is, therefore, reckoned an advantage, as is skill at log-rolling or horse-trading. As important, those who know how to distribute rewards so as to collect pledges of loyalty have their personal clout multiplied by the span of these promises. All of this is encompassed under the rubric of politics. As the art of coalition formation and management, it is at the heart of human stratification.

More broadly, so too are intergroup relationships. Because a person's reputation may depend upon the group (or groups) with which he/she is identified, the corporation for which he works,[26] as well as the ethnic community to which he/she belongs, can establish how he/she will be treated. This may not be fair, but it is how things are.

Already it should be apparent that hierarchy formation is quite complex. But things get worse. Human mental abilities being what they are, people devote their intellects to scheming for hierarchical advantage. When they lose a test of strength, they do not simply quit; they plan ahead for an opportunity to reverse the decision. The horizon for this preparation can cover a lifetime, and beyond. Politics, after all, is a devious game. Prospective leaders spend years laying the groundwork for a run at the top. They even dedicate Herculean efforts to building political capital for the ideologies to which they are committed. Though this may not allow them personally to rise in status, they will have the satisfaction of believing their party will. What is more, the ingenuity occasioned by these plans can be awe-inspiring. Subtle ruses, abstract theories, and multistage conspiracies all contribute to their fruition, so may an ability to think on one's feet. Since victory does not always go to the best-designed strategy, one adjusted to unexpected contingencies can fare best. Flexibility of thought, not raw intelligence or effort, thus becomes the determining factor.

To all this must be added a further layer of complexity which applies specifically to social-class systems. In the hierarchies characteristic of hunter-gatherers, all of the players know one another. Their reputations for power are personal reputations and their alliances are finite combinations. Because the number of players is small, all are observable to all. This capacity vanishes once a community's size passes a certain threshold. In societies in which social class operates, the limit has long since been surpassed. The anonymity of these communities has already been noted, but its implications have not. In a world of strangers, it is impossible for everyone to be familiar with everyone else. It is, therefore, also impossible for them to compare their personal strengths directly. They depend instead upon appearances. Symbols of strength substitute for demonstrations of potency, as may symbols of party affiliation for visible attachments. In creatures with as finely tuned communicative skills as ourselves, refinements of language, variations in fashion, and the material opportunities of wealth are adapted to send messages about relative positions. As we know, the accents with which a person speaks, the labels on a shirt collar, and the horsepower of an automobile can all declare the social stratum to which one belongs. Yet, as we also know, these symbols can lie. They may be used to indicate powers and associations that do not exist. Is this not what snobbery is about? It exists because an ability to put on airs makes it difficult to establish the correct rankings. Nevertheless, this sort of manipulation is part of the game. Nature imposes no rules against deceit or impression management in establishing status. Indeed, it provides the instruments for doing so.

It must also be noted that symbols are related to signs. Some social theorists suggest that the symbols of rank are arbitrary.[27] They complain that the upper classes routinely invent indicators of supremacy in order to lord it over their subordinates. This, however, reverses the order of appearance. Most symbols of power arise from signs of power. That which is associated with strength—sometimes even causative of it—can be confounded with power itself. To be more concrete, during the Middle Ages, members of the aristocracy owed their positions largely to a monopoly on military leadership. Born to be warriors, they often made their rounds armed with the tools of their trade. These were eventually transmuted into symbols of status. Wearing a sword, which began as a sign of one's noble occupation, transmuted into a symbol of membership in the upper class. When merchants ultimately acquired the means to aspire to titles, they, too, took to girding themselves in swords. It mattered not that these were irrelevant to their trade; they made a statement nonetheless. Even less directly associated with power were epaulets. These shoulder boards were originally used as protection against sword strokes. As such, they too were a sign of military connections. When, however, they came to symbolize power, the affectation spread far beyond its initial rationale.

Another common error is depicting emblems of power as symbols of violence. Critics of status are offended by the implied coercion, yet this is an overreaching. Being able to quote Shakespeare might convey the message that one is culturally sophisticated, and, ergo, of higher status, but it is not intended to inflict physical injury.

The central goal is to intimidate, not destroy. Symbols of power are designed to produce victory in tests of strength. If an opponent can be convinced that the way one speaks betokens aptitudes and alliances that cannot be surmounted, he may back down without resorting to a confrontation. The idea is to avoid violence. If the loser feels injured after such a clash, this pain remains less than would be that of the alternative. Indeed, many animals use symbols of strength to limit the need for jarring battles. Baboons, for instance, show off their formidable canine teeth before they sink them into an opponent's flesh. Better for all concerned if the loser decides to back off from this alone.

The strengths that decide status, and their symbolic manipulations, have varied with the historical period. Clearly, neither swords nor epaulets wield the powers they once did. The underlying notion of relative power has not changed, but how this is expressed has been dramatically modified. Some authorities insist that status is socially constructed and from this they erroneously draw the conclusion that it can be reconstructed any way they wish. In the sense that tests of strength create realities that did not exist before them, they are correct. But in the sense that they can independently and arbitrarily alter the results of these contests, they are not. As theorists, they imagine that they stand outside the fray directing traffic within it, but they cannot. Like anyone else, they are able to revise hierarchies to the extent that they are contingent upon the powers brought to bear. If these are inferior to those who oppose them, the odds are they will fail. Nor can they redefine the symbols of power to accommodate their personal whims. Merely declaring these to have been "reconstructed" does not impose new meanings. Actual historical contexts are responsible for such amendments.

The question that must now be considered is what constitutes strength in a society dominated by the middle classes. Clearly, what predominates in an industrial society will not be the same as what did among hunter-gatherers. Neither will what constitutes power be identical within every segment of such a society. That which earns status among professional baseball players is not what produces respect among college professors.[28] Complex societies, including social-class societies, are composed of multiple overlapping hierarchies. In fact, people can simultaneously belong to many different ranked communities. Thus, one might be a person of great consequence among one's lodge brothers but of little moment on the loading dock. Power is not indivisible; hence neither is relative power. Someone can be influential in one area but not in another. This may be confusing, but it provides opportunities to rescue one's self-respect from defeat in one area by compensating with a victory elsewhere.

What this means is that there is a fundamental indeterminacy in the ranking systems of large-scale societies. Even an omniscient observer could not precisely locate every participant. Despite this, there is a tendency to crave exactness in a way that is only superficially possible. Because people want to know where they—and others— stand, they make arbitrary divisions that are at best approximations. Social class is, in reality, a dynamic continuum. People may be higher or lower in specific respects at selected moments, but there are no official barriers separating their statuses. Individuals talk of there being just two classes (the rich and everyone else) or of three classes (the upper, the middle, and the lower), but these are provisional political demarcations. A Marxist might prefer to defend the twofold division since it implies that almost everyone can be recruited to overthrow the capitalists. Someone proud of personal accomplishments might, on the other hand, insist on a middle rank to which that individual can belong. As has often been remarked, the way things look depends upon where one stands. But it can also depend on one's objectives. Republicans and Democrats see things differently, in part, because their incomes differ but more so because they view voting patterns differently. Since each side wants to win and doing so depends on assembling far-reaching coalitions, they perceive these potential assemblages through polarized prisms. They figuratively divide the territory they observe based on their hopes not merely on their personal resources, the one party discerning a nation of haves and have-nots, the other decrying class warfare. In any event, the underlying continuities of social class should not be forgotten. Their ambiguities will have an impact irrespective of whether these are acknowledged.

Sources of Power

The sources of hierarchical strength have modified over time, but their outlines are fairly clear. Primary among these is military strength. People hate the idea that might makes right, but there is a sense in which it does. Those who can compel others to do their bidding also exercise control over how they think and feel. The respect they extract surrounds them with an aura that makes them appear righteous no matter how much pain they inflict. Hitler[29] was genuinely loved before his Wehrmacht was dismantled. So was Stalin,[30] even as his policies starved millions of Kulaks to death. It has become a cliché that the victors rewrite history in their favor, but their advantage kicks in long before that. Their raw ability to threaten harm draws admiration from those forced to look up at them. This may at first be grudging, but in the end it is often whole-hearted.

Power is the ability to get people to behave in specified ways even if they wish to do otherwise. It can be exercised gently, as through persuasion, but when the crunch comes, it can be brutal. If coercion is possible, and nothing else works, it is likely to be employed. Tests of strength may not be about violence, yet, when all else fails, aggression is frequently the only source of intimidation at hand. The problem with physical force, of course, is that it can be met with countervailing force. People get hurt when someone decides to impose his will no matter what the cost. The victim of violence may be its target, but it can also be the assailant. Initiating a battle does not inoculate an attacker against defeat. Nor are innocent bystanders guaranteed free passes. Violence has a way of spilling over in every direction. In fact, it may intentionally be focused on the innocent in the expectation that their defeat will send a signal to one's competitors. Despite their prospective damage, military confrontations are a constant. As far as it is possible to tell, belligerent skirmishes long preceded the advent of recorded history. Death and destruction were the fall back position in tests of strength, even when inflicted by spears and arrows.

Physical strength continues to be a fact of everyday life. People judge one another on their apparent ability to trounce others. Feminists are fond of pointing out that, in a mechanized world, muscle power is not as indispensable as it once was. This may be true, but it is still a sign of power to which people react. Tall people are at first glance assumed to be stronger and smarter than more petite colleagues. Should the long and the short walk into a room side by side, it is the long that invites attention. Yet, experience can reverse this judgment, as occurred with the Civil War's Phil Sheridan.[31] No more than five foot, four inches in height, Sheridan was not initially perceived as officer material by President Lincoln. However, after Sheridan's dashing cavalry victories in the Shenandoah Valley, Lincoln opined that he was just the right size. Actual physical success impresses people. This is so much the case that during the Middle Ages legal disputes were sometimes settled in trials by combat. He who could best an opponent in a test of military skill was assumed to have earned a divine imprimatur.

Before the arrival of agriculture, a community's best fighter might be regarded as a hero and rewarded with leadership in battle and deference afterwards. Even later, as recorded in the Bible, pastoral peoples regarded their champions as special, hence the tale of David and Goliath. Still retold with admiration, this chronicle of how a boy felled a giant exemplifies the bravery that is a steppingstone to kingship. Unfortunately for the cult of the lone Hercules, more organized military prowess soon gained hegemony. Because personal power pales in comparison with the armed energies of a community, organized warfare became the standard of hierarchical superiority. The Greeks[32] could regard themselves as a natural aristocracy after inflicting decisive defeats on the Persians at Salamis and Platea. Their phalanxes and fleet operations proved capable of repelling far greater numbers.[33] More impressive yet were the conquests of Julius Caesar.[34] Caesar was able to overcome Celtic hordes despite their large personal size and imposing broad swords. His legions, armed as they were with the shorter gladius, could prevail on the battlefield thanks to superior discipline. Well trained and intelligently led, they could cooperate to a degree their more individualized foes could not. Blue war paint and ferocious demeanor did not compensate for shields stubbornly held alongside one another, especially when accompanied by sword thrusts from below. This ability to bring dependable alliances to the battlefield made the Romans masters of Europe and Caesar the dictator of an empire. It even produced a month of the year named after him. In this case, collaborative military prowess elevated the Italics to cultural dominance over a continent and their commander-in-chief to dominance over the state and historical imaginations.

Later, the Romans would fall to the resurgent barbarians. No longer able to impose coercion over now better-organized antagonists, they fell victim to alliances more potent than their own. Notably, the military power of these invaders constituted the foundation of later European nobility. The descendants of these adventurers might attribute their ascendancy to divine favor or bluerblood than their villeins, but their actual supremacy was won in a more sanguine manner. Indeed, they could not have maintained their paramount status were they unable to sally forth from their castles to cut down peasants foolhardy enough to challenge them.

Another source of individual and collective power is religion.[35] Stalin may have inquired of his Western allies how many divisions the Pope commanded, but this grossly underestimated the strength of shared beliefs. Compared with the vast expanse of nature, human beings are puny. Small and weak measured against with the forces of a hurricane, we are worse because we are aware of the disparity. Ironically, superior cognitive abilities have the drawback of alerting us to our inferiority. Much as we hate it, sooner or later, everyone learns that he cannot dictate to destiny. Things happen—often quite terrible things—that we cannot forestall. Loved ones die; famines devastate entire nations; and dreams crumble to dust. At such moments, we look for help from those who stood by us in the past, but often they too prove frail. Our parents cannot protect us from the death of child; our spouses cannot forestall layoffs in an industry in decline; and trusted politicians cannot forecast a secret attack on Pearl Harbor. Surrounded by such reverses, we long for a powerful defender. We want someone who can rescue us as our parents once did when we were small.

This someone is typically personified as a deity. God (or the gods) is conceived as supernaturally powerful. Whether depicted anthropomorphically or not, He/she is imagined to be strong enough to intimidate any potential foe. Able even to call forth miracles, this deity possesses such power that no ordinary rival can withstand his/her might. An individual with God as an ally is, therefore, a formidable adversary in a test of strength. As a result, he/she can attain status by terrifying others into submission. When particular persons are perceived to be on good terms with heaven, these favored few may thereby claim social precedence. Priests and prophets, not just kings, can demand subservience on this basis. In promising to visit the wrath of a hidden world on obdurate opponents, they compel believers to do as they desire. Rather than go to hell, these others kneel before the bishop, bequeath their riches to his church, and sacrifice their lives in a crusade aimed at liberating their holy land. Lest it escape notice, a theological ability to command obedience is readily convertible into military power. The pope may not lead organized legions, but he can inspire sanguine battles. Stalin's successors discovered this when a Polish pope motivated resistance among communist Eastern European vassals. So did Saladin when he sought to evict the Franks from the Levant. The knights with whom he jousted wore crosses on their chests, but they were inspired by faith in their hearts. Though ultimately forced to retreat, these champions put up a stout resistance that was only overcome by warriors motivated by a counterbelief.

Beyond the physical power that is thought to cling to the supernatural, there is the potency of the normative.[36] Religion is not just about gods, it is also about moral imperatives. While still at their mothers' knees, children are taught that some behaviors are unacceptable. They learn that eternal punishments await them for violating these crucial rules. Such prescriptions then become internalized to guide subsequent actions. Do not tell a lie is transformed from an external command into a personal commitment. Guilt subsequently arises at the mere thought of telling a falsehood and prevents one from yielding to temptation. Because morality, even when detached from religion, creates standardized obligations, it can also create anonymous alliances. Individuals become more powerful than their personal assets warrant when they can depend on others to back them. This is precisely what happens in the case of morally inculcated norms. The wife who has been betrayed by an unfaithful husband can count upon members of her community to frown upon a man who violates the commandment against adultery. She will be considered the good one and (historically, at least) receive the greater honor. The same applies to theft, where the power of the group can come to bear in defeating the machinations of the crook.

Indeed, a moral consensus can even provide the impetus to combat. The Japanese learned to their sorrow that attacking the United States before declaring war was regarded as an immoral stab in the back that cried for retaliation. They also discovered that in losing this conflict they could no longer maintain the pretense of being a master race.

Lastly, economic potency lends itself to prevailing in tests of strength. As with physical and religiomoral potency, it can persuade an opponent to accept defeat. In the days of the hunter-gatherers, the more successful hunter garnered kudos for bringing home more meat than his fellows. He was respected for his prowess and sought after as good provider. When matched against his rivals, he cowed them with a competence they could not match. Oddly enough, expertise, too, is intimidating. When people go head-to-head over a skill, the one who is more proficient demonstrates a strength that can be as frightening as muscle power. It is disconcerting to be confronted with an aptitude that makes one look weak, which is why people hate to play tennis with someone who is better at the game and it is why the poor feel uncomfortable being friends with the rich.

Human beings have become our planet's dominant species, not because we are physically stronger than other animals, but because we can overpower them with our skills. Intelligent tool use is our hallmark. It is the means through which we acquire the resources to survive. Demonstrable economic prowess is thus a sign of this supremacy.[37] It is of value for what it can produce but also because of the respect it commands. In any event, the economically successful have surplus resources with which to influence the behaviors of others. In a direct confrontation over power, the economically superior can bribe their opponents to desist. These poorer others may be offered goods as an incentive to break off challenges and rewards for assisting in rebuffing third parties. In a sense, even formerly neutral bystanders can become mercenaries in the incessant battles over status. This is what happens to the employees of a corporation when, in consideration for a paycheck, they find themselves defending the interests of their bosses.

Nor should economic power be considered divorced from military power. Dwight D. Eisenhower[38] warned of the dangers of a military-industrial complex. On departing office, he explained that businessmen could control government decisions by bribing generals to favor their plans. This is nothing new. The bankers who lent them the wherewithal to pay for their armies thereby exercised influence over medieval monarchs. Then, as now, soldiers sometimes fought because a charismatic hero inspired them, sometimes from a transcendent spiritual cause, but often because they received compensation for doing so. On occasion, the rewards came from confiscating the property of the enemy; nevertheless, more dependable benefits derived from paymasters with the means to afford their services. As Red Barber might have said, this put the economically successful in the catbird's seat. The wealthy, to be blunt, can buy military power. To this day, they finance the weapons upon which battle depends. In the Middle Ages, these resources allowed kings to purchase the cannons necessary to reduce the castles of recalcitrant barons; in contemporary times, they have allowed the United States to become the world's dominant superpower.

To sum up, human power has many bases. As we will shortly see, even military, religious, and economic potencies themselves have numerous starting points. Today it has become commonplace to refer to social capital.[39] Some people, or groups, are said to get ahead because they possess more of this mysterious something. Economic capital, in contrast, is easy enough to understand. This concept has been in use long enough for us recognize the machinery, the technologies, and the financial resources to which it refers. Social capital, however, is more opaque. It seems to have something to do with the democratic principles that enable modern nation states to function and also with the educational assets that enable persons to prosper within them. The problem is that the requisite norms and skills, and indeed the social networks, to which it refers, are not specified. No doubt there are some conditions that allow individuals and communities to rise above others to permit them to function at higher levels. In a sense, talk of social capital is functionalism for nonfunctionalists. It enables critics of capitalism who wish to deny it success to admit that some qualities facilitate social and personal survival without having to acknowledge that the winners might somehow be better. They can thus be egalitarian in their pronouncements while admitting competition to their pantheon under another name. What follows will be more direct. The specific talents that have enabled the middle classes to become dominant will be identified for what they are. Moreover, how economic power gets transmuted into hierarchical supremacy will be examined in detail, for unless these issues are confronted head on, their mysteries will remain.

Forms of Alliances

Over the course of history, the types of alliances that have fostered hierarchical success have succeeded one another with a dizzying but, in retrospect, is a predictable regularity. What has constituted military, religious, and economic power has been modified according to the kinds of coalitions that have been brought to bear. Not surprisingly, as the ways people have lived were transformed, what determined who was likely to associate with whom did likewise. Specifically, as social, environmental, and economic conditions evolved, so did the sorts of bonds that made a difference. People were thrown together in diverse circumstances where they discovered that what enabled them to do well in tests of strength had correspondingly changed.

In the beginning was the family. Evolutionary psychologists have made a fetish of explaining how genetic bonds influence altruistic behavior.[40] Fascinated with the metaphor of selfish genes that are dedicated to perpetuating themselves, they argue that a relative helping another relative to survive is almost the same as perpetuating one's own chromosomes. On these grounds, the closer the genetic relationship, the greater the DNA overlap and, therefore, the stronger the motivation to be of assistance. Although this sounds fairly mechanical, elementary observations confirm a tendency to family solidarity. Those who share parents and grandparents may fight like cats and dogs, but when an outsider threatens a member of the clan, they close ranks. In moments of danger, they function as allies.[41] Personal relationships based on kinship thus channel individuals into coalitions that enable them to overcome threats from other coalitions. The bonds based on these connections can also set preemptive strikes in motion. Individuals who trust one another based on shared biological roots can collaborate in asserting dominance over others. In combination they can claim, and defend, hierarchical priority.

Family relationships would seem to have been a prime source of status in hunter-gatherer societies. Who was whose son and who married whom helped determine who rose to a dominant position. This was so within the local band, where the prestige of a parent might rub off on a child or the support of one's brothers could overawe a rival who had only sisters. This was also so between bands, in which primitive politics could establish interfamily alliances capable of defending favorable territories. Family connections were so important within small-scale communities that the details of kinship became highly formalized. Anthropologists have discovered that preliterate societies have more complex classifications than do technologically advanced ones. Given their greater political, economic, and social import, this makes perfect sense.

But family relationships do not lose their value as societies increase in scope. They are also crucial within estate systems. In societies such as medieval Europe,[42] the elite stratum was controlled by family lineages. Who was related to whom determined who inherited what lands and which titles. The isolated individual was as good as vanquished in a world where the primary duty was to blood. Even more so than in less elaborate communities, alliances consummated by marriage were the rule. Kings gave their daughters to the sons of other kings on the principle that this would unite their houses. In due course, a conjoined genetic destiny created a larger political agglomeration that assisted in dominating less astute lineages. By the same token, within one's own lands, a fertile union could enable one's house to keep unruly barons from usurping the prerogatives of their betters. This logic was so compelling that it was replicated down the social ladder. Perhaps the best known example is the vendettas of Southern Italy.[43] Not only did the leading families build towers to fend off the attacks of competing dynasties, peasants too engaged in bitter feuds over apparently minuscule plots of land and seemingly trivial questions of honor. Nor was this propensity confined to the Old World. Americans well into the twentieth century were transfixed by the feuds of the Hatfields and the McCoys. Cut off from the larger society in the remote borderlands of Kentucky and West Virginia, the families were featured in lurid accounts of how they slew each other over profit and jealousy. Neither has this tendency been restricted to the poor; equally mesmerizing was the nepotism of Camelot. The nation followed the rise and fall of the Kennedy[44] clan not only because a glamorous young president headed this procession but because he was accompanied by a multitude of siblings and, eventually, nieces and nephews. Cloistered in their private compounds with their magic only intermittently on display, they could bestow honors on one another almost at will, be it as Attorney General or as Senator.

Closely allied to coalitions based on family are those grounded in comradeship. Going back almost as far as genetic bonds are those related to the hunt. Men who together pursued large game developed durable allegiances. Compelled by circumstances to trust their safety to one another, they became as close as brothers. Emotionally prepared to sacrifice all for the survival of the team, outsiders had best beware. Since these hunting bands were frequently interchangeable with military bands, the same loyalties applied to raiding parties. Fighting as a unit against a determined enemy further solidified the partnership. This, too, as with the family, enabled the parties to promote their separate positions. Their relationships constituted a bulwark available to individual tests of strength. In the case of European nobility, warriors who fought together became comrades in arms in defending their superiority over those they conquered. Even after the initial occupation receded into a mythical past and members of the aristocracy were no longer personal friends, a communal fealty, that is, a pledge of honor, bound them in a network of shared interest.

Indeed, this sort of military comradeship was the forerunner of what evolved into government. Stabilized groups of individuals prepared to impose their will, ultimately through physical coercion, were at the heart of the territorial state. Machiavelli[45] prudently advised his prince that it was better to be feared than loved on the assumption that someday he might need to terrify recalcitrant citizens into submission. In practical terms, this required loyal fighters prepared to jeopardize their lives in order to perpetuate his ascendancy. Generals have long been aware that rock-solid discipline is decisive on the battlefield. Experience taught that the army that can maintain orderliness in the teeth of danger is apt to triumph. Rulers are, therefore, dependent upon military élan for power. Equally vital to maintaining a government's integrity is the political solidarity that guides the actions of its soldiers (or constabulary). In analyzing the sources of social stratification, Max Weber[46] highlighted the significance of party. He theorized that political alliances were often the key to social control. James Madison[47] implied as much when he warned that political factions rise up as naturally as weeds and need to be controlled if tyranny is to be avoided. Personal relationships among political activists are, therefore, fundamental to attaining and perpetuating social superiority. These must possess a constancy of discipline, especially in an environment where alliances shift with the alacrity of television commercials. Because political combinations need not be grounded in biology, factors that cultivate remote loyalties are essential. This glue may be based on personal interest, tradition, greed, or passionately held beliefs; the options are legion, but they are indispensable.

For this reason an entirely different source of social solidarity can become paramount. Alliances that create interpersonal strength derive not only from personal relationships but also from impersonal commitments. Indeed, moral and religious duties often take precedence over family or private political ties. They provide the impetus for coalitions of greater breadth than those that depend on individual attachments. When people have internalized particular rules, beliefs, or rituals, they thereby acquire a loyalty that transcends time and place. Such mental allegiances may even feel eternal. Depending as they do on emotional, cognitive, and volitional factors that are inherently conservative, they persist long after people consciously decide to jettison them. Violating a deeply held conviction can be experienced as a betrayal of one's very existence; hence it occurs less often than treachery toward friends or relatives. This makes moral and religious convictions an appealing source of social coordination. If people believe the same things, they can dependably collaborate on the same projects—even if they dislike each other, even if they do not know each other.

Just as governments and kinship systems formalize coalitions based on personal relationships, churches and ideologies do the same for moralities and cosmologies. They specify the places where members of the same denomination can assemble, and they stipulate the procedures through which they can affirm their solidarity. For many people, religion is their central identity. They would happily sacrifice their welfare for the spiritual community to which they belong. Perhaps convinced of a heavenly reward for their piety, they may also be motivated by a sense of doing what is right. Either way, established creeds identify what is true and what is good. Established churches provide designated prayer leaders, agreed upon scriptures, and inspirational places of worship. In so doing, they furnish formal procedures that instill emotional and communal assurances of faith. The effectiveness of these can be seen in the sweeping reach of Al Qaeda. From the mountains of Morocco to the rice paddies of Indonesia, millions of Muslims root for its victory over the Great Satan. Utter strangers to one another, as communicants of Islam,[48] they are united against outsiders who do not pray as they do. Believers in the Koran, they are prepared to assist in killing foreigners who are not.

An equivalent cohesion has underwritten theological states such as Iran. Its ayatollahs command military allegiance from volunteers intent on preserving the one true faith. Many tens of thousands of recruits charged into Iraqi machine gun emplacements with the words of the Prophet on their lips. More spectacular still was the religious enthusiasm that fueled Islam's initial conquests. What to the losers of these encounters would have been experienced as unprincipled aggression furnished the victors with proof of a divine sanction. Whereas the nonbelievers perceived such convictions as fanatical conformity, the believers viewed them as portal salvation.

Many secular individuals find this incomprehensible, yet they place their faith in political ideologies that are every bit as conventionalized. An ideology is a formalized belief system that tells its adherents how the world works and specifies what needs to be done to correct its shortcomings. The Communist Party, just as might a church, has functioned as such a quasitheological communion. Its faith, namely communism, explained that the evils of the world owed not to the devil but to the oppressive machinations of capitalists. It similarly promised that all this could be undone, not by being transported to paradise after death, but by constructing a heaven on earth after instigating a sweeping revolution. Arthur Koestler condemned this movement as a "God that failed," and it is more than a metaphor.[49] The Communist Party has had its prayer leaders, sacred texts, and spiritual shrines every bit as much as have the Roman Catholics. Civic morality too can be formalized. In the United States, obeisances are paid to democratic values with as much fervor as the encomia once offered to Lenin. Even the free-market system has been the object of moralized tributes. Libertarians, for example, are fond of extravagant praise of unrestrained market activities. The entrepreneurial heroes of Ayn Rand[50] have been as lavishly glorified as any Christian saint. Weber described this sort of hierarchical priority as status which operates by elevating people for demonstrating deeply admired qualities. Moral champions thus receive prestige for embodying the principles to which their communities are committed. They are respected and, therefore, obeyed. Such power comes not from coercing those below them but from eliciting their voluntary compliance. Moral exemplars, as it were, tap into internalized springs of motivation. They draw upon deeply inculcated drives. As a consequence, people can become social winners if they hit upon ways to instill these impulses. As counterintuitive as it may appear, the divine messenger and the brilliant social forecaster can hold as much sway as the conquering general.

Which brings us to the economic aspects of alliances. People can agree to follow a leader, not merely from fear or inspiration, but for instrumental reasons. If they believe they can profit from joining the winning side, merging with it may indeed tip the balance in its favor. When hunting was the primary source of wealth, the skilled hunter could gain power by distributing his surplus to those who offered support in exchange. When agriculture took over, control of land became more important than mastery of a weapon.[51] Those individuals who could bestow acreage upon which crops could be grown were rewarded with gratitude and fealty. The same applied to those who could protect the harvest from raiders or who could increase the yield by organizing irrigation projects. In each of these cases, a magnate could offer patronage that encouraged loyal adherents. On one level, allegiance was being traded for a straightforward reward, but, on another, this devotion was to become traditional. The squire was the squire, not necessarily because he conferred a benefit but because he and his father had always been squires. His ownership of the land and, therefore, his ability to legitimize a peasant's control over his portion of it was unquestioned. It emanated not from a demonstrated ability to protect or distribute property but from a widespread perception that it was his to allocate. To those born into such a system, it would seem natural. They may even have attributed it to divine providence.

Once the commercial revolution began to accelerate, settled relationships based on land tenure came under challenge. Profits drawn from doing business could be used to purchase estates from an impoverished gentry. Here, too, patronage could come into play, but the benefits to be dispersed derived from commercial opportunities. Merchants whose wealth and connections enabled them to dominate the marketplace could exchange their goodwill for devoted submission. Those with fewer assets conformed for the privilege of sharing in the reflected glory of such a benefactor. Ultimately, clients became employees whose fate was closely attached to the person who paid their wages. This world of the entrepreneur and his associated workforce was the one Marx knew. The goal, as a result, was to disrupt the attachments that provided the boss his social clout. Without compliant subordinates, he would merely be a bloated imposter who could not hold his own in a brawl with the lowliest laborer.

Marx came on the scene just as the Industrial Era was picking up steam. Large-scale factories were coming into existence, but their implications remained uncertain. A growing impersonality was beginning to have a disquieting effect, yet the consequences of mass production and technological progress could not be predicted. That these would change the relationships between bosses and their workers, and hence the shape of their social alliances, was not evident. Amazingly, Marx could not discern the impending preeminence of the middle classes.[52] They, too, seemed to be low-level employees open to as much exploitation as any machine operator. He could not perceive that a dependence on their expertise would change the conditions of their association with their bosses. As far as he was concerned, they remained relatively weak, whereas, in truth, they were accumulating the strengths to alter the balance of power with their superiors.

The alliances of the marketplace were to be further destabilized by the advent of a postindustrial economy. By the time of its arrival, the volume of commerce had expanded to such an extent that keeping its arteries flowing required additional expertise. Complex professional skills,[53] not merely a knack for bookkeeping, were now in demand.

This often put the putative employee in control of the enterprise. Out of touch with what needed to be done to keep their coffers full, bosses depended upon knowledgeable subordinates to direct their businesses. Many of the old alliances remained intact but not on the same terms. The emergence of the middle classes dramatically altered the contours of social dominance. There was still an upper class, but its writ did not extend as far as it had. Weber, like Marx, was aware that class was a crucial determinate of social stratification; nevertheless, he too missed these developments. Focused on the advent of bureaucratic organizations, he perceived these as fashioning an iron cage that would hold employees immobile. The formalized regulations constraining their jobs would prevent them from exercising initiative. But this was not how things turned out. The arrival of extensive professionalization[54] would once again change the ground rules. It would offer freedom and creativity on a scale perhaps dreamt of but never before realized. A self-directed expertise would guide the development of coalitions that literally remade the world. Hierarchy would not disappear,[55] but power would be more broadly diffused than ever, that is, at least since hunter-gatherer times. Despite a rising chorus complaining about oppression, the opposite was more nearly true.

Middle Class Powers

In the entrepreneurial universe that Mills suggests preceded the nation's descent into a white-collar nightmare, individual proprietors controlled private businesses. They owned their tools, places of employment, and profits. Ben Franklin was a prototype of this sort of businessperson. Starting from nothing, he accrued the funds to purchase a printing press and to finance its operation. A few journeymen and apprentices worked for him, but he was in control of the enterprise. Franklin believed in hard work. Because the fruits of his labor were exclusively within his control, what he did was for himself and his family. Though notoriously thrifty, through perseverance he acquired the resources to achieve a stout independence. In his world, ownership spurred initiative. It motivated him to do well because he was in charge of his exertions and was the chief beneficiary of performing them well. On top of his own little mountain, he ruled his domain to suit himself.

This was all well and good several hundred years ago, but how can responsible authority endure in today's less personalized world? In an industrial and now post-industrial economy, is it possible to motivate leaders to do competent jobs when they do not own their companies? Given the emergence of huge impersonal agglomerations in which ownership is detached from management, why do people not slough off? If acquisitive proprietors do not directly supervise them, why do they not cover their tracks by doing just enough to escape blame? In fact, most do not. Productivity is higher in the modern world than it has ever been. The solution to this paradox is found in the progress of the middle classes. Their power derives largely from an ability to be self-motivated. Not only do they know what they are doing, but they can be trusted to do it without close supervision. Important social decisions have been delegated to them because they make good choices followed up by sound implementation.[56] But why is this so? Why, if they are not proprietors, do they care?

First, let us consider today's managers. For the most part not proprietors, they regard themselves as professional administrators.[57] Corporations organized as bureaucracies hire them to occupy these positions. They do so in the conviction that they are self-starters who will pursue the organization's interests with as much dedication as would its titleholders. In this, their superiors are rarely disappointed. For the most part, modern executives pride themselves on producing healthy bottom lines and growing market shares. Although the majority is scions of the middle and working classes, they spend years grooming themselves for the responsibilities of command. Having, often from childhood, dreamt of becoming successes, they are unwilling to wreck their opportunities through neglect or ineptitude.

Particularly revealing is how prospective supervisory personnel prepare for their roles. Even those who attain their positions through family connections are likely to have been formally instructed in their duties. Contemporary managers are generally the product of college educations. Many boast not just bachelor's degrees, but a masters in business administration. Working one's way up to the executive suite from an apprenticeship on the shop floor was once the stuff of romantic legend, but no more. A mania for professionalism has swept into the front office, as it has in most seats of power. Fredrick

Taylor's[58] Scientific Management is today accepted gospel. A century ago it may have been necessary to proselytize on its behalf; nowadays, it is assumed that leadership requires an expertise analogous to that of an electronic engineer.

The paradigm of the professional is the physician.[59] Medical doctors habitually rank toward the top of surveys of occupational prestige. They are admired and trusted so greatly that stereotypical mothers routinely urge their children to study hard enough to get into medical school. Physicians actually occupy one of the first jobs designated a profession. The concept comes from the notion that theirs was a calling. God instilled the motivation to help mankind into their souls, and they responded to his command. As a result of this divine mandate, they could be counted upon to devote their abilities and energies to doing their best. When one went to the doctor, one did not have to worry that the level of service would be commensurate with the fee paid. Though one was feeling vulnerable from disease, the doctor voluntarily risked his life rather than do harm. One did not need to fear that he/she would depart in the middle of an operation on a beautiful day for golf.

This sort of dedication was implanted via an extended period of socialization. To begin with, physicians underwent an extraordinary technical education. The knowledge needed to become a competent healer was so all embracing and so demanding that it took years of devoted study to acquire. In its current manifestation this entails four years of college, four years of medical school, and perhaps another four years of training in a board-certified specialty. Even afterwards, the learning continues. Physicians are expected to read professional journals, to attend seminars in new techniques, and to participate in conferences of like-minded practitioners. Many also contribute to advances in medical knowledge by engaging in research. They are not allowed to rest on their laurels but must remain on the cutting edge of science.

More than this, the discomfort of their education is so great as to constitute rites of passage. Years of arduous scholarship and long hours of stressful practice are not for the faint of heart. Only the most committed persist in the quest, and, when they complete it, they discover that their personal identity has been transformed. Much as the rigors of an initiation ceremony convert college freshmen into steadfast members of fraternities, so having survived the harsh demands of medical training modifies a person's mindset. Emotionally and intellectually reoriented, the newly minted physician feels the part. He/she has internalized the goals of the profession and now pursues them as a matter of course. A failure to do so would henceforth violate his/her sense of self and be perceived as an intolerable breakdown. This newfound motivation is what enables physicians to be trusted. Technical skills, without the commitment to apply them conscientiously, are useless. Alone they would not warrant the authority bestowed on professionals.

Other professionals partake of a similar, if less painstaking, socialization.[60] They too develop technical competence and internalized motivation. Lawyers, college professors, and mechanical engineers are all allowed to operate independently on the assumption that they are prepared to make the decisions within their span of control. To be concrete, engineers are relied upon to make the mathematical calculations regarding whether a bridge can endure the stresses to which it will be subjected. Having studied how materials such as steel stand up to wind and weight, they are expected to come up with the correct answer. This they generally do because they were thoroughly indoctrinated in their specialties and because they are loath to surrender their reputations to momentary lapses in judgment.

Professionals are also participants in professional communities; a primary source of social support comes from members of their vocation. These peers are the best adjudicators of their competence and the most strongly motivated to provide solidarity. In the same boat, they have an interest in guarding hard-won prerogatives. Principally through professional associations, they maintain the contacts that enable them to coordinate the defense of their separate and joint welfare. Natural allies, their individual powers, when linked in a common cause, can be fearsome. Should their goals coalesce in the same direction, they possess the power to make their wills felt throughout society. Indeed, they generally have the clout to make their desires felt within the local organizations in which they are increasingly embedded. The bureaucrats who are their official bosses tend to listen. Whether in hospitals, HMOs, colleges, or law firms, they have considerable influence over their daily routines. Despite legitimate complaints over a loss of autonomy, their voices are more persuasive than those of nonprofessionals. All of this translates into muscle that elevates their status over those who cannot compete with their authority.

To return to managers, as noted above, their middle-class power also benefits from professionalization. The point of becoming better educated is to acquire a comparable expertise and a similar reputation for reliability. Having more or less achieved this, executives are as likely to identify with their fellow professionals as with old-line entrepreneurs. This increases middle-class influence overall. Even the salespersons that Mills so casually dismissed benefit from these trends. He portrays them as shallow ciphers, but fewer of them are clerks in charge of ringing up retail transactions. Merchandising, especially on the industrial level, has become a specialty operation. Its practitioners not only need an expertise in their products but skill in communicating with potential customers. They must have the sophistication to understand others' goals and the patience to deal with their psychological quirks. This is not easy. It involves far more than smiling vacantly and repeating a sales pitch transmitted from a distant proprietor. Getting a liberal college education goes a long way to producing the personal flexibility necessary to cope with the uncertainties of face-to-face commerce with strangers.

Ironically even entrepreneurs have been professionalizing. They, too, understand that they must operate within a middle-class milieu. This requires that they sometimes play the games of those upon whose services they depend. If they somehow escaped exposure to the language and ethos of the Middle Class Revolution, they would soon find themselves adrift in a sea of consumers whose needs they could not fathom and of production assistants whose skills remained a mystery. Under these conditions, how would they make money? Who would buy what they manufactured or operate the machines that assemble their products? As a result, they, too, get college educations or, failing this, rely on their family ties to socialize them in middle-class mores. Bill Gates[61] famously dropped out of Harvard, but his compulsive envelopment in a computer culture, plus a father who was a successful lawyer, provided what was necessary to launch Microsoft. Better educated, but part of the same community of influence, were the founders of Federal Express and Amazon.com.

They too exercised middle-class powers honed in academic settings to rise to the top.

Endnotes

[1] Marx, K. and F. Engels. [1848] 1935. *The Communist Manifesto,* in Selected *Works.* London: Lawrence and Wishart.

[2] de Tocqueville, A. 1966. *Democracy in America,* translated by George Lawrence. New York: Harper & Row.

[3] Madsen, A. 2001. *John Jacob Astor: America's First Multimillionaire.* New York: John Wiley & Sons.

[4] James, H. 1909. *The Portrait of a Lady.* New York: Modern Library.

[5] Packard, V. 1959. *The Status Seekers.* New York: D. McKay Co.

[6] Fussell, P. 1983. *Class: A Guide Through the American Status System.* New York: Simon & Schuster

[7] Epstein, J. 2002. *Snobbery: The American Version.* Boston, MA: Houghton Mifflin Co.; Epstein, J. 2003. *Envy: The Seven Deadly Sins.* New York: Oxford University Press

[8] de Waal, F. 1989. *Peacekeeping Among Primates.* Cambridge, MA: Harvard University Press; de Waal, F. (Ed.) 2001b. *Tree of Origin: What Primate Behavior Can Tell Us about Human Social Evolution.* Cambridge: Harvard University Press.

[9] de Waal, F. 1982. *Chimpanzee Politics.* New York: Harper & Row.

[10] Bendix, R. and S.M. Lipset. (Eds.) 1953. *Class, Status, and Power: Social Stratification in Comparative Perspective.* New York: The Free Press; Giddens, A. 1973. *The Class Structure of the Advanced Societies.* New York: Harper & Row; Gilbert, D. and J.A. Kahl. 1993. *The American Class Structure.* Fourth Edition. Belmont, CA: Wadsworth Publishing.

[11] Montefiore, S.S. 2004. *Stalin: The Court of the Red Tsar.* New York: Alfred A. Knopf; Payne, R. 1965. *The Rise and Fall of Stalin.* New York: Avon Books.

[12] Jagger, A.M. 1988. *Feminist Politics and Human Nature.* Totowa, NJ: Rowman & Littlefield.

[13] Cronk, L. 1999. *That Complex Whole: Culture and the Evolution of Human Behavior.* Boulder, CO: Westview Press; Cronk, L., N. Chanon, and W. Irons. (Eds.) 2000. *Adaptation and Human Behavior: An Anthropological Perspective.* New York: Aldine de Gruyter; Boehm, C. 1999. *Hierarchy in the Forest: The Evolution of Egalitarian Behavior.* Cambridge, MA: Harvard University Press; de Waal, F. 2001a. *The Ape and the Sushi Master: Cultural Reflections of a Primatologist.* New York: Basic Books.

[14] Toennies, F. 1966. (1887) *Community and Society.* New York: Harper Row; Lofland, L.H. 1973. *A World of Strangers.* New York: Basic Books.

[15] Malthus, T.M. 1926. [1798] *First Essay on Population.* New York: St. Martin's Press.

[16] Tiger, L. 1970. *Men in Groups.* New York: Vintage Books.

[17] Tiger, L. and H.T. Fowler. (Eds.) 1978. *Female Hierarchies*. Chicago, IL; Beresford Book Service; Fisher, H. 1982. *The Sex Contract: The Evolution of Human Behavior*. New York: William Morrow and Co.; Tannen, D. 1990. *You Just Don't Understand: Women and Men in Conversation*. New York: William Morrow and Co.

[18] Diamond, J. 1997. *Guns, Germs, and Steel: The Fates of Human Societies*. New York: W.W. Norton and Co.

[19] Schama, S. 1989. *Citizens: A Chronicle of the French Revolution*. New York: A. Knopf.

[20] Smaje, C. 2000. *Natural Hierarchies: The Historical Sociology of Race and Caste*. Oxford: Blackwell Publishers; Dumanont, L. 1980. [1966] *Homo Hierarchicus: The Caste System and Its Implications*. Chicago, IL: University of Chicago Press; Willie, C.V. 1979. *Caste and Class Controversy*. New York: General Hall.

[21] Collier, P. and D. Horowitz. 1976. *The Rockefellers: An American Dynasty*. New York: Holt, Rinehart & Winston.

[22] Epstein, J. 2002. *Snobbery: The American Version*. Boston: Houghton Mifflin Co.

[23] Eisenstadt, S.N. 1971. *Social Differentiation and Stratification*. Glencoe, IL: Scott, Foresman; Kerbo, H.R. 1996. *Social Stratification and Inequality*. Third Edition. New York: McGraw-Hill; Hurst, C.E. 1995. *Social Inequality: Forms, Causes, and Consequences*. Second Edition. Boston, MA: Allyn and Bacon; Kahl, J.A. 1967. *The American Class Structure*. New York: Holt, Rinehart and Winston; Diehl, M.W. (Ed.) 2000. *Hierarchies in Action: Cui Bono?* Carbondale, IL: Center for Archeological Investigations; Sidanius, J and F. Pratto. 1999. *Social Dominance: An Intergroup Theory of Social Hierarchy and Oppression*. Cambridge: Cambridge University Press; Tumen, M.M. 1985. *Social Stratification: The Forms and Functions of Inequality*. Upper Saddle River, NJ: Prentice-Hall.

[24] Barnes, B. 1988. *The Nature of Power*. Chicago: The University of Illinois Press; Boone, J. 1992. "Competition, Conflicts and the Development of Social Hierarchies," in E. Smith and B. Winterhalter, (Eds.) *Evolutionary Ecology and Human Behavior*. New York: Aldine de Gruyter; Ludwig, A.M. 2002. *King of the Mountain: The Nature of Political Leadership*. Lexington: University of Kentucky Press; Fein, M. 2001 *Race and Morality: How Good Intentions Undermine Social Justice and Perpetuate Inequality*. New York: Kluwer/Plenum; McClelland, D. 1975. *Power: The Inner Experience*. New York: Irvington Publishing; Whyte, W.F. 1943. *Street Corner Society*. Chicago, IL: University of Chicago Press; Anderson, E. 1999. *Code of the Street: Decency, Violence, and the Moral Life of the Inner City*. New York: W.W. Norton & Co.; Banfield, E.C. 1961. *Political Influence: A New Theory of Urban Politics*. New York: The Free Press; Clausewitz, C. 1908. *On War*. New York: Penguin Books; Sun-tzu 1988. (6th Century BC) *The Art of War*, translated by Thomas

Cleary. Boston, MA: Shambala; Dye, T.R. 1975. *Power and Society: An Introduction to the Social Sciences.* Belmont, CA: Wadsworth Publishing; Lenski, G. 1966. *Power and Privilege: A Theory of Social Stratification.* New York: McGraw-Hill.

25 Potter, J.M. 2000. "Ritual, Power, and Social Differentiation in Small-Scale Societies," in Diehl, M.W., *Hierarchies in Action: Cui Bono?* Carbondale, IL: Center For Archaeological Investigations; Goffman, E. 1959. *The Presentation of Self in Everyday Life.* Garden City: Doubleday and Co.

26 Hughes, E.C. 1958. *Men and Their Work.* New York: Free Press of Glencoe.

27 Bourdieu, P. 1990. *The Logic of Practice.* Stanford, CA: Stanford University Press; Lorenz, K. 1966. *On Aggression.* London: Metheun.

28 Larson, M.S. 1977. *The Rise of Professionalism: A Sociological Analysis.* Berkeley: University of California Press.

29 Shirer, W.L. 1960. *The Rise and Fall of the Third Reich.* New York: Simon & Schuster.

30 Montefiore, S.S. 2004. *Stalin: The Court of the Red Tsar.* New York: Alfred A. Knopf.

31 Williams, T.H. 1952. *Lincoln and His Generals.* New York: Alfred A. Knopf.

32 Hamilton, E. 1958. *The Greek Way.* New York: W.W. Norton & Co.; Herodotus 1954. *The Histories,* translated by Aubery de Selincourt. Harmondworth, UK: Penguin Books; Thucydides. 1998. *The Peloponnesian War,* translated by Walter Blanco. New York: W.W. Norton & Co.

33 Hanson, V.D. 2001. *Carnage and Culture: Landmark Battles in the Rise of Western Power.* New York: Doubleday.

34 Caesar, J. [1967] *The Civil War,* translated by Jane Gardner. New York: Dorset Press.

35 Durkheim, E. 1915. *The Elementary Forms of Religious Life.* New York: The Free Press; Armstrong, K. 1993. *A History of God: The 4000-Year Quest of Judaism, Christianity and Islam.* New York: Ballantine Books; Armstrong, K. 2000. *The Battle for God.* New York: Alfred A. Knopf; Augustine, Saint. 1961. *Confessions,* translated by R.S. Pine-Coffin. New York: Dorset Press; Thomas, R.M. 1997. *Moral Development Theories—Secular and Religious.* Westport, CT: Greenwood Press.

36 Sumner, W.G. 1960. *Folkways.* New York: New American Library.

37 Crozier, M. 1964. *The Bureaucratic Phenomenon.* Chicago: University of Chicago Press.

38 Morin, R. 1969. *Dwight D. Eisenhower: A Gauge of Greatness.* New York: Simon & Schuster.

39 Swartz, D. 1997. *Culture and Power: The Sociology of Pierre Bourdieu.* Chicago, IL: University of Chicago Press.

[40] de Waal, F. 1996. *Good Natured: The Origins of Right and Wrong in Humans and Other Animals.* Cambridge, MA: Harvard University Press; Katz, L.D. (Ed.) 2000. *Evolutionary Origins of Morality: Cross-Disciplinary Perspectives.* Bowling Green, OH: Imprint Academic.

[41] Boone, J.L. 2000. "Status Signaling. Social Power, and Lineage Survival," in Diehl, M.W. *Hierarchies in Action: Cui Bono?* Carbondale, IL: Center For Archaeological Investigations.

[42] Manchester, W. 1992. *A World Lit Only By Fire: The Medieval Mind and the Renaissance.* Boston, MA: Little, Brown & Co.; Pirenne, H. 1936. *Economic and Social History of Medieval Europe.* New York: Harcourt, Brace & World; Duby, G. 1983. *The Knight, The Lady, and the Priest: The Making of Modern Marriage in Medieval France.* New York: Pantheon Books.

[43] Putnam, R.D. 1993. *Making Democracy Work: Civic Traditions in Modern Italy.* Princeton, NJ: Princeton University Press.

[44] Collier, P. and D. Horowitz. 1984. *The Kennedys: An American Drama.* New York: Summit Books.

[45] Machiavelli, N. 1966. *The Prince,* translated by Daniel Donnos. New York: Bantam Books.

[46] Weber, M. 1947. *The Theory of Social and Economic Organization.* New York: Free Press; Gerth, H. and C.W. Mills. (Eds.) 1946. *From Max Weber: Essays in Sociology.* New York: Oxford University Press.

[47] Madison, J, A. Hamilton, and J. Jay. 2000. *The Federalist Papers.* London: Phoenix Press.

[48] Mortimer, E. 1982. *Faith and Power: The Politics of Islam.* New York: Random House; Spencer, R. 2003. *Onward Muslim Soldiers: How Jihad Still Threatens America and the West.* Washington DC: Regnery Publishing.

[49] Crossman, R.H. (Ed.) *The God That Failed.* 1963. New York: Harper& Row.

[50] Rand, A. 1966. *Capitalism: The Unknown Ideal.* New York: New American Library; Rand, A. 1992. *Atlas Shrugged.* New York: Dutton.

[51] Wittfogel, K.A. 1957. *Oriental Despotism: A Comparative Study of Total Power.* New Haven: Yale University Press.

[52] Hughes, E.C. 1958. *Men and Their Work.* New York: Free Press of Glencoe.

[53] Larson, M.S. 1977. *The Rise of Professionalism: A Sociological Analysis.* Berkeley: University of California Press.

[54] Vollmer, H. and D. Mills. (Eds.) 1968. *Professionalization.* Englewood Cliffs, NJ: Prentice-Hall.

[55] Tilly, C. 1998. *Durable Inequality.* Berkeley: University of California Press.

[56] Simon, H.A. 1947. *Administrative Behavior.* New York: MacMillan.

[57] Greenwood, E. 1957. "Attributes of a Profession." *Social Work*, II, 3, July.

[58] Taylor, F.W. 1911. *The Principles of Scientific Management.* New York: Harper and Brothers.

[59] Starr, P. 1982. *The Social Transformation of American Medicine.* New York: Basic Books.

[60] Hall, R.H. 1975. *Occupations and the Social Structure.* Englewood Cliffs, NJ: Prentice-Hall, Inc.

[61] Klein, M. 2003. *The Change Makers; From Carnegie to Gates.* New York: Times Books; Wallace, J. 1993. *Hard Drive: Bill Gates and the Making of the Microsoft Empire.* New York: HarperBusiness.

Chapter 3

A Way of Life

You could not step twice into the same rivers, for other waters are forever flowing in to you. (Heraclitus, <u>On the Universe</u>)

Socrates: A Simple thing enough; just what is commonly said, that a man should be temperate and master of himself, the ruler of his own pleasures and passions. (Plato, <u>The Gorgias</u>)

A decent boldness ever meets with friends. (Homer, <u>The Odyssey</u>)

What Do You Want to Be?

The choices used to be simple. When asked what they wanted to be when they grew up, children would answer a policeman, a cowboy, or a mommy. Later on were added the options of an astronaut, an athlete, a rock star, or the first woman president. Adults, of course, knew that this menu was too short. Having been forced to make a concrete selection, they learned firsthand how broad the span of potential employments is. They also discovered that most of the available selections were not visible from their earlier vantage points. When they were children, a few of the most salient professions attracted their attention. The simple, the dramatic, and the newsworthy got noticed despite limited experience, whereas most of the positions they would one day occupy were not so much as suspected. Only as they grew older did they ascertain their existence of these new roles or their attributes.

Ours is a world filled with hundreds of thousands of distinct occupations. Indeed, the federal register, <u>The Dictionary of Occupational Titles</u>,[1] is the size of a phone book. Many thousands of distinct trades crowd its pages and boggle the mind with surprising details. This multiplicity began to attract attention years ago. As sociology was becoming a separate discipline, pioneers such as Herbert Spencer[2] and Emile Durkheim[3] discerned the degree to which modernization had swollen the number of specialties. Spencer even theorized that this was a driving force behind emerging forms of social organization. He explained that newfangled spheres of expertise required more sophisticated means of integration, which, in turn, changed the nature of how people lived. Durkheim elaborated upon this insight by discussing the implications of a convoluted division of labor. He insisted that vocational interdependence altered the way that people networked. They now cooperated with each other not merely because they were similarly motivated but because what they contributed to the whole was dependent upon what their peers added to the mix. Without an awareness of, and a respect for, this mutual dependence, all would suffer. Like a large multicelled animal, society was composed of separate organs each of which collaborated with the others so that the entire organism could survive. Farmers refusing to feed city folk or city folk declining to assemble tractors, would be as if the heart refused to pump blood to the lungs or the lungs declined to aerate the blood for the heart.

The extent of this mutual reliance can be determined from an overview of the health professions. Ensconced in one of the fastest growing segments of the economy, these have proliferated in manifold directions. Increasingly, technologically advanced, they reveal a pattern of integration replicated many times over in other occupations. Among the pursuits enumerated by the Bureau of Labor Statistics[4] under the heading of Healthcare Practitioners are

> *Chiropractors, dentists, dieticians and nutritionists, optometrists, pharmacists, anesthesiologists, family and general practitioners, internists, obstetricians and gynecologists, pediatricians, psychiatrists, surgeons, physician assistants, registered nurses, audiologists, occupational therapists, radiation therapists, recreational therapists, respiratory therapists, speech-language pathologists, veterinarians, medical and clinical laboratory technologists, medical and clinical laboratory technicians, dental hygienists, cardiovascular technologists and technicians, diagnostic medical sonographers, nuclear medicine*

technologists, radiological technologists and technicians, emergency medical technicians and paramedics, dietetic technicians, pharmacy technicians, psychiatric technicians, respiratory therapy technicians, surgical technologists, veterinary technologists and technicians, licensed practical and licensed vocational nurses, medical records and health information technicians, dispensing opticians, orthotists and prosthetists, occupational health and safety specialists and technicians, and athletic trainers.

As extensive as this inventory is, it does not include personnel such as nursing aides. These are listed elsewhere under healthcare support occupations. Nor does it itemize the jealously guarded subspecialties found among internists and laboratory technologists. Podiatrists, sports doctors, dermatologists, plastic surgeons, or serologists are not among these enumerated. Nor does this compendium indicate the vigor with which distinct turfs are defended. A tour of any psychiatric hospital would reveal that psychiatrists insist on maintaining a separate identity from psychologists and that psychologists grow huffy when confused with social workers. For that matter, diagnostic specialists are as adamant about distinguishing themselves from clinicians as PhDs are from EdDs. Those unfamiliar with this minefield of distinctions can set off skirmishes by trampling on the sensibilities of competitors intent on protecting the dignities of their own terrains.

This endless expansion of specialties has several consequences. One is that the occupants of each niche become expert in their domain of operation. Individuals whose attentions are concentrated within a narrow scope can become quite skilled. They have the time and the energies to uncover obscure facts that might escape the notice of others. They also have the space to become proficient in their applications. A full-time cardiovascular surgeon is sufficiently intimate with the architecture of the heart to achieve the dexterity to replace a defective valve. In order to maintain control over their domains, these specialists are also motivated to stay ahead of potential rivals. New knowledge and skills are developed to insure that chiropractors or hypnotists do not encroach on medical territories with their nonsurgical techniques. Specialization, in other words, provides the impetus to professionalization. An ever-elaborating division of labor is a spur to increased expertise and superior performance.

Another consequence of more finely divided occupational territories is the need to harmonize activities among adjacent specialties. The surgeon who does not know how to join forces with an anesthesiologist is likely to be incompetent. This means that the players must possess rudimentary knowledge about one another's contributions. As role partners,[5] they learn that this is the only way to be responsive to one another's tasks. Moreover, with knowledge goes respect, and this respect goes a long way toward fostering good will. Those who are too provincial in their interests tend to become isolated and ineffective. Put another way, a professionalized world is of necessity a cosmopolitan one.

Besides enhanced expertise and improved cooperation, a highly developed division of labor tends to produce internalized motivation. Because the participants are engaged in tasks that few others comprehend, they must be their own supervisors. If the manufacturers do not care about turning out quality products, they would lack the impetus to do so would be lacking, and the entire social edifice might collapse. As a result, the incentive to internalize personal determination is very strong. Society as a whole has an interest in ensuring that practitioners such as physicians are individually driven to serve their patients hence the comprehensive training demanded of them. Hence also social licensure, which can be subject to withdrawal in cases of demonstrable ineptitude. Not all occupations are sensitive to personal incompetence, but even the motormen who operate subway trains need to be alert to their duties. If they do not care enough to refrain from substance abuse, the potential for carnage is acute. As a consequence, individuals are vetted to determine their private habits before they are hired for these positions.

With so many jobs subject to elaboration, the modern world is ablaze with change. So great is the turnover that it has become a cliché to bemoan its instability. At the beginning of the Commercial Revolution, the Greek sophist Heraclitus taught that one could not step in the same river twice. Before one had an opportunity to lift one's leg, the water rushed past and could not be brought back. In this, he was warning of a social environment in constant flux. As a wise man for hire, he had a job to teach clients to cope with the requirements of emerging democracies. Since many of them, as citizens, would be obliged to plead cases before courts composed of their fellow citizens, they needed to understand things from their judges' perspectives. Were they inflexible, they might offend the very people upon whom their fate depended.

Commerce and competition having progressed far beyond that of Ancient Greece, and the scale of change has grown apace.[6] Technologies and merchandizing techniques mutate before our eyes. No sooner has one become accustomed to soft cream cheese than it is flavored with onions and chives. Merchandisers are ever intent upon moving the fruits and vegetables around the produce section of the supermarket. They have discovered that if they shift their locations, customers are forced to pay closer attention and, in the process, alight on items they had not intended to purchase. All this unrest, amazingly, is for relatively unchangeable products. Other commodities have the added fillip of themselves mutating. With electronics, the rate of discovery produces innovations almost hourly. Virtually everyone old enough to vote can remember when mobile phones were a novelty, yet each year they keep getting smaller. These days many cell phones boast the ability to transmit voice and pictures, a capacity beyond Dick Tracy's once magical wrist radio. So common have these contraptions become that they have modified how people conduct business. Salespersons, for instance, can have instant communications with their front offices even while driving, so can mothers with their children and wives with their husbands. Spouses are now effortlessly instructed to pick up Chinese takeout on their ways home from work.

All this turmoil has placed a premium on being able to adjust. There was a time when every son knew he would grow up to be a farmer and every daughter that she would raise children and keep house. More recently, factory workers understood that once hired by U.S. Steel, they would enjoy steady employment for the rest of their careers. On the home front, they correspondingly recognized that marriage was for life. Expected to be loyal both to their companies and to their spouses, they expected reciprocal loyalty. Today, of course, corporations relocate to foreign climes, and love lasts as long as it takes one of the partners to crave self-discovery. Those who cannot distinguish when the earth has moved beneath their feet or who lack the suppleness to move with it find these dislocations painful. Unwavering in their resolve to live by the rules of their childhood, they may, as a result, descend into poverty and isolation.

Another kind of change derives from the omnipresence of diversity. Society has become a patchwork quilt of disparate cultures, ethnicities, and races. Those conversant with history will be aware of previous eras when ethnic migrations changed the composition of Europe. The collapse of the Roman Empire[7] signaled a period of unrest during which Germanic tribes, such as the Lombards, Vandals, and Visigoths, removed from homelands adjacent to Scandinavia and took up residence in Italy, Spain, and Tunisia.[8] This passage is still recorded in place names such as Lombardy and Andalusia. Ours is an era of even greater transience. More people are moving than ever before. They are going longer distances and staying put for shorter durations. The difference now is that they are moving as individuals and families rather than as tribal units.

In a world in which the demands of commerce have improved transportation and communication to previously unrecognizable levels, emigration has become normal. People not only move from one country to another but also within the same one. Clearly, the African diaspora altered the complexion of the New World, as did a European diaspora before it.[9] These brought Negroids and Caucasoids to a continent formerly inhabited solely by Mongoloids. Today, Hispanics are moving north from Mexico and South America, and Asians are traveling east from India and China. Americans have grown accustomed to migrants crossing their borders, but so have the Spanish, Germans, and British. Where once it was French colonialists who overran Algeria, and British sahibs who lorded it over Indians, the direction of traffic has reversed. Nor is the volume of resettlement declining. Mestizos continue to be smuggled over the Mexican border, and Muslims persist in entering Christian strongholds.

Yet, internal migrations dwarf this international traffic.[10] At the time of the American Revolution, New York City had a population of barely twenty thousand.[11] Its numbers were soon swamped by a comparable number of invading British troops. Today's overflowing urbanism is a gift of the Industrial Revolution. This upheaval prompted an urban stampede that has now been replaced by suburban sprawl. Rural populations have long since decamped for places where there were jobs. To illustrate, between World War II and the end of the twentieth century, the sleepy depot town of Atlanta grew more than ten times in size. Because of its location at a transportation hub, as commerce increased, so did the need for those who managed the traffic. This transformed the North Georgia mountains from an Appalachian backwater into a supplier of human capital. More than this, once it became customary to move from the farm to the city, it became acceptable to move from one city to another in search of a better job. These days, Atlanta is inhabited by hordes of damn Yankees who have transformed its ambience. Likewise, throngs of former Southerners have emigrated to Los Angeles to return the favor. The United States has become a nation of gypsies who, on average, move every seven years, often going much farther afield than from one neighborhood to an adjacent, more affluent one.

The resultant diversity has placed a strain on those comfortable only with their ancestral environments. Contemporary Americans require a more expansive view. Living and doing business with people who were formerly strangers demands flexibility. Fortunately, the qualities needed to adjust to a multitude of intersecting occupations are useful in accommodating a swarm of exotic neighbors. People talk of becoming tolerant when they really mean they are becoming ecumenical. Southerners now understand that Northerners can be decent people, and vice versa. Nor do Mexicans, despite linguistic differences, seem subhuman. Just as a greater division of labor prompted broader horizons, so has the mixing of populations. Bigotry is universally condemned, but its comparative rarity is not fully appreciated. Nor is it recognized that middle class dominance has contributed to this achievement. People who are concerned with amassing money and power cannot afford to reject potential customers, or coworkers, merely because they are superficially different.

To sum up, the modern world is astonishingly more complex and varied than its predecessors.[12] Filled with surprises and uncertainties, it exemplifies the fact that that which can instantly change presents significant challenges. Under these circumstances, people are often compelled to act without knowing what is best. Those who would be their leaders are, therefore, hard-pressed to provide reliably constructive plans and coordination. Yet, to do less would risk injury to themselves and to those dependent upon them. This is the social emergency the middle class way of life has evolved to meet. The skills, attitudes, and values it promotes were adopted within this diversified, ever-mutating milieu.[13] Furthermore, were its members unable to cope with these complexities, they could not sustain their own status. Power derived from competent marketplace stewardship would vanish were it overwhelmed by unpredictable exigencies. What then are the capacities required to survive such difficulties? Though these are varied, central among them is an ability to be self-directed.[14] Those who would specialize in contemporary leadership must be able to make independent determinations even when they are not certain of what is optimal. To do so, they must be confident and competent; but above all, they must be their own people. Each must possess an internal compass and the emotional and intellectual resources to follow it.

Self Direction

Mark Twain is reported to have declared that golf is a good walk ruined. He could not understand why anyone would want to contaminate the beauty of a park like setting by indulging in one of the most frustrating pursuits ever invented. Nevertheless golf has become the favorite diversion of American presidents. Even duffers like Lyndon Baines Johnson felt compelled to take to the links, if for no other reason than to heighten the perception of the presidential qualities. Certainly, since Dwight Eisenhower, it has been recognized that golf is the quintessential middle-class activity. Unlike bowling, which has more plebian connotations, golf is indelibly associated with the country-club set and the informal business meeting. Somehow, the sorts of behavior called forth by hitting a small sphere down a well-manicured lawn is regarded as an indicator of status. It appears to bespeak a decorum that goes well with power.

This is in stark contrast with how things were during the Middle Ages.[15] The kings of yore felt obliged to demonstrate their credentials by periodically participating in joust. They would don richly embellished plate armor and enter the lists, as might any self-respecting member of the aristocracy. So enticing was the prospect of demonstrating military prowess that they risked death to achieve it. Some, in fact, died in the process. This was the fate of Henry II of France, who perished when a lance pierced his helm and lodged a splinter in his brain. These days, this sort of bravery is no longer honored. Presidents do not have to prove their military courage. They may be commanders-in-chief of the armed forces, but they are not expected to lead from front lines. Instead required to exercise sound judgment, these must show the nerve to look danger squarely in the eye; that is what is venerated. That is what brings victory now.

Golf is associated with these qualities because it requires internalized controls. Just as Twain intimated, it can be an enormously frustrating endeavor. Hitting the little ball exactly right takes both skill and an ability to maintain one's equilibrium. Even becoming slightly flustered can result in an errant shot. Moreover, one must be patient. One shot may be followed by another, but only after an interval of catching up to its predecessor. This leaves plenty of time to think and plenty of time to second-guess. Bowling, in contrast, offers instant gratification. This working class pastime allows its players the satisfaction of sending wooden pins careening into a backstop. It also offers the pleasing sound of plastic on wood contact and an almost tangible feel of power. Bowling, while it requires personal control, does not do so for nearly as long or under as exasperating conditions. It is golf that tests the mettle of the man or woman; golf that pushes self-control to its limits.

Some years ago Melvin Kohn[16] conducted a series of studies relating work and personality. These began as inquiries into the sorts of values parents expected of their children. He wanted to know if the kind of demands varied with social class. It happens that they do. His investigations uncovered consistent, internationally corroborated correlations. The world around mothers and fathers seeks to instill the same sorts of attitudes that they possess, that is, depending upon their occupational status. Roughly speaking, those in the upper-middle classes favor self-direction, whereas those in the working classes prefer conformity. In diametric opposition to the speculations of C. Wright Mills,[17] Kohn showed that the middling sorts selected innovation over conventionality and personal autonomy over blind obedience.

What Kohn found was that higher status respondents wanted their children to be considerate of others, to be interested in how and why things happened, and to exercise self-control. Lower status parents, however, placed more emphasis on children who had good manners, were neat and clean, and obeyed their parents. Because the former occupied jobs that demanded an understanding of what they did, they groomed their young to deal with similar pressures. The latter, in contrast, found themselves subservient to bosses who demanded compliance, and they unconsciously passed this requirement onto their offspring. While they would never have admitted to promoting conformity, their personal frustrations drove them to issue preemptory commands within the confines of their families.

Let us consider the working conditions of a physician. Kohn describes occupations such as this one as involving substantive complexity and hence intellectual flexibility. On most days, a medical doctor cannot know what problems he/she will encounter. Patients come in with an assortment of complaints that must be diagnosed on the spot. To achieve this, the physician must internalize encyclopedic knowledge about the body and the maladies to which it is prone. This can never be complete, but it must be sufficient to know where to search should further information be needed. Surgeons are under even more stress. Beyond specialized knowledge, they must also possess the manual dexterity to wield scalpels. There may be other specialists in the room to assist in operations, but what is to be cut is at the surgeon's discretion. A surgeon cannot call time out or suddenly plead for a supervisor to take over. In short, surgeons must be personally competent. They may engage in consultations with other surgeons, and those with whom they confer are also professionals. A mere hierarchical superior would be an inappropriate source of advice. What, indeed, could a hospital administrator contribute to an anatomical procedure?

At home, these same surgeons want the best for their children. They understand that professional success depends on developing individualized competence. Because they recognize that discrete credentials allow entry to particular employments, they emphasize getting a good education. But it is also understood that a professional must perform proficiently once on the job. These professionals have learned that being interested in how and why things happen instills a curiosity that pays off in a comprehension of facts that may some day be useful in deciding what to do when the answers are not obvious. Clearly, the more complex the task, the greater the uncertainties; whereas the more knowledgeable the practitioner, the more diverse the options from which to choose. Higher status jobs also require complex interactions with other human beings. One's role partners may be peers or subordinates, but in either case successful coordination is apt to depend on understanding them. Recognizing their motives and capacities facilitates cooperation. Being considerate is thus not merely a matter of respect. Taking account of who people are when soliciting their assistance is crucial. This is, therefore, the sort of psychosocial sophistication middle class parents encourage.

Self-control is also essential for applying knowledge to people and things. A middle class organizer must be suitably self-contained so as to think when thinking is appropriate and to be considerate when consideration is demanded. Going off half-cocked was problematic when this phrase referred to flintlock rifles; it is more so amidst knotty social situations. Kohn, for that reason, suggests that middle class parents support sound judgment, responsibility, and an ability to face facts. They want their progeny to survive under pressure. If a military hegemony celebrated physical courage, middle class endeavors favor social courage. In this case, grace under pressure means keeping one's wits despite the possibility of being blamed should things go wrong. A contemporary leader must be able to look someone in the eye without panicking, irrespective of encircling confusions. This courage with people is not about being physically fearless but about being able to function even when others are upset. Indeed, tests of this facility occur daily within commercial spheres. Under these conditions, individuals who freeze when their authority is questioned cannot be effective planners.

Working class occupations occur under markedly different circumstances. As representative, let us consider an ordinary machine operator. His job may be to stamp out automobile fenders on a huge hydraulic press. Unlike the physician, when he comes to work, he is not in control of his activities. Others, namely his bosses, tell him how many units are required. They also inspect the quality of his work and make suggestions about improving his techniques. Although he may have years of experience, a fresh-faced engineer straight out of college can countermand his decisions. As might be imagined, this is rarely appreciated. It makes a person feel not respected. But what is someone located toward the bottom of the pecking order to do? The answer is very little. He may seethe internally, but this venom cannot be directed above without serious ramifications. As a result, it tends to be displaced downward. Lest it escape notice, downward are to be found his spouse and children. They are subordinate to the man who has endured eight hours of enforced inferiority. Kohn describes the feeling as alienation, but it is also humiliation. No one likes to be on the bottom; no one enjoys feeling like a loser. It is these frustrations that are unleashed upon the family.

The workman who is required to obey a boss all day naturally wants his child to obey him. It would be degrading to feel subordinate to one's offspring. As a consequence, the son or daughter who is too independent is reined in. Doing what one is told, when one is told to do it, is the order of the day, every day. Insolence, even the appearance of insolence, is insufferable; hence the vigor with which impudence is punished. Conformity is inculcated, not for its own sake, but as a means of enforcing deference. Ironically, those who are subservient on the job hate to conform. They do not consciously wish this on their children either, but they impose it, as it were, in self-defense. By the same token, they enforce good manners and neatness and cleanliness, not because they love etiquette, but because they want their youngsters to display the symbols of higher status. Good manners and cleanliness are associated with white- , not blue-collar, jobs. Strangely, middle-class parents are less concerned with these matters, not from a tolerance of filth, but because they expect them to be learned automatically. It is those with dirty jobs and surly coworkers who hope to reverse their destinies.

Surprisingly, Kohn also found lower-status parents more committed to teaching respectability, truthfulness, and success. In addition, they want their children to perform many tasks well. As counterintuitive as this seems, this too is a consequence of relative failure. Those who are not respected crave deference; those surrounded by defensive lies seek truth (from others); those trapped by limited success lust after more; and those constrained by a narrow expertise value an all-encompassing adroitness. They fantasize, as it were, being James Bonds who are at ease in any potential crisis. The trouble is that it is the appearance of these things that is desired. Just as the poor dream of large houses and fancy cars, it is the external signs of success, rather than its internal proficiencies, that are treasured. This is confirmed by the self-conceptions of the respective classes. Those toward the top of the scale exude self-confidence, do not engage in self-deprecation, and are not fatalistic, anxious, or conformist. Meanwhile, those toward the bottom, in marked contrast, do not feel in control. Troubled by self-doubts and haunted by a sense of impotence, they try to compensate by affecting the accoutrements of success at least for external consumption.

Within the privacy of their homes, the self-confidence of social winners is communicated to their young whereas in the houses of losers doubts are transmitted to their progeny. The mechanisms through which this occurs are too numerous to recount, but a sample should do. The middle-class parent, when asked a difficult question, patiently attempts a logical answer couched in terms appropriate to a child's age. The working-class parent, when confronted with a similar query, is more likely to dismiss it as impertinent. In this case, the child is either ignored or attacked for placing his parent in an awkward position. Similarly, the middle-class parent punishes a misdeed by requiring a child to retreat into his/her room to ruminate about it. Told not to come out until she understands why she has been disciplined, she is concurrently being taught how to introspect. The working class parent, in comparison, is apt to resort to a heavier hand. Her child will be struck across a sensitive body part and ordered to desist. He probably will do so, but the resentment will linger. A desire for revenge, rather an understanding of what went wrong, results. The upshot is that the middle-class child internalizes a desire to comply, whereas his inferior is primed to be rebellious. Paradoxically, an education in conformity instills an oppositionalism that makes for mutinous employees. An excessive demand for obedience breeds not leaders but rebels without a cause. Yet, none of this is planned. Neither middle- nor working-class parents are fully conscious of the long-term effects of their actions. They simply react as their life circumstances have prepared them to react.

The self-direction of the middle-classes has the effect of sustaining the decentralization implicit in a social class system. Decision making could not be broadly distributed without a large proportion of the population prepared to make competent, independent determinations. Moreover, many skills and attitudes must be inculcated in childhood if they are to be reliable. Only deeply ingrained orientations provide the steadfast motivations and spontaneous expertise upon which proficiency depends. This applies particularly to emotional and moral dispositions. These may seem trivial, yet without them, the flexibility essential to an advanced commercial society is not possible. What is involved in moral and emotional maturity requires a closer look. But, first, some more general skills must be examined. The question of how the various skills that underwrite middle-class dominance arise must also be resolved.

People Skills

During his travels through the United States, Alexis de Tocqueville[18] was fascinated by the tendency of Americans to be joiners. Unlike in France, here ordinary people spontaneously gathered together to perform acts intended for the common good. Without a government official to order their participation, they might decide to build a school because they collectively concluded one was needed. This was the sort of volunteerism for which Ben Franklin was renowned. Not alone in organizing libraries and fire companies, he exemplified civic initiatives that bespoke the virtual mania for self-help that gripped the nation. De Tocqueville thought this significant. He speculated that these associations were seedbeds of democracy in that they provided opportunities for average people to practice the skills of interpersonal compromise. Communal endeavors demanded that conflicting positions be negotiated, and a knack for this could be transferred to governmental operations where it could allow a wider distribution of authority.

The political scientist Robert Putnam,[19] in studying democratic reforms in Italy, came to the conclusion that the provinces that adapted them most readily were the ones with a tradition of civic involvement. Tuscany, which had long enjoyed self-rule, surged ahead of Sicily, a region that had suffered under despotic aristocrats. Tuscan citizens were better versed in individual initiative and, therefore, more effective in creating grass roots institutions. Turning his attention to his homeland, Putnam[20] argued that a history of civic associations indeed had the effects de Tocqueville theorized. The problem, as

Putnam saw it, was that these habits were eroding. As society grew in size, people were less inclined to join communal projects. The nation was being transformed into an agglomeration of strangers, which boded ill for its democratic foundations. Emblematic of this decline was what seemed to be happening to bowling. Bowling leagues were falling on hard times and he concluded that more people were bowling alone. Instead of coming together with regular associates, they indulged in private pleasures.

In investigating this phenomenon, Putnam speculated that this was a generalized occurrence that everything from religious attendance to participation in the PTA was contracting. For a while, the scholarly debate was heated. In time, however, other investigators found not an absence of civic participation but a shift in its focus.[21] Bowling leagues might have declined in enrollment, but the number of children participating in soccer leagues was increasing. Similarly, main-line churches might be losing their adherents, but evangelical congregations were flourishing. Even the PTA figures were deceptive. This organization turned out to have been captured by the teachers' union; hence, many parents organized competing PA associations that were expanding. The swing seemed to be not so much moving away from combining with others toward going it alone as moving toward associating in ways more appropriate to changed circumstances. One of these circumstances was none other than the burgeoning of the middle classes.

Members of the middle classes remain joiners. They belong to professional organizations, political parties, chambers of commerce, book clubs, sports clubs, neighborhood associations, social clubs, ethnic societies, labor unions, veterans groups, public interest organizations, the Boy and Girl Scouts, and local churches. Volunteering and charitable giving are up, not down. The most popular collaborative efforts no longer back teetotalers or suffragettes but have migrated to the Sierra Club and the American Association of Retired Persons. If bowling went down and soccer went up, it was because soccer was more congenial to a middle class ethos. People also continue to participate in local government. They go to zoning board meetings and vote for school bonds in record numbers. They even run for and were elected to grass-roots institutions such as local school boards.

Civic associations, it must be observed, are noncoercive alliances. People enlist in them not from compulsion, but from personal desire. In so doing, they augment their personal strength in quest of goals they find mutually significant. Nevertheless, they can win struggles of supremacy with competing associations, associations that may have different objectives, only by maintaining cohesion. What makes this solidarity problematic is that these alliances are largely among strangers. Where once hunter-gatherers stood shoulder to shoulder because they were like-minded relatives, modern Americans need to cooperate with people with whom they only share interests. In a mass-market society most affiliations are perforce with relatively unknown associates. Unless these people can find common ground under these conditions, they are destined to fragment. Instead of achieving their goals, they will split into smaller units whose energies will be dissipated in fruitless squabbling.

Francis Fukuyama,[22] another political scientist of note, has emphasized the role of interpersonal trust in these affairs. He argues that in countries like the United States people exhibit a high degree of trust in strangers,[23] whereas in more traditional societies, such as China, they do not. The Chinese, and for that matter the Sicilians, place their confidence in their families. Unfortunately, this interferes with doing business in a market-oriented economy. If people are only willing to engage in commercial transactions with those whom they have known for decades, the scope of their operations will be limited. In this setting, the mass production of an industrial society is impossible. Happily, people with social-class-dominated civilizations routinely make purchases in supermarkets from others with whom they are only casually acquainted. They know that they may occasionally be cheated when a sale price has not been entered into the store's computer, but they also know that these errors are relatively trivial. For the same reason, they are prepared to deposit their paychecks over the Internet. Were they reluctant to do so, the financial infrastructure of the economies on which they rely would unravel, and they would soon find themselves out of work.

What are some of the interpersonal skills that enable people to collaborate in a world full of strangers? One is relatively simple. If they are to organize and inspire one another, they must be able to communicate with each other. In the highlands of New Guinea, tribes living within miles of one another are mutually suspicious, in part, because they speak incomprehensible languages.[24] Multiculturalists dismiss the utility of a lingua franca, but those who would be social mobile must be able to converse with a larger community. Absent a common idiom, they can not make their opinions known beyond their home territory. They definitely can not be persuasive before audiences unable decipher their messages. But from a middle-class perspective, even this is not enough. Those who hope to lead broad coalitions must be articulate. They must command a vocabulary and a clarity of expression that renders them credible. To be well spoken is to be admired, and to be admired is to be influential.

It has become commonplace to refer to ours as an Information Age. But, since most data are transmitted by means of language, information implies competence with words. Furthermore, language is disseminated through channels of communication. One reason information is characterized as central to modernity is that it is conveyed more widely, and effortlessly, than before.[25] The telegraph, the telephone, the radio, the television, and the computer provide instant, worldwide connections. Those who command these can, therefore, commandeer a larger constituency than was previously available. This has thrust the media into the forefront of alliance formation. Those who have access to its channels and are skilled in their manipulation, become opinion leaders. They can persuade strangers to unite behind a popular war or to undermine the prosecution of an unpopular one. It was through these channels that pre-existing commitments to democratic values were appropriated to turn feminism into an intoxicating juggernaut. It was also journalists that convinced millions of viewers that diversity[26] is distinct from affirmative action.[27] Less well appreciated is the fact that the skills to perform this sort of magic is, in large part, cultural skills. They depend on a familiarity not merely with language but with conventionally credible symbols. And as we shall later see, an acquaintance with the subtle connotations of culture is intimately tied with educational and entertainment institutions.

But people skills are also intimate. Individuals become proficient at influencing others when they know where they are coming from. In sociology, this ability is called role taking.[28] Role partners typically coordinate their activities by imaginatively placing themselves in one another's shoes. Thus, a husband who knows that his wife hates to peel onions can do this for her before she asks, thereby gaining her gratitude. Likewise a teacher who detects a student's confusion over algebra can facilitate the learning process by intervening at a critical moment. This roletaking, in turn, depends on a bevy of skills. In order to be responsive to another's intentions, one must first be able to perceive them. To provide a simple example, everyday conversations would be impossible without turn taking.[29] Lest they step on each other's words, speakers must be able to recognize when the other party is about to relinquish the floor. Yet, discerning this depends on having a sense of what the other is saying, in other words, on seeing things from another's perspective. This standpoint cannot be a complete mystery if one's response is to exhibit good timing or a semblance of relevance.

But responsiveness itself is a complex skill one that begins with self-knowledge. Before a person can decode another, he/she must possess insights into the human heart. This, however, commences with self-awareness.[30] Young children tend to be selfish because they act on impulse. If they want something, they want it now, irrespective of the desires of others. Many parents teach them to overcome this egotism by asking how it feels when someone takes a cookie from them. Once children recognize their own potential chagrin, they can be queried about how another child would feel were this is done to them. Obviously the older we get, the more we learn about our own psychodynamics and thereby about the dynamics of those with whom we interact. Some, of course, are better at introspection than others, which gives them a subtle entry into the worlds of their role partners. Long ago, at the beginning of the Commercial Revolution, Socrates recommended self-knowledge to those who would be wise. Even then he understood the value of personal awareness in social relationships.

But, in a world of strangers, self-knowledge is not enough. There are ways in which all humans are alike, but others in which they differ. The more extended the community, the more likely individual motives will vary.[31] Multiculturalists insist on the need to respect diversity, and in this they have a point.[32] They also recommend that people be nonjudgmental, but they take this too far. People need standards. They cannot refuse to make distinctions, for to do so is tantamount to being amoral. Nevertheless, understanding that cultures can be at odds is crucial. Individuals have competing religious beliefs, diverse family arrangements, and conflicting values. One may not agree with a neighbor's love of shish kebab, but a failure to recognize this preference can inevitably result in squabbles. Even the personal circumstances of another's life can produce incomprehensible responses when perceived out of context. A friend's hatred of being confined in tight spaces might appear irrational if it were understood that in growing up he was punished by being confined to a closet. Recognizing these factors permits us to allow for idiosyncrasies. Indeed, one of the more salient differences between adults and children is that the former have a broader range of experiences from which to draw nuanced interpretations.

This subtlety comes in handy in the complex negotiations[33] that permeate contemporary social relations. With so many people pursuing divergent agendas, finding common ground takes extraordinary competence. Engaging in these mediations requires both flexibility and problem solving. If two people are to join in collaborative efforts, they must somehow agree on a unified plan that may vary from what either at first contemplated. Personal flexibility allows for these adjustments. Only if a person's cognitive understandings and emotional commitments are malleable can that person make the requisite compromises. This suppleness permits the person to perceive another's requirements and make appropriate concessions. In the end, people cooperate because they derive something from the deal. Flexibility allows them to recognize that what is relinquished is compensated for by what is gained.

Closely related to this plasticity is a problem-solving orientation. Individuals who enter a negotiation intent on resolving emerging difficulties have a greater opportunity to work things out. Those who insist that their demands are nonnegotiable not only put their adversaries on the defensive, but they close their eyes to potential solutions. They cease looking for unanticipated options and can precipitate a contagious rigidity. As it happens, people who feel like winners are less likely to insist on total victories. Confident in their ability to elicit respect, they do not need to destroy their opponents. The result is a willingness to cede a portion of the pot to others. This, in turn, educes good will and cooperation. As a consequence, a combined effort can contribute to a larger pot from which all can draw. In short, competent negotiations launch spirals of success. For this reason, they are integral to middle-class dominance. They are also derivative of it. Success generates the confidence that permits the flexible bargaining that produces further success.

Technical Skills

People skills are clearly germane in an environment dependent on social alliances. But, this does not mean that technical skills should be slighted. They, too, are pertinent in a society dominated by the middle classes. As professionals, or professionalizers, their members obtain much of their power from their technical proficiency. Our civilization has produced technological wizardry that could not be sustained without scientifically and methodologically proficient personnel. People must be able to operate the wondrous machines upon which they depend and to fix them when they break down. They must also make sure that the transportation links keeping their bounty flowing are in good repair. As the sociologist Michel Crozier[34] has demonstrated, an important source of interpersonal power is an ability to control these uncertainties. Those who understand how to keep the goose laying its golden eggs receive deference in exchange for the benefits they confer. Once more, the middle classes emerge as the guardians of our collective prosperity and, therefore, as virtual titans in the battle for social prestige.

Among the economic sectors dependent on technological expertise are manufacturing, marketing, agriculture, entertainment, communications, transportation, government, health maintenance, and science. Millions of people would starve to death if fertilizers and pesticides did not get to the farms. Many millions more would perish if the harvest did not arrive at customers' door. Disease, too, would be rampant without modern medicine; poverty, unendurable without well-administered welfare programs, and daily life, infinitely more stressful without labor-saving machinery. Even our daily routines would be pallid without readily accessible amusements. The ordinary person may not know the difference between alternating and direct current, but someone must if the television set is to turn on when the button on the remote is pressed.

The density of what must be known is apparent in the case of medicine.[35] It was not until about the time of World War I that going to the doctor improved one's chances of recovering from an illness, but, since then, the quality of life has improved enormously. Today, people take it for granted that infants will survive to a span of almost four score years. They also expect that these will be active years, free of debilitating disorders. The physician is expected to insure this. If not, a malpractice suit may well ensue. To preclude this, doctors are required to endure a rigorous technical training before they are licensed. Just how demanding this is can be confirmed by anyone who has taken courses in organic chemistry, anatomy, or physiology. So much must be committed to memory, and so much of this is contingent upon superior analytical skills, that doctors are renowned for their intelligence.

Yet, the extent of technological expertise is better demonstrated by what has happened to policing. Historically, the police were of blue-collar origin. They were expected to be burly men who, when placed out on the street, dressed in uniforms equipped with guns and nightsticks, could keep social order. Being physically intimidating and reasonably honest were about the only job requirements. Today, this definition would be considered laughable. Although most law-enforcement agents are still of working-class origin, they are rapidly professionalizing. More and more, they are expected to obtain college educations. Criminal justice has graduated into a quasi-science.[36] As with business-school graduates, criminology majors aim to acquire a rationalized approach to their jobs. Future police officers are instructed in the rudiments of criminal procedures, forensic sciences, abnormal psychology, substance abuse, domestic violence, comparative legal systems, criminal law, profiling techniques, sexual deviance, white collar and Internet crime, and community policing. They are required to know what constitutes a legal arrest, how to testify in court, and the best ways to deal with a diverse public. Those who cannot exercise personal control or think on their feet are not deemed good candidates. They are less likely to benefit from the sort of education now considered mandatory across the board.[37]

This is apparent in the explosion of formal education. Only recently have politicians taken to promising a college education for almost everyone.[38] Slogans such as "leave no child behind" have extended to providing bachelors degrees to some of the least academically adept pupils. Based on the premises that everyone should be equal and that no one can compete without advanced schooling, the goal is to turn everyone into an expert. Ironically, this has produced little more than grade inflation. The notion that supplying everyone with an express elevator to the top can eliminate social ranking is discredited by differences in personal aptitude. Some are simply better learners than others, hence when the time comes to contend for precedence in the real world, they can invoke the know-how to prevail. One of the qualities of the members of the middle classes is that they tend to be disciplined learners. They make the effort to read assigned materials and to study for impending tests. They are also lifelong learners. When experience indicates that they need additional information, they go out to get it. In essence, they do their homework. In contrast, those who fall behind frequently come from backgrounds where going through the motions is regarded as sufficient. They do not understand that expertise requires not an appearance of proficiency but the real thing.

Needless to say, technological expertise is also conditional on scientific competence. The insights provided by a disciplined search for knowledge are essential to what has been achieved. Without the discoveries of physics, chemistry, and biology, industrialization could not have occurred. There would have been no steam engine, no television sets, no antibiotics, no CDs, and no rockets to the moon. Yet the ascendancy of science emerged from a hard won struggle. During the medieval period, human dissections were not permitted; hence, it was not known that the heart is a pump rather than a furnace. Similarly, during the Renaissance, the Church was scandalized that the earth might revolve around the sun; so it refused to allow Galileo[39] to publish The Starry Messenger. Accepted truth, that is, truth based on faith or authority, was not to be challenged. As a consequence, it could not be disconfirmed. But as Karl Popper[40] has taught, unless an assertion can in principle be shown to be false, it does not convey truth-value. It is, in essence, a tautology. Science is, therefore, concerned with carefully testing truths, even when they are unpopular. This takes courage, not only because scientists can be censured, but because they can be wrong.

Here, too, status plays a role. First, in being the custodians of the truth, the middle classes acquire an edge in tests of strength. By using science to make it less likely that these assertions will be disproved, their assertiveness is thereby enhanced. Second, the clout that comes with status enables them to defend the very enterprises from which they obtain legitimacy. Though others may wish to forbid scientific investigations that might prove embarrassing to their pretentions, these naysayers can be overruled, and progress proceeds. As an example, feminist ideologues were not able to prevent psychologists from confirming biologically based gender differences. Despite their strenuous objections, they could not outlaw the neurological studies they feared. The scientists, those who funded their inquiries, and the universities that employed them would have none of this. Their own reputations were dependent on breaking new intellectual ground; hence, they persevered despite the opposition.

Emotional Maturity

So far, the middle class way of life has been associated with both interpersonal and technical skills. Nowadays, part of attaining higher rank clearly depends upon learning to deal with people and with obtaining good practical educations. Yet, there is something more fundamental to success. This is personal discipline. Those who cannot control their impulses are not able to concentrate their assets on the fitnesses needed to work in these other areas. They cannot acquire the necessary skills nor apply them appropriately. As a consequence, they are not capable of exercising the internalized restraints upon which decentralized societies rely. Unqualified to make good decisions without supervision, they are not given the leeway to do so.

Yet personal discipline is itself dependent upon emotional maturity.[41] Unless a person can control his or her strong feelings, that person is vulnerable to rash actions. Instead of thinking through the best way to cooperate with role partners, a person will allow intemperate desires to take over. Rather than concentrate on acquiring difficult skills, an individual takes the easy way out and settles for shortcuts. The emotionally immature are like children; they want what they want when they want it. Theirs is not a world of resolution or determination. When they are hurt, they cry;

when they are frightened, they run; when they are angry, they try to get even. As a result, little gets done, certainly little that must be done cooperatively. Not surprisingly, those who exhibit emotional incompetence are not respected. They are not sought out as allies nor held in awe as adversaries whose enmity is to be dreaded.

Several decades ago Edmund Muskie was expected to be a shoo-in for the Democratic nomination for president. As Hubert Humphrey's running mate four years earlier, he had made so solid an impression that the respect lingered. Then, one inopportune day, he mounted a soapbox in front of the offices of the Manchester, New Hampshire, Union-Leader and decried its editor's attack upon his wife's integrity. Affirming that although he had not been personally injured, he considered it his duty to defend her honor, he proceeded to unleash a tirade. So far, his words were unobjectionable, but then Muskie broke down and cried. His voice choked up, and tears streamed down his face. Until that moment, he had exuded an aura of craggy manhood, but suddenly he was revealed to be a crybaby. The nation gave a collective shudder and came to the conclusion that this man was too delicate to be entrusted with the stresses of its highest office. Almost immediately, his approval ratings sank, and within weeks he was forced to withdraw his candidacy. He had demonstrated emotional incompetence, which was judged incompatible with the strength needed in a paramount leader. Decades later, Governor Howard Dean of Vermont, addressing his supporters at a campaign rally after losing the Iowa caucuses, made a comparable blunder. Intending to fire up his troops, he gave what came to be called the "I have a scream" speech. Delivered with such fire that it confirmed the worst fears about his inability to control his temper, his speech also drove his candidacy out of contention.

An analogous fate had earlier befallen Joseph McCarthy.[42] After several years as the scourge of Communist agents in government employ, the senator was cornered by his enemies during what came to be called the Army-McCarthy hearings. His chief interlocutor, Joseph Welch, was the Army's counsel. A folksy New Englander, he came loaded for bear. But this experienced attorney confronted a lawmaker who had already been unnerved. Long denounced as an unprincipled fascist, McCarthy had grown unsure of his ground. In an effort to manage his doubts, he had taken to drink. That morning, evidently suffering from a hangover, he was relentlessly quizzed about the names of a gaggle of alleged Communists. Finally driven to respond, he informed Welch that one of his own younger colleagues had such ties. To this came the famous rejoinder, "Sir, at long last have you no decency." Thrown back on his heels, McCarthy could offer nothing but a whiny denial. The contrast could not have been more stark. On one side sat a genial, grandfatherly defender of justice, and on the other, a shrill bully intent on destroying the career of an innocent. Welch was obviously a sensitive adult, whereas McCarthy was an emotional cripple. That, alone, would be sufficient to decide the issue. An emotional weakling could not be allowed to set the nation's agenda. Within years, a media vendetta crumpled tail-gunner Joe into a pathetic shadow of his former self, and he was soon dead, too.

Emotions matter. They are at the heart of tests of strength. These contests are, after all, usually won by means of intimidation. Accordingly, feelings are vital to attaining interpersonal, and even technical, skills. Over the last several decades psychologists and educators have come to recognize this. One popular concept to emerge from this ferment has been that of EQ. A coinage of Daniel Goleman's,[43] it refers, imitating the intelligence quotient or IQ, to a postulated Emotional Quotient. Drawing upon theories of multiple intelligences, it suggests that possessing emotional competence is equivalent to being smart. Although there is no accepted measure of this faculty, Goleman alleges that without it, a person may get hired but will have difficulty keeping a job. On paper a person might have the qualifications to do what is required, but, in practice, a prickly personality would prevent participation in a team.

The crucial element in this, one that is confirmed in actual relationships, is emotional maturity.[44] Just as human beings are born with a capacity to learn languages, they come equipped with an aptitude to experience a wide range of emotions. But, as with language, the ability to apply these develops over time. For competent speech, there is a vocabulary to be learned and a syntax to be mastered. For emotions, there are communication and motivation factors to be managed. Feelings must be socialized. Children must learn how and when to express them. More importantly, they need to discover how to apply them to achieve desired goals. The passions that send convulsions coursing through infantile frames are primitive in operation. They are stereotyped and virtually automatic. Thus, when angry, a baby issues an aggravated cry. The face screws up, and a bitter hoarseness conveys displeasure. In most cases, the mother recognizes this irritation and tries to assuage it. Yet, were an adult to be as inarticulate, the confusion would be general. A mature person is expected to verbalize sources of displeasure and, in the best circumstances, to indicate what would diminish them.

Primitive, childish emotions simply erupt. They are what they are. The very young do not control them because they have not yet learned how to control them. The problem is that many adults do not master them either. Especially when feelings become intense, they overstep their boundaries. In this situation, anger becomes rage, and fear becomes panic. Even love can become obsessive. Yet, chronological maturity does not guarantee that someone will have discovered how to suppress what is inappropriate. Under these conditions, an individual's influence will shrink. Impulsively berating the wrong person, at the wrong moment, is a sure ticket to defeat. Uncontrolled passions reveal an internal defect that is interpreted as weakness, and weakness, of course, invites attack. It is a sign that a person is a loser who will buckle under pressure. Thus adults who are given to temper tantrums are regarded as puerile. The louder they become, the more they are ignored. Though their histrionics at first gain attention, this soon degenerates into farce. Controlled emotions, in contrast, are effective and powerful. They induce others to act as one hopes.

One of the most dependable indicators of interpersonal strength is emotional courage. Physical courage is appropriate in a militarized society, but an ability to deal with emotional confrontations is more functional in a commercial one. Both in the marketplace and the political arena, people seek to intimidate others through expressive displays. They issue protests, make demands, and convey disappointment, all in an attempt to motivate compliance. Those who are sufficiently self-confident can withstand such face-to-face coercion, whereas those who are not either back off or overreact. In so doing, they signal a relative frailty, with predictable consequences. A renewal of affective attacks then serves to reduce their confidence further. In the end, people sort themselves out according to their emotional reserves with the tougher going to the top and the hypersensitive bottoming out. To compound the trouble of the emotionally fragile, anxious about interpersonal confrontations, they hang back when in quest of people or technical skills. Intuitively aware that acquiring these competences might expose them to further emotional tests, they fail to apply themselves adequately. Particularly with respect to people skills, they shy away from developing the capacities that might discredit their excuses for not asserting themselves. Deliberately, if not intentionally, they fail to learn about themselves or others, expecting that they need not employ what they do not understand. This, sad to say, has been one of the factors holding back progress among African Americans who refuse to study Euro-American customs on the grounds that these are irrelevant to their personal experience.

In any event, emotional socialization[45] is not evenly distributed. Though it is the *sine qua non* of self-direction, members of upper social classes are much more adept at inculcating these disciplines than are those in lower orders. Themselves under control, as parents, they both model and enforce affective restraint. Winners tend to beget winners. Because they are less frustrated than losers, they can afford to be more deliberate. On the assumption that they are in good shape, they take their time before reacting. By the same token, higher-status parents are more patient with their children. When the latter lose control, they understand that this can be a temporary condition. Having personally experienced control, they know it is possible. They also know how valuable it is. They, therefore, expend considerable effort to teach self-discipline. In so doing, they explain what is needed, provide opportunities for timeouts, and exert moderate, albeit persistent, pressures to maintain composure. Even the pastimes they favor support emotional control. Reading novels, listening to classical music, and playing golf all promote self-restraint. Take golf; it does not reward the intemperate. Those who throw tantrums on the links find it difficult to stand quietly over their ball as they adjust their swings. By the same token, players who learn how not only lower their scores also find it easy to cope with change and with difficult people. Having discerned the secret of mastering uncomfortable emotions, they inadvertently discover how to manage external uncertainties. In essence, having discovered how to remain calm under stress, they possess an advantage over those who have not.

Those from the lowest quarter of the social spectrum find powerful feelings problematic. Years of enduring failures leave them not nearly as optimistic as the more fortunate. Often frustrated to the point of distraction, they fear the worst and chafe at the prospect of repeated impotence. Their tendency is to react immediately and, therefore, impulsively. Primitive emotions rise to the surface and spew forth indiscriminately. An obstreperous child becomes an occasion for rage; a bad report card, from a teacher an occasion for panic; a disappointed spouse, an indicator of betrayal. Instead of focusing on what their children need to learn, they convert them into objects of corporeal punishment. A parent's need for emotional release supersedes all else, and this is the lesson which is transmitted. To compound the difficulty, the child who must endure the back of a father's hand becomes further enraged. His goal will now be to get revenge, whether or not this entails additional violence. Ultimately, such training produces an adult who is suspicious of almost everyone's intentions. No one seems capable of control, and, therefore, all must be kept at bay, often with preemptive strikes. This, of course, intensifies the internecine warfare among friends, relatives, and coworkers, and with it the anger and fear of those trapped in such hostilities. Powerful emotions are more likely to be expressed in primitive forms and, consequently, to reinforce a cycle of defeat. The end product is that losing begets more losing. It produces offspring who are uncomfortable with change, with confusing subtleties, and with unfamiliar role partners. In short, it grooms them to be future members of the lower classes.

None of this should be construed as indicating that higher status individuals are less emotional than those below them. Emotions, including intense ones, are universal. The primary hierarchical distinction is in how they are expressed. The emotionally mature can be simultaneously passionate and intelligent. They learn to turn down the heat before they act so that when they do, they can calculate the best strategies for success. By directing their feelings where they will do the most good, they derive added power from them. Thus they may vent their displeasure at a subordinate, while concealing it from a superior, knowing full well where it will have the desired impact. The immature, in contrast, are liable to explode when touched off. If not, they simmer with impotent rage. In a sense, they embody the sound and fury warned in the play, Macbeth, as signifying nothing. Unguided missiles frequently land in their own backyards. Nowadays, it is conventional to assert that crime, including violent crime, is distributed evenly throughout society, but the truth is that its ferocity is concentrated at the lower end. It is there that violence is most destructive.

Middle Class Values and Virtues

So far we have discussed the means through which the middle classes exercise their dominance. Emotional controls, interpersonal skills, and technical competence all contribute to superior performances. They enable people to best others by being more effective in activities that matter. Yet, which goals claim their attention? What are they aiming to achieve? The means people employ are important, but so are the ends to which these are harnessed. Of special significance are the generalized ends called values. A value is a moral objective.[46] It is an end state deemed particularly worthy of consummation. Some goals may seem unconditional, but they, in fact, evolve over time. The sorts of values that animated theocratic or militaristic societies are different from those that permeate commercial ones. More specifically, middle-class values dominate contemporary societies. Moral objectives, such as honesty and freedom, having been found essential within market-oriented environments, become everyone's standards. Closely related to these are middle class virtues. A virtue is an internalized disposition to seek particular goals. In moral terms, a virtuous person is inclined to pursue what is good, not because others demand it, but because the motivation to do so is deeply ingrained. Middle-class virtues include such familiar qualities as responsibility, individualism, and tolerance.[47]

Among the ancient Greeks who gathered beneath the walls of Troy to avenge Helen's abduction, a different set of appraisals governed.[48] Theirs was largely a pre-commercial society. Trading did occur among the Mycenaeans and Minoans, but it was small scale compared with what followed. Indeed, the distinction between a merchant and a pirate was still evolving. Theirs was a world of adventurous souls who took to their small wooden vessels in search of profit or booty. Often at the mercy of dangerous seas, when they came to call on a foreign port, they could not expect commodious accommodations. Since hotels had not yet been invented, these people depended upon the hospitality of the natives, and since a welcome would be extended only if it were reciprocated, hospitality became highly valued. Those who provided it were respected, whereas those who did not were reviled. Today, with commercial establishments available everywhere, this attitude seems quaint. Nevertheless, within its own context, it was the height of ethical behavior. Hospitality was a sacred goal, and those who provided it were men of virtue. Correspondingly, those who accepted it were bound not to abuse this goodwill by kidnapping their host's wife.

Cheek by jowl with this protocommercial outlook subsisted a military tradition that prided itself on courage. The hero was a man who exhibited unusual physical bravery. He charged, unafraid, into battle and cut a swath of destruction in his path. During the epoch preceding the development of the Greek phalanx, individual valor counted most. Muscle power and skill with weaponry won the day and hence, were admired. To back down from a challenge was considered cowardly and would ruin a warrior's reputation. The quality valued above all others was honor. A man, to be a man, had to be honorable. Much as a Star Trek Klingon would rather be dead than display weakness in battle, so might ancient Greeks. They would rather perish than live as dishonored nobodies. This attitude survived up to the first days of the American experiment. Alexander Hamilton[49] preferred to face death in a duel than refuse to accept Aaron Burr's challenge. The middle-class dominance of the contemporary frame of mind is no better demonstrated than by the puzzlement nowadays registered at this decision. Contemporary Americans cannot understand why honor would demand such a course of action. Because their values do not contain a similar code of conduct, they find it incomprehensible.

The values to which people subscribe are tested in the crucible of their experiences. Although social goals change over time, their origins can be ascertained and their ramifications charted. We are, in point of fact, in the midst of a period of turmoil regarding social standards. Over the preceding decades, there has been much talk of culture wars. Conservatives have been pitted against liberals in symbolically sanguine battles over what is best. Each side describes itself as defending truth and decency and condemns the other for fomenting what is opposed. So pregnant is this with social-class implications that the nature of this struggle deserves close attention. As we shall see, much of this controversy can be interpreted as a consequence of cultural lag, which merits a full analysis. In the meantime, the core values and virtues of the commercial middle classes can be examined. Most of these are familiar, but their repercussions may be less so.

One might assume that wealth would hold the place of honor within a commercial society, yet paradoxically it does not. People do aim to get rich, and they admire those who excel in this quest, but this admiration is grudging, with exceptional wealth often equated with greed. Acquisitiveness *per se* is not deemed a moral quality. It is, if anything, associated with the upper classes, especially the *nouveau riche*. Thus, it is considered gauche and frequently disguised with a patina of middle class respectability. One buys a Bentley, not a Rolls Royce, because one intends to be appropriately modest. The truly wealthy are even expected to give away a substantial portion of their assets. Unless they are avid philanthropists, they are dismissed as social parasites.

A more solidly middle-class virtue is responsibility. If Alan Wolfe[50] is to be believed, most Americans hold this attribute to be almost sacred. In his national survey of values, he found almost total agreement that this quality is highly valued. Why it should be is not a mystery in a society in which most people aspire to make important decisions. They understand that being entrusted with this assignment is contingent upon making first-rate choices. They also realize that responsible people are committed to such choices. Prepared to accept the blame when things go wrong, they stick by the efforts they put into deciding them well. If a decentralized system is to work, that is, if leadership is to be widely dispersed, a professionalized dedication to accountability is essential. Were decision makers casually to slough this duty off onto others or automatically to shift the blame in times of trouble, the community would be plagued by incompetence. Those who seemed to be leaders would melt into the scenery, and the nation would be without direction.

Going hand in hand with responsibility is a dedication to merit. In a market-oriented society, individuals compete for preeminence. On the most basic level, they vie to see who can produce the most desirable products. Some goods are reckoned to be better than others, and some producers are superior to others; otherwise such struggles would make no sense. The winners meet the higher standards. To be sure, critics of capitalism complain that this is a fraud. They contend that merchants seek to defraud their customers and, therefore, their alleged merit is a sham. Obviously, this is sometimes true. But were it the norm, the technical improvements that so clearly tower over the current landscape would never have emerged. Max Weber's[51] analysis comes close to the truth. Rationality, which he considered the central characteristic of modernity, is essentially a means of pursuing merit. It utilizes careful calculations in an attempt to achieve designated aims efficiently. Part of this process is obviously a commitment to science. Its deliberate efforts to unravel nature's secrets are integral to the enterprise. The point of science is to focus empiricism, accumulated knowledge, and a careful logic on determining what is best. As with merit, were it not assumed that there is a best (or at least a better), it would make no sense to rank the competent over the less able. Nor would it make sense to value responsibility if its outputs were indistinguishable from those of the bungling.

In the United States, the pursuit of merit has intimate ties to pragmatism. For centuries its citizens have taken pride in a practical know-how. Across the land, a tinkerer mentality hatched battalions of home-schooled inventors. Utilizing what they would have described as common sense, they sought what worked, not what academics considered valid. Before William James or John Dewey[52] lent their prestige to this philosophy, Thomas Edison, more proud of his perspiration than his inspiration, tested hundreds of materials to find a suitable filament for an electric light. Contemporaneously, John Roebling set his sights on straddling New York City's East River. His Brooklyn Bridge became the world's longest suspension span because he and his son Washington dared to adjust their methods as they went along. Experience also mattered to the Wright brothers. They could never have flown at Kitty Hawk had they not previously built a wind tunnel to explore the best wing shape. Even American politicians have joined the bandwagon. John Kennedy was celebrated for his pragmatic approach to dealing with such problems as the race issue.

All of this has lent an ambivalence to American attitudes toward education. More highly prized than ever, education still leaves most Americans uncertain about intellectualism. The benefits of suitable credentials are obvious to all, but individuals too dedicated to scholarship are dismissed as nerds. Ordinary people are suspicious of a lack of practicality and apparent narrow interests. Nonetheless, middle-class parents encourage their children to become accomplished learners. Parents want their children to be intellectually nimble enough to grasp what is needed to in order to move ahead. Emotional maturity, providing clear heads, accompanies an orientation toward reading and inquisitiveness.

Another virtue linked to responsibility and merit is individualism. Middle class Americans like to think of themselves as sturdy loners. As with the cowboys to whom Henry Kissinger compared them, they perceive themselves as self-reliant non-conformists. Out riding the range on their own, they make unaided decisions for which they are happy to take the credit or blame. This, say Robert Bellah[53] and his associates, has characterized them since frontier days. When the continent was an expanse of under-populated forest and plain and one's next-door neighbor could be miles away, one had to fend for oneself. Carried into a corporate context, this orientation continues to allow for innovation and idiosyncrasy. Novelty persists in the marketplace because many individuals remain unafraid to be different. Asked why they go their own way, most refer to a legacy of freedom. Freedom is probably the master American value. It was written into the nation's founding documents and lingers on the lips of children at play. Jealously guarded by volunteer armies over the centuries, the liberty to say what one thinks, to pray as one desires, and to vote as one pleases is taken for granted. The country has never had internal passports or I.D. cards, enforced occupations, or noble privilege. What this adds up to is social mobility. People have an opportunity to select their own pathways, including those that result in increased chances for success. Equality, on the other hand, is less valued. Class warfare may have been imported from Europe, but it never got too far. Americans like the prospect of standing out from the crowd. As long as the game is not rigged in favor of particular players, they are prepared to live with the outcome. The equality they endorse is Jeffersonian. It sanctions an equality of rights, not of conclusions. Jefferson[54] himself supported an aristocracy of merit and was not contradicted by his fellow citizens. If anything, most of them decry class jealousies as petty.

This, however, does not mean that the middle classes approve of oppression. They wish to protect the underdog. To do less would be to become a bully. Still, theirs is not a dedication based on equivalence; rather it is grounded on tolerance. As Wolfe indicates, they believe in a live-and-let-live attitude almost as much as in responsibility. If people wish to be different, as long as this does not interfere with the rights of their neighbors, they do not mind. Originally associated with religious forbearance, as in George Washington's[55] recommendation that each be allowed to pray under his own fig tree, the attitude has expanded to include ethnic differences in the wake of massive foreign immigration. It has also come to encompass racial variation. The Civil Rights Movement may not have brought complete integration, but it did lift a yoke of de jure segregation from the necks of African-Americans. They are now believed to have a right to social mobility. If they choose not to associate with European-Americans, this is considered their choice.

Not long ago, most Americans left the doors of their homes unlocked.[56] They assumed that their neighbors were trustworthy. In this, they were usually justified. Even today when surveys indicate that dishonesty is expected of politicians, most people presume something better from of their personal acquaintances. As important, they generally offer something better themselves. Fukuyama's counsel that trust is essential to civic cohesion is heeded in action, if not belief. Most people still attempt to be respectable. They may bend the truth when advertising a new product or occasionally cheat on a college term paper, but they usually keep their promises. Strangers still approach one another to ask directions and are rarely led astray. Similarly, members of the opposite sex go on unescorted dates, with few terminating in rape. Drivers sometimes drive too fast, but the overwhelming majority stops for traffic lights. Despite Cassandras, the sky has not fallen. People still step outside without fear of being mugged and do business without fear of being cheated. Riots do not break out when the electric grid fails or when a hurricane devastates the coast. Trust and integrity have not disappeared; they have merely undergone a cultural assault.

The middle classes have also maintained a tenacious hold on family values. Divorce might have escalated passes levels once thought imaginable, but romance and personal loyalty are still respected. People want to fall in love and stay in love. They want to have children with faithful spouses and to raise their youngsters to be responsible adults. Irrespective of media clucking about multicultural families, old traditions have been remarkably resilient. The heterosexual nuclear family is still the norm and promises to remain so. Even if, with tolerance, variations are allowed, the old standbys are privately encouraged. Those who are able to remain faithful are prized for their examples. When some succumb to something less, this is seen as failure. It is not the paradigm but an uncomfortable reality. Only the determinedly postmodern would demur.

In recounting its ideal type, Weber[57] described bureaucracy as overcoming the limitations of earlier forms of organization. Its motto was, he declared, *sine ira et studio*. Usually translated into English as "without fear or favor," the expression declares that a rational system would not sanction coercion or favoritism. To be more precise, it would not enforce coordinated action via the terror of military regimes nor the partiality of family based ones. Competent personnel needed to be enlisted and motivated by the reasonableness of working efficiently together for the benefit of all. Because this coordination would be to their advantage, it would suppress centrifugal tendencies. In the end, expertise would rise to fill the positions that only expertise could manage. Unlike previous systems, terror or genetic ties would not distort assessments of who was best. Such alliances that developed would be based on calculated gain, not the accidents of birth or physical aggression.

Adam Bellow[58] has recently suggested that this is wrong. The son of the novelist Saul Bellow, he argues that nepotism has always contributed to social welfare that, in point of fact, favoring one's family need not entail favoring the incompetent. Yet, he makes a distinction between new and old nepotism. In the prejudicial variety, relatives are hired irrespective of their abilities, whereas in the new version one's children are groomed for success because they are one's children. Without a doubt, the offspring of the successful have an unearned advantage over the progeny of the unsuccessful. Their status does tend to be inherited. Nevertheless, whereas status was once directly bestowed in terms of a job, property, or wealth, it is now bequeathed through social training. Higher-status children get a better education for the demands of the marketplace than do their more deprived peers. They are, therefore, better prepared to prevail in the tests that await them. This is not so much a consequence of going to better schools as of having ingested superior habits and values. They are more likely to acquire the assets of a good education, self-discipline, and personal responsibility. Thereby prepared by precept and example to be competent learners and leaders, they perceive themselves as their own loci of control. The opposite of fatalists, they eventually assert themselves to good effect. Justifiably more confidant than their competitors, they take risks that pay off.

The practice of parents preparing their children for independent success should, in fairness, be distinguished from nepotism. This propensity is, as Bellow acknowledges, a biological legacy. Not only is it natural, it is essential to a social-class system. Stable social strata could not exist were social mobility chaotic. The fact that the odds are stacked in favor of the offspring of the middle classes prevents anarchy. It encourages the perpetuation of the qualities necessary for social survival. Instead of merit emerging willy-nilly, it surfaces within a social network prepared to shepherd it to where it is needed. Few would argue that society suffers when Bobby Bonds or Ken Griffey, Jr., profit from having a father who was a talented baseball player. The example and sponsorship that came from within their families helped their careers, but they would have meant nothing if these players had not been able to stand on their own feet. Then, again, keeping operational control within the family has probably hurt the New York Times. Pinch Sulzberger turned out to be much more ideological than his father Punch. Under his stewardship, what was once the nation's newspaper of record has arguably become a partisan broadsheet. Insulated from competing opinions, he has been able to dilute the quality of a once proud journal.

The campaign against nepotism is in many ways a movement in favor of weak as opposed to strong social ties. Family relationships do not preclude effective alliances, but if these were exclusive, they might rule out others. In a commercial society, so much talent is required that it must come from diverse sources. The point of a social class, such as the middle class, is that it has many members and room for many more. Most of these do not know each other; they are certainly not family. Nevertheless, they may be associates. They are affiliated in networks of acquaintances. Because these linkages are far more ramified than family ties, they provide a broader venue from which to draw talent. When contemporary members of the middle class declare that the job should go to the best qualified, not to the best connected, they are asking for more open competition, not an absolute one. They recognize that not everyone can be considered for every position; hence they accede to some narrowing of the pool so long as merit is a significant factor in hiring. In discouraging nepotism, they in essence promote weak ties, not because these always provide superior candidates, but because the strong might otherwise swamp the weak. Norms of fairness are just that. If they are stacked against favoritism, it is because favoritism can take care of itself. A modern economy must, in essence, protect against a bias toward family preferences.

Endnotes

[1] U.S. Dept. of Labor, Bureau of Labor Statistics. 2000. *Dictionary of Occupational Titles*. Washington, DC: Government Printing Office.

[2] Spencer, H. 1891. *The Study of Sociology*. New York: Appleton; Spencer, H. [1899] 1969. *The Principles of Sociology* (3 Vols.) (S. Andreski, Ed.) New York: MacMillan.

[3] Durkheim, E. 1933. *The Division of Labor in Society*. New York: The Free Press.

[4] U.S. Dept. of Labor, Bureau of Labor Statistics. 2001. *2001 National Occupational Employment and Wage Estimates*. Washington, DC: Government Printing Office.

[5] Biddle, B. 1979. *Role Theory: Expectations, Identities and Behaviors*. New York: Academic Press; Sarbin, T. and V. Allen. 1968. *Role Theory*, in Lindzey, G. and Aronson, E. (Eds.), Handbook of Social Psychology. Boston, MA: Addison- Wesley.

[6] Tilly, C. 1997. *Roads from Past to Future*. Lanham, MD: Rowman & Littlefield Publishers.

[7] Gibbon, E. [1963] *The Decline and Fall of the Roman Empire*. New York: Dell Publishing.

[8] Owen, F. 1960. *The Germanic People: Their Origin, Expansion and Culture*. New York: Dorset Press.

[9] Rose, P.I. 1997. *Tempest-Tost: Race, Immigration, and the Dilemmas of Diversity*. New York: Oxford University Press; Sowell, T. 1996. *Migrations and Cultures: A World View*. New York: Basic Books.

[10] Griswold, W. 1994. *Cultures and Societies in a Changing World*. Thousand Oaks: Pine Forge Press.

[11] Johnson, P. 1997. *A History of the American People*. New York: HarperCollins Publishers.

[12] Adams, B.N. and R.A. Sydie. 2001. *Sociological Theory*. Thousand Oaks, CA: Pine Forge Press; Coleman, J.S. 1990. *Foundations of Social Theory*. Cambridge, MA: Harvard University Press; Merton, R. 1949. *Social Theory and Social Structure*. New York: Free Press; Parsons, T. and E. Shils. (Eds.) 1951. *Toward a General Theory of Action*. New York: Harper and Row.

[13] Harrison, L.E. and S.P. Huntington. (Eds.) 2000. *Culture Matters: How Values Shape Human Progress*. New York: Basic Books; Rochon, T.R. 1998. *Culture Moves: Idea, Activism, and Changing Values*. Princeton: Princeton University Press; Hatab, L.J. 1990. *Myth and Philosophy: A Contest of Truths*. La Salle, IL: Open Court.

[14] Kohn, M.L. 1969. *Class and Conformity: A Study in Values*. Homewood, IL: The Dorsey Press.

[15] Le Goff, J. 1980. *Time, Work, & Culture in the Middle Ages*. Chicago, IL: University of Chicago Press.

[16] Kohn, M.L. 1969. Ibid.; Kohn, M.L. and C. Schooler. 1983. *Work and Personality: An Inquiry Into the Impact of Social Stratification*. Norwood, NJ: Ablex Publishing.

[17] Mills, C.W. 1951. *White Collar; The American Middle Classes*. New York: Oxford University Press; Galbraith, J.K. 1958. *The Affluent Society*. Boston, MA: Houghton Mifflin.

[18] de Tocqueville, A. 1966. *Democracy in America*, translated by George Lawrence. New York: Harper & Row.

[19] Putnam, R.D. 1993. *Making Democracy Work: Civic Traditions in Modern Italy*. Princeton, NJ: Princeton University Press.

[20] Putnam, R.D. 2000. *Bowling Alone: The Collapse and Revival of American Community*. New York: Simon & Schuster.

[21] Ladd, E.C. 1999. *The Ladd Report*. New York: The Free Press.

[22] Fukuyama, F. 1995. *Trust: The Social Virtues and the Creation of Prosperity*. New York: Free Press; Bruhn, J. 2001. *Trust and the Health of Organizations*. New York: Kluwer/Plenum.

[23] Lofland, L.H. 1973. *A World of Strangers*. New York: Basic Books.

[24] Diamond, J. 1997. *Guns, Germs, and Steel: The Fates of Human Societies*. New York: W.W. Norton and Co.

[25] Starr, P. 2004. *The Creation of the Media: Political Origins of Modern Communications*. New York: Basic Books.

[26] Wood, P. 2003. *Diversity: The Invention of a Concept*. San Francisco, CA: Encounter

[27] Bergmann, B.R. 1996. *In Defense of Affirmative Action*. New York: Basic Books.

[28] Turner, R.H. 1962. "Role Taking: Process vs. Conformity?" in Rose, A.M. (Ed.), *Human Behavior and Social Processes*. Boston, MA: Houghton Mifflin.

[29] Garfinkel, H. 1967. *Studies in Ethnomethodology*. Englewood, NJ: Prentice-Hall.

[30] Fein, M. 1990. *Role Change: A Resocialization Perspective*. New York: Praeger; Fein, M. 1997. *Hardball Without an Umpire: The Sociology of Morality*. Westport, CT: Praeger.

[31] Suttles, G.D. 1972. *The Social Construction of Communities*. Chicago, IL: University of Chicago Press.

[32] Bernstein, R. 1994. *Dictatorship of Virtue: Multiculturalism and the Battle for America's Future*. New York: Alfred A. Knopf.

[33] Strauss, A. 1978. *Negotiations: Varieties, Contexts, Processes and Social Order*. San Francisco, CA: Jossey-Bass; Pruitt, D.G. 1981. *Negotiation Behavior*. New York: Academic; Zartman, I.W. 1978. *The Negotiation Process: Theories and Applications*. Beverly Hills, CA: Sage Publications; Wolff, K.H. (Ed.) 1950. *The Sociology of Georg Simmel*. New York: The Free

Press; Levine, D.N. (Ed.) 1971. *Georg Simmel on Individuality and Social Forms.* Chicago, IL: University of Chicago Press.

[34] Crozier, M. 1964. *The Bureaucratic Phenomenon.* Chicago, IL: University of Chicago Press.

[35] Starr, P. 1982. *The Social Transformation of American Medicine.* New York: Basic Books.

[36] Schmalleger, F. 2002. *Criminology Today: An Integrative Introduction.* Upper Saddle River, NJ: Prentice-Hall.

[37] Wilson, J.Q. 1975. *Thinking About Crime.* New York: Basic Books.

[38] Good, T.L. and J.S. Braden. 2000. *The Great School Debate: Choice, Vouchers, and Charters.* Mahwah, NJ: Lawrence Erlbaum Associates.

[39] Galileo. 1997. *Galileo on the World Systems.* Berkeley: University of California Press; Sobel, D. 1999. *Galileo's Daughter: A Historical Memoir of Science, Faith, and Love.* New York: Walker & Co.

[40] Popper, K.R. 1959. *The Logic of Scientific Discovery.* London: Hutchinson & Co.

[41] Goleman, D. 1995. *Emotional Intelligence: Why It Can Matter More Than IQ.* New York: Bantam Books.

[42] Coulter, A. 2003. *Treason: Liberal Treachery from the Cold War to the War on Terrorism.* New York: Crown Forum.

[43] Goleman, D. 1995. *Emotional Intelligence: Why It Can Matter More Than IQ.* New York: Bantam Books; Scheff, T. 1990. *Microsociology: Discourse, Emotion, and Social Structure.* Chicago, IL: University of Chicago Press.

[44] Fein, M. 1993. *I.A.M.*: A Common Sense Guide to Coping with Anger.* Westport, Conn.: Praeger.

[45] Lewis, M. and C. Saarni. (Eds.) 1985. *The Socialization of Emotions.* New York: Plenum Press; Wentworth, W. 1980. *Context and Understanding: An Inquiry into Socialization Theory.* New York: Elsevier; Clausen, J. (Ed.) 1968. *Socialization and Society.* Boston, MA: Little Brown; Glendon, M.A. and D. Blankenhorn. (Eds.) 1995. *Seedbeds of Virtue: Sources of Competence, Character, and Citizenship in American Society.* Lanham, MD: Madison Books.

[46] Fein, M. 1997. *Hardball Without an Umpire: The Sociology of Morality.* Westport, CT: Praeger; Fein, M. 1999. *The Limits of Idealism: When Good Intentions Go Bad.* New York: Kluwer/Plenum.

[47] Bennett, W.J. (Ed.) 1993. *The Book of Virtues: A Treasury of Great Moral Stories.* New York: Simon & Schuster; Greer, C. and H. Kohl. 1995. *A Call to Character.* New York: Harper-Collins; Hearn, F. 1997. *Moral Order and Social Disorder: The American Search for Civil Society.* New York: Aldine de Gruyter.

[48] Lattimore, R. (Trans.) 1951. *The Iliad of Homer.* Chicago, IL: University of Chicago Press.

[49] Brookhiser, R. 1999. *Alexander Hamilton: American*. New York: Simon & Schuster.

[50] Wolfe, A. 1998. *One Nation, After All: What Middle-Class Americans Really Think*. New York: Viking. For an alternative view see: Himmelfarb, G. 1999. *One Nation, Two Cultures*. New York: Alfred A. Knopf; Himmelfarb, G. 1995. *The De-Moralization of Society: From Victorian Virtues to Modern Values*. New York: Alfred A. Knopf.

[51] Gerth, H. and C.W. Mills. (Eds.) 1946. *From Max Weber: Essays in Sociology*. New York: Oxford University Press.

[52] Dewey, J. 1943. *The School and Society*. Chicago, IL: University of Chicago Press.

[53] Bellah, R.N., R. Madsen, W.M. Sullivan, A. Swindler, and S.M. Tipton. 1985. *Habits of the Heart: Individualism and Commitment in American Life*. Berkeley, CA: University of California Press; Gans, H.J. 1988. *Middle American Individualism: Political Participation and Liberal Democracy*. New York: Oxford University Press; Gerson, M. (Ed.) 1996. *The Essential Neo-Conservative Reader*. Reading, MA: Addison-Wesley Publishing; Lipset, S.M. 1996. *American Exceptionalism: A Double-Edged Sword*. New York: W.W. Norton.

[54] Ellis, J.J. 1996. *American Sphinx: The Character of Thomas Jefferson*. New York: Alfred A. Knopf.

[55] Brookhiser, R. 1996. *Founding Father: Rediscovering George Washington*. New York: The Free Press.

[56] Fukuyama, F. 1999. *The Great Disruption: Human Nature and the Reconstitution of Social Order*. New York: Free Press.

[57] Gerth, H. and Mills, C.W. (Eds.) 1946. *From Max Weber: Essays in Sociology*. New York: Oxford University Press.

[58] Bellow, A. 2003. *In Praise of Nepotism: A Natural History*. New York: Doubleday.

Chapter 4

Origins

To be ignorant of what occurred before you were born is to remain always a child. For what is the worth of human life, unless it is woven into the life of our ancestors by the records of history? (Cicero, <u>Orations</u>)

They [the Greeks] were the first Westerners; the spirit of the West; the modern spirit, is a Greek discovery and the place of the Greeks is in the modern world. (Edith Hamilton, <u>The Greek Way</u>)

I know of no safe depository of the ultimate powers of the society but the people themselves; and if we think them not enlightened enough to exercise their control with a wholesome discretion, the remedy is not to take it from them, but to inform their discretion. (Thomas Jefferson, "Letter to William Charles Jarvis")

Waves of Change

The expression that one cannot see the forest for the trees has become a commonplace because distinguishing the whole from the part is difficult to do. Distracted by what is immediately before them, people often miss the context in favor of the particular. This is especially so with respect to historic trends.[1] Grounded in the present, people are apt to regard the past as irrelevant. That our ancestors lived differently from how we do seems impossible. That these differences might have been a prelude to what now appear to be eternal verities sounds ridiculous. Nevertheless, that which is could not have been without that which went before. This is as true of middle-class dominance as anything else. It could not have come to fruition had not earlier achievements preceded it. The consequences of these steppingstones cannot, however, be perceived if they are not viewed in perspective. A long-term outlook, literally over many millennia, is necessary to appreciate what has happened and why. As significant, such a view is crucial if we are to see where we are going.

The current status of the middle classes did not arrive fully formed resembling, as it were, some conventional Venus on a clamshell. Their prominence has been part of an incoming commercial tide, but this tide was itself comprised of a series of waves. Advances have occurred and been challenged and consolidated, then swept away in an undertow of reaction. These periodic reversals of fortune have been temporary but compelling. Still, time and again, however deep the trough, the ineluctable power of the marketplace has reasserted itself and in so doing reinforced the power of the middling orders. The very utility of social class mobility and decentralized decision making eventually contributed to a commercial eminence. As a result, the value of their services thrust self-directed doers into leadership positions, and in the process, transformed the foundations of social power. Where family and military alliances, then religious associations, were in their turn supreme, relatively impersonal economic forces ultimately moved to the fore. Hierarchy has remained crucial throughout, but its outlines metamorphosed beyond what would once have been considered possible.

By the same token, the skills and attitudes underlying the Middle Class Revolution have evolved more slowly and inexorably than many social critics care to contemplate. Political reformers, in particular, tend to be oriented toward ideas. They develop a mental conception of what society should be and then assume that if they can convince others to adopt it, their ideal will swiftly emerge. Nineteenth-century anarchists, to cite one instance, truly believed that murdering heads of state would bring about total, government-free, equality. These deeds, as they called them, would be all the impetus needed to restructure society. Yet actual social circumstances proved otherwise. Real life entails relationships too complex to be fully fathomed and too unyielding to command instant compliance. Indeed, much of what happens can only be comprehended in retrospect. Even then, the human mind is too blunt an instrument to assimilate all of its contradictory elements.

Especially confusing are conflicts over supremacy. Human tests of strength are, of course, ubiquitous, as are the shifting alliances of the combatants. Despite episodes of apparent stability, rebellion and strife always lurk just below the surface. These insurgencies are, in fact, the stuff of history. So multifaceted are their political crosscurrents that historians continuously reevaluate their details to ascertain what really happened. Nevertheless, because most of these skirmishes are shrouded in a haze of obfuscation, the truth is elusive. The players lie to themselves and to others as an integral part of their stratagems for success. Even the scholars who assess these matters are enmeshed in webs of lies. Because they too are human, they cannot be completely disinterested observers. Biased by their own political, personal, and moral commitments, they frequently misperceive what they see. History is then reinterpreted because the inconsistent preconceptions of its chroniclers impel them to uncover additional evidence to bolster their favored explanations. Since no one is free of these limitations, what is momentarily asserted must, in consequence, be taken as tentative, including what follows.

Social progress, if that is the appropriate term, generally comes by way of unconscious experiments.[2] Individuals try out new ideas, not in the controlled manner of laboratory trials, but helter-skelter as the mood and opportunities take them. It is not that they do not think things through so much as that their narrow viewpoints prevent them from perceiving the shape of things to come. What occurs is, therefore, a naturalistic separation of the wheat from the chaff. Some things work, and others do not. Some developments fill in the gaps left by previous experiments, while others float like orphans until time passes them by. The innovators, some of whom are not even aware that they are innovating, rarely do this from altruism. More usual, they perceive a problem within their own lifespace, and they attempt to correct it. The results are frequently beneficial, that is, with respect to those innovations that are perpetuated, but this is not the motivating force. A cultural survival of the fittest ultimately crafts a structure made of many incremental advances, which only in retrospect appear intentional.

During their own eras, players may overextend their victories, engage in irrational oppositionalism, and pursue collective fantasies. They habitually imagine that they understand what they are doing, even as they are hopelessly out of touch with reality. W.I. Thomas[3] cautioned that what people perceive to be real can be real in its consequences. Even the most outrageous visions, if they are believed, influence what individuals do. Nonetheless, identifiable mechanisms do seem to underlie what is at work. The nature of human hierarchies, the facts of the physical and biological environment, and the laws of economic transactions are a given. They are the substantial sculptors of events, whether or not this influence is recognized. The question is how do these work in practice. The potential permutations are so vast that no supercomputer is capable of working them through; hence the best that can be done is to achieve a rough impression through a rearview mirror.

Another word of caution is in order. The account presented below is largely drawn from a Western perspective.[4] The same sorts of pressures that influenced European developments also affected the Middle East,[5] India,[6] and China[7] but with disparate implications. Similar patterns can be discerned across their spectra, but diverse conditions produced diverse outcomes. In China, for instance, the Tang and Sung dynasties fashioned something comparable to the West's Industrial Revolution. Nevertheless, this did not terminate with the ascendancy of commercial interests. The power of a centralized agricultural state could apparently countermand the aspirations of uppity merchants however great their temporary successes. The European experience and its subsequent American extension do not indicate what was inevitable but what was possible. All the same, they are germane to the Middle Class Revolution because this upheaval was an outcome of what happened there. Like it or not, the supremacy of the West is fundamental to the triumph of the contemporary professional class. Northern Europe and the United States were not merely where this journey began but also where it reached its apex. It was here, especially in the United States, that the middle classes took a lead they have thus far refused to relinquish.

The Monetary Nexus

Money matters.[8] This has been said many times before, but it remains true. Cash may be crass, but it has been a potent force since its inception. In the West, the starting point was approximately 650

B.C.[9] Coinage was invented in Asia Minor and quickly spread to the Mediterranean littoral zone.[10] Croesus may have been renowned for his wealth, but it was the Greeks who were first infected by the displacements inherent in a rampant commercialism. Inhabitants of a rocky and agriculturally stingy terrain, they abutted a great sea that beckoned as a highway for traders. Blessed with good harbors, they could sail their cargo-laden vessels from the far reaches of the Black Sea to beyond the Pillars of Hercules. Very quickly, it became apparent that reliably weighted pieces of gold, silver, and electrum could make these ventures more flexible and, therefore, more profitable. Citystates quickly began to flourish because urban areas were the natural abodes of commerce. Their concentrated populations facilitated business by allowing merchants to engage in the face-to-face exchanges then necessary to close deals. Thus was born the agora that became the heart of the Greek civilization.[11]

Nourished by this upsurge in traffic were the previously tiny outposts of Athens, Corinth, and the Ionian Islands. In retrospect, Athens has become emblematic of this transformation. As business increased, the town's human density soared, and the nature of its economy was made over.[12] Subsistence farming declined in importance to be replaced by commercial olive farming, silver mining, pottery making, and shipping. Merchants flocked to cities in search of riches and excitement. The settlements changed their complexions, becoming far more cosmopolitan. Not only did strange Greeks come to call, but so did visitors from other nations. Moreover, the Athenians themselves ventured forth. Their worldview grew immensely larger as they sought potential markets. Forced to explore unfamiliar shores, they were also compelled to interact with unfamiliar cultures.

Commerce is frequently depicted as philistine, that is, as insensitive and money-grubbing. Its practitioners are considered uncultured boors, who, in their materialism, overlook the finer things of life. The irony is that it is commerce that made cultural advances possible. Traders must, of necessity, cease being provincial.[13] Because they deal with strangers, they need to accommodate them. They cannot afford to be shocked when they encounter alien languages or exotic religions. Were they to reject what is different out of hand, they would also close the door to profits. They must, instead, tolerate perplexing differences. More than this, they need to understand them. Merchants tend to be most successful when they are familiar with their customers. If they recognize their sensitivities and perceive their needs, they can furnish what is desired without offending their sensibilities.

Nevertheless, the human mind is uncomfortable with contradictions. As Leon Festinger[14] has pointed out, people dislike cognitive dissonance and attempt to resolve it. This is what happened as commerce burgeoned. What was strange provoked attempts to come to terms with it. People were forced to think about things previously taken for granted. What was the nature of the gods? Which was the most satisfactory way to live? Most basic of all, Why was the world the way it was? All this provoked introspection and a questioning of conventional wisdom. The marketplace became alive with conversations regarding these pressing issues. Socrates[15] was but one of many who indulged in this enterprise. The simple answers, such as the idea that the gods were the same albeit with different names in different places, were soon found wanting. In due course, this ferment produced a sophistication that even now inspires admiration. The classical culture studied in contemporary universities was taking shape, not as a means of confusing future generations, but of satisfying its own.

In the arts, in philosophy, and in the sciences[16] a recognizable modernity emerged. The plays that entertained the ancient Greeks continue to entertain us. Aeschylus, Euripides, Sophocles, and Aristophanes touch our hearts just as they did those of their times. Because the characters these plays portray are recognizably human and their dilemmas timeless, they remain instructive. Having engaged in an honest examination of the human condition for audiences also interested in this subject, playwrights were able to analyze predicaments in a way that is useful for another community also absorbed in developing interpersonal skills. Greek philosophers were likewise studying what made humans unique. Best known today are Socrates, Plato, and Aristotle,[17] but they were preceded by the Sophists,[18] who also were philosophers. These itinerant scholars were much in demand as tutors. Well versed in a myriad of subjects, including rhetoric, they are remembered for preaching that man is the measure of all things. In other words, their attention had transferred from the divine to the mundane. Emboldened by the worldly achievements that made their profession possible, they conceived of themselves not only as understanding their environment but as modifying its shape. Less dependent on religion and more on their own efforts, they reflected a middle class hubris.

The contemporaneous scientists, including physicians and astronomers, correspondingly assumed they could encompass all of creation. Archimedes even speculated about his ability to move the earth if given a lever long enough and a place to stand. Theories abounded about the elements composing matter and the structure of the celestial spheres. Aristotle, well known for having proclaimed that men are rational animals, was a compulsive systematizer. Everything needed to be labeled and assigned its place by a scholar shrewd enough to comprehend them. Earth, air, fire, and water, and in some circles, atoms, could be reconfigured to produce all things in heaven and on earth. Crude observations also taught that objects moved in straight lines and went up and down in search of their proper places in the firmament. Hippocrates[19] took science a step further and applied it to the human body. He taught that people became diseased when critical elements were out of balance. As long as blood, phlegm, yellow bile, and black bile were in equilibrium all would be well. When they were not, treatments such as bloodletting were required.

Also, historians came to prominence. Herodotus[20] and Thucydides[21] are read to this day for their accounts of the Amazons and the Peloponnesian wars. Their interest in these events was no doubt sparked by the upsurge in political activity in which they partook. One of the reasons the Greek experience has remained relevant is that it is acknowledged as the source of Western democracy.[22] Athens, in particular, is recognized as a font of this ideal. But this form of government did not come to prominence until the Commercial Revolution upset preexisting arrangements. One of the first changes is attributed to Solon, who in 594 B.C. (after the introduction of coinage), freed the serfs. Almost a century later in 506 B.C., Cleisthenes[23] established the city's first democracy. During the preceding period, the economy had expanded so rapidly that ordinary artisans achieved prosperity. It was their unhappiness at living under a tyranny that contributed to a successful political revolt. This was then ratified by extending the franchise. The power a former rabble possessed simply became too great to ignore, even by the aristocratic class.

In modern terms, an elite still ran Athens.[24] Neither women nor slaves nor foreigners could vote, but the political class had enormously increased. Because the city was small compared with today's metropolises, it was possible for the citizens to gather together in a single place to decide significant issues. They could also be assembled in huge juries of many hundreds to determine the fate of individuals under arrest such as Socrates.[25] The broad consent this allowed permitted them to support Pericles'[26] policies. His building program during the height of Athenian power turned temporal success into stone monuments. The elegance of the city's Acropolis and Parthenon are attributable to these communal decisions. So, too, is the humanism of their sculptures. Previous to the works of such artists as Phidias, who was commissioned to create a representation of Athena, statues had a stiffly artificial mien. After the democratic reforms, people were portrayed as people, and gods were, too. They might be idealized, but they were unmistakable likeness of individuals who were proud of themselves and their accomplishments.

As important was the effect that commercial prosperity and democracy had on warfare. The initial defeat of the Persians at Marathon was owed to the valor of the Athenian phalanx. Ordinary Athenians, that is, their version of the middle classes, trained to fight in concert in armored ranks of spearmen. The effectiveness of this tactic depended upon physically conditioned combatants who were sufficiently disciplined to hold their place in line. This was insured, first, by citizens who voluntarily participated in gymnastics to keep fit and, second, by their motivation to cooperate. Were they less committed or less able to exercise personal control, their lines would have wavered, and they would have been put to flight. As it was, they were able to destroy the cohesion of a larger enemy's coercively recruited troops.

Victor Davis Hanson[27] provides an even better example of this democratic solidarity in his discussion of the evolution of Western military power. The battle of Salamis, which decisively crushed Persian sea power in its second, more extensive excursion to conquer Greece, was impressive. Before this decisive encounter, opinions had been divided. Some Athenians wanted to fight the invaders in the city, while others wanted to withdraw to the safety of the Corinthian isthmus. Themistocles wanted to gamble all on a naval ambush. As the military commander of this enterprise, he was able to convince his fellow citizens that trapping a numerically superior fleet within the confines of a narrow channel would throw the odds in their favor. Upon agreeing to this plan, the men abandoned the city and took to their boats. Despite their earlier disputes, the fact that they had en masse participated in determining the strategy stimulated them to heroic exertions. Citizens who felt that they controlled their own destinies were able to inflict one of the most fateful defeats on record. At the close of the day, tens of thousands of Persians had drowned off their coast, and Athenians had affirmed that they were their own masters.

In sum, a commercial people had asserted its individualism and worth. Having been trained in making decisions as merchants and artisans, these people acquired the skills to make cooperative determinations and to carry them out with vigor. Not so much bound by family or religious ties as by an awareness that their liberties and achievements depended upon voluntary collaboration, they had triumphed. Able to think independently and to value this accomplishment, they were able to overcome daunting odds. In this, they set the stage for what was to come.

What came immediately thereafter were the Romans. The Greeks had learned to harness their individualism in the arts, the sciences, and the battlefield but not in the disputes among rival city states. Notoriously fractious, as revealed in the fragile inter-communal alliances of the Peloponnesian Wars, a pride in their own polities prevented them from joining with their neighbors. In essence, their middle-class mentality had narrow boundaries. They might tolerate foreigners, but they were not about to meld into a single extended community. Nor could they do so and maintain their democratic institutions. Since common consent depended upon gathering together at a defined location, this would be impossible when multiple locations were involved. In the end, the Hellenes were overthrown by a mini-nation state, Macedonia. Subsequently, a mighty empire, Rome, would swallow both.

Rome too began as a city-state.[28]   Indeed, its initial source of prosperity was agriculture, and an aristocracy dominated its youthful political structure. Yet, in the early stages to becoming a continental superpower, it was fortunate to absorb lessons from the more commercial Greeks and Etruscans.   Afterwards, it was to surpass them both in its genius for the eclectic. Assembling bits and pieces of what was available, it created a composite civilization that lasted several hundred years.   The first Romans lived under a king, but these rugged farmers did not begin to prosper until they emulated their enemies by collaborating in well-disciplined legions. These citizen soldiers, much to their own surprise, were able to throw off the suzerainty of the Gauls, the Greeks, and the Etruscans.   Under a republican constitution, they collectively defended, then enlarged, what they perceived to be their own nation.   Like the Athenians before them, they also moved to a more commercial economy by taking advantage of their Mediterranean location to dominate its marine trade.   Initially out-competed by the Carthaginians, after trouncing them in the Punic Wars, they became the undisputed masters of an essentially maritime empire.

One of the peculiarities of this domain, at least from a modern perspective, was its reliance on slave labor.[29]   A side effect of commercialization was an increased demand for material products and, in a society based on muscle power, the necessary industrialization depended on human beasts of burden.   In their marches and counter-marches across Europe, North Africa, and the Middle East, the Roman armies converted many of their humbled foes into bondsmen.[30]   The Roman attitude was that those who were defeated in battle essentially forfeited their lives. Slavery was, in Roman minds, more humane than summary executions.   These captives could then be put to any sort of employment their owners found profitable.   The movies have taught us that many became household servants and gladiators, but they also worked in the mines, as longshoremen, in the brothels, and in industries such as the linen trade.   Bondsmen were even a primary source of tutors for the rich and scriveners for the government bureaucracy.

Status was quite important among the Romans.[31]   Slaves were on the bottom of the heap, whereas the aristocracy remained on top.   On the one hand, becoming entrepreneurs, in imitation of the Greeks, these patricians augmented their wealth by dominating business. On the other, they politically dominated first the Republic, then the Empire. Able to buy elections, only they could serve in the Senate or hope to rise as high as a consulship. Nevertheless, there were local elections that were open to participation by other citizens. More than this, citizenship was extended to conquered peoples as they were assimilated. In acquiring the common language of Latin, they could interact with the centers of power, albeit as provincials. This allowed for wide public involvement, notwithstanding at unequal levels. One of the tensions that plagued the system was the ambition of the lowly to rise. Freedmen, in particular, were considered troublesome. These former slaves, once liberated, could take advantage of the marketplace to make money and afterward aspire above their station. Much of the literature of Rome is concerned with keeping these parvenus in their place.

Concomitant with this was the development of Roman law. The courts and lawsuits flourished in an environment where commercial regulation became more specific. The Greeks too had rules for doing business, but these guidelines became both more institutionalized and more rationalized under the Romans. In hindsight, the Romans seem more practical and the Greeks more creative. The former were, in fact, pragmatic systematizers, more technologically sophisticated than artistic. They, too, had their authors, philosophers, and scientists, but these were largely derivative. Terrence, Ovid, and Horace were talented, but less universally focused or applicable than their predecessors. Virgil's Aeneid likewise, some might say, is a pale reflection of the Iliad. The same applies to historians such as Livy, Tacitus, and Plutarch,[32] and to philosophical movements, as exemplified by Marcus Aurelius's Stoicism. The Romans were builders rather than visionaries. They constructed roads to facilitate the movement of their troops, but these also facilitated trade. They erected aqueducts to bring water to their cities, which enabled them to grow larger. They invented concrete to aid in all sorts of construction, which permitted them to construct domes as impressive as the Pantheon's.

Yet the greatest Roman achievement was maintaining political dominance for so long. This was contingent on a variety of social adhesives. Some of these were family oriented, as with the continuing influence of the aristocratic clans, but others depended on military fraternity.   Once the state grew too large for quasidemocratic institutions, the Empire reverted to legionary authority. Augustus,[33] the first Emperor, was the adopted son of Julius Caesar, but he won his own ascendancy on the battlefield. Styled both a Caesar in honor of his family connections and an Emperor in recognition of his military leadership, he was able to bequeath his position to less able descendants largely through skillful political manipulations.   But this did not last. Once the Praetorian Guard discovered the power of assassination, the generals realized they could seize the throne through force of arms. With no established middle class to resist and a tamed aristocracy willing to play this power game, there seemed no alternative. Bribery and cronyism became the order of the day, with pitched battles among rival claimants often deciding the matter. In time, the commander best loved by his troops or more accomplished on the battlefield came to the forefront. Observers might bewail the chaos, but they could not dispel it.

One of these contestants, Constantine,[34] found another avenue to success. Almost accidentally, he alighted upon religion as a source of anonymous allies. He discovered that his soldiers were better disciplined as Christians than as pagans. For some time, the old Gods had gradually been losing their legitimacy as contending faiths from the periphery sought to invade Rome. Cults of Isis and the Gnostics and followers of Jesus all claimed to be best. What the Christians had going for them was their monotheism and their promises of redemption. A single god could be a universal god and a redemptive divinity could offer peace in an empire riven by dissension. Constantine's innovation was in harnessing this hopefulness to the interests of the state. Believers in a single religion, convinced of its efficacy, could work in harmony against skeptical heretics. Determined to solidify these nonpersonal alliances for his own purposes, he convened the Counsel of Nicaea to endorse a shared orthodoxy. Out of this came the doctrine of the trinity, and shortly to follow was a standardized Bible. Together these constituted the foundations of a Church that was to outlast the Empire.

Unfortunately for the Romans, their nation was afflicted with terminal arteriosclerosis. Its successful militarism had been underwritten by circumstances that were eroded by this very success.

Conquests that became too large to be managed by the existing administrative instruments became burdens. Distant borders had to be guarded by legionnaires who needed to be paid for their services as more patriotic motives evaporated. But now by abutting deserts, impenetrable forests, and competing empires, opportunities for expansion had disappeared. This meant that as the supply of slaves dried up, so did fresh lands with which to reward the troops. Long gone were the citizen soldiers of the Republic, now replaced by barbarian auxiliaries. So too was the robust commercialism of the early Empire. It had been driven to its knees by taxation. In desperate need of funds for their mercenaries, the emperors froze the economy and squeezed it to its limits. This made entrepreneurship impractical and encouraged a reversion to local subsistence. Eventually the turmoil of barbarian incursions thoroughly interrupted commerce and sent city dwellers scurrying for the protection of the latafundia.

For all its magnificence, Rome never evolved an independent middle class. With business and government dependent on chains of patronage, that is, with quasifamilial alliances, a self-sufficient professionalism never came to the surface. Ultimately, the parochialism of this familism, battered by an increasingly unstable militarism, sounded the death knell of a vibrant marketplace. The bonds of religion were able to forestall this decline for a while, but in the West this was not very long. With the arrival of the Germanic hordes, the first great flowering of the Commercial Revolution was at an end. Soon to follow were Dark Ages during which wealth and learning were in retreat throughout most of Europe.

The Medieval Revival

The second wave of the Commercial Revolution took centuries to gather. When the continent's new masters arrived on the scene, they were a combination of agriculturists and pastoralists.[35] Seminomadic tribesmen, they knew almost nothing of the ways of merchants. Despite their skills as metalworkers, their primary orientation was to the land and secondarily to battle. As a result, while they stood in awe of Roman technical accomplishments, they did not comprehend them. Neither literate nor bound in complex political federations, they could not emulate the achievements of a faltering empire. What attracted them most was the opulence of the Roman estates.[36]

Never themselves urbanites, they saw no point in moving to centers of commerce. But large manor houses surrounded by productive fields were another matter. These remnants of the latafundia could be converted into the beginnings of medieval fiefdoms. On these intensely local establishments, the natives who had previously sought rural protection could be turned into serfs[37], thenceforward tied to the land and dedicated to serving their overlords. The emerging nobility meanwhile depended upon family ties and pledges of military fealty to maintain their advantage over those they had come to rule.

What did not persist was long distance trade.[38] The roads fell into disrepair, ships were no longer built; and money was driven out of circulation. Gold was used for decoration rather than for exchange, with much of it bequeathed to the Church as a sign of devotion. Literacy and technology skills also declined. Few large buildings were attempted, and only churchmen kept the art of reading alive. Beyond this, with no central authority to maintain order, brigandage became endemic. Even if there had been merchants who wished to maintain trade, their goods would have been looted by the highwaymen who infested the few tracks that remained open between now isolated communities. If there was a source of large-scale cohesion, it came from the Church. With the invaders themselves converted to Christianity, a common faith became the lingua franca. In a literal sense, it was the Latin kept in circulation by clerics that enabled the nobility to communicate with distant brethren.

Into this disarray, impulses toward power and order continued to arise. The kings, though they were often reduced to the level of local warlords, pressed ahead in quest of supremacy, and, in the case of Charlemagne,[39] achieved considerable success. So too did the Church, initially in the form of monasticism. For a while, however, all this was put in peril by external invasions that a decentralized nobility was hard pressed to repel. Vikings from the north, Magyars from the east,[40] and Muslims from the south penetrated to the heart of the continent. Eventually a wave of castle building provided a parochial bulwark against these aggressors.[41] This created the image of feudalism with which most modern people are familiar. With armored knights ensconced in fortifications from which they could sally forth to maintain control over the adjacent lands, the fortunes of the elite were affected by isolation. The stability thereby established convinced even the Northmen to settle down and become traders instead of raiders. Small hamlets began to huddle together for protection under the castle walls and from these grew vigorous commercial entities. Unplanned from above, urbanism and long distance exchange gradually revived to become counterweights to the powers of the aristocracy.

Part of this progression was owed to the Church.[42] In its effort to survive the commotions of the darkest periods, it invested in monasticism. Establishments such as those of the Benedictine, and later those of Cluny became self-sufficient reservoirs of economic activity.[43] Eventually the Cistercians would consolidate these efforts in a commercialized agriculture, thereby helping to generate the capital from which more secular efforts would benefit. Also implicated in this revival were fairs such as those near centrally located Champagne. Once or twice a year each of these drew merchants from the north and the south, the east and the west. Ultimately all of this stimulated a dynamic urbanism that in time spurred what has been called the medieval Industrial Revolution. In places like Flanders, towns such as Bruges sprouted to importance. Dominated by merchant guilds, they grew rich from businesses that included the textile trade. During this period it was proudly said that city air made one free. Serfs who escaped from rural servitude could find employment and self-governance in these enclaves. If they did sufficiently well, they could even become the masters of their own shops, employing journeymen and apprentices to magnify their personal efforts. As the towns grew, the newly prosperous might move to neighborhoods created by extending the municipality walls outward. These so-called bourgs became the home of the bourgeoisie; which by this means produced the title of infamy future members of the middle-class would bear.[44]

Simultaneous with these developments was a restoration of coinage.[45] Money was as necessary under the evolving conditions as it had been for classical commerce. Arts too began to flourish, with the newfound affluence channeled into guildhalls, town halls, and cathedrals. Gothic elegance replaced Romanesque heaviness, both in architecture and sculpture. Part of this owed to developments in technology. As during the earlier wave of commercialism, an increased demand led to efforts to provide what was desired. Although the Middle Ages is generally considered to be backward times, it boasted many advances over what the Romans[46] wrought. This was the period when waterwheels and windmills came into their own and, therefore, the first period when mechanical energy made a significant contribution to production. This was also a time when small improvements such as the pocket and the button made their appearance, and likewise when the wheelbarrow, the crane, and mechanical clock[47] entered construction sites. It was, in addition, the historical moment when universities were started. First dedicated to training the clergy for a resurgent church, the university quickly became a place where scholars and lawyers could prepare for their callings. This was consequently when the liberal arts came to the fore and established the rudiments of what it meant to be an educated person—even if one were a layman.

One of the unique aspects of the medieval revival was the degree to which military, religious, and commercial forms of organization interpenetrated one another.[48] Family/military alliances[49] remained active throughout the period, grounded in agriculture but borrowing funds from newly affluent commoners. The Church too prospered under these conditions. Still benefiting from contributions from parishioners who were genuine believers, it also drew recruits from the younger sons of the nobility. With secular inheritances preserved by devices such as primogeniture, the disinherited members of aristocratic lineages could nevertheless receive appointments as bishops and abbots. This connection culminated in the Crusades.[50] Popes could rouse their devoted to shunt an unruly young generation of warriors into attempts to conquer Jerusalem. The most universal institution of the era, the Roman Catholic Church, thereby generated cooperation among individuals more usually dedicated to usurping one another's prerogatives. Then, too, even the merchants were believers. They were happy to contribute to the endeavor. As aficionados of the Robin Hood saga will realize, it was they who supplied the ransom to rescue Richard the Lion-hearted from captivity on his way home from the Holy Land.

Proud though this presocial class world was, its heyday was short-lived. During its expansion, it recruited trading towns as far east as Poland under the umbrella of the Hanseatic League, but this association seems[51] to have been in defense of an impending retrenchment. For reasons not completely understood, this period saw a weakening so profound that Barbara Tuchman[52] dubbed it "the calamitous 14th century." One source of the collapse was probably overexpansion. Then as now, businessmen were prone to overoptimism. In creating supplies greater than what the market could absorb, they may have undermined their own prosperity. There was also the disaster of the Black Death. During the middle of this interlude of curtailment, the bubonic plague entered the continent, probably disembarked from a trading ship arrived from the Black Sea, and promptly propelled rings of despair rippling north. Within a decade, perhaps a third of the population was wiped out—especially in the towns. Utterly unaware of the germ theory of illness, their inhabitants had no way of knowing that this disaster was spread by rats infested with diseased fleas. To many, the devastation seemed divine retribution for the sin of pride.

Also practically invisible to the afflicted were the tribulations instigated by the Little Ice Age. Unbeknownst to all, the weather had taken a turn for the worse. For several centuries, the snow belt had drifted south with catastrophic consequences for agriculture. Crops failed, and people starved for reasons that could not be apparent to those innocent of meteorology. What they could see was the generalized conflicts that accompanied these calamities. England and France entered a war that lasted, on and off, for over a hundred years, and Italy, thanks to its internecine conflicts, invented the condottiere. These were mercenaries who, when released from employment, took to freebooting. For the better part of a century, they visited destruction so widespread as to make commerce too hazardous to maintain at its previous levels. Even the Church was not exempt from these disorders. In order to escape the wrath of the Roman mob,[53] a French-born Pope removed the papacy to Avignon. This Babylonian Captivity eventuated in a Great Schism, with a Pope and an Anti-Pope—one in France and the other back in Rome—competing for the allegiance of the faithful. This low point in prestige reduced the Church to virtual irrelevance. It also constitutes a convenient marker for the end of the second wave of the Commercial Revolution.

The Renaissance

The third phase of the Commercial Revolution is traditionally called the Renaissance, which means rebirth.[54]   In many ways, it was.   Daniel Bell[55] traces the beginning of capitalism to this period. He points to the development of Italian financial institutions as the origin of the accumulation of resources that enabled large investments in new enterprises.   Another hallmark of this epoch was the invention of printing.   In the middle of the 15th century, Johann Guttenberg developed movable type and a press that could turn out reams of materials for outrageously low prices.   Prior to this, books were laboriously copied by hand, which meant that only the rich could afford them and that only the most sacred texts would be reproduced.   Printing meant not only cheap bibles, but an unprecedented diffusion of knowledge.   This advance was associated with humanism.[56]   Scholars discovered in the ancient classics, as reproduced by entrepreneurial ventures such as Venice's Aldine Press, a dedication to secular, as opposed to purely religious, knowledge.[57] Works newly imported from a collapsed Byzantine Empire[58] and a reconquered Spain also expanded acquaintance with Greek and Roman sources.   No longer was Aristotle the limit of awareness.   The old myths about the Olympian gods and the emotional subtleties of the Athenian playwrights came to attention with a profound effect on consciousness.   Educated people now began looking toward themselves in the present, rather than focusing merely on the afterlife.

Fundamental to these innovations, beginning first in Italy, was a remarkable resurgence of commerce.   Cities such as Amalfi, Florence, Venice, and Genoa became beehives of mercantile activity.[59]   Located hard by the Mediterranean, as had been their classical predecessors, they too were sovereign urban entities.   Unfettered by the suzerainty of a monarch or an emperor, they controlled their own affairs, as had the Athenians before them.   Sandwiched between a reviving continent and the opulence of the Muslim Levant, they served as a conduit for goods that originated farther east.   Moreover, this increased activity acted as a spur to improvements in trading technology.   Foremost among these was the invention of banking. The Italians learned how to manage credit.   Although the Church forbade usury, these merchants made profits by charging interest on paper transactions. While they did not know it at the time, present-day economists could have told them that credit expands the money supply. Because multiple loans can be based on the same collateral, the effect is as if more coins have been put in circulation. And since additional currency means a greater ease in commercial dealings, the volume of trade can swell. So advantageous were the Italian money-management skills that they were able to set up remote outposts as far afield as London. To this day, Lombard Street commemorates the time when Northern Italians dominated the city's banking. With this extra trade, of course, came greater wealth. And with wealth came power.

Among the chief beneficiaries of this munificence were the Italian merchant princes. The Medici of Florence and the families that dominated the council in Venice were exemplars of how business success could be converted into political domination. Operating in compact territories, they translated their assets into military power ample to maintain status. Influential beyond their borders, they served as models for the magnates of Genoa[60] and the Fuggars[61] of southern Germany who were to grow so rich that they eventually became indispensable creditors to nation states. Within their own boundaries, the Italian commercial princes were affluent enough to emulate the sumptuousness of these monarchies. Despite their diminutive size, they eagerly participated in international diplomacy. Florence was soon to fall to the more numerous French and Spanish, but tiny Venice, thanks to the navy it acquired for its trading interests, was able to ally with Spain to defeat the Turks at the battle of Lepanto.[62] Indeed, for a while, the city was able to defend holdings, such as the island of Crete, against this formidable foe.

So wealthy were the Italian city-states that they were able to patronize the artists and scholars that made the Renaissance synonymous with culture. Beginning with Dante Alighieri's <u>Divine Comedy</u>,[63] a growing self-assurance enabled them to sponsor literature in the vernacular. Previous to this, the languages of the ordinary people did not have a sufficient audience to merit artistic use. Hopes for the favor of his ruler also encouraged Nicolo Machiavelli[64] to jump start political science by writing a how-to guide for princes. Often mistakenly thought of as a craven opportunist, this skilled diplomat intended to promote Italian unification by assessing how power was actually wielded. More congenial today, of course, are the achievements of the painters and the sculptors. Together with the humanism that epitomized the period came a pictorial realism that echoed the achievements of the classical period. Thus a Michelangelo[65] could both paint and sculpt people that looked like actual human beings, rather than stylized tributes to biblical stories. Deeply immersed in the use of perspective, Renaissance masters placed their heroes in a physical world that modeled the one they saw outside their windows. They could also emulate the autonomy of their patrons. Although dependent upon the rich and powerful for commissions, they became recognizable figures in their own right, celebrated in a way that the architects of the Gothic cathedrals were not. Michelangelo, for instance, was able to wrangle with Pope Julius II about how to render the ceiling of the Sistine Chapel. In this we see the glimmerings of the bohemian sensibilities that were to drive Victorian sponsors to distraction. Both groups of artists were cultural specialists whose talents enabled them to exercise power over their own endeavors.

Also associated with Renaissance commercialism was a plethora of mundane technologies. Not tangible *per se* but readily convertible into income was double-entry bookkeeping. One of the imports from the East had been Arabic numbers.[66] This Hindu invention made it possible to calculate profits and losses more precisely than Roman numerals allowed. So cumbersome were Roman numerals that during the medieval revival national budgets were worked out by manipulating piles of coins on checkerboards. The rationalization of financial computations subsequently made it possible to evaluate investments more efficiently. Also crucial to mercantile effectiveness was a dependable system of laws. Trade inevitably entails conflicts, the frictions of which, unless they are resolved, interrupt business. This stimulated a further evolution of Roman based jurisprudence. Not only were classical regulations and procedures reintroduced, but they were extended to meet emerging conditions.

On a more tangible level, the technological advances were epitomized by the advent of the mechanical clock and the vacuum pump. Now commonplace, the clock then seemed miraculous. Its numerous finely machined gears, meshing as closely as they did, came to seem an analog for the universe itself. The instrument's introduction not only prompted a rash of mechanical toys, but the more precise scheduling of business transactions. Once people could coordinate their meetings by consulting a shared apparatus, they did not need to waste time unproductively. The pump meanwhile became the model for how blood circulates through the body. Were it unavailable as a paradigm, William Harvey might never have conceived of the heart as impelling a liquid through tubes. Progress also came through medical dissections. Only after secular power was sufficient to challenge the Church's supremacy were restrictions against cutting into the body loosened. This made anatomy possible and eventually a rationalized surgery. Even the invention of spectacles, which helped reading, was to play a part in the establishment of modern science. Experience in grinding lenses was furthermore to lead to the invention of both the telescope and the microscope, which in their turn opened unimagined vistas to closer observation.[67] Nor should the achievements of Leonardo da Vinci[68] be neglected. Although most of his inventions remained unbuilt speculations, much of his reputation rested on the military devices he did construct for ambitious lay rulers. His paintings deserve the acclaim they have received, but his output in this area was too small to have warranted his contemporary repute. Copernicus, too, deserves a mention.[69] Though a Polish cleric, he was infected by the temper of the times. Were it not for the concurrent upsurge in scholarship, it is doubtful that he would have hypothesized a heliocentric universe.

Competing with this commercially based turmoil was the emergence of the nation state. If a rekindled expansion of trade enhanced social coordination via marketplace relations, political power grounded in agricultural domination and military alliances had not disappeared. In larger continental territories such as France[70] and Spain, the kinds of relationships that prevailed in city-states could not succeed. Neither communication and transportation nor the political institutions of representative democracy were adequately advanced to foster cohesion over long distances. It was instead necessary to impose order by the sword. Only the sorts of coalition capable of dictating their desires on the battlefield could command the obedience of far-flung barons. Yet because the parochial remnants of the Germanic invasions continued to hold sway over remote counties, they could still launch challenges to their overlords. These had to be met, and only leaders capable of commanding personal respect could get the job done.

Nation building did not begin during the Renaissance, but it reached a milestone at this time.[71]   In the midst of the medieval revival, the primary underpinnings of later unification were already perceptible. Foremost among these was the appearance of military and judicial dominance. On the military side, kings and emperors had long been able to assert periodic dominance. The example of Charlemagne lingered within the memories of those who wore the crown; hence, they too hungered for the glory of extending their territory. The problem was that what could be won in battle could as easily be lost in it. Nevertheless, some regal victories foreshadowed the national entities to follow.   In France, for instance, Philip Augustus was able to revive the fortunes of his domains by defeating the Plantagenet challenge.[72] For a time it appeared that Henry II, though based in Anjou, Acquitaine, and England would be able to displace his legal sovereign. To the surprise of most, with the aid of Henry's sons, most of what afterward became France was recovered. Somewhat later, Philip the Fair would further strengthen the throne by increasing its revenues and asserting its power over the Church. It was he who was able to tame the Pope by offering him the protection of an Avignon residence.

Later still, and more decisively, Charles VII reasserted national integrity by expelling the English from the northern part of his territory. Assisted by the inspirational Joan of Arc, he became the embodiment of the state. One of the reasons the English lost this struggle was that their Burgundian allies deserted them.[73] This prosperous tributary of France sought a separate identity by assembling the provinces from Italy in the south to the Netherlands in the north into an independent state. Were this to have come to fruition, it might have been one of the more potent states in Europe, for it would have join the most important commercial centers of the continent and would have possessed the resources to finance its powers. Unfortunately, its king, Charles the Bold, was humbled by Louis XI of France[74] and then undone at the hands of the Swiss. In one of his campaigns for territorial aggrandizement, he ran into their halberds and lost his life. The Swiss, who had hitherto been considered unsophisticated yokels, in defending their independence from the Austrians discovered the value of disciplined battle formations. Like their Greek antecedents, they could hold off more heavily armored foes by maintaining the integrity of lines of spear points.

The importance of military discipline had earlier been demonstrated by the English in their startling victory over the French at Agincourt. Henry V was able to defeat a much larger force via control of his archers. These yeomen were renowned for their skill with the longbow. But what made them more than the match of fully armored French knights was the latter's disorder on a narrowing battlefield made treacherous by acres of mud. As a result, a handful of commoners cut down the flower of an unruly nobility by the thousands. Strangely, no other army emulated this achievement because the training requirements were too stringent. What could be copied, and this was the embryo of the national army, was hiring qualified specialists loyal to a king who paid them. Because his national treasury was larger than that of his rivals, he could employ a greater number of mercenaries. The coffers of his centralized counting houses, not incidentally, were simultaneously being filled from taxes levied on the rehabilitated commercial interests. These same monies could also be used to purchase the recently perfected cannon. One of the reasons Da Vinci and other scientists were prized was that they could calculate how to fire them. Accuracy was important in order to blast holes in the fortifications protecting local barons from an overlord's displeasure. Once these barriers could be breached with ease, organized resistance to a national sovereign became less practical. In time, the disciplined use of gunpowder was to extend to battalions of musketeers and grenadiers, with even greater benefits to state formation.

The judicial element in the creation of nation states goes back at least as far as Henry II of England.[75] His attempts to consolidate his hold over the country he inherited entailed an effort to supplant local justice with his own. Provincial cases were generally settled in baronial courts, until Henry II sent judges out in circuit courts. The trouble had been that what happened in these baronial castles was not standardized. Arbitrary, and often biased, these institutions were supplanted by Henry's appointees who were instructed to avoid being capricious or to curry favor by being fair and judicious. They were also empowered to impanel groups of local citizens to act as witnesses in individual cases. Herein lay the beginnings of juries and the common law. In time, this systematized justice was to provide an ingredient in the monarch's authority. As convener of the courts of last resort, he thus had the last say. Moreover, in successfully applying legitimate coercion within his borders, he gained prestige. Rather than have unpredictable personal brawls decide differences of opinion, order was maintained by convincing a broad constituency to defer to his less subjective procedures. Subsequently stabilized by tradition and a paid constabulary, this mode of civic regulation replaced personal allegiances with more homogeneous, impersonal bonds.

As earlier occurred in citystates, the King's justice facilitated trade within his larger territories. Brigandage was less of a problem when highwaymen feared the monarch's troops, and fraud was more manageable when charlatans dreaded the verdicts of his judges. So dependent did commerce become on these developments that Shakespeare's Henry VI's quote is often cited: "The first thing we do, let's kill all the lawyers." Lawyers were hated by the bard's time because they had become integral to conducting ordinary business. Members of one of the first professions, these legal specialists might be reviled, but they were also respected. Representing power in a world where written contracts increasingly defined interpersonal relations, they had an influence that mattered. Kings even conscripted them in managing national affairs. Where once only clerics such as Thomas Becket could rise to be Lord Chancellor, by the time of the Renaissance, a lawyer, Sir Thomas More, might be selected for the position.[76]

The Church too had undergone sweeping dislocations in response to the resumption of commerce. Within Italy, once the Pope returned from his French sojourn, the Papal States became a player in local power politics. Julius II was more enthusiastic a warrior than a patron of the arts. In a world where money talked, secular supremacy held a greater appeal than did the sacred. Indeed, Alexander VI became infamous for using his election to the seat of St. Peter to feather his family's nest. His children, Cesare and Lucrezia Borgia, are still remembered for the ferocity with which they sought temporal power. This was because Alexander not only believed the papacy was to be enjoyed he also wished to establish inheritable domains for his progeny. If this entailed assassinations and treachery, so be it. In fact, the term <u>nepotism</u> came into currency during this period. Based upon the Italian word for "nephew," it alluded to bestowing benefits on illegitimate children who, for purposes of decency, were referred to as "nephews." Paradoxically, both the ease with which Church doctrines were violated and the disapproval with which this illegal favoritism was met were signs of a rising commercial tide. Nepotism had not been considered a problem when family connections were the primary source of alliances. It became a threat when it promised to undermine business dealings based on profit. If genetic ties were allowed to count for more than reliable streams of revenue, then bankruptcy and a descent from grace might be in the offing for unconnected tradesmen.

Once the Church became entangled in these contradictions, its legitimacy too was in question. One of the ways popes attempted to generate the funds needed to erect the symbols of their power was through the sale of indulgences.[77] These passes to get out of purgatory could become objects of commerce only in a society where the marketplace had ascended to prominence. They would never have sold had not ordinary people resources to spare. Still, the fact that they were for sale offended religious sensibilities. Martin Luther was one who had such sensibilities.[78] He could not abide what he perceived as a betrayal of faith. His resultant challenge to the Church led to the Protestant Reformation because many others felt as he did. They were not willing to be associates of a religious institution that did not respect their commitments. Fortunately for Luther, this dissatisfaction coincided with several other developments. One of these was a growing north-south split in Europe. Another was the fracturing of the Holy Roman Empire. A third was the spread of literacy.

If Italy was the font of the Renaissance, within a century its economic ferment spread to the former seat of medieval industry. Bruges might be in decline, but Antwerp had risen to replace it. In so doing it became a financial center to rival its Mediterranean precursors.[79] But in time, it would be supplanted by Amsterdam. The Low Countries, like the Italians citystates had access to water borne transport. Located at the confluence of the Rhine River and the North Sea, once the lateen sail was developed, they could participate in Atlantic traffic. The lateen sail, which is triangular in shape, permitted a ship to sail at an angle into the wind. This facilitated oceanic voyages. In the more placid Mediterranean, oars could make up for what the wind did not do, whereas in the heavier seas of the Atlantic human power was inadequate. After this changeover occurred, the north too became prime commercial territory. With this, the Flemings and Dutch joined the pursuit of riches.[80] The Germans, incidentally, benefited as well. Also connected to the sea by rivers, they were eager to do business with their Hollander cousins.

Luther, a loyal German, was appalled by the avarice of the Romans. So too were German merchants and princes who perceived the Italians as political and commercial rivals. Happily, declaring their religious independence would provide a dividend in autonomy and market reach. This declaration, however, would not have been possible had there been as potent a German state as there were French and Spanish states. The Holy Roman Empire, which during the height of feudalism was reckoned a superpower, in an era of incipient nationalism was an anachronism. Fragmented beyond the power of an elected emperor to unite, individual duchies and electorates vied with one another for an hegemony that none had the strength separately to impose. This allowed some to defy the central authority of an emperor such as Charles V. A ruler might be a loyal son of the Church, yet his military prowess depended not on taxes but the voluntary cooperation of vassals who were not prepared to cooperate. War, when it occurred, was, therefore, inconclusive. In the end, Luther and his allies survived the wrath of those who would have liked to have condemned him as a heretic. Unlike those of previous reformers, his innovations outlasted him, thanks to the resources mustered on his behalf. A rise in commerce, coupled with a decline in feudalism, made possible the alliances that tipped in his favor. Paradoxically, although Luther was very much devoted to spiritual solutions, his success skewed events against religious power. The Catholic Church was to lose much of its dominion, and the emerging Protestant denominations were too numerous for any one of them to exercise a comparable authority.

There were also the effects of literacy. Printing made books readily available. Not surprisingly, Guttenberg's first project was a Bible.[81]

This enabled Protestants to urge their adherents to read the good book for themselves. Instead of having priests interpret its meaning, they could develop personal relationships with the deity. This allowed for an autonomy of spirit that had not previously been encouraged. Max Weber emphasized a Protestant Ethic that urged communicants to seek riches as a sign of being one of God's elect. This motivation, grounded in a submission to divine providence, theoretically provided the discipline needed to generate the capital for economic growth. Perhaps more important, however, was the rigor needed to confront eternity on one's own. Beginning with the internal controls necessary to read a ponderous book unaided, consciously coming to Christ likewise required a level of introspection that was useful in confronting other independent operators in the marketplace. If good Christians could be entrepreneurs in interpreting a sacred text, why not be entrepreneurial in seeking commercial opportunities?

As the Renaissance upsurge of the Commercial Revolution approached its conclusion, the Netherlands and England, two Protestant nations, rose to prominence. Henry VIII of England began his reign slavishly devoted to Italianate fashions but ended as an implacable foe of the Pope.[82] The winds of reform would soon eventuate in Puritan excess, but in the meantime they inspired collective efforts to preserve an independence from Rome. In other words, the disciplines of Protestantism were social as well as personal. This was obvious in John Calvin's Geneva, which decreed strict adherence to a common code of conduct and a dogmatic set of beliefs. This would unexpectedly provide practice in establishing voluntary interpersonal bonds. One day, civic associations and industrial corporations would dominate the landscape, but for the moment the protomiddle classes were caught between the marketplace and a need to protect their eternal souls.

The Enlightenment

The starting point of the next[83] wave of the Commercial Revolution is difficult to pin down. In many ways the Enlightenment was an acceleration of the Renaissance. It was a period during which the emphasis resolutely shifted from the Mediterranean to the Atlantic littoral. The historian Ferdinand Braudel[84] chronicles an ever-quickening rotation of the wheels of commerce, wherein capitalism became a recognized phenomenon and the tentacles of trade spread across the globe. This was the era during which the West asserted its dominance over the rest of the world. In 1529, immediately before hegemony began, the Turks besieged Vienna in a near-run thing. When they retreated, they nevertheless remained the terror of the Balkans. By 1683, in contrast, conditions had drastically changed. A renewed invasion was still able to put Vienna in jeopardy, but this time once the city was relieved, the Ottoman Empire[85] began its fateful decline. The Austrians, although they were on the fringe of European civilization, were able to liberate Hungary on the way to eventually freeing almost all of Turkey's Christian dependencies. The cause of this reversal was nothing less than the relative prosperity of a market driven economy. In making money ever more effectively through trade, the West had stolen a march on everyone else. What had been a forested backwater when the Romans arrived was about to leap ahead of all its rivals.

Every schoolchild is taught about Columbus' voyages of exploration.[86] Undertaken during the Renaissance, they would revolutionize the ground rules within a century. When the Portuguese under the direction of Henry the Navigator began their cautious descent down the African coast, they did so in caravels capable of carrying cargo. Soon the Portuguese would outflank the Venetians in the spice trade. The Spanish were so eager to follow, they inadvertently discovered the New World. But it would take time before this venture was profitable. Initially what followed was the gold and silver fever of the Conquistadors, but presently the West Indies would be found to be ideal for raising sugarcane. This crop encouraged the development of a sweet tooth back home that could be satisfied at a generous return. So lucrative was this trade that other European powers joined the quest. England, France, and the Netherlands rapidly established their own Caribbean outposts. Thanks to the importation of black slaves from Africa, these investments also paid off handsomely. Ironically, the dominance of capitalism kick-started an institution that later proved at odds with its central ethos.

In the late Renaissance and early Enlightenment industrial power was still largely provided by muscle power, whether of humans or draft animals. Because sugar cultivation turned out to be intensive, in order for it to be practicable cheap labor was needed to cut the stalks and press them into juice. Once introduced, slavery unfolded according to a logic of its own. Thus, when the English decided to exploit the North American mainland, they too acquired bondsmen to grow tobacco, cotton, and indigo.[87] Originally intending to take advantage of the lumber and turpentine trade, the speculators who funded these operations switched to where the money was. In so doing, they sought to emulate the fortunes being made to their south. These riches also had an impact on the mother country. They enabled the adventurous to go abroad relatively impoverished but to return with the wherewithal to invest in homegrown commerce. A favorite outlay of these parvenus was in land and its improvements. Still living in the shadow of feudalism, the objective was to imitate the accoutrements of aristocracy while continuing to derive an income from the marketplace.

The Enlightenment would also receive an impetus from the evolution of absolutism. As nation states developed, the temptation to centralize became profound. Newly established kings sought to enlarge their dominions. Even before the Renaissance, Edward I of England attempted to consolidate his rule by claiming Wales and Scotland. In Spain, Ferdinand and Isabella united the crowns of Aragon and Castile, but they also expelled the Moors from Granada. Flush with Middle Age devotion, they also initiated the Inquisition designed, to cleanse their realm of heresy. Not yet commercial in mentality, they assumed that a common religion was essential to social cohesion. After Spain captured Mexico and Peru, this attitude became evident in the hidalgos who led the occupation, who saw little reason to treat pagan Indians with compassion and less to encourage commerce. Later, Philip II inherited a Spain distinct from the Hapsburg regions in central Europe in which he cultivated a Spanish nationalism.[88] While the centralized unity he achieved might have facilitated an economic self-sufficiency, he, and his subjects, were too dedicated to an anachronistic glory to pursue such an objective.

In France, Francis I consolidated his rule in opposition to that of Charles V of the Holy Roman Empire and Henry VIII of England. He was sufficiently powerful to devote huge expenditures to chateau building and sufficiently attuned to scientific developments to induce Leonardo to come to work for him. Nevertheless, it was not until his successors Louis XIII[89] and Louis XIV in the 17th century that absolutism fully flowered. Louis XIV[90] is still remembered as the Sun King who declared that he was the state. The builder of Versailles, he planned his vast palace complex as a place where his nobility could be forced to reside under his watchful presence.[91] As long as they were in his company, he could rest assured that they were plotting social conquests, not his overthrow. Among those upon whom Louis bestowed his munificence and his personal control were the nobility of the sword and the nobility of the robe. Those of the sword traced their eminence to the military aristocracy of medieval times, whereas those of the robe gained their ascendancy from service to the king. Often of merchant origin, they helped gather taxes and administer justice. Even more than affluent Englishmen, they aspired to aristocratic status. Louis cultivated this propensity by investing in luxury industries. Instead of being oriented toward commerce, he found his inspiration in competition with Spain. Rather than capitalize on the peace his absolutist rule brought, he preferred to patronize the manufacture of mirrors and tapestries.

In stark contrast were the developments unfolding within the Netherlands.[92] Mercantile prosperity had prompted the Dutch first to seek independence from the Spanish and then to defend it from encroachments of the French. Sturdy burgers, as opposed to foppish aristocrats, they were prepared to take to their ships as beggars of the sea rather than submit to foreign domination. Though theirs was a tiny territory, they were the most advanced naval architects of the time. Masters of a fleet that could be dedicated either to war or to peace, they had the tenacity to outlast all comers. As a result, these burgers became the vanguard of a transition to the Enlightenment. Despite their small numbers, they ventured across the globe on business. Ferocious competitors, they wrested the Spice Islands from the Portuguese and used the proceeds to fund a middle class lifestyle. Although they paid deference to the local nobility, the prevailing ambience was that of the merchant class. Those of noble descent might lead them into battle, but associations of prominent citizens undertook most of the ordinary business of governing. These sensibilities are still on display in the art that they financed. Rembrandt van Rijn was one they patronized and paintings such as his <u>Night Watch</u> demonstrate the pride they took in regulating their affairs. A miller's son, Rembrandt also provided a wonderful portrayal of a surgeon guild's satisfaction in its members' skills. Prominent too among the works of the Dutch masters were evocations of domestic life. Rembrandt depicted the <u>Jewish Bride</u>, while Frans Hals presented a gallery of merchant portraits commissioned for their own glorification. Perhaps the best of the middle-class chroniclers was Jan Vermeer. His intimate interiors give a glimpse of ordinary life among the comfortably affluent. Some have suggested that he achieved the striking realism of his compositions by utilizing a recent scientific innovation, the camera obscura. If so, both his subject matter and his methods reflect the advances of the moment.

The Dutch became legendary not merely for their prosperity but also for their tolerance. Like their Greek counterparts, they understood that accepting the idiosyncrasies of one's customers was good business. As a result, their nation became a refuge from the religious storms that ended the Renaissance, attracting among others, Spinoza[93] from Spain and Descartes[94] from France. Also renowned for their financial speculations, the Dutch originated what became stock markets. As with the invention of banking, this promoted commerce by providing the funds for dicey opportunities. Taking risks is a defining characteristic of commercial societies. Because they cannot be certain where the profits lie, business types must possess the confidence to take the well-researched plunge. An ability to assume calculated gambles, despite their uncertainties, is thus a keystone feature of the middle classes.

Across the channel in England an intermediary series of events was unfolding. Somewhere between the absolutism of the French and the mercantile common sense of the Dutch was the predemocratic turmoil of this island realm. Building on the political unity and financial reserves established by his father, Henry VIII began his rule with absolutist aspirations.[95] Almost by accident, his desire for a male heir and, therefore, for a divorce produced the conditions for an upheaval. Strong enough to confiscate the wealth of the Roman Catholic Church on his way to instigating an Anglican Protestantism, he unleashed a sequence of currents and countercurrents that remade his domain. The fight over whether England would remain Protestant or return to Roman Catholicism eventuated in a constitutional monarchy. Bloody Mary was succeeded by Elizabeth I, who, in part to retain her position, remained the Virgin Queen. This opened the way for James I, who relocated from Scotland, could never hope to restore Henry's supremacy. His son Charles I[96] intended to do so, but by then it was too late. The Puritans had developed a taste of autonomy they were not about to relinquish. Eventually, led by Oliver Cromwell,[97] their Parliamentary party acquired the clout to win a civil war. Once Cromwell died, the executed king's son, namely Charles II,[98] resumed sovereignty. Yet there were conditions. He was to rule together with parliament with the stipulation that he be a Protestant. This he did with such aplomb that the nation backed him in a victorious war against the Dutch.[99] His brother James II, who succeeded him, was a different story. He was the Duke of York, the man for whom New York was named, but he was a miserable failure as king. His high-handed tactics in attempting to restore Roman Catholicism were so offensive that they prompted his removal. The Dutch stadtholder, William of Orange, the husband of James's daughter Mary, succeeded his father-in-law in what came to be called the Glorious Revolution. But the price of this victory was a further reduction in the monarch's power. Scattershot, the nation achieved a parliamentary unity, and this novel, democratized stability provided the conditions for the coming Industrial Revolution.

The English experience has been recounted in some detail because its innovations were crucial to the evolution of the middle classes. Under Henry VIII and even Elizabeth I,[100] the sovereign could control the economy by conferring mercantile monopolies on favored subjects. This was the inspiration of the colonial ventures in Virginia and Pennsylvania. Yet, as Protestantism grew, parliament became less indulgent in such matters. Even so, because its members too wished to distribute largesse, there gradually arose a Whig squirearchy dedicated to serving its own interests. Local magnates, in concert, asserted their ascendancy largely through control of parliament. Some of the resources that brought them prominence came from the West Indies, but much of these were the result of an enclosure movement. England had long been a commercial backwater. It was a supplier of raw materials rather than a trading depot or industrial hub. The enclosure movement, therefore, fenced in common lands that had once been open to the public so that they could be devoted to crop cultivation. This provided surpluses for the marketplace. At the same time wool previously shipped to Flanders was rerouted to local production. Previously, sheep, after being shorn, provided wool shipped to Flanders. This brought the landowners into a money economy and gave them a stake in safeguarding market institutions. Irrespective of the desires of the weakened monarchy, they had an interest in promoting legislation to protect their property rights.

Into this world burst the Scientific Revolution that constituted the intellectual underpinnings of the Enlightenment. Galileo may have been Italian, but before the 17th century ended the center of gravity for scientific discoveries had shifted to London. The home of the Royal Society, it became the switching center for the latest developments. With English ships beginning to establish the hegemony that would allow succeeding generations to sing of Britannia ruling the waves, the need to facilitate these journeys was acute. This turned eyes skyward in the belief that the stars might provide the key to navigational accuracy. The titan of the age was Isaac Newton,[101] preceded by Francis Bacon and Rene Descartes, champions of empiricism and analytic geometry. Newton created a breathtaking synthesis based on accurate observations and advanced mathematics. His theory of gravity, coupled with the laws of motion and the discovery of integral calculus, explained the movements of the planets. Johannes Kepler had revealed that planetary orbits were elliptical, but Newton educed why. He calculated the moons' wanderings so precisely that eclipses could be predicted and patterns of tides illuminated. So exact were his measures that Edmond Halley could forecast that the comet named after him would return in seventy-five years. For good measure, Newton even explained the refraction of light into rainbows. So impressed were his contemporaries that Alexander Pope[102] penned the immortal couplet, "Nature and Nature's laws lay hid in night/God said, *Let Newton be!* And all was *Light.*"

It is difficult to imagine a more pithy expression of the awe in which his achievements were held. One also gains a sense of the emerging prestige of science.[103] When, as recently as the lifetime of Galileo, the Church had been able to assert that empiricism was trivial compared with revelation, observation now loomed supreme. In essence, the rationality of business had triumphed. Numbers used to bring order to commercial transactions were doing the same for the universe. Others besides Newton joined the hunt for secular knowledge. Robert Hooke, secretary of the Royal Society, was his competitor in investigating gravity and optics; Robert Boyle was making progress regarding the compressibility of gasses; and across the channel, a draper, Anthony van Leeuwenhoek, had taken time from his shop to peer into a drop of water at the tiny animalcules swimming there. Amateurs, later to be regarded as dilettantes, were on the cutting edge of this enterprise.[104] Instrument makers, lawyers, and soldiers were involved. Nothing less than a societywide mental reorganization had occurred, one that prefigured the professional expertise of the future.

Concurrent changes took place in philosophy, literature, and the law. In philosophy, Thomas Hobbes[105] pioneered a social contract theory of political relations. Caught up in the turmoil of the English Civil War, he speculated that only a monarch could keep order among unruly individualists. John Locke[106] writing at the time of Glorious Revolution was, in contrast, an apologist for the parliament, not for the king. A personal friend of Newton's, he postulated thought processes based on mental associations. As a confirmed empiricist, he provided a rationale for popular sovereignty. Across the water in France, and almost a century later, Jean-Jacques Rousseau[107] became the prophet of revolution. Postulating a loving human nature,[108] he declared that government, which on the continent was still in the hands of the nobility, corrupted the innocent. He preferred that general will guided communal decisions. Either profoundly democratic or inchoately fascistic, this placed ordinary people at the center of the equation. Philosophy too was on the verge of entering the marketplace. Rousseau might be preaching to the aristocracy in their salons, but he was also selling pamphlets to a populace eager to hear of its prospective liberation.

Much of what was occurring had political implications. France's Voltaire[109] was every inch the iconoclast, but also a friend of Frederick the Great of Prussia. Meanwhile Jonathan Swift,[110] an Anglican prelate in English-held Ireland, perfected the art of the satire. More significantly, Scotland's Adam Smith[111] was heralding the advent of laissez-faire economics. The cornerstone theorist of supply and demand, he perceived wealth as created in market transactions.[112] Denis Diderot, back in France, was trying to systematize all this into a massive Encyclopedia, while William Blackstone was attempting to bring order to the perceived anarchy of English law. Law, it should be noted, as emphasized by Montesquieu,[113] was a theme of the time. His <u>Spirit of the Laws</u> underlined the desire for the neutrality of objective regulations. Instead of the personal whims of the ruler deciding who received what, formal standards applied equally to all. This rule of law, as opposed to a rule by men, eventually made democracy possible, but, as important, provided predictability within the marketplace. Commerce was inherently uncertain; it did not need to be further complicated by the caprices of the powerful. Reason needed to prevail everywhere, not just in the countinghouse.

Out in the field, innovations were piling up with dizzying alacrity. Overland transportation had been revolutionized by road construction. For the first time since the days of Rome, new corridors were being blazed for both stagecoaches and cargo wagons to wend their way. Of still greater value to merchants were the canals being cut through the countryside. Inland barge traffic could now carry volumes of freight previously confined to rivers and seas. All this made for larger urban agglomerations. Cities like London and Paris grew past their earlier limits, because their populations were fed from a broadened countryside. Within their precincts further novelties promoted an explosion of business. Thus coffeehouses sprouted to provide venues for discussing mutual interests and innovative ideas, such as the provision of insurance, were exchanged among patrons who sought to reduce the risks of the road. These facilities also provided the foundations for a democratic chatter similar to that which once animated the Athenian agora.[114]

Coming in at the tail end of the Enlightenment was the American experiment. Planted on the shore of a veritable wilderness but in communication with the old world by way of the sea, it produced a synthesis of European traditions and frontier improvements. By its very nature populated by risk-takers, these colonials needed to find a way to tame their backwoods while simultaneously reproducing the amenities of the mother country. Once more Benjamin Franklin is an exemplar of what was evolving. Walter Isaacson[115] describes Franklin's antecedents thus: "During the late Middle Ages, a new class emerged in the villages of rural England: men who possessed property and wealth but were not members of the titled aristocracy.

Proud but without great pretension, assertive of their rights as members of an independent middle class, these freeholders came to be known as franklins, from the Middle English word 'frankeleyn' meaning freeman." Largely autonomous artisans and shopkeepers, these men (and women) managed their own affairs, often with considerable dignity. Adam Smith was to refer to England as a nation of shopkeepers, and though this appellation was derisively hurled back at him, it denotes an admirable self-reliance. It was this, rather than aristocratic pretensions, that were transplanted into the wilds of a new continent.

Franklin, it will be recalled, was a printer. In this, he copied his brother in establishing a newspaper. Both, however, were imitating earlier journals published in London, such as Joseph Addison's The Spectator.[116] In this, they revealed that a literate populace was in place on both sides of the Atlantic. Evidently schooling sufficient to make reading common was of value in societies where books and pamphlets were readily available. Education and the knowledge it provided were helpful within a commercial environment. Information about what was for sale, what was on the political horizon, and where fresh opportunities might be found was eagerly sought. Ordinary people wanted to know what was going on and what their neighbors were thinking. So inquisitive they, so ravenous for data, they turned Franklin's Poor Richard's Almanac into a runaway bestseller. He became the herald of the middle classes, not merely because to this was his community, but because tens of thousands of others shared his aspirations. Theirs was a world of initiative and personal responsibility. Franklin was well loved for the on-point advice he offered via deft, non-preachy, humor. Unlike the nobility of old, he did not force his ideas on readers but allowed them to adopt what they would.

An anecdote told about Franklin illuminates what was happening to a nation on the threshold of becoming substantially middle class. Between 1739 and 1741, George Whitefield toured the colonies sermonizing on behalf of Methodism. In one of the crowds attracted to his Philadelphia crusade stood Franklin himself. At the time a deist not much enamored of organized religion, the great man was nevertheless mesmerized. According to his own account he was so charmed that, much against his inclinations, he ended up prepared to empty his pockets into the collection plate. His fellow Americans felt the same way. Calls to comply with strict moral rules revitalized their faith during a colonywide episode labeled The Great Awakening.[117] John Wesley had previously instigated a religious reform that provided a reason to trust strangers. To the degree that they were evangelized into following his method, they could be expected to keep their promises and to refrain from cheating. Essentially a step in inculcating the internal disciplines critical to maintaining a continentwide marketplace, this converted his admirers into members of the same moral fraternity.

Not long afterwards, Thomas Jefferson[118] participated in solidifying the foundations for political trust. In the Declaration of Independence, following the lead of John Locke, he affirmed that ordinary people had the right to replace their ruler if he violated the compact wherein he promised them protection. Tyrants could be overthrown because God had created everyone with equal rights to life, liberty, and the pursuit of happiness. Indeed, when these were infringed upon, citizens had a duty to rectify the situation. Jefferson almost went as far as Locke in declaring that they had a right to property as well. Private ownership was so integral to the commercial communities in which both lived that it was unimaginable that the government could peremptorily violate that right. With these assurances in place, both the merchant class and ordinary landowning citizens could rely on elected officials to refrain from despotism. Having grown accustomed to regulating their daily affairs without undo intrusion, they had no intention of replacing one autocrat with another.[119]

Endnotes

[1] Sanderson, S.K. 1995. *Social Transformations: A General Theory of Historical Development.* Oxford, UK: Blackwell; Rice, L. and Greenberg, L. (Eds.) 1984. *Patterns of Change.* New York: Guilford Press.

[2] Boorstin, D.J. 1983. *The Discoverers: A History of Man's Search to Know His World and Himself.* New York: Vintage Books; Boorstin, D.J. 1987. *Hidden History: Exploring Our Secret Past.* New York: Harper & Row.

[3] Thomas, W.I. and Thomas, D.S. 1928. *The Child in America: Behavior, Problems and Progress.* New York: Knopf.

[4] Grun, B. 1979. *The Timetables of History: A Horizontal Linkage of People and Events.* New York: Simon & Schuster.; McNeill, W.H. 1963. *The Rise of the West: A History of the Human Community.* Chicago: University of Chicago Press.

[5] Lewis, B. 2002. What Went Wrong: Western Impact and Middle Eastern Response. New York: Oxford University Press; Mortimer, E. 1982. *Faith and Power: The Politics of Islam.* New York: Random House.

[6] Tharpa, R. 1966. *A History of India. (Vols. I & II.)* London: Penguin Books.

[7] Eberhard, W. 1977. *A History of China.* London: Routledge & Kegan Paul; Peyrefitte, A. 1977. *The Chinese: Portrait of a People.* New York: Bobbs-Merrill Co.

[8] Ferguson, N. 2001. The Cash Nexus: Money and Power in the Modern World, 1700 – 2000. New York: Basic Books.

[9] Rawlinson, G. 1993. *Ancient History: The Great Civilizations from 3000 B.C. to the Fall of Rome.* New York: Barnes & Noble Books.

[10] Finley, M.I. 1973. *The Ancient Economy.* Berkeley: University of California Press.

[11] Hamilton, E. 1958. *The Greek Way.* New York: W.W. Norton & Co.

[12] Fornara, C. 1991. *Athens from Cleisthenes to Pericles.* Berkeley: University of California Press.

[13] For a contrast see: Forrest, W.G. 1968. *A History of Sparta 950-192 B.C.* New York: W.W. Norton & Co.

[14] Festinger, L. 1957. *A Theory of Cognitive Dissonance.* Evanston, Ill.: Row, Peterson.

[15] Plato 1928. *The Works of Plato.* (Jowett translation) New York: The Modern Library; Plato 1941. *The Republic.* (Jowett translation) New York: The Modern Library.

[16] James, P. and Thorpe, N. 1994. *Ancient Inventions.* New York: Ballantine Books.

[17] Aristotle 1941. *The Basic Works of Aristotle.* Edited by R. McKeon. New York: Random House.

[18] Nahm, M.C. (Ed.) 1934. *Selections from Early Greek Philosophy.* New York: Appleton-Century-Crofts.

[19] Cumston, C.C. 1987. The History of Medicine: From the Time of the Pharaohs to the End of the XVIII Century. New York: Dorset Press.

[20] Herodotus 1954. *The Histories* (Translated by Aubery de Selincourt) Harmondworth, UK: Penguin Books.

[21] Thucydides. 1998. *The Peloponnesian War*. (Translated by Walter Blanco) New York: W.W. Norton & Co.

[22] Hanson, V.D. 2003a. Ripples of Battle: How Wars of the Past Still Determine How We Fight. How We Live. And How We Think. New York: Doubleday.

[23] Fornara, C. 1991. *Athens from Cleisthenes to Pericles*. Berkeley: University of California Press.

[24] Kagan, D. 2003. *The Peloponnesian War*. New York: Penguin Books. Note that even when they went into battle the Athenians still identified themselves by lineage.

[25] Stone, I.F. 1988. *The Trial of Socrates*. Boston: Little, Brown, & Co.

[26] Plutarch [1959] *Lives of Noble Greeks* (Edited by Edmund Fuller) New York: Nelson Doubleday.

[27] Hanson, V.D. 2001. Carnage and Culture: Landmark Battles in the Rise of Western Power. New York: Doubleday.

[28] Matthews, K.D. 1964. *The Early Romans: Farmers to Empire Builders*. New York: McGraw-Hill.

[29] Carcopino, J. 1940. *Daily Life in Ancient Rome*. New Haven: Yale University Press; Cowelll, F.R. 1961. *Life in Ancient Rome*. New York: G.P. Putnam's Sons.

[30] Caeasar, J. [1980] *The Battle for Gaul*. Boston: David R. GodinePublisher.

[31] Tacitus [1977] *The Annals of Imperial Rome*. New York: Dorset Press.

[32] Plutarch [1959] *Lives of Noble Romans* (Edited by Edmund Fuller) New York: Nelson Doubleday.

[33] Tacitus [1977] *The Annals of Imperial Rome*. New York: Dorset Press.

[34] Straus, B.R. 1987. *The Catholic Church*. London: David & Charles.

[35] Owen, F. 1960. *The Germanic People: Their Origin, Expansion and Culture*. New York: Dorset Press.

[36] Bachrach, B.S. 1972. *Merovingian Military Organization 481-751*. Minneapolis: University of Minnesota Press.

[37] Dockes, P. 1979. *Medieval Slavery and Liberation*. (Translated by Arthur Goldhammer) Chicago: University of Chicago Press.

[38] Barraclough, G. 1976. The Crucible of Europe: The Ninth and Tenth Centuries in European History. Berkeley: University of California Press.

[39] Munz, P. 1969. *Life in the Age of Charlemagne*. New York: G.P. Putnam's Sons.

[40] Grousett, R. 1970. *The Empire of the Steppes: A History of Central Asia* (translated by Naomi Walford). New Brunswick: Rutgers University

Press; Dvornik, F. 1962. *The Slavs in European History and Civilization.* New Brunswick: Rutgers University Press.

[41] Keen, M. 1969. *The Pelican History of Medieval Europe.* Baltimore: Penguin Books.

[42] Brooke, C. 1965. *Europe in the Central Middle Ages 962-1154.* New York: Holt, Rinehart and Winston.

[43] Ranke-Heinmann, U. 1990. *Eunuchs for the Kingdom of Heaven.* New York: Doubleday.

[44] Scott, M. 1964. *Medieval Europe.* New York: Dorset Press.

[45] Duby, G. 1973. *The Early Growth of the European Economy.* Ithaca, NY: Cornell University Press.

[46] Pirenne, H. 1936. *Economic and Social History of Medieval Europe.* New York: Harcourt, Brace & World.

[47] Crosby, A.W. 1997. The Measure of Reality: Quantification and Western Society 1250-1600. Cambridge, UK: Cambridge University Press.

[48] Le Goff, J. 1980. *Time, Work, & Culture in the Middle Ages.* Chicago: University of Chicago Press.

[49] Duby, G. 1980. The Three Orders: Feudal Society Imagined. Chicago: University of Chicago Press; Duby, G. 1983. The Knight, The Lady, and the Priest: The Making of Modern Marriage in Medieval France. New York: Pantheon Books; Gies, F. and Gies, J. 1987. *Marriage and the Family in the Middle Ages.* New York: Harper & Row.

[50] Setton, K.M. (Ed.) 1969. *The History of the Crusades.* Madison: University of Wisconsin Press.

[51] Manchester, W. 1992. A World Lit Only By Fire: The Medieval Mind and the Renaissance. Boston: Little, Brown & Co.

[52] Tuchman, B.W. 1978. *A Distant Mirror: The Calamitous 14th Century.* New York: Ballantine Books.

[53] Gregorovius, F. 1971. *Rome and Medieval Culture.* Chicago: University of Chicago Press.

[54] Plumb, J.H. 1961. *The Italian Renaissance.* New York: American Heritage.

[55] Bell, D. 1978. *The Cultural Contradictions of Capitalism.* New York: Basic Books.

[56] Nauert, C.G. 1995. *Humanism and the Culture of Renaissance Europe.* New York: Cambridge University Press; Davies, T. 1997. *Humanism.* New York: Routledge.

[57] Gould, S.J. 1996. *Full House: The Spread of Excellence from Plato to Darwin.* New York: Three Rivers Press.

[58] Diel, C. 1969. *The History of the Byzantine Empire.* (Translated by George B. Ives) New York: AMS Press.

[59] Braudel, F. 1972. The Mediterranean and the Mediterranean World in the Age of Philip II, Vols. I & II. New York: Harper & Row.

[60] Braudel, F. 1972. The Mediterranean and the Mediterranean World in the Age of Philip II, Vols. I & II. New York: Harper & Row.

[61] Strieder, J. 1984. *Jacob Fugger The Rich: Merchant and Banker of Augsburg 1459-1525.* (translated by Mildred Hartsough) Westport, CT: Greenwood Press.

[62] Hanson, V.D. 2001. Carnage and Culture: Landmark Battles in the Rise of Western Power. New York: Doubleday.

[63] Alighieri, D. 1955. *The Divine Comedy.* (Trans. By Thomas G. Bergin) New York: Appleton, Century, Crofts.

[64] Machiavelli, N. 1966. *The Prince.* (Translated by Daniel Donnos) New York: Bantam Books.

[65] Goffen, R. 2002. Renaissance Rivals: Michelangelo, Leonardo, Raphael, Titian. New Haven: University Press.

[66] Crosby, A.W. 1997. The Measure of Reality: Quantification and Western Society 1250-1600. Cambridge, UK: Cambridge University Press.

[67] Sobel, D. 1999. Galileo's Daughter: A Historical Memoir of Science, Faith, and Love. New York: Walker & Co.

[68] Payne, R. 1978. *Leonardo.* Garden City, NY: Doubleday.

[69] Harre, R. 1964. *Matter and Method.* London: MacMillan and Co.

[70] Briggs, R. 1977. *Early Modern France 1550-1715.* Oxford: Oxford University Press.

[71] Strayer, J.R. 1970. *On the Medieval Origins of the Modern State.* Princeton: Princeton University Press.

[72] Kelly, A. 1950. *Eleanor of Aquitaine and the Four Kings.* Cambridge, MA: Harvard University Press; Warren, W.L. 1961. *King John.* Berkeley: University of California Press.

[73] Hutchinson, H.F. 1967. *King Henry V: A Biography.* New York: Dorset Press.

[74] Kendall, P.M. 1971. *Louis XI: The Universal Spider.* New York: W.W. Norton & Co.

[75] Tilly, C. (Ed.) 1975. *The Formation of National States in Western Europe.* Princeton, NJ: Princeton University Press; Strayer, J.R. 1970. *On the Medieval Origins of the Modern State.* Princeton: Princeton University Press.

[76] Ridely, J. 1982. Statesman and Saint: Cardinal Wolsey, Sir Thomas More and the Politics of Henry VIII. New York: The Viking Press.

[77] Chamberlain, E.R. 1993. *The Bad Popes.* New York: Barnes & Noble Press.

[78] Erikson, E. 1958. *Young Man Luther.* New York: W.W. Norton.

[79] Braudel, F. 1972. The Mediterranean and the Mediterranean World in the Age of Philip II, Vols. I & II. New York: Harper & Row.

[80] Braudel, F. 1979. The Structures of Everyday Life: Civilization & Capitalism 15th-18th Century Volume 1. New York: Harper & Row.; Braudel, F. 1979. The Wheels of Commerce: Civilization & Capitalism 15th-18th

Century Volume 2. New York: Harper & Row.; Braudel, F. 1979. The Perspective of the World: Civilization & Capitalism 15th-18th Century Volume 3. New York: Harper & Row.

[81] Barzun, J. 2000. *From Dawn to Decadence: 500 Years of Western Cultural Life.* New York: HarperCollins Publishers.

[82] Bindoff, S.T. 1950. *Tudor England.* Baltimore, MD: Penguin Books; Ridely, J. 1982. *Statesman and Saint: Cardinal Wolsey, Sir Thomas More and the Politics of Henry VIII.* New York: The Viking Press.

[83] Sanderson, S.K. 1995. Social Transformations: A General Theory of Historical Development. Oxford, UK: Blackwell.

[84] Braudel, F. 1979. The Structures of Everyday Life: Civilization & Capitalism 15th-18th Century Volume 1. New York: Harper & Row.; Braudel, F. 1979. The Wheels of Commerce: Civilization & Capitalism 15th-18th Century Volume 2. New York: Harper & Row.; Braudel, F. 1979. The Perspective of the World: Civilization & Capitalism 15th-18th Century Volume 3. New York: Harper & Row.

[85] Kinross, L. 1977. The Ottoman Centuries: The Rise and Fall of the Ottoman Empire. New York: Morrow.

[86] Morison, S.E. 1978. *The Great Explorers: The European Discovery of America.* New York: Oxford University Press; McNeill, W.H. 1963. *The Rise of the West: A History of the Human Community.* Chicago: University of Chicago Press.

[87] Erickson C. 1983. *The First Elizabeth.* New York: Summit Books.

[88] Elliott, J.H. 1968. *Europe Divided 1559-1598.* London: Fontana Press.

[89] Parker, G. 1984. *The Thirty Years' War.* New York: Military Heritage Press.

[90] Durant, A. and Durant. W. 1963. *The Age of Louis XIV.* New York: MJF Books; Goubert, P. 1966. *Louis XIV and Twenty Million Frenchmen.* New York: Vintage Books.

[91] Elias, N. 1982. *Power and Civility.* New York: Pantheon Books; Elias, N. 1983. *The Court Society.* New York: Pantheon Books; Elias, N. 1998. *On Civilization, Power, and Knowledge.* (Edited by Stephen Mennell and Johan Goudsblom) Chicago: University of Chicago Press.

[92] Tracy, J.D. 1990. Holland Under Hapsburg Rule 1506-1566: The Founding of a Body Politic. Berkeley: University of California Press; Price, J.L. 1994. Holland and the Dutch Republic in the Seventeenth Century: The Politics of Particularism. New York: Oxford University Press.

[93] Wild, J. (Ed.) 1958. *Spinoza Selections.* New York: Charles Scribner's Sons.

[94] Eaton, R.M. (Ed.) *Descartes Selections.* New York: Charles Scribner's Sons.

[95] Ridely, J. 1982. Statesman and Saint: Cardinal Wolsey, Sir Thomas More and the Politics of Henry VIII. New York: The Viking Press.

[96] Watson, D.R. 1972. *The Life and Times of Charles I.* London: Weidenfeld and Nicolson.

[97] Howell, R. 1977. *Cromwell.* Boston: Little, Brown & Co.

98 Fraser, A. 1979. *King Charles II*. London: Weidenfeld and Nicolson.

99 Lantham, R. (Ed.) 1983. *The Illustrated Pepys: Extracts from the Diary*. Berkeley: University of California Press.

100 Erickson C. 1983. *The First Elizabeth*. New York: Summit Books.

101 Gleick, J. 2003. *Isaac Newton*. New York: Pantheon Books.

102 Gleick, J. 2003. *Isaac Newton*. New York: Pantheon Books.

103 Jardine, L. 1999. *Ingenious Pursuits: Building the Scientific Revolution*. New York: Doubleday.

104 Sobel, D. 1995. Longitude: The True Story of a Lone Genius Who Solved the Greatest Scientific Problem of His Time. New York: Walker & Co.

105 Hobbes, T. 1956. *Leviathan; Part I*. Chicago: Henry Regnery Co.

106 Locke, J. 1959. (1765) *An Essay Concerning Human Understanding*. New York: Dover Publications.

107 Cranston, M. 1982. *Jean-Jacques*. New York: W.W. Norton & Co.; Rousseau, J.J. 1968. (1762) *The Social Contract* (Translated by Maurice Cranston) New York: Penguin Books; Rousseau, Jean-Jacques [1762] 1979. *Emile*. Trans. A. Bloom. New York: Basic Books; Rousseau, J.J. 1992. *The Discourse on the Origins of Inequality*. (Edited by Roger D. Masters and Christopher Kelly) Hanover, NH: University Press of New England; Durant, A. and Durant. W. 1967. *Rousseau and the Revolution*. New York: MJF Books.

108 For a closer look at the reality see: Boswell, R.B. 1988. *The Kindness of Strangers*. New York: Pantheon Books.

109 Tallentyre, S.G. 1969. *The Life of Voltaire*. New York: Kraus Reprint Co.

110 Swift, J. 1948. *The Portable Swift*. (Edited by Carl Van Doren) New York: Viking Press.

111 Smith, A. 1776. *An Inquiry into the Nature and Causes of the Wealth of Nations*. London: W. Strahan & T. Cadell.

112 See also the enlightenment skepticism of David Hume, especially as it applied to morality. Hume, D. 1739. *A Treatise on Human Nature*. London.

113 Montesquieu, C. 1977. *The Spirit of the Laws*. Berkeley: University of California Press.

114 Kirk, R. 1997. *Edmund Burke: A Genius Reconsidered*. Wilmington, Del: Intercollegiate Studies Institute.

115 Isaacson, W. 2003. *Benjamin Franklin: An American Life*. New York: Simon & Schuster.

116 Isaacson, W. 2003. *Benjamin Franklin: An American Life*. New York: Simon & Schuster.

117 Andrews, D. 2000. *The Methodists and Revolutionary America 1760-1800*. Princeton: Princeton University Press.

[118] Mapp, A.J. 1987. *Thomas Jefferson: A Strange Case of Mistaken Identity.* Lanham, MD: Madison Books.; Ellis, J.J. 1996. *American Sphinx: The Character of Thomas Jefferson.* New York: Alfred A. Knopf.

[119] Morris, R.B. 1985. *Witnesses at the Creation: Hamilton, Madison, Jay, and the Constitution.* New York: New American Library; Ellis, J.J. 2000. *Founding Brothers: The Revolutionary Generation.* New York: Alfred A. Knopf.

Chapter 5

Industrialization

So naturalists observe, a flea
Hath smaller fleas that on him prey;
And these have smaller still to bite 'em;
And so proceed ad infinitum.
(Jonathan Swift, <u>On Poetry</u>)

All systems of either preference or of restraint, therefore,
being thus completely taken away, the obvious and simple
system of natural liberty establishes itself of its own accord.
Every man, as long as he does not violate the laws of
justice, is left perfectly free to pursue his own interest his
own way, and to bring his own industry and capital into
competition with those of any other man or order of men.
(Adam Smith, <u>The Wealth of Nations</u>)

The Great Depression was a government failure, brought
on principally by Federal Reserve policies that abruptly cut
the money supply.... High unemployment lasted as long
as it did because of New Deal policies that took money out
of people's pockets, disrupted the money supply, restricted
production, harassed employers, destroyed jobs, discouraged
investment, and subverted economic liberty needed for
sustained business recovery. (Jim Powell, <u>FDR's Folly</u>)

Art is a revolt against fate. (Andre Malraux, <u>Voices of</u>
<u>Silence</u>)

The Industrial Revolution

Evidently based on Leeuwenhoek's observations, Swift's[1]
understanding of fleas upon fleas neatly fits the nesting waves
characteristic of the Commercial Revolution. It also corresponds

with the many oscillations manifest within the Industrial Revolution.[2] Often reckoned to be a single cohesive movement, this period can be resolved into a series of succeeding intervals. The details may be debated, but that there was a multistage progression cannot. The social capital today so palpable within middle class was not a unitary achievement. Rather, there were regular and advancing stages.

The self-direction and internalized discipline that allow for commercial and political decentralization did not appear spontaneously. They grew out of a sequence of innovations. Emotional maturation, for instance, could only have evolved through a long series of shared experiences. Adam Smith was wrong in asserting that a simple system of natural liberty establishes itself of its own accord. An invisible hand may direct the marketplace, but even it could not operate without the preexistence of appropriate interpersonal conditions. To be more precise, whereas systems of preference and restraint are universal, the controls that keep them within specific channels take time to evolve. Unfairness and coercion never completely fade away; hence, no one is ever perfectly free to pursue his unhampered interests, but how these interests express themselves depends on the rules and personal assets the players bring to the table. The norms, values, and beliefs of societies and their members are significantly amended over time. What is not possible in one era may become the conventional wisdom of another. In truth, both internal and external controls mutate in accord with emerging social conditions, such that everyone, not just members of bureaucracies, live in quasi-iron cages. Of particular interest to the Middle Class Revolution is the normative emotional restraints that facilitate or deter particular forms of economic and political cooperation. Of these, the evolution of expressive self-control was crucial to the emergence of bourgeois authority. Only its arrival enabled ordinary human beings to work harmoniously on ever more complex tasks without submitting to tyrannical external constraints.

The unfolding of the Industrial Revolution was integral to this succession. As the need to work with machines progressed, it imposed unprecedented demands. These unfamiliar challenges nevertheless took many years to understand and assimilate. It took decades and sometimes centuries for norms, values, and beliefs to make the unknown routine.[3] It also took time for newly formed alliances and institutions to tame apparently threatening innovations and to tamp down the extreme feelings that accompanied them. Until fear, overreaction, and denial could be overcome, mistakes were inevitable. Daniel Chirot[4] has speculated that this developmental sequence unfolded in a series of upheavals that succeeded each other as new technologies came forward. The first wave began in England about the middle of the 18th century.[5] It was launched because the preceding commercial explosion had dramatically increased the call for goods. Not unnaturally, the suppliers of these commodities sought more effective means to take advantage of this opportunity. Among the innovations that sprang up were the use of coal to replace depleting stores of wood, iron smelting to replace more fragile non-ferrous materials, and the steam engine to replace muscle power. Of these, the steam engine was of paramount significance. For the first time in history, a means had been found to inject almost boundless reserves of energy into the economy. Prior to this, the number of human beings required to accomplish a task limited how much of it could be achieved. Now, mindless pieces of machinery worked the day around. People were relieved of traditional drudgery but in the process were reduced to tending these devices. Some thought this a demotion; nevertheless, it allowed each worker to turn out far more goods than was possible previously.

James Watt[6] brought the steam engine, which began with Newcomen's more inefficient contraption for pumping water out of mines, to commercial fulfillment. Fueled by abundant coal and fabricated of newly available iron, it liberated production from the marginal locations to which industrialization had been confined. Previously, factories had been situated adjacent to rapidly flowing streams needed to turn millwheels. These, not surprisingly, tended to be in upland regions where transportation was difficult. Watt's newfangled devices made it possible to build industrial plants in cities where labor was plentiful and where canals could bring in raw materials and carry away finished products. Once more, the volume of trade took a leap forward. The earliest applications of this advance were in the textile industry. England had historically supplied wool to continental manufactories, but now James Hargreaves's spinning jenny, Richard Arkwright's water frame, Samuel Crompton's mule, and Edmund Cartwright's power loom introduced change. With this technology, raw fiber could be processed more efficiently at home than abroad. As a result, the country quickly became the center of cloth manufacture for the entire world.

All this triggered a profusion of social changes.[7] The growing output turned Midland towns like Manchester into booming cities and converted farm laborers into factory workers. Textile production had previously depended on a putting-out system. Individual entrepreneurs carried unfinished materials to individual contractors who performed their discrete tasks in their own homes. But because the new machines required a central location, employees now had to journey to them, with home and work thereby separated as never before. Likewise, the capitalists, that is, those who invested in the machines and organized their operations, became substantial personages. As the nexus of production, they exercised more influence than had their predecessors. Flushed with success, they unleashed further waves of entrepreneurial spirit. Ambitious individuals now sought the main chance in the marketplace rather than the battlefield. These formerly anonymous souls hoped to grow rich and powerful by coming up with ingenious ideas. Ordinary life was similarly revolutionized. To begin with, the new cheaper cloth supplanted the homespuns of yore. Average people could now purchase store-bought materials for less, thereby elevating the quality of their daily lives. No longer were they limited to the products they could produce with their own hands.

Over in France, another sort of revolution was brewing.[8] The French looked with envy toward England, hitherto deemed inferior.[9] Across the ocean in the United States, they also perceived the rapid advances of an upstart democracy they had helped install. Unfortunately, bankrolling American independence had put a strain on French finances. This exacerbated an economic dip that energized a growing discontent with the country's governing absolutism. Sparked at first by an entrepreneurial aristocracy that hoped to benefit by restricting the monarchy, this dissatisfaction was soon appropriated by the bourgeoisie. Through the agency of the Estates-General, it managed to topple the ancient regime. Although inexperienced in the ways of democracy, these ambitious parvenus manipulated the Paris rabble into becoming the cannon fodder for their coup. In the process, cartloads of heads were severed from their bodies, and the nobility was sent scurrying for the safety of the borders, all in the name of liberty, equality, and fraternity.[10]

Into this turmoil rode Napoleon Bonaparte.[11] After taming the passions of the street, he directed his fellow's interests and energies outward toward the conquest of an empire. Since the efficacy of his armies depended on harnessing an insipient patriotism, perhaps his greatest achievement was getting ordinary Frenchmen to identify with the interests of the nation. Without millions of individually motivated citizens ready to die to expand their nation's borders, he could not have swept away the detritus of European autocracy. As Emperor, he also ostensibly made the rule of law supreme by means of the Code Napoleon. Not he, but the people, were now theoretically in charge. A nation of former peasants came to perceive itself as on the vanguard of democratization. This idea, if not its reality, was clearly implanted in the collective psyche. In fact, it was nationalism that had been firmly established. The individual French became the collective French and not merely a collection of disparate provincials. Concomitantly, the glory of their subsequent victories instilled a nascent nationalism among the defeated Germans and Italians.

England meanwhile had been drawn into this continentwide conflict. Regarded by the Emperor as his chief adversary, it was able to sustain the struggle in part due to its industrial and financial superiority. The British had earlier created a national bank to oversee its currency. This could now be turned to generating the loans that kept its military in the field. Contemporaries were terrified of the debt thereby acquired, but the cumulative effect was to keep the economy and government running. Once more, by inadvertence, an innovative means of sustaining commerce had come into being. In addition, Britain's parliamentary institutions were found more resilient than their French counterparts. They, and not their more radical continental competitors, were the genuine pioneers of democracy. After the dust of the Napoleonic period settled, the French too realized the virtues of industrialization, if not of democratization. Though briefly returned to a monarchial government, old-line aristocrats such as Saint-Simon[12] advocated science and technology as a method for catching up with their old enemy. The trouble was that he, and many of his countrymen, took a romantic approach to this task. Instead of the pragmatics of the marketplace, they were fascinated with utopian communities where an idealized spirit of cooperation would provide the edge.

On the other side of the Atlantic, more sweeping innovations were occurring.[13] Almost every contemporary who contemplated these matters was convinced that the new nation would forever remain an agricultural storehouse. Blessed with what seemed unbroken horizons, there was too much cheap land to make industry feasible. It would clearly be more economical to import finished goods from Europe. One small ripple of dissent was furnished by cotton. This inexpensive fiber had become enormously profitable as the Midlands textile mills cranked up their operations. But it also became more plentiful once Eli Whitney's cotton gin could remove the seeds from unprocessed bales. Since the trading interests of the East Coast did not want to be left behind, they clamored for textile factories of their own. These shortly make New England a facsimile of its namesake.

The patron of these protoindustrialists was Alexander Hamilton.[14] The emergent government's first Secretary of the Treasury, he anticipated the eventual arrival of prosperous manufactories. To prepare their way, he insisted that the federal government assume the debts incurred by the separate states during the American Revolution.[15] His rationale was that fiscal responsibility would create strong credit and that this was good for business. In his view, financial stability would enable businessmen to borrow the money they needed to expand and provide the permanence to predict market conditions.[16] In short order, Hamilton was proved right. The budding American industries emulated, and even stole, British technology. Among their best moves was to develop techniques for fabricating interchangeable machine parts. This allowed the assembly of mechanically superior and, therefore, competitive products—among which were to be breach loading rifles.

Within two decades, a member of the French nobility reported on what he observed in the former colonies. Alexis de Tocqueville[17] ventured across the ocean ostensibly to study the new nation's prison system. His real concern, however, was in determining what made American democracy successful.[18] Uncomfortably aware that equality had not taken root in his own country, he was obsessed with discovering the cause. Too young to have witnessed his nation's revolution, he was nevertheless infected with its liberal aspirations. In his travels across the United States, the young man encountered a myriad of surprises. One was the egalitarian comportment of the population. Even ordinary workers would approach him as a peer. Unlike their French counterparts, they would shake his hand and greet him like a long lost brother. Evidently, believing that all men were created equal had spilled into their politics. De Tocqueville sourly noted that even an illiterate backwoodsman such as Davy Crockett could get elected to Congress.

Another phenomenon commented upon by de Tocqueville was that these people were addicted to self-help associations.[19] Much in the manner of Ben Franklin, they, on their own initiative, united to solve common problems. They became members of fraternal organizations, the Grange, the Masons,[20] political parties, chambers of commerce, and school boards. If, in rural Michigan, there was no school for their children to attend, they came together to build one. They did not wait for the central government to act but inaugurated the enterprise themselves. Evidently, in a nation as large as theirs, excessive dependence on a central authority would have been unproductive. Washington was simply too far away. This decentralization had several other effects. First, in cooperating to help themselves, ordinary people gained experience in democratic action. They learned how to negotiate with one another and to make the concessions to get things done. Second, they developed a sense of independence. The frontier, in requiring them to face dangers with the resources on hand, promoted both cooperation and a sturdy individualism.[21] Third, this need for self-reliance encouraged pragmatism. Americans came to pride themselves on their know-how. Since most jobs got done only when they did them, they made sure that what they did worked.

Closely related to this orientation was a rampant commercialism.[22] The shipping interests on the east coast needed to be assertive if they were going to carve out markets in a world dominated by more powerful nations. As a result, they took delight in an entrepreneurial spirit that contributed to their reputation as Yankee traders. Out in the hinterland a similar disposition was taking shape. Speculation in land, and the products that came from it, was rife. Everyone dreamed of striking it rich long before the advent of the California gold rush.

This produced the side effect of muting jealousy of the wealthy. One day they too would move from their present homestead, to where they would build the mills that would make their fortunes. Crockett attempted this and nearly succeeded. Social mobility was a universal birthright. People did not passively accept their fates, but actively prepared for better ones.

De Tocqueville was also much taken by the common culture that enabled people to move a thousand miles from home and still interact with their neighbors. North and South, East and West, all spoke the same language. Being able to understand what strangers said made everyone feel part of a single extended family. As significant were shared values. In addition to a common desire to grow rich, they honored a common religious tradition. More than their Protestantism, they had inherited a legacy of religious toleration. With no established church (as there had been in France) people enjoyed a freedom of conscience they were pleased to extend to others. Most were quite sincere in their faiths, but also sincere in their respect for a plethora of distinct denominations. Then, too, there was litigiousness. Americans were prepared to sue one another at the drop of a hat. This might seem to betoken an antidemocratic divisiveness, but as Tocqueville recognized, it indicated the opposite. Ordinary Americans had faith in their courts. They believed that their laws were just and fairly administered. Able to participate as jurors, they readily submitted their grievances to outsiders for resolution. This had the effect of containing potential conflicts. In a mobile country continuously becoming more populous, these traditions enabled its populace to live in peace without everyone's belonging to the same church or acquiescing to a shared overlord.

Occurring at about the time of Tocqueville's journey was The Second Great Awakening.[23] This religious revival was evangelical in the manner of its predecessor but more ecumenical. As industrialization spread across the land, a more secular-oriented religion began to assert an internal discipline more appropriate to the changed conditions. In places like Rochester, New York,[24] factories were growing commonplace. By the 1820s this upstate town was one of the fastest developing cities in the country, its fortune founded on an auspicious location astride the falls of the Genesee River. Surrounded by flat plains perfect for cultivating wheat and intersected by the newly constructed Erie Canal, it was ideal for grinding grain into flour, then shipping it to the trading centers down the Hudson. The transformation that began this voyage occurred in mills powered by water which were reasonably large operations the profitability of which was contingent upon keeping the machinery running. Like most factories, they required workmen who arrived on time and preformed their duties dependably. They could not be drunk, lest they fall into the gears and clog the works.

The trouble was that imbibing alcohol had been a frontier tradition. With transportation limited, turning grain into spirits, then consuming roughly three times as much as modern Americans do, was the norm. This is where the interests of evangelicals appeared. They were invited to towns by business interests to preach temperance. Workers who went to church instead of the saloon would be better for the bottom line. This began a century-long alliance between industrialists and the religious. Because industrialization required internal controls not only from the capitalists but also from the workforce, sacred motives were used to instill secular virtues. These commercially requisite emotional restraints did not arise because those involved recognized their rationality. Quite the reverse, for preexisting emotional commitments were redirected into novel channels.

At its early stages, many thought industrialization could not be tamed.[25] The thinkers theorized about a need to withdraw into family-like utopian communities.[26] Not only Saint-Simon,[27] but Charles Fourier in France and Robert Owen in Britain attempted to organize such ventures. Fourier's ideal inspired Brook Farm and Owen's prompted the founding of New Lanark in Scotland and New Harmony in Indiana. Each of these places seemed at first to be a refuge for souls determined to salvage human decency from the hard-heartedness of the marketplace. If the goal of making money was to convert human beings into extensions of the machine, perhaps it was better to renounce the whole project. The Luddites[28] might have been too extreme in attempting to destroy Nottingham's knitting machines, but peaceful cooperation among like-minded individuals might prove the epitome of what seemed to be a reasonable idealism. Sadly, these experiments in anti-industrialism collapsed. Members simply could not cooperate for the long run. Nevertheless, they heralded a romantic reaction to the march of commercialism. The Industrial Revolution had so disturbed social relationships that a widespread desire to undo it had emerged, one that has reverberated into the twenty-first century.

The Victorians

Queen Victoria[29] came to the British throne at the end of the 1830s. By this time, industrialism was firmly established in her country. Though she surely did not intend it, she was to become the symbol of the next stage of its evolution. In 1840, just having entered her twenties, she married her first cousin, Prince Albert of Saxe-Coberg-Gotha. Though she was at first reluctant, she settled into a committed domesticity that became an example for her middle-class subjects. A devoted wife and mother, she ceded many of her powers to her consort. When Albert died in 1861, her grief was inconsolable. She immediately withdrew from public life, dressed in black for the rest of her life. When she reemerged into view, after a prolonged period of mourning, she came to be regarded as an affectionate mother figure.[30] She was the embodiment of respectability, and her dedication to moral behavior became synonymous with her era. Victorianism, now thought of largely as sexual restraint, was in its time more closely associated with family values.

Also symbolic of her reign was an undertaking of Prince Albert's. He planned and implemented the Crystal Palace Exposition in 1851. Essentially a World's Fair, it was a celebration of the nation's industrial achievements. By this time, Great Britain was far ahead of the rest of the world; hence, the idea was to showcase its ingenuity and productivity.[31] The building in which the exhibitions were situated, i.e., the Crystal Palace, was itself a singular demonstration of power. Built of cast iron and glass, it would not have been possible without recent advances in technology. It would not even have been possible to amass that much iron. Another aspect of the extravaganza was equally revealing. One of the public's favorite attractions was a garden featuring sculptures of dinosaurs. These were crude affairs, not really representative of the huge reptiles upon which they were supposedly modeled. Nevertheless they made an enormous statement. Not only had technology been stimulated by industrialization, so had science. Everywhere people were digging into the earth for construction projects, but also from curiosity. Indeed, curiosity was the hallmark of an age in which prosperity opened a wider world to individuals who increasingly felt able to master it. When they unexpectedly encountered huge bones, they had the confidence and the knowledge to identify these as belonging to long deceased animals. Where pious ancestors suspected similar finds belonged to biblical giants, geology now taught them better.

Approximately twenty years before the Exposition there had been a glitch in the march forward. Before industrialization, periods of economic distress had plagued society, but these were generally associated with events such as famines and wars. Now, the business cycle swung into operation. As Daniel Chirot[32] explains, one of the worst of these reversals occurred when the market for textiles was temporarily saturated. Entrepreneurs had simply produced more than the market was prepared to absorb. Watching this event, a German university student named Karl Marx observed the suffering of workers who were losing their jobs, and he concluded that this was due to contradictions inherent in capitalism.[33] In their greed, business owners had attempted to wring excess profits from the sweat of their wage slaves' brows. Against all reason or justice, the actual producers of wealth were left to absorb the pain of their bosses' mistakes. Marx's solution was to encourage laborers to throw off the yokes of their oppressors.[34] Once they realized they were being exploited, they could band together to eliminate the property ownership that was the underlying cause of their discomfort. Then, they could exercise joint ownership through the good offices of a government they controlled. After this, thanks to their intrinsic goodwill, they would cooperate for the benefit of all. The increased productivity initiated by the bourgeoisie would thereby be channeled to its true creators, and everyone would gain access to what was necessary for personal comfort. Machines would finally be harnessed to the needs of human beings, rather than the other way around.

Marx's message resonated with his contemporaries because the dislocations of economic progress discomfited so many of them. The proliferating factories and cities displaced millions from traditional employments. No longer living in the countryside, people found that the cultural imperatives that had dictated the tempo of their daily routines lost their authority. As we shall also see with respect to the middle-class developments of the twentieth century, changes in lifestyle have a cultural lag. The old rules cease to apply to what people are doing or how they are interacting before newer, more appropriate ones have yet to emerge. This leaves individuals adrift. They are uncertain where to turn but clamor for answers that might provide a sense of security. The collectivist visions of the communists and socialists furnished consolation. They explained, with what was declared to be scientific exactitude, what was happening and where it was destined to lead. They also provided an enemy to hate. Because it is easier for people to cope with human malice than with economic and sociological imperatives, vast numbers were happy to embrace a story that focused their wrath in a tangible direction. In the long run, this might not help them adjust to the emergent circumstances, but it supplied temporary relief.

In any event, the economy was about to roar forward once again. A new wave of technological innovations provided the impetus for further growth. Foremost among these developments were those in transportation[35] and communication.[36] Earlier in the century, the steam engine had been applied to running cars on rails and powering boats through the water. Toward the middle of the century, the train and the steamboat came to prominence. They opened vast markets within continents and ultimately across the seas. Fulton's[37] invention converted the Mississippi River into a broad avenue of commerce and coastal waters into conduits of produce. Where before barges could float raw materials down to New Orleans, it now became possible for paddleboats to carry finished goods up river to Cincinnati and St. Louis. A flurry of railroad construction extended this activity. With tracks stretched from the east coast to Kansas, cattle were driven from the Texas plains all the way to New York City's Delmonico's Restaurant. Americans acquired a taste for beef and for mechanical inventions—such as reaping machines. Since these could be shipped anywhere by rail, markets mushroomed everywhere and, with them, the potential for profits. One who took advantage of these opportunities was Commodore Cornelius Vanderbilt.[38] From his beginnings as a poor boy in Staten Island, New York, he assembled a fleet of ferries, then one of oceangoing craft, and finally a network of railroads. In the end, he became synonymous with wealth.

Another innovation of the age was the telegraph.[39] It allowed immediate communication over huge distances, which was to come in handy in coordinating the operations of the railroads. Later came the telephone, which permitted voice communication over vast expanses. That device seemed so miraculous that it was featured at Philadelphia's Centennial Exposition of 1876. This celebration of a hundred years of independence was modeled on the Crystal Palace and was America's proclamation that it had come of industrial age. All sorts of mechanical inventions were on display. Of equal note, however, was the coming of steel. This tougher version of iron, which could now be cheaply smelted, was more versatile. Its introduction led to a frenzy of skyscraper construction. Likewise, crude oil, extracted from the ground, now replaced whale oil. Initially refined into kerosene for lamps, it contributed the fuel for internal combustion engines. In the process, Andrew Carnegie[40] and John D. Rockefeller[41] came to rival Vanderbilt in their fortunes.[42]

With this rush of commercialism came a multiplication in scale. Back in Franklin's day, business was conducted from storefronts.[43] Tradesmen's goods were displayed and vended in spaces open to the streets, while journeymen in the back rooms fabricated the products. Upstairs, the families of owners and his family had their apartments. With burgeoning production came not only a separation of the factory from the home, but of the salesroom from the factory. The centers of what came to be much larger cities sprouted business districts replete with department stores. Ordinary people could now take streetcars to patronize multistory structures dedicated solely to marketing a widening variety of items. Clothing, food, and sundries of all sorts were suddenly available in one location. This enabled millions of people to reside within the same municipalities. Both in Europe and the United States, Westerners were becoming urbanites.

Unfortunately, cities had historically been sinks for disease.[44] People in close proximity transmitted communicable diseases with frightening speed. In the past, the solution had been for prosperous citizens to retreat to country estates, but now there were too many people of modest or smaller means. Increasingly, lethal epidemics needed to be controlled. In this, the scientific advances accompanying the technological ferment provided the answers. Intentional investigations demonstrated that pestilences such as cholera were spread by infected water supplies. With innumerable outhouses leaching germs into the soil and this witches' brew trickling into rivers and wells from which public drinking water was drawn, a cycle of death was inevitable. Once this was understood, city fathers began investing in sewer systems to conduct the offending agents elsewhere. Good hygiene became the order of the day.[45] It was at this point that people began saying that cleanliness was next to godliness. Where previously baths were the exception, and even grandees covered their body odor with generous doses of perfume, now everyone including working people began to take weekly soakings.

Hygiene also extended to medicine. At the turn of the century, physicians ridiculed midwives for washing their hands before delivering infants. They considered this insistence on sanitary conditions a superstition and saw no difficulty in moving with bloodstained fingers from one operation to the next. Paradoxically, as science became more prominent, this meant that a greater proportion of middle class women went to the hospital to give birth. The result was a rise in rates of septicemia. This epidemic provided a stimulus for the rise of the germ theory of disease. Animalcules had long been known to pervade the environment, but their connection with illness had been dismissed out of hand. Now a variety of investigators, some with medical and others with chemical credentials, postulated such a linkage. A Hungarian physician named Ignaz Semmelweis sounded the alarm about puerperal fever and agitated for doctors to wash their hands. Meanwhile, Louis Pasteur,[46] a Frenchman whose pasteurization preserved his nation's beer industry, disproved the spontaneous generation of microscopic creatures, while also demonstrating their agency in causing rabies. Robert Koch, a German country practitioner, likewise invented stains to make visible the bacterial sources of tuberculosis and cholera. In short, modern medicine was born, with all its ensuing benefits for life expectancy and personal comfort.

Other biological breakthroughs also occurred. The cell theory of large creatures became well established, with its implications for anatomy and physiology. As important was the introduction of a viable theory of evolution. For more than a century there had been speculations that complex animals developed from simpler ones. This made sense in light of concurrent advances in geology.[47] A close inspection of the rocks convinced prudent observers that the earth was older than the six thousand years Bishop Ussher had proclaimed. The up-and-coming gradualist hypotheses proposed that features such as river valleys came into existence by being continuously and uniformly eroded. Divine interventions would not be necessary if one judged from the perceptible environmental processes. These hypotheses also made the geological strata of alternating stone formations explicable. This, in turn, called for an elucidation of the fossils that kept turning up. These seemed to be stacked as in a layer cake, with the simple at the bottom and the more complex near the top. If this sequence was related to time, and common sense said there must be millions of years of time involved, then, animal morphology would likely be modified. The problem was that there did not seem to be a mechanism for bringing about these changes. It was this dilemma to which Charles Darwin[48] addressed himself. The suggestion that a competition for survival weeded out some creatures, while bolstering the existence of others, was electrifying. Natural selection is what Darwin called this process, and it converted the mysterious into the palpable.

Also mysterious were the myriad peoples discovered in remote corners of the globe. Unbridled commercialization sent traders to formerly inaccessible regions. At the beginning, there strange inhabitants were treated as nuisances. With the advent of imperialism, however, such consideration was impractical.[49] The natives could not all be exterminated; they had to be governed. But to be governed, they had to be understood. No longer were travelers' tales of faraway wonders sufficient. Science must be brought to bear,[50] as it was with the invention of anthropology.[51] Meticulous scrutiny of unfamiliar ways of life provided insights beyond those held by the ancient Greeks. Of particular utility was the concept of culture.[52] Preliterate people could now be understood as possessing techniques for coping with diverse environments. Instead of being dismissed as savages, their humanity could be appreciated in context. By the next century, this would progress to ideas of cultural and ethical relativism. All perspectives then would be declared equally valid, with no overarching criteria available to discriminate among them.

Also laying the foundation for developments was modern chemistry.[53] The Greeks had introduced an atomic theory of matter, but it was during the Victorian era that the modern atomic theory took root, leading to veritable land rush to discover new elements. Having determined that recognizable materials joined together in measurable ratios to form compounds with emergent properties, scientists scrutinized the details of these chemical reactions. As significant were associated advances in electricity. Franklin was celebrated for having elucidated the nature of electrical currents, and Luigi Galvani had invented the electrical battery, but now Humphrey Davy connected the two with his investigations into electrochemistry. Hard on his heels came Michael Faraday's invention of the electric motor and, later, James Clerk Maxwell's discoveries regarding electromagnetism. Most exhilarating of all was Thomas Alva Edison's[54] fabrication of a practical electric light. The arc light and the limelight had already made appearances, but they were not suitable for domestic employment. Edison's was, and it revolutionized society. Here was another fundamental source of non-human energy. For the moment, mostly a curiosity, within decades it was to contribute momentum for another wave of industrialism.

All of these changes had repercussions for how business was done. The glimmerings of industrial discipline present during the Second Great Awakening became a roaring bonfire as the factory system accelerated. Definitely in America, but also in England, reforms piled upon reforms, generally with the goal of developing a more reliable workforce. Isolated objections to imbibing alcohol escalated to crusades against demon rum.[55] Before the century was out, the temperance movement was a regular feature of middle-class sobriety. Neither businessmen who calculated figures nor laborers who ran machines could afford the sloppiness which accompanied intoxication. Drunkenness was not rational; it was not profitable. Nor was alcoholism good for family life. This most salient of Victorian institutions was threatened by bibulous husbands who would not uphold their responsibilities as breadwinners nor refrain from beating their wives when under the influence. This was proclaimed society's foremost problem,[56] especially when immigrants[57] from across the sea or the surrounding countryside began to congregate in inner cities. Everyone knew these communities were rife with drunkenness.[58] It was, therefore, imperative to civilize their inhabitants by teaching the rudiments of abstinence.

Also of momentous import was abolitionism.[59] Holding slaves was the birthright of the United States[60] and the foundation of the British textile industry. In America, the founding fathers contemplated abolishing the institution,[61] but the greed of Southern aristocrats forbade it. Nevertheless, the logic of commercialism militated against slavery. Both in Britain and in its former colonies, the swelling ranks of factory workers resented the competition from unpaid labor. In order to get people from the land and working the machines, they had to be compensated. Bondsmen could not be machine tenders because they were not motivated to be vigilant. Slave labor had always been notoriously inefficient, but this did not matter when there was no alternative.[62] But mechanical energy changed this situation. Conscientious freemen working for wages in steam-driven factories could produce far more than sullen chattel driven by the whip. The very success of the marketplace in increasing the demand for goods undercut the source of power. As a consequence, there was agitation against slavery. Ordinary workers loathed the peculiar institution[63] because they saw it as a menace to their earning power. But even the commercial elites were arrayed against it. They might like the idea of cheap cotton, but they knew that real wealth was being generated on the factory floor, not on the Southern plantation.

Like temperance, a religious ideology impelled the abolitionists.[64] Despite biblical references honoring slavery, people now interpreted shackling others in bondage as against God's will.[65] In America, sermons were preached all across the North. This moral indignation motivated the efforts that provided the muscle for the Civil War.[66] What is as interesting was the nature of this religiosity. A more homogenized and secularized Christianity had evolved to lead the attack. Today religion has often been thought of a conservative force, but this was not the case in the 19th century. Activists modified the fire-and-brimstone tirades of Puritan forebears to serve a more worldly purpose. As is common in human history, these people adapted the tools at hand to novel circumstances. Their new civic religion employed generalized spiritual objectives to promote secular goals. A universalized belief in a merciful God, one that fit comfortably into most Protestant denominations, could be publicly proclaimed without offending particular doctrines. As significantly, it could tap into a desire to do good that had been reoriented toward an innovative definition of what was good.[67]

This malleable religiosity was also directed toward the centerpiece of Victorian morality.[68] As earlier mentioned, the 19th century is now identified with a prudish sexuality.[69] Husbands and wives were certainly urged to remain faithful to each other and their children. The use of sexualized language, the promulgation of nude pictures, and, most especially, the practice of prostitution were discouraged. Truly strenuous efforts, extending to those by England's Prime Minister Gladstone,[70] were undertaken to reform prostitutes and to close down the houses of ill repute. Even masturbation was suppressed. Children were told that playing with themselves led to blindness or insanity. Only wholesome sex within marriage was sanctioned. The missionary position was the lone honorable one, and women, as everyone knew, were to participate in coitus from duty, not for pleasure. Marriage was sanctified by God.[71] This meant that having children out of wedlock was strictly forbidden. Though hampered by their poverty, the poor too believed in marital fidelity and actively sought the prestige of respectability. This was promoted from pulpits, by politicians, and by neighbors. Sexual restraint was considered a sign of broad restraints. It indicated that a person was self-disciplined and, therefore, trustworthy. Critics of the Victorians tend to disparage this public virtue as hypocritical, but the level of illegitimacy during this period was, in fact, dramatically reduced from what it had been.

The family became sacrosanct because it was the anchor of capitalistic achievement. Victoria, and her apparently straight-laced brood, were symbols of domestic stability.[72] They modeled the calm dependability needed if budding industrialists were to keep their fortunes intact. Money earned could not safely be bequeathed to a raucous crowd of bastards. It had to be conferred on progeny who knew what to do with it. In former times, land could be willed to rowdy heirs who kept the lineage going merely by being its caretakers. The complexity of industrial operations made this strategy impossible. Children needed to be groomed in the internal disciplines necessary to direct these agglomerations.[73] Only a close-knit family characterized by love and careful supervision could instill what was required. Thus conventional wisdom held that families that ate together, interacted together, and socialized together, stayed together. Sunday mornings were to be spent in the family pew, while evenings were to be dedicated to singing lively songs beside the family piano. Ironically, the family home simultaneously became a bastion for personal privacy. The goal was to have what Virginia Woolf[74] later celebrated as a room of one's own in which one could think private thoughts, privately defended. This was epitomized by a fad for diary-keeping.[75] In these precious volumes pubescent young women and ambitious older men alike poured secret sentiments, thereby both elevating their importance and enabling them to analyze their significance. The ultimate objective of all of this was not merely to pass along technical knowledge but also to infuse an emotional attachment to upholding family dignity in individuals who were eventually to be their own people. Only this sort of demonstrative intimacy could produce the level-headed loyalties and independent decision making that had become so imperative.

An obsession with personal dignity was likewise expressed in the clothing styles of the period.[76] The now familiar distinction between white- and blue-collar workers originated among the Victorians. Not unexpectedly, both the new entrepreneurs and their middle-class minions performed most of their tasks in offices. As such, they prided themselves on a clean environment. Whereas factory workers became greasy, stainless raiments declared that office workers did not. Always neatly starched, their detachable collars remained spotless. Also emblematic of status was the wearing of suits and ties. So significant were these external advertisements of prominence that many upwardly mobile families dressed formally for dinner. Female fashions too mirrored a desire for formality. Elegant dresses, fitted over corseted bodies, bespoke a dedication to following the rules, irrespective of the discomfort in doing so. A high point of this trend was the bustle. Uncomfortable in the extreme, it did not allow for ease in sitting. Nevertheless it was proof of a Victorian gentleman's financial success that his wife and daughters did not have to engage in manual labor in order to add to their income. Likewise the tassels in their overstuffed living rooms confirmed prosperity and decorum. The level of maintenance these items demanded demonstrated the presence of substantial resources and also the absence of the wild behavior that might destroy their delicate orderliness.

Marx would have us believe that the nascent middle classes consisted of ink stained clerks who were becoming impoverished, but the evidence is otherwise.   One sure marker of the growing power of these classes was the spread of democracy.   It was not for naught that the Statue of Liberty became emblematic of an entire nation.   If Napoleon needed to inspire his soldiers by giving them the appearance of liberty, industrial workers required something more substantial.   If they were to care about their jobs, they needed an assurance of independence.   Laborers who lacked a feeling of autonomy performed with as little diligence as slaves.   Roman citizenship earlier put the steel into redoubtable legions; democratic citizenship did the same for growing industries.   The result was a dispersal of the franchise.   Where pre-Revolutionary America insisted upon property ownership for voting rights, suffrage became universal on both sides of the Atlantic in the 19th century.   Political leaders might still be drawn from the elites, but they needed to widen their appeal to get elected.   Soon enough, the wealthy would find themselves seeking public influence through the mediation of more modestly born politicians.

Women, too, were becoming aware and involved.   Their suffrage did not come to fruition immediately, but agitation in its favor was vigorous.   With larger numbers of women working outside the home, suffrage was to become a practical necessity.   The more their contributions were required in commercial ventures, the more likely they were to insist on independent voices.   The changing of the gender guard began with teenaged females in New England textile plants, but in short order spread to factory offices.   The invention of the typewriter gave the impetus to the rights of the distaff secretary, exemplified by the superior fine motor skills of women.   Similar reasons brought married women to work in the garment trades.   In this case, it was the introduction of the sewing machine that placed a premium on manual dexterity.   Women also began to migrate into the teaching professions as an expansion of education demanded more teachers.   Added to this was the bicycle.   As the historian Gertrude Himmelfarb[77] points out, its appearance facilitated female autonomy by permitting unfettered movement.   Cheaper than carriages, and more compact, bicycles enabled a woman to jump on board and pedal to the market without asking her husband's permission.

Also fundamentally democratic was the introduction of the civil service.[78] When governments were small and their contributions to prosperity marginal, many jobs were allocated as patronage plums. In the United States, this translated into positions for individuals who helped politicians get elected. This, however, was inadequate for technologically sophisticated tasks. Hiring friends and cronies likewise imperiled fiscal responsibility. The all-purpose label for these nepotistic shenanigans was corruption[79] and it was increasingly despised. Alliances within a commercial society, and all the more in an industrial one, were contingent on competence. What was being discovered was that graft and competence were largely incompatible. The consequence of public contempt for these abuses were civil-service reforms that made employment conditional on passing appropriate examinations. Qualifications were to be tested, not assumed. Objectively certified abilities would allow people to rise to the positions for which they were prepared.

So hectic did economic activity become that the era immediately succeeding the Civil War became known as the Gilded Age.[80] Speculation was so intense that within a few years the United States overtook England as the world's richest industrial state. The Rockefellers and the Fisks gained the reputation for being robber barons who accumulated obscenely large fortunes. Their monopolies were so inclusive that it seemed their power would eclipse that of the government. The upshot was a competition between laissez-faire policies and a desire to tame the trusts. Capitalistic affluence seemed to endorse Adam Smith's[81] belief that complete liberty for businesspeople meant liberty and prosperity for everyone. However, the ability of Rockefeller to dictate oil prices was manifestly dangerous.[82] One man, however well intended, could not be allowed to be that arbitrary and potentially vindictive. It was, therefore, imperative to set limits on private enterprise. The initial efforts at this restraint were provided by the labor unions.[83] Ordinary workers, manipulated by their bosses, exposed to unconscionable dangers, and marginally remunerated, manifested the Marxist impulse to unite. During this stage of development, their numbers were small and they were outmuscled by their employers, but they laid down a marker that would eventually be picked up. Some of what they achieved was obstructionist, but their movement eventuated in a respect for employees that redounded to the benefit of all.

Much of the Victorian opposition to capitalist domination came from the bohemians.[84] A prominent faction of the Romantic reaction to industrialization, these artistes were among its most passionate critics. Romanticism[85] is a term that came to be applied to a literary, artistic, and musical movement that celebrated emotion and personality. Its chief architects were stereotyped as being antibusiness, antiscience, antidiscipline, antirational, and antifamily. Their quintessential hero was the loner dedicated to self-expression and aesthetic rapture. John Keats,[86] one of the first of their number, wrote, "'Beauty is truth, truth beauty' —that is all/ Ye know on earth, and all ye need to know." Although when taken out of context, this is literally nonsensical, the evident purpose this proclamation was to rejoice in the dominion of art over science, in personal responses over practical achievements. The Romantics evidently did not want to be submerged in the economic advances of the era. As such, they were rebels, albeit not political ones. By their very nature, they were disorganized. Along with Jean-Jacques Rousseau,[87] some admired the noble savage. Primitive though many of them were, they were respected for an honesty that refused to knuckle under to emerging industrial elites.

Among the more colorful of the Romantics, the bohemians wrote or painted emotionally arousing works in lonely garrets in places such as Paris's Left Bank. Determined to be beholden to no one, they scorned the patronage earlier generations of artists had eagerly cultivated. As a result, they could produce works that repudiated the bourgeoisie. Their agents might sell their productions to the middle classes, but they personally resisted associating with them. Novelists such as Honore de Balzac,[88] Gustav Flaubert,[89] and Victor Hugo[90] vented their spleens at the follies and oppression of the moneyed class. Portrayed as amorously inept or terminally avaricious, these emerging capitalists were condemned as congenitally disposed to hunting good men down for the mere offense of pilfering a loaf of bread. Even death seemed preferable to being trapped in the loveless social embrace of their hangers-on. Meanwhile, painters such as Edouard Manet and Claude Monet founded Impressionism[91] in opposition to the cloying realism of the officially sanctioned artists displayed by the academic salons. Probably in antipathy to the fidelity of the newly developed photography, they attempted to capture the transient of everyday life. Vincent Van Gogh carried the trend to a likely conclusion. Unable to sell his works during his lifetime, he recorded the madness consuming him on canvasses that suggest the torture that one might experience in an overly routinized society. In music, similar accomplishments were achieved by the more mainstream Richard Wagner,[92] Peter Tchaikovsky, and Frederic Chopin.[93] Composing for the public at large, they renounced the formalism of the chamber music that was originally intended for the amusement of effete aristocrats. Throwing decorum to the winds, they might alternately be loud and commanding or soft and amorous. Wagner, for instance, became the lyrical voice of a resurgent German nationalism, while Tchaikovsky voiced Russian feelings. That someone as gifted as Chopin or Keats wasted away from consumption only added to their exotic reputations.

The Proud Tower[94]

In 1893, Chicago hosted the Columbian Exposition. Intended to honor the five hundredth anniversary of the discovery of America, its high point was The White City. One hundred fifty buildings constructed of a marble-like material and executed in Romanesque, Renaissance, and Greek styles shimmered when illuminated by electric light. The effect was startling. Like the Eiffel Tower of by four years earlier, this was a proclamation of economic might and broadcast to the world at large that the United States had genuinely arrived. An advertisement of the country's industrial triumph, it suggested that this nation's accomplishments surpassed those of the ancients. The event was thus steeped in optimism and self-satisfaction. All of these wonders proved that the modern world had mastered the idea of progress and was poised to ride it into a future of unexampled marvels. The control of its destiny seemed to lie in its own hands. Others had dreamt of such grandeur, but none before had managed to grasp it. Visitors to the fair were convinced that this was not arrogance that it was merely the truth. They could not predict that within decades their world would be shaken by a series of seismic shocks. Industrialization had not reached its culmination. More was to come. Though people did not realize, painful adjustments were in the offing.

In the meantime, the prosperity was unprecedented. No previous generation had ever been as rich or as powerful. After some dips in the business cycle, the Gilded Age was replaced by the beginnings of modernism. The industrial order was again kick-started by a fresh wave of innovations. As in the past, technology was part of this cavalcade. Leading the way was the internal combustion engine. Lighter than its predecessors, it could power self-propelled vehicles. Within years the automobile replaced the horse and carriage, and the dream of flying heavier-than-air machines became a reality. That which had seemed impossible not only had occurred, it had proliferated. Thanks to Henry Ford's[95] assembly lines, streets formerly mined with manure became crowded with Model T's. While the skies were not as quickly congested, the Wright brothers inspired a host of imitators, creating airplanes with specifications more complex than their own. The heavens were also being challenged by a race to erect the tallest skyscraper. Steel had proven able to provide sturdier skeletons for tall buildings than had cast iron. Coupled with Otis's safety elevators, downtowns became canyons of stone and glass.

Among the other major technological advances were those in chemistry. In this area, the Germans stole a march on the rest of the world. As trivial as it seems in retrospect, their mastery of the test tube produced coal-tar-based dyes that enabled textiles to boast a rainbow of color. Coal, incidentally, became easier to extract from the earth after the invention of dynamite. Mining, in general, benefited from Alfred Nobel's[96] development of an explosive that was safer and more powerful than gunpowder. To be sure, this same material could also be exploited on the battlefield. Bombs filled with this substance inflicted more damage than did solid metal balls. Less lethal was the introduction of vulcanized rubber. Before tires were fabricated of this plastic material, iron-rimmed wheels on cobblestone roads had made riding a jarring experience. Afterwards, automobile passengers could travel comfortably at amazing speeds.

Among the nontechnological advances that multiplied production was the corporation. As industrialization proceeded to concentrate the manufacturing and distribution of goods, companies became bigger. In Karl Marx's imagination, individual capitalists owned and controlled individual enterprises. But this picture was rapidly going out of focus. The level of investment in the steel industry or the railroads was too great for even the wealthiest entrepreneur to muster. If a company was instead turned into a trust that could be owned by multiple stockholders, pooled resources could meet these greater challenges. As importantly, stockholders could share the risks. Newly invented legal arrangements provided this limited liability, which made it easier to gamble on untried markets and products. All this elevated the position of bankers and financiers. Men like J.P. Morgan[97] did not run specific companies; they merely oversaw those who did. Many, such as Morgan himself, made a career of rationalizing enterprises by assembling them into conglomerates that could take advantage of the economies of scale. Morgan's crowning achievement was U.S. Steel. Not quite a monopoly over this industry, it was still large enough to dominate it. For providing this service, Morgan grew enormously wealthy.

These newfangled corporations were to have another effect. Because they were so large, they demanded rationalized forms of control. No individual, no matter how smart or energetic could understand the operations of U.S. Steel. The company itself had to be organized in a way that made coordination possible. This was achieved through the invention of bureaucracy. Protobureaucracies had been around since Roman times. They had been incorporated into the Roman Catholic Church and national armies, but their structures were now to be perfected. Max Weber,[98] who chronicled their emergence, provided an idealized description of their elements. First, there had to be an organizational goal.[99] Unless the entire entity shared a mission, it would be torn by irreconcilable crosscurrents. Second, there had to be a functional division of labor. Multiple, necessary tasks could not be efficiently accomplished if they were not broken down into interlocking duties. Third, these duties could not be performed effectively if they were not assigned to specific individuals. Such defined offices would indicate who was to do what and, therefore, allowed people to be assigned according to individual expertise. Fourth, there needed to be a hierarchy of authority. Unless the participants understood who was in charge of what, they might spend more time competing for power than in doing their jobs. Hierarchy was not a novel idea, but specifying its dimensions this precisely was. Fifth, specific tasks were to be performed, not according to the whim of the individual, but according to the most effective procedures. Standard forms of operation replaced idiosyncratic adventurism, to better the bottom line. Six, strict records would be kept of what had been done and who owed what to whom. As the memory of the organization, these files would enable the business to keep running even if the personnel changed. Together, these six dicta constituted a control mechanism so potent that Weber dubbed it an "iron cage." No individual player could be responsible for the whole, but neither could those involved extract themselves from its mandates without penalty. If they attempted to do so, the mass of stabilized relationships in which they were entangled would bring them back into alignment.

Fundamental to this bureaucratic machinery was its managers. Most of those who gave orders were not classical capitalists. They did not own the corporation nor independently decide its directions. On the contrary, they were professionals. Making executive decisions was their job; it was not a consequence of possessing the means of production. They were hired because they were self-motivated and self-directed, and they proved their worth by increasing the profitability of the whole.[100] No wonder these administrators found Frederick Taylor's[101] scientific management so attractive. It promised to promote efficiency by discovering the optimal procedures. This would enable expertise in defined offices and authoritative directives. Subsequently, instead of ambitious children hoping someday to establish their own businesses—although many did—a greater proportion aspired to become presidents of corporations operating under the mandates of boards of directors. In their imaginations, they would become Horatio Alger[102] heroes recognized, and rewarded, for meritorious contributions to the organization.

Science, too, continued to provide new understandings. Thus, physics reasserted its centrality with a vengeance. New fundamental particles were discovered within the atom and the range of electromagnetic waves was extended to cover X-rays and gamma rays. All of a sudden, physicians could peer into living human tissue and astronomers out into a more capacious universe. But what really concentrated attention was Albert Einstein's[103] theory of relativity. Not since Newton had there been such a profound reorganization of how nature was understood. Quite unexpectedly, matter and energy were connected in an equation that has had momentous implications. Yet, science also looked inward. Until this point, psychology had been slow to develop because no one could figure out how to measure something as ephemeral as the workings of the mind. Now Pavlov introduced the idea of the conditioned reflex and Freud[104] that of the unconscious. It would not be long before psychoanalysis and behaviorism were the rage. In the competition between these, there would develop a tug-of-war between introspection and objective manipulation. Sociology, too, was being organized as an independent discipline. Plagued, as had been psychology, by measurement difficulties, Emile Durkheim[105] provided a rationale for social facts and Weber[106] catalogued many of these. Not surprisingly, as the social division of labor continued to differentiate, investigators were stumbling onto its implications.

The political world too was under renovation. Progress was not confined to the business or scientific realms. Nation states were more powerful than ever. A shining example was the <u>Dreadnaught</u>. The first truly modern battleship, it was steam powered, heavily armored, propeller driven, and studded with countless heavy guns. Britain led the way to naval modernization, but even the isolationist United States followed suit. Now able to project power around the world, Teddy Roosevelt[107] commissioned its circumnavigation by the Great White Fleet. Roosevelt also arranged for Panama to proclaim its independence so that it could serve as the site for a canal uniting the Atlantic and Pacific. In an era when economic power had been converted into imperial power, he wished his nation to play. Not to be outdone were the political journalists. Given an increasingly literate public, newspapers became more influential than ever. This enabled William Randolph Hearst[108] to incite the Spanish-American War. With little provocation, his version of jingoistic yellow journalism portrayed the Spanish as murderers. When the battleship <u>Maine</u> was blown up in Havana harbor, he convinced his readers that this was a deliberate act, which, as a powerful people, they were required avenge. As a consequence of the ensuing victory, his country acquired imperial outposts in Puerto Rico and the Philippines.

All in all, people were acquiring greater control over their universe.[109] And they were enjoying it. The rich certainly learned how to celebrate. Thorstein Veblen[110], in 1899, wrote <u>The Theory of the Leisure Class</u> based on his observations of the wealthy. One of his lasting contributions was the concept of conspicuous consumption. He noticed that the wealthy (and, to a lesser extent, the middle-classes) made purchases in order to make an impression. That which visibly cost large sums of money demonstrated the power relative to those who lacked such resources. J.P. Morgan[111] exemplified this attitude in remarking that someone who needed to inquire about the price of a yacht evidently could not afford one. Also opulent were the cottages being erected in places like Newport, Rhode Island.[112] In actuality, they were palaces furnished with the leftovers of their European forerunners and were designed as stagesets for lavish social gatherings. Maintained by corps of servants, they emulated the noble establishments of times past. Though the middle classes were growing, they were still subservient to this moneyed elite. This was why the superrich looked above historic models and not below in deciding how to disperse their resources.

The working classes, too, improved their condition.[113] Marx postulated that they would be reduced to privation, but industrialization furnished a significant portion of its bounty. Better clothed, fed, and housed than their ancestors, they also had more leisure time. Instead of working from dawn to dusk, they were on their way toward the eight-hour day and the five-day week. This meant that, during good weather, they had the freedom to picnic in city parks or, in summer, to take streetcars to newly opened amusement parks. In order to drum up business, the trolley tracks were extended to places like New York's Coney Island.[114] An early prototype of Disneyworld, its Dreamland enticed average workers with rides and games of all sorts. Dressed in finery once reserved for church, shopgirls flaunted hats decorated in exotic feathers while invisible breezes blew their dresses up over their ankles. They even dared to put on bathing suits to enter the surf and show off their nubile figures.

At home, there were also improvements. Labor saving devices proliferated to make housekeeping less burdensome. Iceboxes became commonplace. Perishables, such as milk, could be purchased in advance, without fear of spoilage. Gas ranges replaced fireplaces. This made it possible to cook exotic dishes without danger. Indoor plumbing also made its appearance. With indoor flush toilets, no longer was it necessary to traipse to the outhouse in the dead of winter. For a lucky few, there were even washing machines. Scrubbing clothes by hand had always been one of a housewife's most tedious chores. Now a mechanical device could eliminate this drudgery. However, families were larger. Because of medical advances, children were no longer dying as frequently as they had. In this case, a cultural lag kept the birth rate higher than the death rate. As a result, women often had eight or more offspring under their care. At the same [115]time, families were making increased investments in their children. With economic success more than ever contingent on expertise, the goal was to prepare the young for good jobs. This was achieved by supporting education. Instead of sending them out to apprenticeships or to work on factory floors, young people were encouraged to go to high school. As a result, they were less responsible for contributing to family finances and could loiter with peers. In this, society witnessed the appearance of the teenager.

Still, there were nagging problems. Industrialization had not been an unmixed blessing.[116] The cities, teeming as never before with slums, blighted on the landscape. Hearst might be encouraging of boosterism, but other reporters were investigating society's dirty underbelly. The muckrakers had arrived on the scene. One of them, Upton Sinclair,[117] wrote a novel, <u>The Jungle</u>, in which he exposed the sanitary shortcomings of the meatpacking industry. This so appalled the nation that, with the aid of a progressive president, reform food and drug legislation quickly passed. Ida Tarbell[118] added to the political ferment by exposing John D. Rockefeller's predatory business practices. This, too, created an uproar that led to the enforcement of antitrust laws. Standard Oil was broken up into smaller companies, none of which could threaten to monopolize commerce. Meanwhile, Lincoln Steffens[119] focused on local government corruption in <u>The Shame of the Cities</u>. Together with the goo-goos (i.e., the good government reformers), efforts were made to prevent ballot stuffing and under-the-table payoffs. The result was increased democratization. Control was redistributed between the government and the private sector to diminish the likelihood of a dangerous concentration of power.

Progressivism,[120] as this movement was called, was closely related to populism. It added a concern for the welfare of the little man to the public agenda. As prosperity became widespread, it seemed unconscionable that the poor be left out. Jacob Riis's[121] pictorial reportage revealed the squalor of slums. Union busting, in which hired goons shot unarmed strikers, offended the sense of fairness held by ordinary Americans. Likewise, a terrible fire at the Triangle Shirtwaist Factory[122], in which 146 young immigrant women workers burned to death, underlined the dreadful conditions that prevailed in sweatshops. Because many of these victims died as a result of locked exits (in order to reduce pilferage), calls for enforce humane working standards were sounded. For similar reasons, child labor became a target of concern, ultimately to be prohibited. Even outside the workplace, efforts to support the poor, e.g., by providing free milk to mothers, were proliferating. Much of this campaign culminated in the professed socialism of Eugene V. Debs.[123] This onetime leader of the American Railroad Union ran for President several times, at one point attracting the support of nearly a million voters.

The art scene too was radicalized. The bohemians graduated from Impressionism to Post-Impressionism and from Cubism to the Fauve Movement. The Impressionism of Renoir, Degas, and even, in retrospect, of Cezanne, was replaced by the eccentricities of Picasso, Kandinsky, and Mondrian.[124] Regarded as wild animals by the establishment, they competed with one another to see how impertinent they could be. Even in music atonality became a fad. Arnold Schoenberg's radical experiments may have confused many of those who counted themselves as among the avant-garde, but "pretty" music, art, and literature were nevertheless spurned as bourgeois sentimentalism. A new breed of creators would not be bound by the self-satisfaction of the more affluent. They would instead rub people's noses in the hypocrisies of the time.

The worst shock to the pride of the self-satisfied came with the outbreak of World War I.[125] Unchecked imperialism led to a conflagration that consumed much of what had been built. The multiplying jealousies between Germany[126] and the Western powers were to be resolved in battles made horrendous by the application of industrialism. Machine guns, poison gas, effective artillery, submarines, and airplanes inflated the death rolls. Trench warfare in which the combatants stood statically from whence they periodically emerged to mow each other down took a terrible toll. Before the slaughter ended, millions of corpses lay rotting in the mud.[127] The effect was to traumatize those involved. Before the outbreak of hostilities, people thought they were in control. Afterwards, they discovered they were not. The politicians, the generals, and the ordinary doughboys were all proved wrong. This left lasting doubts that were not assuaged by the inconclusive Treaty of Versailles.[128]

Reprise and Collapse

Once the Great War concluded, peace did not descend on an exhausted world.[129] The confusions, disappointments, and desires for vengeance of the combatants were played out over the next quarter century. Industrialization too underwent a period of turmoil. Instead of marching forward with the determined progress of the preceding decades, movement was hesitant, sideways. Perhaps an evocative description of the interlude would be "manic-depressive." Within the space of a few years, Western society had experienced enormous highs and devastating lows. At one point, individuals assumed the millennium was at hand, but within short order they were plunged into a despair that looked like hell itself. In the United States, an incoming president campaigned on a platform of a return to normalcy.[130] For a while, it appeared that he would deliver on this,[131] but events went seriously awry. Since no one understood the foundations of prosperity, once things did not go as predicted, no one knew how to fix them.

Another successful candidate for the American presidency had promised a chicken in every pot and two cars in every garage. In light of the concurrent increases in productivity, it seemed that these could happen. Certainly, automobiles had replaced from horse-drawn transportation.[132] Even more symbolic of the economic advances were changes in the media. Beginning with the World War, movie making had come into its own. The blatantly racist The Birth of a Nation was praised by Woodrow Wilson as "history written with lightening."[133] Distorted though it was, this film demonstrated the power of moving images to deliver emotional messages. By the 1920s, a habit of going to the cinema overtook the entire Western World.[134] Quite unexpectedly, public consciousness was being shaped by entertainments guided by uncultivated entrepreneurs. The logo of Metro-Goldwyn-Mayer claimed, "Art for art's sake," but the motive power was satisfying the pubic taste for excitement and titillation. The same was happening in radio. Before the war, it had been an invention in search of an application. Afterwards, it was broadcast music, news, and comedy to a multitude of nations and millions of listeners. Because the technology was inexpensive, most families could afford to gather beside their own sets to hear what advertisers believed would capture their attention. The result was an unanticipated cultural unity. Hearing the same songs, listening to the same jokes, and being exposed to the same news stories homogenized social perspectives beyond anything imaginable in the 19th century. It soon enabled politicians to mold public opinion as well.

But before this could occur, the Roaring Twenties saw countless social experiments.[135] This was the Flapper Era. A joy at having survived a brush with death in the World War unleashed a manic exuberance. Dances, such as the Charleston, were wilder and more sexual than the sedate foxtrot of an earlier day. Dresses were shorter and more revealing than the floor-length models of their mothers' generation. Moreover bathtub gin flowed freely in the speakeasies to which Prohibition[136] had driven partygoers. This was the period during which the idea of the teenager came to prominence. Wearing raccoon-skin coats and taking hip flasks to football games became the epitome of a good time. Having fun became an international obsession. In Germany, the Berlin nightlife became celebrated for its decadence. In France, American expatriates such as Hemingway wrote about bullfights and sexual peccadilloes. In the United States, huge crowds screamed themselves hoarse as Babe Ruth pursued the home run record. Free love was in the air and criminals were in the street. Poets and philosophers were proclaiming that marital fidelity was a form of bourgeois slavery, while Al Capone[137] was exciting Chicago with his latest audacious murder. This was the era of the Tommy gun, with which gangsters sprayed bullets in multiple directions. As might be expected, art too was indulging in excess. Modern art meant abstract art and that meant in-your-face rebellion.

But then the U.S. stock market crashed, following sky-high levels of speculation. Ordinary workers had purchased their pieces of corporations on margin. Since the sky appeared to be the limit, there was no reason why they, too, should not leverage their resources into substantial fortunes. When the prices began to fall, panic set in. No one, including the professionals, knew how to stem the tide. Attempts at imposing stability by raising interest rates had the opposite effect. By removing liquidity from the market, deflation was instituted, which had hideous consequences for business. So dreadful was the impact that within the year the United States entered the Great Depression.[138] Millions of people lost their jobs. At one point, over twenty percent of the workforce stood idle. Nothing like this had ever been seen before. The business cycle was not new, but its troughs had never been as deep nor lasted as long. It would not be until the Second World War that there would be a definitive turnaround. A full decade would transpire before the factories were once again operating up to their potential.[139]

As bad as this was, it paled in comparison with the German experience. In the wake of its defeat, the nation experimented with democracy in the guise of the Weimar Republic. Yet this, despite its noblest intent, was a miserable failure. The country had no history of democracy upon which to draw; hence when things went wrong both the elite and the populace longed for familiar trappings of stability. And things did go terribly wrong. Inexperienced politicians precipitated a roaring inflation that left the deutschmark nearly worthless. It soon took wheelbarrows of cash just to purchase a loaf of bread. In this environment, people desperately sought a savior. And potential saviors were not in short supply. On the left, the Communists touted the Bolshevik Revolution as the vanguard of an international Communism.[140] Nationalization of the country's industries, accompanied by local soviet-style governing councils, would return money to the pockets of the people. Theoretically, on the right but also collectivist in mentality, were the National Socialists, i.e., the Nazis. They promised to undo what had lost the war and to reintroduce social discipline. Rival gangs ran wild in the street, but thanks to the backing of veterans groups, Adolf Hitler[141] and his cronies gained power. Eventually, they won enough seats in the Reichstag to make Hitler Chancellor and, within a year, Fuehrer. Totalitarianism had come to Germany,[142] as it earlier had to Russia and Italy, and soon would to Spain.[143] In England and France, democratic institutions held on, but socialists, who wished to nationalize industry, also dominated. Traumatized by memories of the late war and labor unrest, politicians promised constancy at any price.

Across the Atlantic, conditions were not so desperate. Franklin Roosevelt[144] was elected president and he promised his countrymen a New Deal. Something had to be done to prevent banks from collapsing and businesses from closing. People needed to be put to work and their confidence restored. Roosevelt and his team did their best.[145] They introduced a blizzard of legislation and the president himself went on the radio to give reassuring fireside chats. Part of the plan called upon the government to provide jobs and another to offer a financial safety net. Out of this welter of initiatives came Social Security. Widows and orphans would receive checks directly from the U.S. treasury, while older Americans would participate in an insurance program to provide for retirement. Unemployment benefits too were improved.[146] Most important, people were given hope. A nation that had always prided itself on its individualism made a decisive turn toward governmental solutions. Many were convinced that capitalism had run its course.[147] and that the depression was the fulfillment of Marxist prophesies.[148] Since the system's contradictions had evidently caught up with it, it was doomed to destruction. A communist utopia was inevitable; hence it made sense to support its introduction. For many, this meant joining the communist party and cheering for the Stalinist regime. For others, it meant becoming a social democrat, following the Western European model.[149] Yes, they were socialists, but they wanted preserve democratic government. Roosevelt, according to many academics, acted just in time. Had he not touted his reforms, the pessimism of the average American might have grown to critical proportions. In this case, a German-style revolution might well have come to the nation's shores.

The Depression, it must be added, also had a profound impact on the family. All of a sudden, the levels of fertility dropped. Parents who had expected to educate their children no longer possessed the resources to do so. Committed to having smaller families, the average number of offspring dropped to two, just enough for replacement purposes. The age of marriage simultaneously increased, so that child bearing was postponed until it could be afforded. During this economic catastrophe, people scraped by. They settled for smaller living quarters and accepted almost any jobs that came along. Contributing to the welfare of the group became a way of life. Since there did not seem to be any hope in sight, most people lowered expectations, purchased only what was needed, and soldiered on. Even the movies reflected this mood. Some were saccharinely sweet; others, intensely gloomy. In the former, battalions of singers and dancers lauded the good times to come, whereas in the latter regiments of gangsters shot each other dead. Banished from sight was the sunny sexuality of the twenties. Even clothing became less revealing, perhaps in an effort to hide that of which people had become ashamed.

Then came World War II. As unwelcome as it was, this conflict did not arrive as a shock. Pacifist strains had pressured for the first war to be a genuine war to end all wars, but the appeasement policies derived from this wishful thinking encouraged would-be aggressors. Japan attacked China, and Italy invaded Abyssinia, and no one did anything to stop them. Woodrow Wilson[150] envisioned a League of Nations as a guarantor of peace, but it degenerated into a debating society. When Spain became the testing ground for Nazi and Soviet weaponry, the League of Nations did nothing. By this time it was apparent that unless the major powers had the will to act, there would be no action. Hence, when Hitler marched in to Austria or broke the promises he had made at Munich, the lack of an assertive response was foreseeable. That, upon the invasion of Poland, the allies finally issued a warning they were prepared to honor was a surprise to many. This event ushered in the greatest conflagration in the history of armed quarrels. By the time it concluded, over fifty million people, most of them civilians, had been butchered. So great was the slaughter than it instituted permanent changes. In many ways, the First World War was the opening salvo of a struggle that did not cease until after the bombing of Hiroshima. But when it did, the participants were not the same. The crisis of industrialization at its heart was resolved by an extraordinary bloodbath—and then the world would move on.

World War II was a case of unequaled horror for several reasons.[151] One was the technology of battle. Inventions which had been in their infancy twenty-five years earlier, reached a dreadful maturity. The tank, for instance, formerly a lumbering failure in smashing through defensive trenches, was transformed into the spearhead of the blitzkrieg. It could swiftly move into the rear echelons of an enemy, sowing panic as it went. Thanks to its brutal efficiency, the battles of France and Poland were over within weeks. Much the same can be said of the airplane. In the first war it was almost a toy. Swashbuckling aces dueling each other in romantic dogfights thrilled earthbound observers, but did little actual damage. In the second war, fleets of bombers turned peaceful cities into flaming funeral pyres. First London, then Dresden and Berlin, and finally Tokyo and Nagasaki were flattened and their populations incinerated. Even under the oceans, the techniques for inflicting death had become more advanced. Modern submarines could wander farther, stay under the surface longer, and launch more lethal torpedoes. The loss in shipping was, in consequence, calamitous. Everywhere one turned, massive death awaited, even without the reintroduction of chemical weapons.

Worse still was the intentional butchery imposed by politicians. Nazis, Soviets, and Japanese made terror an official policy. Able to command the efficiency of modern weapons and modern bureaucracies, they could order the execution of millions of innocents. The Nazis, of course, were the instigators of the Holocaust. Hitler made it his mission to exterminate Jews, Slavs, and Gypsies. Coming to power on the premise that there had been a Jewish conspiracy, he pledged to get even. Few imagined the lengths to which he would go, which eventuated in the concentration camps. Millions were gassed to death; many of them were reportedly flayed to turn their skins into lampshades. So well organized was this killing machine that Hitler also had millions of Poles and Russians shipped into its maws. Not to be outdone, Stalin ordered thousands of his enemies shot or imprisoned. Already an expert in mass murder, having starved millions of Ukrainian kulaks and executed thousands of former colleagues in show trials, he was prepared to visit his vengeance upon German prisoners of war and his own troops who dared to surrender to his enemies. Around the globe in Asia, the Japanese warlords had taken on similar delusions of national grandeur. Heirs to a samurai tradition, they scorned those who surrendered rather than perish in battle. They, therefore, kept their POWs in subhuman conditions, often starving them to death. Lesser mortals, such as the Chinese, were treated with unimaginable brutality. During the rape of Nanking, hundreds of thousands of civilians were slain by the sword and the bayonet. In order to give their troops practice with these weapons, soldiers were ordered to toss babies into the air and skewer them on the way down. And just as in Hitler's camps, prisoners were subjected to medical experiments that were more torture than science.

Thus had industrialization reached its nadir. Visions of peace and prosperity were being drowned in blood and gore. The technology that erected skyscrapers and bridged broad rivers was turned to blasting these to bits. Medicine, which had finally learned to save lives, was reduced to preventing them from being taken. Superior forms of organization that had delivered products to remote locations now arranged to send battalions to distant battlefields fully equipped to deal out mayhem. Worst of all, democracy was under siege. Ordinary people had been making strides in governing themselves, but now the dictators asserted a counterrevolution. Utilizing the very tools that made representative governments feasible, they controlled vast armies and intimidated huge populations. The same disciplines that turned factories into the engines of prosperity were redirected into engines of destruction. In the midst of this twisted pandemonium, it was not clear that civilization would survive. Industrialization seemed bent on self-immolation. The commercial revolution that began millennia earlier in a few Greek harbors apparently contained the seeds of its demise. The critics had said so, and for the moment only the hardiest optimists dared to contradict them.

Endnotes

[1] Swift, J. 1948. *The Portable Swift*. (Edited by Carl Van Doren) New York: Viking Press.

[2] Doty, C.S. (Ed.) 1969. *The Industrial Revolution*. New York: Holt, Rinehart and Winston.

[3] Fein, M. 1997. *Hardball Without an Umpire: The Sociology of Morality*. Westport, CT: Praeger.

[4] Chirot, D. 1994. *How Societies Change*. Thousand Oaks: Pine Forge Press.

[5] Ashton, T.S. 1962. *The Industrial Revolution 1760-1830*. New York: Oxford University Press.; Speck, W.A. 1977. *Stability and Strife: England, 1714-1760*. Cambridge: Harvard University Press.

[6] Sanderson, S.K. 1995. *Social Transformations: A General Theory of Historical Development*. Oxford, UK: Blackwell.

[7] Porter, R. 1982. *English Society in the Eighteenth Century*. New York: Penguin Books; Kirk, R. 1997. *Edmund Burke: A Genius Reconsidered*. Wilmington, Del: Intercollegiate Studies Institute.

[8] Rude, G. 1964. *Revolutionary Europe 1783-1815*. London: Fontana Press.

[9] Pocock, T. 1988. *Horatio Nelson*. New York: Alfred A Knopf.

[10] Schama, S. 1989. *Citizens: A Chronicle of the French Revolution*. New York: A. Knopf.

[11] Englund, S. 2004. *Napoleon: A Political Life*. New York: Scribner.

[12] Collins, R. and Makowsky, M. 1993. *The Discovery of Society, Fifth Ed*. New York: McGraw-Hill.

[13] Huntington, S.P. 2004. *Who Are We?: The Challenges to America's National Identity*. New York: Simon & Schuster.; Bailyn, B. 1992. *The Ideological Origins of the American Revolution*. Cambridge, MA: The Belknap Press.; Bailyn, B. 2003. *To Begin the World Anew: The Genius and Ambiguities of the American Founders*. New York: Vintage Books; Churchill, W. 1958. *A History of the English-Speaking Peoples*. New York: Dorset Press.; Johnson, P. 1997. *A History of the American People*. New York: HarperCollins Publishers.

[14] Brookhiser, R. 1999. *Alexander Hamilton: American*. New York: Simon & Schuster.

[15] Morris, R.B. 1985. *Witnesses at the Creation: Hamilton, Madison, Jay, and the Constitution*. New York: New American Library.

[16] Madsen, A. 2001. *John Jacob Astor: America's First Multimillionaire*. New York: John Wiley & Sons.

[17] de Tocqueville, A. 1966. *Democracy in America*. Trans. by George Lawrence. New York: Harper & Row.

[18] Lipset, S.M. 1996. *American Exceptionalism: A Double-Edged Sword*. New York: W.W. Norton.

[19] Putnam, R.D. 2000. *Bowling Alone: The Collapse and Revival of American Community.* New York: Simon & Schuster.

[20] Kelly, C. 1974. *Conspiring Against God and Man.* Boston: Western Lands.

[21] Lipset, S.M. 1996. *American Exceptionalism: A Double-Edged Sword.* New York: W.W. Norton.; Bellah, R.N., Madsen, R., Sullivan, W.M., Swindler, A., and Tipton, S.M. 1985. *Habits of the Heart: Individualism and Commitment in American Life.* Berkeley, CA: University of California Press.

[22] Ellis, J.J. 1979. *After the Revolution: Profiles of Early American Culture.* New York: W.W. Norton & Co.

[23] Andrews, D. 2000. *The Methodists and Revolutionary America 1760-1800.* Princeton: Princeton University Press.

[24] Johnson, P.E. 1978. *A Shopkeeper's Millennium: Society and Revivals in Rochester New York 1815-1837.* New York: Hill and Wang.

[25] Dickens, C. 1884. *Barnaby Rudge: Hard Times.* Boston: Perry Mason & Co.

[26] Mannheim, K. 1936. *Ideology and Utopia.* New York: Harcourt, Brace, and World, Inc.; Mannheim, K. 1940. *Man and Society.* London: Routledge and Kegan Paul.

[27] Collins, R. and Makowsky, M. 1993. *The Discovery of Society, Fifth Ed.* New York: McGraw-Hill.

[28] Bailey, B.J. 1998. *The Luddite Rebellion.* New York: New York University Press.

[29] Richardson, J. 1977. *Victoria and Albert.* New York: The New York Times Book Co.

[30] Bradford, S. 1982. *Disraeli.* New York: Stein & Day.

[31] Cannadine, D. 1999. *The Rise and Fall of Class in Britain.* New York: Columbia University Press.

[32] Chirot, D. 1986. *Social Change in the Modern Era.* New York: Harcourt, Brace, Jovanovich.: Chirot, D. 1994. *How Societies Change.* Thousand Oaks: Pine Forge Press.

[33] Collins, R. and Makowsky, M. 1993. *The Discovery of Society, Fifth Ed.* New York: McGraw-Hill.

[34] Marx, K. and Engels, F. [1848] 1935. *The Communist Manifesto.* (In: *Selected Works*) London: Lawrence and Wishart.

[35] Taylor, G.R. 1951. *The Transportation Revolution 1815-1860.* New York: Rinehart.

[36] Starr, P. 2004. *The Creation of the Media: Political Origins of Modern Communications.* New York: Basic Books.

[37] Knox, T.W. 1886. *The Life of Robert Fulton.* New York: G.P. Putnam.

[38] Auchincloss, L. 1989. *The Vanderbilt Era: Portraits of a Gilded Age.* New York: Scribner.

[39] Starr, P. 2004. *The Creation of the Media: Political Origins of Modern Communications.* New York: Basic Books.

[40] Klein, M. 2003. *The Change Makers; From Carnegie to Gates*. New York: Times Books.

[41] Collier, P. and Horowitz, D. 1976. *The Rockefellers: An American Dynasty*. New York: Holt, Rinehart & Winston.

[42] See also: Colby, G. 1984. *DuPont Dynasty: Behind the Nylon Curtain*. Secaucus, NJ: Lyle Stuart Inc.

[43] Bridenbaugh, C. 1964. *Cities in the Wilderness: Urban Life in America 1625-1742*. New York: Capricorn Books.: Blumin, S.M. 1989. *The Emergence of the Middle Class: Social Experience in the American City 1760-1900*. New York: Cambridge University Press.

[44] Diamond, J. 1997. *Guns, Germs, and Steel: The Fates of Human Societies*. New York: W.W. Norton and Co.; Zinsser. H. 1935. *Rats, Lice and History*. Boston: Little, Brown, Co.; McNeill, W.H. 1977. *Plagues and Peoples*. New York: Doubleday.

[45] Starr, P. 1982. *The Social Transformation of American Medicine*. New York: Basic Books.

[46] Holmes, S.J. 1961. *Louis Pasteur*. New York: Dover.

[47] Gohau, G. 1990. *A History of Geology* (Trans. by Albert Carozzi and Marguerite Carozzi). New Brunswick, NJ: Rutgers University Press.

[48] Darwin, C. 1979. *The Origin of Species*. New York: Avnel Books.; Darwin, C. 1974. *The Descent of Man, and Selection in Relation to Sex*. Detroit: Gale Research.; Bowlby, J. 1990. *Charles Darwin: A New Life*. New York: W.W. Norton & Co.

[49] Rice, E. 1990. *Captain Sir Richard Francis Burton*. New York: Scribner's Sons.

[50] Kuhn, T.S. 1970. *The Structure of Scientific Revolutions; Second Edition*. Chicago: University of Chicago Press.; Laudan, L. 1977. *Progress and Its Problems: Towards a Theory of Scientific Growth*. Berkeley: University of California Press.

[51] Boas, F. 1928. *Anthropology and Modern Life*. New York: Dover Publishers.

[52] Dunbar, R, Knight, C. and Power, C. 1999. (Eds.) *The Evolution of Culture*. New Brunswick, NJ: Rutgers University Press.; LeVine, R. 1973. *Culture, Behavior and Personality*. Chicago: Aldine Publishing.; Benedict, R. 1934. *Patterns of Culture*. Boston: Houghton Mifflin; Cronk, L. 1999. *That Complex Whole: Culture and the Evolution of Human Behavior*. Boulder, CO: Westview Press

[53] Boorstin, D.J. 1983. *The Discoverers: A History of Man's Search to Know His World and Himself*. New York: Vintage Books.

[54] Baldwin, N. 1995. *Edison: Inventing the Century*. New York: Hyperion.

[55] Johnson, P.E. 1978. *A Shopkeeper's Millennium: Society and Revivals in Rochester New York 1815-1837*. New York: Hill and Wang.

[56] Burns, E. 2004. *The Spirits of America: A Social History of Alcohol*. Philadelphia, Pa.: Temple University Press.

[57] Gans, H.J. 1962. *The Urban Villagers: Group and Class in the Life of Italian-Americans.* New York: The Free Press; Gambino, R. 1975. *Blood of My Blood: The Dilemma of the Italian Americans.* Garden City, NY: Doubleday; Howe, I. 1976. *The World of Our Fathers.* New York: Harcourt, Brace, Jovanovich, Publishers; Handlin, O. 1951. *The Uprooted.* Boston: Little, Brown and Co.; Thomas, W.I. and Znaniecki, F. 1918/1958. *The Polish Peasant in Europe and America.* New York: Dover Publications; Sowell, T. 1981. *Ethnic America.* New York: Basic Books.

[58] Rossi, A.S. (Ed.) 1973. *The Feminist Papers: From Adams to de Beauvoir.* New York: Bantam Books.

[59] McFeely, W.S. 1991. *Fredrick Douglass.* New York: W.W. Norton Co.; Blauner, R. 1972. *Racial Oppression in America.* New York: Harper & Row.

[60] Patterson, O. 1982. *Slavery and Social Death: A Comparative Study.* Cambridge, MA: Harvard University Press.: Stampp, K.M. 1956. *The Peculiar Institution: Slavery in the Ante-Bellum South.* New York: Knopf.

[61] West, T.G. 1997. *Vindicating the Founders: Race, Sex, Class, and Justice in the Origins of America.* Lanham, MD: Rowman & Littlefield Publishers. Thomas, H. 1997. *The Slave Trade: The Story of the Atlantic Slave Trade: 1440-1870.* New York: Simon & Schuster.

[62] Blassingame, J.W. 1979. *The Slave Community: Plantation Life in the Antebellum South.* New York: Oxford University Press.

[63] Stampp, K.M. 1956. *The Peculiar Institution: Slavery in the Ante-Bellum South.* New York: Knopf.

[64] McFeely, W.S. 1991. *Fredrick Douglass.* New York: W.W. Norton Co.

[65] Stampp, K.M. 1965. *The Era of Reconstruction: 1865-1877.* New York: Vintage Books.

[66] Thomas, B.P. 1952. *Abraham Lincoln: A Biography.* New York: The Modern Library.

[67] Bannister, R.C. 1979. *Social Darwinism: Science and Myth in Anglo-American Social Thought.* Philadelphia: Temple University Press.

[68] Hunt, A. 1999. *Governing Morals: A Social History of Moral Regulation.* New York: Cambridge University Press.

[69] de Riencourt, A. 1974. *Sex and Power in History.* New York: Delta Books; Himmelfarb, G. 1995. *The De-Moralization of Society: From Victorian Virtues to Modern Values.* New York: Alfred A. Knopf.

[70] Biazine, E. 1992. *Liberty, Retrenchment, and Reform: Popular Liberalism in the Age of Gladstone 1860-1880.* New York: Cambridge University Press.

[71] Seward, K. 1978. *The American Family: A Demographic History.* Beverly Hills: Sage Publications.

[72] Richardson, J. 1977. *Victoria and Albert.* New York: The New York Times Book Co.

[73] James, H. 1909. *The Portrait of a Lady.* New York: Modern Library.

[74] Woodring, C. 1966. *Virginia Woolf.* New York: Columbia University Press.

204 *The Great Middle Class Revolution*

75 Gay, P. 2002. *Schnitzler's Century: The Making of Middle-Class Culture 1815-1914*. New York: W.W. Norton & Co.

76 Veblen, T. 1967. (1899) *The Theory of the Leisure Class*. New York: Viking Penguin.

77 Himmelfarb, G. 1995. *The De-Moralization of Society: From Victorian Virtues to Modern Values*. New York: Alfred A. Knopf.

78 Hoogenboom, A.A. 1968. *Outlawing the Spoils: A History of the Civil Service reform Movement 1865-1883*. Urbana: University of Illinois Press.

79 McFeely, W.S. 1981. *Grant: A Biography*. New York: W.W. Norton & Co.

80 Twain, M. 1915. *The Gilded Age*. New York: Harper.

81 Smith, A. 1776. *An Inquiry into the Nature and Causes of the Wealth of Nations*. London: W. Strahan & T. Cadell.; Heilbroner, R.L. 1980. *The Worldly Philosophers*. New York: Simon and Schuster.

82 Collier, P. and Horowitz, D. 1976. *The Rockefellers: An American Dynasty*. New York: Holt, Rinehart & Winston.

83 Dulles, F.R. 1966. *Labor in America: A History*. Arlington Heights, Ill.: Harlan Davidson.

84 Seigel, J.E. 1999. *Bohemian Paris: Culture, Politics, and the Boundaries of Bourgeois Life, 1830-1930*. Baltimore: Johns Hopkins Press.

85 Talmon, J.L. 1985. *Political Messianism: The Romantic Phase*. Boulder: Westview Press.

86 Mayhead, R. 1967. *John Keats*. Cambridge: Cambridge University Press.

87 Rousseau, J.J. 1968. (1762) *The Social Contract* (Translated by Maurice Cranston) New York: Penguin Books.

88 Balzac, H. 1960. *The Works of Honore de Balzac*. New York: Crowell.

89 Flaubert, G. 1959. *Madame Bovary*. New York: Bantam.

90 Hugo, V. 1887. *Les Miserables*. Boston: Little, Brown and Co.

91 Blanquet, Y. 1995. *The Impressionists*. New York: Chelsea House.

92 Millingham, B.M. 1984. *Wagner*. London: J.M. Dent.

93 Liszt, F. 1963. *Frederic Chopin*. (Trans. By Edward N. Waters) New York: Free Press of Glencoe.

94 Tuchman, B.W. 1966. *The Proud Tower: A Portrait of the World Before The War: 1890-1914*. New York: MacMillan.

95 Collier, P. and Horowitz, D. 1987. *The Fords: An American Epic*. New York: Summit Books; Lacey, R. 1986. *Ford: The Men and the Machine*. Boston: Little, Brown and Co.

96 Gray, T. 1976. *Champion of Peace: The Story of Alfred Nobel, the Peace Prize, and the Laureates*. New York: Paddington Press.

97 Forbes, J.D. 1981. *J.P. Morgan Jr*. Charlottesville, VA: University of Virginia Press.

[98] Weber, M. 1958a. *The Protestant Ethic and the Spirit of Capitalism*. New York: Charles Scribner's Sons.

[99] Gerth, H. and Mills, C.W. (Eds.) 1946. *From Max Weber: Essays in Sociology*. New York: Oxford University Press.

[100] Bannister, R.C. 1979. *Social Darwinism: Science and Myth in Anglo-American Social Thought*. Philadelphia: Temple University Press.

[101] Taylor, F.W. 1911. *The Principles of Scientific Management*. New York: Harper and Brothers.

[102] Garder, R.D. 1978. *Horatio Alger: or the American Hero Era*. New York: Arco Publishers.

[103] Lanczos, C. 1965. *Albert Einstein and the Cosmic World Order*. New York: Interscience Publishers.

[104] Freud, S. 1953-1974. *The Standard Edition of the Complete Psychological Works of Sigmund Freud*. (Edited by J. Strachey. London: Hogarth Press and Institute for Psychoanalysis; Gay, P. 1988. *Freud: A Life for Our Time*. New York: W.W. Norton & Co.

[105] Durkheim, E. 1915. *The Elementary Forms of Religious Life*. New York: The Free Press; Durkheim, E 1933. *The Division of Labor in Society*. New York: The Free Press; Durkheim, E 1961. *Moral Education*. New York: The Free Press.

[106] Weber, M. 1947. *The Theory of Social and Economic Organization*. New York: Free Press; Weber, M. 1958a. *The Protestant Ethic and the Spirit of Capitalism*. New York: Charles Scribner's Sons Weber, M. 1958b. *The City*. New York: The Free Press.

[107] Morris, E. 2001. *Theodore Rex*. New York: Random House.

[108] Nasaw, D. 2000. *The Chief: The Life of William Randolph Hearst*. Boston: Houghton, Mifflin.

[109] Warner, W.L. et al. 1949. *Democracy in Jonesville*. New York: Harper & Brothers.

[110] Veblen, T. 1967. (1899) *The Theory of the Leisure Class*. New York: Viking Penguin.

[111] Forbes, J.D. 1981. *J.P. Morgan Jr*. Charlottesville, VA: University of Virginia Press.

[112] Veblen, T. 1967. (1899) *The Theory of the Leisure Class*. New York: Viking Penguin.

[113] Howe, I. 1976. *The World of Our Fathers*. New York: Harcourt, Brace, Jovanovich, Publishers; Gatrell, P. 1986. *The Tsarist Economy 1850-1917*. London: B.T. Batsford.

[114] McCullough, E. 2000. *Good Old Coney Island*. New York: Fordham University Press.

[115] Bowles, S. and Gintis, H. 1976. *Schooling in Capitalist America: Educational Reform and the Contradictions of Capitalist Life*. New York: Basic Books;

Ravitch, D. 1974. *The Great School Wars: A History of the New York City Public Schools.* New York: Basic Books.

[116] Frankel, N. and Dye, N.S. (Eds.) 1991. *Gender, Class, Race and Reform in the Progressive Era.* Lexington, KY: University of Kentucky Press.

[117] Sinclair, U. 1988. *The Jungle.* Urbana: University of Illinois Press

[118] Tarbell, I. 1904. *The History of the Standard Oil Co.* New York: McClure, Phillips.

[119] Steffens, L. 1957. *The Shame of the Cities.* New York: Hill and Ward.

[120] Link, A.S. 1954. *Woodrow Wilson and the Progressive Era 1910-1917.* New York: Harper; Frankel, N. and Dye, N.S. (Eds.) 1991. *Gender, Class, Race and Reform in the Progressive Era.* Lexington, KY: University of Kentucky Press.

[121] Meyer, E.P. 1974. *"Not Charity, But Justice," The Story of Jacob A. Riis.* New York: Vanguard Press.

[122] Sherrow, V. 1995. *The Triangle Factory Fire.* Brookfield Conn.: Millbrook Press.

[123] Salvatore, N. 1982. *Eugene V. Debs: Citizen and Socialist.* Urbana: University of Illinois Press.

[124] Shone, R. 1979. *The Post Impressionists.* London: Octopus Books.

[125] Tuchman, B.W. 1962. *The Guns of August.* New York: MacMillan.

[126] Taylor, A.J.P. 1987. *Bismarck: The Man and the Statesman.* New York: Vintage Books.

[127] Toland, J. 1980. *No Man's Land: 1918, The Last Year of the Great War.* New York: Ballantine Books.

[128] MacMillan, M. 2001. *Paris 1919: Six Months that Changed the World.* New York: Random House.

[129] Kennedy, P. 1987. *The Rise and Fall of the Great Powers: Economic Change and Military Conflict from 1500 to 2000.* New York: Random House.

[130] Lynd, R. and Lynd, H. 1929. *Middletown.* New York: Harcourt, Brace, Jovanovich.

[131] Lewis, S. 1922. *Babbitt.* New York: Harcourt. Brace & Co.

[132] McShane, C. 1994. *Down the Asphalt Path: The Automobile and the American City.* New York: Columbia University Press.

[133] Loewen, J.W. 1995. *Lies My Teacher Told Me: Everything Your American History Textbook Got Wrong.* New York: The New Press.

[134] Gabler, N. 1988. *An Empire of Their Own: How the Jews Invented Hollywood.* New York: Random House.

[135] Fishman, R. 1987. *Bourgeois Utopias: The Rise and Fall of Suburbia.* New York: Basic Books; Freeman, D. 1983. *Margaret Mead and Samoa: The Making and Unmaking of an Anthropological Myth.* Cambridge, MA: Harvard University Press.

[136] Cashman, S.D. 1981. *Prohibition: The Lie of the Land.* New York: Free Press.

[137] Kobler, J. 1971. *Capone: The Life and World of Al Capone.* New York: Putnam.

[138] McElvaine, R.S. 1984. *The Great Depression: America 1929-1941.* New York: Times Books; Lynd, R. and Lynd, H. 1937. *Middletown in Transition.* New York: Harcourt, Brace, Jovanovich.

[139] Freidel, F.B. 1973. *Franklin Roosevelt: Launching the New Deal.* Boston: Little, Brown.

[140] Fischer, L. 1964. *The Life of Lenin.* New York: Harper & Row.; Courtois, S, Werth, N., Panne, J-L., Paczkowski, A., Bartosek, and Margolin, J-L. 1999. *The Black Book of Communism: Crimes, Terror, Repression.* Cambridge, MA. Harvard University Press.

[141] Hitler, A. 1972, *Mein Kampf.* Translated by Ralph Manheim. Boston: Houghton Mifflin Company.

[142] Shirer, W.L. 1960. *The Rise and Fall of the Third Reich.* New York: Simon & Schuster.

[143] Chirot, D. 1994b. *Modern Tyrants.* Princeton, NJ: Princeton University Press; Ludwig, A.M. 2002. *King of the Mountain: The Nature of Political Leadership.* Lexington: University of Kentucky Press.

[144] Goodwin, D.K. 1995. *No Ordinary Time: Franklin and Eleanor Roosevelt.* New York: Simon & Schuster.

[145] Powell, J. 2003. *FDR's Folly: How Roosevelt and His New Deal Prolonged the Great Depression.* New York: Crown Forum.

[146] Dulles, F.R. 1966. *Labor in America: A History.* Arlington Heights, Ill.: Harlan Davidson.

[147] Farley, R. 1996. *The New American Reality: Who We Are, How We Got Here, Where We Are Going.* New York: Russell Sage Foundation.

[148] Steinbeck, J. 1986. *The Grapes of Wrath.* New York: Penguin Books.

[149] Ebenstein, A. 2001. *Friedrich Hayek: A Biography.* New York: Palgrave.

[150] Clements, K.A. 1987. *Woodrow Wilson: World Statesman.* Boston: Twayne.

[151] Colville, J. 1985. *The Fringes of Power: 10 Downing Street Diaries 1939-1955.* New York: W.W. Norton & Co.

Chapter 6

The Tipping Point

That which in England we call the middle class is in America virtually the nation. (Matthew Arnold, A Word About America (1882))

The best political community is formed by citizens of the middle class. (Aristotle, Nicomachean Ethics)

Wealth is not without its advantages, and the case to the contrary, although it has often been made, has never proved widely persuasive. (John Kenneth Galbraith, The Affluent Society)

The Middle Class Ascendancy

The first atomic bomb sent a plume heavenward that was also an exclamation point. Its mushroom shape bespoke a fantastic power. The genie of the subatomic particle had been let out of the bottle so violently that over a hundred thousand people lay dead or dying. Suddenly mankind had the means of wiping itself out. A collective shudder swept across the planet as billions of individuals wondered what was in store for them. Would this illustration of triumphant science usher in a renewed prosperity or did it forecast their personal destruction? For the moment, the United States was this apparition's sole custodian, but how long would it exercise a monopoly? Democratic politicians would likely be moderate in its employment, but would others be as responsible? One good thing that could be said of this was that it punctuated a temporary American hegemony. This upstart nation had been the prime mover in the Axis defeat; now its mastery of this astonishing weapon demonstrated that it had become a superpower.

One of the consequences of the recent war was that the continental United States had been left untouched by destruction.

Most of the other belligerents, both in Europe and Asia, sustained enormous damage to their infrastructures. Their cities and factories had been bombed into rubble, and their people, turned into refugees. Dislocations in their social fabric abounded, whereas in America the joy of victory was undiluted. The nation had fought a just war and won a resolute peace. Even its citizens were impressed by their ability to fabricate and mobilize so potent an arsenal. Pleased that fewer than half million of their own had perished, the man in the street was horrified that so many others were exterminated in Hitler's concentration camps. Abraham Lincoln[1] almost a century beforehand had called their land the last best hope of mankind, and more than ever, they believed his words prophetic. Their nation had just delivered humanity from an extraordinary peril, and, as when one saves another's life, they felt responsible for maintaining international security.

One worry, however, was the economy. After the last war there had been a recession when the troops came home. Would jobs be available for the conquering heroes this time once they were decommissioned? The women who had manned the factories during the conflict would have to return to being domestic engineers, but would this be enough? Memories of the Great Depression lingered.[2] People realized that full employment had not been restored until the demands of battle compelled the government to resort to massive deficit spending. Could a civilian economy take up the slack? No one knew for sure because the situation was unprecedented.[3] During the war, a competition to outdo the other side resulted in a myriad of technological innovations. Would these advances prove useful in peacetime? Once again, no one knew for sure. Bigger planes had proved they could drop tons of bombs on the enemy, but could they be converted to carrying passengers across the continent? Only time would tell.

In fact, there was a slight hiccup when the GIs returned home, but fortunately it did not last long. An innovation not contemplated after the previous war was to fill the gap. This was the GI Bill.[4] The last time, the veterans had been promised pensions; this time a grateful nation decided to provide a good education. Most of its soldiers had come from blue-collar backgrounds; hence, they had been to neither college nor technical school. Now, it was decided that improving their academic expertise would benefit both them and their fellow citizens. They could get better jobs, and the economy would become more robust. To the surprise of many, those eligible for these benefits took up the offer in overwhelming numbers. Of about twelve million servicemen, approximately eight million signed on, and, of these, several million opted for college[5]. In one fell swoop, the educational level of the nation surged upward. The sector of the population crucial to further commercial development would now be better equipped to handle these demands. Sobered by their battle experiences, these men (and women) were prepared to dedicate themselves to doing their best. A little hard work would be nothing as compared to facing death. The result was a massive infusion of professionalism[6] into the work force.[7] People who in former times would have been satisfied being ordinary working stiffs were given a leg up the ladder and, as a result, made a tentative entry into the middle class. For most of them, this was a momentous step. For society, too, it was an earth-shattering event. Few could see it coming, but an historical landmark was about to be reached. The threshold into a middle class world would soon be crossed. Though the consequences could not be foreseen, a tipping point[8] had arrived and a long-building social revolution had entered upon a period culmination.

What was in the process of evolving has been characterized as a "service" economy or alternatively as a "post-industrial" one. The social commentator Daniel Bell[9] has pointed out that the kinds of jobs about to be available would mutate as manufacturing processes were automated. During the earlier part of the century something similar had occurred. The body politic had then been traumatized as multitudes of farmers were forced from the land. As a corollary of agricultural mechanization, what had been seventy percent of the population engaged in farming would be reduced to a scant two percent. This transformation was so shocking that it was met with a variety of policies intended to stem the tide. As is usual with social change, a cultural conservatism dictated that people would demand a restoration of the status quo ante. One means attempted for achieving this was the imposition of price supports. Family farmers would presumably be kept on the land by paying them not to grow crops. Theoretically, by artificially lowering productivity, more labor would be required. Continued increases in productivity, however, militated in fact against this solution, but an idealization of the pioneer spirit prevented a widespread recognition that failure was inevitable. The resultant government programs probably did ease the transition for some individuals, but for many others they merely held out a false hope. In the end, all that was accomplished was to slow the transformation.

With regard to industry, something similar seemed to be occurring in the postwar environment. Here, too, the number of people required to run the operations declined as the machinery, and the means of controlling it, became more sophisticated.[10] Far more goods could now be produced at a lower price with fewer people at the controls. Would this entail an increase in unemployment? Would it mean that millions of veterans would descend into poverty? Despite battalions of Cassandras, this did not happen. The nation did not slide into a renewed Depression as the manufacturing payrolls declined. People merely transferred from one sort of employment to another. On a personal level, this could be disconcerting. Individuals forced to change jobs had to confront the insecurity of developing new skills and the humiliation of losing seniority. They might even be compelled to move from one part of the country to another. Yet from the point of view of the whole, these developments prefigured a huge step forward. None could know it at the time, but the next half century would experience no commercial declines as severe as those recently experienced. The business cycle would not be repealed, but the post-industrial economy would be much less volatile. There were to be periodic recessions, but none of these would be as deep or tenacious. Instead a regular upward slope would transform the nation into the undisputed economic colossus of the planet. By the end of the century, the United States would be its only military superpower and its sole enduring economic superpower. People would say that when its marketplace caught a cold, the rest of the world's financial systems got pneumonia.

Nevertheless, to call this emerging economy service-based would be misleading. The sorts of jobs Americans were assuming varied enormously in scope. The division of labor was not merely to be between blue- and white-collar workers but encompassed a veritable rainbow of shades. The recipients of the GI Bill found themselves training for a wide variety of tasks. Not only this, but many of their assignments were more intricate, with many of these required to be self-directed. No longer did employees merely carry materials to and from machines. Much of the time, they would not even be tending machines. Rather, working with people and data was to become the norm. Yet, to achieve this effectively required that the participants attain internal discipline and a substantial expertise. To put the matter succinctly, they would have to become middle class. Although their own families had not prepared them for this eventuality, they would have to find a way to muddle through. No matter how much they might hunger for the simpler lifestyles of their romanticized youths, their jobs would oblige them to make changes.

An Occupational Survey

Why this was so can only be appreciated by exploring the complexity of the evolving division of labor.[11] It was not only enormously ramified, but it also included extremely complicated activities. At the risk of becoming tedious, it is essential to review its particulars. To begin with, the U.S. Department of Labor and its Bureau of Labor Statistics (BLS)[12] were mandated to keep track of what was happening in the workplace. In order to fulfill this obligation, their specialists found it necessary to categorize the tasks being performed. This turned out to be a Herculean endeavor. They discovered that no simple classification could be fully consistent in how it represented the myriad of intertwining relationships. In spite of this, an overview of the resultant schema is illustrative of why self-direction became standard.[13] At the top of their list of occupations are those that pertain to management. These are the ones that specialize in higher-level supervision. As corporations and government agencies grew larger,[14] the number of people needed to coordinate their activities multiplied. These organizations required not just owner/managers, but chief executives and middle managers, legislators and legislative assistants.[15] The sorts of activities that begged for centralized direction varied from advertising to marketing, from public relations to human resources, from purchasing to real estate. Their divergent bosses, therefore, needed to know how to work with people in order to get the most out of them and also the technical details of the assorted businesses of which they were to be in charge.

Closely aligned to these employments are those in the second category listed by the BLS. The heading for this group is Business and Financial Operations Occupations. It includes business agents, buyers, claims adjusters, insurances appraisers, recruiters, benefits specialists, accountants, bankers, auditors, budget analysts, underwriters, and tax examiners. In a market economy where money matters, numerous specialists are required to keep track of its flow. Banks, corporations, insurance companies, department stores, and the Internal Revenue service employ them to oversee their operations. Marx's contingents of clerks were no longer sitting, a la Charles Dickens,[16] on spindly stools wielding quill pens on ink-stained ledgers. They were now making important decisions about what would be spent, how this would be recorded, and what was likely to be profitable. Far from being ciphers, they were a semi-visible army of puppeteers who often determined what others would be able to do. Anyone who knows how the federal government operates understands that the Office of the Budget is often where the power lies. In deciding how the available pot of funds will be divided, its denizens get to establish who will have the most clout. Nowadays, experts in computer management have supplemented these fiscal operatives. As computers assumed control over day-to-day transactions, programmers, database administrators, statisticians, and systems analysts achieved prominence. Since it is often only they who understand how things can be done, they are frequently the ones put in charge.

Next down the line in the BLS compendium are architectural and engineering occupations. The list of these is truly impressive. Within the architectural area, they include architects, landscape architects, cartographers, and surveyors. It is within the engineering grouping that things get more interesting. These jobs include aerospace engineers, agricultural engineers, biomedical engineers, chemical engineers, civil engineers, computer-hardware engineers, electrical engineers, electronic engineers, environmental engineers, health-safety engineers, industrial engineers, marine and naval engineers, materials engineers, mining and geological engineers, nuclear engineers, and petroleum engineers. Responsible for translating science into practical operations, these professionals are the experts in what is functional. Hardheaded realists, they are the modern incarnation of traditional American know-how. Clearly, what they do requires thought and accountability. Unless they are personally dedicated to making good decisions, bridges fall down and people perish. Nevertheless, they are not lone rangers. They work in teams supported by architectural and civil drafters, electrical and electronic drafters, mechanical drafters, aerospace technicians, civil engineering technicians, electrical and electronic technicians, environmental engineering technicians, industrial engineering technicians, and mechanical engineering technicians. These latter, too, though less responsible, must be skilled at what they do. One small slip of the pen (or computer) can have as dire an impact on a project as a faulty overall conception.

More directly people oriented are many of the life, physical, social-science, and social-service occupations. As commercialization has pushed the technological bubble forward, the sciences underlying these developments have grown more critical. Research and development has become crucial to modernization. Both with regard to the products that make it to the marketplace and to the social policies that are implemented to solve human problems, intentional efforts at expanding the knowledge base tend to precede practical applications. Scientists of all sorts are employed by commercial, academic, and governmental organizations. Agricultural scientists, biologists, biochemists, microbiologists, zoologists, epidemiologists, astronomers, geographers, physicists, chemists, hydrologists, economists, psychologists, anthropologists, sociologists, and political scientists all seek answers to questions that may, or may not, prove useful down the road. The embodiment of self-direction, they must first figure out what to ask before they even begin to look for solutions.

More pragmatic in their orientation are those dedicated to social service. Substance-abuse, vocational, marriage and family, mental-health, and rehabilitation counselors and social workers of various stripes, including those oriented toward family, mental-health, and school, deal directly with individuals in trouble. The answers they provide must, therefore, be tailored to the dilemma of the moment. In a sense, the engineers of the social sciences, they bear a similar burden of responsibility. Also listed in this grouping by the Bureau of Labor Statistics (BLS) are clergymen and religious directors. They too have become specialists in the human condition and are frequently summoned to intervene in personal and interpersonal crises. Where ministers were once expert only in the scriptures, they are now being called upon to provide valid answers about marriage, business ethics, and personal growth.

De Tocqueville[17] long ago suggested that stable commercialized relationships are contingent upon a legitimate legal system. Apparently the larger the marketplace the greater the need for dependable means of settling disputes among strangers. Still, even he would probably be surprised to learn that by the end of the twentieth century the United States boasted almost a million persons working in legal occupations and that, of these, more than half were lawyers. Besides the attorneys, there are judges, hearings officers, arbitrators, mediators, paralegals, court reporters, and law clerks. Not all of the lawyers, of course, are trial lawyers, nor are most of these criminal lawyers. A larger proportion is, in fact, engaged in corporate or civil law. Moreover, despite the histrionics for which fictional lawyers are famed, most remain under secure emotional control. Indeed, the legal system specializes in emotional control. It is where people go when their own disciplines break down. As such, it is another venue characterized by self-direction. Lawyers must be able to figure out what to say, and how to say it, without undue reliance on external supervision. They have to be first-rate at thinking on their feet.

So, too, must educators. When they appear before a group of students, they must know that which they wish to convey. If they are unfamiliar with the subject matter, they may not know where to begin. Teachers must likewise be expert in how to convey information. Those who are knowledgeable, but inarticulate, are nearly useless. In addition, when asked a question, they need to have a sufficient store of knowledge to provide a relevant response. All this is done while standing alone in front of what may be a hostile audience. Like lawyers, or, for that matter, counselors, they are typically unable to consult a colleague before they reply. They need, in short, to know their stuff and to possess the confidence to deliver it. So voracious has the quest for knowledge become that, as of 2001, the BLS estimated that there were over seven and a half million teachers and those in related occupations in the United States. These individuals teach business, computers science, mathematics, architecture, engineering, agricultural sciences, forestry, meteorology, chemistry, environmental sciences, physics, anthropology, philosophy, economics, social science, nursing, criminal justice, law, social work, English, foreign languages, and history at primary, middle, and secondary schools and at colleges, universities, and proprietary schools. Joining them in this endeavor are special-education, adult literacy and remedial, and self-enrichment teachers, archivists and museum curators, librarians, audiovisual specialists, and teacher assistants. Many of these would be considered semiprofessionals by sociologists,[18] but with each passing year they become more professionalized. The levels of knowledge and skill they bring to bear have far surpassed what the core professions would have found acceptable a mere two centuries ago.

Next on the list of jobs are the arts, design, entertainment, sports, and media related occupations. Not long ago, these would have been denied professional recognition. During the gay nineties, actresses, for instance, were considered painted ladies and, therefore, next to prostitutes. Nor would bohemian artists have merited professional respect. Their work was admired, but their genius was reckoned akin to madness. But, times have changed, and now artists and entertainers receive extensive training in the refinements of their undertakings. According to the BLS, fewer than ten thousand individuals earn their living as fine artists, i.e., painters, sculptors, and illustrators, but twice as many are employed as art directors and three times as many work as multimedia artists and animators. Also employed in substantial numbers are commercial and industrial artists and fashion, floral, graphic, and interior designers and merchandise displayers and set designers. Besides having talent, to be good at what they do, these people must possess independent aesthetic judgments. The same applies to actors, producers, directors, dancers, choreographers, musicians, composers, and musical directors. Most of them would be happy to consider themselves performing artists and would, no doubt, insist on their internalized contributions to their craft. Athletes, though nowadays regarded as entertainers and labeled as professionals when they get paid for their sport, do not possess the technical knowledge that is the hallmark of the traditional professions. They must nevertheless be dedicated to honing their skills, or they would be consigned to short careers. Media people, too, have come close to being entertainers, especially when they are on-the-air personalities, but most have higher ambitions. Whether they are reporters, correspondents, editors, writers, authors, or photographers, they claim a journalistic status. Styling themselves members of the "fourth estate," they claim special privileges and unique insights. Clearly most go to college to learn the subtleties of soliciting, interpreting, and conveying the news.

Nowadays outstripping the educational occupations in membership are the health related occupations. Even in the wake of the Second World War, they were a presence to be reckoned with. As society became more prosperous, people insisted on first-rate care. Wonder drugs, most notably antibiotics such as penicillin, convinced ordinary Americans that physicians both understood the causes of illnesses and possessed the tools to defeat them. Everything from the mumps to heart disease, from indigestion to polio, seemed capable of a cure. Once medicine demonstrated a reliable competence, laymen began trooping to doctors' offices or the hospital. Actually, before the 1950s, it was the physician who visited when people were sick. With further progress, however, preventive medicine came to the fore. Patients, especially those who possessed health insurance, went to offices for routine checkups and prophylaxis. Chapter 3 has already presented a summary of the proliferation of medically associated jobs. These range from the quintessential professionalism of brain surgeons to the less exalted contributions by pharmacy technicians and licensed practical nurses.[19] Not included in that compendium are the less prestigious positions of home-health-care and nursing aides, hospital orderlies, occupational and physical-therapy assistants, massage therapists, dental assistants, medical transcriptionists, pharmacy aides, and veterinary assistants. What is notable is that even these lower-status occupations have been professionalizing. The levels of knowledge, training, and dedication required of them have all escalated. No longer merely jobs, they have become career orientations that demand special training.

As earlier remarked, this same phenomenon has asserted itself within the protective service occupations. Police officers,[20] detectives, sheriffs, transit and railroad police, fire fighters, correctional officers, fish and game wardens, animal-control workers, private detectives, and also security guards have been impelled to professionalize.[21] They are expected to get better educations than their predecessors did and to exercise self-control when on the job. Self-direction and an allegiance to democratic standards are presently considered the norm. Whereas skill with a nightstick was once admired, it has become a potential indicator of abuse as a sign that an officer prefers to act first and think later. Yet, thinking has become mandatory for protective positions. Their occupants are not merely expected to exercise control but to shelter people from harm. As such, they must understand individual rights and personal vulnerabilities.

Even the sorts of white-collar workers that C. Wright Mills[22] discussed have been professionalizing. There are now an immense number of office and administrative support personal. The equivalent of the nineteenth century clerks, by the end of the twentieth century the BLS estimated that there were almost 23 million of these adjunct staffers. Of these, a million and a half were supervisors of administrative-support workers. These, of course, required the people skills of supervisors. Among the first-line workers they oversaw were switchboard and telephone operators; bill and account collectors; billing, bookkeeping, and auditing, payroll, and procurement clerks; bank tellers; brokerage, correspondence, and court clerks; customer-service representatives; eligibility interviewers; file and hotel and motel desk clerks; loan interviewers; library assistants; new accounts and order clerks; human resource assistants; receptionists; reservation and ticketing clerks; cargo and freight agents; couriers and messengers; police, fire, and ambulance dispatchers; meter readers; postal service clerks; postal carriers; postal sorters; production and expediting, shipping and receiving, and stock clerks; weighers; measurers and checkers; executive secretaries and administrative assistants; legal and medical secretaries; computer operators; data-entry keyers; word processors and typists; insurance-claims, mail, and general office clerks; office-machine operators; proofreaders; and statistical assistants. This is quite a list and obviously quite varied. Nevertheless, what should jump out from the page is how many of these are responsible positions. Executive and legal secretaries, billing clerks, and police dispatchers make decisions involving a great deal of money and sometimes life and death. Moreover, some of these workers, notably those employed by the post office, would be insulted were they not referred to as professionals. In any event, they are expected to exercise some degree of self-direction and often quite a bit of skill. Far from being mindless robots tremulously fulfilling every request of their superiors, they must be able to engage in independent problem solving. Mills would probably be discomfited to learn that a large proportion of them have at least a two-year college education. Like their more educated chiefs, they have been upgrading their expertise in the expectation that this will lead to greater responsibilities.

Mills might also be astonished by the skills exercised by those in sales related occupations. With almost 15 million people occupying them by century's end, over a million more engage in supervisory roles. In other words, many of those in supposedly subservient posts are, in fact, expected to exhibit leadership. While on the job, they are not under constant supervision but are mandated to exercise discretion. Some of their subordinates, such as cashiers, perform fairly simple tasks, but even these need to do so with care. Others, such as sales representatives for wholesale, manufacturing, and technical and scientific products, need a detailed understanding of their merchandise, their customers, and the logistics of joining the two. The same can be said of insurance, advertising-sales, travel, and securities, commodities, and financial sales agents and real-estate brokers. All require a sensitivity to customer needs that is inconsistent with vacuous conformity. Here, too, Mills might be surprised at how many have gone to college to obtain degrees in marketing or psychology.

Although Daniel Bell[23] characterized the emerging economy as service oriented, the BLS estimates that less than three million people are currently employed in personal care or service occupations. Those who are include animal caretakers, gaming dealers, motion-picture projectionists, ushers and ticket takers, amusement and recreation attendants, funeral attendants, barbers, hairdressers, manicurists, skin-care specialists, baggage porters and bellhops, concierges, tour guides, flight attendants, child care workers, personal and home care aids, fitness trainers and aerobics instructors, and recreational workers. Of these, there are only some 12 thousand barbers, 330 thousand hairdressers, and 115 thousand flight attendants. The point is that there are fewer in classical service jobs than might be supposed, and these are varied in their level of prestige, responsibility, and remuneration. As the United States passed the middle-class tipping point, the number of personal servants did not mount to astronomic levels. Once upon a time, in preindustrial England, maids and individual private servants were common occupations; middle-class Americans, in contrast, are offended by sycophantic attention. Themselves determined to be no one's servant, they are loath to impose this status on others. The closest they come to accepting fawning attention is from those in the food preparation and serving occupations. As members of the middle classes acquired money, they began to eat out more frequently. This was reflected in the century's end tabulation of nearly ten million workers in these employments. Chefs, cooks, bartenders, and waiters and waitresses proliferated in taking on these roles, though, they did not deign to become menials. Some chefs became television stars, and many servers earn enough to support a plush suburban lifestyle. Bowing and scraping to customers, as opposed to being polite, are deemed déclassé. Often, it is the customers who are intimidated by the insouciance and knowledgeability of their attendants.

So far, most of the jobs discussed are at least tangentially white-collar. Yet to be mentioned, however, are the traditionally blue-collar occupations. These too have metastasized into thousands of subspecialties. Moreover, they, too, have been infected by the professionalization mania.[24] Although these trades continue to be largely manual in nature, their practitioners no longer work merely with things. More and more, they, too, deal with data and people. Even in their hands-on aspects, their work has become increasingly complex. A strong back is no longer a sufficient qualification for most of their occupations. The BLS enumerates only six categories that may be considered traditionally blue-collar. These are building and grounds cleaning and maintenance, farming, fishing, and forestry, construction and extraction, installation, maintenance, and repair, productions, and transportation and material-moving occupations. Before examining these further, it should be noted that among the cleaning and maintenance occupations fewer than a million are reported to be maids or housekeepers. Another two million are janitors. This agrees well with the notion that personal service has gone out of style.

The most central blue-collar occupations are those that entail production. These are the manufacturing positions, the ones historically associated with the Industrial Revolution. By century's end there are little over 12 million of them, including their supervisors and foremen. What is astonishing, however, is the multitude of distinctions among what these people do. The reader is warned that the following inventory, while incomplete, is staggering in its tedium.

The effect of reading this registry would be overwhelming. It makes it clear that skill and conscientiousness are not confined to the traditional professions. Many of the enumerated positions would qualify their holders as artisans. A significant number of these workers have spent years learning their crafts and take pride in being able to perform operations that others cannot. Take machinists; their ability to shape obdurate materials into complex forms entails more than turning on a switch or pushing a few buttons. In order to achieve tolerances often measured by micrometers, each must possess a good eye, a superior mechanical aptitude, and a disciplined attention span. This work obviously demands far more expertise than did that of a medieval plowman. To some minds, production workers are associated with an innate churlishness, that is, with a peasant's mentality. With the coming of the middle-class revolution, this has ceased to be true. Classified by most sociologists as perched somewhere within the lower middle class, they rightly consider themselves as among the middling orders. They surely have a jurisdiction over their own lives that a medieval serf would envy.

One more of the BLS categories should be sufficient to document the growth in the division of labor and the professionalization that has accompanied the middle class ascendancy. The transportation and material moving occupations are also a hodgepodge of the simple and the complicated, the conformist and the responsible. They embrace airline pilots; air-traffic controllers; ambulance, bus, long-distance truck, light delivery, and taxi drivers; locomotive engineers; railroad conductors; sailors and marine oilers; parking-lot and service-station attendants; conveyor operators and tenders; crane and tower, excavating and loading-machine, and industrial truck and tractor operators; hand laborers and freight and stock movers; hand packers and packagers; and refuse collectors. Needless to say, the distance between an airline pilot and a refuse collector is considerable. Both in terms of social prestige and occupational complexity, they are worlds apart. Yet, even long-haul truckers have increased their levels of responsibility and remuneration. They are accountable for the safe operation of vehicles that have intensified in sophistication and ability to do harm if they are not faithfully, and independently, managed.

Lastly, and without resort to cataloging occupational divisions of labor, construction and repair occupations deserve mention. Construction workers can no longer be stereotyped as ditch diggers or as human mules to carry loads for others. Carpenters, masons, electricians, and plumbers are almost semiprofessionals. The tools they wield and the plans they follow are intricate and, therefore, a mystery to the uninitiated. Road builders and heavy construction workers also employ machinery that cannot be mastered by sitting in a seat and turning a wheel. As for repair occupations, whether these are in telecommunications, avionics, automobile repair, air conditioning, or factories, the very nature of this work enables their providers to control uncertainties. This becomes a source of power. Workers are not mere plebeians. Because they can figure out what others cannot, they can regulate the resumption of important operations. Consider the plumber who comes to restore what caused a flooded basement. The job must be done; hence the homeowner, who probably knows little about plumbing, is at the mercy of a technician in dirty overalls. In most cases, he/she must accept the plumber's diagnosis of the problem on faith and in the hope that, when given the bill, he/she won't be gouged.

One more indicator of the momentous change that has occurred must be addressed. This is what happened to the labor movement. From its inception in the nineteenth century with the Knights of Labor, labor organizing had been envisioned as a shield to protect the workingman from capitalist incursions. Labor unions decisively replaced guilds when industrialization moved people into factories where they could compare the multifarious indignities to which they were subjected.[25] As industrialization advanced, the impetus to join together increased. While the particulars of this movement varied from country to country, within the United States it reached its apotheosis during the Great Depression. The National Labor Relations Act, more familiarly known as the Wagner Act, protected the right of workers to become members of these organizations, thereby expanding union rolls dramatically. C. Wright Mills,[26] a dedicated collectivist, was encouraged that this trend extended well into the 1940s. He noted that, in 1900, only 2.5% of white-collar workers and 8.2% of wageworkers belonged to unions. These figures grew during the 1920s but at first dipped in the 1930s. By 1948, however, 16.2% of white-collar workers and 44.1% of wageworkers had joined the fold. At this point, it looked as if unionism would dominate the foreseeable future. Mills hoped that white-collar employees would choose solidarity with their greasier brethren, and it appeared his wish might be fulfilled.

In the late 40s and earlier 50s unions seemed unstoppable. John L. Lewis[27] ran the coal miners union with an iron hand and could bring the country to its knees by threatening a strike. So potent did these threats appear that, Harry Truman, albeit a Democrat, threatened to nationalize the steel industry in order to forestall a labor action. Nevertheless, a reverse trend had already begun. Though controversial, Republicans had pushed through Congress the Taft-Hartley Act, which outlawed wildcat strikes and, under specific circumstances, mandated collective bargaining. The Landrum-Griffin Act, which further constrained union activities, would eventually augment this. Union abuses were also under attack in Congress, where Jimmy Hoffa was forced to answer the questions of the McClellan Committee as it investigated racketeering among the Teamsters Union. The most significant change, however, came courtesy of the middle class tipping point. As the nature of jobs changed, so did the composition of the unions. Coal miners, for instance, lost their clout as automation came to the mines. With far fewer miners and with those who remained more technically proficient, power could be exercised by monopolizing skills rather than by instituting shutdowns. Steel workers also lost leverage through automation and competition from other materials. They could not lock the nation in a chokehold once plastic was able to substitute for steel.

In general, as industrial occupations declined, the number of industrial unionists declined.[28] By 1990, only 16% of all American workers belonged to a union. What changed more emphatically was who belonged to unions. In 2002, only 13% of miners and a scant 15% of manufacturing workers did. Those in financial and sales occupations had even lower concentrations: 3% and 5%, respectively. The largest gains had been among government workers. In this area, 42% were members, and many of these were professionals, or at least semiprofessions. One of the most heavily unionized groups has been the teachers. Unionism has decisively altered its complexion. Thanks to the middle class revolution, burly laborers have been replaced on picket lines. Standing where they once had stood, were females. They, too, might walk off the job despite laws against this, but their most potent tool is political influence. Backing the right candidates could get favorable treatment at the bargaining table. After all, politicians ran government, and government was their employer. Unionism, therefore, came to reflect the professionalization of the workforce. Many of its strongest adherents no longer thought of themselves as blue collar but as members in good standing of the middle class. Far be it for them to bring the system down.

The Eisenhower Consolidation

Dwight Eisenhower[29] was a national father figure. A few short years before he became president, he had led millions of troops in a desperate crusade to save civilization from the Nazi challenge. He was safe; he was solid; he could be trusted. Ike might sometimes be boring, but he was never threatening. In retrospect, it is conventional to assert that his presidency was a period during which nothing happened. Thought of as placid and without turmoil, the times are deemed as uninspiring as was the nation's leader. The truth is quite different. To begin with, there was massive conflict; its dimensions were merely different from those of later years. The 50s was fundamentally a decade of consolidation. The middle-class tipping point had just been reached, and it was now being knit into the social fabric. In short, a social revolution was in the process of being solidified. The Sturm und Drang might be muted, but this was largely because legitimation required agreement, not discord. Too many strident voices of dissent might indicate that the new social order had not been accepted. An apparent consensus signaled to everyone that what had been achieved would not easily be reversed.

One of the things for which the period is remembered is the moment when Charles E. Wilson, Eisenhower's Secretary of Defense designate, allegedly said that what was good for General Motors was good for the nation. The outgoing president of GM, he was defending the profits his corporation made on defense contracts. What is significant about this incident is that it symbolized the legitimation of the corporation. Once a new-fangled innovation that had inspired resistance, it now had growing dominance as an organizational form made normal.[30] Most people had come to accept the fact that such business entities strode the economy like colossi. They might be criticized, but very few expected, or even intended, to dismantle them. To do so would kill the goose that lay the golden eggs. On the contrary, the idea was to tame the giants. People wanted to work for them, and to move up within them, not to supersede them. They could perhaps stand to be regulated, but their destruction was unnecessary. All that was required was legislation to limit their powers.

Similar sentiments applied to those who worked for these corporations. They were organization men; they wore gray flannels suits; they were cut from the same cookie-cutter mold.[31] Garbed in copycat white shirts, uniform ties, and felt hats, they were proud of the white-collar conformity Mills so roundly condemned. The economist John Kenneth Galbraith[32] described theirs as an affluent society and they cheerfully accepted this portrayal. Viewing themselves on the cutting-edge of prosperity, they were too busy pursuing success to worry that materialism was unseemly. Seen from the inside, they were innovators and go-getters. Job advertisements from the period routinely sought individuals who were "self-starters." The term "self-direction" might not have been a prominent part of their vocabulary, yet its reality was. The business uniforms so frequently ridiculed were the external symbols of an internalized discipline directed toward progress.[33] The corporate types truly wanted to make things better. Indicative of their attitude is another cliché from contemporary advertisements. Virtually every product was extolled as "new and improved." Otherwise, it was not keeping up with the competition. Nothing could be static. Those doing the pacesetting could always find superior ways to do things. This was the overriding orientation of these supposedly mindless clones.

Nor should it be forgotten that this was the era of the Cold War. The Soviet Union had become a strategic adversary.[34] Also a nuclear power, it presented itself as the wave of a very different future. Trumpeting the inevitable destruction of capitalism, it offered totalitarian communism as a more advanced alternative. Many intellectuals of the period were convinced this was true. They believed that centralized planning was more rational than the confusions of the marketplace and that, therefore, it would be economically, and militarily, more efficient. They also alleged that socialism, and ultimately communism, were potentially more democratic than representative institutions arguably controlled by business interests. In the end, Marx would be vindicated and an egalitarian prosperity would be triumphant. But neither American politicians, nor members of the public, were convinced of this. They feared that their hard-won freedoms might be overrun by dictatorial aggressors. The result was an arms race and attempts at containment. Vast sums of money were expended to prevent Europe and Korea from slipping behind the Iron Curtain. Eventually the competition concerned intercontinental ballistic missiles. The object was to see who could build better rockets to carry nuclear warheads to the other's territory. Mutually assured destruction (MAD) became the watchword of security, and it scared nearly everyone to death.

At home, this confrontation opened with a renewed red scare.[35] People began to worry that Russian spies had infiltrated the government. At first the House Un-American Activities Committee (HUAC), then Senator Joseph McCarthy,[36] began to investigate a bevy of suspects.[37] Many, indeed, turned out to be Soviet collaborators, notably Alger Hiss and the Rosenbergs,[38] but the seeds for a culture war were being sown. Overreaction in the form of blacklists was countered by furious denials of treason. In later years, this episode gave the era a reputation for being ultraconservative. Once more, the reality was subtler. The Eisenhower administration did not turn back the clock. It did not attempt to undo most of the New Deal's social legislation. Social Security remained intact, as did unemployment insurance. The social-welfare safety net had become as much a part of the nation's institutional fabric as had the corporations. Even McCarthyism lost its cache. Eisenhower himself found it too extreme for his tastes.

On the domestic front, progress was also evident. [39]One of the mechanisms of consolidation was television. Invented in the 20s and perfected in the 40s, it did not enter most living rooms until the 50s. Radio had earlier fertilized a national culture, but moving pictures that could be summoned at the turn of a dial signaled a new dimension in entertainment. From coast to coast, ordinary people saw the same situation comedies, the same variety shows, and the same newscasters. Everyone loved Lucy;[40] everyone found Ed Sullivan a poker-faced presence on a family friendly program; and everyone was impressed with Edward R. Murrow's[41] mellifluous tones and ever-present cigarette. Another mechanism of consolidation was the highway system. Eisenhower sponsored a plan for interstate highways partly because his military experience demonstrated the utility of being able to move men and equipment across the country, but the major benefits were nonetheless civilian. Now, truckers could move merchandise more efficiently than by rail. Steel tracks could not be built into every small town, but asphalt roads could. Nor were trains effective in delivering small loads; trucks were. This gave commerce as much an infusion as had canals many years before.

This expanded highway network had an even more direct influence on individuals. Ford had made automobiles affordable; Eisenhower gave them a place to go.[42] Before his concrete strips crisscrossed the land in emulation of Hitler's autobahns, intercity transportation had been tortuous. Roads were narrow, winding, and sometimes unpaved. They certainly did not tempt people to take pleasure trips far from home. The interstates transformed this.[43] They made every corner of the country accessible to every other corner. This prompted a slew of innovations to facilitate these journeys. Motels sprouted like mushrooms. Holiday Inn was not any longer just the title of a movie; it designated a chain of motor hotels to which families could repair in the assurance that they would be provided ample comfort. Likewise, a bevy of standardized restaurants arose to feed these travelers. Kentucky Fried Chicken and McDonald's became household names.[44] "Finger licking good" and the "golden arches" signaled dependable, if not exhilarating, cuisine. In the process, these changed the nation's eating habits. Because they had to be uniform if they were to guarantee consistency and quick if they were to be profitable, they became the progenitors of fast food. Even at home, a TV dinner hastily removed from the freezer and eventually popped into the microwave became the standard of convenience. People on the move still expected nourishing food, but they did not have the time to be fancy.

Their families too had become compressed. During the Depression, families were postponed for financial reasons, but, after the war ended, there was a burst of fertility characterized as The Baby Boom. By the 50s, however, parents were voluntarily confining themselves to two children. In essence, the nuclear family was legitimated. Its flexibility was perfectly suited to the agility needed to take advantage of a market economy. Middle-class families, accordingly, no longer participated in extended families in order to tend to their immediate needs.[45] If anything, they relied more on friends who had similar interests than on relatives. The lesson a better educated,[46] and more affluent, generation has absorbed is that childrearing is an intensive endeavor. If the young are to be prepared for self-directed success, family resources must be directed their way.[47] Sending parental attention or financial reserves elsewhere, including to extraneous siblings, might shortchange them. One consequence has been the widespread practice of setting up college trust funds. Savings are specifically designated for higher education on the premise that it is inevitable and obligatory. Children are not asked whether they want to go to college, but what they expect to study once they get there. The new understanding is that, absent this preparation, they will be unmitigated failures.

Yet college is not the start of this preparation. Parents have to make certain that their children go to first-rate primary and secondary schools. One way to ensure this is to move to the suburbs.[48] Inexpensive automobiles make it possible to live outside the city limits,[49] and the assembly-line style construction of houses make these domiciles affordable. The Levittown phenomenon has arrived.[50] Those boxy residences, for which their inhabitants were so roundly censured, are cozy affairs that enable people to practice the watchword of the modern family, namely "togetherness."[51] Mother, father, and their children are expected to comprise a mutually supportive household. Those who play together, and perhaps pray together, will stay together. Their love will be an umbrella to shelter them from the hazards of a world filled with unpredictable strangers. The models for this friendly perfection are <u>Ozzie and Harriet</u> and <u>Father Knows Best</u>. Their gentle conversations, during which family members discuss their various dilemmas, are how it is supposed to be. Sweet reason and mutual concern provide encouragement for their younger members to stand on their own feet. Parents are there to furnish guidance, not dictatorial orders, and children, who in their immaturity might bridle at this assistance, would eventually incorporate these lessons into their personal repertoires. Television, the very essence of modernity, thereby became an academy for social advancement.

Another of the changes that occurred within suburban abodes was how discipline was exercised. During the 30s, John B. Watson[52] had been the guru of childrearing.[53] His central recommendation was that children not be spoiled. They must be put on a strict schedule, not unlike that found in the contemporary factory. By the 40s and into the 50s, Dr. Spock[54] asserted a contrary expertise. He recommended a gentler regime. Children were not to be exposed to corporal punishment; they were to be patiently and carefully instructed. When they misbehaved, they were to be sent to their rooms so that they could reflect on their misdeeds. Although this sometimes verged on permissiveness, the central intent was explored by Melvin Kohn. [55] The underlying goal transmuted from obedience to internalized discipline. Children needed to understand why they should do what their parents required. These external objectives had to become their own if they were to be pursued when no external authority was available. The young were, in short, to become middle class paragons, capable of emotional restraint and competent decisions. Even in school, discipline was directed toward internalized learning.[56] Gone were the hickory stick and the "board of education." A trip to the vice principal for a good talking-to replaced a rap across the knuckles. All of this was reinforced by suburbanization wherein a group of like-minded parents migrated to the same location to ensure that their offspring could attend good schools. They would thenceforth insist that quality education meant a progressive, nonpunitive, education.

While this was happening, a newly middle-class public was insisting that the rules of the game be universal. They wanted equality of opportunity truly extended to all with equivalence before the law. Consumed with a desire to participate in the upward mobility[57] they saw around them, they were adamant that no one receive special favors. This applied on the job, in the schools, and in the courts. Merit and justice were to govern how things turned out. People were supposed to get what they earned. At work, expertise was to be rewarded with promotions; at school superior scholarship would be recompensed with good grades, and within the legal system no one would to be railroaded because of lowly origins. Television too reinforced these ideals. On its ubiquitous western and detective programs, justice always prevails in the end. The good guy gets the girl, and the bad one is arrested and locked up.

While the Eisenhower era has a reputation for conservative stasis, it was actually the springboard for the reforms that flowered in the next decade.[58] One of these was the Civil Rights Movement.[59] The Supreme Court's Brown v. Board of Education ruling was published in 1954.[60] It launched the movement toward desegregation and then integration. Eisenhower might reluctantly dispatch U.S. marshals to Little Rock to enforce the Constitution, but he did dispatch them. And at this time, Rosa Parks began the Montgomery bus boycott when she refused to move to the back of a bus. The conventional wisdom dismisses this period as a dark age, without noticing that a sea change had occurred. A half century earlier, the Supreme Court had ruled that separate could be equal and had acquiesced in routine lynchings of assertive blacks. At the time of these outrages, the public did not object. Keeping blacks as second-class citizens seemed the normal order of things. By the time of the middle class tipping point, this was no longer so. Middle-class values dictated fairness for all, irrespective of skin color.[61] If social mobility were open to talent, then talent could not be denied whatever its shade. Blacks, too, had to be allowed to take advantage of the rules, if these rules were to mean anything. Northerners, who became middle class before Southerners, were offended when they saw the law perverted to enforce segregation. It was this attitude, one that also infected the South as it extricated itself from its agricultural slumber, which made the Civil Rights Movement possible. "Negroes" too were to be inducted into a social class system that could not function if it did not reward merit wherever it was found.[62]

Similar considerations applied to the gathering feminist movement. Nowadays, it is conventional to mock primitive television commercials that presented housewives as glorying in their sparkling bathrooms, but this was not all that changed. The togetherness of the suburbs celebrated the roles of mother and housekeeper, yet in this it was behind the times. The cleanliness that was so highly regarded was handed down from earlier days, reinvigorated by a flurry of technical developments. Electric refrigerators, washing machines, dishwashers, and even sponge mops made sanitation more easily accomplished.[63] So did a host of detergents and grease-cutting agents. Nevertheless, the myth of the housewife trapped in her lonely suburban prison was never fully valid. Rosy the Riveter supposedly pioneered the progress of women in the workplace, but her wartime contributions were a blip on a much longer continuum. Women had been gradually entering the labor force for over a century, and the trend now accelerated. Wives and mothers were going to work in greater numbers, not so much to supplement the family's budget as for personal fulfillment. With so many of their traditional tasks superseded by technology, they needed an opportunity to perform respected work. Better educated than their mothers, they craved situations where they could demonstrate their abilities. Having gone to coeducational schools and, often, colleges, they languished when restricted to domestic ghettos. It was these women, and their daughters, who were to provide the audience for a looming feminism.[64]

Dissent, such as it was during these years, was marginalized. Most famous from the time were the beatniks.[65] They affected scruffy beards, ill-fitting berets, and embarrassing poetry. Contemptuous of the materialistic surrounding them, they were ostentatiously poor. Styling themselves intellectuals, they sounded the tocsin of impending dehumanization. Updated bohemians, they gathered in coffee-houses to admire one another's work and to curse organizational types. Mothers cautioned their children not to become such wastrels, but for the moment they need not have worried. The Beat Generation might have been an object of curiosity, but it was also one of ridicule. While the middle-class consolidation was at its peak, people were too focused on business to be attracted by its message. They would have agreed with Calvin Coolidge that the business of America was business.

The Hippie Eruption

The 60s began with John F. Kennedy.[66] When he stood with his head uncovered by the customary top hat to deliver his ringing inaugural address, it was as if there really was a New Frontier. By general consensus, he represented a fresh generation, one untainted by war or Depression. In his campaign, he promised to get the country moving again. Implying that nothing much had happened under Ike, he pledged social as well as economic progress. What seems to have been forgotten over the succeeding decades is that he was elected on a platform dedicated to prosecuting the Cold War more effectively. In his debates with Richard Nixon,[67] he promised he would close a "missile gap" with Russia and protect Quemoy and Matsu from Communist Chinese expansion. Even the famous peroration in which he said, "And so my fellow Americans, ask not what your country can do for you, ask what you can do for your country," has, as its goal, patriotism.

Before these oft-quoted words, Kennedy had also declared, "Let every nation know, whether it wishes us well or ill, that we will pay any price, bear any burden, meet any hardship, support any friend, oppose any foe, to insure the survival and success of liberty." Protecting freedom, the quintessential middle-class value, was the central aim of his presidency. But the packaging was new. Thus, he began his address by asserting, "Let the word go forth from this time and place, to friend and foe alike, that the torch has been passed to a new generation of Americans, born in this century, tempered in war, disciplined by a hard and bitter peace, proud of our ancient heritage, and unwilling to witness or permit the slow undoing of those human rights to which this nation has always been committed...." The theme was clear: it was idealism in service to standards already set by the American experiment. Kennedy's signature program, the Peace Corps, underlined this direction. It would spread middle class values across the world. Youths committed to doing good would travel to third-world countries, for little or no pay, where they would teach the lessons they had learned at home. In this, they would convert their moral aspirations into action.

The actual accomplishments of JFK's administration are very much mixed. He had stared down Big Steel,[68] flubbed the Bay of Pigs landings, recouped during the Cuban Missile Crisis, pledged to send men to the moon, instituted a tax cut, and begun inserting advisors into Viet Nam.[69] The war on poverty was not yet off the drawing board, and it would not get started until after he was assassinated. What must strike the neutral observer is the idealism apparent in most of these programs. The youthful vigor of Camelot reverberated around the land, especially among the young. They wanted to save the world, not merely to aspire to suburban affluence. This attitude was to erupt in full blossom in the hippie generation. These children of the children of depression had been raised on tales of frustrated idealism. Their parents wanted to change the world but had been diverted into rescuing it from a barbarian invasion. Now the young were chafing at the bit to fulfill their parent's aborted missions. They would not sell out just to attain personal comfort. Since the millennium was visibly within reach, they would see things through regardless of the obstacles blocking the way.

Some of these ambitious youths were red diaper babies.[70] Their parents had been Depression era revolutionaries from whence they imbibed a Marxist legacy. Most, however, came from families with a liberal bent, or, if from conservative ones, they were in rebellion against a reactionary heritage. A majority of the activists were college educated. Members of the first cohort of middle-class children where a higher education was considered mandatory, they believed themselves to be intellectually superior to their forebears. As such, they were certain that their idealism was grounded in an enhanced understanding of the human condition. Despite their youth and inexperience, they were persuaded they knew best.[71] Their book learning and good intentions ensured that this was so. If their elders would simply listen to their prescriptions with an open mind, they too would realize that the problems of the past were amenable to solution. All that was needed was the will to implement reforms.[72]

The hippie ideal was fairly simple.[73] The Beatles[74] were soon to capture its essence in a hit song. "All you really need is love" went their mantra. The key to universal happiness wasn't a mystery; it was a matter of dedication. Another popular song advised: "If you are going to San Francisco, you're going to meet some gentle people there. If you are going to San Francisco, be sure to wear a flower in your hair." The Haight-Ashbury district of San Francisco, along with New York City's East Village, became the capitals of a peace-oriented movement. Along their urban streets wandered bona-fide converts to the cause. Dressed in tie-dyed tee shirts and sporting granny glasses, they preached a message of universal love to all comers.[75] "Make love, not war!" and exercise "flower power" were among their observations. If people would just be nice to one another, there would be no need for a confrontation with the Soviets. If everyone pursued beauty, as opposed to avarice, there would likewise be no need for the rat race. People of every shade and description could join hands and lift their voices in song. At long last recognizing their inherent brotherhood, they would automatically seek to help, rather than hurt, their neighbors.

Among the other slogans making the rounds were "Don't trust anyone over thirty"; "If it feels good, do it"; and "Do your own thing." The idea was that the children knew best. Uncorrupted by the need to earn a living, or to prove how powerful they were, they reincarnated Rousseau's noble savages.[76] Often financed by their parents, they would nevertheless seek to achieve dignified objectives. Art, for instance, was high on their list. But this was not the art of their parents. It was more vibrant and more rebellious. Some of it was psychedelic. Bright, otherworldly colors replaced less adventurous shades. Some of it was pop art. Andy Warhol led the way in appreciating the beauty of ordinary objects. The catch here is that these objects are simultaneously being satirized. They are kitsch, not true art. Although many hippies emulated the beards and long hair associated with the bohemians of old, few were practicing artists. They merely copied the poverty of these long-ago rebels. If they lived in lofts, this was by choice, not necessity. The best they could do by way of artistry was to engage in handicrafts. Personally made objects, whether clothing, jewelry, or furniture, took on a status significantly more elevated than that of manufactured goods. The very imperfections indicated that they were more honest.

Most important was their rejection of the middle class discipline of the older generation. These young people would not play the commercial game. Money did not matter. One of their mentors, Abbie Hoffman,[77] went so far as to entitle a book Steal This Book. The objective was to undermine the market, not to participate in it. They preferred to be like Neil Diamond, "forever in blue jeans." If they had anything to say about it, their privileged childhoods would never end. Work would not be necessary because they would never make the mistake of assuming its responsibilities. They knew that spontaneous feelings are what really counted. Getting in touch with one's inner self, rather than obtaining a huge bank account, earned the respect of one's peers. This made it attractive to pursue shortcuts. One of these was song. Folk music and, to a lesser extent, rock and roll touched the soul. With a guitar in one's hand, one could share an expression of intense emotion with others. All could communicate a joint appreciation of the poignant question: Where have all the flowers gone? The answer was "the graveyard," but this generation would never personally join in the slaughter. Striving for universal peace was the core of what it meant to be a loving individual. It's what flower power was about. As its partisans also said, one should "make love not war," for if everyone did, there obviously would be no war.[78]

Another shortcut was drugs. It was a simple matter to zone out with a joint in one's hand. The Depression-era generation sought discipline by avoiding narcotics, but this generation was too sophisticated to be fooled by the propaganda that beguiled its parents. The young people knew that pot was not the killer depicted in Reefer Madness. Marijuana did not make a person crazy; it only made one feel good. Passing roaches around at a party was an expression of solidarity, love, and even creativity. More potent still was LSD. The Harvard psychologist Timothy Leary[79] was then touted it as the perfect gateway to self-understanding. He described trips illuminated by vivid colors and deep insights. "Tune in, turn on, drop out" was his rallying cry. The world of inner beauty thereby released was far more valid than crass materialism of the marketplace. It, and not mere things, was what life was about. Heroin too was out there in the streets, but most of the hippies knew that it was deadly. They also passed along the word that "speed (i.e., amphetamines) kills." They would use drugs, but recreationally rather than addictively.

A third shortcut was sex. It was love made tangible by the act of coitus. <u>Pippin</u>, one of the era's Broadway plays, promulgated the message that sex was fun. It was no more harmful than pot and had been denied these youngsters by their parents because they were envious of youth. Like the actors in <u>Hair</u>, they would take off their clothes and do what came naturally. Sex was not dirty; it was a biological function. Unlike the Victorians, one should not be prudish. One should be proud of one's body, not ashamed of it or the pleasure it gave. Nor was marriage a necessary prerequisite for doing the deed. This too was a superstition inherited from less enlightened times. Why did people need a piece of paper in order to express their affection for one another? It was perfectly all right to shack up. By the same token, it was okay to take advantage of crash pads. Sleeping on the floor of a total stranger's apartment, where what happened happened, was a sign of generosity, rather than of immorality. The apotheosis of this occurred at Woodstock. This open-air celebration of music was characterized by several days of mud and nudity. Reckoned to be a milestone of the up-to-the-minute mindset, in later years people could prove they were hip by recounting how they made the trek to this Catskill Mountain extravaganza.

Nevertheless, the hippie generation was also typified by ennui. Many young people were bored. Most of their days were spent just hanging around and doing nothing. They literally did not know what to do with their lives or where to look for clues about how to find out. There was a genuine sense of being adrift. Deep down, they hoped things would work out, but they were not sure things would. Despite all the idealism, there was a nagging emptiness akin to that experienced by the beatniks. Because so much of what was valued was determined by what would offend parents, these young people were not sure what they personally wanted. They were certain they were morally superior and that it was their duty to inherit the world; they were not definite about what to do with this bequest.

Not surprisingly, this fragile bubble burst when confronted by harsh realities.[80] Another of the era's clichés proclaimed that those who were not part of the solution were part of the problem. In spite of this, unfocused loved turned out a poor mechanism for problem solving. The first great shock was Kennedy's assassination.[81] He was so much an icon that most people did not believe that his murder was possible. He was too vibrant to be snatched away at so appallingly early an age. The result was a cottage industry in conspiracy theories. Because it did not seem reasonable that a single misfit could change history, the idea that Lee Harvey Oswald was a lone assassin was rejected out of hand. Something more sinister had to be responsible. Despite the fact that there was little evidence to this effect, many concluded that members of the elite were to blame. Perhaps LBJ was too eager to become president. Perhaps, the CIA, or was it the FBI, did not want Kennedy to discontinue the Viet Nam project. Never mind that he was the one who initiated it. Never mind also that the proof of these nefarious plots kept changing. That Jack Ruby shot Oswald and that some witnesses thought they heard shots from the grassy knoll were too suspicious not to be expanded.

When within years Robert F. Kennedy, the deceased president's equally charismatic brother and Martin Luther King Jr.,[82] the compelling leader of the Civil Rights Movement, were also assassinated, it was too much to bear. Naïve love had not been able to stay the hand of evil. Sense could not be made by those who believed that love would conquer all. Sadly, they could find no comforting explanations. Several other of their fondest hopes were also running into trouble. The Viet Nam War had turned into a quagmire,[83] the war on poverty was spinning its wheels,[84] and riots had broken out in urban streets. Flower power turned out to be an illusion. The hippies of Haight-Ashbury were easy marks for muggers; the drug scene mutated into a killing zone; and commercial interests ripped off their art. Worst of all were the Tate-La Bianca murders. The work of the infamous Manson family, these nailed the lid on hippie coffins.[85] Even the name of Charles Manson's ill-assorted clan gave the lie to hippie ideals. This group of unrelated individuals fancied itself a family. Living, and having sex together, its members thought of themselves as the embodiment of selfless love. Charmed by Manson's story-telling abilities and his personalized attentions, these middle-class throwaways felt that they had found unconditional positive regard. Charlie cared. Charlie would watch out for them. All he asked in return was their loyalty. Going out to kill people to start a race war was thus a reasonable request. They would do it in the name of their love for Charlie and for the good of humanity.

This facile brutality was too much, save for the most hard-bitten of the love children. The hippie kingdom succumbed to reality. It dissolved as a product of its own unfulfilled promises. Most of those who participated moved on to more conventional lives, but its central aspirations would no more disappear than had those of the Depression. They were incorporated within the liberalism that became a standard middle class affectation. The former hippies did not renounce their youthful indiscretions; they looked back upon them with nostalgia. For many, these were the most exciting times they would ever experience. Never again would they know the heady feeling of saving the world. Never again would they be embryonic geniuses for whom all things were possible. If their odysseys had not ended as they had anticipated, at least they had tried.

The irony of the hippie interval is that it is a parody of middle-class ascendancy. The superannuated teenaged heirs to unprecedented social mobility did not know what to do with this heritage. In fact, most of their parents were first generation members of a higher social status. Not quite sure of how to inhabit an unaccustomed lifestyle, they were even less sure of how to transmit it to their offspring.[86] As a result, they requested that their young be successful; they provided them with material well being; and they bundled them off to college. What they could not manage was teaching them how to be self-directed. Consumed with coming to grips with the difficult task of becoming effectively middle-class, they asked their children to learn the how and why of things without providing them the keys to doing so. The upshot was that the 60s generation was left to experiment without the guidance of clear directives. Confronted with a myriad of uncertainties, they pounced on simple answers. Pampered when they were young, they retrogressed to the uncomplicated remedies of their halcyon days. With little personal experience of the ways of the world, they substituted fantasy for practicality.

More specifically, the hippie cohort exhibited a caricature of self-direction. Without putting effort into attaining emotional maturity or acquiring certified expertise, they made decisions based on whim or anxiety. Expected to perform better than their parents but unconvinced of their ability to accomplish this, they renounced hierarchy as a species of immoral exploitation. Theirs would be a world of perfect cooperation and total equality. The only thing necessary to validate one's worth would be one's humanity. And since nothing was more human than one's emotions, these were sufficient to make everyone equal to everyone else. To be honest to one's inner core, rather than to put on airs as did their parents, was to demonstrate one's superiority. Rather than seek empty symbols of success, or kowtow mindlessly to insensitive bosses, they would seek to be genuine and independent. The trouble was that everyone had feelings. To be true to oneself, and no more, left one indistinguishable from the common ruck. This might be fundamentally democratic, but to be this undistinguished was essentially to be a failure.

One of the contradictions that the hippies could not resolve was that between merit and equality. In asserting an allegiance to art, they were aspiring to a particular form of excellence, whereas in denouncing independent achievement, they were abrogating efforts at being outstanding. The hippies believed in tolerance, but as idealists, they took tolerance to an extreme. Everything was as good as everything else; therefore nothing was better than anything else. Daniel Patrick Moynihan[87] in another context talked about society's "defining deviance down." He suggested that outrageous behavior had become more commonplace because people were no longer offended by conduct once considered disgraceful. Hippie tolerance was one of the starting places of this decline. In adopting styles of dress and standards of action expressly designed to outrage the older generation, this generation lowered the bar for those who would follow them. In their rejection of discipline, these young also rejected efforts to do well. Since doing good, or even being good, is contingent upon meeting standards, to discard these out of hand is to eschew both quality performances and social decency.

At least as serious was the mutiny against responsibility. If the middle class specializes in making social decisions, to be worthy of this designation, it must execute this assignment earnestly. It cannot be frivolous or sloppy nor can it indiscriminately slough off blame. Above all, its members must try to do a good job. To put momentary pleasure above responsibility would be to condemn others to harm. Yet in playing the victim, rather than acting as a locus of personal control, the hippies failed to do what could be done. They did not believe in their power to shape events. Instead, they cast the future to the winds of chance. For them, planning for what was not yet present was anathema. Theirs was a here-and-now universe in which mental images substituted for solid achievements. Determined not to hold down nine-to-five jobs, they considered a drug-induced haze the equivalent of productive activity. Almost constitutionally opposed to following rules, they celebrated anarchistic impulsivity. They not only rejected discipline in terms of the standards they honored but also in terms of the efforts they exerted. With short attention spans and a restricted event horizon, they could not mobilize themselves for long-term projects. Nothing mattered enough to apply that much energy. As a result, they did not accomplish a great deal. Looking back, they left no substantial monuments except their romantic attitudes. Not even in art did they produce timeless masterpieces.

The hippies, of course, preached cooperation. Loath to be competitive, they mouthed platitudes about working together in harmony. In fact, given their lack of discipline, they were poor allies. Whatever their promises, they could not be relied upon to fulfill them. The consequence was that they could not band together to assert their power against straight society.[88] Aggressively nonpolitical, they treated exercises in seeking hierarchical advancement as sinful. To be ambitious was to be selfish; to join with others in asserting social control was oppressive. Nor would they descend to being pragmatic. This would require them to contaminate their hands with mundane occupations, and they were above this. Essentially immature egoists, they gloried in their own isolation and uselessness. In their own minds, they were pure and unsullied and, therefore, exceptional human beings. The antithesis of what it meant to be middle class, they were bent on disassembling the social class structure. The way that this was expressed was to claim that the system was at fault. Exactly in what the system consisted, they were unprepared to say. Undisciplined even in their intellectual life, the details of history, sociology, or political science left them cold. Nor could they explain the future in concrete terms. As they never tired of reminding their critics, love was all one needed.

This love, however, did not extend to marriage. Marriage and children and a lifelong commitment were for the more conventional. Worried primarily about the present, their plans did not encompass the next generation. Primarily concerned with rebelling against their parents, they suffered from a Peter Pan complex. In their own terms flower children, they took pride in a resistance to growing up. Although many continued their lifestyle well into their twenties, they refused to equate their sexual promiscuity with potential parenthood. Farthest from their thoughts was any conception of how to prepare the young to meet future middle-class responsibilities. Tireless in their complaints about what their own parents had done wrong, they were remarkably hazy about how such mistakes could be corrected. Defiantly young in spirit, it seemed enough that they should get their own way, without figuring out the implications of this direction. Convinced of their moral worth, they were certain that their instincts would be infallible. Not unexpectedly, utterly excluded from their consciousness were thoughts of returning to the suburbs. For many, this was the scene of their former incarceration. That a detached home, surrounded by a manicured lawn, might prove a suitable environment for raising their own children was inconceivable. This would be the epitome of selling out. It would betray the sources of their moral supremacy for the monotony of responsibility.

After Kennedy's death, his promise of a New Frontier was followed by the specter of Barry Goldwater.[89] The Republican candidate who opposed Lyndon Johnson, he promised the nation a choice, not an echo. Uncompromisingly conservative, he unabashedly championed a return to a market-oriented economy. For the hippies, despite their lack of political passion, this was a joke. Capitalism had been thoroughly discredited; hence a return to its middle-class standards was unthinkable. Everyone knew that Goldwater was a madman dedicated into nuking the Communists back to the Stone Age. Ineffably dangerous, he was the personification of an extremist. Thus, when he stood before the Republican convention to accept its nomination and opined, "Extremism in the defense of liberty is no vice. And…moderation in the pursuit of justice is no virtue," they were persuaded that their fears were vindicated. Four short years earlier, Kennedy had vowed to "pay any price, bear any burden, [and] meet any hardship" in defense of liberty, but that was then. The revolt against the middle-class ascendancy was now at full cry, and anyone who suggested that this might be an ill-advised adventure was obviously a less than competent counterrevolutionary.

Endnotes

[1] Thomas, B.P. 1952. *Abraham Lincoln: A Biography*. New York: The Modern Library.

[2] Powell, J. 2003. *FDR's Folly: How Roosevelt and His New Deal Prolonged the Great Depression*. New York: Crown Forum.

[3] McCullough, D. 1992. *Truman*. New York: Simon & Schuster.

[4] Rudolph, F. 1990. *The American College and University: A History*. Athens: University of Georgia Press.

[5] Rudolph, F. 1990. *The American College and University: A History*. Athens: University of Georgia Press.

[6] Vollmer, H. and Mills, D. (Eds.) 1968. *Professionalization*. Englewood Cliffs, NJ: Prentice-Hall.

[7] Hughes, E.C. 1958. *Men and Their Work*. New York: Free Press of Glencoe.

[8] Gladwell, M. 2000. *The Tipping Point: How Little Things Can Make a Big Difference*. Boston: Little, Brown and Co.

[9] Bell, D. 1978. *The Cultural Contradictions of Capitalism*. New York: Basic Books.

[10] Williams, T.I. 1984. *A Short History of Twentieth Century Technology*. New York: Oxford University Press.

[11] Hall, R.H. 1975. *Occupations and the Social Structure*. Engelwood Cliffs, NJ: Prentice-Hall, Inc.; Hall, R.H. 1999. *Organizations: Structures, Processes, and Outcomes*. Upper Saddle River, NJ: Prentice-Hall.

[12] U.S. Dept. of Labor, Bureau of Labor Statistics. 2001. *2001 National Occupational Employment and Wage Estimates*. Washington, DC. Government Printing Office.

[13] Lamont, M. 1992. *Money, Morals, and Manners: The Culture of the French and the American Upper-Middle Class*. Chicago: University of Chicago Press.

[14] Ritzer, G. 2000. *The McDonaldization of Society*. Thousand Oaks, CA: Pine Forge Press.

[15] Blau, P. 1963. *The Dynamics of Bureaucracy*. Chicago: University of Chicago Press.; Crozier, M. 1964. *The Bureaucratic Phenomenon*. Chicago: University of Chicago Press.

[16] Dickens, C. 1884. *Barnaby Rudge: Hard Times*. Boston: Perry Mason & Co.

[17] de Tocqueville, A. 1966. *Democracy in America*. Trans. by George Lawrence. New York: Harper & Row.

[18] Larson, M.S. 1977. *The Rise of Professionalism: A Sociological Analysis*. Berkeley: University of California Press.

[19] Vollmer, H. and Mills, D. (Eds.) 1968. *Professionalization*. Englewood Cliffs, NJ: Prentice-Hall.

[20] Schmalleger, F. 2002. *Criminology Today: An Integrative Introduction*. Upper Saddle River, NJ: Prentice-Hall.

[21] McDonald, H. 2003. *Are Cops Racist? How the Wear Against the Police Harms Black Americans.* Chicago: Ivan R. Dee.

[22] Mills, C.W. 1951. *White Collar; The American Middle Classes.* New York: Oxford University Press.

[23] Bell, D. 1978. *The Cultural Contradictions of Capitalism.* New York: Basic Books.

[24] Vollmer, H. and Mills, D. (Eds.) 1968. *Professionalization.* Englewood Cliffs, NJ: Prentice-Hall.

[25] Dulles, F.R. 1966. *Labor in America: A History.* Arlington Heights, Ill.: Harlan Davidson.

[26] Mills, C.W. 1951. *White Collar; The American Middle Classes.* New York: Oxford University Press.

[27] Van Tine, W. 1977. *John L. Lewis: A Biography.* New York: Quadrangle/New York Times.

[28] U.S. Dept. of Labor. 1991. "Research Summaries." *Monthly Labor Review, December.* Washington, DC. Government Printing Office.

[29] Morin, R. 1969. *Dwight D. Eisenhower: A Gauge of Greatness.* New York: Simon & Schuster.

[30] Grusky, O. and Miller, G.A. (Eds.) 1970. *The Sociology of Organizations: Basic Studies* (Second Edition). New York: The Free Press.

[31] Packard, V. 1959. *The Status Seekers.* New York: D. McKay Co.

[32] Galbraith, J.K. 1958. *The Affluent Society.* Boston: Houghton Mifflin.

[33] Whyte, W.H. 1956. *The Organization Man.* New York: Simon & Schuster.

[34] Montefiore, S.S. 2004. *Stalin: The Court of the Red Tsar.* New York: Alfred A. Knopf.; Payne, R. 1965. *The Rise and Fall of Stalin.* New York: Avon Books.

[35] Courtois, S, Werth, N., Panne, J-L., Paczkowski, A., Bartosek, and Margolin, J-L. 1999. *The Black Book of Communism: Crimes, Terror, Repression.* Cambridge, MA. Harvard University Press.

[36] Coulter, A. 2003. Treason: Liberal Treachery from the Cold War to the War on Terrorism. New York: Crown Forum.

[37] Tanenhaus, S. 1997. *Whittaker Chambers: A Biography.* New York: Random House.

[38] Haynes, J.E. and Klehr, H. 2003. *In Denial: Historians, Communism and Espionage.* San Francisco: Encounter Books.

[39] Seligman, A.B. 1992. *The Idea of Civil Society.* Princeton, NJ: Princeton University Press.

[40] McNeil, A. 1996. *Total Television: The Comprehensive Guide to Programming from 1948 to the Present.* New York: Penguin Books.

[41] Sperber, A,M. 1986. *Murrow: His Life and Times.* New York: Freundlich Books.

[42] McShane, C. 1994. *Down the Asphalt Path: The Automobile and the American City.* New York: Columbia University Press.

[43] Smigel, E.O. (Ed.) 1963. *Work and Leisure.* New Haven: College & University Press.

[44] Jakle, J.A. and Sculle, K.A. 1999. *Fast Food: Roadside Restaurants in the Automobile Age.* Baltimore: Johns Hopkins University Press.

[45] Lindsey, B.B. and Evans, W. 1927. *Companionate Marriage.* New York: Boni and Liverright.

[46] Rudolph, F. 1990. *The American College and University: A History.* Athens: University of Georgia Press.

[47] LeVine, R. 1973. *Culture, Behavior and Personality.* Chicago: Aldine Publishing.

[48] Jackson, K.T. 1985. *Crabgrass Frontier: The Suburbanization of the United States.* New York: Oxford University Press; Fishman, R. 1987. *Bourgeois Utopias: The Rise and Fall of Suburbia.* New York: Basic Books; Alba, R.D. 1990. *Ethnic Identity: The Transformation of White America.* New Haven: Yale University Press; Garreau, J. 1991. *Edge City: Life on the New Frontier.* New York: Random House.

[49] Vidich, A. and Bensman, J. 1958. *Small Town in Mass Society: Class, Power, and Religion in a Rural Community.* Princeton: Princeton University Press.

[50] Gans, H.J. 1967. The Levittowners: Way of Life and Politics in a New Suburban Community. New York: Alfred A. Knopf.

[51] Handel, G. [Ed.] 1967. *The Psychosocial Interior of the Family: A Sourcebook for the Study of Whole Families.* Chicago: Aldine-Atherton.; Nye, F.I. 1976. *Role Structure and the Analysis of the Family.* Beverly Hills: Sage Publications.; Parsons, T. and Bales, R.F. 1955. *Family, Socialization and Interaction Process.* New York: Free Press; Seward, K. 1978. *The American Family: A Demographic History.* Beverly Hills: Sage Publications; Riesman, D. 1950. *The Lonely Crowd.* New Haven: Yale University Press.

[52] Buckley, K.W. 1989. *Mechanical Man: John Broadus Watson and the Beginnings of Behaviorism.* New York: The Guilford Press.

[53] Watson, J.B. 1928. *Psychological Care of Infant and Child.* New York: Norton.

[54] Spock, B. 1957. *The Common Sense Book of Baby and Child Care.* New York: Duell, Sloan and Pearce.

[55] Kohn, M.L. 1969. *Class and Conformity: A Study in Values.* Homewood, Ill.: The Dorsey Press.

[56] Ravitch, D. 2000. *Left Back: A Century of Failed School Reforms.* New York: Simon & Schuster.; Dewey, J. 1943. *The School and Society.* Chicago: University of Chicago Press.

[57] Duncan, O.D. 1965. "The Trend of Occupational Mobility in the United States." *American Sociological Review*, 30: 491-498.; Lipset, S.M. and Bendix, R. 1959. *Social Mobility in Industrial Society.* Berkeley: University of California Press.

[58] Caplow, T., Howard, H.B, Chadwick, B.A. Hill, R., and Williamson, M.H. 1982. *Middletown Families: Fifty Years of Change and Continuity.* Minneapolis: University of Minnesota Press.

[59] Blauner, R. 1969. "Internal Colonialism and Ghetto Revolt." *Social Problems* 16:393-408.

[60] Williams, J. 1998. *Thurgood Marshall: American Revolutionary.* New York: Times Books.

[61] Coleman, J.S., Campbell, E.Q, Hobson, C.J., McPartland, J., Mood, A.M., Weinfeld, F.D. and York, R.L. 1966. *Equality of Educational Opportunity.* Washington: U.S. Government Printing Office.

[62] Rubin L. B. 1972. *Busing & Backlash: White Against White in an Urban School District.* Berkeley: University of California Press.

[63] Caplow, T., Hicks, L. and Wattenberg, B.J. 2001. *The First Measured Century: An Illustrated Guide to Trends in America, 1900-2000.* Washington, D.C.: AEI Press.

[64] Friedan, B. 1963. *The Feminine Mystique.* New York: W.W. Norton & Co.

[65] Raskin, J. *2004. American Scream: Allen Ginsberg's Howl and the Making of the Beat Generation.* Berkeley: University of California Press; Cassidy, C. 1991. *Off the Road: My Years with Cassidy, Kerouac, and Ginsberg.* New York: Penguin Books; Ginsberg, A. 1972. *The Gates of Wrath: Rhymed Poems.* Bolinas, CA: Grey Fox Press.

[66] Collier, P. and Horowitz, D. 1984. *The Kennedys: An American Drama.* New York: Summit Books.

[67] Ambrose, S.E. 1987. *Nixon: The Education of a Politician 1913-1962.* New York: Simon and Schuster.

[68] Hall, C. 1997. *Steel Phoenix: The Fall and Rise of the U.S. Steel Industry.* New York: St. Martin's Press.

[69] Halberstam, D. 1969. *The Best and the Brightest.* New York: Random House.

[70] Horowitz. D. 1997. *Radical Son: A Generational Odyssey.* New York: The Free Press.

[71] Erikson, E. 1968. *Identity: Youth and Crisis.* New York: W.W. Norton.

[72] Schlafly, P. and Ward, C. 1968. *The Betrayers.* Alton, IL: Pere Marquette Press.

[73] Riech, C.A. 1971. *The Greening of America.* New York: Bantam.

[74] Davies, H. 1968. *The Beatles.* New York: Dell Books.

[75] Hoffman, A. 2001. *The Autobiography of Abbie Hoffman.* New York: Four Walls Eight Windows; Partridge, W.L. 1973. *The Hippie Ghetto: The Natural History of a Subculture.* New York: Holt, Rinehart and Winston; Van Hoffman, N. 1968. *We Are the People Our Parents Warned Us Against.* Chicago: Quadrangle Books.

[76] Orwin, C. and Tarcov, N. (Eds.) 1997. *The Legacy of Rousseau.* Chicago: University of Chicago Press; Rousseau, J.J. 1968. (1762) *The Social Contract* (Translated by Maurice Cranston) New York: Penguin Books.

[77] Hoffman, A. 2001. *The Autobiography of Abbie Hoffman.* New York: Four Walls Eight Windows.

[78] Chatfield, C. 1992. *The American Peace Movement: Ideals and Activism.* New York: Twayne Publishers.

[79] Leary, T. 1983. *Flashbacks: An Autobiography.* Boston: Houghton, Mifflin Co.

[80] Halberstam, D. 1986. *The Reckoning.* New York: William Morrow Co.; Magnet, M. 1993. *The Dream and the Nightmare: The Sixties Legacy to the Underclass.* New York: William Morrow & Co.; Tipton, S.M. 1982. *Getting Saved from the Sixties.* Berkeley: The University of California Press.

[81] Posner, G.L. 1993. *Case Closed: Lee Harvey Oswald and the Assassination of JFK.* New York: Random House.

[82] Pyatt, S.E. 1986. *Martin Luther King, Jr.: An Annotated Bibliography.* New York: Greenwood Press.

[83] Joes, A.J. 1989. *The War for South Viet Nam 1954-1975.* New York: Praeger.

[84] Piven, F.F. and Cloward, R.A. 1977. *Poor People's Movement's: Why They Succeed, How They Fail.* New York: Vintage; Howell, J.T. 1973. *Hard Living on Clay Street: Portraits of Blue Collar Families.* Prospect Heights, IL: Waveland Press, Inc.

[85] Bugliosi, V. 1975. *Helter Skelter: The True Story of the Manson Murders.* New York: Bantam Books.

[86] Bettleheim, B. 1987. *A Good Enough Parent; A Book on Child-Reaing.* New York: A. Knopf.

[87] Moynihan, D.P. 1993. "Defining Deviancy Down." *American Scholar.*

[88] Lasch, C. 1979. *The Culture of Narcissism: American Life in an Age of Diminishing Expectations.* New York: Warner Books.

[89] Goldwater, B.M. 1964. *Conscience of a Conservative.* New York: MacFadden-Bartell Corp.

Chapter 7

The Reaction

For every action there is always opposed an equal reaction.
(Isaac Newton, Principia Mathematica)

Attack is the reaction; I never think I have hit hard unless it rebounds. (Samuel Johnson, from Boswell's Life of Johnson)

Every reform, however necessary, will by weak minds be carried to an excess, that itself will need reforming. (Samuel Taylor Coleridge, Biographia Literaria)

The Reform Impulse

The middle class ascendancy threw up a series of challenges. As the world changed, an unanticipated crop of conundrums arose to puzzle society.[1] This new stage of the Commercial Revolution was not a walk across an untroubled upland meadow. The way was littered with conflicts, abuses, and even stupidities.[2] People had always dreamt that progress would culminate in greater happiness and fewer uncertainties, but its realization was fraught with anxieties and the consciousness of human limitations.[3] Rain clouds surrounded the heads of the inexperienced. Unequivocal happiness was apparently not to be the lot of mankind. The more people got, the more they wanted and the greater their power, the more numerous their frustrations. Or, so it seemed. Observers were transfixed with what had gone wrong, rather than what was going right. It is a journalistic cliché that good news is no news. The unexpected predicament, not the ordinary accomplishment, is what captures public attention. When a man bites a dog, especially when there is not supposed to be any biting, bystanders take notice. This sort of event requires concentration. If it is to be assimilated, it is imperative to figure out what happened and why.

Likewise, the more revolutionary the change, the more intense the reaction to it.[4] That which is exceedingly different from what preceded it feels uncomfortable merely because it is different. When people do not possess the routines with which to cope with a new situation, they feel impelled to respond. This novel circumstance is sensed as problematic and, therefore, as in need of a solution. The stumbling block lies in finding an appropriate answer. Given that the Middle Class Revolution was a seismic event, it called forth a series of momentous, if not always appropriate, rejoinders[5]. Although hardly remarked upon as it occurred, the transformation traumatized the social structure. Commentators were aware of the dislocations of the Industrial Revolution[6] but were less cognizant of the tribulations intrinsic to so great a success. Nevertheless, many crucial relationships were not what they had once been. In point of fact, the social hierarchy was shaken to its foundations. Those who now got to the top of the greasy pole were not the same ones who got there before. Nor were the strengths that once produced success identical with those of the past. The professionalization of society had changed the ground rules. Technological expertise, for instance, counted for much more than it ever had previously. Nor were the types of jobs people performed the same. The division of labor fractured into so many anomalous pieces that it was difficult to grasp how they fit together. Occupations were changed, their associated statuses were altered; political techniques were revised; educational demands were amended; and even family interactions were under siege. Something had to be done, but no one could be certain of what.

The hippies, in their own immature and inarticulate way, had sought answers.[7] Unfortunately, their remedies, though striking, were soon found wanting.[8] What was presently to emerge in their place was a sequence of politicized solutions. The nation, and indeed the world, would be rocked by a succession of political earthquakes in what amounted to an outburst of reform mania. As people felt driven to deal with the displacements in their lives, they got caught up in an uncomfortable cycle of disguised cultural lag. Intending to keep moving forward, their problem solving inclinations unexpectedly betrayed them. In place of developing truly innovative answers, they inadvertently recycled those of a bygone age. As might be expected, in a civilization increasingly populated by middle-class strivers, it would not take long for the nouveau riche to apply their talents to the conundrums elicited by their triumphs. They were, after all, professional decision makers. Accustomed to utilizing their expertise to organize productive activities, they assumed this approach would be appropriate to their current predicament. On balance, the tactic had surely worked well within the industrial arena—hadn't it? Techniques for scheduling the arrival of raw materials to cleverly designed machines undoubtedly resulted in a cornucopia of goods stocking suburban shopping malls. Why couldn't this same stratagem be applied to interpersonal dilemmas? If these too were addressed in an orderly manner, they too should prove amenable to resolution. Even as astute an observer as Max Weber[9] depicted this method as "rational." It was simply what made sense. Not surprisingly, those who extrapolated from this supposition presumed that, if the government were assigned the task of correcting social injustices, it could manage the mission. With greater resources available than any combination of individuals and kept within reasonable bounds via democratic oversights, it could, without question, be trusted to do what was best for all concerned. The sticking point was that government would have to perform this magic blindly. In a world that had never before undergone a middle-class revolution, no one could accurately predict what would be required.

The resultant line of attack is generally referred to as social engineering.[10] Patterned on tangible forms of manipulation, it theoretically converts social knowledge into enlightened plans of action. Deliberate, disciplined, and well motivated, how could it not achieve desirable ends? As with other varieties of engineering, this one is steeped in efforts at control. Grounded in rationality, it is expected to take the mystery out of human misery and enable the community to implement shared objectives. Yet, asserting control does not, of itself, provide control. It is one thing to declare mastery of a situation, quite another to master it. Sadly, social engineering did not live up to its billing. Time and again, it has failed to produce the promised results. What has really rankled is that problems meant to be corrected have frequently been exacerbated. Instead of efforts at improving a situation making things better, they often made them worse.

The reason is not hard to fathom. Social engineering takes for granted three prerequisites.[11] First, it assumes that the target problem is understood. Clearly, people must know what is wrong before they can fix it. Second, the solution to the difficulty is believed to be readily at hand. It is imagined that the experts can always devise an ingenious means of overcoming a problem. Third, when the solution is known, it is presupposed that it can, and will, be implemented. The authorities, and the people, will do what needs to be done, and the issue will evaporate. The trouble with this scenario is that in most cases, one, or more, of these preconditions is not met. People do not understand the source of their discomfort and/or how this distress can be relieved and/or how the appropriate resources can be brought to bear. Activists speak glibly of root causes without evidence that these are the actual sources of difficulty. Similarly, they routinely proclaim insights into the ideal intervention. Swearing up and down that a favorite policy will do the trick, they rarely produce facts to back this up. Likewise problematic is mobilizing the appropriate actions. Politicians engrossed in petty squabbles often find it impossible to develop a well-timed consensus. Too little too late is a common failing, but just as frequently the requisite resources cannot be assembled, irrespective of good-faith efforts. To illustrate, if personal therapy is deemed a sovereign cure for individual unhappiness, this does not mean that there will be enough qualified therapists. Nor does it mean that there are sufficient funds to pay them. Indeed, the facts of social life are such that the players are usually ignorant of what is transpiring. Worse yet, they are often congenitally incapable of executing that to which they are consciously committed. Merely to get from day to day, human beings have a knack of fooling themselves about their fundamental circumstances.

The gap between action and intention is regularly filled by idealism.[12] People genuinely want to do good, but their ideas regarding what is good are often based more on hope than practicality. Ignorant of what is taking place, they substitute visions of a romanticized future for a bleaker reality. Things will work out for the best if only others will strive toward this perfect endpoint. How, indeed, could they not? All the same, where this ideal came from is, nine times out of ten, itself troublesome. Potential reformers habitually refer to a future they are convinced is within their grasp, yet its outlines typically owe more to the past than to their prophetic powers. Peering over the horizon is notoriously ticklish. No one can literally foresee what is to come. More common is extrapolating from what is known to what is unknown, from the familiar to the unfamiliar. Generally what is recognizable is reworked to serve as a model for what is desired. One reason why cultural lag is so prevalent is that people unintentionally tighten their hold, on what used to be in the very process of trying to cope with what is materializing. They literally look toward what once succeeded for hints about what is to come.

The reforms that were about to take center stage in response to the middle-class ascendancy had their inception in idealizations of this sort. Their backers were working from visions generalized from past events. Promised cures were based, not on demonstrable results but on purified ideals. Indeed, the nature of these ideals depended on mentally cleaning messy realities. That which had been was simplified and its rough edges smoothed out Eyeliner made the outlines of the eyes more distinct and rouge produced cheekbones that stood out. The ideal glowed with promise precisely because it had been made extreme. More intense than real life, as with many mental constructs, it did not suffer from mundane gaps or nagging imperfections.

An ideal is by definition perfect.[13] It is what people would want if they could manipulate the world as they wished. As such, it is a bright beacon that derives its allure from deeply buried fantasies. Yet fantasies are inherently immoderate. They tend to go farther than the facts allow because they are not impeded by facts. Nevertheless, being fantasies, they may be impossible to achieve. However much they are desired, often they cannot come true. People may approach them and assume that, with a little more effort, they can be reached, but this is apt to be an illusion. The worst part about uncritical objectives is that they offer false hope. In convincing people that improbable tactics can solve their troubles, they divert efforts from what is possible. The perfect becomes the enemy of the good, and people wind up with less than they might have had were they not so credulous.

With regard to the middle-class reaction to its preeminence, the sorts of ideals sought derived largely from factors perceived as contributing to this dominance. One of these was a veneration of peace. As the wheels of commerce began to accelerate, the kind of warfare in which medieval knights gloried became unproductive. Hand to hand combat did not add to the output of factories or hasten goods to market. Rather, it placed all this in jeopardy. To put the matter crudely, violence was not good for business. The result was that physical aggression declined. Highwaymen disappeared from the arteries of commerce, and successful capitalists refused to wear swords in emulation of a vanished aristocracy. Peace came to be seen as a good in its own right. Thus Benjamin Franklin[14] was widely quoted as saying, "There never was a good war or a bad peace." Himself an architect of revolution, he nonetheless preferred the comforts of home and hearth. Pacifism had come into vogue. "No wars ever, for any reason," became a guiding principle for would-be social saviors. Certainly, this made sense. Since war is harmful to living things, no sane person could possibly favor it.

Another idealized goal is equality.[15] As the commercial revolution rushed forward, so did social mobility. Those who had been poor could reasonably expect to grow rich, whereas those who had been rich, if they were careless, might slide into obscurity. In any event, the ranks of those in the middle of the pack expanded immeasurably. This meant that the distance between the top and the bottom had been reduced. The direction of this change was evident for all to see and, if it were projected into the future, might eventuate in the space between the best and the worst closing into nothingness. To many, it seemed clear that the endpoint would be complete equality. Hierarchy would disappear and be replaced by an egalitarian brotherhood. The result would indisputably be true democracy. Not only would there be equality before the law and equality of opportunity but also an equality of results. Material resources would be distributed uniformly, as would social power. No one would have any more than anyone else; hence all jealousies and conflicts would abate.

A third ideal that arose in tandem with the middle classes was rationality. Businesspeople needed to make careful calculations in order to insure a profit, but this rationalism could be utilized for other purposes. One of these was science.[16] In this field, especially within the physical sciences, mental discipline proved invaluable.

Its projected application to the social sciences was, therefore, a no-brainer. The same could be said of social engineering. Employing the computations of the sciences to solve irritating social predicaments made sense. That this might not be automatic was regarded as trivial. Surely, given sufficient diligence, every significant problem would one day be amenable to systematic solution. On the other hand, those who hated what they perceived as the cold, dead hand of science idealized its opposite. Unprepared to allow passionless prognoses to dominate social events, these romantics celebrated emotion. Feelings, rather than precise measurements, were their standard of value. It was these that made people human; these that had to be intensified and allowed to determine communal dealings.

Part of what made the middle-class revolution unique was that these ideals were not allowed to sit on the shelf. Previous generations had had their own moral ambitions, which they attempted to bring to fruition, but this time these efforts were to be more methodical. The medieval knights, when they first set out to rescue Jerusalem from the infidels, did so haphazardly. They took to the highways with sketchy maps of their itinerary. Contemporary Westerners launched their crusades in a more orderly fashion. Carefully crafted social and political policies guided their steps. Purposefully they set out to implement reforms scientifically. Or, so it was hoped. In the event, this journey turned out to be more disorganized than expected. Although even the most romantic of the reformers conceived of themselves as intellectuals, they exercised less conscious control than they had imagined. Disoriented by an inability to distinguish the ideal from the real, their intentions were, time and again, frustrated by an obdurate universe.

The Reforms

War is not good for business; as a consequence it is not good for the middle- classes. It disrupts their orderly lives and throws their plans for success into a cocked hat. Instead of children marching off to college and then on to commercial triumphs, they are drafted into a meat-grinder from whence they can not escape unharmed. The difficulty is that pacifism is not good for business either. Antiwar advocates complain that capitalists are warmongers because they make a profit from the arms trade, whereas the actual merchants of death are a tiny sliver of that number. The real reason that war can be of benefit to the bourgeoisie is precisely because they are rich. Relative to others, they possess attractive resources. Were they unprepared to defend these, by the sword if necessary, they would soon find themselves stripped of all they have. The new middle classes, like it or not, also developed a stake in this wealth. They too have much to lose to the envious. If they lived in a world where selflessness was the norm, they might not have to worry. Similarly, were the less affluent content to stay in their places, the middle-class need not dread coercive attempts to appropriate their goods. In fact, the poor are not so inclined. Given the opportunity and the belief that they would encounter no opposition, many of them would act in what they perceived to be their best interests.

These opposing impulses, that is, in favor of peace but also approving of self-defense, have resulted in ongoing squabbles within the middle classes. What has exacerbated this conflict and made pacifist reformers more insistent are the unprecedented dangers that surfaced during the twentieth century. This was an era during which warfare graduated to incalculably lethal dimensions. The First and Second World Wars truly were world wars. Nations in every corner of the planet were drawn into bloodbaths of unparalleled scope. Advances in communication and transportation made it possible for countries separated by thousands of miles to participate in different theaters of the same hostilities. And when they did, advances in technology and productive capacity made the carnage all the greater. This peril was further escalated when science unleashed the power of the atom. In short order, there was reason to fear that rockets tipped with hydrogen bombs could within minutes traverse broad oceans to deliver death on a massive scale. No one would be safe, no one immune.

The peace movement was a response to this specter.[17] In the wake of the Great War it gathered momentum toward outlawing aggressive militarism. Unfortunately this contributed to the appeasement policies that provided Hitler his opportunity for expansion. Nonetheless, after the bombing of Hiroshima and Nagasaki,[18] the need for general disarmament seemed imperative. When Russia, too, developed the bomb, and the Cold War arose between former allies, a desire to prevent a universal conflagration animated efforts to impose sanity. Reformers first asked both sides to renounce their arsenals, but when this call went unheeded, they turned to agitating for unilateral disarmament. Of course, the Soviet Union was not a democracy, but the Western powers were. If only their people put pressure on their governments to dismantle these weapons, the Russians might feel less threatened and follow suit. This, of course, did not happen. However, by the 60s the Students for a Democratic Society (SDS)[19] was a potent force on American college campuses. The organization made pacifism seem both acceptable and intellectual. Reasonable people could surely agree that it was the duty of the most advanced industrial nation on earth to set a good example. Marching and singing songs (in emulation of the hippies), the young sought to educate their elders to the dangers—and the opportunities.

When the Viet Nam War intervened to complicate this picture, the peace activists knew where they stood.[20] They were convinced that politicians were disingenuously arguing that hostilities were an attempt to prevent a domino effect, that if an aggressive communism were allowed to succeed in one area, its appetite for hegemony would be whetted. Conservatives mistakenly claimed that other nations would soon be invaded and, in their increased anxiety, be less prepared to defend their independence. In the long run, the United States and Western Europe would be encircled and overthrown. The Korean War had laid down a marker; now it was time to lay down another. Communists must be sent a message this time, that aggression would not be appeased. While the public seemed to buy this argument, the students knew better. The United States was becoming an imperialist power, and they would have none of it. The domino theory was a myth, as was the idea of a monolithically aggressive Communism. In order to get the word out, they organized teach-ins. The facts would be put forward to counter the hysterical fictions emanating from Washington. Eventually the ordinary voter must recognize that Southeast Asia should be left to the Southeast Asians.

This antiwar initiative was to rise to national proportions when the media joined the effort.[21] Reporters who at first filed heroic stories about the deeds of the Green Berets became increasingly skeptical. A conflict that dragged on for years with ever-larger casualty lists began to feel like a quagmire. As more of the combatants came home in body bags, journalists, both in the field and at home, became cynical. The youth refused to believe in the accuracy of the body counts issued by the military brass. With their own eyes they concluded that the struggle was unwinnable. Images of death became routine thanks to a television technology that allowed ordinary citizens to view the battlefield from their living rooms. In time, the pacifist demonstrators, at first regarded as kooks, were given sympathetic coverage. The critical point was reached during the Tet Offensive. Once the Communists committed themselves to overrunning southern cities, the disturbing effects of combat were perceptible. Prominent newscasters such as Walter Cronkite interpreted this as a loss. Although the Viet Cong suffered a crushing defeat, the American people were informed otherwise. This increased the pressure exercised on politicians to refrain from incursions into the enemy's bases. North Viet Nam, Cambodia, and Laos became off-limits; hence when they were bombed a hullabaloo arose in the nation's streets. Critics of the war burned their draft cards; peace marchers converged on the capital; and members of Congress began to demand a peaceful resolution. Some advised the president simply to declare victory and pull out. Others cringed when the protestors chanted, "Hey, hey, LBJ, how many kids have you killed today," but then did nothing. Even when Jane Fonda flew to the North Vietnamese capital to praise Ho Chi Minh and condemn America, she escaped prosecution for treason upon her return home.

The accumulated effect of this was to persuade President Johnson[22] not to stand for reelection. Likewise, responding to these strains, his successor Richard Nixon,[23] felt impelled to sue for peace. Eventually, after a treaty was signed, the southern armies were left to fend for themselves. The United States pledged to provide support should the North violate its undertakings, but once these transgressions occurred, Congress refused to honor the promised of aid. Soon the South fell, and the images of refugees being helicoptered from Saigon rooftops convinced millions of viewers that the war had been futile. It had not accomplished anything, and, therefore, war should never again be attempted. In the future, no American children should be sacrificed to the arrogance of power. As far away as Western Europe, the public reached the same conclusion. Anti-Americanism became fashionable. The world's greatest superpower was told it must learn to mind its manners. Power was inherently oppressive, and the only way to keep it from doing harm was to keep its sword permanently sheathed.

Another reform that emerged in America in tandem with pacifism was the Civil Rights Movement. Achieving racial equality became as imperative as achieving worldwide peace. The seeds of this crusade were planted early in the twentieth century. Although American slaves had been officially liberated by the events of the Civil War, they did not acquire anything like parity with whites. Almost universally regarded as of inferior ability, they were relegated to second-class citizenship. Neither in the marketplace nor in politics nor in the courts were they accorded equal weight. Agitation to fulfill the Declaration of Independence's objective of equality for all had survived in the abolitionist cause, but just barely. Slowly, however, African Americans were allowed to do more. Booker T. Washington[24] was invited to have dinner in the White House;[25] the resurgent Ku Klux Klan[26] of the 1920s was driven into disgrace; and the NAACP began to institute lawsuits to widen access to public accommodations.[27] Nevertheless, it was not until after World War II, that is, after the middle-class revolution had reached its apogee that civil rights became visible. It was an issue at the Democratic nominating convention, when Harry Truman[28] issued a presidential order mandating the desegregation of the military and when the Supreme Court decided <u>Brown v. the Board of Education</u>.[29]

The court's decision that "separate is inherently unequal" signaled an acceleration in the efforts to provide racial justice. Building upon a change in attitudes that had already stimulated scientific research into the ill effects of discrimination, the justices promptly ordered that desegregation occur with "all deliberate speed." The law was to be obeyed, which meant that black students were to be allowed into the same classrooms as whites. Subterfuges designed to postpone the inevitable would not be tolerated. Soon thereafter, the nation, outside of the South, cheered when Central High School in Little Rock, Arkansas was integrated.[30] Millions saw the hatred on the faces of the parents opposed to this measure and were appalled. They did not understand how children could be treated so barbarically. This was not the American way. In middle-class America, everyone is to be given the benefit of our society. In a democracy, whatever your origins, you deserve an opportunity to prove yourself. Several years later, when Bull Connor, Commissioner of Public Safety in Birmingham, Alabama, unloosed dogs on peaceful demonstrators, the aversion was palpable.[31] It reminded people of the Nazis, and they would not tolerate it.

Initially this movement was very much about civil rights.[32] The objective was to enforce the equal application of the law. Everyone, regardless of race, was to be allowed to go to publicly funded schools,[33] to ride publicly subsidized buses, to use public restrooms, to be served at public restaurants, and to vote in civic elections. *De jure* segregation was to be dismantled, that is, the laws were to be changed when they were unfair and were to be equally applied when they were mandated to be equal. The culmination of this was the civil rights legislation that passed following Kennedy's assassination. It was only subsequent to this that the call also went up for an end to *de facto* segregation.[34] If the proportion of the races in different schools was different, not because legislation required this, but because the neighborhoods in which the children lived were segregated, this too was deemed to be unacceptable.[35] As a result, efforts at integration moved north. Students were to be redistributed within school systems according to their percentages in the larger community. If this could not be achieved by redistricting, forced busing would impose it. Despite the resistance of parents eager to preserve neighborhood schools, the government moved to compel the desired outcome.[36]

The culmination of this policy was the advent of affirmative action.[37] Gradually, but with increasing momentum during the Nixon administration, the government used race to manipulate social phenomena. Rather than allow the marketplace, or individual choice, to determine how individuals were distributed, various agencies intervened to coerce an idea of fairness. Generally, this meant that the final result would be in line with group representation within the total population.[38] Anything less was deemed racist and subject to rectification by a quota system. Since quotas are anathema in a democracy, these preferences usually went by another name, e.g., "diversity"[39] or "multiculturalism."[40] On the job, in schools, and in the dispersal of government contracts, one's group membership became the deciding factor, with lower standards typically applied to black, and later to Hispanics.[41] The public at large believed these techniques unjustified, but for the activists they were so crucial that they made their influence felt at the ballot box.[42]

Another change occurred in the sorts of pressure employed to achieve these goals. Initially, under the tutelage of Martin Luther King, Jr.[43], the Civil Rights Movement was dedicated to passive resistance. Inspired by Mohandas Gandhi's efforts in liberating India from the British Raj,[44] people pursued their objective through moral suasion to convince Americans to liberate African Americans. Sit-ins, boycotts, marches, and freedom rides were determinedly nonviolent. The protesters held hands and sang about overcoming injustice while they were beaten by batons or soaked by fire hoses. In fact, this strategy worked as intended. When properly publicized, these incidents had the expected effect. Ordinary middle-class Americans were morally offended by the exercise of excessive force against innocent protesters. So outraged were they that they demanded reform. Nevertheless, as these developments gathered impetus, they were deemed insufficient.[45] Their very success whetted the appetite of the activists for more and faster. Persuasion was replaced by "nonnegotiable demands." The authorities, or whoever was the target, had to comply instantly and completely. There was no room for equivocation or compromise. What the militants decided was moral did not permit of adulteration.

All too quickly, this intransigence erupted into violence.[46] Across the country, inner cities erupted into riots. The phrase "long, hot summer" became a commonplace as flames and bloodshed swept over the North and West.[47] Embittered firebrands now demanded power rather than civil rights.[48] They wanted to be in control. Even though more African-American politicians were winning elections, activists found the pace too slow. Soon gun-toting, beret-wearing revolutionaries were out on the streets. Led by the Black Panthers,[49] they insisted upon control of their neighborhoods. The police, disparagingly referred to as "pigs," were regarded as an occupying army even as many more of them were black. Some suggested that whites be cleared out of Mississippi so that it could become an entirely black enclave. Gone now were calls for integration. Separation became the order of the day, that is, so long as minorities themselves engineered it. By the time the 90s arrived, some colleges were offering segregated dormitories on the premise that oppressed groups were more comfortable living among their own kind. Even some high schools, once the focus of efforts at integration, unabashedly sponsored separate graduations for African Americans and Hispanics.[50]

The victim mentality had become a national obsession.[51] Whites were expected to feel guilty for their continuing acts of oppression, whereas blacks were excused from responsibility on the grounds that they were innocents. Because Caucasians had imposed racism on Negroes, it was assumed that prejudice and discrimination could not flow the other way around. Hypocrisy became a way of life as people refused to say publicly what they privately believed. Whites refrained from criticizing blacks for fear of being branded racist, while blacks concealed negative aspects of their communities on the assumption that the truth would be used against them. The only people that seemed happy with the situation were the liberals.[52] Enduring frictions enabled them to pose as racial saviors and to reap the rewards at the ballot box.

Piggybacking on the Civil Rights Movement was the Feminist Movement. Its pedigree was as hoary as that of the racial activists, but it had lain fairly dormant since the achievement of suffrage. Agitation on behalf of women began with the dawn of the Industrial Age, but its manifestations were at first isolated and sporadic.[53] Not until the middle of the 19th century did it become a force to be reckoned with. Spurred by the entrance of women into factories and then into classrooms and offices, aggrieved spokespersons began to demand civic rights commensurate with their public occupations. Initially, the focus was on the vote. Male resistance to sharing governmental power was so stubborn that seeking it required a concentrated effort. Women were also making their presence felt in fields such as social work. Leaders in the temperance and antiprostitution movements, they sought changes in the areas that affected them most. Desirous of respect, they were able to obtain it in significant measure. Additionally coeducation became available as industrialization progressed.

With the achievement of constitutional amendments regarding Prohibition and the vote, many thought that feminist objectives had been satisfied. There was an evanescent distaff upsurge during the 1920s when so-called flappers flaunted their sexuality in short skirts and agitated dances, but this was to go underground during the 30s. Depression-era virtue, as well as an enforced poverty, kept female vivacity in check. During the Second World War, Rosie the Riveter made her appearance, but she was the product of a national crisis. While many women acquired a taste for the freedom that accompanied earning paychecks, they were nevertheless prepared to return to domestic chores during the 50s. It was not until the 60s that a self-conscious feminism emerged to demand its share of the social pie. Among many contributors to these developments, the opening salvo might be attributed to Betty Friedan.[54] Her book, The Feminine Mystique,[55] sounded a clarion call to battle. Women across the nation responded to her thesis that selfish husbands imprisoned wives in the suburbs. Placed on a pedestal and forced to endure empty lives, women were subservient to a male jurisdiction over important decisions.

As with blacks, the initial quest was for equal rights.[56] Women wanted to be able to sign contracts without obtaining their husbands' permission or to take out loans in their own names rather than under another person's identity. In short, they wished to obtain an independent legal status, with rights that belonged to them personally. The activists saw an opening with the advent of civil rights legislation. If the law was amended to read that both race *and* gender were impermissible criteria for discrimination, women could make effortless gains. This transpired when male legislators could see no reason to deny women what they were prepared to give African Americans. Women, with this one stroke, became an oppressed minority with all the deference this implied. Not initially, but fairly quickly, they too became eligible for affirmative action.[57] Were they for any reason to be denied jobs on account of gender or equal pay for equal work, they too could seek relief in court. So tightly was the concept of gender oppression bound to racial oppression that sociology textbooks were rewritten to include race, gender, and social class as equivalent phenomena.

Still, this was not enough for the reformers. They insisted that absolute equality be written into the fundamental law of the land.[58] Thus were born the lobbying efforts to include an equal rights amendment (ERA) in the Constitution. Women, by law, were to be considered comparable to men in every respect. The critics fretted that such an edict would ultimately impose unisex bathrooms and enlist female infantry soldiers,[59] but its advocates denied these intents. While the amendment was itself never fully approved by all the requisite members of state legislatures, its aspirations gradually began to permeate society. Bathrooms were never fully integrated, but the military increasingly was. Women were mandated to be given basic training alongside men on the grounds that they could do anything their brothers could. The watchword among committed feminists was that everything should be fifty-fifty. All jobs, including the most powerful, were to follow this guideline. No longer would there be a glass ceiling that prevented women from rising to the executive suite.[60] No longer would custom prevent women from becoming construction workers or men from working in nursery schools. There was, these partisans insisted, no biological difference between male and female abilities; therefore, there should be none in the marketplace or home.[61] Housework too should be fifty-fifty, with men becoming Mr. Moms. The endpoint was to be androgyny.[62] Henceforward, gender would be irrelevant. For starters, traditional gender roles were to be deconstructed so that all tasks were open to everyone. Even dating patterns would be reorganized so that women could ask men out. Moreover, just as with race, the final arbiter of success would be an equality of results. Only when gender made no difference,[63] as certified by the equivalence of a color-blindness with regard to sex, would this goal be achieved. Only then would women be free to be whatever they wanted to be.

The ideal of androgyny, however, was impeded by traditional social arrangements.[64] First, as long as children were socialized according to historical practices,[65] they would be trained to perpetuate artificial differences. With little boys given guns or trucks as toys and little girls presented with dolls, boys would continue to aspire to be soldiers and girls, mothers. What was needed was to give each the other's playthings—although on the grounds that they were too violent, guns would be omitted. Eventually, a rationalized nurture would overwhelm obsolete superstitions, and a new, more humane division of labor would arrive.[66] Second, male aggression had to be curbed.[67] The reason that gender oppression lasted was that males had grown accustomed to intimidating women into submission. Taking advantage of their larger size, they had persisted in threatening rape should women assert their independence. This had to be stopped.[68] Not merely persuasion, but strict punishment, had to be imposed for violations of female rights. Men needed to be sent to jail if they physically abused their wives. They also had to be chastised, e.g., by being expelled from school, for engaging in any equivalent of rape. Using sexualized language or staring lasciviously at a woman who did not want to be admired qualified for this category. Such behaviors created an impermissibly hostile working environment. Just as physical rape prompted efforts to "take back the night,"[69] it would be necessary for enlightened women to protest pornography and male boorishness. Third, in the catalogue of social changes, female values had to replace their male counterparts. Because competition was destructive, it needed to be supplanted by feminine cooperation. Mutual supportiveness, rather than nasty rivalries, would reduce communal violence and produce a better social environment for all.

In time, at least for a while, a tension equivalent to what had developed among the races arose between men and women. Men no longer knew whether they were expected to be chivalrous or asexual, while women were unsure about whether to be gracious or assertive. Were men supposed to cry in public? Were women to become more bossy? No one knew for sure. There were even intimations from some feminists that marriage, as historically defined, was constitutionally permissive of rape. Perhaps, women did not require male companionship at all. Gloria Steinem[70] indicated as much when she opined that women needed men as much as a fish needed a bicycle. Nor was there a consensus about having children. In many circles, caring for them was deemed oppressive; hence, many thousands of professional women postponed motherhood in favor of careers. All in all, the feminist revolution precipitated a great deal of angst for men, for women, for couples, and for children. Expected to open new vistas of female fulfillment, it inadvertently aroused bewilderment for individuals and families alike.

The last watershed reform associated with middle-class ascendancy was the War on Poverty. [71] Only a middle-class society intoxicated with its own achievements could imagine that poverty might be abolished. John Kenneth Galbraith[72] celebrated America as an affluent society, and people took this to heart. They were evidently so rich that they had the resources to make certain no one would ever be poor again. Clearly, social mobility should be open to everyone. So many individuals had climbed into comfortable positions that it was unconscionable that anyone be left behind. This was unfair and should not be tolerated by a moral community. According to the middle class ethos, if the rules were applied equally to everyone, then everyone should have a shot at doing well. Failing that, provisions should be made to transfer payments to those who could not compete on an equal basis. If a handicap or a social disability impeded success, comfort should still be possible for those owed an opportunity to share in the common good fortune.

For openers, welfare was declared a right and not a privilege.[73] Government agents were instructed to inform those eligible that they need not feel ashamed to apply for that to which they were entitled. When welfare had been instituted during the Depression, the fear was that free handouts would breed dependency. Franklin D. Roosevelt[74] himself was concerned lest people lose the incentive to be responsible for their own well-being. This was to be forestalled by imposing strict guidelines for eligibility. Now, these guidelines were to be relaxed. In some cases, all a person had to do to enter the relief rolls was to sign a form attesting to the lack of resources. Nor would caseworkers act like detectives attempting to sniff out illicit arrangements of men living with the women who were their clients. Teenagers too, if they were in distress, could qualify as independent recipients. This was the case if they were mothers. By the same token, solvent relatives would no longer be compelled to support indigent kin. In particular, children would not be required to contribute to the upkeep of elderly parents. All were to be considered independent of each other and, therefore, entitled to equal treatment.

Another front of the War on Poverty engaged social mobility.[75] The intention here was to empower individuals who had been robbed of their autonomy by an oppressive elite.[76] Heretofore, reformers had concentrated on redistributing physical resources; now, they would attempt to redistribute social power. Democracy was reconceptualized as entailing equivalent interpersonal influence. That some individuals should exercise greater control over their destiny than others was declared unjust. It was, therefore, necessary to train the weaker to become stronger. First, they had to be told that it was their right to be more powerful. Second, they had to delegate authority over their lives. Should they gain practice in making significant decisions, they might be able to apply this to other situations. Third, they had to be instructed in marketable skills. The illiterate would be taught to read and write; high-school graduates would be encouraged to go to college; blue collar workers would be steered toward vocational training. Fourth, they also had to be taught to cooperate rather than to compete. Community organizers would be sent forth to integrate their activities. Only if the poor could pool their power could this clout serve as a counterweight to that of the elites. In the end, it would enable them to join the system and reap its benefits.

Begun with the sincerest of intentions, this crusade was to falter before long. Some blamed this failure on the diversion of resources to the Viet Nam War. They concluded that the nation could not simultaneously finance guns and butter. Others thought that the blame lay with a Republican administration that was not sufficiently committed to the fundamental principles of the War on Poverty. In any event, in little more than a decade, the campaign stumbled into oblivion. Despite the floods of idealism tapped among the young and social scientists, the momentum could not be sustained. By the 1980s, conventional wisdom was ascribing the program's demise to the rise of greed. The latest generation of Americans had evidently stopped worrying about social justice and instead turned its attention to individual enrichment. Early estimates that poverty might be driven to extinction turned out to be premature. The poor were still very much with us; indeed the ranks of those on welfare had grown. Once more, promises of correcting the difficulties exposed by the middle-class ascendancy proved empty. To the question What next? few claimed to know the answer.

Before assessing the issue of these reforms, we should acknowledge their Marxist roots. Obsessed with equality, the reformers sought to impose a collectivist version of parity. Marx envisioned that class conflicts would conclude with the triumph of the proletarians. Once property was eliminated, competition would disappear; hence, there would no way for some to assert superiority over others. Everyone would voluntarily work for the whole and then collect only what they needed from it. Much as on the starship Enterprise, money would no longer be needed in a world where exchange was unnecessary. Neo-Marxists were aghast that in the world as it is competing parties persisted in vying for dominance. The leitmotif of their reforms was the need to resist the oppression this principle generated. Elites, however conceived, were regarded as the enemy. Only after they were overthrown could true equality arise. A genuine egalitarianism, in which everyone was equal, could not prevail so long as the bourgeoisie reigned. This contrasts sharply with Jeffersonian impartiality. The Declaration of Independence asserts that all people have an equal right to life, liberty, and the pursuit of happiness. An equality of results was never contemplated, never mind to be coercively imposed.[77] Indeed, Jefferson was candid in advocating an aristocracy of merit. He hoped that in a free society, the best would rise to the top. They might not be born to command but would earn this distinction through their actions.

The Marxist and neo-Marxist epiphanies imagined a world without hierarchy. Yet if hierarchy is built into human nature, this was a fatuous expectation. To illustrate, most contemporary sociologists recognize that poverty is a matter of relative deprivation. They realize that America's poor are not poor by historical standards.[78] According to the American Census Bureau, as of 2002, 46% of poor households owned their own homes; 76% of them had air conditioning; nearly three-quarters owned a car; 97% had a color television; and 73% possessed microwave ovens. Their poverty did not consist in having to endure squalor or semistarvation. Compared to others in their society, they were not doing well, but this measure was only comparative. Yet, that is the point. What hurts about poverty is not how little you have, but that you have less than the next guy. Since hierarchies always have a bottom, those to be found there feel disadvantaged compared with those above them. Given the logic of this situation, absolute poverty can never be eliminated. The best that can be achieved is to bring more people into the middle by making social mobility available to all.

Power, too, is relative. It is also hierarchical and, therefore, can never be parceled out with complete equivalence. The racial, feminist, and poverty reformers all excoriated oppression in the expectation of deliverance by a utopian equality of results. As romantic idealists, they took an extremist view of equality, one that did not take account of the human condition. The same was true of antiwar reformers. They perceived an arrogance of power even in attempts at self-defense. As long as the United States is more powerful than other nations and, therefore, superior, they would condemn its policies as unilateral. But because its actions always betrayed this greater strength, it was enjoined from exercising them. Only weakness, as imposed perhaps by the collapse of the middle class, would satisfy this particular sense of morality. The same applied to race, gender, and wealth. The only definitive way to cease being oppressively racist, sexist, or financially successful was to become poor and powerless, not an end likely to recommend itself to those who were doing well—or who hoped to do so.

The Great Disruption

The politicized reforms that followed hard on the heels of the hippie eruption backfired. Despite preliminary optimism, these reforms were not well calculated to improve the human condition. Conceived in haste and in reaction to social changes that were difficult to digest, they did not address the actual sources of discomfort. To judge by what occurred subsequent to their imposition, we see that a series of unanticipated complications followed. The timing of these emergent problems, their temporal convergence, and their occurrence in disparate societies suggest a disquieting causal relationship. This was Francis Fukuyama's[79] conclusion. A political scientist by trade, he dubbed what transpired "The Great Disruption." Until this point in its history, the Middle-Class Revolution had been making orderly progress. The Eisenhower consolidation was relatively smooth, and the hippie eruption had been more amusing than alarming. Once the politicized reforms got going, however, small clouds on the horizon swelled into thunderheads. Instead of people's adjusting to success and making it more general, society as a whole and a few of its subdivisions in particular were subjected to significant harm.

Among the indicators of disruption to which Fukuyama alludes is crime. First in the United States, then in Western Europe as it caught up economically, crime rates soared.[80] Starting slowly in the 1950s, but accelerating rapidly by the mid 60s, the violent crime rate multiplied by many times. Assault, rape, and murder all became more common, with, by the 90s, the murder rate almost ten times what it had been at the turn of the century. Both the Wild West and the gangster ridden 30s have worse reputations, but they were eclipsed by later events. Property crimes, such as theft and robbery, also mushroomed. Ordinary people began to worry about being mugged in their own neighborhoods. In New York City, they avoided places like Central Park where they feared this might to take place.[81] The night became more frightening as potential victims contemplated how much easier it was to be attacked after dark. In large cities, the conventional wisdom now declared the streets ungovernable. Despite hiring more police, there seemed no way to stem the torrent.

The family, too, appeared to be under assault.[82] Once reckoned the cornerstone of civilized society, it was falling apart. After the elevated number of births in the Baby Boom, fertility rates declined to fewer than the replacement rate of two per family. In Europe this had long been so, but in the United States it was a novel experience for times of prosperity. By century's end, the population was still rising, but this was due to high birth rates among fecund immigrants. More troublesome was the increase in divorce.[83] Its incidence, too, began to spike in the mid 60s and reached an historically elevated plateau in the 90s. By then, approximately half of all marriages ended in court. This was better than it sounded, but only marginally so. In fact, only a third of first marriages terminated in divorce; the rest of the statistic was based one second, third, and fourth couplings. Most people continued to get married—well over ninety percent—but they did so at later ages,[84] expecting their unions to last, through well aware of the divorce rate. Once upon a time divorce was a deviant act, but those days have receded into antique memory.

More disconcerting still was the growth in the rate of illegitimacy. Divorce was already creating a generation of children raised by single parents.[85] As would be seen, this was stressful for the young, but worse yet was growing up in a family that had never consisted of two parents. Before 1950, fewer than five percent of all births were out of wedlock. The pregnancies of unmarried women had once been considered shameful. Often she would leave home to have her child elsewhere, lest knowledge of her transgression ruin her chances for married respectability. Giving the child up for adoption was a forgone conclusion. When couples shared the prospect of such a birth, they frequently married to provide legitimacy. After such hastily arranged affairs, they explained to friends and relatives that the child was premature. By the 90s, over thirty percent of children were being born to single mothers. In the African-American community, more than two thirds of all youngsters suffered this fate. Nor was it unusual for many to come of age in a family populated by several half-siblings. It was also common to be raised by grandparents, especially for children of teenaged mothers. Sadly unexceptional, these children having children were unprepared for the responsibility of parenthood. Many preferred to continue the party lifestyle that put them in the family way in the first place. To compound this misery, the largest share of illegitimacy occurred among the poor. Those with the least adequate financial and social resources were the ones most likely to bear the burden.

Fukuyama[86] also emphasized the decline in interpersonal trust. He had earlier documented that trust is imperative in gesellschaft societies, and it was within these communities that the decline was most precipitous. As the number of interdependent strangers increased, their confidence in one another declined. People now expected others to lie. They also expected cheating when someone could get away with it. Sadly, surveys have shown, at least in school, most did. Where once people left their front doors unlocked, confident that no one would rob them, multiple lock, kept bolted, became the norm, especially in large cities. Conventional wisdom now stressed that placing temptation in front of others was almost as serious an offense as the theft itself. Leaving one's keys in an unlocked car was condemned an invitation to teenaged joy riding. Ordinary people were also encouraged to buy guns.[87] These might be hidden to keep children from having accidents, but not owning a firearm, nor understanding how to use it, was thought to make families vulnerable. It left them at the mercy of those who might attempt a home invasion. In some towns, such as Kennesaw, Georgia, gun ownership became mandatory. After this law went into effect, as was intended, the volume of crime went down.

This lack of trust extended to particular segments of society. The faith that Americans had in their government's ability to help them eroded badly. They were especially disillusioned with politicians. Cynically convinced that most were liars, they considered their promises with a grain of salt. Amazingly, when Bill Clinton[88] was caught red-handed, a common response was that everyone did what he had done; that everyone lied to and cheated on their spouses.

Although his denial of having sex with Monica Lewinsky was patently false, it was not immoral because everyone told untruths about sex. Sex was a private affair to be judged only by the wife. What had once been considered depraved behavior had transmuted into a justification of itself. [89]

A similar cynicism extended to the media.[90] The journalistic purveyors of bad news became associated with their products, particularly since they were assumed to slant the news to serve their own purposes.[91] Thanks to television, the volume of news to which people was exposed had increased exponentially.[92] Average viewers could now see paparazzi pestering celebrities for photographs, pundits of all sorts wildly spinning the facts to suit ideological preferences, and vulgar sensationalism dressed up as the public's right to know.[93] If the public paid attention, it could also hear pious anchorpersons justifying their latest biases. But many were not listening. They had heard it all before. Even the police and courts were treated to this suspicion.[94] In previous years, before the Great Disruption, the police had been the ordinary citizens' friends and the legal system was assumed to be the world's best. Fairness and integrity were taken for granted.[95] Unfortunately, too many scandals followed. A drumbeat of accusations about police brutality, political corruption, and sexual peccadilloes convinced observers that where there was smoke, there must be fire. They understood that much of what they saw was exaggerated—that hyperbole was the standard means of generating media interest—but they could not believe that none of it was true. Though they knew that it was safer to trust little of what one saw and less of what one heard, some of it registered.

Were this all that resulted from the turmoils following the Great Middle-Class Revolution, it would be noteworthy. But there was more. Not only were there more incidences of crime and distrust; there was also greater disorder.[96] Levels of civility declined along with communal security.[97] People were not as polite as they had once been.[98] Where vulgar language had previously been considered a sign of poor breeding, four-letter words now sprinkled even erudite conversations.[99] Being too persnickety about obscene words came to be interpreted as evidence of artificiality. It was stiff and uptight and far too square for relaxed discourse. People said what was on their minds, even when it was earthy. Real people apparently also wrote choice epithets on the sides of subway cars, abandoned buildings, and unprotected billboards. Graffiti, formerly dismissed as a species of vandalism, was reevaluated as street art. Among the cognoscenti, graffiti came to be widely admired as a form of communication open to those otherwise silenced by social conventions. This pattern of rationalization became the norm in private discussions and public forums; it also became standard fare in the entertainment industry. Words never before heard coming from the silver screen or the television set issued from the mouths of demure heroines. Worst of all was what happened to music. During the 50s most popular songs had been sweet and romantic. There were, to be sure, sexual allusions, but they remained just that, allusions. The language of early rock and roll was more explicit, but its words paled in comparison with those in rap music, heavy metal, grunge, and hip-hop. Vocalists had no difficulty in advocating that the police be murdered or that women be treated as prostitutes. Accompanied by videos that left less and less to the imagination, even young children were bombarded with the next best thing to coitus. When criticized for these improprieties, the entertainment executives and artists did not back down. This, they explained, was real life, and real life needed no apologies.

Overall attitudes toward sexuality had undergone a metamorphosis.[100] In the pre-disruption 50s, television producers were loath even to show married couples sleeping in the same bed.[101] Usually they occupied twin beds and, if seen in an embrace, had at least one foot on the floor. By the 90s, by common consent, there had been a sexual revolution. Almost everyone now admitted that sex was a natural function. People talked openly about it, and television seemed obsessed with it. Scarcely a single episode of most situation comedies could conclude without intimations of musical beds. Consummating even the slighted physical attraction was considered sophisticated. Everyone knew that being abstinent was a religious affectation. Normal people had normal desires, which it was healthy to fulfill. To do less was to be a prude. It indicated a neurotic insecurity that was to be pitied rather than emulated. Virginity was not a virtue; it was almost a psychological disorder. Ever since the promulgation of the birth-control pill, there was no need to worry about unwanted pregnancies. As long as people were careful, and after the spread of AIDS[102] this meant utilizing a condom, casual sex imposed no harm and was, therefore, no foul. Sex was fun, and what was life for if not to extract its pleasures? Even the term "promiscuity" went of fashion. Why not have multiple partners? During the 60s and 70s, there was actually a period in which swinging was extolled. Sharing partners, including in the midst of orgies, was praised for improving relationships and removing guilt. It was just doing what came naturally.

As time progressed, advertisements for casual sex appeared almost everywhere. Besides the testimonials in the media, social dancing became orgiastic. Bodies not only writhed in sexual ecstasy but came to express in a pantomime of sexual collaboration. Clothing, too, became more than suggestive. During the 60s, the miniskirt made its appearance. Rising much higher than its 20's forerunner, it barely covered the crotch. This, however, was to seem modest when compared with the thong. First introduced in bathing suits intended to do bikinis one better, they became undergarment standards. With the buttocks exposed and frequently highlighted by tattoos, the next demand was that the breasts be liberated. Early feminists attempted the feat by burning their bras, whereas later libertines reveled in wet tee-shirt contests and in "girls gone wild" episodes of flashing chests. Men, too, got into the act by discovering the Full Monte of male strippers. The effect of this is to lower standards, albeit not to the degree that it might appear. Yes, it is true that among girls the age of first sexual encounter dropped to the high school years; with virgins often ridiculed for their timidity. It also came to be expected that couples would have sex before they were married. By the same token, many decided to live together before marrying. At first promoted as a sort of trial marriage intended to determine whether formal union would succeed, when this turned out not to improve the chances of a lasting relationship, it was simply accepted for what it was. Couples became comfortable introducing their bed partners as roommates, even to their parents. All the same, there was more private sexual morality than was publicly advertised.

To begin with, the amount of sexual activity did not rise as much as might have been predicted.[103] People, especially women, continued to be selective in their pairings. Frequently ashamed at their own diffidence, they were unaware that others were privately as reserved as they. Nor was cheating as extensive as the media depicted. More men strayed than did women, but the best evidence indicated that this was about 25% for them versus 15% for women. The misreading of what was happening had been encouraged by the fact that the exhibitionists were more visible than more modest folks. Nevertheless there was more experimentation with different sorts of sex and with different sorts of partners. What made this dangerous was that it was the young who were most vulnerable to being seduced into compromising positions.

Also escalating during the Great Disruption was the rate of substance abuse.[104] Some of this increase was relatively modest. Most people did not become confirmed addicts. Nevertheless, in its early appearances marijuana was a gateway drug. Many who experimented with it later turned to heroin and cocaine. There might have been warnings, yet millions succumbed. And when hooked, abusers became shadows of their former selves. Unable to hold down solid jobs and addicted to expensive habits, they resorted to crime and prostitution. This pattern became epidemic when crack cocaine arrived on the scene. It could be smoked, rather than snorted or injected; hence it was easier to use. Besides, it was cheaper. This made it attractive to the poor; consequently they were most devastated by its spread. Ironically, cocaine had begun as a high-status drug with a reputation for being nonaddictive. When it became apparent that addiction was possible, and after the government sponsored a "just say no" campaign, usage among the middle classes declined. Individuals who intended to be socially mobile understood that success was incompatible with zoned-out substance dependence. This left members of the lower classes to wallow in their wretchedness. Already more vulnerable to alcoholism, addicted mothers gave birth to crack babies, needle sharers were susceptible to AIDS, and all were at the mercy of violent drug dealers. Added to this were the miseries inherent in other substances. A plague descended upon many neighborhoods, as amphetamines, quaaludes, ecstasy, angel dust, and designer drugs flooded the market.[105] Some of these recreational narcotics established a foothold among middle-class teenagers, but, in time, they easily made their way to ghettos and barrios.

Ironically, despite the fact that the middle classes flourished with improvements in education, schools were among the most serious casualties of the Great Disruption.[106] Instead of learning becoming more highly developed, the reverse occurred.[107]   Education became more widely spread in the sense that a greater number of children went to school and more of them graduated with advanced credentials, but the amount of information acquired declined. This decline was so substantial that professional educators called it The Great Decline.[108] Among its first indicators were the Scholastic Aptitude Test (SAT) scores.   This gatekeeper test for college admissions was once accounted a landmark of American education. Previous to its arrival, acceptance to prestigious universities depended more upon family connections than academic abilities. Consequently, universities like Harvard and Yale were typified by the intellectual superiority of their student.[109] They became way stations that guided the nation's best and brightest into its most responsible and remunerative positions. As a result, colleges of every description and students of every aptitude scrambled to make use of the SAT. This diluted the talent pool, but the deterioration in scores outstripped what was contained in this explanation. In both reading and math, after the 60s, the college bound did less well. So serious did this become that the Educational Testing Service that owns the test changed its scoring procedures so that the outcomes would be less embarrassing.

Below the college level, the devastation was as general.[110]   In both primary and secondary schools, testing demonstrated that students were less well prepared than earlier generations. Regularly administered achievement tests made it plain that reading and math competences were barely holding their own and that there was about a four-year difference in the accomplishments between majority and minority students. In areas such as science and history, the results were especially discomforting. They revealed levels of knowledge that were incredibly low and getting lower. When these figures were compared with those of other countries, the American students invariably came out toward the lower end of the spectrum. Even students in third-world countries routinely did better in tests of science and math. Much of this was disguised from parents because their children's grades remained high. In fact, they were probably better than the parents' own. This was not because they knew more but because of grade inflation. Teachers were simply giving better evaluations for inferior performances. They knew that to do well their charges had to get into college and that bad averages might ruin their chances. Moreover, in passing nearly everyone rather than in improving their teaching techniques, they more easily satisfied the pressures coming from parents and administrators. Little Johnny had to get good grades to keep these potential critics happy. Long gone too was the technique of tracking students according to their abilities. Because the final results were supposed to be equal, no one was allowed to get special treatment to accelerate learning. This would have been antidemocratic, but could be prevented by the simple expedient of permitting everyone to remain comparably ignorant.

Another of the educational declines was in discipline. In the past, students were expected to heed their elders. When asked to behave themselves, they generally complied—often fearful that if they did not, their parents would inflict dire punishments. This too changed. Middle-class parents became advocates for their offspring. They lobbied teachers to make sure that Johnny was given a fair shake. Lower-class parents were often as adamant. They would not stand to have their children. If Junior complained of an injustice, his parents were certain his obstreperous behavior had been justified. The teacher needed to shapeup, not the student. As a consequence, many inner-city classrooms were reduced to bedlam. The pupils would not sit quietly in their seats for teachers who could not enforce social order. Many youngsters even brought weapons to class. Teachers and administrators became so concerned for their own safety that they refrained from imposing discipline. Instead of teaching the sort of self-control that is a prerequisite of middle class success, they allowed chaos to reign, both externally and internally.

Already mentioned was the increase in the numbers on welfare rolls.[111] More people were getting more money from the federal government than ever before, on the condition that they not make efforts to support themselves. This not only promoted dependence, it also encouraged cheating. Subsequent accountings would demonstrate that double and triple dipping was common. With loosened restraints appearing throughout society, taking advantage of bureaucratic slackness appeared to be the rule. One could, for instance, collect welfare from several venues, get unemployment insurance while working under the table, obtain workman's compensation for fake disabilities, and receive training for a job only to quit it immediately to be trained for something else one also did not intend to do. No one in charge seemed to care about such cheating, so why should the cheaters?

Emblematic of these patterns is the Watergate scandal.[112] Richard Nixon stood before television cameras to declare that he was "not a crook," symbolizing the lowering of standards so characteristic of the Great Disruption. If the president could manipulate the truth, why shouldn't everyone else? It was all a matter of what you could get away with. Besides, the country was rich. It was so rich that none of this mattered. The middle class cornucopia furnished a bounty so enormous that it covered a multitude of sins. Why not scramble for a bigger piece of the pie when there was so much pie to go around? Why not cheat a little when no one would be seriously hurt by this larceny? There was no need to come to honest terms with these disruptions as long as almost everyone was sliding by.

The Culture Wars

The Great Disruption exacerbated what had already been a division between liberals and conservatives. They were now at each other's throats over the most fundamental community values. So ferocious did their conflicts become that they were dubbed a Culture War.[113] Each side was convinced that the other was ruining the republic and, therefore, put up a stiff fight to preserve civilization from destruction. According to the liberals, democracy hung in the balance. Unless the appropriate reforms were put into effect, freedom and equality were in jeopardy. According to the conservatives, these reforms were the real source of jeopardy. They were said to undermine the principles upon which freedom depended. To this charge liberals responded by dismissing the conservatives as rigid troglodytes. They were evidently so opposed to change that they refused to repair what was unequivocally broken. The conservatives did acknowledge a respect for tradition, but they insisted that their goal was to defend crucial institutions.[114] They too wanted things to be better; but they did not want to throw the baby out with the bath water.

Both sides had a point, but they also missed a larger one. Though each would vociferously deny the claim, what both were attempting to do was intimately intertwined with what the other was seeking. Each assumed that it was engaged in an independent activity, while it was, in fact, participating in a social give-and-take. Theirs was a moral negotiation.[115] Most people, including the parties to significant disputes, assume that morality is a matter of eternal truths. They believe it is a set of absolute and inviolable rules. What is good is by definition good, and what is right is inherently right. There can be no ands, ifs, or maybes about such matters. Nonetheless, such dichotomous inflexibility is wrong-headed. Morality is not a compendium of peculiarly obdurate facts. Nor is it something discovered by inspecting the texture of the universe. Morality is a social process. Its rules are socially constructed, socially modified, and socially enforced. As a result, the standards people apply are always of evolving. They never stand still. By their very nature, dynamic, they perpetually trap humankind in a tug-o-war between competing factions.

The nature of moral negotiations is distinctive.[116] Because moral rules are considered exceptionally important, conflicts over their shape are typically animated. Among other things, the parties to any enterprises tend to be polarized.[117] They perceive themselves as the good guys, with their own side always in the right. This places a premium on distinguishing oneself and one's allies from the competing faction. But to be distinct, one has to be distinctive. Both cliques want the differences separating the sides to be so striking that potential converts will have no difficulty in choosing sides. This, however, fosters extremism. Because the real world is pervaded by shades of gray, to provide the desired clarity, divergences have to be enhanced and the lines between them artificially straightened. In other words, the differences have to be simplified and strengthened if the players are to assemble the alliances necessary to promote their positions. Moral goals, therefore, tend to be idealized, with each side regarding its own as perfect and the other's as the opposite. Both are certain that were they to succeed, the world would become a better place, whereas a victory for their enemy would be tantamount to an excursion into hell.

Moral negotiations normally emerge when people are faced with unusual circumstances. They engage in debate about the standards best equipped to mange their discomfort because they are not sure of what will work. Although stated in objective terms, their positions are customarily predicated on individual situations and distinct socializations. In essence, what they conclude has helped them and their allies to prosper is projected as potentially helpful to everyone. Often intransigent in these assertions, the battle can seesaw back and forth for centuries until a compromise is achieved. Because this argument can escalate into warfare, people are often grievously injured in their quests for justice. Nevertheless, this slipshod means of developing a communal consensus ultimately subsumes more information than might a purpose-designed settlement. Just as with economic planning, a centralized version of moral planning would be ill advised. Rather than displaying rationality, it would be coercively unfair—favoring the interests of its designers over those of the community. In morality and, therefore, in moral negotiations no one has the final authority because no one is neutral or objective. Since no individual can discern all that is involved, even the best of intentions can go astray. The upshot is that mistakes are made, sometimes corrected, and then replaced by new mistakes. This is one of the reasons why history proceeds in waves. A push-and-pull of discovery, often based on idealized miscalculations, results in both progress and error. Improvements tend to accumulate, but the missteps that occur along the way can send civilization reeling backward.

A contemporary illustration of a moral negotiation is the debate over abortion.[118] Generally this squabble is framed in either/or terms. The pro-choice faction demands that abortion be available to all, including teenaged girls, upon request. The pro-life faction counters that abortion is equivalent to murder and is, therefore, never acceptable. These are extreme positions, but it is usually the extremists who are most active in asserting the virtues of any side. Eventually, a modified position tends to emerge. For abortion, this looks as if it might eventuate in discouraging abortion, while making it legal in most cases. It should also be noted that this quarrel first arose only after modern medicine made it probable most children would grow to adulthood. Before that, natural deaths swept away many babies before anyone could contemplate abortion. Similar considerations apply to euthanasia and alcoholism. Euthanasia was not a moral problem requiring a social solution until medicine made chronic illness more common by increasing life expectancy. Likewise, alcoholism was not regarded as a social difficulty until industrialization demanded workplace discipline. Only then did discussions of temperance and prohibition enter the public domain.

By the time of the middle-class tipping point, liberals had taken the initiative in promoting moral reforms.[119] Their efforts to reduce incidences of racism, sexism, and poverty came to the fore as social mobility became available to more and more people.[120] It seemed to these activists that a variety of impediments were interfering with success based on merit. Those already on top, namely the elite, were oppressively preventing others from supplanting them. One of the first challenges to this form of intimidation developed out of anthropology. These social scientists, in dealing with preliterate peoples, discovered that their subjects too were fully human. Anthropologists also found that, in order to understand these other lifestyles, they had to view the world from that perspective. This practice was eventually codified as "cultural relativism." Soon thereafter, cultural relativism mutated into ethical relativism.[121] Figures such as Frans Boas[122] were appalled when Social Darwinism[123] was utilized to justify eugenics. At the turn of the century, Francis Galton's argument that society should improve its genetic heritage by preventing the poor and disabled from reproducing had won many converts.[124] It seemed reasonable that society should not handicap itself by diverting its surpluses into supporting individuals who could never contribute to the commonweal.[125] What Boas and his colleagues realized was that this theory was being used to excuse the punishment of those on the bottom. In the United States, welfare clients, who were often black, were inaccurately accused of mental retardation and subsequently sterilized. This was not only barbaric, it was also a depraved form of discrimination.

Ethical relativism, however, went further; it argued that moral rules were culturally specific. Each society constructed its own standards, and, therefore, no group was entitled to criticize the imperatives of another. Each was right unto itself. Thus, if Muslims practiced polygamy, it was valid for them, whereas monogamy was correct for Americans. In due course, this relativism was idealized to promote non-judgmentalism. The intellectually sophisticated were to refrain from judging how any others chose to live. This was their own business, not those of the busybodies. By the 1940s, Carl Rogers[126] had imported this attitude into psychotherapy.

His client-centered therapy taught that every individual deserved "unconditional positive regard." Parents and therapists distinguished between the person and the deed so that the individual was always accorded loving support. In psychotherapy, this had the advantage of putting vulnerable clients at ease, but within society as a whole it justified universal tolerance. No one was to be punished for misdeeds but rather to be presented with an opportunity for rehabilitation. This would enhance a miscreant's self-esteem so that he/she would never be motivated to repeat mischief. People who loved themselves, because others loved them, would pass this attitude along to still others. Ultimately, unqualified kindness would be the rule. Social mobility would, in effect, become universal because cooperation would replace competition.

By the end of the century, this philosophy had mutated again. Now it was identified with multiculturalism and diversity.[127] Not only were women and minority groups to be accorded respect, their differences were to be celebrated. Society as a whole would benefit from cultivating their unique contributions. One of the means through which this was expressed was "rights talk."[128] Sooner or later most political conversations devolved into assertions of individual or group rights. Formerly, civic-minded persons were concerned with promoting duties. Now, the issues are what is due the claimant. Activists never tired of presenting women and blacks as victims entitled to protection from the more powerful. Only this could insure that there would be no social losers. Only this protection could guarantee that all would share in the advantages of freedom. Far from imposing social or personal discipline, punishment and violence were to be outlawed. Even symbolic violence, that is, making people feel uncomfortable by treating them unwelcomely, was to be banished.[129] Merely to express a hatred or sexual attraction toward protected groups was intolerable. Denying the right to feel good personally was considered the equivalent of punishment.

Competition, too, was seen as punitive. Because competition required some to win and others to lose, it imposed pain on the weak. Instead of accepting the weak as they were, competition consigned them to failure. In response to this abuse, efforts were instituted to eliminate the circumstances productive of invidious comparisons. Dodge-ball was banned from the schoolyard on the grounds that it was both violent and discriminatory. By the same token, many Little League teams decided not to keep score. At the end of the season, everyone would get a trophy regardless of efforts or talent. Enlightened persons began to say—and mean—"it's not whether you win or lose, but how you play the game." Actually, it was not even how you played, but merely whether you showed up—and sometimes not even that. Anything less was oppressively unequal and, therefore, the opposite of genuine freedom.

It was this moral entrepreneurship that sparked a revival of conservatism.[130] Largely in retreat through the 50s and 60s, by the 70s, referring to oneself as a "conservative" once more became respectable. This appellation, however, had undergone a transformation. The political turf was now crowded with fiscal conservatives, social conservatives, neocons, religious fundamentalists, and libertarians.[131] All claimed an allegiance to tradition in one form or another, but what made them allies was a shared revulsion at what liberalism had become.[132] They looked at the reforms accelerating into extremism and demanded a halt. Blacks might deserve a color-blind society, but not quota-oriented affirmative action. Women were entitled to equal pay for equal work, but not androgyny. The poor were worthy of a chance to get ahead, but not to excessively generous transfer payments that robbed them of their independence. Leading the charge in this culture war were the religiously committed. More deeply offended by the assault on family values than most, they had a faith which gave them the courage to stand up and say so. When the multiculturalists asserted that single parenthood was just as legitimate as the traditional family, they bridled at the suggestion. This was not what the Bible said, and they would not be persuaded otherwise.

Conservatives, in general, asserted an adherence to the primacy of the nuclear family. What many did not realize was that this was less traditional than they imagined. While household consisting of a man, woman, and their children was of ancient lineage, the companionate marriage is a recent innovation. Though the gospels urged women to be subordinate to the husbands, this was not how contemporary fundamentalists regarded the message. They, too, emphasized mutual respect between spouses. There was to be a division of labor between the two, but this was not the same as it had been. Essentially, middle class standards were being grafted onto old texts. The fundamentalists, while quick to defend school prayer, had no intention of instituting a Christian theocracy. As democratically committed as their fellow citizens, they found nondenominational messages perfectly acceptable. Indicative of their attitude were attempts to place copies of the Ten Commandments in courtrooms. These, they argued, were representative of no particular church, but were part of the Judeo-Christian, and even the Muslim, tradition.

Among the values conservatives defended most vociferously were "responsibility," "merit," and "discipline."[133] They believed in old-fashioned standards and wanted to see them respected. This mind-set was exemplified in their approach to law and order. Exasperated by the legalistic exploitation of excuses to relieve malefactors of blame, they wanted hold them accountable for their misdeeds.[134] If this meant that murderers deserved capital punishment, so be it. As to the major liberal reforms, conservatives were ambivalent. Most believed passionately in fairness, but they were convinced that benefits targeted for oppressed minorities were a mistake. Unimpressed with claims that one had to tilt in order to restore balance, conservatives insisted that the same rules be applied to all. Committed to a market economy and interpersonal competition, they wanted people to earn what they received. Nevertheless, in return for upholding this version of fairness, conservatives were castigated as racists, sexists, and classists. According to the liberals, they were merely protofascists determined to turn back the clock.

The liberals, despite a professed dedication to being nonjudgmental, held strong opinions about conservatives.[135] Although prepared to leap to the defense of fascists and Marxists, the fact that conservatives might be able to impose their values made them too dangerous to disregard. Tolerance was acceptable for embattled minorities, not for potential majorities. These could not be accorded unconditional positive regard but must be converted to the correct viewpoints. Nor was this to be done gently. Conservatives offended liberals. Liberals grew indignant at conservative attitudes and were unwilling to allow those to prevail. In this, liberals were prepared to utilize political coercion. After all, that which was immoral had to be suppressed. Thus, laws needed to be instituted to make certain that hate crimes were extinguished. Those who used drugs recreationally might find their habits decriminalized, whereas those who murdered minority members would be treated more harshly than those who killed members of the majority—with women, numbering more than men, of course, defined as a minority. Likewise, men who battered their wives would no longer be warned to desist but immediately would be carted off to jail. Moreover, cultures that engaged in female circumcision would be ostracized for their barbarity. To the extent possible, in the name of female liberation, pressures would be exerted to criminalize what had been a religious rite.

Remarkably, liberalism reverted from universalistic to particularistic standards. During the Middle Ages, members of the nobility were subject to different laws than others were. The ax rather than the noose, for instance, was used to execute them. With the dominance of commercialism and its resolve to level the playing field, equality before the law became a central aim. Contemporary liberalism reversed this trend. Some people would receive special benefits because of their classification, whereas others were to receive harsher punishments. Even the weight one's testimony was accorded in courts would vary with group membership. Women, to provide a salient example, were allowed to judge whether they had been sexually offended. The standard of what was permissible was their reaction, rather than a more objective standard. Instead of a color-blind or gender-blind society, a socially engineered equality became the goal.

Endnotes

[1] Corey, L. 1935. *The Crisis of the Middle Class.* New York: Columbia University Press; D'Souza, D. 2000. *The Virtue of Prosperity: Finding Values in an Age of Techno-Affluence.* New York: The Free Press.

[2] Hughes, R. 1993. *Culture of Complaint: The Fraying of America.* New York: Oxford University Press.

[3] Samuelson, R. 1996. *The Good Life and Its Discontents: The American Dream in the Age of Entitlement 1945-1995.* New York: Times Books.

[4] de Botton, A. 2004 *Status Anxiety.* New York: Pantheon Books; Skocpol, T. 2000. *The Missing Middle: Working Families and the Future of American Social Policy.* New York: W.W. Norton & Co.

[5] Wolfe, A. 1996. *Marginalized in the Middle.* Chicago: University of Chicago Press.

[6] Lipset, S.M. and Bendix, R. 1959. *Social Mobility in Industrial Society.* Berkeley: University of California Press.; Dahrendorf, R. 1959. *Class and Class Conflict in Industrial Society.* Stanford, CA: Stanford University Press.; Doty, C.S. (Ed.) 1969. *The Industrial Revolution.* New York: Holt, Rinehart and Winston.

[7] Riech, C.A. 1971. *The Greening of America.* New York: Bantam.

[8] Collier, P. and Horowitz, D. 1989. *Destructive Generation: Second Thoughts about the '60s.* New York: The Free Press.

[9] Gerth, H. and Mills, C.W. (Eds.) 1946. *From Max Weber: Essays in Sociology.* New York: Oxford University Press.

[10] Fein, M. 2001 Race and Morality: How Good Intentions Undermine Social Justice and Perpetuate Inequality. New York: Kluwer/Plenum.

[11] Fein, M. 1999. The Limits of Idealism: When Good Intentions Go Bad. New York: Kluwer/Plenum.

[12] Fein, M. 1999. The Limits of Idealism: When Good Intentions Go Bad. New York: Kluwer/Plenum.

[13] Fein, M. 1999. The Limits of Idealism: When Good Intentions Go Bad. New York: Kluwer/Plenum.

[14] Isaacson, W. 2003. *Benjamin Franklin: An American Life.* New York: Simon & Schuster.

[15] Fein, M. 2001 *Race and Morality: How Good Intentions Undermine Social Justice and Perpetuate Inequality.* New York: Kluwer/Plenum.; Myrdal, G. 1944. *An American Dilemma: The Negro Problem and American Democracy.* New York: Harper & Row.

[16] Laudan, L. 1977. *Progress and Its Problems: Towards a Theory of Scientific Growth.* Berkeley: University of California Press.

[17] Gray, T. 1976. *Champion of Peace: The Story of Alfred Nobel, the Peace Prize, and the Laureates.* New York: Paddington Press.; Chatfield, C. 1992.

The American Peace Movement: Ideals and Activism. New York: Twayne Publishers.

[18] Hersey, J. 1946. *Hiroshima.* New York: Bantam Books.

[19] Sale, K. 1973. *SDS.* New York: Random House.

[20] Halberstam, D. 1969. *The Best and the Brightest.* New York: Random House.: Halberstam, D. 1986. *The Reckoning.* New York: William Morrow Co.; Joes, A.J. 1989. *The War for South Viet Nam 1954-1975.* New York: Praeger.

[21] Kohn, B. 2003. *Journalistic Fraud: How The New York Times Distorts the News and Why It Can No Longer Be Trusted.* Nashville: WND Books.

[22] Goodwin, D.K. 1971. *Lyndon Johnson and the American Dream.* New York: Harper & Row.

[23] Ambrose, S.E. 1987. *Nixon: The Education of a Politician 1913-1962.* New York: Simon and Schuster.; Wicker, T. 1991. *One of Us: Richard Nixon and the American Dream.* New York: Random House.

[24] Washington, B.T. 1901. (1985) *Up From Slavery.* New York: Oxford University Press.

[25] Morris, E. 2001. *Theodore Rex.* New York: Random House.

[26] Lowe, D. 1967. *Ku Klux Klan: The Invisible Empire.* New York: W.W. Norton.; Allport, G. 1954. *The Nature of Prejudice.* Boston: Beacon Press.

[27] Park, R. 1950. *Race and Culture.* Glencoe, Ill: Free Press.

[28] McCullough, D. 1992. *Truman.* New York: Simon & Schuster.

[29] Williams, J. 1998. *Thurgood Marshall: American Revolutionary.* New York: Times Books.

[30] Morin, R. 1969. *Dwight D. Eisenhower: A Gauge of Greatness.* New York: Simon & Schuster.

[31] Pyatt, S.E. 1986. *Martin Luther King, Jr.: An Annotated Bibliography.* New York: Greenwood Press.

[32] Thernstrom, S. and Thernstrom, A. 1997. *America in Black and White: One Nation, Indivisible.* New York: Simon and Schuster.

[33] Coleman, J.S., Campbell, E.Q, Hobson, C.J., McPartland, J., Mood, A.M., Weinfeld, F.D. and York, R.L. 1966. *Equality of Educational Opportunity.* Washington: U.S. Government Printing Office.

[34] Rieder, J. 1985. *Canarsie: The Jews and Italians of Brooklyn against Liberalism.* Cambridge MA: Harvard University Press.

[35] Coleman, J.S., Campbell, E.Q, Hobson, C.J., McPartland, J., Mood, A.M., Weinfeld, F.D. and York, R.L. 1966. *Equality of Educational Opportunity.* Washington: U.S. Government Printing Office.

[36] Rubin L. B. 1972. *Busing & Backlash: White Against White in an Urban School District.* Berkeley: University of California Press.

[37] Bergmann, B.R. 1996. *In Defense of Affirmative Action.* New York: Basic Books.; Skrentny, J.L. 1996. *The Ironies of Affirmative Action: Politics, Culture, and Justice in America.* Chicago: University of Chicago Press.

[38] Schlesinger, A.M. 1992. *The Disuniting of America.* New York: W.W. Norton & Co.; Kinder, R.R. and Sanders L.M. 1996. *Divided by Color: Racial Politics and Democratic Ideals.* Chicago: University of Chicago Press.; Connerly, W. 2000. *Creating Equal: My Fight Against Race Prejudices.* San Francisco: Encounter Books.

[39] Wood, P. 2003. *Diversity: The Invention of a Concept.* San Francisco: Encounter Books.

[40] Glazer, N. 1997. *We are All Multiculturalists Now.* Cambridge: Harvard University Press.; Bernstein, R. 1994. *Dictatorship of Virtue: Multiculturalism and the Battle for America's Future.* New York: Alfred A. Knopf.

[41] Thernstrom, S. and Thernstrom, A. 2003. *No Excuses: Closing the Racial Gap in Learning.* New York: Simon and Schuster.

[42] Deveaux, M. 2000. *Cultural Pluralism and Dilemmas of Justice.* Ithaca, NY: Cornell University Press.

[43] Pyatt, S.E. 1986. *Martin Luther King, Jr.: An Annotated Bibliography.* New York: Greenwood Press.

[44] Erikson, E. 1969. *Gandhi's Truth: On the Origins of Militant Nonviolence.* WE.W. Norton.

[45] D'Souza, D. 1995. *The End of Racism: Principles for a Multiracial Society.* New York: The Free Press.

[46] Brownstein, H.H. 2000. *The Social Reality of Violence and Violent Crime.* Needham Heights, MA: Allyn and Bacon.

[47] Sears, D.O. and McConahay, J.B. 1973. *The Politics of Violence: The New Urban Black and the Watts Riot.* Boston: Houghton Mifflin.

[48] Cleaver, E. 1967. *Soul on Ice.* New York: McGraw-Hill.

[49] Horowitz. D. 1997. *Radical Son: A Generational Odyssey.* New York: The Free Press.

[50] Entwisle, D.R., Alexander, K.L. and Olson, L.S. 1997. *Children, Schools & Inequality.* Boulder, CO: Westview Press.

[51] Steele, S. 1990. *The Content of Our Character: A New Vision of Race in America.* New York: St. Martin's Press.; Steele, S. 1998. *A Dream Deferred: The Second Betrayal of Black Freedom in America.* New York: HarperCollins Publishers.

[52] Ball, T. and Dagger, R. 1999. *Political Ideologies and the Democratic Ideal.* New York: Longman.

[53] Rossi, A.S. (Ed.) 1973. *The Feminist Papers: From Adams to de Beauvoir.* New York: Bantam Books.

[54] Horowitz, D. 1998. *Betty Friedan and the Making of the Feminine Mystique.* Amherst: University of Massachusetts Press.

[55] Friedan, B. 1963. *The Feminine Mystique.* New York: W.W. Norton & Co.

[56] Becker, S.D. 1981. *The Origins of the Equal Right Amendment: American Feminism between the Wars.* Westport, CT: Greenwood Press.; MacKinnon, C.A. 1987. *Feminism Unmodified: Discourses on Life and Law.* Cambridge, MS: Harvard University Press.

[57] Epstein, C.F. 1970. *Woman's Place: Options and Limits in Professional Careers.* Berkeley: University of California Press.

[58] French, M. 1992. *The War Against Women.* New York: Summit Books.

[59] Gutmann, S. 2000. *The Kinder, Gentler Military: Can America's Gender-Neutral Fighting Force Still Win Wars?* New York: Scribner.

[60] Faludi, S. 1991. *Backlash: The Undeclared War Against American Women.* New York: Crown Publishers.

[61] Lorber, J. 1994. *Paradoxes of Gender.* New Haven: Yale University Press.

[62] Jagger, A.M. 1988. *Feminist Politics and Human Nature.* Totowa, NJ: Rowman & Littlefield.

[63] Baron-Cohen, S. 2003. *The Essential Difference: The Truth about the Male and Female Brain.* New York: Basic Books.

[64] Blankenhorn, D. 1995. *Fatherless America: Confronting Our Most Urgent Social Problem.* New York: Basic Books.

[65] Clausen, J. (Ed.) 1968. *Socialization and Society.* Boston: Little Brown.

[66] Gilligan, C. 1982. *In a Different Voice.* Cambridge, MA: Harvard University Press.

[67] Brownmiller, S. 1975. *Against Our Will: Men, Women and Rape.* New York: Bantam.

[68] Gelles, R.J. 1997. *Intimate Violence in Families (3rd Edition)* Beverly Hills: Sage Publications.; Gelles, R.J and Straus, M.A. 1989. *Intimate Violence: The Causes and Consequences of Abuse in the American Family.* New York: Touchstone Books.

[69] Roiphe, K. 1993. *The Morning After: Sex, Fear, and Feminism On Campus.* Boston: Little, Brown, & Co.

[70] Steinem, G. 1992. Revolution From Within: A Book of Self-Esteem. Boston: Little, Brown.; Fein, M. 1999. The Limits of Idealism: When Good Intentions Go Bad. New York: Kluwer/Plenum.

[71] Humphrey, H.H. 1964. *War on Poverty.* New York: McGraw-Hill.; Zarefsky, D. 1986. *President Johnson's War on Poverty.* University, Ala: University of Alabama Press.

[72] Galbraith, J.K. 1958. *The Affluent Society.* Boston: Houghton Mifflin.

[73] Murray, C. 1986. *Losing Ground: American Social Policy.* New York: Basic Books.

[74] Powell, J. 2003. *FDR's Folly: How Roosevelt and His New Deal Prolonged the Great Depression.* New York: Crown Forum.

[75] Piven, F.F. and Cloward, R.A. 1977. *Poor People's Movement's: Why They Succeed, How They Fail.* New York: Vintage.

[76] Lewis, O. 1966. *La Vida: A Puerto Rican Family in the Culture of Poverty.* New York: Random House.; Valentine, C. 1968. *Culture and Poverty.* Chicago: University of Chicago Press.

[77] Mill, J.S. 1863. *On Liberty.* London.

[78] Stein, H. and Foss, M. 1999. *The Illustrated Guide to the American Economy, Third Edition.* Washington, D.C.: AEI Press.

[79] Fukuyama, F. 1999. *The Great Disruption: Human Nature and the reconstitution of Social Order.* New York: Free Press.

[80] Garbarino, J., Schellenbach, C.J. and Sebes, J. 1986. *Troubled Youth, Troubled Families.* New York: Aldine De Gruyter.

[81] Giuliani, R.W. 2002. *Leadership.* New York: Miramax Books.

[82] Coontz, S. 1992. *The Way We Never Were: American Families and the Nostalgia Trap.* New York: Basic Books.

[83] Whitehead, B.D. 1998. *The Divorce Culture: Rethinking Our Commitments to Marriage and the Family.* New York: Random House.

[84] Cherlin, A.J. 1992. *Marriage, Divorce, and Remarriage.* Cambridge, MA: Harvard University Press.

[85] Wallenstein, J.S., Lewis, J.M. and Blakesee, S. 2000. *The Unexpected Legacy of Divorce: A 25 Year Landmark Study.* New York: Hyperion.; Coltrane, S. 1996. *Family Man: Fatherhood, Housework, and Gender Equity.* New York: Oxford University Press.

[86] Fukuyama, F. 1995. *Trust: The Social Virtues and the Creation of Prosperity.* New York: Free Press.

[87] Lott, J.R. 1998. *More Guns, Less Crime: Understanding Crime and Gun Control Laws.* Chicago: University of Chicago Press.

[88] Schippers, A. 2000. *Sellout: The Inside Story of President Clinton's Impeachment.* Washington, DC: Regnery Publishing.; Lowery, R. 2003. *Legacy: Paying the Price for the Clinton Years.* Washington, D.C.: Regnery Publishing.

[89] Baker, P. 2000. *The Breach: Inside the Impeachment and Trial of William Jefferson Clinton.* New York: Scribner.

[90] Goldberg, B. 2002. *Bias: A CBS Insider Exposes How the Media Distort the News.* Washington, DC: Regnery Publishing.; Goldberg, B. 2003. *Arrogance: Rescuing America from the Media Elite.* New York: Warner Books

[91] Blyth, M. 2004. *Spin Sisters: How the Women of the Media Sell Unhappiness and Liberalism to the Women of America.* New York: St. Martin's Press.

[92] Bozell, L.B. 2004. *Weapons of Mass Distortion: The Coming Meltdown of the Liberal Media.* New York: Crown Forum.

[93] Kohn, B. 2003. *Journalistic Fraud: How The New York Times Distorts the News and Why It Can No Longer Be Trusted.* Nashville: WND Books.;

McGowan, W. 2001. *Coloring the News: How Crusading for Diversity Has Corrupted American Journalism.* San Francisco: Encounter Books.

[94] McDonald, H. 2003. *Are Cops Racist?: How the Wear Against the Police Harms Black Americans.* Chicago: Ivan R. Dee.; Rothwax, H.J. 1995. *Guilty: The Collapse of Criminal Justice.* New York: Random House.; Boot, M. 1998. *Out of Order: Arrogance, Corruption, and Incompetence on the Bench.* New York: Basic Books.

[95] Campos, P.F. 1998. *Jurismania: The Madness of American Law.* New York: Oxford University Press.; Cantor, N.F. 1997. *Imagining the Law: Common Law and the Foundations of the American Legal System.* New York: HarperCollins Publishers.

[96] Farber, D.A. and Sherry, S. 1997. *Beyond All Reason: The Radical Assault on Truth in American Law.* New York: Oxford University Press.

[97] Carter, S.L. 1998. *Civility: Manners, Morals and the Etiquette of Democracy.* New York: Basic Books.; Lasch, C. 1979. *The Culture of Narcissism: American Life in an Age of Diminishing Expectations.* New York: Warner Books.

[98] Elias, N. 1982. *Power and Civility.* New York: Pantheon Books.

[99] Sheed, W. 1975. *Muhammad Ali: A Portrait in Words and Photographs.* New York: Crowell.

[100] Jones, J.H. 1997. *Alfred C. Kinsey: A Life.* New York: W.W. Norton & Co.

[101] Lichter, S.R., Lichter, L.S. and Rothman, S. 1994. *Prime Time: How TV Portrays American Culture.* Washington, DC: Regnery Publishing.

[102] Shilts, R. 1988. *And the Band Played On: Politics, People and the AIDS Epidemic.* New York: Penguin Books.

[103] Michael, R.T., Gagnon, J.H., Laumann, E.O. and Kolata, G. 1994. *Sex in America: A Definitive Study.* New York: Warner Books.

[104] Glass, I.B. (Ed.) 1991. *The International Handbook of Addiction.* New York: Tavistock/Routledge.; Morgan, H.W. 1981. *Drugs in America 1800-1980.* Syracuse: University of Syracuse Press.

[105] Glass, I.B. (Ed.) 1991. *The International Handbook of Addiction.* New York: Tavistock/Routledge.

[106] Brimelow, P. 2003. *The Worm in the Apple: How the Teacher Unions Are Destroying American Education.* New York: HarperCollins Publishers.

[107] National Center for Educational Statistics. 2001. *Digest of Educational Statistics, 2001.* Washington, DC. Government Printing Office

[108] Kramer, R. 1991. *Ed School Follies: The Miseducation of America's Teachers.* New York: The Free Press.

[109] D'Souza, D. 1991. *Illiberal Education: The Politics of Race and Sex on Campus.* New York: The Free Press.

[110] Zigler, E. and Valentines, J. (Eds.) 1979. *Head Start: A Legacy of the War on Poverty.* New York: Free Press.

[111] Sommers, P.M. (Ed.) 1982. *Welfare Reform in America: Perspectives and Prospects.* Boston: Kluwer and Nijhoff.

[112] Bernstein, C. and Woodward, B. 1974. *All the President's Men.* New York: Simon and Schuster.

[113] Hunter, J.D. 1991. *Culture Wars: The Struggle to Define America.* New York: Basic Books.

[114] Gerson, M. (Ed.) 1996. *The Essential Neo-Conservative Reader.* Reading, MA: Addison-Wesley Publishing.

[115] Fein, M. 1997. *Hardball Without an Umpire: The Sociology of Morality.* Westport, CT: Praeger.

[116] Fein, M. 1997. *Hardball Without an Umpire: The Sociology of Morality.* Westport, CT: Praeger.

[117] Fein, M. 1999. *The Limits of Idealism: When Good Intentions Go Bad.* New York: Kluwer/Plenum.

[118] Cook, A.E., Jelen T.G. & Wilcox, C. 1992. *Between Two Absolutes: Public Opinion and the Politics of Abortion.* Boulder: Westview Press.

[119] Kramer, H. and Kimball, R. 1999. *The Betrayal of Liberalism: How the Disciples of Freedom and Equality Helped Foster the Illiberal Politics of Coercion and Control.* Chicago: Ivan R. Dee.

[120] Feagin, J.R. and Sikes, M.P. 1994. *Living with Racism: The Black Middle-Class Experience.* Boston: Beacon Press.

[121] Westermarck, E. 1960. *Ethical Relativity.* Paterson, NJ: Littlefield, Adams, and Co.

[122] Boas, F. 1928. *Anthropology and Modern Life.* New York: Dover Publishers.

[123] Bannister, R.C. 1979. *Social Darwinism: Science and Myth in Anglo-American Social Thought.* Philadelphia: Temple University Press.

[124] Newnan, H.H. 1969. *Evolution, Genetics, and Eugenics.* New York: Greenwood Press.

[125] Betzig, LL. 1986. *Despotism and Differential Reproduction: A Darwinian View of History.* New York: Aldine.

[126] Rogers, C. 1951. *Client Centered Therapy.* Boston: Houghton Mifflin.; Rogers, C. 1961. *On Becoming a Person.* Boston: Houghton Mifflin.

[127] Lynch, F.R. 1997. *The Diversity Machine.* New York: The Free Press.

[128] Glendon, M.A. 1991. Rights Talk: The Impoverishment of Political Discourse. New York: Free Press.

[129] Bourdieu, P. 1990. *The Logic of Practice.* Stanford, CA: Stanford University Press.

[130] Goldwater, B.M. 1964. *Conscience of a Conservative.* New York: MacFadden-Bartell Corp.

[131] Ball, T. and Dagger, R. 1999. *Political Ideologies and the Democratic Ideal.* New York: Longman.

[132] Bork, R. 1996. *Slouching Toward Gomorrah: Modern Liberalism and American Decline.* New York: Regan Books.

[133] Bennett, W.J. (Ed.) 1993. *The Book of Virtues: A Treasury of Great Moral Stories.* New York: Simon & Schuster.

[134] Boot, M. 1998. *Out of Order: Arrogance, Corruption, and Incompetence on the Bench.* New York: Basic Books.

[135] Farber, D.A. and Sherry, S. 1997. *Beyond All Reason: The Radical Assault on Truth in American Law.* New York: Oxford University Press.

Chapter 8

Bobos in Limbo

The inherent vice of capitalism is the unequal sharing of blessings; the inherent virtue of socialism is the equal sharing of miseries. (Winston Churchill, Saying)

CONSERVATIVE. n. A statesman who is enamored of existing evils, as distinguished from the Liberal, who wishes to replace them with others. (Ambrose Bierce, The Devil's Dictionary)

What a chimera then is man! What a novelty! What a monster, what a chaos, what a contradiction, what a prodigy! Judge of all things, feeble earthworm, depository of truth, a sink of uncertainty and error, the glory and the shame of the universe. (Blaise Pascal, Pensees)

Bobos

David Brooks[1] is owed a debt of gratitude for introducing the term "bobo" into our lexicon. Related to the concept "yuppie," the appellation places a critical segment of the middle class in historical context. The yuppies were young, upwardly mobile professionals. They were go-getters on the rise, whereas the bobos are defined as "bourgeois-bohemians." This clever elision calls attention to the artistic connections of many of the recently successful. Brooks begins his ethnography of what is mistakenly labeled "the new upper class" by exploring changes that occurred in the New York Times society section. During the 1950s, the paper routinely identified couples about to be married by the prominent families to which they belonged. The WASP establishment was then very much intact. It took pride in its heritage and the nation's most prominent newspaper was happy to collude in this. To quote Brooks, one such notice read: "She [the bride] is descended from Richard Warren, who came to

Brookhaven in 1664. Her husband, a descendent of Dr. Benjamin Treadwell, who settled in old Westbury in 1767, is an alumnus of Gunnery School and a senior at Colgate University."[2] The towns in which the parties lived, and the fortunes to which they were heir, clearly took precedence over personal achievements. And, as clearly, the longer their pedigree, the better.

By the 60s, this had begun to change and by the 90s the style was radically different. Not only had ethnics, such as Jews and Italians, replaced the Episcopalian elite,[3] but their claims to higher status rested on other grounds. They were part of an emerging educated class. Instead of families of recent immigrant origin taking pride in their roots, the new wedding notices featured the couple's own accomplishments. The bride might be described as a graduate of Yale University who was employed as a buyer by Bonwitt-Teller, whereas the groom would be recognized as having received a degree from Princeton and now working for a Wall Street law firm. Again to cite Brooks, as of 1999 a reader of the wedding section "learned that Stuart Anthony Kingsley…graduated magna cum from Dartmouth and got an MBA from Harvard on the way to becoming a partner at McKinsey & Company. His father was a trustee of the National Trust for Historic Preservation, and his mother an overseer of the Boston Symphony Orchestra…"[4] Thus, even the WASP elite had begun to justify their inclusion by personal or family achievements. Their lineages might be long, but it was education, expertise, and service that earned them notice.

The bobos, who edged their way to privileged status, were very much a product of the middle class. Prominent, not because of their fortunes, or those of their ancestors, they were instead eager to be portrayed as "the best and the brightest."[5] Theirs was a dominance predicated on the exercise of power, and this power was predicated on what they knew. As a result, they were not given to ostentatious display[6]. Long gone were the palatial estates of the Robber Barons.[7] The bobos might have multi-million dollar apartments just off Park Avenue and even more expensive ski lodges in Aspen, but they were not fawned over by battalions of servants. Like President Jimmy Carter,[8] they were prepared to carry their own luggage. Flagrant luxuries struck them as pretentious. They were just ordinary folks whose jobs happened to provide a comfortable living. Painfully aware that they were not Vanderbilts,[9] or Astors,[10] most did not want to be. They were content to be hard-working professionals whose prestige derived from their social contributions.

If the bobos were not into luxuries, they were into lavish necessities. Brooks presents what he calls the bobo "code of financial correctness." According to this list of conventions, it is virtuous to spend $25, 000 on one's bathroom, but not $15,000 on a sound system. Top of the line leather patent leather shoes are a no, no, whereas pricey hiking boots are not. Kitchen equipment is definitely okay, no matter the cost, but purchasing a Corvette, rather than an SUV, is tasteless. It is also "perfectly acceptable to spend lots of money on anything that is of 'professional quality,' even if it has nothing to do with your profession."[11] Paying $300 for a "multi-purpose industrial-strength toasting system," therefore makes more sense than paying $30 for an ordinary toaster. These pretend journeymen often congregate together in "Latte Towns" such as Boulder, Colorado and Burlington, Vermont, where they revel in upscale coffee shops and arts and craftsy main streets. Dedicated to the games of their youth, they flaunt a healthy physicality. Much like over-grown college students, they enjoy demonstrating that they can still play tennis or skipper a sailboat. Then too, they love nature. They dote on climbing mountains to appreciate their beauty. Dedicated environmentalists, they are committed to saving virgin forests, rather than cutting them down. Besides, this naturalness is good for one's health. Jogging around the reservoir in the morning and eating greens for lunch preserves one into a vigorous old age. Evidently not only are the bobos smart in business; they are smart in their personal lives.

Emblematic of the bobo mentality are Ben and Jerry of Ben and Jerry's Ice Cream. Vermont based refugees from New York, they learned how to make their product from a library book. They then proceeded to name their politically correct flavors for their culture heroes, e.g. Cherry Garcia. More importantly, they have been ostentatious in supporting liberal causes. The bobos may be successful professionals, but they harbor an antibusiness mentality. Comprehending themselves as erudite specialists, they resent the managers they perceive as the real bosses. In their view, they are hardworking employees, whereas these executives are the loutish heirs of the old bourgeoisie. Even when self-employed, the bobos regard themselves as oppressed under-dogs. They, as opposed to more business-oriented types, are creative in their approach. Definitely not power-hungry parasites, they contribute their ingenuity for the good of mankind. Self-expression, not insensitive control, is their forte. Though they make innumerable business decisions, they reject any association with a profit motive. Theirs is the world of the intellectual and the artist, not of the avaricious capitalist.

Bobos, whether they understand it or not, are cultural specialists. Because their power derives from their education, they identify with pursuing knowledge and beauty for their own sake. The old-line bohemians[12] clustered on the fringe of polite society, yet were aggressively excluded from it. Prosperous capitalists might patronize their productions, but these unconventional creators themselves lived in scruffy poverty. The new bohemians, in contrast, find themselves smack-dab amongst the bourgeoisie. Living upscale lifestyles, their self-conceptions are nevertheless those of the impoverished outsider. While not aesthetic innovators on anything like the scale of their forebears, they aspire to this standing. Decidedly not organizational conformists, most are nevertheless tied to corporate giants, either as employees or contractual providers. Apt to depict themselves as hierarchically feeble, regardless of their poormouthing, they set the standards for these establishments. They dictate what is tasteful, what is linguistically appropriate, and what is morally acceptable. As the lawyers, the doctors, and the artistic directors of untold companies, they determine what is within bounds and what is doable. In this, they are guided by cultural principles derived from the bohemian past. What they believe is proper often has more to do with what these antecedents thought than with what works in the here and now.

The chief innovation of the bobos is in how they manage self-direction.[13] Avowed enemies of bureaucratic institutions, they loathe the technical rationality it theoretically embodies. Max Weber dissected organizations he thought were tightly controlled by scientifically validated procedures.[14] In the quest for efficiency, these institutions ostensibly sought to banish the human factor in favor of impersonal rules. Such rigidity does not, however, appeal to individuals invested in creative autonomy. Having majored in the arts, the humanities, and the social sciences, they are not about to defer to the authority of MBAs or engineers.[15] When they make decisions, they wish these to be in flagrant disregard of systematic rationality—or so it would seem. Bobo self-direction is grounded more in aesthetics, emotion, and self-expression. They go with their gut-feelings, not with cut-and-dried regulations. In fact, energetic and competitive, they affect an easy-going cooperativeness. From their mouths roll forth collectivist platitudes, yet their behaviors speak a different language. The situation is exemplified in an episode of the television program Law and Order, where a Hollywood executive explains that she works with people who talk like hippies, but who act like members of the Sicilian mob. Utterly cutthroat in their tactics, as they twist in the knife, they justify what they are doing in artistic and humanist terms.

Caught in a time warp, many bobos feel more controlled than controlling. Excruciatingly aware of their personal limitations, they appropriate an historical rationalization to vindicate their shortcomings. Part of being a social leader is dealing with uncertainties, which means making some choices that will not work out. Being able to blame these on the wayward foolishness of uncouth managers can, therefore, be psychologically comforting. Obviously the greed and narrow-mindedness of these supreme leaders is at fault. The bobo, however, is guided by an impeccable sense of what is appropriate. Individual feelings and tastes cannot go wrong, especially when these are imputed to moral sources. In this, the cultivated bobo is in touch with the natural, and perhaps spiritual, springs of correct behavior. Much as the old bohemians were certain of their muses, their cultural descendents are as romantically inspired. This means that they cannot be wrong; nor be blamed for what goes wrong. The problem must be with the system, or those in charge of it—never themselves. Though, in fact, responsible for many critical decisions, they do not feel responsible.

Politically, the bobos have become the standard-bearers of liberalism. Flamboyantly in sympathy with progress, this is conceived of in antiestablishment terms. Because they do not pride themselves on being pillars of the system, but rather as its victims, they feel justified in agitating for its dismemberment. Indeed, the bobos and modern liberalism were born in the same crucible. They both came to prominence as the hippie eruption subsided. When the blatant bohemianism of the flower children proved a disappointment, its aspirations were transferred to more politicized objectives. Members of the middle class who were disillusioned with the oppressive discipline of their jobs appropriated this reformist reaction for their own purposes. Uncomfortable both with internalized rules and restraints on their social mobility, they adopted a philosophy opposed to both. They too would fight for a world in which social stratification was abolished, but would do so using the tools of the middle class. Well educated, and familiar with the means of social organization, they would turn these skills to the task of achieving complete equality. Though they would be appalled by the suggestion, their liberalism was a variety of political romanticism. With their goals largely determined by emotional reactions, they were even given to theatrical politics. For them, dramatic promises replaced careful evaluations in deciding public policy. It became enough for office seekers to indicate that they "cared" about the welfare of their constituents; they didn't actually need to do anything to promote it. Likewise, as long as they proclaimed their approval of cooperation, they could be as competitive as they pleased.

Brooks describes the bobos as living in paradise.[16] He notes both their political ascendancy and the comfort in which they live. He also suggests that they have achieved a stable adjustment to contemporary conditions. According to him, "we are not living in an age of transition. We are living just after an age of transition. We are living just after the culture war that roiled American life for a generation. Between the 1960s and the 1980s the forces of bohemia and the force of the bourgeoisie launched their final offensives.... But out of that climactic turmoil a new reconciliation has been forged. A new order and a new establishment have settled into place...."[17] This new order is the bobo order. It supposedly combines the bohemian and the bourgeois in a stable compromise that satisfies both sides of the dispute—and the nation as well. The new elite, namely this culturally dominant middle class, can, owing to its ingenious rationalizations,[18] exercise leadership responsibilities without having to acknowledge them. It can apply its skills and energies for the common good, without anyone admitting that the old elite has been superceded.

Nevertheless, there is reason to believe this is overly optimistic. The culture wars are not yet over; they have not even taken a respite. Today's sulfurous politics do not include the riots of yesteryear, but they hardly bespeak a renewed "era of good feelings." The antagonisms continue to run deep because a durable settlement has not been achieved.[19] Rather than the bobos being in paradise, they are more accurately described as hovering in limbo. Caught between a bohemian lifestyle they cannot truly emulate and leadership responsibilities they have not fully embraced, they do not rest easy. Theirs is a temporary stopping place. Because it sits on a foundation of contradictions, the so-called "bobo reconciliation" promises to be torn asunder. Since much of what is being attempted is impossible, it cannot come to fruition. For similar reasons, camouflaged resentments directed toward the old establishment portend difficulties. Eventually these hatreds must be seen for what they are and resented. The current resolution runs only along the surface, with oppositionalist policies frequently breaking through. Many of the players persist in doing things designed to injure their enemies rather than to accomplish positive objectives. Thus they press for regulations to hamper despised business interests or they promote a sexual promiscuity that cannot be good for the next generation, irrespective of the consequences. Sooner or later this must redound against community interests and motivate fresh efforts to find a workable solution. Despite Brooks's assurances, the transitional period has not ended. Still a work in progress, much remains to be done. Where this middle class reaction will come to rest is not certain, but that it is not yet reached this place is.

The Liberal Hegemony

Liberalism has a reputation for being the wave of the future,[20] whereas it is actually an undertow from the past. While its champions claim that is the herald of things to come, it reverberates with ideas derived from times long gone. Although liberalism has not lived up to its promises, it has nevertheless become the dominant force in contemporary politics.[21] In the United States and Western Europe it is currently the default position. In both of these middle class societies, criticisms of the market economy, and of those at its apex, have become standard fare. This is a fact of life. The momentary state of the cultural wars may obscure this verity, but it needs to be explained. Even though liberals present themselves as an embattled minority, while conservatives assert that the liberal advantage is merely temporary, this is because both are embroiled in a desperate battle. Each side is seeking to define the situation in tactically advantageous terms. Thus, liberals derogate their favorable position lest their allies grow complacent, whereas conservatives boast of modest victories to inflate their apparent strength.

Still and all, liberalism is the contemporary gold standard. It declarations are widely considered pure and free from the taint of avarice. Although what conservatives advocate was traditional within the recent past, nowadays it is castigated as "extremist."[22] Amazingly, should the traditionalists come to the defense of the market system, they are immediately suspected of greedily oppressing the disenfranchised. Or if they argue on behalf of merit, they are dismissed was favoring their associates. Meanwhile, liberal promises of total equality are assumed to be realizable. The conditions they endorse may never have existed among human beings, but these are regarded as what would prevail if opposing forces did not intervene. Moreover, liberals are assumed to favor "progress." They want to bring about changes for the better, whereas conservatives, in Ambrose Bierce's[23] memorable words, "are enamored of existing evils." Apparently suffering from inborn anxieties, they are too apprehensive to experiment with up-to-the-minute solutions. Unlike the liberals, they do not possess the courage to peer into the future or to conceive of substantial improvements.

Liberalism has become the international orthodoxy wherever the industrial revolution has triumphed. In Western Europe conservatives have occasionally prevailed at the polls, but they have scarcely been able to undo the nationalizing impulses that convulsed the continent immediately following the last World War. Deeply steeped in welfare economics, their governments continue to tax their citizens for "essential" services. More particularly, national medical programs tend to be state run and vacations centrally mandated. Likewise traumatized by Nazism and the Cold War, ordinary people have opted for a civilized pacifism. They do not want to see their homes or families devastated, hence when conservatives urge them to take defensive measures, they reject these out of hand. Even when the United States, an ocean away, was shaken into an anti-terrorist resolve and decided to invade Iraq, they were outraged. Perhaps an embargo might do, but once this was demonstrated to be ineffective, actual combat remained unthinkable. Much preferred was hand wringing about the environment and global warming. The Green parties, not the neo-fascists, created the stir in the streets.

In the United States, despite the successes of Richard Nixon and Ronald Reagan,[24] liberalism has continued to set the agenda. Nixon,[25] on account of his earlier anti-communist grandstanding, was commonly reckoned to be a die-heart conservative, but that was not how he governed. Not only did he preside over the opening to Communist China,[26] but he instituted significant extensions to affirmative action and, when inflation arose, he imposed price controls. Reagan was more conservative, but found that the only way to control government spending was to create budget deficits. This was necessary because congress continued to enact programs aimed at solving a raft of imagined problems. The best he was able to achieve was a political stalemate. With each new electoral cycle politicians continued to promise legislation to satisfy the latest political itch. Their proposals to end racism, sexism, poverty, or medical inequality regularly crowded the legislative calendar. The public might hate higher taxes, but it clung to its love affair with government-sponsored benefits. Nonetheless, there arose a split between the urbanized coasts and the less professionalized heartland. So-called "blue" states like New York[27] and California became reliably liberal in national elections. The bobos that increasingly populated their voter lists hailed government initiatives and tilted toward candidates who supported them. They even contributed record amounts to their campaigns. From their perspective, liberalism was enlightened self-interest. Conservatives were, in comparison, consigned to a holding operation. The best they could usually muster was to slow the liberal impetus.

Another indicator of the supremacy of the liberal establishment was the spread of political correctness (PC).[28] Despite the ridicule such super-sensitivities elicited among ordinary people, its prohibitions became a national obsession. Formerly unexceptional words were no longer allowed—on pain of ostracism. Women could not be called girls or airline stewardesses "stewardesses." They were now "flight attendants."[29]   The greatest sensitivities dealt with race. Though a host of four-letter words began to seep past the censors, this did not include the "N-word." It was strictly off limits. Talking about "Negroes" or "colored people" is impolite, but alluding to "niggers"[30] is vicious. So malicious was this considered that when detective Mark Fuhrman was discovered to have employed it in private eight years before the O.J. Simpson trial,[31] this was taken as prima facie evidence that he was a racist and, therefore, that his testimony could not be trusted. Without any additional proof, jurors jumped to the conclusion that he must have planted the incriminating glove. As a result, they acquitted a person that the nation perceived to be a cold-blooded killer.

Liberals tend to believe in the inevitability of their dominance. Just as Marxists at one time boasted that they were on the side of history, these semiMarxists sense that impending developments are ineluctably trending as they prefer. Liberalism promises a bobo millennium. Once the cold hand of capitalism is lifted from the throats of workingpersons, everyone will be free to be his/her self. The "system" will no longer repress self-expression; hence along with complete equality will come complete freedom. What they fail to add is that they will be in control[32] of these events. As their sponsors, they intend to preside over the implementation of the required reforms. The bobos also claim that they will eliminate competition. In their future, cooperation will win out because fair-mined people will recognize its virtues. What is not mentioned is the parallel between their situation and that of the early capitalists. Adam Smith[33] is famed for remarking that no one hated competition more than business people. They realized that unbridled struggles over market share could result in bankruptcy. In response, whenever they got together, they colluded to fix prices. Best of all was monopolistic control of the marketplace. This guaranteed profits without the anxiety of trying to out-do one's competitors. Bobos too despise the uncertainties of scuffling for success. Their goals may be more cultural, entailing the triumph of ideas or aesthetics, but these too are open to defeat. Abolishing competition would, at least in their imaginations, preserve them from this fate. In their future, there will be no losers—especially among themselves.

Paradoxically, liberalism is more reactionary than liberal. For the better part of a century, liberalism has been identified with social change. High school civics classes routinely define it as the political doctrine that promotes prudent reforms. Thought to be inherently forward-looking, it has been described as the opposite of conservative. Nevertheless, liberalism would reinstall ancient social structures if it could. The names may change, but the patterns are of primordial vintage. Just because people proclaim an allegiance to progress does not prevent them from looking backwards. Thus Joseph Stalin[34] described the collective farms he was imposing on the rural Soviet Union as a prelude to communist democracy, whereas they were like nothing so much as a reincarnation of the old-time estates of the Russian boyars.[35] In both cases, the peasants were ruled from above. The only difference is that under Stalin, the effective owners were the party apparatchiks. A similar allegation can be lodged against Napoleon Bonaparte.[36] Although he proclaimed himself the embodiment of the French Revolution,[37] he had himself crowned Emperor. To the end of his days he portrayed himself as the champion of liberty, whereas he had in reality attempted to reinstate a draconian form of absolutist rule.

Liberals too are absolutists. In their love of government programs, they continuously press for centralized rule. Remarkably like the communists, they assume that they are smarter than other people and, therefore, that they know what is good for them. Better educated than their peers, they readily imagine themselves in the role of "philosopher king."[38] Once triumphant, they would surely work for the benefit of their fellow citizens. In this, they would also be uncannily effective. As a natural "intelligentsia," they would accurately assess their constituents' true interests. And because contemporary technology permits improved communications, as the central planners, they would implement these more efficaciously than did a Louis XIV.[39] Instantly transmitted orders would be quickly monitored regarding their results and the information revolution would make the ensuing decisions more relevant. Added to this, an unparalleled command of the facts would enable them to determine the most cost-effective ways to achieve communal goals. Given the advantages of this sort of centralized command, it was their duty to quash opposing forces. Where the Sun King was once preoccupied with drawing the fangs of the French nobility, their destiny was to reduce the power of commercial interests. Forever on the alert to corporate corruption, they needed to minimize the resources available to bourgeois leaders. Among the tools for achieving this would be crippling taxes and complex regulations. By imposing either or both, they would prevent greedy plutocrats from doing further mischief. Left out of these calculations, however, was the mischief of an unopposed liberal dominion. That it too might become corrupt was unimaginable.

Liberals are also romantic naturalists. They want to turn back the clock to a time before human interference distorted Nature. Rousseau's[40] noble savages never existed, but today's college educated observers are aware that there was a time when our ancestors were hunter-gatherers. During this Golden Age, people presumably dealt with each other as their biology decreed that they should. Men and women were total equals; and no one was the paramount chief. Humankind lived in large, extended families where they treated each other like honored relatives—because they were. Inherently loving, they had not yet been crippled by the competitive pressures of commercialization. This is taken as an article of liberal faith; one redeemable only by dismantling the machinery sustaining the Industrial Revolution. How could it be doubted that if people get back to nature, they would thereby get back to their true selves? This was clearly what the Unabomber thought. Albeit a grotesque offshoot of the liberal ideal, in his manifesto justifying random killings he vilified industrialism as heartily as might any nature child. Leaning upon his mathematical training, he was simply more explicit in drawing out the implications of this thesis than most.

In many ways liberalism represents a fusion of Marxism and bohemianism. Though the "liberal" designation has been around for many years, in its current manifestation it is relatively recent. At the dawn of the twentieth century, what was to become modern liberalism was associated with progressivism[41] and socialism.[42] The excesses of rampant industrialization had already become apparent, as had the discomforts of urbanization. Progressives like Theodore Roosevelt[43] wished to fix these by tinkering with the system. They sought legislation to curb the abuses of the monopolists and to insure healthful products in the marketplace. The socialists, however, sought bolder solutions. They wanted the government to control all property. This, they insisted, was the only way to enforce economic justice. Nevertheless—although Eugene Debs did well in the voting booth—most Americans were fearful of such dramatic change. They preferred to be cautious, especially after the Russian Revolution sent a shudder through elite circles. In fact, it was not until the 1916 presidential campaign that the editors of The New Republic, in an effort to distinguish their position from the fading progressives, popularized the "liberal" label.[44] This term had international cachet because of its prior use in Europe, but it now took on more democratic overtones. Soon, however, the prosperity of the roaring twenties was to make an enormous social upheaval, in any form, seem superfluous.

The Great Depression[45] changed all this, and incidentally made liberalism more respectable. With capitalism falling apart, the do-nothing Republicanism of Coolidge seemed insufficient. Something had to be done. Franklin Roosevelt[46] did his best to administer the appropriate medicine. Himself a scion of the upper class, he did not intend to destroy his country's heritage. Nonetheless his administration was riddled with activists who did. As a consequence, socialist, and to some extent communist, solutions found their way into his policies. These did not, however, dominate. A sort of compromise was reached. The New Deal blend of capitalism with collectivism was to prove the underpinning of modern liberalism.[47] The role of the government was significantly enhanced, but it did not assume an ownership function. For ordinary people, there was the safety net of social security, for workers support for unionization; for business people regulation to prevent speculation and profiteering. The government would be the final arbiter of what was fair and under dire circumstances would provide the stimulus to restart the economy.

This compromise was to outlast the return of normalcy under Eisenhower.[48] Although a Republican, he made few efforts to undo the policies that underwrote confidence in the system. Yet liberalism in its ascendant format was really to take shape during the 1960s. First under Kennedy,[49] but more decisively under Johnson,[50] it became political dogma. The movement from the hippie reaction to political romanticism has already been outlined, but how this resulted in a fusion of Marxism and bohemianism has not. The bohemianism of the hippies is patent, as was their idealistic inefficiency. Indeed, it was this inefficiency that the emerging Marxist element sought to rectify. If there were to be genuine reforms, *i.e.*, if complete parity was to come to fruition, the activists would need more than flower power—they would require well-planned interventions. At the time, conventional wisdom held that centralized planning was inherently more effective than unsupervised market transactions. Communists might be mean-spirited, but they were also supremely rational. Thus, if the lingering socialism of the 30s were combined with the warmheartedness of the hippies, it might be possible to correct the defects of both. What the Europeans called "social democracy" could then come into being, with ordinary people protected by a government that genuinely cared about them. Racism, sexism, and poverty[51] would succumb to social engineering presided over by an educated middle class that retained the idealism of the flower children. Some might describe this as governmentally enforced love, but reformers intoxicated by visions of universal ecstasy were undeterred. They had seen the light at the end of the tunnel, and it was a liberal light.

Liberalism[52] glowed with such vivacity because it incorporated, or seemed to incorporate, crucial middle class values. Peace, equality, and rationality were the apparent bedrock of democratic prosperity. To enhance and intensify these could only be good. Marxism, in piggybacking on these, made its projections seem compassionate. No war for any reasons, equality in all things, and rationality administered by intellectuals would make a good thing better. These themes did not include freedom because it seemed to Americans raised on assurances of liberty that this was a foregone conclusion. It did not occur to them that equality and freedom might sometimes be at odds. Nor could they imagine that equality would be coercively imposed. They were not that kind of people. They were Americans; *i.e.*, they were nice!

Universal niceness has indeed been one of the most enduring themes of liberalism. Forged in hippie friendliness, it assumed that if one is nice to others, they will reciprocate by being equally nice. There is no need to be coercive because everyone wants to be friendly if given the opportunity. The origins of this attitude can be found in children raised in middle class prosperity. Taught to share their toys, they were also instructed that when they did, their playmates would return the favor. It did not occur to middle class types that a propensity to share was contingent upon possessing surplus resources. They sincerely believed that even the meanest person would desist from evil if confronted with a broad smile and a welcoming handshake. This sort of niceness essentially combined the goals of peace and equality. In refusing to threaten others and, in treating them with respect, it sent the message that their aspirations toward parity would not be challenged. No one was going to force those on the bottom to settle for less; there was, consequently, no need to resort to defensive force. Everyone could be friendly because no one was going to exhibit any animosity. So compelling was this logic that even criminals could be rehabilitated once they were showered with ample doses of love and compassion.[53]

This was peace and equality as advanced by emotional means. Primarily a hippie, rather than a Marxist contribution, the role of warm feelings was raised to heroic proportions thanks to the Bohemian legacy. It created what some have dubbed a "social Marxism,"[54] *i.e.*, a Marxism based on Herbert Marcuse style love and sex.[55] The pivotal thesis was that if what was inside a person made him/her what he/she was, then surely placing this in contact with others would alter what they were. At a minimum, it would draw out emotional truths hidden deep within. No longer would there be tests of strength between individuals; only communication between kindred spirits. Gone too would be an impulse toward competition; replaced by a firmly entrenched commitment to be non-judgmental.[56] Also firmly installed would be a desire to be compassionate. People would want to feel empathy for others and this would impel them to help those in need of assistance. Furthermore, once their insides were exposed to each other, they could not help but experience sympathy. And once they were sympathetic, they would act benevolently.

One of the forms this compassion took was a defense of the underdog.[57] Those who did not have the power[58] to safeguard themselves could be equal only if others came to their rescue. Niceness demanded efforts at such universal protection. Left out of this assessment, however, was whether such interventions would be just. It was assumed that evening out differences was automatically fair.   Unfortunately, the reflexive emotionality of this attitude has been visited upon the Israelis, with results they would not consider appropriate.[59]   When the Jewish state was first established, most western nations supported its independence.   A couple of million Jews pitted against many tens of millions of Arabs did not seem to be a principled contest.   Initially it appeared that these refugees from the Holocaust might be pushed into the sea, but when they managed to hold their own, they were roundly applauded for their courage. For a while, they looked like an heroic David, who had felled an aggressive Goliath.   Then came the Six Days War and the Yom Kippur War.   During these, a well-equipped Israeli military soundly defeated Egypt, Jordan, and Syria.   This too seemed like the underdog coming out on top and was at first welcomed.   But as the years passed, the odds were turned on their head.   The longer the misery of the Palestinian refugee camps appeared on television screens, the more the losers began to seem like the real underdogs.   The Jews had been transmuted into an army of occupation and, in some eyes, into racist oppressors.   Despite the fact that Islamic fundamentalists still threatened to throw them into the sea, and the small detail that both sides were Semitic, they were scolded for taking repressive measures against suicide bombers.   Now depicted as terrorists for resisting terror, their capacity to protect themselves deprived them of their earlier sympathy, and converted many liberals into the allies of their foes.   The lesson was that niceness was accorded the weak rather than the strong; irrespective of the moral implications.

A second enduring theme of liberalism has been its adherence to centralization.   Planned economies, and cradle-to-grave welfare programs, appear rational to those who obtain their status from a cultural expertise.[60]   Intent on exercising these skills, they are certain the man on the street is too ill informed and too selfish[61] to make sound choices.   Despite protestations of being social democrats, they distrust democratic institutions; especially those of the marketplace. One of the clichés of American politics is that having to meet a payroll equips businesspeople with both a sense of responsibility and the personal discipline to oversee governmental budgets.   This surely goes too far—as the success of any number of nonbusiness politicos can testify.   Nevertheless, those who learn their administrative skills from ideological sources can be sadly deficient.   Cultural leaders, who develop their plans of action in bull sessions with their peers, easily go astray if they never get to test these in practice. They may believe that a perfectly balanced scheme for achieving a particular objective cannot help but succeed, only to discover too late that it will not. This has been one of the unwelcome lessons of social engineering. Programs, such as Head Start,[62] looked unstoppable on paper. How could providing minority children with personalized instruction before they entered grammar school not enable them to keep up with better-prepared peers? The only problem was that experience proved it did not. Though these youngsters made initial gains, these did not last past the fourth grade. This, however, did not prevent liberals from proposing a federal take-over of the nation's medical system. They were certain that they could manage one seventh of the country's economy more efficiently by placing it under the direction of a bevy of public agencies. Not even the experience of Medicare costs escalating wildly beyond the original predictions cautioned them to be modest.

Centralization is good for many things. When coordination and/or uniformity are called for, it is frequently the best approach. Nevertheless centralization does not automatically confer insight or wisdom. Because planners are subject to the hubris of power, they tend to over-estimate what they understand or can control. There is also a tendency to underestimate the appropriateness of socially negotiated outcomes. Indeed, processes in which no one has a preponderant voice strike them as anarchic. Combined with the liberal certitude in their innate goodness, there is an unwillingness to consider decentralized solutions. To the political romantics allowing others to address their own problems seems to tantamount to abdicating their duty to save their inferiors from themselves. It is to do nothing in the face of a palpable obstacle, which is equivalent to allowing problems to spiral out of control. That their proposed interventions might be irrational makes no sense to those bred to be proficient problem-solvers.[63]

A third enduring theme of liberalism is its ambivalence toward social rules.[64] On the one hand, rules are perceived as an essential tool of centralization. Those who sit in the middle of the social web know they must often implement decisions by promulgating laws and/or administrative regulations. Unless others are ordered to take action on pain of a specified sanction, they may not respond. Moreover, centralized rules, that is, approved forms of standardized behavior, are supposedly superior because those best able to determine what is for the common good have formulated them. Were individuals to go off on personal tangents, they would make grievous errors. They might, for instance, behave in a bigoted or unfair manner. On the other hand, standardized rules impose personal constraints. They prevent people from acting as individuals and convert them into virtual automatons. Such obligations are definitely inimical to creativity or self-expression. Nor do externally imposed controls allow people to be guided by their feelings or aesthetic sense. Intrinsically judgmental, uniform regulations provide no outlet for unconditional positive regard. They are, to be blunt, the diametric opposite of tolerance. In enforcing one-size-fits-all solutions, differences are submerged and conformity is demanded. Which is definitely not nice.

This, however, does not prevent liberals from endorsing some rules; or from doing so enthusiastically. If they believe that significant moral principles are at stake, they are eager to see them enforced. This was the case with the Supreme Court's decisions regarding integration. Whether or not "separate is inherently unequal" is literally true, they supported the use state power to act as if it were. The same is the case with Roe v. Wade.[65] When more democratic institutions failed to pass legislation making abortion legal, they turned to an un-elected court to do their bidding. After a mere majority of appointed justices eventually found a previously undiscovered constitutional right to privacy, they applauded its discernment. In their view, this protected freedom and was, therefore, an exception to their antipathy toward external directives. The same applies to the constraints of political correctness. Whether these standards are enshrined in university codes of permissible language, or are less formally enforced via ridicule, they are deemed justified omissions vis-à-vis the consecration of self-expression. Indeed, because they are intended to protect people, they are not regarded as rules, but as elementary common sense. This enables their advocates to engage in mental gymnastics to vindicate whatever they want. To illustrate, burning an American flag gets interpreted as a form of protected speech, whereas calling someone the N-word is regarded as a hostile act worthy of being banned. The liberal antagonism toward rules is thus managed by particularizing them. Instead of the universalization dominant within market relationships, a tactic more reminiscent of absolutism is preferred. The only way to predict which rules liberals will approve is first to distinguish between their friends and enemies. Despite unending protestations of an allegiance to principle, this is trimmed to fit the political exigencies of specific alliances. A Clarence Thomas[66] could surely explain why he, but not a Bill Clinton,[67] was condemned as sexist. Apparently making an off-color joke is more culpable than is engaging is sex with an intern, that is, if one is also opposed to Roe v. Wade.

Sitting cheek by jowl with particularized rules is liberal permissiveness. In the name of being nice, it is considered imperative not to offend people by demanding that they do what they are not inclined to do. This attitude has, first and foremost, been applied to the family.[68] Liberal parents frequently decide that it is better to be a child's friend than an authority figure.[69] Children who are allowed to get their way are placates their offspring when they protest against being punished. This way, their brood will love, rather than fear them. Spouses too are allowed free reign.[70] The object is to demonstrate that they are not pierces of property, but free to pursue pleasures in their own fashion. In perhaps the most bizarre manifestation of this phenomenon, partner swapping[71] has been advocated as the ultimate expression of interpersonal trust. The same approach also extends beyond the home, *e.g.*, to the school.[72] No longer is it to be regimented, but it must become a place dedicated to cultivating free expression and creativity. Children are not to be forced to sit silently in their seats, but are encouraged to decide what they want to learn and how they want to learn it. Old style discipline is rejected as tantamount to imprisonment.[73] Even dress codes are discarded as too restrictive. In essence, the liberal solution to an ambivalence regarding rules is that they are okay for others, but not for themselves or their friends. They (and their allies) are loving people who do not require external constraints to keep them in line.

Contradictions of Liberalism

Among liberals, it is an article of faith that capitalism is riven with contradictions.[74] A system based on decentralized commercialism and representative democracy is regarded as inherently unstable.[75] This analysis goes back at least as far as Marx.[76] He assumed that the same mechanisms that made the industrial order distasteful would eventually force its demise. One of the reasons the market-based system generated unprecedented prosperity was that its entrepreneurs were driven by greed. It was because they were seeking to accumulate as much as they could that they implemented profitable efficiencies. At the same time, in their unrelenting pursuit of riches, the fruits of their achievements were concentrated in ever fewer hands. This would ultimately alienate the workers who made this possible. Once they understood that they were being exploited, they would overthrow their masters. Out-numbered, and grown effete from luxury, the bourgeois hegemony would disappear as unconditionally as had the dominion of the dissolute Romans.

Undiscouraged by the failure of this prediction, the neo-Marxist element in liberalism still expects capitalism to crumble. Marx had not anticipated the rise of the middle class, nor its dominance within representative democracies, but this has not deterred his acolytes from uncovering fresh reasons for its imminent downfall. Daniel Bell,[77] who describes himself as a socialist in economic matters, is among these. He perceives an intrinsic conflict between the avariciousness of modern materialism and the asceticism necessary to finance economic growth. In the old days, when the Protestant Ethic[78] was operative, entrepreneurs willingly postponed gratification in order to invest in their enterprises. Fully expecting their reward in heaven, they could control their desires in the here and now in favor of was needed by their businesses. With affluence, however, came decadence. Those grown unimaginably rich could not refrain from indulging their private dreams. As some of their number began to say, "when you've got it, flaunt it."[79] Why not fly the Concorde to Europe to save a few hours? Why not purchase a sports car that can go one hundred and fifty miles an hour? What else is money for? This attitude effectively diverted them from commerce. It made the governing classes lazy and sidetracked their resources from more productive purposes.

In this, however, Bell is wrong. First, as to their laziness, this has no more occurred than did the impoverishment of the working classes. The middling orders, including the bobos, are, for the most part, very hard workers. They put in long hours and do so in a disciplined manner. Religious asceticism is evidently not necessary for commercial effort. People can be motivated by professionalism as well as by a desire to please God. Second, other ways to finance capital formation than through personal savings have been developed.[80] Contemporary capitalism invented numerous such mechanisms. To state but a few, stocks, bonds, and government programs all proved effective in concentrating the necessary funds. Corroboration of this is found in a constantly growing economy. Thus when computers were invented, they were not consigned to a back shelf because companies were strapped for cash. Nor did self-satisfied executives refuse to learn how to use them.

Bell[81] also suggests that there is a conflict between bureaucratization and a desire for self-expression. He characterizes the modern corporation as hide-bound by a devotion to detailed procedures and picky records keeping. This, he laments, contrasts sharply with the predilections of an educated workforce preoccupied with its emotional well-being. There is, to be sure, this sort of tension, but it is not true that the market has found no ways to cope with it. Just as Marx over-looked the emergence of the middle class, Bell discounts the emergence of a professionalized middle class. The specialization inherent in postindustrialization called forth an individuation that is indeed inconsistent with idealized forms of bureaucracy. Nevertheless professional workers are capable of a decentralized organization in which they control much of their own efforts. They, thereby, escape the close supervision that characterized early industrialization. Since their expertise and internal motivation permit more creativity and emotional independence than Bell imagined, they get to call the shots.

This said, adjusting to the on-going evolution of the Commercial Revolution entails more than an appeal to tradition. Because the past cannot be an infallible guide to the future, the ideals appropriate to primitive capitalism are insufficient to its more recent professionalized form. The nature of interpersonal honesty, social responsibility, and family relationships cannot be identical in a mass society. A certain level of social experimentation has, therefore, been inevitable. So has a conflict between increasingly divergent moral perspectives. Indeed, this is essential as a means of testing revised solutions. Liberalism itself has put forward an assortment of such social innovations, while traditionalists have challenged the validity of these proposals in an effort to find something better. Each side of this culture war is convinced of its correctness, but the eventual resolution is likely to differ from what either would find ideal. That which works under emergent conditions is invariably beyond the ability of the participants to foresee.

What is clear is that the liberal solutions have proved no more satisfactory than would have an unalloyed traditionalism. To judge from the nascent disorders of the Great Disruption,[82] they too failed to resolve the dilemmas thrown up by the Middle Class Revolution. Questions about how to handle prosperity, a revised division of labor, and self-direction among professionals have not yielded to their idealism. Specifically, they have not reconciled the conflict between emotional spontaneity and rational calculation. If anything, the contradictions of liberalism are more serious than those of traditional capitalism. Ideologues who attempt to execute their visions verbatim are in for grievous disappointments. Because their dreams always include inconsistencies, they can never deliver precisely as promised. As an example, more often than not, the centralized and naturalistic mechanisms said to promote peace, equality, and rationality are incapable of doing so. They certainly cannot promote these simultaneously. To illustrate, liberalism implies that it can supply both equality and freedom. But this is a vain assurance. The situation is rather like that to which Winston Churchill[83] alluded after Neville Chamberlain came back from Munich promising "peace in our times." Churchill observed that the prime minister had chosen peace over honor, but would eventually have neither. Liberals likewise tend to choose equality over freedom and are destined to achieve neither.

Liberalism, in shunning market-oriented values such as responsibility, merit, and discipline, does not help professionals adjust to their newfound powers.[84] Instead of assisting them in applying their expertise and motivation, it offers comfort via a fictitious, never-never land of pipe dreams. Far from being compassionate, or even moral, it undermines its aspirations through its grandiosity. Taking idealism too far ensures the opposite of what is desired. A platitude most children learn is that the road to hell is paved with good intentions. This is as true of the liberals as it was of the hippies. Despite their hopes, a resort to Marxist embellishments did not provide rationalism so much as an additional layer of fantasy. Paradoxically, liberals go on to denounce conservatives as mean-spirited and cold-hearted. Their adversaries are assumed either to be callous computing machines or greedy monsters. Alleged to suffer from a condition analogous to that of the Conquistadors when Cortez told the Aztecs that his Spaniards had a disease that could only be cured by gold, they too are labeled terminally avaricious. Nevertheless, in believing this, liberals demonstrate their own emotional immaturity. In refusing to see people, including their enemies, as complex human beings, they confirm an idealistic short-sightedness.

To begin with, liberals specialize in "invidious goodness."[85] They condemn their moral competitors as "bad," that is, in comparison with themselves.[86] Instead of modestly performing good works, they ostentatiously proclaim a dedication to these in order to put others down. As they tell it, they are the ones that care about the poor and downtrodden; whereas the traditionalists do not. They compassionately feel other's pain, whereas conservatives are self-involved egoists. In essence, their opponents are censured for not living up to liberal standards. But in making this claim, they engage in the very behavior of which they theoretically disapprove. Ironically, they are the ones being "mean" when they insist on rubbing in their goodness. Were they truly moral, they would let their deeds speak for themselves.

Nor is liberal relativism inherently moral.[87] Those who tolerate everything, including the intolerable, have no standards. When they accept whatever is as right, because they are not prepared to judge anything as wrong, they perforce accept conditions others would recognize as morally abhorrent. Thus, were some people to find slavery, human sacrifice, or genocide to their taste, on what grounds could these be criticized? The consistent relativist must desist from outlawing cannibalism or ethnic cleansing should those who commit these deeds believe them valid. If unconditional positive regard cannot be withheld for any reason, the true relativist is barred from expressing disagreement. Deep down most liberals know this. In fact, they do disagree with many practices—often vehemently. Rather than stand quietly aside while others engage in racism or sexism, they protest. Nor are they troubled by Emerson's[88] criticizing the "foolish consistencies" as "hobgoblins of little minds." Inconsistent though they may be, they are addicted to particularizing. Regularly making ad hoc judgments about their opponent's shortcomings, they exempt conservatives from their strictures of tolerance. As the bad guys of their moral universe, those on the right side of the aisle are admonished for their purported callousness. Meanwhile, their friends, *e.g.*, the feminists, are not allowed to languish without assistance. Like other human beings, liberals delight in hurling verbal barbs at their foes, while regaling their allies with praise. Theirs is thus a selective compassion. They may feel for the agony of the street junky, but they gloat when a Rush Limbaugh reveals he is addicted to painkillers. For them, the anguish of the "little guy" is far more repugnant than that of an articulate opponent.

Worse still is the immorality of the short horizon. Liberals tend to make extravagant promises without fretting about their long-term consequences. It matters less to them whether their programs work than whether they promise to work. If increasing the minimum wage is intended to put money in the pockets of the poor, but, in fact, results in their becoming unemployed, they will continue to advocate for it. If bi-lingual education[89] is sold as facilitating the assimilation of immigrant children, but produces a generation incompetent in English, at least they tried. The difficulty with this approach is that ignoring predictable consequences is equivalent to not caring about what happens to people. It is to live in a fantasy world where actual pain counts for less than imagined pleasures. After all, in the Antebellum South, slaveholders justified their peculiar institution by insisting that they were intent on civilizing their property. They did not consider themselves immoral because they overlooked the many injuries thereby inflicted. In contemporary America, something analogous occurs with regard to school discipline. It is anathematized as inflicting force on the powerless without regard to the implications of abolishing social control. Samuel Bowles castigates classroom order as a means of channeling poor children into work as factory laborers. Yet were he to peer further into the future, he would perceive that these external disciplines instigate the internal disciplines vital for social mobility. Merely letting children do whatever they please implicitly consents to their ignorance and subsequent failure. Similarly, advocating multicultural families on the grounds that this permits individual freedom is to doom the poor to single parent households that cannot prepare them for economic advancement. It is to promote short-term expediency over the long-term happiness of millions of innocents.

Nor is liberalism particularly nice.[90] Coercion is alleged to be the domain of traditionalists who believe in such things as spanking small children. Yet there is more than one way to be coercive. One can also inflict force indirectly. One can, for instance, impose it without overt acknowledgement. Liberals proclaim that they are always kind, but because they want to win, they frequently play rough. Human experience is such that everyone learns that excessive niceness is an invitation to exploitation. People who never stand up for themselves are habitually relegated to the leftovers. The result is that most individuals discover how to be assertive. Some disguise their aggressiveness by accusing others of being nasty, but upon closer inspection themselves inflict pain. Thus throwing conservatives out of academic positions on the grounds that they are not being collegial surely qualifies as unkind. So does destroying the newspapers of campus Republicans when they publish unwelcome editorials. Name-calling, which has become a liberal staple, is likewise not very nice. Sticks and stones break bones, but names break spirits. Even so, deadly violence is not excluded from the liberal arsenal. The lengths to which they can go—and this is admittedly an atypical case—was demonstrated by the Weather Underground.[91] An offshoot of the Students for a Democratic Society,[92] this faction of urban terrorists came to the conclusion that peace would never arrive through persuasion alone. When politicians failed to heed their warnings, they decided to bomb them into compliance. Sadly, peaceful demonstrations also have a way of escalating into violent confrontations. When frustrated, idealists have a way of mutating into Molotov cocktail-throwing thugs.

Contrary to expectations, a less direct means of liberal coercive is tolerance itself. One of the contradictions of naïve niceness is that it is impotent against the truly nasty. When everything is treated as equal and, therefore, as deserving of the same protection, the intolerant are given a helping hand in becoming dominant. This is an unintended implication of multiculturalism. Contemporary democracy did not come into being full-blown.[93] It evolved through an accretion of norms, values, and attitudes. A tolerance of political differences, for instance, emerged from innumerable street clashes and many contested elections. To be more specific, the Irish, when they arrived on American shores were initially regarded as heretical bog-hoppers. They later earned respect, in part, when urban riots made them a force to be reckoned with. On the other hand, they were only gradually recruited into democratic practices.[94] It took time for them to resort to the ballot box, and even longer to desist from stuffing it. Yet nowadays the progeny of these once squalid outsiders are as horrified by electoral fraud as any native Protestant. They too reckon electoral honesty intrinsic of the structure of democracy; that, were it not widespread, would dictate elections counting for naught.

Yet multiculturalists show little reverence for this normative infrastructure. In advocating tolerance and equality, they simultaneously advocate the rights of minorities who are opposed to democratic traditions. As good relativists, they are apologists for groups like the Black Panthers when they aim to impose their will at gunpoint. While they oppose the KKK[95] and skinhead militias, they readily find excuses for draft card burners. The Palestinians, in particular, are given a free pass for their suicide bombers and Islamists, in general, are excused for promoting Jihad.[96] What seems not to be appreciated is that were these minorities to get their way, democratic traditions would erode and with them the protections they offer. Idealists who loathe coercion, therefore, pave the way for coercion imposed by those currently too weak to impose it. On behalf of equality, they empower precisely the sort of people who do not accept the equality of others.[97] Paradoxically, in their unsophisticated niceness, they assume that egalitarian pluralism is possible in a world where not everybody is benevolent; in one where hierarchy is a biological imperative and not a momentary aberration.[98]

By the same token, to be against internal discipline is implicitly to favor random violence. As per Rousseau,[99] human beings may be born with kindly impulses, but they also come equipped with angry and vengeful ones. As any mother knows, frustrated infants are capable of temper tantrums. Were these to go unsocialized, in the hands of adults, they could prove fatal. Like Ivan the Terrible,[100] who in a towering rage stuck down his own son, ordinary parents might kill their youngsters over trivial disagreements. Ivan, as Czar of all the Russias, grew up believing that he could do whatever he wished. Most ordinary people learn otherwise. They are taught to feel guilt when their anger passes certain bounds. As a result, they become their own keepers. Though they may have violent thoughts, they develop the means of keeping these under wraps. Advocates of unrestrained niceness inadvertently open the cage containing the monsters from the id. Despite their pipe dreams, because everyone is both nice and nasty, everyone must learn to encourage one and restrain the other.

When liberals heap scorn upon the traditional family because they perceive it as an impediment to self-expression, they inadvertently encourage impulsive violence.[101] Likewise, when they describe the nuclear family as a prison that should be breached by sponsoring other formats, they interfere with inculcating personal discipline. Every society has some form of family because every society has found it essential to socializing its young. Unless children acquire basic rules, including emotional rules, they become the enemies of social order.[102] In the contemporary middle class universe, neither an orderly marketplace nor peaceful democracy would be possible without them. The virtue of the family is that it provides the emotional supports and the close instruction crucial to instilling what is needed. Self-discipline is a significant accomplishment that is facilitated by loving relationships and expert counsel. The insecure and the uninstructed are unguided missiles. They become indiscriminately coercive because they are incapable of better. This makes the family, as it were, the workshop of civilization. To suppose that it might be supplanted by public education or government transfer payments is wishful thinking. For moral rules to mean anything, they must be enforced, and to be externally enforced, they must first be internally enforced.

Liberalism for all its vaunted moralism undermines its own aspirations. It is not rational if rationality implies utilizing facts and logic to achieve stated aims.[103] By disguising what it is doing, and failing to acknowledge the implications of its policies, it encourages the opposite of what is sought. Instead of eliminating social conflicts, it incites them. Despite protestations of universal love, it stimulates antagonisms. Yet in its stubborn refusal to engage in honest negotiations with its foes, it ensures that these hostilities will continue. As incongruously, by insisting on total equality, it prevents those at the bottom rung from rising as quickly as they might. Attempts at social engineering that ignore the realities of tests of strength or alliance formation deprive the poor of the skills and emotional strengths needed to get ahead. Because equality cannot come by way of social fiat, to deny the realities of social mobility is to impede it. Finally, in opposing merit and responsibility, it undercuts the sources of social prosperity and representative democracy, *i.e.*, in demanding a utopian whole loaf, it attacks the conditions that make ordinary decorum possible.

Marx thought that communism could come about because industrialization would produce the surpluses needed to provide everyone with comfort.[104] He did not understand that the machinery of a commercial system would not run itself and that once market institutions were dismantled this excess of wealth would vanish. Present-day liberals make a similar mistake. They assume that values such as merit and responsibility produce destructive competition without recognizing that they also generate efficiency and interpersonal restraint. Were these standards no longer to be passed to the next generation, the post-modern edifice would collapse. The products liberals expect to redistribute would cease coming from the factories and the power they hope to equalize would evaporate in an explosion of anarchism. To sum up, liberalism promises peace, but serves up conflict; it promises equality, but keeps the poor powerless; it promises rationality, but is mired in childish emotionalism and a myriad of contradictions.

Foremost among these contradictions is the conflict between liberalism's absolutist and egalitarian impulses. The draconian coercion of one and the sentimental warn-heartedness of the other are not compatible. While they are easy to reconcile on a conceptual level, they cannot coexist in practice. Karl Marx and 60's style hippies make uncomfortable bedfellows. As long as they are in agreement, they can share a love-fest. Yet should they have a falling out, there will be hell to pay. Unconditional love and centralized planning must clash when economic quotas are unfulfilled. Furthermore, the only way to believe that the victims of centralized penalties are equal is to pretend they are not in distress. Like it or not, freedom and equality are incompatible so long as freedom leads to inequalities. But in the real world it does. Unequal inputs create unequal results; hence the only way to prevent this is through coercion. In a world where the lottery of birth favors some over others, this demands that the winners be cut down to size. Plato[105] thought stealing babies from their mothers and raising them by nurses could achieve this. Liberals think they can do it through universal education and democratic regulations. They are both wrong. Because their goals cannot be accomplished without opposition, this opposition must be stilled by means of force.

Sources of Power

Liberalism denies the implications of social power.[106] In their niceness, its advocates pretend they neither have, nor seek hegemony. They are merely individuals in quest of universal justice. Peaceful and non-hierarchical, they would instantly return to their creative endeavors if the political situation allowed it. Like George Washington,[107] or Cincinnatus before him, they are generals who would happily go back to plowing their fields once the battle against the reactionaries is won. It is only the exigencies of the moment that rouse them to fight as energetically as they do. Yet liberalism, like any other political movement thrives on power. Those who would foist their ideas on others could not achieve this without the ability to be persuasive, or failing this, to be coercive. Leadership, including ideological leadership, is a species of authority.[108] Liberals may renounce any intention to obtain superiority, but, in their eagerness to be influential, they give the lie to this assertion.

One more paradox of liberalism is that the sort of power it exercises is retrogressive. Instead of grounding itself in a commercially oriented professionalism, it turns to absolutist and religious sources. As the Middle Class Revolution gathered momentum, internalized controls transferred power to individuals.[109] People made more decentralized decisions as increasingly complex institutions demanded that expertise and motivation be concentrated in their hands. Liberalism reverses this trend by attempting to re-centralize control. As per the absolutists,[110] it employs government coercion to impose its dictates.

Whatever the perceived problem, the solution is a state administered program. Nor is liberalism averse to using coercion on a personal level. Those who oppose its plans find their reputations besmirched and their careers interrupted. In essence, liberalism finds much of its support in personal relationships.[111] In particularizing the sting of its sanctions, or the benefits of its support, it acts as might a military brotherhood. Within the community of its own interest, love is all that matters; whereas outside this family, the politics of personal destruction are allowed free reign.

Nevertheless the most important source of liberal power derives from quasi-religious sources.[112] Despite being adamantly secular, the movement is also profoundly ideological. Time and again, unsubstantiated beliefs trump facts. Strange to say, one of the reasons for the antipathy between liberals and fundamentalists[113] is that they are remarkably similar. Both exhibit a certitude based on moral commitments. Though they would be aghast at the suggestion, many of their central allegiances are nearly identical. Liberals believe in universal niceness, whereas Christian fundamentalists believe in universal love. Liberals believe that niceness breeds niceness, whereas fundamentalists are urged to turn the other cheek. Both likewise have collectivist tendencies. They believe in cooperation, rather than competition, and would like to implement something akin to primitive communism. Moreover, each is grounded in a community of the faithful. Within their own confines they impose an intense loyalty and a strict orthodoxy. Durkheim[114] argued that the power of the sacred derives from the united devotion of the true believers and one sees this operating in both locals. Theirs is each a solidarity validated by holding fast to those within the fold, while execrating the heretics. Then too, both sets of communicants share a grandiosity of spirit. The fundamentalists promise their followers entrance to heaven for reliable devotion; the liberals counter with a utopian heaven on earth. Convinced of their respective righteousness, they both have no doubt they will reap tangible rewards. The difference between them is, of course, that one believes in a deity and the other does not; one is avowedly spiritual and the other obstinately secular. But this is sufficient to guarantee mutual revulsion.[115] Precisely because they are so similar, they assert their uniqueness by reviling the other. What might seem minor discrepancies are elevated to heroic proportions, with one side anathematized as Godless humanists and the other as mindless dogmatists.

In fact, both are faiths.[116] Many have asserted this as a metaphor, but it is much more than that. Freud[117] speculated that monotheism of the Judeo-Christian variety depended upon the projection of a strong and protective father figure upon the heavens. The faithful imaginatively, if unconsciously, created their deity as an answer to their hopes and fears. Utopians of the neo-Marxist variety rely instead upon the projection of a kind and protective family upon the future.[118] They mentally conjure up an imminent society based on good will and total equality that will one day redeem them from the tribulations of social conflict. In each case the intellectual consensus upon which they rest depends not on evidence, but an implacable allegiance to shared beliefs. Furthermore, these beliefs are not subject to disconfirmation. No matter what facts come to light, they cannot shake true believers of their central commitments. Karl Popper[119] argued that an ability to disconfirm its hypotheses was the distinctive element of science. Scientists examined the world, proposed an explanation of what was going on, made predictions based on this thesis, then modified their theories in light of what turned out to be true or false. Religious beliefs, in contrast, cannot be falsified. If they seem to be erroneous, it is only because people have misinterpreted them. For the faithful, that which has been promulgated by an eternal authority, be it natural or super-natural, cannot be abrogated by human perception.

Some years ago Festinger, Riecken, and Schacter[120] did a study of a cult that had predicted the end of the world. In <u>When Prophesy Fails</u>, their account of what happened when this forecast was apparently disconfirmed, these investigators initially registered surprise when this did not result in the sect's demise. On the contrary, after a period of disappointment, the event was interpreted as reinforcing the group's articles of faith. According to its affiliate's revised view, the world continued because of some miscalculations had been made. What was needed to insure the millennium was to recalculate the date and reinvigorate their commitment. This tendency to excuse failure by converting it into proof of an accepted revelation has a long pedigree. The ancient Hebrews routinely indulged in it.[121] When something terrible happened, that is, when their God failed to protect them, a prophet arose to explain that this was because they were guilty of some religious infraction. Jehovah was punishing them because they had been derelict in their duties. They must, therefore, rededicate themselves to his service in order to receive a renewed blessing.

The same tendency is found in liberalism. It too makes predictions, which when they fail to come to pass are reworked to demonstrate the fundamental correctness of the central assertions. The unity of liberalism is rooted in this inability to disconfirm its premises. It is, therefore, a faith. The list of events that might have been taken as disproving its contentions is long. That these have not had this result, suggests the absence of a scientific point of reference. A partial inventory follows:

- A generous welfare system was supposed to foster social mobility; it did not.

- Tighter restrictions on welfare would surely to produce more misery; they did not.

- Unionization was to be the wave of the future; it was not.

- Poverty levels were said to be been increasing; they have not.

- The minimum wage was alleged to reduce poverty; it does not.

- Healthcare is described as in crisis; but life expectancy keeps rising.

- The poor are said not to receive health care; they do, albeit not through employer paid insurance.

- Race relations were to be improved by affirmative action; they have not been.

- Affirmative action was to produce social mobility; it did not.

- Easy divorce was to produce solid marriages; the reverse is closer to the truth.

- Casual sex was to be a liberating experience; it was not.

- Stay-at-home moms have been called traitors to their gender; they are not.

- Multicultural families were supposedly more supportive of children; they are less so.

- Rape was assumed be epidemic; it is not.

- Men, in general, have been condemned as innate rapists; they are not.

- The suburbs are depicted as a living hell; they are a middle class utopia.

- Most members of the middle class are portrayed as insensitive louts; they are not.

- Instilling unearned self-esteem in children would make them more successful; it did not.

- Bi-lingual education would stimulate minority assimilation; it does not.

- Stereotypes caused racism; they do not.

- Acid rain would destroy the forests; it did not.

- DDT would contaminate the environment; thanks to its discontinuation millions of children have died from malaria.

- Arsenic in the water supply was an imminent threat; it is not.

- Criminals could be reformed via rehabilitation; they were not.

- Police brutality is on the rise; it is declining.

- Profiling is ineffective and racist; it is not.

- FDR's reforms shortened the Great Depression; they lengthened it.

- Rent control would guarantee affordable housing; it did not.

- Price controls would prevent inflation; they never do.

- Alger Hiss was not a communist spy; he was.

- The Rosenbergs did not steal secrets for the Russians; they did.

- Increasing the defense budget could not defeat Communism; it pushed the Soviet economy into bankruptcy.

- The United States's arrogance brought terrorism on itself; it did not.

- America is an imperialist power; it is not.

- International trade bankrupts rich countries and exploits poor ones; it provides wealth for nearly all.

- Star-wars was a fiasco; it brought the Soviet Union to its knees.

- Training programs would end poverty; they have not.

- Kneeling buses would provide independence for the disabled; they did not.

- Socialist planning produces prosperity; it does not.

- Mental illness could be controlled by deinstitutionalization; it increased homelessness.

- Protecting homosexuals from public ridicule was more socially beneficial than aggressively testing for AIDS; it was not.

- Women would be happier becoming superwomen; most did not.

- Women should be more aggressive daters; they find this awkward.

- Military intelligence was an oxymoron; it is not.

- Progressive education would improve reading scores; it did not.

- Government housing could eliminate homelessness; it could not.

- Guaranteeing jobs through strict employment laws would reduce insecurity; it breeds conflicts.

- Lauding it as street art would control graffiti; it did not.

- Aggressive policing does not reduce crime: it does.

- Political correctness instills interpersonal respect; it promotes social dishonesty.

- Community policing would lessen crime; it did not.

- North Korea could be trusted to dismantle its nuclear program; it could not.

- Castro would renounce Communism if treated respectfully; he did not.

- Civilization is intrinsically anti-human; it is not.

- Everyone lies and cheats (except liberals); they do not.

These are more than a handful of anomalies.[122] The presence of this many represents a pattern; a pattern some might equate with the extreme spasms of a moment in its death throes. Whatever the reason, liberalism plainly exhibits an inclination to disregard the truth. So egregious has this tendency been that political spinmiesters do not hesitate to stand before the television cameras to proclaim the demonstrably ridiculous. In one amusing case, a Democratic spokesman explained that Arnold Schwartzenegger's victory in California's recall election was actually a defeat for the Republicans. Because the loser, Gray Davis, was an incumbent, this was surely bad news for incumbents such as George W. Bush. By the same logic, if liberal programs have not been successful, all this proves is that they haven't been given a chance. Not enough money was invested; too little skill was applied to administering them; insufficient confidence was placed in them. What is necessary is to go back and do things the right way. Triple the budgets, make the regulations more inclusive, employ harsher punishments, and all will go well. In any event, the liberal paladins fought the good fight, for which they deserve credit. They did their best to improve the world and conditions would surely have been worse had they not.

Die-hard liberals claim the reason they have not prevailed is attributable to a determined, and powerfully immoral, opposition. When the Bolsheviks were attempting to communize Russia, they blamed their difficulties on "counter-revolutionaries."[123] If a production quota was not met or famine hobbled the grain belt, the cause was sabotage. Those who wished to restore the Czars patently conspired to make the system look bad. Since these villains were beyond redemption, the only way to terminate their interference was to extirpate them root and branch. They had to be removed from their jobs, sent to the Gulag, and most likely killed. So must their relatives, lest they pass on a lethal infection. Only after millions of such souls were eliminated would good communists be able to implant genuine socialism. For parallel reasons, the traditionally religious, ascribe their failures to the devil. Were it not for him, mankind would never have been seduced away from following God's will. A supernatural rebel, he diligently continues to proselytize for his empire of darkness.

For liberals, conservatives and traditionalists are the devil. Their intransigence prevents a collectivist utopia from actualizing; their seductions divert good people from supporting necessary reforms. Were they physically removed progress would certainly accelerate. This is why they must be resisted. This is why they have to be barred from positions of power. Were they allowed a bully pulpit of any sort, they would utilize it to corrupt the defenseless. Given this menace, liberals have nothing for which to apologize; nothing to retract. If they have mistakenly asserted something that is not true, even acknowledging this might present evil with a weapon with which to bludgeon the good. All that is necessary is to move on without comment. Or if a lie promotes the good, *e.g.* by inflating the number of homeless[124] and, therefore, the resources devoted to them, it may still be promulgated because it represents a deeper truth. This strategy places them in exactly the same situation as the Popes when they forbade the teaching of a heliocentric universe that might elicit doubts about the Bible.

The faith-saturated moralism of liberals is further confirmed by the manner in which they engage in moral negotiations. Their vociferousness betrays an almost spiritual confidence in their rectitude. When the religious fundamentalists were riding high, they were as strident. God-besotted ministers would hurl fire and brimstone thunderbolts from the pulpit. Those who dared question their orthodoxy were promised an eternity in hell. Indeed, during the Middle Ages, the insufficiently conformist might be accused of witchcraft and purged of their corrupted souls by way of searing flames. Contemporary liberals are not so vulgar. They too attack their adversaries, but not with threats of immolation. Name-calling is generally deemed adequate.[125] Those who disagree are accused of being ignorant fascists. Instead of having their arguments examined, they are dismissed by means of ad hominem assaults. Judge Kenneth Starr[126] is transmuted into a priggish extremist, George W. Bush is seen as a stupid party-boy (or is that a diplomatic cowboy), and Clarence

Thomas is converted into an ungrateful mediocrity who owes his elevation to affirmative action. Not merely maligned as inept or evil, they are ridiculed for a plethora of putative absurdities. George Bush's malapropisms are proof of dimwittedness, Dan Quayle's difficulties with spelling "potato" demonstrate mental limitations, and Gerald Ford's stumbles derive from years of playing football without a helmet. Liberals, it must be understood, are exempt from such mockery. When Edward Kennedy misidentified Sammy Sosa after he set a home run record, his lack of knowledge was passed over in silence.

This attack dog spirit is supplemented by a penchant for supporting liberal initiatives by way of sob stories. The problems their reforms are intended to rectify are invariably elaborated upon in heartrending illustrations. If drug costs are said to be too high, Aunt Minnie from Oshkosh is trotted out explain that she was reduced to eating cat food because her social security did not cover her medical expenses. Or if racism is alleged to be virulent, the tragic dragging of a black man to his death is asserted to be the norm in race relations. The objective is not to investigate the extent of a difficulty, but to arouse an emotional response. People need to be motivated to do good; not merely to understand its nature. In traditional religions, evil was painted in as evocative terms.[127] Were this not so, people might sit on their hands as opposed to joining the war against immorality. Action, not disinterested thought, is what wins moral contests.

After raising the specter of evil, the old-line religions explained what the forces of light needed to do in order to triumph. Among the recommended actions were prayer, good works, regular church attendance, and belief in the catechism. The liberals, as confirmed secularists, put forth a different agenda. Their salvation is not aimed at a heavenly reward, but a more mundane one. Drawing on their Marxist core, they invariably propose governmental solutions. Whatever is wrong, a state organized program can fix it. A new bureaucracy and/or more money are the sovereign remedies for any difficulty. The details of these programs are never fully elaborated; nevertheless their intended purposes are sufficient to overcome all barriers. Nor are the results honestly evaluated. Because their sponsors and administrators have vested interests in success, whatever the actual outcome, it is celebrated as surpassing expectations. Head Start may not have improved the academic performance of minority students, but look at the many millions it served. At least they were not labeled retarded.

Whatever the outcome of these programs, the time comes to move on. Liberal moralizing is contingent on promises, not results. Sooner or later the subject is changed and a new sob story is put forward for the edification of the voters. When the traditionalists question this account, they are attacked for their insensitivity and the game is once again afoot. Even successes may be bypassed on the way to a freshly embellished future. Sad to say, old triumphs, such as social security, are boring. They may be cited as in need of defense from reactionaries, or as evidence of liberal compassion, but on their own are not sufficient to elicit support. Faith-based impulses are not satisfied by what is, but only by what might be. Whether via heaven, or an earthly utopia, hope is what animates communal solidarity. Either that, or terror of a vividly limned devil.

Nowadays the bobo faith has nearly transmuted into nature worship. A desire to protect the environment has become the signature cause of the cultural middle class. According to the standard cliché the ecology is "fragile" and must defended lest it go out of balance.[128] If one small part is disrupted, the whole will lose its equilibrium. Humankind itself is threatened by such unenlightened tampering. In their greed, people will destroy the very factors that make survival possible. They must, therefore, be educated to become environmentalists and conservationists. Instead of wasting the precious resources upon which they depend, they must limit their consumption. Rather than infringe on nature's eternal wisdom, they must work in conjunction with it.

This is a gentle, lyrical philosophy, one befitting the college educated, but it is based on a tautology. Every eco-system is fragile because every one represents a particular equilibrium. If something is altered, the old balance is gone, but this does not mean that doom is imminent. What happens is that a new equilibrium comes into being. A priori, this development is neither better nor worse than the one that preceded it. Since the world is always changing, a succession of equilibria is a fact of nature. Once upon a time the North American skies were blackened by flights of passenger pigeons. For over a century now these birds have been gone; hunted into premature extinction. This is sad, but it did not result in the desolation of the continent. Non-native birds such as sparrows and starlings took over some of their environmental niches, but then so have European immigrants vis-à-vis Amerindians. Treating that which is as intrinsically sacred is not a scientific necessity, but a moral imperative. Despite the reputation of liberals for being progressive, they make a fetish of stability.

An illustration of the mindset of this naturalistic faith is the fight over drilling for oil on the North Slope of Alaska.[129] A Republican administration, in order to lessen dependence on imported oil, proposed opening the area to exploration and utilization.   An uproar immediately ensued among the environmentalists.   This, they groaned, was one of the few untouched regions in the nation. Moreover, it was particularly fragile. Bringing in heavy equipment would irreparably damage the permafrost and put endangered species, such as the caribou, in jeopardy. This objection sent oil industry experts scurrying to their drawing boards. They came up with several solutions. One was to use a single platform to house multiple directional wells. This would mean that only a few acres would be necessary for production purposes. Another was to bring in equipment over ice roads in the dead of winter. By summer these thoroughfares would melt without any impact on the underlying soil. As was also pointed out, even more intrusive techniques had proven caribou friendly. The trans-Alaska pipeline, in particular, had not decreased their numbers. They had actually increased.

All of this made no impression on the environmentalists. It was the purity of the North Slope they were defending, not its physical integrity.   Any intrusion was too much for their liking. No matter how their concerns were addressed, the rhetoric remained the same. Arctic Alaska was a pristine wilderness that must not be desecrated for commercial purposes. What they did not emphasize is that even tourism would have impacted the land. Feet on the ground, housed in heated facilities, and brought in by modern transport might profoundly injure the ecosystem. This too would be intolerable. Therefore, in order to maintain Nature unspoiled, it could neither be drilled nor viewed. It would just have to lie there off-limits to any human involvement. This, it must be noted, is the perfect definition of what it is to be sacred. It demonstrates that the environmentalists were no so much seeking to protect against catastrophe, as to safeguard an emotional ideal.

Environmental excesses have proliferated in many directions. No matter what the cost, streams and rivers must be cleaned up, toxic dumpsites returned to absolute purity, miniscule the traces arsenic removed from water supply, and carbon dioxide and sulfur oxide scrubbed from the air. Global warming and environmental poisoning need to be prevented despite the fact that these remain theoretical possibilities. The worst possible computer models, as opposed to hard data, are publicized to alert the population to speculative hazards. Even if this creates an economic decline, the health benefits must come first. Left out of these calculations is that a prosperous economy might produce the resources and technology to address other problems. Also not considered is the misery of poverty.[130] The reason for these oversights is that the environmental religion is fundamentally antibusiness. Time and again, the changes demanded are in how commerce is conducted. The villain is industrial production and the salvation lies in relieving industrialists of their profits so that these can be sunk into restorative programs. Herein one sees the bobo revenge. They are using the appearance of science to get even with their hated superiors. Conceiving of themselves as powerless workers exploited by callous managers, they seek to turn the rationality of industrialism against itself. As cultural experts, they use their facility with language to coordinate an alliance of the disaffected. The way they tell it, catastrophe lies just over the horizon—the numbers prove it—and we must all hasten to stave it off. Yet this is being done with mirrors. Mysteries are created out of symbolic distortions in order to recruit allies to equally mysterious solutions. Some bobos apparently believe that if they are not running the show, they can at least leverage the insecurities of others to enhance their influence.

Endnotes

[1] Brooks, D. 2000. *Bobos in Paradise: The New Upper Class and How They Got There*. New York: Simon & Schuster.

[2] Ibid.

[3] Barone, M. 2001. *The New Americans: How the Melting Pot Can Work Again*. Washington, DC: Regnery Publishing.

[4] Brooks, op cit.

[5] Halberstam, D. 1969. *The Best and the Brightest*. New York: Random House.

[6] Brooks, D. 2004. *On Paradise Drive*. New York: Simon & Schuster.

[7] Collier, P. and Horowitz, D. 1976. *The Rockefellers: An American Dynasty*. New York: Holt, Rinehart & Winston.

[8] Morris, K.E. 1991. *Jimmy Carter, American Moralist*. Athens: University of Georgia Press.

[9] Auchincloss, L. 1989. *The Vanderbilt Era: Portraits of a Gilded Age*. New York: Scribner.

[10] Madsen, A. 2001. *John Jacob Astor: America's First Multimillionaire*. New York: John Wiley & Sons.

[11] Brooks, D. 2000. Bobos in Paradise: The New Upper Class and How They Got There. New York: Simon & Schuster.

[12] Seigel, J.E. 1999. *Bohemian Paris: Culture, Politics, and the Boundaries of Bourgeois Life, 1830-1930*. Baltimore: Johns Hopkins Press.

[13] Brooks, op. cit.

[14] Gerth, H. and Mills, C.W. (Eds.) 1946. *From Max Weber: Essays in Sociology*. New York: Oxford University Press.

[15] Taylor, F.W. 1911. *The Principles of Scientific Management*. New York: Harper and Brothers.

[16] Brooks, D. 2004. *On Paradise Drive*. New York: Simon & Schuster.

[17] Brooks, D. 2000. *Bobos in Paradise: The New Upper Class and How They Got There*. New York: Simon & Schuster.

[18] Freud, A. 1966. *The Ego and the Mechanisms of Defense*. New York: International Universities Press.

[19] Farley, R. 1996. *The New American Reality: Who We Are, How We Got Here, Where We Are Going*. New York: Russell Sage Foundation.

[20] Marx, K. and Engels, F. [1848] 1935. *The Communist Manifesto*. (In: *Selected Works*) London: Lawrence and Wishart.

[21] Ball, T. and Dagger, R. 1999. *Political Ideologies and the Democratic Ideal*. New York: Longman.; Bork, R. 1996. *Slouching Toward Gomorrah: Modern Liberalism and American Decline*. New York: Regan Books.

[22] Kirk, R. 1993. *The Politics of Prudence*. Wilmington, DE: ISI Books.

[23] Bierce, A. 1911. *The Devil's Dictionary.* New York: Thomas Cromwell Publishers.

[24] Morris, E. 1999. *Dutch: A Memoir of Ronald Reagan.* New York: Random House.

[25] Wicker, T. 1991. *One of Us: Richard Nixon and the American Dream.* New York: Random House.

[26] Hersh, S.M. 1983. *Kissinger: The Price of Power.* London: Faber and Faber.

[27] Stein, H. 2000. *How I Accidentally Joined the Vast Right-Wing Conspiracy (And Found Inner Peace)* New York: Delacorte Press.

[28] Leo, J. 1994. *Two Steps Ahead of the Thought Police.* New York: Simon & Schuster.

[29] Hochschild, A.R. 1983. *The Managed Heart: Commercialization of Human Feeling.* Berkeley: University of California Press.

[30] Kennedy, R. 2003. *Nigger: The Strange Career of a Troublesome Word.* New York: Vintage Books.

[31] Rice, E. 1997. *The O.J. Simpson Trial.* San Diego, CA: Lucent Books

[32] Gibbs, J. 1989. *Control: Sociology's Central Notion.* Chicago: University of Illinois Press.

[33] Smith, A. 1776. *An Inquiry into the Nature and Causes of the Wealth of Nations.* London: W. Strahan & T. Cadell.

[34] Payne, R. 1965. *The Rise and Fall of Stalin.* New York: Avon Books.

[35] Troyat, H. 1984. *Ivan the Terrible.* New York: E.P. Dutton.

[36] Lyons, M. 1994. *Napoleon Bonaparte and the Legacy of the French Revolution.* New York: St. Martin's Press.

[37] Schama, S. 1989. *Citizens: A Chronicle of the French Revolution.* New York: A. Knopf.

[38] Barone, M. 2004. *Hard America Soft America.* New York: Crown Forum.

[39] Durant, A. and Durant. W. 1963. *The Age of Louis XIV.* New York: MJF Books.

[40] Rousseau, J.J. 1992. *The Discourse on the Origins of Inequality.* (Edited by Roger D. Masters and Christopher Kelly) Hanover, NH: University Press of New England.

[41] Frankel, N. and Dye, N.S. (Eds.) 1991. *Gender, Class, Race and Reform in the Progressive Era.* Lexington, KY: University of Kentucky Press.

[42] Salvatore, N. 1982. *Eugene V. Debs: Citizen and Socialist.* Urbana: University of Illinois Press.

[43] Morris, E. 2001. *Theodore Rex.* New York: Random House.

[44] Starr, P. 2004. *The Creation of the Media: Political Origins of Modern Communications.* New York: Basic Books.

[45] McElvaine, R.S. 1984. *The Great Depression: America 1929-1941.* New York: Times Books.

[46] Powell, J. 2003. *FDR's Folly: How Roosevelt and His New Deal Prolonged the Great Depression.* New York: Crown Forum.

[47] Freidel, F.B. 1973. *Franklin Roosevelt: Launching the New Deal.* Boston: Little, Brown.

[48] Morin, R. 1969. *Dwight D. Eisenhower: A Gauge of Greatness.* New York: Simon & Schuster.

[49] Collier, P. and Horowitz, D. 1984. *The Kennedys: An American Drama.* New York: Summit Books.

[50] Goodwin, D.K. 1971. *Lyndon Johnson and the American Dream.* New York: Harper & Row.

[51] Howell, J.T. 1973. *Hard Living on Clay Street: Portraits of Blue Collar Families.* Prospect Heights, IL: Waveland Press, Inc.

[52] Gans, H.J. 1988. *Middle American Individualism: Political Participation and Liberal Democracy.* New York: Oxford University Press.

[53] Olasky, M. 1992. *The Tragedy of American Compassion.* Washington, DC: Regnery Publishing.

[54] Flynn, D.J. 2004. *Intellectual Morons: How Ideology Makes Smart People Fall for Stupid Ideas.* New York: Crown Forum.

[55] Marcuse, H. 1966. *Eros and Civilization: A Philosophical Inquiry into Freud.* Boston: Beacon Press.

[56] Rogers, C. 1961. *On Becoming a Person.* Boston: Houghton Mifflin.

[57] Robinson, R. 2000. *The Debt: What America Owes to Blacks.* New York: Dutton.

[58] Barnes, B. 1988. *The Nature of Power.* Chicago: The University of Illinois Press.

[59] Roth, C. 1961. *A History of the Jews: From Earliest Times Through the Six Day War.* New York: Schocken Books.; Bard, M.G. 2001. *Myths and Facts: A Guide to the Arab-Israeli Conflict.* Chevy Chase, MD: AICE.

[60] Hayek, F.A. 1988. *The Fatal Conceit: The Errors of Socialism.* Chicago: The University of Chicago Press.; Barone, M. 2004. *Hard America Soft America.* New York: Crown Forum.

[61] Lasch, C. 1979. *The Culture of Narcissism: American Life in an Age of Diminishing Expectations.* New York: Warner Books.

[62] Entwisle, D.R., Alexander, K.L. and Olson, L.S. 1997. *Children, Schools & Inequality.* Boulder, CO: Westview Press.

[63] Chong, D. 2000. *Rational Lives: Norms and Values in Politics and Society.* Chicago: University of Chicago Press.

[64] Howard, P.K. 1995. *The Death of Common Sense: How Law Is Suffocating America.* New York: Random House.

[65] Cook, A.E., Jelen T.G. & Wilcox, C. 1992. *Between Two Absolutes: Public Opinion and the Politics of Abortion.* Boulder: Westview Press.

[66] Thomas, A. 2001. *Clarence Thomas: A Biography*. San Francisco: Encounter Books.

[67] Baker, P. 2000. *The Breach: Inside the Impeachment and Trial of William Jefferson Clinton*. New York: Scribner.

[68] Lindsey, B.B. and Evans, W. 1927. *Companionate Marriage*. New York: Boni and Liverright.; Eberstadt, M. 2004. *Home-Alone America: The Hidden Toll of Day Care, Behavioral Drugs, and Other Parent Substitutes*. New York: Sentinel,

[69] Bettleheim, B. 1987. *A Good Enough Parent; A Book on Child-Reaing.*. New York: A. Knopf.

[70] Coontz, S. 1992. *The Way We Never Were: American Families and the Nostalgia Trap*. New York: Basic Books.

[71] O' Neill, N.O. and O'Neill, G.O. 1972. *Open Marriage: A New Life Style for Couples*. New York: M. Evans.

[72] Rochester, J.M. 2002. *Class Warfare: Besieged Schools, Bewildered Parents, Betrayed Kids and the Attack on Excellence*. San Francisco: Encounter Books.

[73] Kramer, R. 1991. *Ed School Follies: The Miseducation of America's Teachers*. New York: The Free Press.

[74] Bell, D. 1978. *The Cultural Contradictions of Capitalism*. New York: Basic Books.; Schumpeter, J.A. 1942. *Capitalism, Socialism and Democracy*. New York: Harper & Brothers.

[75] Elshtain, J.B. 1995. *Democracy on Trial*. New York: Basic Books.

[76] Marx, K. 1967. *Das Capital*. Edited by F. Engels. Translated by Samuel Moore and Edward Aveling. New York: International Publishing.

[77] Bell, D. op cit.

[78] Weber, M. 1958a. *The Protestant Ethic and the Spirit of Capitalism*. New York: Charles Scribner's Sons.

[79] Epstein, J. 2002. *Snobbery: The American Version*. Boston: Houghton Mifflin Co.

[80] Ferguson, N. 2001. *The Cash Nexus: Money and Power in the Modern World, 1700 – 2000*. New York: Basic Books.

[81] Bell, D. op cit.

[82] Fukuyama, F. 1999. *The Great Disruption: Human Nature and the reconstitution of Social Order*. New York: Free Press.

[83] Colville, J. 1985. *The Fringes of Power: 10 Downing Street Diaries 1939-1955*. New York: W.W. Norton & Co.

[84] Ellis, R.J. 1998. *The Dark Side of the Left: Illiberal Egalitarianism in America*. Lawrence: University of Kansas Press.; Horowitz, D. 2003. *Left Illusions: An Intellectual Odyssey*. Dallas, TX: Spence Publishing Co.; Kramer, H. and Kimball, R. 1999. *The Betrayal of Liberalism: How the Disciples of Freedom and Equality Helped Foster the Illiberal Politics of Coercion and*

Control. Chicago: Ivan R. Dee.; Sleeper, J. 1997. *Liberal Racism.* New York: Viking.

[85] Fein, M. 1997. *Hardball Without an Umpire: The Sociology of Morality.* Westport, CT: Praeger.

[86] As a possible explanation see: Epstein, J. 2003. *Envy: The Seven Deadly Sins.* New York: Oxford University Press.

[87] Knight, R.H. 1998. The Age of Consent: The Rise of Relativism and the Corruption of Popular Culture. Dallas TX: Spence Publishing.; Norris, C. 1997. Against *Relativism: Philosophy of Science, Deconstruction and Critical Theory.* Oxford, UK: Blackwell Publisher.

[88] Meyerson, J. (Ed.) 1982. *Emerson Centenary Essays.* Carbondale, IL: Southern Illinois University Press.

[89] Crawford, J. 1981. *Bilingual Education: History, Politics, Theory, and Practice.* Trenton, NJ: Crane Publishing Co.

[90] Sleeper, J. 1997. *Liberal Racism.* New York: Viking.; Bruce, T. 2001. *The New Thought Police: Inside the Left's Assault on Free Speech and Free Minds.* Roseville, CA: Prima Publishing.; Ellis, R.J. 1998. *The Dark Side of the Left: Illiberal Egalitarianism in America.* Lawrence: University of Kansas Press.; Flynn, D.J. 2004. *Why the Left Hates America: Exposing the Lies That Have Obscured Our Nation's Greatness.* New York: Three Rivers Press.; Charen, M. 2003. *Useful Idiots: How Liberals Got It Wrong in the Cold War and Still Blame America First.* Washington, DC: Regnery Publishing.; Coulter, A. 2002. *Slander: Liberal Lies about the American Right.* New York: Crown Forum.

[91] Jacobs, R. 1997. *The Way the Wind Blew: A History of the Weather Underground.* New York: Verso.

[92] Sale, K. 1973. *SDS.* New York: Random House.

[93] Benn, S.I. and Peters, R.S. 1959. The Principles of Political Thought: Social Foundations of the Democratic State. New York: The Free Press.

[94] Ignatiev, N. 1995. *How the Irish Became White.* New York: Routledge.

[95] Lowe, D. 1967. *Ku Klux Klan: The Invisible Empire.* New York: W.W. Norton.

[96] Mortimer, E. 1982. *Faith and Power: The Politics of Islam.* New York: Random House.; Lewis, B. 2002. *What Went Wrong: Western Impact and Middle Eastern Response.* New York: Oxford University Press.

[97] Deveaux, M. 2000. *Cultural Pluralism and Dilemmas of Justice.* Ithaca, NY: Cornell University Press.

[98] Schlesinger, A.M. 1992. *The Disuniting of America.* New York: W.W. Norton & Co.

[99] Orwin, C. and Tarcov, N. (Eds.) 1997. *The Legacy of Rousseau.* Chicago: University of Chicago Press.

[100] Troyat, H. 1984. *Ivan the Terrible.* New York: E.P. Dutton.

[101] Coontz, S. 1992. *The Way We Never Were: American Families and the Nostalgia Trap.* New York: Basic Books.

[102] Lewis, M. and Saarni, C. (Eds.) 1985. *The Socialization of Emotions.* New York: Plenum Press.; Richards, M. 1974. *The Integration of a Child into a Social World.* London: Cambridge University Press.

[103] Green, D.P. and Shapiro, I. 1994. *Pathologies of Rational Choice Theory: A Critique of Applications in Political Science.* New Haven: Yale University Press.

[104] Marx, K. 1967. *Das Capital.* Edited by F. Engels. Translated by Samuel Moore and Edward Aveling. New York: International Publishing.

[105] Plato 1941. *The Republic.* (Jowett translation) New York: The Modern Library.; Edman, I. (Ed.) 1928. *The Works of Plato.* New York: The Modern Library.

[106] Bierstadt, R. 1950. *An Analysis of Social Power.* American Sociological Review.

[107] Brookhiser, R. 1996. *Founding Father: Rediscovering George Washington.* New York: The Free Press.

[108] Eckstein, H and Gurr, T.R. 1975. *Patterns of Authority: A Structural Basis for Political Inquiry.* New York: John Wiley & Sons.

[109] Hunter, F. 1953. *Community Power Structure: A Study of Decision Makers.* Chapel Hill: University of North Carolina Press.

[110] Durant, A. and Durant. W. 1963. *The Age of Louis XIV.* New York: MJF Books.

[111] Etzioni, A. 1993. *The Spirit of Community: Reinvention of American Society.* New York: Simon & Schuster.

[112] Hoffer, E. 1951. *The True Believer: Thoughts on the Nature of Mass Movements.* New York: Harper & Row.; Bork, R. 1996. *Slouching Toward Gomorrah: Modern Liberalism and American Decline.* New York: Regan Books.

[113] Sandeen, E.R. 1970. *The Roots of Fundamentalism: British and American Millinarianism* 1800-1930. Chicago: University of Chicago Press.; Armstrong, K. 2000. *The Battle for God.* New York: Alfred A. Knopf.

[114] Durkheim, E. 1915. *The Elementary Forms of Religious Life.* New York: The Free Press.

[115] Carter, S.L. 1997. *The Culture of Disbelief: How American Law and Politics Trivialize Religious Devotion.* New York: Basic Books.

[116] Hoffer, E. 1951. *The True Believer: Thoughts on the Nature of Mass Movements.* New York: Harper & Row.

[117] Freud, S. 1953-1974. *The Standard Edition of the Complete Psychological Works of Sigmund Freud.* (Edited by J. Strachey. London: Hogarth Press and Institute for Psychoanalysis.

[118] Mannheim, K. 1936. *Ideology and Utopia.* New York: Harcourt, Brace, and World, Inc.

[119] Popper, K.R. 1959. *The Logic of Scientific Discovery.* London: Hutchinson & Co.

[120] Festinger, L. Rieken, H.W. and Schacter, S. 1964. *When Prophesy Fails*. New York: Harper & Row.

[121] Friedman, R.E. 1987. *Who Wrote the Bible?* New York: Summit Books.

[122] Anderson, M. 1992. Imposters in the Temple: American Intellectuals are Destroying Our Universities and Cheating Our Students of Their Future. New York: Simon & Schuster.; Barlett, D.L. and Steele, J.B. 1996. America: Who Stole the Dream? Kansas City: Andrews and MaMeel.; Bernstein, R. 1994. Dictatorship of Virtue: Multiculturalism and the Battle for America's Future. New York: Alfred A. Knopf.; Best, J. 2001. Damned Lies and Statistics: Untangling Numbers from the Media, Politicians, and Activists. Berkeley: University of California Press.; Blankenhorn, D. 1995. Fatherless America: Confronting Our Most Urgent Social Problem. New York: Basic Books.; Bruce, T. 2001. The New Thought Police: Inside the Left's Assault on Free Speech and Free Minds. Roseville, CA: Prima Publishing.; Caplow, T., Hicks, L. and Wattenberg, B.J. 2001. The First Measured Century: An Illustrated Guide to Trends in America, 1900-2000. Washington, D.C.: AEI Press.; Charen, M. 2003. Useful Idiots: *How Liberals Got It Wrong in the Cold War and Still Blame America First*. Washington, DC: Regnery Publishing.; Collier, P. and Horowitz, D. 1989. Destructive Generation: Second Thoughts about the '60s. New York: The Free Press.; Courtois, S, Werth, N., Panne, J-L., Paczkowski, A., Bartosek, and Margolin, J-L. 1999. *The Black Book of Communism: Crimes, Terror, Repression.* Cambridge, MA. Harvard University Press.; Demott, B. 1990. *The Imperial Middle: Why American Can't Think Straight about Class.* New Haven: Yale University Press.; Ellis, R.J. 1998. *The Dark Side of the Left: Illiberal Egalitarianism in America.* Lawrence: University of Kansas Press.; Flynn, D.J. 2004. *Why the Left Hates America: Exposing the Lies That Have Obscured Our Nation's Greatness.* New York: Three Rivers Press.; Freeman, D. 1983. *Margaret Mead and Samoa: The Making and Unmaking of an Anthropological Myth.* Cambridge, MA: Harvard University Press.; Friedman, M. 1962. *Capitalism and Freedom.* Chicago: University of Chicago Press.; Gelles, R.J and Straus, M.A. 1989. *Intimate Violence: The Causes and Consequences of Abuse in the American Family.* New York: Touchstone Books.; Graglia, F.C. 1998. *Domestic Tranquility: A Brief Against Feminism.* Dallas, TX: Spence Publishing Co.; Hayek, F.A. 1988. *The Fatal Conceit: The Errors of Socialism.* Chicago: The University of Chicago Press.; Hewitt, J.P. 1998. *The Myth of Self-Esteem*: Finding Happiness and Solving Problems in America. New York: St. Martins.; Hollander, P. 1992. Anti-Americanism: Critiques at Home and Abroad 1965-1990. New York: Oxford University Press.; Horowitz, D. 1998. Betty Friedan and the Making of the Feminine Mystique. Amherst: University of Massachusetts Press.; Horowitz, D. 2003. Left Illusions: An Intellectual Odyssey. Dallas, TX: Spence Publishing Co.; Howard, P.K. 2001. The Lost Art of Drawing the Line: How Fairness Went Too Far. New York: Random House.; Hughes, R. 1993. Culture of Complaint:

The Fraying of America. New York: Oxford University Press.; Hunter, J.D. 1991. *Culture Wars: The Struggle to Define America.* New York: Basic Books.; Huntington, S.P 1996. *The Clash of Civilizations and the Remaking of World Order.* New York: Simon & Schuster.; Jencks, C. 1992. *Rethinking Social Policy: Race, Poverty and the Underclass.* Cambridge, MA: Harvard University Press.; Jencks, C. 1994. *The Homeless: Rethinking Social Policy.* Cambridge, MA: Harvard University Press.; Jones, J.H. 1997. *Alfred C. Kinsey: A Life.* New York: W.W. Norton & Co.; Kors, A.C. and Silverglate, H.A. 1998. *The Shadow University: The Betrayal of Liberty on America's Campuses.* New York: The Free Press.; Kramer, H. and Kimball, R. 1999. *The Betrayal of Liberalism: How the Disciples of Freedom and Equality Helped Foster the Illiberal Politics of Coercion and Control.* Chicago: Ivan R. Dee.; Lomborg, B. 2001. *The Skeptical Environmentalist: Measuring the Real State of the World.* New York: Cambridge University Press.; MacDonald, H. 2000. *The Burden of Bad Ideas: How Modern Intellectuals Misshape Our Society.* Chicago: Ivan R. Dee.; Magnet, M. 1993. *The Dream and the Nightmare: The Sixties Legacy to the Underclass.* New York: William Morrow & Co.; Olasky, M. 1992. *The Tragedy of American Compassion.* Washington, DC: Regnery Publishing.; Rubin L. B. 1972. *Busing & Backlash: White Against White in an Urban School District.* Berkeley: University of California Press.; Samuelson, R. 1996. *The Good Life and Its Discontents: The American Dream in the Age of Entitlement 1945-1995.* New York: Times Books.; Satel, S. 2000. *PC, M.D.: How Political Correctness is Corrupting Medicine.* New York: Basic Books.; Smith, H. 1988. *The Power Game: How Washington Works.* New York: Random House.; Sommers, C.H. 1994. *Who Stole Feminism: How Women Have Betrayed Women.* New York: Simon & Schuster.; Sowell, T. 1999. *The Quest for Cosmic Justice.* New York: The Free Press.; Stein, H. 2000. *How I Accidentally Joined the Vast Right-Wing Conspiracy (And Found Inner Peace)* New York: Delacorte Press.; Tanenhaus, S. 1997. *Whittaker Chambers: A Biography.* New York: Random House.; Thernstrom, S. and Thernstrom, A. 2003. *No Excuses: Closing the Racial Gap in Learning.* New York: Simon and Schuster.; Tipton, S.M. 1982. *Getting Saved from the Sixties.* Berkeley: The University of California Press.; Wilson, J.Q. 2002. *The Marriage Problem: How Culture Has Weakened Families.* New York: HarperCollins Publishers.; Zarefsky, D. 1986. *President Johnson's War on Poverty.* University, Ala: University of Alabama Press.; Zigler, E. and Valentines, J. (Eds.) 1979. *Head Start: A Legacy of the War on Poverty.* New York: Free Press.; Entine, J. 2000. *Taboo: Why Black Athletes Dominate Sports and Why We're Afraid to Talk About It.* New York: Public Affairs.

[123] Montefiore, S.S. 2004. *Stalin: The Court of the Red Tsar.* New York: Alfred A. Knopf.

[124] Jencks, C. 1992. *Rethinking Social Policy: Race, Poverty and the Underclass.* Cambridge, MA: Harvard University Press.; Jencks, C. 1994. *The*

Homeless: Rethinking Social Policy. Cambridge, MA: Harvard University Press.

[125] Coulter, A. 2002. *Slander: Liberal Lies about the American Right.* New York: Crown Forum.

[126] Schippers, A. 2000. *Sellout: The Inside Story of President Clinton's Impeachment.* Washington, DC: Regnery Publishing.

[127] Armstrong, K. 1993. *A History of God: The 4000- Year Quest of Judaism, Christianity and Islam.* New York: Ballantine Books.; Armstrong, K. 2000. *The Battle for God.* New York: Alfred A. Knopf.

[128] Mathiesen, M.M. 2000. *Global Warming in a Politically Correct Climate.* San Jose: Writers Club Press.

[129] Lomborg, B. 2001. *The Skeptical Environmentalist: Measuring the Real State of the World.* New York: Cambridge University Press.

[130] Dalrymple, T. 2001. *Life at the Bottom: The Worldview that Makes the Underclass.* Chicago: Ivan R. Dee.

Chapter 9

Temples of Liberalism

By education most have been misled;
So they believe, because they so were bred
The priest continues what the nurse began,
And thus the child imposes on the man.
(John Dryden, <u>The Hind and the Panther</u>)

Journalists say a thing that they know isn't true in the hope
that if they keep saying it long enough, it will be true.
(Arnold Bennett, <u>The Title</u>)

Men never do evil so completely and so cheerfully as when
they do so from religious conviction. (Blaise Pascal,
<u>Pensees</u>)

Cultural Institutions

As if the middle-class revolution has not been difficult enough, adjusting to it has been made more difficult thanks to the resistance provided by the institutionalization of reactionary liberalism. Institutions, whether theocratic or ideological, are the bane of self-direction. They are also the enemy of unbiased expertise. Institutions specialize in providing and enforcing standard answers. In this respect, the institutionalization of liberalism is no different. It focuses on facilitating anti-middle class power plays grounded in a self-righteous moral consensus. It insists upon collectivist orthodoxies and furnishes reliable anti-middle class coalitions to impose these orthodoxies; coalitions for which, not incidentally, C. Wright Mills' characterization of middle class foibles remain valid. As such, it has attempted to derail the middle class ascendancy.

To begin with, religions are institutionalized.[1] This enables societies to develop the cultural and structural means of perpetuating themselves. Consisting of stabilized belief systems and formalized social relationships, these much respected spiritual establishments are able to carry recognizable ideological systems forward; often for millennia. Through their agency, communities hold on to their core ideas with a tenacity, and a uniformity, that prevents their disintegration. The Jewish faith has managed this feat for almost three thousand years,[2] the Christian for two thousand,[3] and Islam for well over a thousand.[4] We call these institutions "churches" and they posses a solidity that can make them seem like facts of nature. They are, in essence, a method for conserving shared norms, values, and viewpoints.

Among the assets institutionalized religions typically possess are communal belief systems. Included within these are cosmologies that explain how the world was created and moral codes that specify how communicants should live. These concepts are normally promulgated within an accepted format; *e.g.*, a set of scriptures. As some point, it is officially decided which beliefs count as orthodox and these are set forth in an authorized configuration. For Christians, the Council of Nicaea was instrumental in certifying that God was to be considered a Trinity. For Jews, their Rabbis decided that some books belonged in the Bible,[5] whereas others were apocryphal, decisions made by Christian authorities are often vested in particular persons. These individuals constitute a designated leadership; hence their opinions are accorded extra weight. Sometimes these "holy" ones are arranged in a hierarchy. The Roman Catholic chain of command is a case in point. Other religions are less formal, with status established by individual merit. Both Judaism and Islam come closer to this model. There are also designated times and places where worship occurs. Whether in cathedrals, synagogues, or mosques, the faithful gather at predictable moments to celebrate what they jointly regard as sacred. In this, they reinforce their connection to a powerful communion, thereby enhancing their individual feelings of control.

Quasireligions, such as liberalism, are also institutionalized, yet their cultures and structures are not as formal. As cultural ideologies, they too require a stabilized consensus in order to perpetuate themselves. Nonetheless this need not be as strict as that exhibited by their spiritual counterparts. Secular communicants require an emotional bond to observably similar beliefs,[6] but not necessarily one stabilized by a scriptural format. Most get by with a conventional wisdom that is sustained by a common literature and regularized communications. It is enough that people read the same things, praise interchangeable opinions, and condemn familiar heresies. Nor do they need an official leadership. Here it is sufficient that there be recognized opinion leaders. Individuals noted for their intelligence, energy, and/or communication skills articulate positions that are later dispersed by unofficial means. Communicants read what they write, listen to what they say, and then repeat this within their own social circles at their own initiative. These off the record contacts are essential; hence they are facilitated by occurring at predictable locations. Liberals, for instance, are not uniformly distributed throughout society.[7] There are particular places where they constitute a majority and thus where they feel free to exchange their beliefs. Nowadays, the universities are one of these sites. They provide a comfort zone for jocular self-congratulation and joint derision of outsiders. Moreover, these gathering places provide the resources necessary for their continuation. True believers can, therefore, be assured that these locations will be available tomorrow and ten years from tomorrow. This provides them the confidence to make the moral, emotional, and intellectual commitments that sustain their faith.

Some quasireligions are more institutionalized than others. Until recently the Communists boasted an official party hierarchy upon which they could rely for leadership and a sense of security.[8] A central command dictated an official party line adhered to by card-carrying members. There were also authorized texts written by Marx,[9] Lenin,[10] and Mao[11] that could be consulted to determine eternal truths. Needless to say, the party possessed a bureaucratic configuration, not unlike that of the Vatican, in which apparatchiks sought to establish a rewarding career. This provided a shared discipline, a common agenda, and a party headquarters. In places like the Soviet Union, countless splendid buildings were essentially party property.

Meanwhile, in the United States, political organizations, such at the Democratic Party, did not approach this level of structure. Back in the 1920s, Will Rogers[12] could joke that he did not belong to an organized party—that he was a Democrat. He knew that his party had squishy political positions, a constantly shifting panoply of local and national alliances, and a headquarters that floated upon the political tide. There might be temporary platforms, daily talking points, and successful candidates for office, but no single individual, or idea, could claim exclusivity. While Democrats could distinguish themselves from Republicans, the boundaries between them were porous.[13] People joined or left their ranks via private declarations of intention. The same could be said about the convictions they represented. Although Democrats prided themselves on being the party of the little people, how these were to be represented varied with the electoral cycle. Entrepreneurial candidates routinely modified their policies and rhetoric to conform to public opinion. Democrats could not even boast that their primary constituency consisted of working people. Contrary to a widely held perception, by the end of the twentieth century almost half of the nation's wealthiest voters were casting ballots for them.

When one considers liberals, the state of their institutionalization is still more tenuous. Although associated with the Democratic Party, not all Democrats are liberals[14] and not all liberals are Democrats. More a diffuse cultural orientation than a concretely identifiable faction, liberalism is dominated by the bobos. They provide the outlook's most articulate spokespersons and its more powerful defenders. Indeed, it is their institutional connections that give the perspective its backbone and its megaphone; *i.e.*, they who provide its stabilized points of transmission. To add to the confusion, the central tenets of liberalism are not codified in an identifiable sourcebook, nor sanctioned by an official convocation. Its wellsprings are instead found in a loose consensus of culture-based professionals. People, whose jobs entail manipulating ideas, coordinate their beliefs over the water fountain or the dinner table. They also do so while playing tennis, during intermission at the symphony, or when standing before paintings at the art gallery. Because they are plugged into the same scuttlebutt at work, consistent sermons at church, and congruent psychological theories, they tend to see things the same way. Likewise, having gone to the same schools, watched the same news programs, and read identical books, they can predict what their peers will find persuasive. Theirs is not a conspiracy, but what Bernard Goldberg[15] characterizes as a "bubble" of opinion.

Eventually there arises a "canon" to which most remain loyal.[16] Once upon a time the literature sophisticated people perused and the music to which they listened were determined by upper class tastes. In the English-speaking world, to be unfamiliar with Shakespeare was to be a cultural clod; to never have attended a chamber music concert was to be déclassé. With the initial arrival of the middle classes, allusions to popular novels became the currency of cultivated conversation, while sentimental songs could be found on most lips. The bobo ascendancy dramatically changed this. A liberal oppositionalism rejected anything associated with the traditional bastions of power. That which was produced by dead white males became anathema. Now works created by former outsiders set the tone. A Rigoberta Menchu,[17] not a John Milton, received their kudos. Often it was enough that an author was a member of a minority or a musician was uncommonly vulgar to obtain public acclaim. The liberal establishment consistently certified that that which offended conservative sensibilities was intrinsically valuable.

Liberals do not, however, possess a formal hierarchy. No single person directs their opinions. Nevertheless they know whom they are expected to admire. Some sources of information are considered reliable, whereas others are not; some persons trustworthy, and others not. Individually in quest of reputations for credibility, many prize the status of a "guru." Little surpasses the honor of being regarded as an expert by one's peers or as creative force by future generations. As representational specialists, they cherish being persuasive over being intimidating. Liberals may thus be thought of as secular preachers. In their own minds, custodians of "the truth," they compete to garner acclaim for their lay sermons. This makes liberalism a venue for almost non-stop moralizing.[18] Indeed, the crux of the movement's institutionalization is located in an atmosphere of shared, and vigorously projected, testimonials.

Where these homilies occur is not a trivial matter. Liberalism has appropriated many of society's junction boxes to broadcast its messages. Virtually monopolizing centers of communication and education, its devotees control "mainstream" viewpoints.[19] Primary and secondary schools, higher education, the media, and entertainment outlets have all become their strongholds.[20] So have philanthropical foundations, agencies providing research grants, and professional societies. While no underlying plot directs what is taught in colleges or transmitted over the evening news, a community of views holds sway as if one did. Professors and students, editors and reporters, participate in feedback loops that rein them in as tightly as any party line. Most know that the punishment for apostasy is severe; that to deviate too far from the established consensus risks ostracism. Friends and acquaintances will look at a renegade askance and are suddenly unavailable for lunch. This sort of isolation may sound trivial, but it is the lifeblood of human sociality. Most people want to "belong" and will do almost anything to maintain their social contacts. Over and above this are the more substantial matters of careers and their concomitant material rewards. Those who do not conform to the approved attitudes find themselves out of a job or no longer in line for promotion.[21] In many cases, they never receive the initial appointment. The gatekeepers who do the hiring, or determine what gets published, do not overtly condemn their deviations; they merely find others more qualified. Members of the faith, not defectors, get the big houses, the fancy cars, and the corner offices. They are the ones who obtain prizes for their books, face time before the camera, and elective office in professional societies.

Progressive Education

Education was once the province of the church, the nobility, and prosperous merchants, but with the arrival of the middle classes formal learning was democratized. Schools grew in number and the period of instruction in length. Ultimately education was to be universal.[22] Even the children of the lower classes were tutored in the rudiments of what every citizen should know. This would provide the foundation for a representative democracy and a technologically based commerce. The questions then arose as to what should to be taught and how would this to be realized. The old liberal education of the Middle Ages was designed for the clergy and a smattering of professionals, but advances in the sciences and scholarly achievements made this obsolete. Moreover, it was essential that these newly valuable subjects no longer be taught by rote. If students were to be flexible thinkers, they had to cultivate more than a good memory. They would have to become proficient in something other than the once pervasive Greek and Latin—as taught to the tune of the hickory stick.

Ideas for liberating pupils from the tyranny of aristocratic conformity go back hundreds of years. Jean-Jacques Rousseau[23] was one of the more influential exponents of what came to be called "progressive education." He asserted that young children must be allowed to follow their instincts. Tutors might arrange their environments so that these would lead them to important discoveries, but their insights had to come from the youngsters themselves. That which failed to excite their interests or enlist voluntary experimentation was an epiphenomenon that would be lost once the teacher's discipline was removed. What was needed instead was something more practical; something related to the world in which the child would one day operate. Rousseau was himself of the old school. Emile, his major excursion into educational theory, revolved around a single tutor mentoring a single child. Its model was the aristocratic household and the purpose hired scholar. Once education became more democratized, these did not apply. The sort of close supervision possible in a one-on-one relationship was impossible is a schoolroom where one teacher confronted dozens of students.

By the dawn of the twentieth century, the appropriate alterations in perspective had been made. At this point, the leading theorist of progressive education was John Dewey.[24] A pragmatic philosopher by background, in time his focus shifted to preparing children for modernity. One of his primary concepts was that of "experience." Instead of being artificially intellectual, he wanted the young to interact with the world. It was by doing, and not simply absorbing verbal lessons, that they would acquire a genuine understanding of their environment. This perspective was institutionalized in the "project method." Either individually, or in groups, students would engage in pieces of independent research, art, or social intervention. They would choose their own goals, and their own means, and implement these with the assistance, not the oppressive direction, of the teacher.[25] In this, not only would they develop the initiative needed to control their own lives; they would also learn how to be creative. In essence, they would discover the secrets of being self-directed. Given this head start on personal growth, they would be prepared continually to expand their horizons once they entered the professionalized world of their future.[26]

This, at least, was the theory. The practice was very different.[27] An example of what happened was the "open classroom."[28] In order to introduce freedom to the grammar school curriculum, the traditional classroom was torn down. Gone were fixed seating arrangements and solid walls separating classes. Taking their place were movable seats and impermanent partitions. This way, children could move around from one project to another and one work group to a second. The teacher would no longer stand before the collected group to deliver a boring one-size-fits-all lecture. Instead, she would move between individuals providing personalized instruction as she went. All would, therefore, move at their own pace and come out ahead of where they would have with an enforced conformity. This sounded heaven-sent and a perfect fit for a middle class dominated society.

The problem was that not everyone was from the middling orders. Most of the children who went to public schools did not come from upper middle class backgrounds.[29] Those who did had already been taught to be considerate of others, to be interested in how and why things happened, and to exercise self-control. They had also been trained to think things through and to take personal initiative. Thus, when presented with an opportunity to choose an individual learning project and then to follow it up, they possessed the internalized disciplines to succeed. Lower class children, however, came from homes where their parents placed more emphasis on good manners, being neat and clean, and obeying those in authority. Primed to conform, they had no practice in how to exercise independent judgment. When asked to take control over their own activities, they were more apt to seek an easy way out. Having already encountered oppressive power, their primary concern was to evade it. Few took advantage of the opportunity to learn how to be self-directed. In the end, this form of progressive education ratified the pre-existing social class structure. Platitudes about sponsoring social mobility were contradicted by the reality making families responsible for inculcating both internal discipline and the value of knowledge. Instead of freeing lower class children from oppression, it insured that they would one day be subject to the external discipline of the workplace.

The same considerations applied to other educational reforms.[30] One of these was the "whole word" means of learning to read. Gone were the phonics of yesteryear. Ascertaining the pronunciation of individual letters and sounding them out in words was supposedly too monotonous to sustain student attention. Simply jumping in and recognizing combinations of words as embedded in stories would be more enticing. In fact, it was more confusing; particularly for lower class children. Less likely to have been introduced to books at home, this facsimile of being thrown into the deep end of the pool was decidedly not reassuring. Nor was it helpful when they were told that spelling didn't matter and that grammar was old-fashioned. Starting with less preparation in reading, and with parents whose linguistic skills were wanting, this was a formula for remaining permanently handicapped. Because they were also instructed, when asked to write stories, that whatever came naturally was acceptable, they never developed the vocabulary or the disciplined approach to linear organization necessary to handle professional communications. Then too, "modern math" was equally debilitating.[31] Where once children were drilled in their times tables, it became fashionable to introduce them to conceptual themes. Instead of calculating twelve times twelve in their heads, an approximate answer was deemed good enough. Teachers believed that understanding the rudiments of symbolic logic was more important. The difficulty here was that students who relied upon calculating machines, rather than internalized mental operations, never became comfortable with numbers. As a result, they never pursued the higher mathematics for which a familiarity with set theory was ostensibly to prepare them. Once more, it was the offspring of the higher classes whose parents had instilled these skills who surged ahead. It was they, because they were less intimidated, who took the advanced classes in these topics.

As sadly, students who were forced to serve their own teachers could not turn for assistance to adult pedagogues who knew much of anything.[32] Those delegated to supervise their education might be skilled in motivating, but not in instructing them. The educators of potential educators believed it imperative that soon-to-be teachers care more about the welfare of their students, rather than acquire something to share with them. Liberalism had come to the classroom.[33] What mattered were good intentions, emotional rapport, and creative aspirations. Schools of education were no longer places dedicated to promoting knowledge. They sought instead to imbue politically correct attitudes. Teaching was presented as more akin to social work than to an academic enterprise.[34] Children were to be furnished with self-esteem,[35] rather than intellectual tools. Presumably, if they learned to feel good about themselves, they would automatically be able to achieve what was later expected of them. For similar reasons, they were to learn to be cooperative rather than competitive. Modern society was represented as a place where love would predominate over conflict, that is, if everyone learned to be nonviolent. In this vein, students were to celebrate the differences that existed in a multicultural society. They must be indoctrinated to believe that everyone was as good as everyone else. Only this would expunge sexism, racism, and classism.[36] By this logic, if children studied history, it must be as a cautionary tale against oppression.[37] They needed to learn about the horrors perpetrated by their ancestors so as never to repeat them. Likewise, if they read literature, it was to be as an object lesson in tolerance and universal love. Only stories that showed women, gays, and minorities as active winners would be allowed on the reading list. Rather incongruously, this watered down curriculum sat well with novice teachers. Most of them had never been very good students; hence they appreciated a program that was not intellectually demanding. Far from intending to pass along a love of learning, they were satisfied to be well-meaning babysitters.

Given these objectives, contemporary schools of education focus on teaching methods, not content. They insist on fostering an absolute equality of results,[38] rather than academic excellence. Neo-Marxist as it was possible to be without proclaiming oneself a Marxist and as bohemian without retiring to a Montmartre loft, they promote egalitarian techniques ad nauseum.   Rita Kramer,[39] while taking a national tour of Ed schools, overheard numerous exhortations of the prevailing philosophy. Coast to coast, she was privy to sentiments inimical to "meritocracy." Thus, working hard at on one's lessons was frequently dismissed as totalitarian, for as one student opined, "if it doesn't work, if you don't succeed, you think, What's wrong with me? [And] because it doesn't always work" this is terrible for the losers. This suggests that a failure is the student's fault, blaming the victim, which is equivalent to a death sentence.[40] It also fosters hierarchical thinking, and that too would be wrong. Clearly, suggesting that one child might be better than another harmed both.[41] As one professor insisted in explaining the rationale of multicultural education, "The central and overriding [objective] is to promote equity in student achievement." Everyone must come out the same. But Kramer, herself, had doubts. She comments that, "the real losers in this situation are the ones they profess to be concerned with helping. In their determination to avoid the charge of 'elitism' by providing the same education in the same classroom for everyone, they ignore not only the needs of those youngsters with an academic bent but those with more practical interests as well." Paradoxically, in this rush for equality, no one gets much of anything.

What tends to happen with extreme egalitarianism is that the lessons get "dumbed down."[42] Since the only way for everyone to do equally well is for the best to do less well than they can, the emphasis is on fun rather than on effort. Courses are geared to the lowest common denominator and are expected to be more enjoyable than enlightening. Under these circumstances, arts and crafts and visual aids drive out the more challenging currency of lectures and homework dwindles to the vanishing point. And because no one is allowed to fail, grade inflation becomes the rule. Every student is expected to get an A or a B, whether or not this is earned. Even a B is considered an insult to students who expect to receive a college-bound average just for showing up. Nor are textbooks allowed to be challenging. The slightest hint of controversy might insult, and, therefore, damage the scholarship of sensitive students. Although this generates boredom, the teacher is delegated to find a way to sustain interest. There is also an antitest bias. Since time immemorial, students have been reluctant to take examinations. These produce enormous anxiety because it is possible to fail them. Try as one might, one can still come out worse than others. This has produced a cottage industry in derogating tests. First, they are alleged not to reveal what matters. As artificial assessments, they are said to leave out what the student really knows. Second, other means of evaluation are declared superior. Personal journals and portfolios are thought to be better at disclosing creativity. The problem is that there are no standardized means of evaluating these alternative indicators. There is the additional difficulty that the traditional methods have a documented ability to predict academic success, whereas their replacements do not.

Many liberal educators have come to the conclusion that what matters most are credentials. Since it is degrees that allow students to obtain employment, these must be equally available to all. Much as the Wizard of Oz's scarecrow had his ability to think confirmed by a diploma, all students are to be allowed their "piece of parchment." This has at least two consequences. One is an escalation in the degrees sought. If everyone is a graduate, then the only way to distinguish one's competence is to obtain a yet higher degree. There is also the phenomenon of mainstreaming. Every student, irrespective of ability or motivation, is said to deserve to be in the same classroom. To isolate anyone because of low intelligence or obstreperous behavior is to stigmatize him or her. This "labeling"[43] will surely convince the victim that he/she is unable to keep up. Such practices as tracking are, therefore, tantamount to oppression in that they sponsor some for success and others for the opposite. Particularly reviled is providing extra help for gifted students. Since they already have an advantage, giving them further assistance is unfair. If this leaves them bored, and society deprived of their abilities, this is a small price to pay for promoting democracy.

Exceptionally large sums have been devoted to helping mentally retarded students. Both in terms of funds and time, attentions have been lavished on them that might have been more productively invested elsewhere. The concept of "normalization"[44] holds that if intellectually disabled children are placed in ordinary classrooms and treated as normal, they will function close to normal levels. This, in fact, is massive denial in service to an egalitarianism fantasy. Retarded children are biologically handicapped and can never keep up with their undamaged peers. That middle class parents agitate for them to achieve comparable results is understandable in terms of the middle class need for success. Less understandable is diverting social energies that would have a greater payback if directed toward those with superior abilities. The results have, in fact, been meager. Educational budgets have swollen and class sizes have decreased, but this has had little impact on overall achievement. As foolishly, because ordinary teachers are not experts in special education, those students who do require expert attention are deprived of it.

Romantic egalitarianism has also been unproductive with respect to racial differences and classroom discipline. Instead of comparable demands being made of all students, African-American and Hispanics have been allowed to languish.[45] The continued existence of discrimination has been invoked as an excuse for lowering the standards they are expected to realize. This has resulted in large disparities in achievement tests, with the importance of these instruments written off as an artifact of segregation, lesser funding, or cultural bias. No matter how often these causes are disproved, minority students (excepting, of course, Asians) are permitted to slack off. Although the advocates of special attention for blacks contend that they are promoting equality, they do not seem to believe black abilities are equivalent to those of whites. Somehow, sitting beside a white is supposed to substitute for reading books or doing homework.[46] With respect to maintaining classroom order, it is similarly argued that imposing discipline is indistinguishable from racial repression. Those from different cultures are said to require approaches unique to them. If they are made to sit still, this theoretically deprives them of the advantages of a more dynamic heritage. To suggest that all students, irrespective of their backgrounds, require peace and quiet to absorb their lessons is dismissed as ethnocentric. Somehow "street smarts" are thought a viable alternative to what must be read and tranquilly assimilated.

Teachers unions have promoted much of this agenda.[47] Their leaders have become the de facto bishops of liberal, multi-cultural education. Incessantly agitating for the progressive program, they contend that additional money and more personalized instruction are the answers to all questions. Asserting a professional expertise that trumps the demands of disappointed parents, their hierarchies remain unfazed by evidence of failure. Whenever testing indicates that gains have not been made, it is alleged that classes are too large or that private schools are creaming the best students. Particularly anathema to an oligarchy that derives its power from the shear numbers of public school teachers are proposals for voucher systems.[48] Giving parents monies directly might enable them to utilize the power of the purse to discipline unsuccessful schools and this is unacceptable to those who wish to retain control. In essence, a pseudo-professionalism is employed to resist efforts toward a more genuine professionalization of education.

Higher Education

One of the consequences of the Middle Class Revolution is the belief that every child deserves a college education.[49] With so many good jobs contingent upon the expertise and motivation inculcated in higher education, everyone is expected to have the opportunity to acquire these. Whether or not an individual demonstrates an academic bent, he/she is urged to go beyond high school; often at public expense. Even functional illiteracy is not a disqualification. As most colleges and universities have learned, they are now expected to compensate for lessons not previously learned; thus almost all have remedial programs designed to provide the foundation for more traditional courses. Even so, the results have been disappointing. A large proportion of students admitted to college never complete a degree. Despite the aid of grade inflation,[50] they drop out.

As unhappily, higher education has been subject to the pressures from progressive forces.[51] Equality of results is supposed to apply in this instance too. Once again, however, the only way to achieve absolute parity is to demand less from all. Knowledge that was previously considered the inevitable outcome of university training is never broached, never mind attained. Moreover, as with their lower status peers, many college professors and administrators have come to believe that their primary task is social reform. Dedicated liberals, they dismiss an accumulation of facts as of secondary importance. Far more significant is becoming a tolerant, peace-loving person. Far from encouraging merit, their aim is a non-judgmental altruism that fosters egalitarianism; albeit one with a creative tinge. Cooperation, not competition, is their aspiration, with emotional spontaneity, not intellectual incandescence, the sign of accomplishment. Just as in the lower grades, the traditional canon is dismissed as sterile, whereas political correctness has become de rigueur. This means that grade inflation,[52] non-traditional assessment formats, and affirmative action have become the norm.[53] Anything that might discourage tender souls is off limits, especially in the arts, humanities, and social sciences. All must be allowed into the tent and all graduate with the same degree, irrespective of their shortcomings.

Much of this is a consequence of the faculty's gatekeeping tendencies.[54] During the 60s, and especially at the height of the Viet Nam War, colleges became a sanctuary from the real world.[55] As long as one was a student, one did not need to get a real job or submit to military discipline. The university campus was also the perfect nexus for a social consciousness. Much better to prepare oneself for enlistment in the War on Poverty than for the paddy fields of Southeast Asia. The effect was to produce a generation of liberal Ph.D.s. So great was their dominance that by 2002 a survey by the American Enterprise Institute revealed an overwhelming liberal hegemony.[56] In elite universities such as Harvard and Brown literally 95% of the faculty were registered to vote as affiliates of "parties of the left." In general, across the academic spectrum the ratio of Democrats to Republicans tended to be roughly 10 to 1.

Evidently convinced that their pacifism and selflessness were intellectually justified, these enthusiasts had devoted themselves to remaking their disciplines in the image of their political commitments. Gone was the academic rigor of previous cohorts; in its place arose a self-congratulatory moralism. Emblematic of this transformation was the ascendancy of post-modernism.[57] Even more modern than modernity, it preached that there was no such thing as truth. No one could be more correct than anyone else, because there are no absolute standards of correctness. Nevertheless, these same post-modernists felt justified in indoctrinating students in their own moral viewpoints.[58] More genuine and principled than their predecessors, in tearing down the remnants of the old order, they were paving the way for a kinder, more democratic, future.

This neo-Marxist,[59] bobo inspired, liberalism became the conventional wisdom in fields such as history,[60] English literature,[61] and sociology.[62] Each of these cultural-based disciplines sought to contribute to an emerging canon. But first they needed to "deconstruct" the existing intellectual edifice.[63] As per Marx, they had to demonstrate that people believed what they did because a "false consciousness" propagated by the capitalists obscured their vision. Old-fashioned ideas such as truth, merit, and responsibility were evidently rationalizations for concentrating power in the hands of the rich. If one looked past what was said to what was done, it became obvious that the intention was to handicap the poor. Historians contributed to this interpretation by emphasizing how pervasive sexism and racism had been.[64] Instead of delving into the activities of politicians and industrialists, they shifted their gaze toward their innocent victims, *i.e.*, the women and minorities. Where once the Civil War was understood in terms of what Abraham Lincoln had done, Sojourner Truth emerged as a major player. Almost invisible now were the contributions of Thomas Edison, exchanged for the depredations of Joseph McCarthy.[65] What mattered was to show how ordinary people lived. Also essential was demonstrating how vicious the oppression had been. George Washington was to become more renowned for being a slaveowner than as the Father of His Country. That contrary to the wishes of his relatives, he, on his deathbed, freed his bondsmen was not as well publicized, for this might contradict the image being purveyed.

In literature, the transformations were more dramatic.[66] The authority figures decided that Standard English was too confining.[67] Ruled the arbitrary creation of a predatory elite, students needed to be taught that other forms of expression were equally valid. They were now allowed to sprinkle their writings with what would once have been thought vulgar. They could likewise collaborate in committees to produce original works of art. Thanks to the computer, groups of individuals were encouraged to contribute to common ventures. If asked to analyze literature, this was intended either to deconstruct the biases of the past or to explore the authenticity of once marginal figures. Charles Dickens was still acceptable as a spokesperson for the downtrodden, but Mark Twain was uncomfortably addicted to the n-word.[68] Jane Austin was a wonderful example of female genius, whereas Samuel Johnson was a misogynist buffoon. William Shakespeare was definitely out of date, while obscure authors from Africa and Latin America enjoyed a vogue. Students might themselves read Ayn Rand, whereas in class they poured over John Steinbeck's[69] The Grapes of Wrath in order to determine how the reserve army of the unemployed had been used to keep workers impotent. In 1989 The Wall Street Journal[70] described the curriculum of Stanford University's course in Western Civilization thus: "Dante's 'Inferno' is out...but 'I...Rigoberta Menchu' is in...Aquinas and Thomas More are out, but "Their Eyes Were Watching God" by feminist Zora Neale Hurston is in…Locke and Mill go down the memory hole, replaced by the U.N Declaration of Human Rights and Rastafarian poetry… [while] Virgil, Cicero, and Tacitus give way to Frantz Fanon…."

In sociology, as in most of the social sciences, the emphasis shifted to exposing oppression to the antiseptic effects of intellectual sunlight.[71] Students needed to become familiar with the continuing universality of exploitation. Understanding how societies were put together thus took a backseat to revealing the means whereby they perpetuated immorality.[72] Once upon a time functionalists sought to determine the prerequisites of community survival, but by the 70s conflict theorists had defiantly supplanted them. Neo-Marxists in all but name, they were preoccupied by issues of inequality. On the grounds that race, class, and gender were all about disparities in power, these were taught in the same courses. It did not matter that social class had more to do with hierarchical relationships and gender relations with heterosexual intimacy. Furthermore, much of what was covered was treated as problematic. Marriage was revealed to be an institution dedicated to suppressing women and children,[73] and schools a mechanism for instilling industrial uniformity.[74] Time and again, the answer to human misery was seen as liberating people from the despotic grip of greedy capitalists. According to authoritative professors, when business people spoke of responsibility, they meant an allegiance to themselves. When they praised merit, this was a code word for that in which they excelled. Since many who gravitated to sociology had been involved in social reforms, they were also fascinated with social movements.[75] Essentially "movement" people, they were not so much interested in studying how morality operated as in determining the means of making their interventions successful. This might not be social science as originally conceived, but it was in line with their liberal dispositions.

This moral certitude produced classrooms of stifling conventionality.[76] The correct answers might not be representative of the larger society, but they were the ones students were expected to proselytize once they exited the halls of academe.[77] In former times, professors had been committed to exposing students to all sides of important issues in a relatively dispassionate manner. The students were to be introduced to the facts and to canons of logic, and then make up their own minds. This was now history. Despite protestations of promoting "critical thinking,"[78] the only critiques allowed were of the old order. A deconstruction of the particulars of the liberal establishment was strictly off limits. Its faith was to be the guiding faith, not the target of a disinterested investigation. So virulent was this new orthodoxy that ridicule was deemed an appropriate means of enforcing its tenets. Professors literally failed students who expressed the wrong views about race or gender. Moreover, they did so unabashedly. With upwards of ninety percent of faculty members in the humanities and social sciences of elite institutions avowedly liberal (or left of liberal), there was little dissent when they taught or graded ideologically. In sociology, for instance, it was routinely assumed that the science dictated liberal conclusions. This meant that only liberal texts were assigned and only liberal speakers invited to speak on campus. "Only" may be too strong a term, but one study indicated that, when it came to commencement speakers, if a political orientation was demonstrable, it was liberal by a ratio of sixteen to one.

Something more sinister occurred to the nature of science. Dispassionate science, one of the hallmarks of industrialization, made its mark by utilizing disciplined observations to push out the boundaries of knowledge. In areas such as physics, chemistry, and biology this continued to be the situation. In the social sciences, however, political correctness became the standard of truth. The moral agendas of investigators determined what would be studied and how this would be interpreted. Because committed ideologues dominated subjects like sociology, they did not even pretend to go beyond this. Theirs became advocacy research. The goal was to disseminate what was already believed, but to do so with the authority of science. Unconscious biases had always been the bane of social science, but keeping them unconscious was no longer a priority. The post-modernists[79] argued that since everyone had a bias, Max Weber's notion of value neutrality was naïve. The only question was how persuasive one could be in propagating one's views. Given that the liberals were on the side of justice,[80] it was incumbent upon them to be as convincing as possible. Not the truth of their observations, but their righteousness was what counted.

"Scientism," as opposed to science, exploited the trappings of rational investigation.[81] Though it employed the language of science, and often such valid techniques as statistical analysis, it did this without a genuine commitment to discovering important truths. The prestige of science, not its motivating spirit, was appropriated to serve moral interests. This enabled the advocacy researchers to distort their activities with a clear conscience. They could, for example, exaggerate the positive impact of affirmative action[82] or detract from negative effects of divorce without qualms. Some pieces of research could be totally ignored if they contained unwelcome implications. This was the fate of James Coleman's[83] massive study on education. When he found that parental values mattered more for student success than did school resources, his conclusions were hushed up. Sometimes the measuring rods were manipulated to produce the desired inferences. This is what occurred with respect to sexual abuse. Because conventional liberal opinion demanded that males be guilty of overwhelming abuse of women, what was regarded as "abuse" was expanded beyond its ordinary meaning. Merely casting an admiring glance at a female could be viewed as the equivalent of rape, that is, if its object found it objectionable. Sometimes interpretations were massaged after the fact. One set of investigators reported that teachers were paying more attention to boys than girls and that this was injuring the self-esteem of the girls.[84] What they failed to divulge was that most of this attention was negative. The boys were being told to shut up because they were more disruptive than the girls. How this was supposed to enhance their self-images was a mystery. Also left unsaid was that the girls were doing better in school. Despite questioning their abilities, they got better grades and entered college in larger numbers.

Much of this distortion of science took the form of statistical manipulations.[85] Both in college classes, and on the political hustings, impressive figures were manufactured because they proved persuasive. This made it advantageous both to inflate the numbers and to misinterpret their implications. To wit, although the census bureau could only find three hundred thousand homeless persons, homeless advocates, including academic sociologists, cited three million as the actual count. This was no more than a seat-of-the-pants estimate, yet it was treated as an absolute fact. For a while it was also taken on faith that strangers annually kidnapped over two million children, although the true number was under a few hundred. Even when the figures were correct they could be given a deceptive spin. Percentages, for instance, might be ignored in favor of raw numbers. To illustrate, it was said that crime and welfare were not concentrated among African-Americans because there were in fact more Caucasians in jail or on the dole than blacks. This was true, but to get the appropriate incarceration figures they had to combine the white and Hispanic census. More importantly, they had to disregard the minor detail that blacks were only thirteen percent of the population. What mattered were proportions, not absolute numbers, but stating this would have produced the wrong impression. People might have realized that per capita blacks were committing more than seven times as many murders as whites. They might also have recognized that per capita many more members of minorities are on welfare. This perpetuates a debilitating dependence, but to acknowledge it might induce the public to come to racist conclusions. The same statistical smoke and mirrors applied to marriage. Academics who found the institution outdated produced articles that suggested that less than ten percent of families consisted of the traditional husband, wife, and their two children. What they neglected to add was that most of these households were either still childless, or past the child rearing period, or composed of single individuals. Despite divorce and out-of-wedlock births, most children continued to be raised by married couples.

Higher education had become infested with these "just so" stories.[86] As with more traditional religious institutions, what was disseminated was chosen for its moral effect, not its truth-value. Faculty members and administrators had come to think of themselves as trustees of the next generation. Intent on making sure that the young were protected from corrupting influences, they censored that to which they were exposed. Some of this as overt, but much of it was accomplished via a community of opinion. Just as what was considered beautiful has been determined by a cultural zeitgeist, so was that which was deemed intellectually valid.

Journalists

Journalism and democratic politics shared the same cradle.[87] Both came into being dependent upon the other. If free citizens were to elect suitable representatives, they needed to know who these persons were and for what they stood. As importantly, they had to keep track of their activities once in office. In fact, the most important function of the first newspapers, and more recently the electronic media, has been electioneering. From the beginning candidates were not content to leave their fate to chance.[88] If they could, they would stage-manage pubic attitudes to their advantage. What made it into the journals, and how this information was construed, was critical to their interests. Sometimes these manipulations were quite sophisticated, as when the Federalist Papers[89] were used to agitate for ratification of the American Constitution. Sometimes they were evocative, as with Thomas Paine's[90] proindependence pamphlet Common Sense. At other times, they were merely scurrilous, as when Thomas Jefferson[91] was lambasted for having an affair with Sally Hemmings. In retrospect, the origins of the United States may seem sedate, and even dignified, but as they were unfolding they were so raucous that John Adams[92] attempted to muzzle the press with a sedition act that made it illegal to write offensive pieces about public figures.

The partisan nature of the press is, therefore, of ancient lineage. What has changed with the advent of liberal dominance is that this influence became monolithic. The biases of reporters and their editors grew to be so one-sided as to produce an apparent unanimity of opinion. Henry Luce,[93] the founder of Time Magazine, though an outspoken conservative, observed that he was forced to rely on a liberal staff because they were better writers.[94] Unquestionably they were a larger proportion of those from whom he was obliged to draw. Although it has become compulsory to deny that journalists are largely left wing, this has long been the case. Surveys of their voting patterns routinely demonstrate that upwards of ninety percent vote Democratic, yet most reporters insist that as professionals they can separate their private beliefs from their occupational judgments. Even a Dan Rather, whom his colleague Andy Rooney described as transparently liberal, could continue to describe himself as politically neutral after vociferously defending forged documents intended to be detrimental to a Republican president.[95] The truth seems to be that journalism attracts a certain sort of person. Many are idealists, who if they weren't writing about the world, would be attempting to reform it. Indeed, many seem to be attempting both; the quintessential social workers with pens.

Added to this is the reality that journalists are cultural experts. They may seem to know everything, but what they know best is the prevailing conventional wisdom.[96] While many affect an air of detached omniscience, they come closer to being observers with attitudes than disinterested authorities. As a matter of fact, most of the people who turn out to be reporters or editors study communication, rather than technical skills. Some have backgrounds in political science or economics, but many more majored in journalism, English, or the law. Their competence thus lies in how to disseminate a message, not in making certain that it is accurate. Under these circumstances being theatrical is often of more consequence than being honest. Though many in the press portray themselves as pundits, this is a self-proclaimed designation. The platform they have achieved, rather than the insights they possess, lend them their air of legitimacy. Often a stentorian voice or an elegant way with the printed word is their sole claim to public attention. Also of inestimable value in validating their pronouncements is the uniformity of opinion with which they are surrounded. The repetition of bald-faced absurdities, if sufficiently homogeneous, can make almost anything sound plausible. Ordinary consumers, if they do not have access to contrary viewpoints, may have no way of distinguishing truth from falsehood. The liberal dominance has, therefore, converted the press into a Temple of sacrosanct ideas. As soon as technological advances limited the number of newspapers and media outlets, only their propaganda reached the public ear. Standardized reportage accordingly came close to being spiritual indoctrination once contrary voices were muted.

One of the indicators of this development was the metamorphosis of the front page of newspapers into an extension of their editorial pages. Where previously this was considered unprofessional, journalists began to insert personal viewpoints into their stories and headlines. The tipping points for this progression seem to have been the Viet Nam War and the Watergate affair. After Walter Cronkite,[97] by unanimous consent "the most trusted man in America," indicated that the Tet offensive was a terrible defeat, many of his viewers lost their faith in the war.[98] In time, the government was forced to extricate the nation from its commitment. This achievement convinced journalists of their ability to influence events. Shortly thereafter, Richard Nixon's disgrace confirmed this assessment. Reportage by the Washington Post was largely credited with exposing the illegal cover-up of a third rate burglary, thereby driving a president from office.[99] This, in turn, was construed as saving the nation from totalitarian ruin. In this manner, having saved both the peace and democracy, journalism, and particularly investigative journalism, was tinged with romantic potency. Talented journalism students could now project themselves as heirs to the mantle of Woodward and Bernstein. Someday they too would uncover a scandal so great that their names would be imbued with legendary status.

Under these circumstances ordinary newspersons began to think of themselves as adversaries of the political elite. Their job, as the shadow government, was "to tell truth to power," which meant that their goal was to reveal as many lies as possible.[100] News conferences, which had once been sedate venues for obtaining information, became opportunities to embarrass public officials. Even liberal office-holders were subjected to "gotcha" exercises in tripping them up over small matters. During FDR's administration, those who covered him felt obligated to hide his paralysis from the public on the grounds that this was in the national interest. Now national purposes were to be damned when they conflicted with "the public's right to know." When the politician was a conservative, the glee in exposing his feet of clay was palpable. Given that journalists believed that their profession endowed them with both moral authority and technical proficiency, they routinely explained what the news really meant. They not only told their audiences what happened, but why it had happened and what the long-term effect would be. Strange to say, this was habitually consistent with liberal platitudes. In this way, Monday morning quarterbacking was transformed into a seven-day-a-week distraction. Whatever occurred, reporters could elucidate how it could have been done better. During the Nixon administration[101] Spiro Agnew, the soon to be discredited Vice President, drew disdain for labeling these pundits "nattering nabobs of negativity." Yet this criticism stopped no one. Both its message and its alliteration struck those at whom it was aimed as over the top. Themselves emancipated of responsibility for achieving results, they systematically found those who were accountable wanting. Well aware that their own prescriptions were unlikely to be tested, they could paint their consequences in the rosiest of hues without fear of contradiction. Despite the revolving door between the press and office-holding,[102] when journalists were on the outside looking in their disparagement was so strident as to be malicious. An aura of smug self-satisfaction clung to romantic analyses that were never to be tested against the disinterested verdict of reality.

In many ways contemporary journalists have become emotional demagogues. They utilize sentiments to manipulate the perception of policies for which they are not answerable. Theirs is power without consequence. Theirs is the muscle to set the parameters of debate without having to consider the outcomes. The New York Times has demonstrated the degree to which moralistic kibitzing can color events.[103] Widely considered America's most influential newspaper, in the past it prided itself on being the nation's journal of record. In presenting all the news "fit to print," its staff considered itself engaged in presenting the first draft of history. As such, accuracy and even-handed objectivity were the goal. Those days, however, are long gone. With the advent of the liberal hegemony, the Times was transformed into the cathedral of left wing political thought. Though an integral part of the nation's political establishment, it became obsessed with crusading for change. Much as might a small town newspaper seeking to unseat a corrupt mayor, it flooded its pages with stories intended to promote a compassionate collectivism. Thus one of its chief objectives was to promote peace. Writers, as pacifistic as any tied-dyed hippy, rarely found a kind word to say about military adventures. This included efforts to confront terrorism after the devastation of 9/11. In particular, they resolutely sought to undermine the Bush Administration's Iraq undertaking.[104]

Throughout its coverage, the Times depicted the Iraqi situation as analogous to Viet Nam. Within days of launching the ground action, one of its most prestigious columnists used the front page to moan about an impending "quagmire." Wont to quote any public figure remotely critical of Bush's policy, its editors had the temerity to misquote Henry Kissinger about its legitimacy and then to drag their feet before giving a grudging retraction. So far as the Times was concerned, it would be impossible to defeat Saddam Hussein because there was no viable "plan" for doing so. One might have imagined that entering Baghdad within a mere three weeks would have quieted these editorial qualms, but it did not. As Bob Kohn[105] documents, before, during, and after major combat the Times ran a preponderance of negative stories. It began by fearing a "protracted war" and a new "jihad," then it worried that the British "mistrusted" how the U.S. was waging the battle, and it highlighted a "chorus of criticism" that speculated "images of victory overshadow doses of realism." As the climax drew near, it perceived new dangers in the "final push" and described American troops as "weary" from their exertions. Meanwhile the paper stressed that images of the war were "faltering in the Arab world," found disagreement pervading the U.S. Congress, depicted a "trail of death" in the Iraqi capital, and reported the enemy as claiming the U.S push had been "thwarted." Soon it was proclaiming that the "urban war begins: it was real scary," while speculating that the "evidence contradicts rumors of torture." Moreover, "anti-Americanism" was growing in Greece, and an African leader was saying the "Iraq war sets bad precedent." When weapons of mass destruction were not immediately found this prompted loud skepticism about whether they ever existed. Eventually it would be implied that George W. Bush lied about their presence in order to get revenge for his father's earlier fiasco.[106]

One of the more revealing episodes disclosed the lengths to which the Times would go to portray the government as incompetent. After Baghdad fell, looting broke out in the streets. This was quickly blamed on the administration's failure to anticipate disorder or to react expeditiously. Particularly shocking was that the national museum had been robbed of hundreds of thousands of irreplaceable treasures. Obviously this legacy of Mesopotamian civilization should have been protected by the conquering troops. The American military simply stood by while unalloyed greed destroyed a part of everyone's heritage. From the beginning the Times' reporters knew that things were not what they seemed, nevertheless their editors could not resist printing archeological testimony about how horrendous this event was. Within days other outlets were suggesting that the missing artifacts might have been removed by the museum's own staff, but this did not stop the Times' from continuing the assault. Eventually it was found that no more than a couple of dozen items were lost; that most had merely been transferred elsewhere for safekeeping. But the damage had been done. The impression was created that the American military was composed of vulgar philistines led by uncivilized warmongers.

On the home front similar distortions ruled the day. In matters small and large, a tendentious flavor of liberalism and a nagging disdain for its enemies prevailed. One of the longstanding disputes between liberals and traditionalists concerned crime.[107] Those with a conservative bent insisted that law and order must be maintained, whereas "progressives" claimed that rehabilitation and respect for diversity would eliminate the root causes of criminality. For many years, it seemed that there would be no resolution to this controversy. Then Rudy Giuliani appeared on the scene.[108] Once he was elected mayor of New York City, he determined to end the disorder on its streets. The local Democratic establishment, which included the Times, had taken to describing the city as ungovernable. It contended that the crime rates traced an unbroken gradient due to the community's large population and freewheeling spirit; that, and, of course, the bigotry on the mean-spirited Right. Giuliani, however, decided to give the Broken Window Theory a try. He would instruct his underlings to pursue small, as well as large, violations of the law. And this is what happened. Within a couple of years the effects were dramatic. The crime rate tumbled, with the number of murders falling to almost one fourth of what they had been. The streets, and the subways, were measurably safer. People began to talk about the community having been taken back from the criminals. Even the graffiti had been scrubbed off of public property. The environment was literally cleaner than it had been in decades.

One might have thought the Times would celebrate these events.[109] Presumably its editors too preferred safer neighborhoods. From their perspective, however, the price was intolerable. A Republican mayor had achieved what his liberal predecessors only promised. His solution, not theirs, had been demonstrated to be effective. Were this allowed to stand, it might cast doubts on the entire liberal enterprise. Some fly had to be found in the ointment and people convinced that this was serious enough to renew their confidence in the old prescriptions. Providence was soon to provide what seemed the perfect vehicle. A young African street vendor, Amadou Diallo, was gunned down outside his home in the Bronx. Not just this, but the police had riddled his body with over forty shots. This over-kill was unambiguous evidence of brutality. Yes, crime had gone down, but only because a totalitarian regime was allowed to dominate the streets.

The Times quickly went on the offensive.[110] A paper that had historically spurned crime reporting in favor of national and international coverage became obsessed with pursuing justice. Day after day, week after week, often several times a day, it ran stories about the incident. When there was no news, it recruited Al Sharpton to lead protest rallies designed to highlight the incipient racism. Sharpton was a well-known demagogue, but he was also an articulate spokesperson. His antics were sure to draw attention. Through all this, the Times was aware that police brutality had been on the decline. Under Giuliani there were fewer such acts than their had been under an earlier African-American mayor. There were also fewer such incidents than in most large cities. This did not matter. What did was that a graphic episode could make it appear that conservatives were insensitive brutes. Nor were officials at the Times concerned that an investigation showed the killing had been accidental or that the police officers involved were later found innocent in a court of law. This was about appearances, and as the gatekeepers of public perceptions, they could manipulate these to send the appropriate political message. Even when they became aware that their crusade provoked the police to reduce their presence in minority neighborhoods and that this reduction was followed by an increase in crime, they were not apologetic. They could no more admit a mistake than a Pope could express doubts about the resurrection of Christ.

Though they persistently deny it, journalists habitually implement their ideological commitments in their editorial choices.[111] They regularly decide what they will write about and how they will describe it. This both the substance and tone of the media are at their discretion. While these are not always conscious decisions, they are momentous. This is why political correctness continues to flourish.[112] In general, members of the establishment share core beliefs that influence what is considered newsworthy. Almost entirely sympathetic to abortion, its proponents receive a supportive hearing, whereas its foes are portrayed as kooks.[113] Likewise strongly approving of feminism, it is represented as defending the rights of women, whereas traditional views are depicted as oppressive.[114] Also in favor of gun control, they brook no amount of contrary evidence convinces them that gun ownership does not increase murder rates.[115] Similarly, the efficacy of affirmative action is never seriously reviewed.[116] To be against it is assumed to be racist and, therefore, its achievements are exempt from neutral evaluation.[117] Even prayer in schools gets short shrift. Routinely identified with fundamentalism, advocates of school prayer are seen as advancing a religious orientation. The result is that a molehill is presented as a barbaric onslaught against religious freedom.

As arbiters of good and evil, the priesthood of institutionalized journalism exercises the prerogatives of an image-maker.[118] Whose words are quoted, how these are edited, the details chosen to convey their ambiance, what adjectives applied, and the critics selected for provide a rebuttal determine how what is reported will be perceived. If he did not already understand this, Arnold Schwarzenegger discovered it when he ran for California governor. Having previously been considered an open-minded friend of Jewish interests, the Los Angeles Times suggested that he had years earlier made pro-Hitler comments. These were ostensibly cited in full, but subsequent investigations revealed that they had been revised to leave out his anti-Hitler assertions. Corresponding to this libel have been those addressed toward virtually every Republican president. Democrats are praised for their intelligence and compassion, whereas conservatives are ridiculed for stupidity and avarice. George W. Bush was already being dismissed as an intellectual lightweight when a reporter sprung a surprise quiz about obscure world leaders. When Bush missed most of these, this was taken as confirmation of his mental limitations. Needless to say, no Democratic candidate faced similar opprobrium. It cannot be an accident that Ronald Reagan[119] was regarded as a genial dunce, Dwight Eisenhower[120] a dim-witted grandfather, and Gerald Ford[121] a clumsy oaf, while John Kennedy[122] was a brilliant young leader, Adlai Stevenson an intellectual statesman, Al Gore a wooden, but insightful intellect, Jimmy Carter[123] a detailed scientific mind, and Bill Clinton[124] one of the smartest men to inhabit the Whiter House. Even conservatives too bright to be labeled dumb did not escape. Richard Nixon[125] became a villainous crook, Barry Goldwater[126] a troglodyte cold warrior, and George Bush the elder an out of touch elitist who did not understand how supermarket scanner worked.

Needless to say, liberals are presented as paragons of the mainstream, whereas their opponents are dismissed as extremists.[127] Those on the left are likewise victims of McCarthyite slurs, while those on the right perpetrate these. It does not matter that it has been decades since liberals were accused of being communists, the implication of a lack of patriotism remains. Nor does it matter that conservatives are hounded for being racist, sexist, homophobes; they undoubtedly deserve it. Progressives are the "real" democrats, in sharp contrast to these traditionalists, who are closet Nazis. No epithet, not liar, mass-murderer, or warmonger is too severe. The spin is never-ending. Nowadays the accusations have reached a crescendo with the arrival of competing news outlets. Both the Fox network and talk radio have aroused suspicions that the liberal monopoly may not endure. As a result, the rhetoric has heated up with accusations that it is the conservatives who are actually in charge.

It must be noted in passing that liberals also dominate the publishing business. Most of the big houses have a penchant for printing and publicizing works congruent with these preferred beliefs. With most of the larger companies headquartered in New York City, their editors are influenced by the prejudices of the Manhattan intellectuals who are their friends. The neo-Marxism of these thinkers appears mainstream to decision-makers who are exposed to little else when they make their social rounds.

Entertainment

If America's image-makers are concentrated in New York City, its myth-makers are clustered in Hollywood, California.[128] Just as a society's beliefs are shaped by the facts its institutions transmit, so they are molded by the stories they tell. Human beings learn about their world as much from fictional accounts of it as from direct observation. These narratives have the advantage of possessing uncluttered plots and emotional clarity. For the most part, straightforward depictions of who is good or evil, they are the contemporary version of biblical parables. As a result, audiences receive transparent instructions on whom to root for or against. Once, the Christian Church utilized passion plays to tutor the laity on the rudiments of faith. Today, in our more secular times, the entertainment industry has acquired this function. In movies, television dramas,[129] and music it broadcasts its favorite lessons in the form of easy to swallow amusements. People pay attention because they are emotionally enlisted into performances that appeal to their instinctual dispositions. Though they know this is make-believe, they nevertheless care about who wins and loses because they are biologically programmed to care about such things. As it happens, liberals have attained a virtual monopoly within the entertainment industry. In control of the machinery of storytelling, they produce materials uniformly favorable to their point of view.

The cultural dominance of liberalism is revealed by pieces of evidence such as how U.S. presidents are portrayed. In almost every instance, positive renderings are reserved for liberal politicians. From the movie's <u>American President</u> to television's <u>West Wing</u>, conservatives are rendered as heartless villains intent of destroying sympathetic left-leaning heroes. Indeed, it is far more likely that a president will be depicted as a bloodthirsty murderer than as a conscientious traditionalist trying to reduce the size of government in order to preserve freedom. Much more visible are Dr. Strangelove characters who are plotting an anti-democratic conflagration. The attitude is also exposed in depictions of tradition. <u>Pleasantville</u> was one such concoction. This film magically transported teenagers back into a black and white television portrayal of the 1950s. Not only was color gone from this world, so were art, love, and sex. The morals of a half-century ago were thereby pilloried as crimped and antihumanistic. They clearly needed to be loosened up by a large dose of abstract painting and lyrically represented lust. They needed, in short, to be rescued by an injection of liberal values.

One of fiction's specialties is presenting the unreal as true. There may never have been dragons, but novelists and filmmakers routinely construct images that make them appear factual. The same can be said of idealized models of the future. A world in which hierarchy fades away may not be possible, but is on the silver screen. So is one in which indiscriminate sex has no unfavorable consequences.[130] The Pleasantville teens did not fret about becoming pregnant, that is, as long as the producers kept this out of the story line. In the same way, history can be reworked to serve contemporary purposes. Nixon and JFK could identify the scoundrels as whoever their director desired. Yet that which was shown to have happened never really unfolded in that way. Even in a genre as simple as westerns, the staples have been revised to convey liberal shibboleths. Once upon a time the good guys wore white hats and the bad ones black. Once upon a time the Indians attacked the wagon train and the cavalry drove them off. In recent years, this has been reversed. In Dances with Wolves there is no question that the underdogs are morally superior. Their defects are passed over in poetic silence.

A casual glance at the academy awards[131] demonstrates who is in and who out. From Gentlemen's Agreement in 1947, to The Apartment in 1960, to Midnight Cowboy in 1969, to Rocky in 1976, to Platoon in 1986, to the Unforgiven in 1992, the underdogs received compassionate treatment. About the only conservative hero to win an award was Patton in 1970. More recently Bowling for Columbine was honored with the Oscar for best documentary. Blatantly anti-establishment, and riddled with misrepresentations, its awkward filmmaking nevertheless impressed voters in agreement with its central thesis. Less egregious is what happened to made-for-television movies. Though many of these traded in sensationalism for its own sake, another batch were dedicated to illustrating the "problem of the week." Just as liberal politicians specialize in sob stories about whatever grievance they promise to solve, so media moguls feature social conditions that cry out for reform. That they are not able to offer a viable solution takes a back seat to mobilizing social concern for a legislative intervention.

Hollywood has also produced a bumper crop of liberal celebrities. Artists whose only claim to fame is that their occupation provides a larger-than-life image leap to the defense of causes they barely understand. Imbued with the romance of being among the beautiful people,[132] viewers often confuse them with the roles they play. While actors and actresses have as much right to be politically active as any citizen, many nevertheless disingenuously conceal their modest intellectual credentials. For many, a liberal-oriented appearance of compassion is a good career move. It is certainly valuable to politicians who can raise huge donations by associating themselves with well-loved entertainers.

One of the worst effects of the entertainment industry has been on sexual mores. In an effort to attract viewers, conventionalized lasciviousness has become the order of the day. Full frontal nudity, plus simulated sexual intercourse, have migrated from the x-rated movie theater to the television screen. No longer is much off-limits. Worse yet, promiscuity is represented as exciting and sophisticated. To judge from what appears in the cinema or on situation comedies, the beautiful people routinely swap bed partners. They have learned that sex is natural, beautiful, and inconsequential, and like Madonna are trying to liberate others by sharing their insights. When it is objected that this sends the wrong ideas to young people, the response is to lament censorship. Government regulations are denounced as totalitarian impositions that must be resisted lest democracy be imperiled. Even private criticisms of casual sexuality are deplored as smacking of fascism. They are said to portray a narrow-mindedness inimical to art and creativity. The paradox in this is that those who defend a complete freedom of sexual expression also favor broader representation for minority performers. In this case, they argue that the downtrodden need positive role models if they are to move forward. Yet if race relations can be improved by providing such models, why shouldn't sexuality receive analogous treatment? Why isn't casual promiscuity an image that needs to be shunned as much as are Sambo representations of African-Americans?

In fact, a ready access to cavalier sexuality seems to have had grievous consequences. The very individuals liberals claim to be defending are the ones most adversely affected. Youngsters impressed by the glamour of publicly exposed skin conclude that going naked is not so terrible. Less likely to come from families that instill strict standards, they are easily drawn into prostitution and/or relationships based on physical attributes. Instead of being encouraged to seek the professional skills needed to move up the social class ladder, they are seduced into besmirching their reputations. It is as if they have been lured into one-night stands by unscrupulous media Lotharios who promise they will still love the victims in the morning. The same can be said of hip-hop music[133] that substitutes friction between body organs for enduring love. "Shake your booty" and "give it to me baby" and you will be liberated from oppression shout a bevy of half-naked millionaires. And the very young listen. They submit to the importations of their lustful boyfriends and flash their breasts for the television camera. It is all in good fun and in a world were everyone is destined to be equal can have no unfortunate by-products.

Lawyers and Social Workers

A few words must also be said about lawyers and social workers. They too have become pillars of the liberal establishment. In their different ways dedicated to supporting centralized government, they have likewise contributed to the institutionalization of niceness. Both, for example, theoretically fight for the rights of the disempowered. Both also have a vested interest in promoting victimization and collectivist solutions. Although respectively professionals and semi-professionals, they are occupationally committed to discouraging others from becoming professionalized. Neither group would accept this characterization—quite the contrary, they consider themselves compassionate facilitators of social justice—yet they exhibit a bobo mentality that undermines their official intentions.

Lawyering has become a growth industry.[134] Ironically, the more commercialized our society has become, the more de Tocqueville's social peacemakers have taken to tearing at its foundations.[135] Many attorneys dedicate their careers to settling contractual disputes, but many more use the law as a bludgeon to beat the powerful into submission.[136] Casting themselves in the role of a David sworn to fell the capitalist Goliath, they perceive themselves as making democracy work for the little guy. In their own eyes, legal ombudsmen who apply the law to correct grievances for those who have no other recourse, they do so with so a blunt instrument that they are in danger of weakening the social infrastructure undergirding the law.[137] The very market system that produced the values and self-discipline to make universalistic regulations viable is attacked with singular enthusiasm. Instead of genuinely fostering an even playing field, victory at any cost is all that matters.[138]

The primary tool of legal liberals is tort law.[139] Torts are civil wrongs such as negligence. Private citizens suing each other in court to have their differences decided by a judge or jury enforce these statutes. Out of this frequently comes a monetary award intended to correct the adjudicated imbalance. Someone who has been injured by slipping on ice might, therefore, have his medical costs paid by the party held responsible for having cleared that ice. But the tort law goes farther than this. It allows the injured party to collect "punitive damages." This is intended to discourage others from committing the same wrong. Trial lawyers who specialize in negligence suits, as a consequence, regard themselves as a bulwark against iniquity. In their own view, they make sure that doctors avoid malpractice, that manufacturers do not sell defective products, that employers guard against sexual harassment, that motorists exercise due caution, and that schools do not smuggle in Christian prayer under the guise of a moment of silence.

All of this sounds reasonable, yet in the hands of unscrupulous practitioners has been overdone. Once upon a time, the damage awards were relatively modest. Nowadays they have escalated into the billions of dollars. The objective is not merely to send a message, but to drive the villains into bankruptcy. Thus when liberals were unable to pass legislation outlawing tobacco, they did an end run around democracy by seeking to drive the tobacco companies out of business. This has not yet been achieved, but they did destroy the asbestos business. What makes this tactic egregious is that virtually any court can impose these awards. Attorneys are free to do venue shopping.[140] They can bring their suits before jurisdictions sympathetic to their clients. This has the effect of holding the accused hostage to the least common denominator. As a result, the potential quarry is hesitant to engage in actions some unelected vigilantes might find objectionable. Corporations, in general, fearing that they might be detested for their commercial success often avoid risky enterprises in the expectation that these might draw unwanted fire. The outcome is to play it safe and retard progress.

Another result of this is a spate of frivolous suits brought for profit rather than to redress injustices. In legal circles it is well understood that some actions are brought only because the defendant has "deep pockets." Another reason for these cases is that they can be brought at no cost to the accuser. Because victory can be so profitable, lawyers are prepared to work for contingency fees, that is, they agree to work for a proportion of what they can later extract

from the target. This technique has become so prevalent that it has
driven up medical costs to unconscionable levels. In order to engage
in practice, physicians must carry malpractice insurance that costs
them hundreds of thousands of dollars. They must also engage in
defensive medicine, ordering unnecessary, but expensive tests, lest
they afterward be accused of failing to do so. All of this provides trial
lawyers with a financial incentive to make sure there exist regulations
others can be sued for violating. In favor of big government because
it is good for their business, they are generous contributors to the
party of Big Government, *i.e.*, the Democratic Party (which even
nominated a trial lawyer for vice-president).

Another devotee of big government is the American Civil
Liberties Union (ACLU).[141] Dedicated to constitutional cases
ostensibly in defense of personal freedoms,[142] somehow the freedoms
protected are never those of conservatives. More apt to be on the
organization's agenda are measures shielding affirmative action than
those challenging reverse discrimination. Remarkably, the ACLU's
idea of free speech is either liberal or crackpot speech. It never seems
to get involved when a college president refuses to protect a student
newspaper from being vandalized, that is, if the paper's editorial
policy is right of center. Here too the institutionalized "niceness" is
highly particularized.

Still more associated with niceness is social work.[143] It too has
been a growth industry in a society that considers itself affluent enough
to rescue everyone from any conceivable disability. Much of the
social engineering that liberals have sponsored is understood in social
work terms. As was mentioned above, many educators today regard
themselves as social reformers. They believe in neo-Marxist changes
and expect that in instituting an equality of academic results they
are laying the foundation for broader social equalities. Professional
social workers have similar aims. Given an enormous boost both by
the war of poverty and the advent of psychotherapy, they have long
since surpassed their origins in assimilating immigrant populations.
Professionally nice, they believe that compassion dictates a quest for
complete equity.

The primary recipients of social work attention have always
been the poor. This has naturally engendered a commiseration with
their condition. Social workers get an up-close and personal view of

the devastation poverty can impose. Were they able to they would wave a magic wand to raise everyone's social status. Given the facts of social hierarchy, however, this is not possible. Improvements can be made, but these are always limited and, therefore, to some degree frustrating. For many, solace is found in liberal idealism. Its extravagant promises are supported in the belief that they can be redeemed. That they are impractical contradictions, which cannot come to fruition, is suppressed. As true believers, social workers are among the most persuasive advocates of programmatic solutions.

Psychotherapy too has provided a wedge to produce change.[144] The Freudian discovery that analyzing emotional impediments could facilitate personal growth had by the 1940s created a therapeutic craze among the well heeled. Financially, the only way the poor could participate in this treatment was to avail themselves of therapists less expensive than the physicians who introduced the procedure. Social workers fit this bill. For the most part, less intensively trained, they were prepared to work for less. The irony is that they performed this so well that the demand for their services outgrew the ability of insurance companies to afford long-term interventions. The result was that instead of well-motivated clients receiving services that could in fact promote social mobility, they were shunted into brief therapies that more or less maintained the status quo. Liberalism having over-promised, it delivered almost the opposite of what it promised. In the hands of social work, it became a rationalization that legitimized the reverse of what its supporters hoped.

The Working Class Counterattack

The Middle Class Revolution has produced many winners, but not everyone can be counted among their numbers. Those who remain on a lower rung have benefited materially, yet they understand that many others outrank them. As disturbingly, they recognize that they are subject to direction from above. Trapped in relatively conformist occupations, they may be more self-directed than their ancestors, but are less so than their bosses. This can be so irritating that it impels them toward rebellion. They become oppositionalists who decide what to do on the basis of what will exasperate those with greater power. Feeling relatively weak, they go out of their way to embrace purported symbols of strength.

How this strategy operates can be seen in the wrestling ring.[145] In almost every corner of the country, gigantic blue-collar bruisers can be found standing before huge crowds shouting their defiance toward the world. With muscles pumped up to grotesque proportions, they threaten to wreck violence on anyone who gets it their way. To this, their audiences respond with vicarious delirium. They too shout their insubordination toward anonymous others; thereby engaging in a symbolic mutiny they could never sustain on the job. Among their other forms of disobedience are the self-mutilations of tattoos and body piercing. As visible evidence that they are willing to endure physical pain, these disfigurements are boasts of being stronger than effete corporate executives. So too are song lyrics that promise to shoot law officers and rape uppity women. Those who sing them out at rock concerts know full well that they offend law-abiding sensibilities. And this is the point—to get away with being vulgarly offensive.

Throughout most of history, the trendsetters have come from the higher social classes. The ways that they have dressed and spoken have usually established the models for those below them. Not surprisingly, in their desire to improve their situation, the poor have emulated what they could. Yet with the ascendancy of the middle class, there has been a partial role reversal. Today many styles have bubbled up from below. Music, fashions, and even tattoos and piercings started among the lower orders have become chic among middle class adolescents. This is partly due to the rebelliousness of teenagers, but it also to the dynamics of social class politics. Amazingly bobos have been instrumental in spreading styles that are inimical to their interests, or, at least, to the interests of their children. They too have enthusiastically ratified lower class over upper class practices.

As cultural specialists, liberals control most of the companies that market communal fashions. Were they, in fact, opposed to vulgar sexuality or defiant rebelliousness, these would not show up in the magazines, television programs, or college classrooms they command. Yet they do provide them a social imprimatur. Instead of condemning graffiti as vandalism, it is encouraged as "street art."[146] Instead of rejecting pornography as exploitive, it is promoted as free speech. The reason for this counter-intuitive behavior is as old as the belief that "the enemy of my enemy is my friend." In seeking allies against the traditional middle class, bobos have courted those below them in the pecking order. Because, like the bourgeois politicians who sponsored Adolf Hitler,[147] they are convinced they can manage the antics of their inferiors, they advance activities detrimental to social mobility. But since most of their own children only dabble in this sort of raucous rebellion, they are not seriously hurt, whereas the children of the poor take these adventures seriously. They believe that becoming tattoo billboards identifies them as sophisticates. Much to their surprise they will one day discover that they have been excluded from positions of authority. The victims of another group's assault on the bastions of conventional middle class supremacy, they are apt to be the last to recognize it. The bobos, the ones who support the institutionalization of this folly, may be the only winners—if only temporarily. They gain the profits and the political capital, but perhaps at the expense of their own long-term security.

Endnotes

1 Armstrong, K. 1993. *A History of God: The 4000- Year Quest of Judaism, Christianity and Islam.* New York: Ballantine Books.; Olson, R.E. 1999. *The Story of Christian Theology: Twenty Centuries of Tradition and Reform.* Dowers Grove, IL: Intervarsity Press.

2 Roth, C. 1961. *A History of the Jews: From Earliest Times Through the Six Day War.* New York: Schocken Books.

3 Straus, B.R. 1987. *The Catholic Church.* London: David & Charles.

4 Glubb, J.B. 1963. *The Great Arab Conquests.* London: Quartet Books.

5 Friedman, R.E. 1987. *Who Wrote the Bible?* New York: Summit Books.

6 Hoffer, E. 1951. The True Believer: Thoughts on the Nature of Mass Movements. New York: Harper & Row.

7 Miller, Z. 2003. *A National Party No More: The Conscience of a Conservative Democrat.* Atlanta: Stroud & Hall Publishing.

8 Montefiore, S.S. 2004. *Stalin: The Court of the Red Tsar.* New York: Alfred A. Knopf.

9 Marx, K. 1967. *Das Capital.* Edited by F. Engels. Translated by Samuel Moore and Edward Aveling. New York: International Publishing.

10 Fischer, L. 1964. *The Life of Lenin.* New York: Harper & Row.

11 Terrill, R. 1980. *A Biography: Mao.* New York: Harper & Row.

12 Day, D. 1962. *Will Rogers: A Biography.* New York: D. McKay Co.

13 Smith, H. 1988. *The Power Game: How Washington Works.* New York: Random House.

14 Gans, H.J. 1988. *Middle American Individualism: Political Participation and Liberal Democracy.* New York: Oxford University Press.

15 Goldberg, B. 2003. *Arrogance: Rescuing America from the Media Elite.* New York: Warner Books.

16 Bloom. A. 1987. *The Closing of the American Mind.* New York: Simon & Schuster.

17 Flynn, D.J. 2004. *Intellectual Morons: How Ideology Makes Smart People Fall for Stupid Ideas.* New York: Crown Forum.

18 Blyth, M. 2004. *Spin Sisters: How the Women of the Media Sell Unhappiness and Liberalism to the Women of America.* New York: St. Martin's Press.

19 Goldberg, B. 2002. *Bias: A CBS Insider Exposes How the Media Distort the News.* Washington, DC: Regnery Publishing.; Bozell, L.B. 2004. *Weapons of Mass Distortion: The Coming Meltdown of the Liberal Media.* New York: Crown Forum.

20 Ellis, R.J. 1998. *The Dark Side of the Left: Illiberal Egalitarianism in America.* Lawrence: University of Kansas Press.; Bloom. A. 1987. *The Closing of the American Mind.* New York: Simon & Schuster.

21 Stein, H. 2000. *How I Accidentally Joined the Vast Right-Wing Conspiracy (And Found Inner Peace)* New York: Delacorte Press.

22 Durkheim, E. 1961. *Moral Education.* New York: The Free Press.

23 Rousseau, Jean-Jacques [1762] 1979. *Emile.* Trans. A. Bloom. New York: Basic Books.

24 Dewey, J. 1943. *The School and Society.* Chicago: University of Chicago Press.

25 Neill, A.S. 1960. *Summerhill: A Radical Approach to Child Rearing.* New York: Hart Publishing Co.

26 Bowles, S. and Gintis, H. 1976. *Schooling in Capitalist America: Educational Reform and the Contradictions of Capitalist Life.* New York: Basic Books.

27 Ravitch, D. 2000. *Left Back: A Century of Failed School Reforms.* New York: Simon & Schuster.; Jencks, C. 1972. *Inequality: A Reassessment of the Effect of Family and Schooling in America.* New York: Basic Books.; Barone, M. 2004. *Hard America Soft America.* New York: Crown Forum.; Hanson, V.D. 2003b. *Mexifornia: A State of Being.* San Francisco: Encounter Books.

28 Silberman, C.E. (Ed.) 1973. *The Open Classroom Reader.* New York: Random House.

29 Ogbu, J.U. 1974. *The Next Generation: An Ethnography of Education in an Urban School.* New York: Academic Press.

30 Rochester, J.M. 2002. *Class Warfare: Besieged Schools, Bewildered Parents, Betrayed Kids and the Attack on Excellence.* San Francisco: Encounter Books.

31 Ibid.

32 Kramer, R. 1991. *Ed School Follies: The Miseducation of America's Teachers.* New York: The Free Press.

33 Brimelow, P. 2003. *The Worm in the Apple: How the Teacher Unions Are Destroying American Education.* New York: HarperCollins Publishers.

34 Lortie, D.C. 1975. *Schoolteacher: A Sociological Study.* Chicago: University of Chicago Press.; Waller, W. 1967. *The Sociology of Teaching.* New York: John Wiley & Sons.

35 Hewitt, J.P. 1998. *The Myth of Self-Esteem: Finding Happiness and Solving Problems in America.* New York: St. Martins.; Steinem, G. 1992. *Revolution From Within: A Book of Self-Esteem.* Boston: Little, Brown.

36 Rubin L. B. 1972. *Busing & Backlash: White Against White in an Urban School District.* Berkeley: University of California Press.

37 Ravitch, D. 2003. *The Language Police: How Pressure Groups Restrict What Students Learn.* New York: Alfred A. Knopf.; Loewen, J.W. 1995. *Lies My Teacher Told Me: Everything Your American History Textbook Got Wrong.* New York: The New Press.

38 Coleman, J.S., Campbell, E.Q, Hobson, C.J., McPartland, J., Mood, A.M., Weinfeld, F.D. and York, R.L. 1966. *Equality of Educational Opportunity.* Washington: U.S. Government Printing Office.

[39] Kramer, R. 1991. *Ed School Follies: The Miseducation of America's Teachers.* New York: The Free Press.

[40] Valentine, C. 1968. *Culture and Poverty.* Chicago: University of Chicago Press.

[41] Kurtines, W.M. and Gewirtz, J.L. (Eds.) 1987. *Moral Development Through Social Interaction.* New York: John Wiley & Sons.

[42] Thernstrom, S. and Thernstrom, A. 2003. *No Excuses: Closing the Racial Gap in Learning.* New York: Simon and Schuster.; Crawford, J. 1989. *Bilingual Education: History, Politics, Theory, and Practice.* Trenton, NJ: Crane Publishing Co.

[43] Becker, H.S. 1963. *The Outsiders: Studies in the Sociology of Deviance.* New York: Free Press of Glencoe.; Becker, H.S. (Ed.) 1964. *The Other Side.* New York: Free Press.; Becker, H. 1970. *Sociological Work: Method and Substance.* Chicago: Aldine Publishing Co.; Lemert, E.M. 1967. *Human Deviance: Social Problems and Social Control.* Englewood Cliffs, NJ: Prentice-Hall.

[44] Wolfensberger, W. with Nirje et al. 1972. *The Principle of Normalization in Human Services.* Toronto: National Institute on Mental Retardation.

[45] Thernstrom, S. and Thernstrom, A. 2003. *No Excuses: Closing the Racial Gap in Learning.* New York: Simon and Schuster.

[46] Fein, M. 2001 *Race and Morality: How Good Intentions Undermine Social Justice and Perpetuate Inequality.* New York: Kluwer/Plenum.

[47] Brimelow, P. 2003. *The Worm in the Apple: How the Teacher Unions Are Destroying American Education.* New York: HarperCollins Publishers.

[48] Good, T.L. and Braden, J.S. 2000. *The Great School Debate: Choice, Vouchers, and Charters.* Mahwah, NJ. Lawrence Erlbaum Associates.

[49] Rudolph, F. 1990. *The American College and University: A History.* Athens: University of Georgia Press.; D'Souza, D. 1991. *Illiberal Education: The Politics of Race and Sex on Campus.* New York: The Free Press.

[50] Johnson, V.E. 2002. *Grade Inflation: A Crisis in College Education.* New York: Springer.

[51] Douthat. R. 2005. *Privilege: Harvard and the Education of the Ruling Class.* New York: Hyperion.; Hatab, L.J. 1990. *Myth and Philosophy: A Contest of Truths.* La Salle, IL: Open Court.

[52] Johnson, V.E. 2002. *Grade Inflation: A Crisis in College Education.* New York: Springer.

[53] Kors, A.C. and Silverglate, H.A. 1998. *The Shadow University: The Betrayal of Liberty on America's Campuses.* New York: The Free Press.

[54] Adams, M.S. 2004. *Welcome to the Ivory Tower of Babel: Confessions of a Conservative College Professor.* Augusta, GA: Harbor House.

[55] Kimball, R. 1990. *Tenured Radicals: How Politics Has Corrupted Our Higher Education.* Chicago: Ivan R. Dee.

[56] American Enterprise Institute. 2002. "The Shame of America's One-Party Campuses." *American Enterprise,* September.

[57] Collins, R. 1998. *The Sociology of Philosophies: A Global Theory of Intellectual Change.* Cambridge, MA: Harvard University Press.

[58] Kurtines, W.M. and Gewirtz, J.L. (Eds.) 1987. *Moral Development Through Social Interaction.* New York: John Wiley & Sons.

[59] See the writings of Italian communist theorist Antonio Gramcsi for the justification of a Marxist take-over of higher education. Gramsci, A. 1977. *Antonio Gramsci: Selections from Political Writings.* New York: International Publications.

[60] Cheney, L. 1995. *Telling the Truth.* New York: Simon & Schuster.; Haynes, J.E. and Klehr, H. 2003. *In Denial: Historians, Communism and Espionage.* San Francisco: Encounter Books.; Hoffer, P.C. 2004. *Past Imperfect: Facts, Fictions, Fraud—American History from Bancroft and Parkman to Ambrose, Bellesiles, Ellis and Goodwin.* New York: Public Affairs.

[61] Ellis, J.M. 1997. *Literature Lost: Social Agendas and the Corruption of the Humanities.* New Haven: Yale University Press.

[62] Lopreato, J. and Crippen, T. 1999. *Crisis in Sociology: The Need For Darwin.* New Brunswick, NJ: Transaction Publishers.; Rule, J.B. 1997. *Theory and Progress in Social Science.* Cambridge, UK: Cambridge University Press.

[63] Derrida, J. 1997. *Deconstruction in a Nutshell* (Edited by D. Caputo) New York: Fordham University Press.

[64] Cheney, L. 1995. *Telling the Truth.* New York: Simon & Schuster.

[65] Hoffer, P.C. 2004. *Past Imperfect: Facts, Fictions, Fraud—American History from Bancroft and Parkman to Ambrose, Bellesiles, Ellis and Goodwin.* New York: Public Affairs.

[66] Fish, S. 1989. *Doing What Comes Naturally: Change, Rhetoric, and the Practice of Theory in Literary and Legal Studies.* NC: Duke University Press.

[67] McWhorter, J. 2003. *Authentically Black: Essays for the Black Silent Majority.* New York: Gotham Books.

[68] Twain, M. 1989. *The Adventures of Huckleberry Finn.* New York: Tom Doherty Associates, Inc.

[69] Steinbeck, J. 1986. *The Grapes of Wrath.* New York: Penguin Books.

[70] Anderson, M. 1992. *Imposters in the Temple: American Intellectuals are Destroying Our Universities and Cheating Our Students of Their Future.* New York: Simon & Schuster.

[71] Gouldner, A.W. 1970. *The Coming Crisis of Western Sociology.* New York: Basic Books.; Cole, S. (Ed.) 2001. *What's Wrong with Sociology?* New Brunswick, NJ: Transaction Publishers.

[72] Hamilton, R.F. 1996. *The Social Misconstruction of Reality: Validity and Verification in the Scholarly Community.* New Haven: Yale University Press.

[73] Glenn, N. 1997. *Closed Hearts, Closed Minds: The Textbook Story of Marriage.* New York: Institute for American Values.

[74] Bowles, S. and Gintis, H. 1976. *Schooling in Capitalist America: Educational Reform and the Contradictions of Capitalist Life.* New York: Basic Books.

[75] Hunt, A. 1999. *Governing Morals: A Social History of Moral Regulation.* New York: Cambridge University Press.; Oberschell, A. 1995. *Social Movements: Ideologies, Interests, and Identities.* New Brunswick, NJ: Transaction Press.

[76] Hunter, J.D. 2000. *The Death of Character: Moral Education in an Age Without Good and Evil.* New York: Basic Books.

[77] Shapiro, B. 2004. *Brainwashed: How Universities Indoctrinate America's Youth.* Nashville TN: WND Books.

[78] Cassel, J.F. 1993. *Critical Thinking: An Annotated Bibliography.* Metuchen, NJ: The Scarecrow Press.

[79] Foucault, M. 1965. *Madness and Civilization: A History of Insanity in the Age of Reason.* New York: Pantheon Books.; Foucault, M. 1979. *Discipline and Punish: The Birth of the Prison.* New York: Random House.

[80] Rawls, J. 1971. *A Theory of Justice.* Cambridge, Mass.: The Belknap Press.

[81] Cole, S. (Ed.) 2001. *What's Wrong with Sociology?* New Brunswick, NJ: Transaction Publishers.

[82] Sniderman, P.M. and Carmines, E.G. 1998. *Reaching Beyond Race.* Cambridge, MA: Harvard University Press.

[83] Coleman, J.S., Campbell, E.Q, Hobson, C.J., McPartland, J., Mood, A.M., Weinfeld, F.D. and York, R.L. 1966. *Equality of Educational Opportunity.* Washington: U.S. Government Printing Office.

[84] Sommers, C.H. 2000. *The War Against Boys: How Misguided Feminism is Harming Our Young Men.* New York: Simon & Schuster.; Pollock, W. 1999. *Real Boys: Rescuing Our Sons from the Myths of Boyhood.* New York: Henry Holt and Co.

[85] Best, J. 2001. *Damned Lies and Statistics: Untangling Numbers from the Media, Politicians, and Activists.* Berkeley: University of California Press.

[86] Ravitch, D. 2003. *The Language Police: How Pressure Groups Restrict What Students Learn.* New York: Alfred A. Knopf.

[87] Starr, P. 2004. *The Creation of the Media: Political Origins of Modern Communications.* New York: Basic Books.; Bailyn, B. 1992. *The Ideological Origins of the American Revolution.* Cambridge, MA: The Belknap Press.

[88] Shogan, R. 2001. *Bad News: Where the Press Goes Wrong in the Making of the President.* Chicago: Ivan R. Dee.

[89] Madison, J, Hamilton, A. and Jay, J. 2000. *The Federalist.* London: Phoenix Press.

[90] Paine, T. 1953. *Common Sense and Other Political Writings.* (Edited by Nelson F. Adkins) New York: Liberal Arts Press.

[91] Ellis, J.J. 1996. *American Sphinx: The Character of Thomas Jefferson.* New York: Alfred A. Knopf.

[92] McCullough, D. 2001. *John Adams*. New York: Simon & Schuster.

[93] Swanberg. W.A. 1972. *Luce and His Empire*. New York: Scribner.

[94] Tanenhaus, S. 1997. *Whittaker Chambers: A Biography*. New York: Random House.

[95] Goldberg, B. 2002. *Bias: A CBS Insider Exposes How the Media Distort the News*. Washington, DC: Regnery Publishing.

[96] McGowan, W. 2001. *Coloring the News: How Crusading for Diversity Has Corrupted American Journalism*. San Francisco: Encounter Books.; Murray, D., Schwartz, J. and Lichter, S.R. 2001. *It Ain't Necessarily So: How Media Make and Unmake the Scientific Picture of Reality*. Lanham, MD: Rowman & Littlefield Publishers.

[97] Cronkite, W. 1996. *A Reporter's Life*. New York: Alfred A. Knopf.

[98] Joes, A.J. 1989. *The War for South Viet Nam 1954-1975*. New York: Praeger.

[99] Bernstein, C. and Woodward, B. 1974. *All the President's Men*. New York: Simon and Schuster.

[100] Moore, M. 2001. *Stupid White Men...and Other Sorry Excuses for the State of the Nation*. New York: ReganBooks.

[101] Wicker, T. 1991. *One of Us: Richard Nixon and the American Dream*. New York: Random House.

[102] Smith, H. 1988. *The Power Game: How Washington Works*. New York: Random House.

[103] Kohn, B. 2003. *Journalistic Fraud: How The New York Times Distorts the News and Why It Can No Longer Be Trusted*. Nashville: WND Books.

[104] Woodward, B. 2002. *Bush at War*. New York: Simon & Schuster.

[105] Kohn, op. cite.

[106] Woodward, B. 2002. *Bush at War*. New York: Simon & Schuster.

[107] Gottfredson, M.R. and Hirschi, T. 1990. *A General Theory of Crime*. Stanford, CA: Stanford University Press.; Rothwax, H.J. 1995. *Guilty: The Collapse of Criminal Justice*. New York: Random House.

[108] Giuliani, R.W. 2002. *Leadership*. New York: Miramax Books.

[109] Sleeper, J. 1997. *Liberal Racism*. New York: Viking.

[110] MacDonald, H. 2003. *Are Cops Racist?: How the Wear Against the Police Harms Black Americans*. Chicago: Ivan R. Dee.

[111] Stossel, J. 2004. *Give Me a Break: How I Exposed Hucksters, Cheats, and Scam Artists and Became the Scourge of the Liberal Media*. New York: HarperCollins.; McBride, J. 1996. *The Color of Water: A Black Man's Tribute to His White Mother*. New York: Riverhead Books.

[112] Leo, J. 1994. *Two Steps Ahead of the Thought Police*. New York: Simon & Schuster.; Leo, J. 2001. *Incorrect Thought: Notes on Our Wayward Culture*. New Brunswick: Transaction Publishers.

[113] Blyth, M. 2004. *Spin Sisters: How the Women of the Media Sell Unhappiness and Liberalism to the Women of America*. New York: St. Martin's Press.

[114] Fox-Genovese, E. 1996. *Feminism is Not the Story of My Life: How Today's Feminist Elite Has Lost Touch with the Real Concerns of Women.* New York: Doubleday.

[115] Lott, J.R. 1998. *More Guns, Less Crime: Understanding Crime and Gun Control Laws.* Chicago: University of Chicago Press.

[116] Skrentny, J.L. 1996. *The Ironies of Affirmative Action: Politics, Culture, and Justice in America.* Chicago: University of Chicago Press.

[117] McGowan, W. 2001. *Coloring the News: How Crusading for Diversity Has Corrupted American Journalism.* San Francisco: Encounter Books.

[118] Bruce, T. 2001. *The New Thought Police: Inside the Left's Assault on Free Speech and Free Minds.* Roseville, CA: Prima Publishing.

[119] Morris, E. 1999. *Dutch: A Memoir of Ronald Reagan.* New York: Random House.

[120] Morin, R. 1969. *Dwight D. Eisenhower: A Gauge of Greatness.* New York: Simon & Schuster.

[121] Ford, G.R. 1979. *A Time to Heal: The Autobiography of Gerald R. Ford.* New York: Harper & Row.

[122] Collier, P. and Horowitz, D. 1984. *The Kennedys: An American Drama.* New York: Summit Books.

[123] Morris, K.E. 1991. *Jimmy Carter, American Moralist.* Athens: University of Georgia Press.

[124] Graham, T. 1996. *Patterns of Deception: The Media's Role in the Clinton Presidency.* Alexandria, VA: Media Research Center.

[125] Wicker, T. 1991. *One of Us: Richard Nixon and the American Dream.* New York: Random House.

[126] Goldwater, B.M. 1964. *Conscience of a Conservative.* New York: MacFadden-Bartell Corp.

[127] Coulter, A. 2002. *Slander: Liberal Lies about the American Right.* New York: Crown Forum.; Alterman, E. 2003. *What Liberal Media? The Truth about Bias and the News.* New York: Basic Books.

[128] Gabler, N. 1988. *An Empire of Their Own: How the Jews Invented Hollywood.* New York: Random House. Lichter, S.R., Lichter, L.S. and Rothman, S. 1994. *Prime Time: How TV Portrays American Culture.* Washington, DC: Regnery Publishing.

[129] McNeil, A. 1996. *Total Television: The Comprehensive Guide to Programming from 1948 to the Present.* New York: Penguin Books.

[130] Michael, R.T., Gagnon, J.H., Laumann, E.O. and Kolata, G. 1994. *Sex in America: A Definitive Study.* New York: Warner Books.

[131] Osborne, R.A. 1999. *70 Years of Oscar: The Official History of the Academy Awards.* New York: Abbeville Press.

[132] Marshall, P.D. 1977. *Celebrity and Power: Fame in Contemporary Culture.* Minneapolis, Minn.: The University of Minnesota Press.

[133] Chuck D. with Yusef Jah. 1998. *Fight the Power: Rap, Race, and Reality.* New York: Delta Trade Books.

[134] Olson, W.K. 1992. *The Litigation Explosion.* New York: Truman Talley Books.

[135] Cantor, N.F. 1997. *Imagining the Law: Common Law and the Foundations of the American Legal System.* New York: HarperCollins Publishers.; Howard, P.K. 2001. *The Lost Art of Drawing the Line: How Fairness Went Too Far.* New York: Random House.

[136] Crier, C. 2002. *The Case Against Lawyers.* New York: Broadway Books.

[137] Fish, S. 1989. *Doing What Comes Naturally: Change, Rhetoric, and the Practice of Theory in Literary and Legal Studies.* NC: Duke University Press.

[138] Campos, P.F. 1998. *Jurismania: The Madness of American Law.* New York: Oxford University Press.

[139] Olson, W.K. 1997. *The Excuse Factory: How Employment Law is Paralyzing the American Workplace.* New York: The Free Press.; Olson, W.K. 2002. *The Rule of Lawyers: How the New Litigation Elite Threatens America's Rule of Law.* New York: St. Martin's Press.; Farber, D.A. and Sherry, S. 1997. *Beyond All Reason: The Radical Assault on Truth in American Law.* New York: Oxford University Press.

[140] Boot, M. 1998. *Out of Order: Arrogance, Corruption, and Incompetence on the Bench.* New York: Basic Books.

[141] Markmann, C.L. 1965. *The Noblest Cry: A History of the American Civil Liberties Union.* New York: St. Martin's Press.

[142] Rothwax, H.J. 1995. *Guilty: The Collapse of Criminal Justice.* New York: Random House.

[143] Hollis, F. 1964. *Casework: A Psychosocial Therapy.* New York: Random House.

[144] Fein, M. 1992. *Analyzing Psychotherapy: A Social Role Interpretation.* New York: Praeger.

[145] Mazer, S. 1998. *Professional Wrestling: Sport and Spectacle.* Jackson: University of Mississippi Press.

[146] Redstone, L.G. and Redstone, R.R. 1981. *Public Art: New Directions.* New York: McGraw-Hill.

[147] Shirer, W.L. 1960. *The Rise and Fall of the Third Reich.* New York: Simon & Schuster.

Chapter 10

The Family

MARRIAGE, n. The state or condition of a community consisting of a master, a mistress and two slaves, making in all, two. (Ambrose Bierce, <u>The Devil's Dictionary</u>)

Accidents will occur in the best-regulated families. (Charles Dickens, <u>Dombey and Son</u>)

As powerful as government is, it can only do so much by itself. Government can never take the place of parents in raising children. Government can never take the place of families and churches and synagogues in teaching values. (Zell Miller, <u>A National Party No More</u>)

A Bridge to the Future

When he was running for re-election as President, Bill Clinton promised to build a bridge to the 21st century.[1] He would introduce the reforms necessary to deal with the emerging challenges of postmodernity and lay the foundation for a nearly utopian future. These improvements would, to be sure, be liberal in nature. Those championed by his wife were particularly so. Hillary Clinton[2] had earlier acquired notice for, among other things, arguing that it takes a village to raise a child. Paraphrasing an old African adage, she contended that it was now up to the government to protect the interests of the very young. Only government-sponsored programs could provide the education and security children deserved. In this, neither of the Clintons believed that they were doing damage to the family. Both took it for granted that domesticity in its customary format was outdated. As good bobos,[3] they were certain that federal regulations were inherently more moral than potentially abusive nuclear families.

For some time now, those who proclaim themselves to be the wave of the future have placed their confidence in the quasireligious institutions of liberalism. They have concluded that schools, media, entertainment industry, social-work establishments, and law-enforcement agencies can be trusted to do a better job of raising children than the men and women who brought them into the world. Because the members of these civil bodies are open to rationalization in a way that emotionally biased parents are not,[4] they can be perfected to a degree impossible for nuclear families. It is certainly true that liberals are more alarmed by private, as opposed to, public abuses. They can barely envisage the family as crucial in helping individuals adjust to the Great Middle-Class Revolution. Committed to niceness and centralization, they find it inconceivable that unfettered parents might do better jobs than the enlightened autocracy they propose. Nevertheless, the familial changes presently underway point in the direction of an improved management of the professionalism and affluence so characteristic of the modern world. Contrary to the faith of its devotees, liberalism is riven with so many contradictions, that it cannot overcome the challenges of a complex marketplace or individual self-direction. Families, in contrast, possess an elasticity that enables them to adjust to varying demands.[5] Though imperfect, they can provide more than governments ever will.

Liberals, in their discomfort with the dislocations of the middle-class ascendancy, have insisted upon absolute solutions.[6] In quest of intellectual and aesthetic control, they confuse a yearning for emotionally infused rationality with insights into how to achieve this. Authentically desirous of a better world, they mistake their shared fantasies for what is feasible. That which is actually possible is, in fact, in the process of evolving. Contrary to what they imagine, no single person or group of persons, however, has total control over these emerging realities because no individual or collection of individuals is that formidable. Discoveries are constantly being made as billions of mortals stumble along attempting to deal with their private issues, all the while influencing others engaged in similar attempts. This interlocking web of social negotiations is hammering out the shape of future families. Mistakes have been made and will continue to be made, but a combination of instinctive longings, combined with external pressures, is pushing us toward better answers. These responses become more rational as people learn more, but they are never as pure as are quasireligious visions. Nevertheless, they are bona fide solutions, which are, in addition, emotionally authentic. Derived from experience, they are lived rather than speculative.

To begin with, it must be recognized that liberalism has inherited a hostility toward the family. From both its Marxist[7] and hippie antecedents, it acquires a suspicion of the emotional crucible in which organic relationships materialize. Though both of these ideological precursors romanticize a loving family of all humankind, they have difficulty with the genuine article. Like many reformers, they tend to be more comfortable with people in the abstract than with particular human beings. For their part, the Marxists equate the family with capitalist exploitation. The bourgeois male is depicted as a greedy tyrant who dominates his household for his personal glory. His wife and children are said to be extensions of himself who either display his fortune or are groomed to enlarge it. Since both are essentially conceived of as his property, they are his to do with as he pleased. This converts women into sexual objects whose central tasks are childrearing and conspicuous consumption.[8] His children, though loved, are potential heirs whose primary purpose is to mirror his personal achievements after he is gone. Unless they liberate themselves from this suffocating hegemony, they are doomed never to have independent lives. The best they can hope is to become pampered slaves lashed to the service of his needs.

The Marxists, when they came to power in the Soviet Union, were passionate advocates of free love.[9] Eager to see the bourgeois family consigned to the dustbin of history, they urged women to rebel against commodification by participating in sexual relationships solely from personal desire. Children too were soon redefined as the property of the state. Its preservation was where their first loyalty belonged. In this, their fidelity would be to all mankind rather than to private privilege. As time passed, this orientation became enshrined in schoolrooms where cooperation as opposed to competition is taught. Among today's unacknowledged neo-Marxists, radical feminists remain equally distrustful of heterosexual intimacy and filial piety.[10] They, as Engels[11] taught, perceive women as having been enslaved by men in the wake of the Agricultural Revolution. Marriage, which was designed to hold them in bondage through threats of rape, is regarded as a means of enforcing this tyranny.[12] It provides the legal chains that enable men to implement their diabolical threats. Only when women recognize this as maltreatment and take charge of their lives will they ever be truly free.[13] Only by choosing to live independently will they become the coequals of men.

Nor should women be shackled to childrearing. Anatomy must not be allowed to be destiny.[14] Just because men want women barefoot, pregnant, and in the kitchen does not mean they have to comply. Much more honorable is breaking out to become the CEO of a corporation.[15] As for children, they, too, will benefit from having liberated mothers. This will provide a model for their own manumission and bestow permission to seek independent success.[16] In the feminist universe, loyalty to the family becomes secondary to loyalty to oneself.[17] This same outlook infused hippie sensibilities. Perceiving themselves as eternal children, their primary objective was to engage in recreation for its own sake. They would never settle down to become sellouts like the over-thirty crowd. They would certainly never voluntarily assume the responsibility of starting their own families. Having been tutored in the arts of consumption within households now interpreted as having purloined their souls, they exulted in an autonomous egotism. Not for them commitments to spouses. Such choices were often mistakes that were later transformed into penal relationships. Nor for them the humdrum jobs of those bound to servitude by a need to support children. The hippies[18] preferred the pseudofamily of the crash pad. It allowed them to come and go as they pleased, with the illusion that anyone in momentary proximity could and would provide as much love as might be needed.

Contrasted with this was the misery of the traditional family.[19] Its apotheosis during the Victorian[20] era ushered in a sexual repression that mirrored the more extensive repression of industrialization. Cooped up in isolated households, its victims perforce lived cramped, parochial lives.[21] Contemporary religious people who recommended a return to committed domesticity were thereby championing the imposition of a narrow-minded bondage. Worse still, these pious hypocrites wanted to impose families grounded in antediluvian platitudes.[22] They literally sought to go back to the Bible for inspiration about how men and women should treat one another. Although this text was written thousands of years ago, they intended to utilize it as a model for contemporary relationships. This was absurd. Modern Westerners were no longer shepherds. It made no sense for women to walk a step behind their husbands or to fawn over them as if they were reincarnations of ancient despots. Liberated women neither could nor should be subservient to men who were neither smarter nor more moral than they.

What the critics of traditional family values fail to appreciate is that the fundamentalists[23] are not advocating a literal return to the past. The words might be derived from ancient sources, but the sentiments have been adapted to modern conditions. When these religious defenders of the family speak about preserving the institution, they are concerned about issues such as personal commitment. They want husbands and wives to be faithful to one another and their children. Although there might be disputes among family members, they urge them to work things through without resort to physical or emotional desertion. The parties are to respect one another and their mutual pledges.[24] Thus, when wives are asked to honor their husbands, they are not being asked to become doormats. They are merely expected to treat their spouses with the respect that intimacy requires. Nor was this to be a respect; they, too, are entitled to have their needs valued. The traditionalists further insist that men and women are different[25] and that, therefore, their responsibilities within the family differ, and in this they come closer to reality than did those feminists who argue that there are no biological differences between the genders—at least, none that matter. Furthermore, in encouraging women to concentrate on being good mothers and men on being competent providers, they come nearer to the realities of contemporary domestic relations, even taking into account the sexual and Middle Class Revolutions.

A bridge to the future is, therefore, unlikely to be structurally sound if it does not pay attention to family values.[26] Though these standards are not liable to be what they once were, neither are they apt to be totally different. The Marxist-inspired and bohemian augmented immaturity that captures the bobo imagination, because it totally disregards both human nature and social imperatives, cannot provide viable answers. The idea of totally independent human beings who can meet their needs for love and their children's requirements for social support, without stable attachments, is a chimera.[27] So is the notion that government bureaucrats or impersonal transfer payments can substitute for long-term interpersonal commitments. These are ideological fantasies utterly detached from human experience. Even liberals, it is safe to say, have begun to realize these fairy tales are inadequate.

Tradition, however, is not unconditional.[28] What existed in the past was never perfect, nor can it be the final word for all eternity. Modifications have been made right along and will continue to be made. The importance of tradition is as a starting point. The rules people once lived by, in their time, undoubtedly served significant purposes, even if their functions have been misunderstood. Jettisoning them without qualms would, therefore, be unwise. More prudent is experimenting with reasonable modifications. Small changes that are re-evaluated as people push ahead can avoid catastrophic readjustments. The trouble, of course, is that no one possesses a consistent objectivity. Human beings are always confused by the small slice of reality they personally glimpse. Imagining that each slice is the whole, they generally project it past its the breaking point. They are also hampered by intellectual and emotional boundaries they cannot overcome. No one is as smart as he or she supposes. This produces an inevitable irrationality that is compounded by the turbulence introduced via other people's irrationalities. Being churned in a world of competing demands is inherently disorienting. Often, the best that can be done is to look back upon past social negotiations in order to discern how they evolved. With luck, it may be possible to recognize what people have been dealing with and why.

The Post-Liberal Way of Life

In chapter 3 much was made of the middle class way of life. People are said to be coping with a commercial world in which the division of labor has subdivided to a perplexing degree. Required by technical and social circumstances to adapt to unprecedented complexities, they create a decentralized and professionalized lifestyle contingent upon self-direction and internalized disciplines. They thereby learn to make independent decisions in a fluid environment fraught with uncertainties. This is no mean task, one ultimately betrayed by the normal human tendency toward cultural lag.[29] People who grow up with the customs and social relationships of one way of life find it difficult to convert to another. Frequently, they do not even recognize the pressures they are sustaining. As a consequence, when attempting to adapt to what they think is happening, they revert to reactionary solutions. This is the irony of liberalism. Touted as a progressive development, it is actually retrogressive. Bound to an absolutism and a naïve familism, it depends upon quasireligious alliances to enforce its dictates. When it comes to the family, although it propounds an extended domesticity of all humanity, in practice it seeks to dismantle nuclear families in favor of a government-sponsored hegemony.[30]

This, almost certainly, cannot be the shape of things to come. Interlaced with contradictions and institutionalized falsehoods too unstable to provide a sound foundation, it must collapse. What seems more likely is the establishment of a post-liberal way of life centered on professionalism. Liberalism does offer hope for improvements, and this hope cannot be abandoned, but neither can it be allowed to explode due to romantic idealism. An optimistic, yet realistic, alternative must be found. Fortunately, this transformation is in the process of materializing. Families are being revamped as this is being written. As important, these modifications are not apt to result in its termination. The nuclear family is decidedly not dead.[31] Despite the ravages of divorce and extramarital affairs, an overwhelming majority of people choose. They still dream of finding soul mates and of raising a passel of tow-headed children. What they participate in differs from what their parents knew, but its dimensions would nevertheless be recognizable to earlier generations.

The family emerging from the Middle Class Revolution is one that has been amended to fit the needs of developing circumstances.[32] To begin with, this remains a hierarchical world. It has not become suffused with a quixotic egalitarianism. Social class continues to be a crucial organizing principle, with some individuals winning and others losing. Successful families are, therefore, those capable of promoting social mobility. This means the marital partners must receive the interpersonal support they need in order to win tests of strength.[33] Though the criteria required to come out on top have changed, some couples continue to achieve greater power than others. The family must, as a consequence, keep up with these advances. It has to furnish the resources to meet emerging standards of success. Husbands and wives have to encourage their respective professionalization and, as parents, must collaborate in preparing their children to achieve self-directed futures.[34] All must acquire the skills and emotional reserves to enter and sustain productive alliances in a world full of strangers.[35]

Liberalism fosters a quasireligious orientation toward the family. Its simple faith is in disembodied love and centralized altruism.[36] Yet, upon a closer inspection, it reflects a flaccid immaturity. Parents are asked to be indulgent, friends to their children, and spouses are asked to be open-minded regarding the partner's infidelities. Even single parenthood is celebrated as evidence of multicultural tolerance. None of this, however, has been well thought through. Advocates have not considered the implications of their proposals. What, for instance, would happen to youngsters who did not have parents capable of consistent discipline or marital partners who were continually betrayed by irresponsible mates? Love and good intentions may be alleged to conquer all, but among normal human beings they never do. In fact, the liberal family is about denying the validity of the traditional family, rather than offering a blueprint for a viable alternative. It is an act of defiance, not a prudent effort at innovation.

Not too surprisingly, the professionalizing family is apt to have more in common with professionalized occupations than with colliding billiard balls.   and lawyers and their ilk are trusted to make important decisions because they have demonstrated the expertise and motivation to do so effectively. The same must apply to the family. It has to provide its members with the expertise and motivation to live successful lives. This means its core cannot be bound together by flower power or mindless tolerance. Nor can it be about total independence. Although its members are self-directed and self-disciplined, they must also be committed to a common mission. Individually, they need to know a great deal and to be a great deal. They, likewise, have to possess significant people skills, technical skills, and emotional maturity. Beyond this, they benefit from being committed to middle class values and virtues. The job of the family, as a group, is to inculcate and perpetuate these factors.[37] Both for the marital partners and their children, the family must facilitate the sorts of strength necessary for its members to make independent decisions in an indeterminate world of shifting alliances. An ability to be successfully assertive under these circumstances derives, in part, from biology. Some people are born smarter and more energetic than others. Nevertheless, much of the family comes from the social structure and culture in which a person is embedded. The family is at the center of this infrastructure. It is the framework that gives people their start, in life and that keeps them going in moments of stress.

For a husband and a wife, the family has been described as a haven in a heartless world.[38] It is a place to which they can retreat to lick their wounds and receive aid and comfort from individuals who care about them. Those who do not have such succor face the daunting challenges of fending off the pressures of social competition in isolation. Without someone to love, the individual must find the courage to persist somewhere deep inside. For children, the family can also be a safe home base.[39] It is a place where they, too, can receive acceptance and encouragement. But, it is also their primary source of socialization. It is where lessons are taught in how to cope with what is eventually to come. It is also the starting point for social networking. The child who does not have a supportive family is, as a result, deprived of a ticket into the middle classes. The child will have to scramble to learn how and with whom upward mobility can be accomplished.

The family is critical for instilling and reinforcing people skills, emotional maturity,[40] and middle-class values and virtues.[41] Less focal in teaching technical skills, it may nevertheless be significant in directing children toward the schools and jobs where these can be acquired. Social propaganda to the contrary, formal education is inept at teaching personal competence. If someone wants to study the mathematics of civil engineering, there is no better place than an accredited university. If one wants to discover how to be a responsive role-taker, however, it is virtually useless. One of the reasons liberalism cannot fulfill its promises is that public institutions are dismal at dealing with emotional tasks.[42] As is well known, massive bureaucracies and formal regulations are notorious for impersonality.[43] They may advertise themselves as caring about the little person, but they, in fact, incorporate few individuals assigned to do the caring. Genuine emotional concern occurs among people who know one another and who, typically, have previously bonded.

Massive organizations specialize in an interchangeability of personnel that is inimical to intimate emotional support. No sooner do those who belong get to know one another than they are whisked away to other assignments. They, thus, find themselves subject to rules enforced by individuals who do not know or care about them. This is true even in elementary-school classrooms. Many teachers[44] assume that they will be able to compensate for the love their charges are not getting at home, but this is a vain hope. They can never know most of their students well enough to achieve this, but, what is worse, they can never commit to them for the long haul. However well things go during this school year, their charges will be passed along to someone else next term. And the children know this. They understand that they cannot depend on the long-term availability of the best-intentioned teacher. Their parents, in contrast, will be there next year and the year after that. Parents are the ones children have to worry about and the ones upon whom their fate depends. For better or worse, they are the persons with whom emotional bonding is possible.

With respect to people skills, the intimate intensity of the nuclear family is decisive.[45] A father, a mother, and their children interact regularly and familiarly. They have access to one another when they are at their most vulnerable and most open to influence. Take the issue of communication. Family members converse with one another both verbally and non-verbally. For the young, these dialogues are the place where they learn language and where they discover how to be persuasive. If their parents are inarticulate, it is not likely they will be much different. Members of the middle class, it must be remembered, are cultural specialists.[46] Their jobs typically entail the manipulation of symbols. They are, therefore, well equipped to demonstrate how this is done. This may not be fair, but it is the way it is. If one's parents are not orally expressive or do not value expressivity, they are unlikely to encourage it in their offspring. Middle class mothers and fathers, to the contrary, encourage communication by filling their houses with high-quality books and sophisticated cultural artifacts. The poor generally do not.

Similar considerations apply to role-taking and responsiveness.[47] Parents who are self-involved make it difficult to learn how to see things through the eyes of others. Not only are they inadequate models, but their selfishness tends to elicit defensive counter-measures. This, in turn, makes it difficult to develop subtle negotiation skills. Individuals who do not recognize the needs and goals of their role partners fail to recognize solutions that might meet their concerns.[48] Instead of engaging in problem-solving efforts where both parties emerge as winners, they arouse suspicion and resistance. Should this sort of conflict arise, the chances of building effective alliances are reduced. Since the family is the place where a person's first interpersonal negotiations occur, it is where basic training in deal making occurs. As should be evident, middle-class parents, because they are apt to be better practiced at this skill, make better tutors. Although deal-making routinely occurs among school-yard peers, it is remarkable how closely this follows patterns instituted earlier.

There are also the closely related competencies of self-knowledge and other-knowledge. Because learning to see what is taking place inside dissimilar individuals begins with being able to look inside oneself, children of self-aware parents get a head start over those never exposed to parental introspection. Knowing oneself takes courage. All human beings are more fragile than they would prefer; hence, they can be discouraged from making unwelcome discoveries. If these discoveries are also turned into weapons against a child by insecure parents, the message is obvious. The youngster is thereby instructed on the virtue of becoming an opaque fortress, opaque even to himself. If, on the other hand, parents are sympathetic toward their own and their offspring's mistakes, they can point toward methods for overcoming these. They can instill an honest acceptance of normal human frailties

Once more, middle-class children have an advantage. Because their parents will probably have developed personal insights in their quests for social mobility, they are better able to teach these.[49] They will also have learned more about what makes others tick. People- and data-oriented occupations demand a cosmopolitan sophistication. They force individuals to discover that blindness to cultural and situational differences produces an ignorance that is not conducive to sensitive leadership or valid decision-making. Self-absorbed social organizers virtually beg to be challenged by subordinates who may be required perform what they are not equipped to perform. Such bosses inadvertently violate Chester Barnard's[50] injunction that a manager should only lead where others are already headed, or, at least, where they are willing to head. Parents who deliver this understanding must perforce possess an accurate comprehension of social arrangements. As a consequence, their children will be less naïve than their more sheltered rivals and, therefore, less apt to inspire insurrections by being authoritarian.

People skills can also be reinforced within the marital union. A husband and wife who are both middle class can supplement each other's abilities. Since both are apt to possess independent competences, they can pool their resources such that both are better off than either would be, alone.[51] A woman may, for example, share her superior ability to read emotions by interpreting subtle social cues for her husband, whereas a man may share his more aggressive problem-solving style. As important, in getting to know each other, they can acquire a better understanding of themselves and of outsiders. The mutual responsiveness and role-taking[52] required of them hones their dexterity in dealing with others. Similarly, engaging in the negotiations inherent in an intimate relationship can improve bargaining skills. People who learn to accommodate one another, in the intensity of private liaisons, can productively transfer this forbearance to other circumstances. In learning to get along with one another, they obtain an advantage in getting along with strangers.

Many family-nurtured people skills are closely bound to the emotional maturity that is a product of certain kinds of intimacy. Emotional maturity,[53] that is, an ability to control and utilize strong emotions, is of enormous import. To be emotionally immature is to be a social weakling easily intimidated by others.[54] Those who are overwhelmed by their own feelings are prone to having these used against them. Yet, emotional strengths do not come automatically. All human beings enter the world equipped with roughly the same affective toolbox. Some may perhaps be more passionate than others, but all are imbued with a capacity for anger,[55] fear, love, etc. How to employ these interpersonally must, however, be learned. The primitive emotions of children—the crying, the lashing out, etc.—

come naturally, whereas control and appropriate communication do not.[56] These must be socialized, that is, they must be taught and practiced. Once more, the family, as the locus of interpersonal intimacy,[57] is where this best occurs. It is the place adults who have learned to manage their own feelings can instruct the young on how to manage theirs.

The school, the work site, and the welfare office cannot substitute for the family.[58] They provide neither the continuity nor the intensity to do the task. What goes on behind a family's closed doors is usually supposed to stay there because much of it would be embarrassing in front of outsiders. Most people want to appear more mature and in better control than they are. They, therefore, lack candor with strangers. It is only in the let-it-all-hang-out environment of the private household that they are truly themselves. As a consequence, only some tasks are possible. Learning to deal with strong emotions is impracticable in places where they rarely go wild. Unless passions are sometimes too powerful to be contained, there can be no rehearsal in containing them. Childhood tantrums, to cite one familiar case, must be managed *in situ*. The toddler rolling around the floor in despair discovers during his agony that this condition is not fatal. If parents who are not unhinged by the display immediately confront the child with its vapidity, the child may also learn that this demonstration is ineffective. This should prompt seeking more advanced means of making a point. Were emotions only talked about or indirectly referred to in socially acceptable charades, they could never be successfully resolved. Public pretense is occasionally required, but it does not allow for experiential learning. Family crises, for all their sturm und drang, are, therefore, essential.

Among the emotions with which families deal are anger, fear, and love. Individuals who never learn to deal with rage never find the means to overcome their frustrations. Those for whom terror is more than they can handle never learn to cope with social intimidation. And those for whom intense love is an ineluctable mystery may be swept away by a desire to be cared for by the perfect other. Yet, all of these feelings occur in every family. Some individuals suppress them in an attempt to deny their presence, but no normal child ever escapes their clutches. All that hiding from them achieves is sending the message that they are beyond control. This strategy, for that reason, perpetuates immaturity instead of confronting it. To resort to what has become a familiar mantra, middle-class status can once more make the difference. Because most people- and data-oriented jobs cannot be navigated without emotional maturity, middle-class parents are less likely to feel overmatched by a child's emotionality. Their own work-forged courage comes into play at home and enables them to convey the dependable love that converts passion from an enemy into a friend.

Marital partners may correspondingly find that marriage increases their emotional maturity. Small children often require an adult to mediate their disputes. On their own, the violence of their anger can escalate to insupportable levels. A husband and wife cannot afford to permit this to happen when they disagree. They must independently find the means to restrain their passions. They must learn that, although they will fight,[59] they are capable of resolving these quarrels without inflicting emotional injuries.[60] What is more, if they love each other, they can become allies in increasing each other's internal reserves. Instead of engaging in emotional assaults, they can provide the loving tolerance within which an overexcited partner is allowed to regain control. Couples who establish a reliable domestic anchorage within which both can find safety, thereby, furnish the conditions for further emotional growth. This sort of learning is not something confined to childhood. Fresh dangers, frustrations, and yearnings must continually be confronted and mastered by adults. An intimate friend, *i.e.*, a spouse, who cares and who is present during moments of stress can be crucial in providing the collaboration that makes the difference.

The family is also the place where values and virtues are inculcated into children.[61] Parents instruct their young on which goals are important. As significant, they provide both models of propriety and of negotiating partners for deciding what is acceptable. Because morality is socially constructed, it must be passed along from one generation to the next. One of the ways children learn to be decent human beings is by observing paradigms of moral behavior. Parents who live out these patterns provide the best lessons on virtue. Honest parents are thus unsurpassed at demonstrating that honesty is both valuable and possible. They also offer examples of how truth can be employed. By the same token, they may function as sounding boards against which the young can test variations on moral standards. Since each generation confronts different challenges, its members will need to modify their patrimony. Some sorts of falsehoods, for instance, become less morally acceptable under emerging circumstances. But, which ones in particular need to be altered is determined in negotiations with authority figures. This process occurs within families when parents and children differ on what is appropriate, as they regularly do about such matters as staying out late on dates or experimenting with psychoactive substances.

Among the most important moral traditions transmitted are those entailing personal responsibility,[62] individual merit, and self-discipline. Children, who are rewarded for exercising initiative and for accepting blame, are more likely to take chances and to learn from these experiences. Likewise, when they are praised for their successes and honored for their individuality, they are more apt to value personal achievement. Perhaps as important, children who are loved for themselves are likely to grow into loving adults.[63] Having been raised in a trustworthy emotional environment, they develop into trustworthy role partners, partners who can be relied upon by intimate strangers. Nor need they be naïve in placing their confidence in others. Those who experience trust early on learn to distinguish between genuine reliability and the counterfeit variety.

Finally, marital intimacy can promote moral behavior in a husband and wife.[64] Sociology has taught us that partners who share crucial values have successful heterosexual relationships. If one believes in honesty and the other does not, their interchanges are likely to be fraught with conflict. On the other hand, if both are honest, they reinforce this disposition. Although external forces will batter them with contradictory messages, they can validate their shared commitments and hold fast despite periodic disappointments. They can also discuss their reactions to evolving circumstances. Since they, like their children, continue to negotiate their moral obligations, they can, as well-disposed allies, do so with greater confidence. Because they stand with each other, they are more likely to stand up to those who disagree and, in the process, contribute to social bargains in accord with their own needs.

406 The Great Middle Class Revolution

Feminist (etc.) Lessons

Because the middle-class way of life could not have been foreseen, the way the family developed has been misunderstood. Would-be prophets regularly denounced the institution as antiquated and confining.[65] Later, feminists pinned most of the blame for their personal disillusionments on men.[66] They lambasted males as gender bullies who intentionally imprisoned women in gilded suburban cages. Neither of these perspectives was accurate.[67] Marriage has demonstrated a continuing utility for men, women, and children,[68] whereas most men have been unfairly castigated as protorapists. Nevertheless, there are lessons to be learned from the Marxist and feminist missteps. In their efforts to persuade people of their utopian fantasies, they convinced many of the unwary to pursue their visions. These did not succeed, but their failures revealed what was left out. In this, they also highlighted what the professionalized family of the future must include.

One of the more painful lessons has been provided by divorce.[69] Traditionally, marriages were considered everlasting. After a couple said its "I do's," they expected to live happily ever after, or at least until one of them died. With the advent of widespread prosperity, all this changed. Because the availability of market-oriented jobs enabled both men[70] and women to live independently,[71] many came to the conclusion that it made no sense to remain bound in a loveless union. Divorce became common and even normal, once the laws were changed to facilitate marital dissolution. In the midst of this instability, opinions about divorce underwent a sea change. What was previously regarded as sinful was reevaluated to be beneficial. Dissolving a bad relationship was said to give each partner an opportunity to find a better match and their children a chance to grow up within a loving family. Rather than suffer from emotional or physical abuse, all would be resilient enough to embrace the transformation.

This turned out to be wishful thinking.[72] Most divorces do not produce the expected gains.[73] Ideological promises of a bright future are not redeemed because they are not based on a sound understanding of human-attachment behavior. Those who propounded them believed that people could rationally move from one relationship to another without undue upset. What they failed to reckon with was the emotional aspects of personal bonds. When people get married, they do not merely sign a piece of paper; they also undergo a courtship process that rearranges their internal motivations. Falling in love rewires their brains so that they cannot move on with impunity. Once a relationship has been forged, it can only be torn asunder with difficulty. Almost everyone wants love to be perpetual; hence, when it is not, individuals experience disappointment. They become furiously angry at the partners who, they feel, betrayed them and eventually fall into deep depressions. Divorce is an unhappy event even when the ex-spouse is a miserable human being. The agony of detaching from a former lover takes several years, at minimum. But even then, the acceptance of this catastrophe does not prepare either party for something better. An individuals who has chosen a partner poorly often utilizes the newfound freedom to make another appalling choice. Nor may that person have learned much about how to make intimacy work.[74] There is no guarantee that the person will not make the same mistakes in a new marriage.

One of the discoveries that emerged from the explosion in the rate of divorce is that marriages must be worked at. Love does not automatically exclude conflict. No matter how well suited two individuals may be, they are never a perfect match. They must, therefore, learn how to negotiate their differences. This means they must be committed to hammering their disagreements out. If they are not, if they look for quick exits once they hit a rough patch, they will never salvage a strong bond. During the hippie interregnum, trial marriages, often without benefit of clergy, came into vogue. Couples lived together in sexual cohabitation without agreements to formalize their relationships. This was rationalized as providing information upon which a solid association could arise. If individuals saw firsthand what their partners were like, they could presumably unite their fortunes once they had confirmed their worth. As a result, they would be less likely to divorce. But this is not how it turned out. Partners who lived together for extended periods before marriage are more apt to divorce. This might appear nonsensical, but what researchers found was that those who shacked up before tying the knot tended to be less committed to the institution of marriage. As a result, when things went wrong they invested less effort in working them out. More traditional couples who viewed marriage as sacred stayed together long enough to find solutions.

This said, the greatest victims of precipitous divorce turn out to be the children.[75] These innocents are the most affected by ruptures over which they have almost no say. Before the divorce craze, conventional wisdom urged unhappy spouses to stay together for the sake of the children. Afterwards, it was equally well understood that children were resilient enough to bounce back from the worst breakup. Indeed, they would benefit by being freed from an atmosphere saturated by parental conflict. For a while, the experts agreed with this claim. Unfortunately, they did not have the benefit of longitudinal studies. It took years for the children of divorce to reach maturity and for the hidden injuries of their conditions to come to light. Eventually, social scientists recognized that in almost every measurable category these children are at a disadvantage. Persons whose parents had separated are themselves more likely to divorce. They are also less apt to be well educated or to achieve economic success. Even their health suffers relative to that of their peers. Divorce, it seems, leaves children emotionally isolated and financially at risk. Parents distracted by the pain of their own troubles have less time to recognize or alleviate those of their youngsters. Instead, these children have to suppress their pain lest they further distress their parents. Frequently blaming themselves for what has gone wrong, they have to wait until adulthood to work through losses incurred when they were small.   In the meantime, they endure relative impoverishment and a father who is at best an infrequent visitor. Moreover, because so many men remarried, they were also unlikely to provide assistance in funding college educations.

Perhaps worst off are the children of unmarried parents.[76] As divorce becomes more frequent, many conclude that marriage is an unnecessary frill. As a result, illegitimacy rates have exploded. Feminists argue that a woman alone, unencumbered by masculine oppression, can provide better parenting by herself.[77] Not diverted by a need to ward off abuse, she can offer maternal love in its purest form.   In their view, a heterosexual commitment is not only superfluous, it was positively harmful.   Yet, the research on the children of illegitimacy is even more discouraging than that for those of divorce.[78] They, too, suffer personal and professional disabilities from which they find it difficult to extricate themselves. Far from being the happy recipients of freedom, they tend to be insecure and unsuccessful. Frequently afflicted by mental disorders and inclined to indulge in deviant behaviors, the absence of two loving parents handicaps them by denying them the emotional, financial, and socialization supports that might prepare them to hold their own in a dynamic commercial society.

Marriage has been misconstrued.[79] Visions of unencumbered lust as a practical alternative are always a false ideal. Simply having sex for the mere pleasure of the experience has unanticipated consequences, consequences that leave its practitioners bereft of the expected payoffs. In contrast, marriage, though it ties people down, provides compensation for this restriction. The Great Middle-Class Revolution has not reduced the relevance of the family. To the contrary, it has enhanced it. Both men and women profit from the companionship of stable marriages; both derive comforts from the material rewards of their partnerships; and both can draw pleasure from raising children who will one day grow to be happy, self-sufficient individuals. Far from being the seedbed of despotism, the successful middle-class family provides refuges within which all can pursue their private dreams. While the institution is not an unruffled sanctuary, it is superior to the alternatives.

Nor has feminist male-bashing been productive. Men have never been the despots they have been portrayed to be. Most are certainly not rapists.[80] Indeed, isolating and demonizing them has had disconcerting effects. Ironically, though males have been maligned, those most seriously damaged are not the intended targets. Relieving men of their marital and parental duties does not bankrupt them, nor reduce their power, nor even deprive them of sexual outlets. What it does is to force women into uncomfortable roles and to deprive children of their fathers.[81] Furthermore, because marriages are adversely affected, men, women, and children are denied the benefits of the emotional and financial supports these can provide.

For the moment, let us focus on the damage done the father role. The feminist indictment of men includes their alleged abuse of their children. Said to be inherently violent, the blows they direct at their offspring supposedly harm them more than would living without them. This is demonstrably wrong. Children need their fathers.[82] The limits they set, the goals they encourage, and the models they provide are of inestimable value. Fathers are critical in inculcating the strengths needed to succeed in a competitive society. Even the roughhousing in which they specialize has the effect of making competition fun. If this sometimes frightens the young, it is more than compensated for by the protective buffer they furnish. Should this be doubted, sociologists have established that the children of strong, available fathers do better than those without them. They tend to feel better about themselves and hence are more confident when they strike out on their own. They also have a better understanding of what it is to be a man, both within a family and out in the marketplace. This is better for boys who will become men, and also for girls who may one day want to interact with one.

Feminists, in stark contrast, mistakenly contend that there are virtually no differences between men and women.[83] They find men unnecessary because in their androgynous universe women can perform any service that males can.[84] Women are told that they can have it all. They can simultaneously be lovers, mothers, corporate presidents, and, if necessary, surrogate fathers. All that has to happen is for men to relinquish their hegemony so that women can demonstrate their worth. This transformation is supposed to be utterly democratic and pacifically cooperative. Men are urged to oblige because after they denounce their macho posturing, they too will find solace in the liberation of their own feminine qualities. Equality, in the final analysis, is said to be the ultimate form of freedom. Yet, this prediction has not been fulfilled. Men and women have not become carbon copies of one another. Feminists typically blamed this on male obstructionism, but most people, including women, realize that there are fundamental differences between the genders. Females may want equal pay for equal work,[85] but they do not want to be men.[86] Nor did they want to be superwomen once they realize that this entails the expenditure of more energy than anyone has to spare. If they have to choose where to apply themselves, many decide that being a mother counts for more than running a corporation.

The most fundamental error of feminists, one that has amply been confirmed by modern science, is their assertion that the only differences between the genders are in their sexual plumbing.[87] Some sociology texts[88] persist in making this claim, but psychologists and biologists have demonstrated numerous behavioral and biological discrepancies in this thinking. Whatever the radicals say, men do tend to be more aggressive than women. From infancy, they are predisposed to be more assertive. This is not a matter of learning but of genetic heritage. Similarly, women are more nurturing toward young children. Strongly drawn toward babies and toddlers and gentler in manner, women find this reciprocated by their being preferred as sources of emotional comfort. These differences are not absolute. Were they graphed, they would show up as overlapping normal curves. Just as it is accurate to say the men are taller than women because on average there is a more than five-inch difference, so men are on average more aggressive than women. In particular cases, it might be the woman who is taller or more aggressive, but this does not alter the overall distribution.

Other differences have been revealed in terms of brain structure.[89] Women are verbally more able than men. They have more neurons in the part of the brain that organizes speech. They also have a larger corpus callosum. This means that the communication between their right and left hemispheres is better than in male brains. Magnetic resonance imaging discloses that, when given identical problems to solve, women utilize more areas in different parts of the brain. On a macro level, this is expressed in the intuitive and multitasking abilities in which women have long excelled.[90] Men, on the other hand, tend to be more precise in their orientation, a style that has generally been depicted as logical. For many decades, sociologists, and more recently linguists, [91] have noted that men tend to be instrumental in style, whereas women are expressive.[92] What this means is that men are more intent on getting tasks accomplished, whereas women are more concerned with maintaining tranquil relationships. Closely related to this is the fact that men are more occupied with competition and women with cooperation. Though the genders belong to the same species and, hence, are both enormously competitive and cooperative, the energies they devote to desired ends are not the identical.

Few serious observers today dispute these disparities. To do so, as many feminists continue to do, is to encourage men and women to seek jobs they are unlikely to find satisfying.[93] The feminist ideal, namely androgyny, would have eliminated the gender division of labor.[94] All jobs would be divided 50/50, with women working in equal numbers as machinists and men as primary school teachers. It would not matter that men are better at spatial relationships or that women are superior with young children. To the gender reformers, democracy means not freedom of choice, but absolute equality, even if artificially enforced. Unwilling to allow the chips to fall where they may, they even insist on reorganizing the military to put women on the front lines. Though this requires that the standards of physical training be lowered to accommodate women whose upper body strength does not match that of men, they forge ahead, irrespective of the consequences for national security.

The question naturally arises as to why feminists have made so palpable an error. Paradoxically, the reason seems to be connected with of the Middle-Class Revolution.   Once the Industrial Revolution[95] moved into high gear, men transferred their work from behind the plow onto the factory floor. Women stayed behind to take care of the house and children, yet, as technology advanced, much of their work was taken over by labor-saving machinery. For middle-class women, this eventually reduced their status to that of an indolent symbol of family prosperity. This, however, was boring and unappreciated. By the 1950s, suburban housewives began to feel more useless than is good for anyone's ego.[96] From their perspective, men were monopolizing the fun and glory. Into this void marched the feminists with their hyperegalitarian solution. Since the male jobs were more rewarding, feminists would rectify the imbalance by opening them to women. The women, in short, would do everything their husbands did—and vice versa. What did not occur to these social engineers was that the traditional differences might be transferred to the workplace. Transfixed by an egalitarian Marxist ideology,[97] they could not conceive of a world in which males continued their competitive/instrumental ways, whereas females dominated the expressive roles. Yet, this seems to be what has happened. Women continue to preside over elementary-school education,[98] while men rule the construction trades. This, however, is a matter of choice and divergent skills, not of male hegemony. Men intent on cheating women out of their just heritage have not imposed it on them.

A failure to recognize the differences between the genders has also had untoward outcomes with respect to heterosexual relationships. In as simple an issue as dating,[99] a refusal to admit that male and female sexualities are different has confused how people make contact. When Freud[100] suggested that anatomy is destiny, the feminists scoffed.[101] As far as they were concerned, there did not need to be a double standard. If men could play around, why couldn't they? If their brothers could call women to ask them out, why should they have to wait passively by the phone? Nevertheless, when women did not react as aggressively as was hoped, the reformers did not revise their understanding of the causes. Ideologically prevented from acknowledging the truth, they could not confess that women had more of an investment in pregnancy than men and that, therefore, they needed to be more careful about whom they admitted into their bedrooms. Nor could they recognize that men are more interested in physical beauty because this is a biological sign of female fertility, whereas women are more concerned with male finances because this represents evidence of an ability to protect them and their children. Instead they condemned men for admiring female pulchritude. Against all history, an appreciative glance became evidence of sexual harassment and could get a culpable male fired from his job. Though many women enjoyed being visually prized, those who did not were allowed to define what was unlawful.

All of this amounts to a radical reversal of Victorian standards.[102] Then, it was women who were by common consent seductive hussies. In their lust, they distracted men from their duties. For the feminists, the opposite has been true. It is men who in their lust have terrified women into submission. Threats of rape, rather than feminine wiles, poisoned gender relations.[103] Both of these theories are, of course, absurd caricatures. Men and women are simultaneously different and similar. Though one or the other may specialize in a particular quality, both share enough to understand where the other is coming from. They are also both complex compounds of good and bad. Neither has a monopoly on virtue or vice. Nevertheless, for a while the gender warfare was out of hand, with accusations of perfidy rising to comedic heights. Thankfully, sanity seems to be returning. More people have come to realize that individual men and women need to be appreciated for what they are and not for how they fit into an artificial morality game.

This has happened none too soon because successful families depend on men and women who both understand and approve of their respective uniquenesses. Raising children well begins with parents who not only like, but love, one another. This, however, is difficult in an atmosphere where the partners are encouraged to be suspicious. The gender libels they propagated are probably the worst contribution of the feminists. These have made it difficult for men and women to achieve an accurate assessment of each other. An accomplishment that is inherently difficult is made more so by suggestions that men are devils and women, innocent victims. This encourages, not honest and egalitarian communications, but gender-based posturing. It makes each side feel that it has been wronged and that this injustice might be irreversible.

Voluntary Intimacy

These are serious errors. Heated gender misunderstandings make it seem as if the family is beyond redemption. Nevertheless, under this smokescreen of contempt, a new sort of family has been arising on the foundations of the traditional model. This is a family that is more isolated than its predecessors but, for that very reason, more flexible. The new middle-class family has to be nimble on its feet. A highly commercialized and technologically integrated society is one in which change has become endemic. From moment to moment, the skills demanded have mutated at a dizzying tempo. So have the locations where these are required. Those who cannot keep up, those whose professionalization is stuck in an obsolescent mode, pay the price by falling behind. Families, therefore, have to be supportive of adaptability. They need to help their members stay abreast of changing jobs, postgraduate education, and transcontinental relocations. As a result, they have to be small and self-sufficient.

In former years, extended families were the archetype.[104] If aunts and uncles did not reside under the same roof, they usually lived within walking distance. Nowadays, economic fragmentation has become so routine that families have tendrils in remote locations. Formerly, relatives could drop by one another's homes, but now they rely on long-distance telephone conversations to remain in contact.

This has made the nuclear family the primary focus of allegiance. A man, a woman, and their children have become the center of their own universe. In a decentralized market society, they are the molecules that must be rearranged to make for an efficient whole. As a consequence, there is more stress on the pair bond of the marital couple. Where once their respective families and friends pressured them to dwell together, the responsibility for doing so now falls on their shoulders. Despite the ease of divorce, if they are to remain together, it is because they voluntarily choose to do so.

In this, the family has itself become professionalized. It members, and more particularly the spouses, must possess the expertise and motivation to make their relationships work.[105] Because they reside in a self-sufficient home, making their own decisions about how to live, it is up to them if this is to be done satisfactorily. While they may receive advice from those close to them, their economic and social independence provides the room to act as they desire. Nevertheless, the intimacy and interdependence of this arrangement holds dangers.[106] Unregulated intimacy is fraught with hazards. Adult human beings (whether hetero- or homosexual) who dwell under the same roof, and often sleep in the same bed, hold each other's fate in their hands. Behind closed doors, unsupervised by outside authorities, they can inflict injuries of unparalleled ferocity. Because they are physically close, they have the opportunity to do material harm. They can, if they desire, murder one another. Though this does not occur often, propinquity provides a setting for emotional violence. People who dwell together for extended periods get to know one another's deepest secrets. They observe where their buttons are, and because they are regularly in each other's presence, find the occasion to push them. Those who love one another can utilize intimacy to be mutually supportive, but when they get angry may take advantage of it to gain revenge. If they are emotionally immature, uncontrolled rage can cause inestimable hurt.

If a man and a woman are to collaborate for their own and their children's advantages, they must guard against these hazards. If they are to adjust to shifting circumstances, they must be individually and jointly flexible. To begin with, they need to trust one another. This trust is so important that it is a central feature of the courtship processes that bring them together. Love is not like a faucet that can be turned off and on. It takes time to cultivate and time to be torn asunder. During its development, when a couple is getting acquainted, a crucial duty is assessing their respective trustworthiness. They need to fathom who this previous stranger is and how he or she might react under adverse circumstances. When upset, might this other's fury become destructive? Individuals who are not honest in their appraisals are in for some nasty surprises. If their own immaturity prevents them from obtaining an accurate reading; *i.e.*, if their neurotic needs attract them to dangerous partners, trouble is likely to ensue.

One of the reasons why feminism has been so destructive is that it tarred everyone with the same brush. All men were condemned as vicious rapists and all women exalted as innocent victims.[107] Acceptance of this fantasy made it more difficult to recognize individual differences. In real-life intimacy, two people must open their souls to one another. They must be able to see each other, warts and all, and accept what they see. This, however, is not easy. It takes skill and effort. As the modern family evolves, it becomes essential to pierce the romantic myths of bygone eras. For starters, the parties must understand that men and women are different. If their expectations are out of line with what is possible or if they imagine that they can reconstruct their partners in their own images, they are in for disappointment. Once the feminist or Victorian mythologies are out of the way, it becomes possible to evaluate the other as an individual. This is where knowledge of the self and of other human beings comes in handy. Those who understand themselves and what it is to be human have head starts on determining whether they are apt to mesh with particular partners. They can determine whether their respective goals and values are compatible and what sorts of adjustment might be necessary to make them so.[108]

This perceptiveness does not come automatically, but it comes most naturally to those who are personally mature. Individuals whose socialization has prepared them to control their emotions and to recognize their distinct limitations are not only better equipped to perceive the emotions and limitations of others, they are also better equipped to deal with them. One of life's greater ironies is that persons who grow up within loving families are more able to give and receive love. Less in need of affection, they are better prepared to participate in it. In other words, those who are raised within stable middle-class families are better situated to create their own stable middle-class families. They are more competent in making allowances for other's failures and in reacting to these resiliently. They are also more likely to be constant in their commitments. People who grow up feeling good about themselves have less of a need to pursue emotional balm outside committed relationships. During the height of the hippie efflorescence, sexual fidelity was regarded as old-fashioned. Physical love was deemed fungible. Yet, this was never true. The traditions that lauded sexual commitment have proven remarkably durable. Especially under conditions of voluntary intimacy, marital partners need to trust each other on multiple levels. One of these is the sexual.[109] After they pledge each other their troth, should this not be taken seriously, that is, should they stray, they are engaging in emotional betrayal. They are breaking promises and dishonoring bonds. In direct opposition to the sophisticated philandering of open-minded liberals, the middle-class marriage seeks to maintain its integrity in many dimensions. In this, if not in their naïve sexual fairy tales,[110] the Victorians got it right.

Also fundamental to middle-class intimacy is a secure division of labor.[111] The feminist fable extols gender interchangeability. Total equality is supposed to bleach out all task differences. This has proven inaccurate vis-à-vis the marketplace but also within the family. Contemporary couples rarely divide their domestic duties as did their grandparents, but neither have they established an amorphous egalitarianism. No longer may the woman be the sole cook nor the male the exclusive repairman, but together they decide who will specialize in what. Not all reach the same settlement, but almost all have some settlement. The reason is simple. Intimacy is about cooperation, not competition. If a man and a woman are pursuing exactly the same goals, one is apt to do better in something than the other, and this is bound to elicit envy. If, however, they are pursuing separate but compatible objectives, when one wins, so does the other. This enables them to root for each other. They can be allies, both with respect to the jobs they hold outside the household and the tasks performed within it. In dividing their responsibilities, each obtains authority within a personal sphere of influence, thereby reducing the issues over which they come into conflict.

This, however, leaves open the question of how to arrive at an agreement about what each will do. Voluntary intimacy, if it is to work, requires a mechanism for resolving differences. Because no two individuals are ever in complete accord, there must be a give-and-take that results in concurrence. To put the matter plainly, we can say that they must be good negotiators. Lasting bonds depend in equal measure on shared commitments and shared bargaining skills. Indeed, these aptitudes depend on each other. Individuals who do not work at staying together will not work at resolving their differences, whereas those who do not resolve their differences will have their steadfastness severely tested. Nevertheless, negotiating is a skill. The parties need to be motivated to engage in it, and they need to know how to do it. When they enter into their various wrangles, they must possess a dual-concern attitude; that is, they must be committed to meeting the needs of both parties. If either or both are excessively selfish, the resultant bargain will be too skewed to be durable. The loser will leave, nursing a grievance that is bound to upset the agreement later on.

Beyond this, the negotiators must be competent problem solvers.[112] Their personal professionalism must encompass an ability to be creative in pursuing their aims. The word usually used to express how spouses can come to an agreement is "compromise," but this is inadequate to many circumstances. Obviously, the baby cannot be divided in half. Intimate partners, if they are of good will, collaborate in coming up with ideas that neither would have entertained alone. Instead of agreeing to take their vacation halfway between the mountains and the seashore, they discover a Caribbean island that has a mountain at its center. This ability to envision solutions that allow both to win becomes exceptionally valuable when children enter the scene. With more than two parties to be satisfied, all concerned need the patience of Job to consider unforeseen answers. Life is full of surprises; hence, those with the courage to embrace the unexpected tend to come out ahead.

One of the preeminent qualities of the emergent middle-class family is the complementarity at its heart.[113] The companionate marriage is a relatively new invention. Husbands and wives talking to one another as friendly partners in the same enterprise is a recent innovation. Spouses, to be sure, have always communicated, but the degree of voluntary integration has not always been as great. In the past, the domestic division of labor was laid down along precise cultural lines. Both parties knew what was expected even before they crossed a common threshold. Now, in our commercialized technological world, many of these inherited patterns are obsolete. The invention of the cell phone, for instance, revolutionized how family members keep track of their whereabouts. Who is expected to call whom could not follow previous guidelines because there were none.

Contrary to the feminists or the free-love mavens, the differences between men and women do not need to be a handicap or a source of perpetual discord. Heterosexual intimacy can generate forms of expertise that neither party could manage apart. Gender complementarity is not an empty boast. The father who roughhouses with his children is not necessarily opposed to the mother who worries about an eye being poked out.[114] Their children benefit from both of these attitudes. Their youngsters are simultaneously tutored in risk taking and in prudence, each of which is desirable for a successful life. Men do not need to become more like women, nor women more like men, for them to act in concert. Despite their periodic frictions, the expertise and motivations built into their respective frames can contribute to a whole that is more than the sum of its parts. Furthermore, the full benefits of voluntary intimacy accrue only if innate differences are understood, respected, and exploited. To this end, mythologies that blame one or the other are of less value than clear-eyed acknowledgements of complex truths.

The Children

If the emerging middle-class family esteems and is dependent upon gender differences, it must also acknowledge the nature of children and childhood.[115] Responsible for socializing the young so that they can succeed in a competitive and uncertain environment, it must take advantage of who they are and how they develop to shape them into self-directed adults.[116] Kohn suggests that middle-class parents want their children to be considerate of others, to be interested in how and why things happen, and to exercise self-control.[117] He also indicates that they are less concerned over whether they have good manners, are neat and clean, and obey their parents. In this, they seek to prepare them to strike out on their own. Aware that the most substantial legacy they can provide is not financial but personal, they intend to make them strong and self-reliant. The aim, in short, is to groom the next generation for a professional lifestyle. Both on the job and at home, they attempt to instill the skills and motives to organize complex tasks—both independently and in partnership with reliable allies.

The self-direction and self-discipline to which Kohn refers are not implanted via the obedience that working-class parents prefer, but by more subtle means.[118] Were middle-class parents to assert absolute control over their young, they would prevent them from internalizing controls.[119] Mothers and fathers can inspire, can guide, and can direct their children, but they cannot dictate to them. To do so would arouse oppositionalism, not a desire to acquire personal strengths. Parents who want these to emerge seek to establish the conditions in which they can. They know that they surface only through a child's own efforts. Adult supervision establishes limits, *i.e.*, boundaries beyond which the young are not allowed to go, but not initiatives that, by definition, come from inside. Children can be required to respect the rights of others or to avoid extravagant risks but not to be creative. Because there are dangers adults can anticipate, but children cannot, it is imperative for the former to set terminal points. Yet because of the inevitable novelties, everything can never be completely foreseen.

Middle-class parents explain things to their children and encourage them to think, but they also allow them to internalize their own conclusions. The paradigm for this is found in childhood discipline. In former times, parents were expected to beat the devil out of their offspring.[120] Spare the rod and spoil the child was not an empty phrase; it was a prescription for action. Children were considered inherently sinful and, therefore, in dire need of having their willfulness expunged. Paradoxically, a controlled willfulness is at the core of self-direction. Those who are spanked on the grounds that independent thinking is selfish are thereby instructed not to make autonomous decisions. As a result, spankings, and, ever stronger whippings, have gone out of style. Contemporary discipline is more apt to consist of a stern discussion of what is appropriate or, in extremes, of a time out. Children are sent to their rooms, told to think about what they did, and asked not to emerge until they understand what is right. The objective is not behavior elicited from fear of punishment but internal commitments that operate without parental intervention.

This sort of regime permits children to make mistakes.[121] In the traditional working-class family, a mistake was tantamount to disobedience. Children were expected to get things right the first time and, if they did not, were subjected to corporal punishment. This, not surprisingly, discouraged experimentation. If they knew what was good for them, the young either kept to the straight and narrow or threw over the traces. In contrast, middle-class parents understand that complex lessons entail missteps. The error is not in making a mistake but in failing to learn from it. They, therefore, allow their children to be less self-critical, that is, as long as they keep forging ahead. Because they understand how and why things are complicated, they realize these lessons cannot be instantaneously absorbed. Their own experience having demonstrated that the acquisition of knowledge is a lifelong affair, they not only allow but encourage their children to take their time. They are also pleased when the young exhibit curiosity.[122] Getting into things and creating a mess may be bothersome, but it is better than a lack of interest. Who knows what discoveries a toddler will make. Lower-class parents, in contrast, find unregulated behavior less tolerable. Theirs is a tendency either to allow their children to proceed unattended or to demand conformity to strict standards.

Back in the 1920s and '30s, the behaviorist psychologist John B. Watson[123] counseled Americans that the worst thing they could do was to spoil their children. The son of an alcoholic father who deserted his family, he believed absolute emotional control was urgent.[124] To this end, he advised parents to allow their children to cry themselves to sleep. His belief was that, if babies were picked up and comforted, they would grow into selfish adults. This philosophy fit well in a working-class world where external discipline was the norm. It does not, however, suit middle-class requirements. The sort of responsive love Watson abhorred is precisely what their families must provide. Contrary to the behaviorist model, reacting to a child's discomfort by being warmly solicitous does not create egotism. It makes a child feel important, and also secure. This imparts the confidence to make independent decisions, despite concurrent uncertainties. As an adult, the individual's determinations will arise from a personal psyche, but need not on that account be selfish. The apparent contradiction Watson did not appreciate is that persons who learn to love themselves are also capable of leading others. Having had their own needs attended to, they can better assess and meet external needs.

The evolving middle-class family seems to be discovering that a collaborative interaction between parents and children is essential for the development of the young.[125] It was once said that children should be seen and not heard, but this interferes with the dialogues that build social skills. Because the middle-class way of life entails synergistic alliances, discovering how to negotiate with others is crucial. Practice in this occurs first within the nuclear family. Parents and children of necessity encounter conflicts that must be resolved. Dictatorial controls might prevent these from escalating, but they do not provide training in coming to reasonable bargains. The young, of course, are less powerful than their parents. As a consequence, adults who desire to impose their will can, but does not allow the children to learn how to assert themselves. What is necessary for two-sided negotiations is adult restraint. A parent must be patient with the often maddening immaturity of the biologically undeveloped. This means that neither empty-headed permissiveness nor obdurate authoritarianism is best. An adult who is thinking about a child's future will seek a moving equilibrium. The goal is to be as firm as is needed to match the child's developing ability to be assertive. To overpower the child would crush a fragile spirit, whereas to be a doormat instills a false estimate of the child's worth. More useful are the energy and coherence needed to ensure an honest exchange of ideas, an exchange grounded in a dual-concern model of their respective needs and in flexible problem-solving techniques.

These sorts of negotiations do not simply happen; they too are an achievement. In previous centuries, they were not considered necessary because they were not a normal part of day-to-day functioning. Peasants did not need to work out the intricate bargains characteristic of a commercial environment. Nor did a preindustrial society require the mental dexterity of a technological one. Today's complex decentralized division of labor has, in essence, forced families to conform to its needs. Parents who have themselves been struggling to attain a self-directed, emotional maturity have assumed the supplementary burden of discovering how to pass this along to another generation. After it reached its tipping point, the Middle-Class Revolution demanded personal growth from newly professionalized individuals, as well as modifications in their parenting skills. As we have seen, there was a cultural lag with regard to the former and perhaps a lengthier one with respect to the latter. Those who were actively engaged in the process of ascertaining how to direct their vocational lives might be expected to need additional time to apply these lessons to their families, especially to their children.

The liberal excursions into no-fault divorce and androgynous feminism were time-consuming dead-ends. Sadly, they diverted attention away from exploring better solutions. First, they interfered with developing voluntary intimacy. In rejecting the past root and branch, they made it difficult to build upon evolving family values. This, in turn, made it difficult to provide the direction and support their children required. Parents barely able to negotiate fairly with one another could scarcely be expected do this with their young. To be committed and yet to allow emotional independence entails an apparent inconsistency that was not easy to surmount. Authoritarian models derived from the centuries past certainly did not do the trick. Something else was needed, but those entangled in these events did not understand what. They literally could not perceive the utility of being flexible. Worse still, they had not attained the internal strengths to live by this standard. Voluntary intimacy and responsive childrearing necessitate insights and emotional controls that are themselves achievements. Irrespective of their conscious intentions, individuals who had not mastered their inner environments found it difficult to engage in evenhanded negotiations. Unable to control who they were or what they felt, they had to await internal developmental processes they could not deliberately engineer.

The professionalized middle-class family may ultimately change this. As people gain experience on the job, in their marriages, and with their children, they can be expected to move forward from their mistakes. In time, the conventional wisdom will surpass the reactionary fantasies that seemed to promise salvation. People will nevertheless need to work at what they accomplish, including in their personal lives. The liberal model has suggested that neutral government institutions could protect people from their selfish impulses. It held out the prospect of a nonhierarchical society in which the most important decisions would be codified in centralized regulations. This has proven to be a chimera. There are a variety of tasks that no impersonal bureaucracy, however brilliantly conceived, can manage. No corporate entity can substitute for intimate love or fair-minded interpersonal negotiations. Drained as they are of emotional responsiveness and localized knowledge, these organizations cannot deliver the motivation or expertise to do what is best. The very factors that enabled them to provide the broad social controls that were useful for early industrialization continue to prevent them from exercising personal concern. Yet, without this concern, no society can supply the emotional supports adults require or the guidance the next generation demands. In its rationalistic simplicity, a Big-Brother government can furnish neither the happiness nor the self-directed individuals it needs for its own perpetuation. Here, then, is the central irony of initial attempts to cope with the dislocations of the Great Middle-Class Revolution. The family, which seems so contrary to the large-scale objectification of postindustrialized commercialism, may be the linchpin essential for its survival. Only it provides what human beings need in order to become decentralized decision makers.

Endnotes

1 Graham, T. 1996. *Patterns of Deception: The Media's Role in the Clinton Presidency.* Alexandria, VA: Media Research Center.

2 Sheehy, G. 1999. *Hillary's Choice.* New York: Random House.

3 Maraniss, D. 1995. *First in His Class: The Biography of Bill Clinton.* New York: Simon & Schuster.

4 Stone, L.J., Smith, H.T. and Murphy, L.B. (Eds.) 1973. *The Competent Infant: Research and Commentary.* New York: Basic Books.

5 Nye, F.I. 1976. *Role Structure and the Analysis of the Family.* Beverly Hills: Sage Publications.; Nye, F.I. (Ed.) 1982. *Family Relationships: Rewards and Costs.* Beverly Hills: Sage Publications.; Handel, G. [Ed.] 1967. *The Psychosocial Interior of the Family: A Sourcebook for the Study of Whole Families.* Chicago: Aldine-Atherton.

6 Rossi, A.S. (Ed.) 1973. *The Feminist Papers: From Adams to de Beauvoir.* New York: Bantam Books.

7 Engels, F. 1972. *The Origin of the Family, Private Property, and the State.* New York: International Publishers.

8 Veblen, T. 1967. (1899) *The Theory of the Leisure Class.* New York: Viking Penguin.

9 Fischer, L. 1964. *The Life of Lenin.* New York: Harper & Row.; Russell, B. 1929. *Marriage and Morals.* New York: H. Liveright.

10 Fein, M. 1999. *The Limits of Idealism: When Good Intentions Go Bad.* New York: Kluwer/Plenum.

11 Engels, F. 1972. *The Origin of the Family, Private Property, and the State.* New York: International Publishers.

12 Brownmiller, S. 1975. *Against Our Will: Men, Women and Rape.* New York: Bantam.; MacKinnon, C.A. 1987. *Feminism Unmodified: Discourses on Life and Law.* Cambridge, MS: Harvard University Press.; Wilson, J.Q. 2002. *The Marriage Problem: How Culture Has Weakened Families.* New York: HarperCollins Publishers.

13 de Riencourt, A. 1974. *Sex and Power in History.* New York: Delta Books.

14 Freud, S. 1953-1974. *The Standard Edition of the Complete Psychological Works of Sigmund Freud.* (Edited by J. Strachey. London: Hogarth Press and Institute for Psychoanalysis.

15 Lorber, J. 1994. *Paradoxes of Gender.* New Haven: Yale University Press.

16 French, M. 1992. *The War Against Women.* New York: Summit Books.

17 Horowitz. D. 1997. *Radical Son: A Generational Odyssey.* New York: The Free Press.

18 Partridge, W.L. 1973. *The Hippie Ghetto: The Natural History of a Subculture.* New York: Holt, Rinehart and Winston.

19 Aries, P. 1962. *Centuries of Childhood: A Social History of Family Life.* New York: Vintage Books.

[20] Himmelfarb, G. 1995. *The De-Moralization of Society: From Victorian Virtues to Modern Values.* New York: Alfred A. Knopf.

[21] Friedan, B. 1963. *The Feminine Mystique.* New York: W.W. Norton & Co.

[22] Jones, J.H. 1997. *Alfred C. Kinsey: A Life.* New York: W.W. Norton & Co.

[23] Sandeen, E.R. 1970. *The Roots of Fundamentalism: British and American Millinarianism* 1800-1930. Chicago: University of Chicago Press.

[24] Lindsey, B.B. and Evans, W. 1927. *Companionate Marriage.* New York: Boni and Liveright.

[25] Moir, A. and Jessel, D. 1989. *Brain Sex: The Real Difference Between Men and Women.* New York: Delta.

[26] Bennett, W.J. (Ed.) 1993. *The Book of Virtues: A Treasury of Great Moral Stories.* New York: Simon & Schuster.; Hunter, J.D. 2000. *The Death of Character: Moral Education in an Age Without Good and Evil.* New York: Basic Books.; Wilson, J. Q. 1997. *Moral Judgment.* New York: The Free Press.; Wuthnow, R. 1987. *Meaning and Moral Order: Explorations in Cultural Analysis.* Berkeley, CA: University of California Press.; Fein, M. 1997. *Hardball Without an Umpire: The Sociology of Morality.* Westport, CT: Praeger.

[27] Popenoe, D. 1996. Life *Without Father: Compelling New Evidence that Fatherhood and Marriage Are Indispensable for the Good of Children and Society.* New York: The Free Press.

[28] Kirk, R. 1997. *Edmund Burke: A Genius Reconsidered.* Wilmington, Del: Intercollegiate Studies Institute.

[29] Ogburn, W. 1922. (1966) *Social Change with Respect to Culture and Original Nature.* New York: Heubsch.; Fein, M. 1990. *Role Change: A Resocialization Perspective.* New York: Praeger.

[30] Russell, B. 1929. *Marriage and Morals.* New York: H. Liveright.; Coontz, S. 1992. *The Way We Never Were: American Families and the Nostalgia Trap.* New York: Basic Books.

[31] Waite, C.J. and Gallagher, M. 2000. *The Case for Marriage: Why Married People are Happier, Healthier, and Better Off Financially.* New York: Doubleday.; Cherlin, A.J. 1992. *Marriage, Divorce, and Remarriage.* Cambridge, MA: Harvard University Press.

[32] Seward, K. 1978. *The American Family: A Demographic History.* Beverly Hills: Sage Publications.

[33] Fein, M. 1999. *The Limits of Idealism: When Good Intentions Go Bad.* New York: Kluwer/Plenum.

[34] Garbarino, J., Schellenbach, C.J. and Sebes, J. 1986. *Troubled Youth, Troubled Families.* New York: Aldine De Gruyter.

[35] Lindzey, G. and Aronson, E. (Eds.) 1985. *Handbook of Social Psychology; Third Edition.* New York: Random House.; Lofland, L.H. 1973. *A World of Strangers.* New York: Basic Books.

[36] Russell, op cit.

[37] Wentworth, W. 1980. *Context and Understanding: An Inquiry into Socialization Theory.* New York: Elsevier.

[38] Lasch, C. 1979. *The Culture of Narcissism: American Life in an Age of Diminishing Expectations.* New York: Warner Books.

[39] Bowlby, J. 1969. *Attachment.* New York: Basic Books.; Bowlby, J. 1973. *Separation: Anxiety and Anger.* New York: Basic Books.; Bowlby, J. 1980. *Loss: Sadness and Depression.* New York: Basic Books.

[40] Schaffer, H. 1971. *The Growth of Sociability.* Baltimore: Penguin Books.

[41] Bellah, R.N., Madsen, R., Sullivan, W.M., Swindler, A., and Tipton, S.M. 1985. *Habits of the Heart: Individualism and Commitment in American Life.* Berkeley, CA: University of California Press.

[42] Scheff, T. 1990. *Microsociology: Discourse, Emotion, and Social Structure.* Chicago: University of Chicago Press.

[43] Weber, M. 1947. *The Theory of Social and Economic Organization.* New York: Free Press.

[44] Lortie, D.C. 1975. *Schoolteacher: A Sociological Study.* Chicago: University of Chicago Press.

[45] Handel, G. [Ed.] 1967. *The Psychosocial Interior of the Family: A Sourcebook for the Study of Whole Families.* Chicago: Aldine-Atherton.

[46] Kohn, M.L. and Schooler, C. 1983. *Work and Personality: An Inquiry Into the Impact of Social Stratification.* Norwood, NJ: Ablex Publishing.

[47] Sarbin, T. and Allen, V. 1968. *Role Theory.* In: Lindzey, G. and Aronson, E. (Eds.), Handbook of Social Psychology. Mass.: Addison, Wesley.

[48] Fein, M. 1990. *Role Change: A Resocialization Perspective.* New York: Praeger.; Pruitt, D.G. 1981. *Negotiation Behavior.* New York: Academic.

[49] Herrnstein, R.J. & Murray, C. 1994. *The Bell Curve: The Reshaping of American Life by Differences in Intelligence.* New York: Basic Books.

[50] Barnard, C. 1938. *The Function of the Executive.* Cambridge, Mass.: Harvard University Press.

[51] Waite, C.J. and Gallagher, M. 2000. *The Case for Marriage: Why Married People are Happier, Healthier, and Better Off Financially.* New York: Doubleday.

[52] Mead, G.H. 1934. *Mind, Self and Society.* Chicago: University of Chicago Press.

[53] Goleman, D. 1995. *Emotional Intelligence: Why It Can Matter More Than IQ.* New York: Bantam Books.

[54] Hollingshead, A. and Redlich, F. 1958. *Social Class and Mental Health.* New York: John Wiley.

[55] Lorenz, K. 1966. *On Aggression.* London: Metheun.

[56] Fein, M. 1993. *I.A.M.: A Common Sense Guide to Coping with Anger.* Westport, Conn.: Praeger.

[57] Zeldin, T. 1994. *An Intimate History of Humanity.* New York: HarperCollins Publishers.

[58] Eberstadt, M. 2004. *Home-Alone America: The Hidden Toll of Day Care, Behavioral Drugs, and Other Parent Substitutes.* New York: Sentinel,

[59] Bach, G.R. and Wyden, P. 1968. *The Intimate Enemy.* New York: Avon.

[60] Gelles, R.J. 1997. *Intimate Violence in Families (3ʳᵈ Edition)* Beverly Hills: Sage Publications.; Gelles, R.J and Straus, M.A. 1989. *Intimate Violence: The Causes and Consequences of Abuse in the American Family.* New York: Touchstone Books.

[61] Glendon, M.A. and Blankenhorn, D. (Eds.) 1995. *Seedbeds of Virtue: Sources of Competence, Character, and Citizenship in American Society.* Lanham, MD: Madison Books.

[62] Morris, H. (Ed.) 1961. *Freedom and Responsibility.* Stanford, CA: Sanford University Press.

[63] Cooley, C.H. 1956. *Human Nature and the Social Order.* Glencoe, Ill.: The Free Press.

[64] Fein, M. 1997. *Hardball Without an Umpire: The Sociology of Morality.* Westport, CT: Praeger.

[65] Horowitz, D. 1998. *Betty Friedan and the Making of the Feminine Mystique.* Amherst: University of Massachusetts Press.

[66] MacKinnon, C.A. 1987. *Feminism Unmodified: Discourses on Life and Law.* Cambridge, MS: Harvard University Press. Sommers, C.H. 1994. *Who Stole Feminism: How Women Have Betrayed Women.* New York: Simon & Schuster.; French, M. 1992. *The War Against Women.* New York: Summit Books.; Whittier, N. 1995. *Feminist Generations: The Persistence of the Radical Women's Movement.* Philadelphia: Temple University Press.; Brownmiller, S. 1975. *Against Our Will: Men, Women and Rape.* New York: Bantam.; Faludi, S. 1991. *Backlash: The Undeclared War Against American Women.* New York: Crown Publishers.; Rossi, A.S. (Ed.) 1973. *The Feminist Papers: From Adams to de Beauvoir.* New York: Bantam Books.

[67] Whittier, N. 1995. *Feminist Generations: The Persistence of the Radical Women's Movement.* Philadelphia: Temple University Press.

[68] Waite, C.J. and Gallagher, M. 2000. *The Case for Marriage: Why Married People are Happier, Healthier, and Better Off Financially.* New York: Doubleday.

[69] Whitehead, B.D. 1998. *The Divorce Culture: Rethinking Our Commitments to Marriage and the Family.* New York: Random House.; Wallenstein, J.S., Lewis, J.M. and Blakesee, S. 2000. *The Unexpected Legacy of Divorce: A 25 Year Landmark Study.* New York: Hyperion.

[70] Weiss, R.S. 1990. *Staying the Course: The Emotional and Social Lives of Men Who Do Well at Work.* New York: Free Press.

[71] Epstein, C.F. 1970. *Woman's Place: Options and Limits in Professional Careers.* Berkeley: University of California Press.

[72] Weiss, R.S. 1975. *Marital Separation: Coping with the End of Marriage.* New York: Basic Books.

[73] Whitehead, B.D. 1998. *The Divorce Culture: Rethinking Our Commitments to Marriage and the Family*. New York: Random House.

[74] Fisher, H.E. 1992. *Anatomy of Love: The Natural History of Monogamy, Adultery and Divorce*. New York: W.W. Norton & Co.

[75] Wallenstein, J.S., Lewis, J.M. and Blakesee, S. 2000. *The Unexpected Legacy of Divorce: A 25 Year Landmark Study*. New York: Hyperion.

[76] Moynihan, D.P. 1965. *The Negro Family: The Case for National Action*. Washington, D.C.: U.S. Govt.; Franklin, D. L. 1997. *Ensuring Inequality: The Structural Transformation of the African-American Family*. New York: Oxford University Press.; Landry, B. 1987. *The New Black Middle Class*. Berkeley: University of California Press.

[77] Faludi, S. 1991. *Backlash: The Undeclared War Against American Women*. New York: Crown Publishers.

[78] Blankenhorn, D. 1995. *Fatherless America: Confronting Our Most Urgent Social Problem*. New York: Basic Books.; Wallenstein, J.S., Lewis, J.M. and Blakesee, S. 2000. *The Unexpected Legacy of Divorce: A 25 Year Landmark Study*. New York: Hyperion.; Popenoe, D. 1996. *Life Without Father: Compelling New Evidence that Fatherhood and Marriage Are Indispensable for the Good of Children and Society*. New York: The Free Press.

[79] Waite, C.J. and Gallagher, M. 2000. *The Case for Marriage: Why Married People are Happier, Healthier, and Better Off Financially*. New York: Doubleday.

[80] Roiphe, K. 1993. *The Morning After: Sex, Fear, and Feminism On Campus*. Boston: Little, Brown, & Co.

[81] Graglia, F.C. 1998. *Domestic Tranquility: A Brief Against Feminism*. Dallas, TX: Spence Publishing Co.; Fox-Genovese, E. 1996. *Feminism is Not the Story of My Life: How Today's Feminist Elite Has Lost Touch with the Real Concerns of Women*. New York: Doubleday.; Lynn, D.B. 1974. *The Father: His Role in Child Development*. Monterey Ca.: Brooks/Cole.

[82] Blankenhorn, D. 1995. *Fatherless America: Confronting Our Most Urgent Social Problem*. New York: Basic Books.; Coltrane, S. 1996. *Family Man: Fatherhood, Housework, and Gender Equity*. New York: Oxford University Press.

[83] Moir, A. and Jessel, D. 1989. *Brain Sex: The Real Difference Between Men and Women*. New York: Delta.; Baron-Cohen, S. 2003. *The Essential Difference: The Truth about the Male and Female Brain*. New York: Basic Books.; Tiger, L. 1970. *Men in Groups*. New York: Vintage Books.; Tiger, L. and Fowler, H.T. (Eds.) 1978. *Female Hierarchies*. Chicago; Beresford Book Service.

[84] Lorber, J. 1994. *Paradoxes of Gender*. New Haven: Yale University Press.; Jagger, A.M. 1988. *Feminist Politics and Human Nature*. Totowa, NJ: Rowman & Littlefield.

[85] Epstein, C.F. 1970. *Woman's Place: Options and Limits in Professional Careers*. Berkeley: University of California Press.

[86] Tittle, C.K. 1981. *Careers and Family: Sex Roles and Adolescent Life Plans.* Beverly Hills: Sage Publications.

[87] Lopreato, J. and Crippen, T. 1999. *Crisis in Sociology: The Need For Darwin.* New Brunswick, NJ: Transaction Publishers.

[88] Glenn, N. 1997. *Closed Hearts, Closed Minds: The Textbook Story of Marriage.* New York: Institute for American Values.

[89] Moir, A. and Jessel, D. 1989. *Brain Sex: The Real Difference Between Men and Women.* New York: Delta.; Baron-Cohen, S. 2003. *The Essential Difference: The Truth about the Male and Female Brain.* New York: Basic Books.

[90] Gilligan, C. 1982. *In a Different Voice.* Cambridge, MA: Harvard University Press.

[91] Tannen, D. 1990. *You Just Don't Understand: Women and Men in Conversation.* New York: William Morrow and Co.

[92] Parsons, T. and Bales, R.F. 1955. *Family, Socialization and Interaction Process.* New York: Free Press.

[93] Epstein, C.F. 1970. *Woman's Place: Options and Limits in Professional Careers.* Berkeley: University of California Press.

[94] Fein, M. 1999. *The Limits of Idealism: When Good Intentions Go Bad.* New York: Kluwer/Plenum.

[95] Ashton, T.S. 1965. *The Industrial Revolution 1760-1830.* New York: Oxford University Press.

[96] Friedan, B. 1963. *The Feminine Mystique.* New York: W.W. Norton & Co.; De Beauvoir, S. 1978. *The Second Sex.* New York: Alfred A. Knopf.

[97] Mannheim, K. 1936. *Ideology and Utopia.* New York: Harcourt, Brace, and World, Inc.

[98] Lortie, D.C. 1975. *Schoolteacher: A Sociological Study.* Chicago: University of Chicago Press.

[99] Fisher, H.E. 1992. *Anatomy of Love: The Natural History of Monogamy, Adultery and Divorce.* New York: W.W. Norton & Co.

[100] Freud, S. 1953-1974. *The Standard Edition of the Complete Psychological Works of Sigmund Freud.* (Edited by J. Strachey. London: Hogarth Press and Institute for Psychoanalysis.

[101] Consider too the Darwinian implications. Darwin, C. 1974. *The Descent of Man, and Selection in Relation to Sex.* Detroit: Gale Research.

[102] Himmelfarb, G. 1995. *The De-Moralization of Society: From Victorian Virtues to Modern Values.* New York: Alfred A. Knopf.

[103] MacKinnon, C.A. 1987. *Feminism Unmodified: Discourses on Life and Law.* Cambridge, MS: Harvard University Press.

[104] Zeldin, T. 1994. *An Intimate History of Humanity.* New York: HarperCollins Publishers.

[105] Rebach, H.M. and Bruhn, J.G. (Eds.) 1991. *Handbook of Clinical Sociology.* New York: Plenum Press.

[106] Scarf, M. 1987. *Intimate Partners: Patterns in Love and Marriage.* New York: Random House.

[107] Brownmiller, S. 1975. *Against Our Will: Men, Women and Rape.* New York: Bantam.

[108] Wilson, J. Q. 1993. *The Moral Sense.* New York: The Free Press.; Wilson, J. Q. 1997. *Moral Judgment.* New York: The Free Press.

[109] Fisher, H. 1982. *The Sex Contract: The Evolution of Human Behavior.* New York: William Morrow and Co.

[110] Jones, J.H. 1997. *Alfred C. Kinsey: A Life.* New York: W.W. Norton & Co.

[111] Coltrane, S. 1996. *Family Man: Fatherhood, Housework, and Gender Equity.* New York: Oxford University Press.

[112] Pruitt, D.G. 1981. *Negotiation Behavior.* New York: Academic.

[113] Cherlin, A.J. 1992. *Marriage, Divorce, and Remarriage.* Cambridge, MA: Harvard University Press.

[114] Bettleheim, B. 1977. *The Uses of Enchantment.* New York: Vintage Books.

[115] Whiting, J. and Child, I. 1953. *Child Training and Personality.* New Haven: Yale University Press.

[116] For case studies of the difficulties see: Wead, D. 2003. *All The Presidents' Children: Triumph and Tragedy in the Lives of America's First Families.* New York: Atria Books.

[117] Kohn, M.L. 1969. *Class and Conformity: A Study in Values.* Homewood, Ill.: The Dorsey Press.

[118] Clausen, J. (Ed.) 1968. *Socialization and Society.* Boston: Little Brown.

[119] Bettleheim, B. 1987. *A Good Enough Parent; A Book on Child-Rearing..* New York: A. Knopf.

[120] Foucault, M. 1979. *Discipline and Punish: The Birth of the Prison.* New York: Random House.

[121] Stone, L.J., Smith, H.T. and Murphy, L.B. (Eds.) 1973. *The Competent Infant: Research and Commentary.* New York: Basic Books.

[122] Bergen, D. 1988. *Play as a Medium of Learning and Development: A Handbook of Theory and Practice.* Portsmouth, NH: Heinemann.

[123] Watson, J.B. 1928. *Psychological Care of Infant and Child.* New York: Norton.

[124] Buckley, K.W. 1989. *Mechanical Man: John Broadus Watson and the Beginnings of Behaviorism.* New York: The Guilford Press.

[125] Spock, B. 1957. *The Common Sense Book of Baby and Child Care.* New York: Duell, Sloan and Pearce.

Chapter 11

Toward a Professionalized Society

Now Art, used collectively for painting, sculpture, architecture, and music, is the mediatress between, and reconciler of, nature and man. It is, therefore, the power of humanizing nature, of infusing the thoughts and passions of man into everything which is the object of his contemplation. (Samuel Taylor Coleridge, <u>On Posey or Art</u>)

Science frees us in many ways…from the bodily terror which the savage feels. But she replaces that, in the minds of many, by a moral terror which is far more overwhelming. (Charles Kingsley, Sermon, <u>The Meteor Shower</u>)

Freedom although it has brought [modern man] independence and rationality, has made him isolated and, thereby, anxious and powerless. (Erich Fromm, <u>Escape from Freedom</u>)

A Professionalized Humanism

Society is not in the process of becoming one huge family. Nor is it about to become an extended village encompassing of all humankind, not even in a some fanciful electronic version of democracy. Nor is it likely to revert to a modernized theocracy of born-again souls. Not even a technocratic utopia seems to be in the cards, not to mention a nanny state guided by super-educated philosopher kings. As the Middle-Class Revolution continues to unfold, it promises to move in directions undreamt of by most reformers. Contrary to the proclamations of the culture wars, neither traditional conservatives nor enlightened liberals are apt to emerge victorious. Something else, something neither romantic nor trouble-free, seems to be brewing. In short, we appear to be developing an unprecedented civilization, *i.e.,* a professionalized society.[1] With expertise and internalized motivation more critical than ever before, these, and the conditions that sustain them, are becoming more prominent. Larger numbers of individuals, and the institutions upon which they rely, are transforming into something genuinely middle class. Almost despite themselves, and their ubiquitous misinterpretations of their circumstances, billions of moderns are lurching into a brave new world, not of totalitarianism, but of personal growth and responsibility.

The Great Middle-Class Revolution has been more terrifying than the harbingers of progress could have imagined. Who among them would have thought that growing rich and free might impel battalions of the best and brightest to rush headlong into what F. A. Hayek characterized as a renewal of serfdom?[2] Hayek, and his contemporary Erich Fromm,[3] lived through the horrors of Nazism, fascism, and international communism. They learned firsthand that individuals could choose to submerge themselves in an authoritarian collectivism rather than face the insecurities of coping with a triumphant commercialism. This scared them, as well it should have. Victorian commentators earlier on speculated that art or science would provide the keys to surmounting the challenges of modernization. But few of them predicted that a near universal prosperity would itself be construed as problematic.[4] They would surely have been surprised to learn that unequivocal affluence could prove more fearsome than poverty or political tyranny. Had they lived to see it, they would have been baffled by calls to dismantle the very institutions that delivered unparalleled gains. Yet, this is precisely what bobo liberalism has proposed. It may do so in muted tones, insisting that relief will come by way of the ballot box rather than the barricade; nevertheless, were it to get its wish, the world would undergo a transformation more radical than any previously conceived.

Clearly, the adjustments needed to cope with being middle class have proven more wrenching than might have been predicted. To the astonishment of many, a burgeoning ability to control our individual circumstances inaugurated uncertainties that, from a distance, might seem trivial but which up close appeared insurmountable. So profound did these seem that many would-be saviors recommended a complete social overhaul. They sought to do away with both the marketplace and social hierarchies. In their utopian cosmos, equality and universal love were to become the norm. As members of the same congenial family, everyone would be equivalent. Although their personal experiences were of gesellschaft commercialism and social stratification, in their minds' eyes these crusaders perceived perfection. Thus, without evidence of feasibility, they counseled the elimination of personal property and the imposition of radical egalitarianism. Terrified by the lack of organization inherent in a decentralized society, they rushed to introduce a comforting predictability by forcing everyone to operate on the same plane. Sadly, this anticipated equivalence existed only in their imaginations. Its alleged fairness derived from their psyches, not from reality.

The liberal ideal is a fantasy.[5] It is a chimera summoned up by the emotional insecurities of those unsure about how to manage their independence. Were it to be implemented, its universal love would prove as ephemeral as a morning mist. So, too, would the prosperity and egalitarianism it is said to augment. Paradoxically, those frightened by the advent of a middle-class society do not allow themselves to recognize that both the wealth and liberties they take for granted derive from institutions they despise. They do not understand that the efficiencies of the marketplace are the source of their prosperity or that decentralized decision-making is the foundation of political democracy. Whatever their glorious conjectures, it is indisputable that neither command economies nor anarchistic autonomy have been able to make good on their claims. To the contrary, experience has demonstrated their tendencies to devolve into totalitarian scarcity or murderous discord. Hobbes[6], long ago, was right about the human potential for a war of all against all. Without the boundaries set by the marketplace, people either fail to coordinate their activities or do so via brutal repression. Liberalism, for all its elevated rhetoric, because its pedigree derives from a combination of quasireligious absolutism and romantic familism, would kill the golden goose in order to preserve comforting delusions. Despite the promises of its advocates, their new Zion would halt progress in its tracks. To quote John Hospers,[7] its legacy would be "splendidly equalized destitution" or a sanguine tyranny.

Contrary to what the prophets of egalitarian collectivism say what is needed is more freedom, not less. Instead of mandating an equality of results, people have to be released to pursue individual success. Despite the skeptics, this is not to recommend a Social Darwinism,[8] which authorizes losers to perish in isolated misery. As social creatures, humans must be free to create interpersonal alliances even as they seek private benefits. What the old-style eugenists did not realize is that, just as people can pursue individual aims, they can collaborate on joint ventures. The central point is that, if the Middle-Class Revolution is to expand in scope, its evolving institutions must facilitate a social mobility based on merit. This means that an ever larger a proportion of the population must contribute its talents to furthering the concerns of the majority. A sort of neo-utilitarianism,[9] based not on conscious calculations, but semiconscious social negotiations,[10] has to determine, then implement, the greatest good for the greatest number. Both individually and as members of competing alliances, the participants must reshuffle their social statuses so that superior worth can have the greatest impact. Put another way, we can say that the tests of strength in which people engage should be domesticated rather than outlawed. These contests need to be both fair and flexible if they are to result in what is socially optimal. The upshot is that conflict cannot be eliminated. There will still be winners, and therefore losers, but the overall consequences can be collectively advantageous. As significant, most individuals, by dint of their effort and expertise, will have a greater opportunity to improve their personal lots.

Indeed, complete equality is a procrustean bed. It slices off the legs of those who are exceptional while concurrently stretching those who do not measure up. People are different in both their motives and capacities. They are also hierarchical by nature. Once these facts are put together, efforts to make them otherwise are revealed to be inevitably coercive. Only compulsion can produce a facsimile of uniformity when so many of necessity resist homogenization. More suitable is encouraging people to be their best, which entails promoting professionalization in all its aspects. The more expert and dedicated people are as they play their individual roles,[11] the more they can do for themselves, their loved ones, and humanity in general. Naturally, this would not eliminate conflicts, disappointments, or mistakes.

It would merely militate toward improvements in an inescapably imperfect human condition. Aiming toward this would demonstrate that a greater occupational professionalization allows for more control over one's work,[12] while a greater personal professionalization facilitates greater fulfillments in the private domain. In permitting decentralization, these, in tandem, maximize the application of local knowledge and personal energies to human aspirations.

But to become more professional, people need to become as strong as they can get. They need to maximize their separate abilities. This, of course, is not a unique insight. The modern military long ago learned that the best army is composed of the best-trained soldiers. Bitter experience demonstrated that throwing warm bodies into machine-gun fire was a prescription for slaughter, not victory. The same can be said of civilian pursuits. Those who do not know what they are doing are not apt to do it well. Untrained minds and bodies crumple under pressure. But even this is not enough. To do well, people need to capitalize on their humanity, not just on an abstract rationalism.[13] They have to get in touch with their inner selves and to reinforce what they find.

A model regarding what is possible can be drawn from the past. Thus, during the Renaissance newly discovered documents arriving from Muslim realms hinted at a world beyond medieval scholasticism.[14] Greek and Roman manuscripts written in ignorance of the Bible argued for a way to understand nature other than that expounded by the Doctors of the Church. To be more precise, Greek playwrights revealed a psychological sophistication that set literary minds racing. Their heroes and heroines exhibited scandalous impulses outside the purely religious. Fictional though the characters might be, these ancient forms were more completely human than their biblical counterparts. This provided the impetus for humanism.[15] Suddenly the best and brightest concluded that there was more to life than a preparation for heaven. The here-and-now realities of flesh and blood also deserved attention.

This Renaissance humanism inadvertently accelerated a search for secular knowledge that proved of inestimable value to a revived commercialism. Those prepared to examine mankind firsthand now opened a window on unsuspected truths. Not only could asrtists paint figures that looked like their neighbors, scientists could engage in autopsies to determine human anatomy. Eventually, this expanded enlightenment led academic explorers into virgin territory and launched the West on an adventure that has yet to reach a conclusion. Indeed, we are at the threshold of a new humanism[16] or, more precisely, a social humanism. As social creatures, we are in the process of locating ourselves in a social context. With time and experience, it becomes patent that each of us possesses inescapable connections to others. What these are and how they are established must therefore be appreciated in multifaceted detail. The time to wallow in mythological storytelling is long gone. A genuine social humanism has to include a social anatomy at least as faithful to the ligaments of interpersonal associations as were the renderings of the Renaissance anatomists.

What is more, in our convoluted technocommercial world, it is essential not to deny unpleasant realities. The breath of human experience has to be accepted for what it is, warts and all. Nor should people aspire to perfection. Because our natures encompass disagreeable elements, the best that can be hoped for are improvements. Our aggregate and individual prospects can be enhanced, but not to the point where everyone wins. Like it or not, pain and loss are integral to the human condition. These may be unwelcome, but they are fundamental to the mechanisms that make people people. Paradoxically, they are also crucial to what has made our species successful. This being so, we cannot be rescued by romanticized aesthetics. While art can furnish insights into the human situation, particularly on an emotional level, by itself, it is insufficient. More regretful, its idealized simplifications tend to produce false hope. This is especially true of quasireligious idealizations. Mysticism banishes too many facts to be a reliable guide. Nor can an enlightenment-style physical science provide all the answers. People are more than assemblages of atoms, molecules, and cells. Physics, chemistry, and biology have demonstrated their worth yet, by themselves, are incapable of explicating the social aspects of human existence.[17]

A new professionalism,[18] a humanistic professionalism must, therefore, emerge from the demands of a budding middle-class society. The need to coordinate the complex activities of self-directed individuals, if permitted, will elicit the tools necessary to decipher what is occurring. Just as the need for sailing ships to pilot themselves on trackless oceans once brought forth the chronometer, so a gesellschaft social order can summon the reflexivity needed to determine the combined location of its members. Since the social is human and vice versa, this process can be aided by a social science that provides honest, nonideological accounts of its subject. By candidly examining the mechanisms through which interpersonal associations are created, maintained, and modified, it can strengthen the base of knowledge available for those planning their private and social activities. In illuminating limitations as well as opportunities, ordinary men and women may thereby direct their energies where they can have the greatest effect. As such, the socially well informed can become professional with respect to their personal circumstances.

The enemy in this is an immature romanticism. Good intentions cloaked in a breathless, emotional utopianism venture into the world unclothed. Winston Churchill[19] said that some truths are so important that they deserve to be guarded by a cordon of lies. This was certainly true for allied military secrets. But it is not the case for social realities. Self-deception here is the height of folly. Yet, people habitually fool themselves about their social situations in order to protect against the pain of failure.[20] They would rather bask in the glory of phony triumphs than recognize that they are not sitting atop the hierarchical heap. On an individual level some such balm may be indispensable, but collectively it is a disaster in waiting. A single person walking off a cliff is one thing; an entire society doing so is quite another. This being the case, reorganizing gender roles to conform to feminist mythologies would have been more than a private tragedy. Taken literally, it might have resulted in the sort of communal suicide that overtook the Shakers. These religious zealots thought celibacy provided a route to heaven; and separately it may have, but for an organized community it ushered in their extinction.

Nor was Hobbes, despite his central insight, right about the solution to a war of all against all. He believed a Leviathan who could compel obedience was necessary to curb private ambitions. A man of his times, he conceived this as a monarch with the centralized power to command submission. Yet, such a consolidated authority cannot work in a middle-class society.[21] Notwithstanding the fact that human beings are no more altruistic today than they were during his era, given the upsurge in social complexities, many more of them must partake in controlling their destinies. To do so, however, they must become stronger and more knowledgeable than their ancestors. Instead of relying exclusively on associations based on hierarchical organizers, they must become expert in making role-based decisions. Rather than reflexively defer to one-size-fits-all ideological principles, they must participate in shaping the rules that guide their personal actions. To be succinct, they must become skilled interpersonal role players. This said, an evolving commercialized division of labor must not be rejected from fear of its ambiguities. Indeed, it must be embraced as an honored part of the human condition, then implemented with intelligence and dexterity. This, however, requires that the skills needed to execute it be internalized.

Unfortunately, the data and the internal controls necessary to craft workable role relations are not instinctive. People must today prepare themselves to assume the responsibilities to which they have become heir. They cannot afford to react impulsively in a landscape littered with hidden snares. Effort is, therefore, needed to allocate their respective positions with intelligence, as well as to obtain practice in performing these satisfactorily. The answer to complexity is not an all-powerful genius at the helm; it is informed competence at the periphery. An apt analogy would be a network of billions of personal computers. The introduction of a multitude of interlinked desktops, in place of a single super-mainframe, surprised the experts with its dispersed intellect. A professionalized distribution of specialized roles should do no less. Profoundly human in its architecture, if appropriately expert and flexible, it possesses the potential to handle matters no unified authority ever could.

The Division of Labor Revisited

The power of integrated social roles has been profoundly underestimated. As surprising as it may sound, history seems to be pointing us toward this conclusion. Nevertheless, the hubris of the Marxists in assuming they understood the arrow of history provides a useful caution.[22] Despite what we have learned, the future is not ours to master. Still, an overview of what has already happened suggests where things might be headed. The progression of society from the Symbolic Revolution[23] that set our hunter-gatherer ancestors on a global trek, through the Agricultural Revolution that sent populations soaring, to the Commercial Revolution that drastically improved efficiencies and led to the intricacies of the Industrial and Middle Class Revolutions points to an evolution in organizing principles and sources of interpersonal power. Where once personal relations and face-to-face hierarchies dominated the scene, they have receded in influence. And while religiously inspired structures previously rose to prominence because they could assimilate the swelling numbers in protocivilizations,[24] more empirical principles have taken over. Commercialization has also dictated that social-role configurations become more focal. A complex, yet decentralized, division of labor proved necessary to keep pace with complications too byzantine to be dealt with any other way. What did not occur, however, was the wholesale replacement of one form of organization by another. That which came later built upon what came before, albeit with appropriate modifications to account for altered circumstances. Old traditions and old mechanisms were not abandoned so much as adjusted to meet unanticipated needs.

To reiterate, personal relations and hierarchical command structures did not disappear with the advent of commercial/technological societies. They merely assumed new forms. Where huntergatherers depended almost exclusively on family relations, members of the contemporary middle class rely more on friends and colleagues. Common activities, rather than biological ties, cement their alliances as they navigate novel occupational and avocational crosscurrents. This is not to say that family ties have evaporated. As was explained in the previous chapter, the nuclear family has increased in salience, especially for the middle classes. Though more voluntary than its predecessors, its assigned tasks are no less crucial. As a haven in a heartless world and as the incubator of future self-directed generations, it remains unsurpassed. Even the fingerprints of more extended family relations remain detectable. These are more attenuated than those of former times but are still called upon to solemnize rites of passage and to provide succor in times of crisis. The relatives may gather only for family holidays such as Christmas and Thanksgiving or for weddings, funerals, and graduations, but their incipient presence continues to be a source of security.

A parallel transformation has overtaken social hierarchies.[25] When foraging bands represented the norm, determining which individual was dominant occurred in tests of strength among persons who knew one another. The victory of one and the defeat of the other resulted in inarguable reputations with observable consequences. After societies became too large for these contests to be universal, less personal means for determining precedence developed. Ultimately, social class structures evolved. These relied more upon commercial success but also upon the symbols of this success. Winners and losers remained a part of the scene even though the means of deciding who was who had drastically altered. Today, the distinction between the dominant and the submissive remains significant. Commercialization may have increased social mobility, but it has not eliminated the perquisites of power. Nor will it.

A hierarchical species must continue to generate hierarchical differentiations. It is the shape and the mechanisms of these rankings that have been modified. Clearly social classes and, more particularly, the middle classes have swelled in bulk and prestige. Similarly, what counts as a form of strength has been adjusted, *e.g.*, economic expertise now carries more clout than does physical prowess. So, too, have the abilities to assemble alliances in mass communities torn by a myriad of divisions. Most significantly in their quest of power, the roles individuals occupy and the connections these engender with other players are more critical than in simpler times. Nowadays, the nature of someone's expertise and how it intersects with that of role partners can determine how individually powerful the person is and/or how effective in organizing the activities of others. Moreover, it is not merely the nature of these roles but how nimbly they can be revised that often proves decisive.

Meanwhile, this obligation to manage mounting complexities has also affected religious configurations. Once societies became too large for everyone to be familiar with everyone else, the emerging impersonality of shared systems of faith allowed strangers to coordinate their pursuits. A commitment to common gods and communal myths permitted united fronts when confronting external challenges.[26] Members of the same normative group could rely on the steadfast beliefs of others to enforce a joint set of standards. Indeed, when this normative consensus was grounded in supernatural phenomena, it could achieve a resilience that enabled it to withstand considerable stress. This was an enormous advantage during periods of strife. Thus at the height of the Middle Ages, marauding bands of Vikings might come and go and ambitious aristocrats might scour the countryside for wealth, but the Church and its teachings remained intact. The problem with this form of social integration, however, was that it could also be rigid. Religious beliefs and later political ideologies have undergone more change than most of their adherents imagine; nevertheless their viewpoints are jealously guarded against heresy. The result can be an inability to meet unsuspected difficulties. A Church may, for instance, decree that charging interest is usury and therefore a sin at the very moment when commercial transactions require impersonal forms of financing. By the same token, an ideological social movement can insist that gender differences are a myth, just when isolated nuclear families demand a greater tolerance of gender disparities.

One of the worst consequences of normative rigidity, of course, has been caste systems. When religions declare that particular forms of stratification are sacred, these become virtually impossible to modify. The strengths and abilities of individuals count for little when the weight of the entire community is recruited to prevent organizational innovation. This, as we have seen, runs directly contrary to the requirements of social class systems. These are dependent upon frameworks that stimulate social mobility. Once a religion unbendingly prohibits economic fluctuation, this sort of flexibility cannot exist. The same applies to legal frameworks that attempt to institutionalize fairness too precisely. Mechanisms such as rent-and-price controls typically have side effects that their sponsors do not anticipate. Nevertheless, rigidity can be beneficial in some moral contexts. Murder is an activity that must be unwaveringly prohibited. Religious bans, therefore, make sense in demanding that it be proscribed. Less functional are political ideologies. Refusing even to consider welfare reforms because one insists that transfer payments are rights can bind a commercialized community to counterproductive policies and condemn many of its citizens to blighted dependencies.

What is indispensable within a middle-class society is adaptable moral negotiations.[27] Romantic relativism[28] goes too far in

444 *The Great Middle Class Revolution*

sanctioning normative fluidity, yet a critical relativism that allows rules to be adjusted to novel conditions is also conceivable. In the latter, individuals realistically assess the impact of specific regulations, then work out their differences with others to promote diverse interests or perspectives. In this way, values and virtues are modified to provide support for evolving patterns of interaction. As a result, middle-class societies have been characterized by dizzying debates about values. Politically and socially rent by disputes about what is right or wrong, everyone seems to have a unique opinion about what to do. Eager to vent these in public, they are often hawked as a form of media entertainment. It may sometimes seem that these controversies proceed without purpose, but, viewed longitudinally they are akin to a problem-solving mechanism. Thanks to them, modern societies need not be constrained by behavioral tenets more suitable to their preindustrial precursors. Nor need they renounce the communal standards essential to interpersonal trust. They can have both stability and flexibility owing to bargaining processes that fluctuate between agreement and discord.

Still, of central import to the advent of modernism has been the proliferation of social roles and the evolution of their complexity.[29] More than ever, people occupy highly personalized sets of tasks within an extended, impersonal infrastructure. Despite the apparent contradictions of pursuing individualized activities within a system that treats the players interchangeably, this is what seems to be occurring.[30] The dramatis personae are becoming highly skilled at occupations with which they personally identify even though most of those who rely on their contributions do not recognize their humanity. To compound this irony, the power of these persons and of the societies to which they belong are augmented by this circumstance. As members of cohesive communities, these individuals benefit from the effectiveness inherent in an extremely specialized but nonetheless responsive division of labor. For one thing, their separate needs are more efficiently met by role partners who possess the ramified competences to do so. For another, the community itself becomes more powerful thanks to the integration of roles. Because the various parts mesh to facilitate amazingly intricate activities, the whole is able to achieve complex goals, goals that allow it to prevail vis-à-vis competing societies.

Perhaps unexpectedly, the participants in these complex role structures[31] also gain hierarchical power from being personally crucial to the attainment of specific ends. Though they are theoretically regarded as expendable, once ensconced in particular positions, they may not easily be replaced. This permits them to exercise control over critical uncertainties and therefore over others dependent on having these performed. As the linchpins of particular activities, they can demand personal deference by threatening to withhold their services. In making crucial decisions, they thus require others to alter their behaviors. This is so even though these others may not be consciously aware that their conduct has been manipulated. The secret of how this sort of power is allocated lies in the dynamics of role negotiations[32] and in the conservative nature of role scripts. In essence, the means whereby a social division of labor is created and maintained provide the key to how authority is exercised and why some role players become more powerful than others.

Social roles[33] may not completely replace either social hierarchies or normative standards, but they frequently trump both. In rearranging how these other mechanisms are organized, they permit personalized controls that would not otherwise be available. More particularly, the existence of detailed roles in which some individuals develop an expertise, but others do not, dramatically modifies how ranking systems operate. One of the ways in which hierarchies and divisions of labor intersect is in methods the latter utilize to define power. A simple way to understand what is involved is through bureaucratic offices.[34] A person appointed to a position within a bureaucracy[35] is not only delegated a precise task but also the authority with which to accomplish it.[36] Along with the role assignment to fabricate a circumscribed item comes the right—nay the requirement—to direct specific others in creating it. One is hired not merely as an engineer but as the boss of a particular task group. Others, who also possess assigned roles, roles that Weber[37] called defined offices, become one's designated subordinates. They are, thereby, directed to defer to orders emanating from their superior. The boss, as part of her role, makes identifiable decisions and then oversees their performance. Indeed, the might of the entire organization will come to her aid should an underling defy this arrangement.

What differs between hierarchical power that grows out of face-to-face tests of strength and power mediated by roles is that the latter is more restricted. Roles, which include leadership imperatives, also specify limitations on this authority. They define the perquisites of the boss more clearly than does an unfocused ability to intimidate others. An organizational role might, for instance, demand that a superior set the schedule for his subordinates, but it will be equally definite in precluding his meddling in their home life. Rational-legal power, such as that discussed by Weber, prevents what would today be considered abuses by endorsing some orders, but not others. By the same token, subordinates facilitate role-based authority by recognizing the legitimacy of some commands but not others. The former are accepted as part of the leader's task assignment, whereas the latter are not.

These role arrangements also facilitate power by defining networks of relationships. Oftentimes the allies a would-be decision-maker can call upon are motivated to help because of the roles they occupy. As direct or indirect role partners, they engage in activities which tend to be dependent upon his. Just as parents support one another in disciplining their young because they know that, if they do not, they will soon be open to challenge, so may one bureaucratic boss support the claims of another. This assistance is typically built into the role and is not a matter of conscious choice. Police officers, to cite an important instance, do not ask for the identity of the victim when their radio blares a call to assist an officer in distress—they simply come to his aid as expeditiously as they can. From this point of view, this is what one does if one is a police officer. Less dramatical, one student will disapprove of another who arbitrarily refuses to take a scheduled examination. This is part of what it means to be a student. This predisposition may not be intended to strengthen the teacher's hand, but it has this effect. Indeed, it is so predictable that few students consider challenging this phalanx of intersecting roles.

These phenomena have the consequence of making the exercise of power less arbitrary. In a world populated by millions of strangers, such clarity is essential.[38] Were individuals with few personal relationships unrestrained by internal role structures, an impatience to achieve dominance might lead to the escalation of tests of strength to fatal endpoints. Absent the inhibitions of personal sympathy, some might callously torture those they do not individually know. This is no mere academic possibility. It is the stock-in-trade of tyrants and has been for millennia. Thus, well-defined roles not only permit extensive alliances among strangers, they also temper potential extremism. Indeed, democratic institutions are contingent upon such highly ramified roles structures. They do this, in part, by investing some decisions in their less powerful members by way of the ballot box. Universal suffrage,[39] by endowing ordinary citizens with the right to vote upon their leaders, provides a brake on the more powerful. Elected officials get to make decisions ordinary people do not, but they must make these with an eye to future polls. The same is true within corporations where capricious bosses find that their reputations and, therefore, their promotions, suffer if their subordinates bridle at being manipulated into working outside their job descriptions.

There is also a consequential intersection between norms and social roles. Just as roles help to shape hierarchies, so norms help mold roles. Both personal and interpersonal rules contribute to determining the sorts of tasks particular individuals perform. On a society-wide level, moral standards define how social roles will be negotiated.[40] The sorts of demands that role partners make of one another and how these are pursued are regulated by broadly held commitments. Parents, for instance, are not allowed to impose violent strictures on their children. It may be their responsibility to shape their young into law-abiding citizens, but they are not allowed to do this by beating them with bullwhips. Nor do contemporary communities countenance parents forcing offspring into unwanted marriages. What were once acceptable forms of influence have categorically gone out of style. That which is now permissible has slowly evolved to meet the needs of a socially mobile and frequently self-directed society. Almost second nature, these rules are today considered coterminous with civilization.

Other rules are found within role scripts.[41] These are a part of the machinery that guides role performances. Unlike moral rules, however, these norms and values can be highly specific. More precise, that which is considered moral derives much of its force from a social consensus. Indeed, it would not be considered moral were it not enforced by a significant proportion of the community. Individual roles, in contrast, vary too dramatically for the same parameters to be applicable. To cite one example, the conventions that make for an ethical dogcatcher are not the same as those that make for an ethical politician. Few, except other dogcatchers, would be familiar with the standards appropriate to a humane animal capture. Likewise, few, except other politicians, understand the constraints under which elected officials must operate. This lack of inter-role visibility is on display in recent social disputes over police brutality. Outside observers, who have never had to subdue lawbreakers, are frequently scandalized by the physical restraints professional law officers understand as essential. Never having been personally attacked nor ever having been tutored in what constitutes going too far, countless laypeople find even defensive force too brutal. Fortunately, within a particular role, there may exist internalized directives that keep power within bounds. Law officers really do commit to standards of restraint that are known within their role set, although not beyond it. Matched to local conditions, these imperatives make for greater flexibility than would universal imperatives. At once responsive to restricted circumstances and bounded by suitable constraints, they are derived from generations of street experience. In other words, the rules that apply to particular roles allow for decentralized variation without succumbing to anarchistic license. They are the equivalent of the physician's Hippocratic oath, albeit with less historical fanfare.

When all of this is synthesized, it becomes apparent that the evolution of a social-class society is intimately linked to the evolution of highly diversified yet closely integrated social roles. It is these, grafted onto earlier hierarchical and normative structures, that make middle-class lifestyles possible. They permit people to be both mobile and self-directed within the larger communities upon which they have become dependent. Had they not arrived on the scene, neither the specialized competences necessary within a technocommercial society nor their intelligent combination would have been feasible. Their validity, however, is contingent upon a growing professionalization.[42] These roles would be useless without a concurrent evolution in the expertise and motivation necessary for those performing them. Individuals who have not internalized the skills and commitments to make them work would be placeholders in a pathetic charade. To invoke a familiar Texan cliché, they would be all sizzle and no steak. What is more, the society to which they belonged, to further mix metaphors, would be a house of cards. It is, therefore, vital to understand how proficient roles are created and maintained. Comprehending this is a first step toward facilitating their continued proliferation. Since role negotiations and roles scripts are key, they must be our next area of focus.

Role Negotiations and Role Scripts

Emile Durkheim[43] in confronting the conundrum of why mass societies have remained stable postulated what he called "organic solidarity." People cooperated with one another not because they were relatives or were imperatively compelled to do so or feared eternal damnation but because it was in their interest. Conversely, members of foraging bands were mutually sympathetic as a result of an intimate familiarity with each other's situations. The latter could be reciprocally compassionate because they were able to put themselves in one another's shoes. Members of contemporary nation-states, in contrast, work harmoniously because they recognize their mutual interdependence. Since each receives essential services that only others can provide, they are sensitive to the utility of these exchanges. Moreover, since their own services require consumers, they are alert to the reactions of their patrons, however remote these may be. Their partners in such transactions might be strangers; they might even be unsympathetic personalities; yet it is to their own advantage to be civil and accommodating. Since all benefit from partaking in this division of labor, all profit from maintaining its integrity. They are, in Durkheim's powerful analogy, like the organs of a single body that cannot survive without their joint contributions.

In the century since Durkheim presented this thesis, the division of labor has proceeded apace. The proliferation of specialized roles has become so extensive that direct observation rarely confirms the efficacy of interpersonal collaboration. People know their own jobs and those of their immediate role partners, but the contributions of most others are a blur. They make regular trips to supermarkets to purchase provisions, yet they do not make the mental connection between prepackaged chicken breasts and bib-overalled chicken farmers. How then are they to feel gratitude toward these others? How can they care about their welfare? Worse still, the efficiency of modern institutions has exacerbated an impersonality already evident at the beginning of the Industrial Revolution.[44] This suggests that individuals who never participate in face-to-face exchanges may not literally recognize the value of their interdependence. It may be virtually impossible for them to feel indebted to specific others for services not identified as such. From this, it follows that few are likely to feel solidarity with strangers out of a rational appreciation of their mutual reliance.

Nevertheless, people continue to cooperate. They do so almost as if this were a conditioned reflex. Society has managed to maintain its integration, partly because it continues to incorporate personal and hierarchical relations, partly because it carries forward a normative order, but also because it has evolved a network of detailed and highly personalized role structures. Since these roles could not exist without being reciprocal, they must be mutually obliging. But this is not from a conscious awareness that this is collectively functional. It is the very nature of how social roles are created and maintained that provides their stability. Durkheim did not pay sufficient attention to the mechanisms through which this occurs, but they are of crucial import. They dictate what is possible and what is not. Likewise, they determine how societies can be integrated and who will hold which positions within them.

Just as it is impossible to understand how families function without recognizing the sorts of negotiations that occur between spouses, so it is impossible to appreciate the connections joining less intimate individuals without recognizing the negotiations, some of which are indirect, that occur between them. In the same way that tests of strength were fundamental to understanding how hierarchies are constructed, it is essential to recognize that social roles typically come in pairs. A division of labor implies that tasks will be divided among different individuals and also that these will be linked together in larger social operations. If, as Adam Smith said,[45] in manufacturing pins, one person draws out lengths of wire, another cuts these into pin-sized pieces, and a third sharpens the points, they must all coordinate their actions to make the desired end product. The ultimate goal of each player would be incomplete without the contributions of the others—and indeed of many others besides these. The same is true of husbands who require wives and vice versa and of teachers who require students and vice versa. More than this, these role partners are involved in chains of interlinking partnerships. Spouses have children, children have teachers, teachers have administrators, and so on and so forth. Every person has many role partners, who themselves have multiple partners. Sometimes, these individuals interact with only one at a time, but, at other times, they are simultaneously torn among completing claims. In any event, to be a role player is to be subject to the demands of multiple players who have vested interests in how one acts one's parts.

Furthermore, it is these intersecting demands between multiple partners that constitute the core of role negotiations.[46] For the sake of simplicity, consider the situation of two partners—let us say a pair of spouses. Each has desires about how the other should fulfill assigned tasks. In the traditional household, a husband may have ideas about what he wants his wife to fix for dinner, and she about the domestic repairs on her honey-do list. These will influence what gets done and, more specifically, how the husband decides to be a husband or the wife a wife. But this is a negotiation; hence, each will have ideas about role performances—some of which may have derived from previous role partners and some from personal desires. It is from this complicated give-and-take that relatively well-settled behavior patterns evolve. Despite numerous altercations, eventually a series of compromises is reached. Each party then makes an internalized commitment that more or less stabilizes the partnership. Because each player knows what is expected and is in more or less agreement with this expectation, it can be performed with reasonable regularity.

These internalized compromises become institutionalized as role scripts.[47] When people decide that they will voluntarily execute certain tasks, they do not need constant reminders from their partners. Their interior attitudes are transformed so that they are disposed to act in accord with the designated behavioral patterns. During role negotiations, each party is exposed to demands to think, feel, and act in particular ways. Each will be directed to understand the world in specified dimensions, to react to it with appropriate emotions, and to conduct oneself in accord with identifiable norms and values. These are, respectively, the cognitive, emotional, and volitional aspects of their individual roles. In time, these elements are adopted as personal commitments. They, then, become role scripts in the sense that how the person now thinks, feels, and believes guides future activities without direct consultation with role partners. The person need only consult these inner guidelines before deciding how to behave. Although role partners may continue to provide input, this is not always as decisive as are the internal traces of prior demands.

Much of how people are prepared to behave typically derives from interactions with previous role partners.[48] Those who helped inculcate an earlier repertoire of predispositions retain an influence that expresses itself in subsequent interactions. This is because role scripts tend to be conservative. The ways that people have learned to think, feel, and behave become part of their identities and cannot be altered by the mere expedient of deciding to do so. Central to this conformity are emotions. When these are intense, they can perpetuate themselves for a lifetime. Antique fears, outdated angers, and historic loves frequently continue almost unabated over decades. And since the clashes that occur during role negotiations can be quite passionate, they are ideal for instilling these role-preserving attitudes. Furthermore, since primitive emotions tend to be at their zenith when a person is young, role patterns established in childhood can set the template for adult relationships.

Role conservation via role scripts is thus a two-edged sword. On the one hand, its ability to maintain a division of labor without constant reminders provides for social stability. People can confidently predict that others will uphold their ends of the division of labor because of who they have become. This enables them to plan their activities with confidence. On the other hand, roles can be so constrained that they fail to adjust to altered circumstances.[49] People inflexibly perform actions that are no longer appropriate to their own or their partners' situations. Given the fluidity of modern market societies, this can be a serious drawback. Instead of becoming expert in their specialties, the players continue in their loyalties to ineffective tactics. They can, in a sense, be hobbled by personalized cultural lags.

As commercialization has produced a society that is at once more complex and mobile, the requisite professionalization of roles can be obviated by a reactionary allegiance to obsolete practices. Both individually and institutionally, people can persist in attempting to do things the way they learned they were supposed to long after this is counterproductive. They can literally seek to retain organizational arrangements that hark back to former times. Although they find themselves in a gesellschaft world, they long for intimate communal ties that cannot be revived. Romanticism[50] takes over, and they dream either of a universal extended family or an absolutistic father figure. More particularly, though a dynamic market economy means that businesses grow and contract and that jobs come and go, they fantasize about the security of lifelong employment within a doting familial corporation. On a personal level, they may likewise remain dedicated to archaic skills. Instead of professionalizing, they learn just enough to get by. Rather than dedicate themselves to expanded expertises, they reject challenging innovations. Worst of all, in preference to pursuing emotional maturity, they idealize childish spontaneity. The goal is to be forever young based on the rationalization that this means being forever happy.

What these rigid souls fail to realize is that these practices condemn them to comparative impotence. In a middle-class society, power is usually tied to occupying a middle-class niche.[51] But in a modern market economy, the best decision-making slots are normally allocated to those with the expertise to perform them. Who will get to fill authoritative positions is supposed to depend on who possesses the motivation and abilities to execute them. Not unexpectedly, because some roles are more rewarding than others, disputes arise as to who is appointed to what. Just as with hierarchical priority, people butt heads to determine who will prevail. This means that, as with raw power, role conflicts can be decided by assembling potent alliances. Given that there is no rule obliging role negotiations to be one on one, powerful supporters can give one person's demands more weight than another's. But a major reason why those who exercise clout choose one side over another is that they believe their choice is potentially more competent than the one rejected. Those who demonstrate the skills and inclinations to accomplish the relevant tasks, therefore, elicit the support of those with an interest in having these accomplished satisfactorily. A boss who wants greater profits will, assuming he is rational, favor the applicant for promotion who has demonstrated the best track record. This puts a premium on professionalization for those who are ambitious. They know, or should know, that they can improve their chances to obtain more potent roles by pursuing the appropriate education and personal qualities.

In the end, the marketplace usually determines who rises to the top.[52] What constitutes expertise is not merely a matter of prejudice. Efficiencies in production, distribution, and social organization decide who will have the most power and, in the rawest terms, who will be able to defeat whom. Those who believe in the superiority of cultural appearances essentially commit themselves to the potency of detached interpersonal reputations. On one level, they understand that in the same way that tests of strength are generalized through the reputations earned in victory, symbols of competence can, per se, persuade others to support their role aspirations. Should they articulate popular indicators of role dexterity, they expect to be rewarded with a confidence in their ability to deliver on their promises. In this, they are not totally wrong. People often confuse seductive appearances with underlying substances. Indeed, politicians depend upon this propensity when they appeal for public support. In telling others that they feel their pain or that they have a compelling solution to their problems,[53] politicians rely on a conventional wisdom that can be deceptive. But eventually many of these charlatans are found out. When their schemes fail, they are turned out of office. Substance does matter, and in the long run appearances that outrun their ability to come through tend to be replaced by understandings more in conformity with emerging realities. It may take centuries for this sort of realignment to occur, but that which works is liable at some point to be recognized.

Besides eventually endorsing efficiency, the marketplace tends to reward flexibility. Caste systems[54] were replaced by class systems precisely because of the latter's superior ability to adjust to unforeseen circumstances. The same applies on an individual level. People who can modify their roles to fit emerging conditions have an advantage over those wedded to obsolete methods. One of liberalism's great failings was its attempt to control social behavior through a proliferation of centralized rules. Whether these were the price controls of the New Deal[55] or the political correctness of diversity-based labor regulations, they attempted to coerce people into conforming to utopian visions. In essence, the populace was to be frozen into theoretical versions of perfection. Yet, in their hubris, their advocates overestimated their own levels of expertise. They believed that centralized planning would be more rational than private greed, whereas their inability to assimilate local deviations doomed their decisions to irrelevance. Dedicated more to uniformity than to efficiency, they could not imagine that decentralized role players might make better decisions than they. This, however, has turned out to be the usual state of affairs. Individual role players, in their ability to react to here-and-now discrepancies, have an advantage in suppleness. Operating in accord with role scripts that have a narrower purview than do the absolute imperatives of the centralizers, they can make modifications without throwing entire societies off-kilter. Such individuals must, to be sure, contend with their own inclinations toward role conservation, but these are easier to manage than are the simple-minded prescriptions of large-scale social reforms—and they are less coercive to boot.

Critical Relativism

If role negotiations and role scripts are to live up to their promise, they must occur within a framework of rules that facilitate flexibility and responsiveness. What counts as a strength and what is considered fair must enable people to create divisions of labor that meet individual and collective needs. Those who get to make the decisions should be the ones best suited to do so, as determined by appropriate forms of conflict and association. Adaptable competence is essential in a mass technocommercial society; hence, such communities must possess a moral framework that encourages decentralized and socially mobile self-direction. This framework, however, is not a given. Despite the historically near universal belief that morality should be absolute, it is constantly adjusted to accommodate nascent conditions. Yet, the recent faith in ethical relativism is equally flawed.[56] Moral rules, if they are to mean anything, cannot be so plastic that they are alterable at anyone's whim. These regulations may be subject to modification, but this will be via moral negotiations over which no single person has total control. The consensus that emerges and that provides the clout to impose shared standards will have been tediously hammered out by millions of contributors over what may be centuries of development.[57]

The Great Middle-Class Revolution has been a major incentive toward moral reform. Liberalism[58] has, in fact, been a response to this impetus. So has the reaction of the social conservatives. Together they have participated in Culture Wars[59] that are, in reality, a massive renegotiation of the operative rules. Though the romantic relativists favor a do-your-own-thing philosophy and religious conservatives appeal to divine authority, more appropriate than either of these viewpoints is a critical, that is to say, a realistic relativism. Moral rules need to be evaluated according to their potential impact. Surprisingly, this is what many of the participants are in the process of doing. From their private perspectives they are reacting to the world they, and their associates, experience to demand adjustments that seem to address their concerns. As a result, although often unconsciously achieved and all too often by way of a series of dead-ends that announce their unsuitability in unexpected failures, all sorts of constraints get factored into the final product. People compare evolving alternatives and gradually settle on those that seem the most efficacious.

In the case of the rules guiding role negotiations, this process is ongoing. The very passions that permeate contemporary politics testify to their unsettled status. When liberals accuse conservatives of being fascists or conservatives counter by labeling liberals communists, the resulting anger is a sign of how far they are from agreement. One of the pivotal areas of contention has been society's master values. Since its inception, the United States has been torn by disputes over the relative importance of freedom and equality.[60] Both have been deemed important, as is reflected in the last line of the Pledge of Allegiance. Schoolchildren know that it concludes by praising the nation as standing for "liberty and justice for all." Liberty is obviously synonymous with freedom, whereas justice implies fairness for all. The problem is that the meanings of these commitments have been transformed over the centuries. The language is never stable, and its applications are always in flux.

Equality once meant an equality of rights.[61] People were supposed to be equivalent before the law. This, however, has transmuted into an equality of results. Liberals, under the unacknowledged sway of neo-Marxists, have insisted that a mass society cannot be fair unless everyone participates equally in its rewards.[62] They deny the validity of hierarchy and demand that resources and power be evenly distributed. This dispersal is supposed to be across the board. Thus, they would use the federal government to ensure that jobs are doled out in proportion to the representation of various groups within the larger population.   Women, African Americans, and the disabled, according to this program, are all entitled to what is deemed their rightful shares of the spoils. This proportionality even extends to schoolrooms where grades are to be inflated so that no one feels slighted and also to Little League ballparks where no one is allowed to lose. Conservatives, of course, demur. Where once their forebears distrusted democracy as dangerously egalitarian, today they vigorously defend the principle of one person, one vote, and are as scandalized as any libertarian by pretensions of noble birth. Nevertheless, they continue to believe in an equality of opportunity, rather than of results. They want people be given a comparable chance to prove themselves, not to have the game cancelled by a premature determination to award trophies to all. They know that this will result in an inequality of success, but consider this both fair and essential for social competence.

Beyond this, conservatives place a greater emphasis on freedom.[63] They demand a reduction in government regulations to permit people more control over their lives. Their antecedents among the American Founding Fathers had less to say about these matters because, for them, liberty was still about being released from the indignities of feudal serfdom.   Jefferson, Adams,[64] and their contemporaries worried about a reemergence of royalism, not about imperious federal regulators or imperialistic judges. What troubles modern conservatives is the lack of respect liberals display toward personal liberties.   Although left-leaning reformers continue to express an allegiance to freedom, in favoring government imposed economic and social regulations, they have redefined the significance of personal autonomy. As a case in point, where once individuals were thought completely free to enter or leave employment, present-day labor lawyers argue for strict limitations on how this is achieved. Similarly, where once free speech implied an ability to engage in casual insults, these have been proscribed on the grounds that they create a hostile work environment.[65] Liberals also continue to endorse legacies like academic freedom, whereas in practice they deny right-wing dissenters tenure. One Duke University philosophy professor went so far as to insist that his university did not hire conservatives because they were not sufficiently bright. To this, the conservatives again strenuously dissent. They insist that true freedom must contain the ability to express out-of-favor opinions, even boorish ones. They also insist that the ability to adjust to unpredictable contingencies depends on people being allowed to follow their private inclinations. They would agree with Walter Olson,[66] who concluded in his book on labor law that, "for all its risks and disappointments, liberty—the simple policy of refusing to force others to deal with us against their will and without their consent—turns out to be the best method to elicit the greatest willingness and enthusiasm to cooperate from those who might do us good." This would certainly apply to the ability to construct competent social roles, including those with hierarchical implications.

Besides the master values applicable to contemporary conditions, a myriad of subsidiary values are in dispute. There are genuine disagreements about the goals and norms that should apply to embryonic roles and role negotiations. Liberals have either disparaged or profoundly modified the traditional commitments on the grounds that they are no longer relevant within diverse democracies. Conservatives, in contrast, find many time-honored standards still viable. Indeed, they strongly commend them as sustaining the competence and flexibility essential for a mass-market-based civilization. One of these old-fashioned values is merit. Some personal and social qualities are deemed superior to others and, therefore, deserving of encouragement. These traits are literally thought to be better than others and hence worthy of respect. To this, the liberals demur. They find merit to be either fraudulent[67] or situationally dependent. According to them, elites arbitrarily decide what is best so that this favors their own strengths. Either that, or superior performances are called forth by the demands of individual circumstances and consequently can come from anyone having these. Tests or evaluations that purport to measure merit are, accordingly, illegitimate. They are spurned as excluding the powerless and, therefore, as in need of being superseded by a random selection of jobholders. Let chance, not elite bias, decide who gets the plum assignments.

To this, the conservatives shudder in horror.[68] They do not believe that abilities and skills are randomly distributed. Nor do they agree that everyone will be equally competent when thrown into identical circumstances. For them, knowledge, talent, and motivation have uneven outcomes. For a job to be done right, it is vital to support the processes that increase the probability of competence. This conviction, it should be noted, is crucial to the notion of professionalism.[69] If professionals are those with greater expertise and motivation, then it must be possible for them to exhibit superior proficiency in practice.[70] Support for a complete interchangeability among individuals suggests that skill is automatic, whereas history indicates that this is not the case. Some people are indeed smarter, more diligent, or more insightful than others. If anything, a failure to recognize that some role performances, and individuals, are more accomplished than others provides evidence of an inability to make sound judgments. It suggests that one cannot distinguish quality from rubbish. It also implies an unwillingness to encourage the personal dedication needed for self-improvement. Why try to be better if there is no better? The sad fact is that, were everything as good as everything else, in the end nothing, and no one, would be very good at anything.

This divergence in attitudes has expressed itself in related attitudes toward education. Nowadays, everyone, whether on the left or the right, believes that education is important. The conflicts come from an inability to define education the same way. Because liberals are committed to equality, they are dismayed by manifestations of intellectual superiority. They, therefore, favor curricula that, while universal, are not especially demanding.[71] Learning, they declare, must be fun. It must also be relevant to the student's personal concerns. That which does not come easily is for that reason dismissed as elitist and scorned as beside the point. Conservatives, in contrast, value rigorous standards.[72] They shudder when teachers boast that they learn more from their students than the other way around. Nor are they moved by pleas that a poor grade will ruin a student's chances in life. For them, education is not equivalent to the number of years spent in the classroom or to the credentials amassed but to lessons mastered.

For the traditionalists, education and merit are intimately related to personal responsibility. If people are to be self-directed, if they are to be given the authority to make important decisions, they are expected to be internally motivated to do their best. If they are to manage decentralized roles, they must likewise be prepared to defend their choices and to take the blame when things go wrong.[73] Liberals, too, believe in responsibility[74] but apparently not with the conventional trappings. Since they believe in niceness, they want everyone—with the exception of articulate conservatives—to be rewarded. They are even more adamant that no one be punished. All individuals must be instructed that they are beautiful just the way they are, irrespective of what they may ever achieve.[75] Nor should individuals be held responsible for their personal welfare. This is the bailiwick of the central government. Because the state, in its disembodied wisdom, always knows what is best and everlastingly commands the necessary resources, it is accountable for protecting its citizens from themselves and from almost any potential threat. To this, the traditionalists respond that the fundamental spring of professional motivation is personalized responsibility. They claim that individuals are best situated to know what they need. Were they not to assume responsibility for their decisions, but instead to hide under a mantle of victimization,[76] they would not work hard to get things right. Nor would the results be nearly as good.

This attitude, in its turn, is related to an exaltation of American individualism.[77] Ever since the days of the frontier, a sturdy sense of independence has been admired on the western shores of the Atlantic. People have seen themselves as being in control of their destinies and hence as responsible for their success. This facilitated efforts at innovation and entrepreneurship from which the society as whole gained. Liberals, however, tend to confuse self-determination with greed.[78] They declare it selfish when people wish to stand out from the crowd. Their ideal is cooperation,[79] not free enterprise. People are supposed to submerge their egos in shared endeavors that extol loving relationships over private ambition. The part of this that is on target is that coordination is essential for large-scale activities. Common goals cannot be attained unless the participants are willing to accommodate to joint plans. Nevertheless, the originality that animates these undertakings rarely derives from committees.

Individuals can be obnoxious in the manner in which they stir the pot, yet without provocation they can provide inertia to slow progress to a crawl. For better or worse, market-oriented, social-role-dominated communities could not forge ahead without a fair number of individualists.

By now, also, customary to capitalism is an emphasis on interpersonal trust.[80] Though often honored in the breach, honesty and integrity continue to be widely respected. People understand that, if they are to survive within a community of strangers,[81] they must have confidence in most others most of the time. Yet, if this trust is to endure, they cannot shrug off public untruths as indicative of a culture of deceit. Political expediency has led some to defend lying as the norm, but, were this true, no one could leave his or her back undefended. On the other hand, tolerance is a liberal value that has become more useful as social migrations bring diverse populations into contact. People need to understand the world from one another's point of view if they are to reduce the numbers of superfluous conflicts.[82] Nevertheless, they cannot take this insight to the romantic extent of declaring that no value is superior to any other and no cultural artifact preferable to potential alternatives. This would invite anarchy.

Lastly, family values matter.[83] Standards that uphold intimate relationships and parental obligations are more necessary than ever, given the impersonality and mobility of a middle-class-dominated society. Changes in how families are organized are inevitable, but that families are preferable to a pandemic of promiscuity is irrefutable. In general, it seems certain that the culture wars will terminate in a moral consensus that is closer to the time-honored values than to their liberal replacements.[84] Traditional values may sometimes be too rigid for contemporary purposes, but their provenance bespeaks a different interpretation. Though dismissed as conservative, these tenets have undergone an evolution in conjunction with the spread of commercialization. The evaluation of merit, for instance, has been continually modified to reflect alterations in technology and social organization. Similarly, the estimation of personal responsibility has grown as decentralization forced decision-making to become more widespread.

This said liberalism, too, has contributed essential revisions.[85] Social rules could neither be as flexible nor as professional as they need to be were they not responsive to progressive critiques. Even when they are misguided, these observations introduce elements that require examination. Such has been the case with feminism.[86] Its notions of gender equality are self-indulgent, but they call attention to legitimate gender problems. This has obliged people to expand their knowledge of gender differences and to incorporate this into evolving gender norms. Men and women have been discovered to vary; hence, this must be factored into an updated gender of division labor more in harmony with contemporary requirements. In any event, proposed moral adjustments can be compared with one another to evaluate their implications. An expanded professionalism with respect to social role and hierarchical arrangements depends on achieving an expertise in this sort of moralism. People need to understand how ethical negotiations operate. They must similarly be prepared to examine the consequences of particular norms and values, whether proposed by themselves or their rivals. Facts matter—as do honest appraisals of where these lead.

The Professionalized Self

None of this, however, can be socially constructive without the active participation of a growing segment of the population. As more individuals become middle class, it is incumbent upon them to become professionalized, not just at work, but also in the rest of their lives. As has already been commented upon, middle-class society, because it is decentralized and mobile, distributes decision making ever more broadly. People must, therefore, be prepared to make the requisite choices and to make them wisely. They must develop the expertise and the motivation to assemble determinations about their family life, their civic responsibilities, and their private amusements. It is up to them to choose their own occupations, religious commitments, and friendship patterns. If they do not possess the knowledge and personal qualities to do this well, it is unlikely to be done to their satisfaction—or that of their neighbors. Their personal roles, how these relate to those of their role partners, including in terms of relative power, are more than ever in their hands. If they do not commit themselves to growing into these tasks, they only have themselves to blame for their frustrated ambitions.

A professionalized self, as opposed to a professional career, is not acquired through a professional education. There are no credentials for managing one's own life, no college degrees in choosing a livelihood, a wife, or a residential lifestyle. Plans for raising one's children, techniques for maneuvering through the political shoals of career advancement, or methods for controlling intense emotions in moments of stress do not come neatly packaged in self-help books or university courses. To the contrary, these must be individually crafted to meet unique circumstances. Role players must themselves decide to grow up and, having done so, to turn what they have learned into reality. They need, in sum, to take charge of their futures. Unless they summon the courage to confront life's uncertainties and make preparations to meet its challenges, they, of necessity, consign themselves to exogenous domination. Much to their chagrin, they will find that there are always some individuals eager to govern the timid or the ignorant, and if they qualify as one of the governors, they will one day encounter these others.

Potentially self-directed people need to learn how to participate in isolated nuclear families.[87] They must be able to make good choices about potential spouses and then discover how to live in comfortable intimacy with them and their offspring. This clearly requires competence in role negotiations, and also a knowledge of the potential resolution of private divisions of labor. As significant, those who wish to start families must understand the needs of children and how to prepare them for disciplined, self-directed futures. Negotiating roles with dependent youngsters requires both firmness and restraint. Though these qualities are ostensibly incompatible, they must nevertheless be mastered if children are to internalize a capacity for independent decision-making. Life never offers total satisfaction, but those who know how to love and how to compromise dramatically improve their chances of achieving contentment.

Another skill advantageous for the professionalized self is organizational competence.[88] Successful members of the emerging middle class need to be able to answer questions about what they want to be when the grow up, then realistically to implement their conclusions. Since so much contemporary work is performed within large, impersonal organizations, most will need to understand how bureaucracies operate. Unless they recognize the parameters of the functional divisions of labor, defined offices, hierarchies of authority, rules and procedures, and files and records within these, they will feel adrift in apparently irrational and hopelessly rigid morasses. Once they perceive what is happening, however, they can join the political fray to recruit allies in their quests to negotiate the best possible deals consistent with their personal goals. Moreover, if they wish to be leaders, they will need to understand how power is exercised. If they do not, they are apt to display an aura of weakness precisely when a test of strength requires the opposite. Clearly, those who aim to be influential require the ability to develop authentic strengths. Furthermore, those who would exercise interpersonal control need to incorporate qualities that facilitate authority within the contexts in which they will operate. They have to be able to do something that others value and are willing to exchange for their collaboration or compliance.

Needless to say, in a world where so many alliances depend on coordination through shared norms and values, professional selves have to be capable moral negotiators.[89] They must understand that important social rules are neither absolute nor romantically relative. Many of their commitments will have been acquired during the moral negotiations of their youth, yet many of others will derive from their current living and working conditions. If they are to contribute to the evolution of universalistic standards, they will have to speak up when things seem out of whack and must do so in a manner calculated to recruit the enthusiastic support of people with different points of view. This will require emotional and cognitive flexibility, combined with an appropriate firmness of purpose when they are contradicted. Truly moral individuals possess both personal commitments and the ability to adjust when confronted with evidence that their commitments are counterproductive.

All of this suggests that those who would be professional in their personal lives have to be emotionally mature.[90] They cannot be terrified by the challenges of ordinary living. Nor can they become unyieldingly furious over grievances that should have been overcome in the distant past. They cannot even afford to be so ravenous for love that they will sell their souls for the proverbial mess of pottage. Those who would be strong enough to master the demands of a mutable and confusing technocommercial society must be able to deal with their own fears, rages, and emotional longings. They must, likewise, be able to cope with their personal guilt, shame, and disgust. Individuals who cannot, who are instead swept away in the bewilderment inherent in intense passion, are vulnerable to manipulation by the more clear-headed. They may wish to be strong but are more likely to revert to infantile spontaneity when overwhelmed.

In the end, people who wish to be self-controlled experts in surviving within a middle class environment must be capable of personal growth.[91] Everyone begins life as a frail child, but not everyone learns to overcome the barriers this engenders.[92] Many become fixated in juvenile patterns thanks to severe losses encountered along the way. Having ineffectually sought to assert themselves in hierarchical, social role, attachment relationships, they are thrown back into defensive postures from which they have not discovered the means to extricate themselves. More concerned with getting revenge or with preventing further losses, they are not able to let go of what went wrong in order to move forward to something better. Frequently conceiving of themselves as victims, they do not understand what they must do to get on with their lives. Filled with self-pity, they blame others—or what they may refer to as the system—for weaknesses over which as adults only they have the most control.

Many of these limitations have been rationalized as mental disorders.[93] People are encouraged by the mental-health establishment to interpret their unhappiness as a sign of a functional disease and, then, to ingest medication in order to feel better. Anxieties and depressions that result from the wear and tear of interpersonal conflict are attributed to chemical imbalances and, hence, are never directly dealt with. This is unfortunate because many individuals would be capable of personal growth if they realized what was happening to them. If they understood, for instance, that they were trapped in dysfunctional roles whose point of origination was in childhood, they might choose to engage in role change. They would then comprehend their need to let go of the unsatisfying patterns to which they are emotionally committed to adopt more satisfying ones. They would, in short, decide to engage in resocialization.

Thanks to the dominance of medical ways of thinking,[94] few people appreciate the conservative power of role scripts.[95] When coerced into dysfunctional patterns of behavior, they do not choose to renegotiate them because they do not recognize what is holding them back. Tossed about by strong feelings, they perceive themselves as defective precisely because they cannot voluntarily turn these off.[96] Having never been instructed that the anxiety and depression they are experiencing are normal parts of the processes of attempting to change, they seek to suppress them through chemical means. Their discomforts, rather than their dysfunctional roles, are perceived as problems, and efforts are, therefore, made to eliminate them. In fact, resocialization operates by inducing a mourning process whereby a person reactivates a dysfunctional role, determines that it represents an irretrievable loss, then grieves this defeat.[97] Only then can the role script be modified to meet the present exigencies. Only then can the person adopt patterns of living that are competent and sustainable. Ironically, individuals who are forever sabotaging their life chances rarely realize that they are not allowing themselves to succeed for the very reason that they hate the roles in which they are confined. They do not even perceive these as dysfunctional. Because their energies are being directed toward conquering long departed role partners, they cannot accurately discern the here and now. As a result, they do not recognize that they are neither fully using their brains nor applying their best efforts. Nevertheless, were they to disengage emotionally via resocialization, they would find this potential liberated.

As a bonus, society too would benefit from their liberation. A middle-class world that is dependent upon decentralized decision-making works best when its members are able to respond to their personal circumstances. The whole becomes more flexible when its separate elements are free to adapt to their diverse situations. Since people trapped in dysfunctional roles are unthinkingly conservative; once freed from these, they can apply their intelligence to solving problems that may affect the lives of others beside themselves. Also, once released to meet their own needs, they are apt to be more productive, thereby increasing the size of the pie from which all share. Professionalization has worked well in the economic domain;

it can do the same on other fronts. The more people are able to be themselves, competently, the more likely they are to realize the utilitarian ideal of the greatest happiness for the greatest number.

A genuine social science,[98] rather than one engaged in ideological posturing, is apt to be useful to achieving this end. The answers to the problems generated by an increasingly commercialized, middle-class society are better served by knowledge than by comforting fantasies. Most empty promises are eventually exposed, whereas hard truths, no matter how difficult, can elicit improved coping mechanisms. Life is not fair and never will be, but it can be less unjust the better people understand what is happening. This will permit them to unleash their ingenuity and to pool their resources on joint ventures. Egalitarian collectivism is a chimera, but intelligence and cooperation are not. Conflict and inequality are ineluctable aspects of our social nature; nevertheless, they are not implacably at odds with collaborative ventures. As previously indicated, predicting the future is a fool's errand, but we can still learn from history. A middle-class future need not be resisted. It is not automatically barren or conformist. If we are up to the challenge of adjusting to its many capricious twists, a significant proportion of these may prove exciting and even productive.

Endnotes

1 Vollmer, H. and D. Mills (Eds.) 1968. *Professionalization.* Englewood Cliffs, NJ: Prentice-Hall.

2 Hayek, F.A. 1944. *The Road to Serfdom.* London: Routledge.

3 Fromm, E. 1941. *Escape From Freedom.* New York: Holt, Rinehart and Winston.

4 D'Souza, D. 2000. *The Virtue of Prosperity: Finding Values in an Age of Techno-Affluence.* New York: The Free Press.

5 Hollander, P. 1992. *Anti-Americanism: Critiques at Home and Abroad 1965-1990.* New York: Oxford University Press.

6 Hobbes, T. 1956. *Leviathan; Part I.* Chicago: Henry Regnery Co.

7 Hospers, J. 1953. *An Introduction to Philosophical Analysis.* Englewood Cliffs, NJ: Prentice-Hall Inc.; Hospers, J. 1961. *Human Conduct: An Introduction to the Problem of Ethics.* New York: Harcourt, Brace, World.

8 Bannister, R.C. 1979. *Social Darwinism: Science and Myth in Anglo-American Social Thought.* Philadelphia, PA: Temple University Press.

8 Mill, J.S. 1857. *Utilitarianism.* Indianapolis: Bobbs-Merrill; Bentham, J. 1948. *An Introduction to the Principles of Morals and Legislation.* Oxford: Clarendon Press.

9 Strauss, A. 1978. *Negotiations: Varieties, Contexts, Processes and Social Order.* San Francisco, CA: Jossey-Bass.

10 Zurcher, L. 1983. *Social Roles: Conformity, Conflict and Creativity.* Beverly Hills, CA: Sage Publications

11 Greenwood, E. 1957. "Attributes of a Profession." *Social Work*, II, 3, July.

12 Gardiner, M. 2000. *Did Adam and Eve Have Navels?: Debunking Pseudoscience.* New York: W.W. Norton & Co.; Gardiner, M. 2003. *Are Universes Thicker than Blackberries?* New York: W.W. Norton & Co.

13 Manchester, W. 1992. *A World Lit Only By Fire: The Medieval Mind and the Renaissance.* Boston, MA: Little, Brown & Co.

14 Davies, T. 1997. *Humanism.* New York: Routledge.

15 Sarton, G. 1962. *The History of Science and the New Humanism.* Bloomington: Indiana University Press; Kurtz, P. 2000. *Humanist Manifesto 2000: A Call for a New Planetary Humanism.* Amherst, NY: Prometheus Books.

16 Jardine, L. 1999. *Ingenious Pursuits: Building the Scientific Revolution.* New York: Doubleday.

17 Larson, M.S. 1977. *The Rise of Professionalism: A Sociological Analysis.* Berkeley: University of California Press.

18 Churchill, R. S. 1966. *Winston S. Churchill.* Boston, MA: Houghton, Mifflin; Churchill, W. 1958. *A History of the English-Speaking Peoples.* New York: Dorset Press.

[19] Dawes, R.M. 2000. *Everyday Irrationality: How Pseudo-Scientists, Lunatics, and the Rest of Us Systematically Fail to Think Rationally*. Boulder, CO: Westview.

[20] Hughes, E.C. 1958. *Men and Their Work.* New York: Free Press of Glencoe; Hayek, F.A. 1988. *The Fatal Conceit: The Errors of Socialism.* Chicago, IL: The University of Chicago Press.

[21] Courtois, S., N. Werth, J-L Panne, A. Paczkowski, Bartosek, and J-L Margolin. 1999. *The Black Book of Communism: Crimes, Terror, Repression.* Cambridge, MA: Harvard University Press; Faludi, S. 1991. *Backlash: The Undeclared War Against American Women.* New York: Crown Publishers.

[22] Pinker, S. 1994. *The Language Instinct: How the Mind Creates Language.* New York: William Morrow & Co.

[23] Sanderson, S.K. 1995. *Social Transformations: A General Theory of Historical Development.* Oxford, UK: Blackwell.

[24] Diehl, M.W. (Ed.) 2000. *Hierarchies in Action: Cui Bono?* Carbondale IL: Center for Archeological Investigations.

[25] Armstrong, K. 1993. *A History of God: The 4000-Year Quest of Judaism, Christianity and Islam.* New York: Ballantine Books; Armstrong, K. 2000. *The Battle for God.* New York: Alfred A. Knopf.

[26] Pruitt, D.G. 1981. *Negotiation Behavior.* New York: Academic.

[27] Norris, C. 1997. *Against Relativism: Philosophy of Science, Deconstruction and Critical Theory.* Oxford, UK: Blackwell Publishers; Fein, M. 1999. *The Limits of Idealism: When Good Intentions Go Bad.* New York: Kluwer/Plenum.

[28] Spencer, H. [1899] 1969. *The Principles of Sociology* (3 Vols.) (S. Andreski, Ed.) New York: MacMillan; Durkheim, E. 1933. *The Division of Labor in Society.* New York: The Free Press.

[29] Hall, R.H. 1975. *Occupations and the Social Structure.* Engelwood Cliffs, NJ: Prentice-Hall, Inc.; Hall, R.H. 1999. *Organizations: Structures, Processes, and Outcomes.* Upper Saddle River, NJ: Prentice-Hall.

[30] Sarbin, T. and V. Allen. 1968. *Role Theory.* in Lindzey, G. and E. Aronson (Eds.). Handbook of Social Psychology. Boston, MA: Addison-Wesley.

[31] Zartman, I.W. 1978. *The Negotiation Process: Theories and Applications.* Beverly Hills, CA: Sage Publications.

[32] Biddle, B. 1979. *Role Theory: Expectations, Identities and Behaviors.* New York: Academic Press.

[33] Weber, M. 1947. *The Theory of Social and Economic Organization.* New York: Free Press.

[34] Grusky, O. and G.A. Miller. (Eds.) 1970. *The Sociology of Organizations: Basic Studies* (Second Edition). New York: The Free Press.

[35] Eckstein, H and T.R. Gurr. 1975. *Patterns of Authority: A Structural Basis for Political Inquiry.* New York: John Wiley & Sons.

[36] Gerth, H. and C.W. Mills. (Eds.) 1946. *From Max Weber: Essays in Sociology.* New York: Oxford University Press.

[37] Alba, R.D. 1990. *Ethnic Identity: The Transformation of White America.* New Haven: Yale University Press.

[38] Elshtain, J.B. 1995. *Democracy on Trial.* New York: Basic Books.

[39] Fein, M. 1997. *Hardball Without an Umpire: The Sociology of Morality.* Westport, CT: Praeger.

[40] Fein, M. 1990. *Role Change: A Resocialization Perspective.* New York: Praeger.

[41] Vollmer, H. and Mills, D. (Eds.). Op. cit.

[42] Durkheim, E. 1933. *The Division of Labor in Society.* New York: The Free Press.

[43] Ashton, T.S. 1965. *The Industrial Revolution 1760-1830.* New York: Oxford University Press.

[44] Smith, A. 1776. *An Inquiry into the Nature and Causes of the Wealth of Nations.* London: W. Strahan & T. Cadell.

[45] Pruitt, D.G. Op. cit.

[46] Fein, M. 1990. Op. cit.

[47] Clausen, J. (Ed.) 1968. *Socialization and Society.* Boston, MA: Little Brown.

[48] Fein, M. 1992. *Analyzing Psychotherapy: A Social Role Interpretation.* New York: Praeger.

[49] Fein, M. 1999. *The Limits of Idealism: When Good Intentions Go Bad.* New York: Kluwer/Plenum.

[50] Hughes, E.C. 1958. *Men and Their Work.* New York: Free Press of Glencoe.

[51] Hayek, F.A. 1988. Op. cit.

[52] Loseke, D.R. 1999. *Thinking About Social Problems: An Introduction to Constructivist Perspectives.* New York: Aldine de Gruyter.

[53] Dumanont, L. 1980. [1966] *Homo Hierarchicus: The Caste System and Its Implications.* Chicago: University of Chicago Press; Dollard, J. 1937. *Caste and Class in a Southern Town.* New Haven Yale University Press.

[54] Powell, J. 2003. *FDR's Folly: How Roosevelt and His New Deal Prolonged the Great Depression.* New York: Crown Forum.

[55] Norris, C. 1997. *Against Relativism: Philosophy of Science, Deconstruction and Critical Theory.* Oxford, UK: Blackwell Publishers.

[56] Fein, M. 1997. Op. cit.

[57] Gans, H.J. 1988. *Middle American Individualism: Political Participation and Liberal Democracy.* New York: Oxford University Press.

[58] Hunter, J.D. 1991. *Culture Wars: The Struggle to Define America.* New York: Basic Books.

[59] Fein, M. 2001. *Race and Morality: How Good Intentions Undermine Social Justice and Perpetuate Inequality.* New York: Kluwer/Plenum; Landry, B.

1987. *The New Black Middle Class.* Berkeley: University of California Press.

[60] Mapp, A.J. 1987. *Thomas Jefferson: A Strange Case of Mistaken Identity.* Lanham, MD: Madison Books; Bailyn, B. 1992. *The Ideological Origins of the American Revolution.* Cambridge, MA: The Belknap Press; Bailyn, B. 2003. *To Begin the World Anew: The Genius and Ambiguities of the American Founders.* New York: Vintage Books.

[61] Kramer, H. and R. Kimball. 1999. *The Betrayal of Liberalism: How the Disciples of Freedom and Equality Helped Foster the Illiberal Politics of Coercion and Control.* Chicago, IL: Ivan R. Dee.

[62] Hayek, F.A. 1944. Op. cit.

[63] Bailyn, B. 2003. Op. cit.

[64] MacKinnon, C.A. 1987. *Feminism Unmodified: Discourses on Life and Law.* Cambridge, MA: Harvard University Press.

[65] Olson, W.K. 1997. *The Excuse Factory: How Employment Law is Paralyzing the American Workplace.* New York: The Free Press.

[66] Guy, M.E. 1997. Counterpoint: By Thine Own Voice, Shall Thou Be Known. *Public Productivity and Managment Review,* Vol. 20, No. 3, March, pp.- 237-242.

[67] Bork, R. 1996. *Slouching Toward Gomorrah: Modern Liberalism and American Decline.* New York: Regan Books.

[68] Larson, M.S. 1977. *The Rise of Professionalism: A Sociological Analysis.* Berkeley, CA: University of California Press.

[69] Greenwood, E. 1957. "Attributes of a Profession." *Social Work,* II, 3, July.

[70] Kramer, R. 1991. Ed School Follies: The Miseducation of America's Teachers. New York: The Free Press; Brimelow, P. 2003. *The Worm in the Apple: How the Teacher Unions Are Destroying American Education.* New York: HarperCollins Publishers.

[71] Rochester, J.M. 2002. *Class Warfare: Besieged Schools, Bewildered Parents, Betrayed Kids and the Attack on Excellence.* San Francisco, CA: Encounter Books; D'Souza, D. 1991. *Illiberal Education: The Politics of Race and Sex on Campus.* New York: The Free Press.

[72] Simon, H.A. 1947. *Administrative Behavior.* New York: MacMillan.

[73] Morris, H. (Ed.) 1961. *Freedom and Responsibility.* Stanford, CA: Sanford University Press.

[74] Steinem, G. 1992. *Revolution From Within: A Book of Self-Esteem.* Boston, MA: Little, Brown.

[75] Steele, S. 1998. *A Dream Deferred: The Second Betrayal of Black Freedom in America.* New York: HarperCollins Publishers; Steele, C.M., S.J. Spencer, and M. Lynch. 1993. "Self-Image, Resilience and Dissonance: The Role of Affirmational Resources." *Journal of Personality and Social Psychology,* 66(6): 885-896.

[76] Bellah, R.N., R. Madsen, W.M. Sullivan, A. Swindler, and S.M. Tipton. 1985. *Habits of the Heart: Individualism and Commitment in American Life.* Berkeley, CA: University of California Press; Lipset, S.M. 1996. *American Exceptionalism: A Double-Edged Sword.* New York: W.W. Norton.

[77] Greer, C. and H. Kohl. 1995. *A Call to Character.* New York: Harper-Collins.

[78] Gilligan, C. 1982. *In a Different Voice.* Cambridge, MA: Harvard University Press.

[79] Fukuyama, F. 1995. *Trust: The Social Virtues and the Creation of Prosperity.* New York: Free Press.

[80] Toennies, F. 1966. (1887) *Community and Society.* New York: Harper Row.

[81] Mead, G.H. 1934. *Mind, Self and Society.* Chicago, IL: University of Chicago Press.

[82] Blankenhorn, D. 1995. *Fatherless America: Confronting Our Most Urgent Social Problem.* New York: Basic Books; Popenoe, D. 1996. *Life Without Father: Compelling New Evidence that Fatherhood and Marriage Are Indispensable for the Good of Children and Society.* New York: The Free Press.

[83] Wolfe, A. 2001. *Moral Freedom: The Search for Virtue in a World of Choice.* New York: W.W. Norton.

[84] Bernstein, R. 1994. *Dictatorship of Virtue: Multiculturalism and the Battle for America's Future.* New York: Alfred A. Knopf.

[85] Sommers, C.H. 1994. *Who Stole Feminism: How Women Have Betrayed Women.* New York: Simon & Schuster.

[86] Handel, G. [Ed.] 1967. *The Psychosocial Interior of the Family: A Sourcebook for the Study of Whole Families.* Chicago, IL: Aldine-Atherton.

[87] Grusky, O. and G.A. Miller. (Eds.) 1970. *The Sociology of Organizations: Basic Studies* (Second Edition). New York: The Free Press.

[88] Fein, M. 1997. Op. cit.

[89] Fein, M. 1999. Op. cit.; Goleman, D. 1995. *Emotional Intelligence: Why It Can Matter More Than IQ.* New York: Bantam Books.

[90] Fein, M. 1990. Op. cit.

[91] Henry, J. 1963. *Culture Against Man.* New York: Vintage Books; Laing, R.D. 1960. *The Divided Self.* London: Tavistock.

[92] American Psychiatric Association; Task Force on DSM-IV. 1994. *Diagnostic and Statistical Manual of Mental Disorders; Fourth Edition.* Washington, DC

[93] Szasz, T. 1961. *The Myth of Mental Illness: Foundations of a Theory of Personal Conduct.* New York: Dell; Szasz, T. 1970. *Ideology and Insanity.* New York: Anchor; Valenstein, E.S. 1986. *Great and Desperate Cures: The Rise and Decline of Psychosurgery and Other Radical Treatments for Mental Illness.* New York: Basic Books.

[94] Fein, M. 1990. Op. cit.

[95] Sullivan, H.S. 1953. *The Interpersonal Theory of Psychiatry.* New York: W.W. Norton Co.

[96] Kubler-Ross, E. 1969. *On Death and Dying.* New York: MacMillan.

[97] Krimmerman, L.I. (Ed.) 1969. *The Nature and Scope of Social Science: A Critical Anthology.* New York: Appleton-Century-Crofts.

Bibliography

Adams, B.N. and R.A. Sydie. 2001. *Sociological Theory*. Thousand Oaks, CA: Pine Forge Press.

Adams, J. 1770. Argument in Defense of British Soldiers in the Boston Massacre.

Adams, M.S. 2004. *Welcome to the Ivory Tower of Babel: Confessions of a Conservative College Professor*. Augusta, GA: Harbor House.

Aguirre, A. Jr. and J.H. Turner. 1998. *American Ethnicity: The Dynamics and Consequences of Discrimination*. Second Edition. New York: McGraw-Hill.

Alba, R.D. 1990. *Ethnic Identity: The Transformation of White America*. New Haven: Yale University Press.

Alighieri, D. 1955. *The Divine Comedy*, trans. by Thomas G. Bergin. New York: Appleton, Century, Crofts.

Allport, G. 1954. *The Nature of Prejudice*. Boston: Beacon Press.

Alterman, E. 2003. *What Liberal Media? The Truth about Bias and the News*. New York: Basic Books.

Ambrose, S.E. 1987. *Nixon: The Education of a Politician 1913-1962*. New York: Simon & Schuster.

American Enterprise Institute. 2002. "The Shame of America's One-Party Campuses." *American Enterprise*, September.

American Psychiatric Association; Task Force on DSM-IV. 1994. *Diagnostic and Statistical Manual of Mental Disorders; Fourth Edition*. Washington, D.C.

Anderson, E. 1999. *Code of the Street: Decency, Violence, and the Moral Life of the Inner City*. New York: W.W. Norton & Co.

Anderson, M. 1992. *Imposters in the Temple: American Intellectuals are Destroying Our Universities and Cheating Our Students of Their Future*. New York: Simon & Schuster.

Andrews, D. 2000. *The Methodists and Revolutionary America 1760-1800*. Princeton, NJ: Princeton University Press.

Aries, P. 1962. *Centuries of Childhood: A Social History of Family Life*. New York: Vintage Books.

Aristotle 1941. *The Basic Works of Aristotle*, edited by R. McKeon. New York: Random House.

Armstrong, K. 1993. *A History of God: The 4000-Year Quest of Judaism, Christianity and Islam*. New York: Ballantine Books.

Armstrong, K. 2000. *The Battle for God*. New York: Alfred A. Knopf.

Ashton, T.S. 1965. *The Industrial Revolution 1760-1830*. New York: Oxford University Press.

Auchincloss, L. 1989. *The Vanderbilt Era: Portraits of a Gilded Age*. New York: Scribner.

Augustine, Saint. 1961. *Confessions*, translated by R.S. Pine-Coffin. New York: Dorset Press.

Bach, G.R. and P. Wyden. 1968. *The Intimate Enemy*. New York: Avon.

Bachrach, B.S. 1972. *Merovingian Military Organization 481-751*. Minneapolis: University of Minnesota Press.

Bailey, B.J. 1998. *The Luddite Rebellion*. New York: New York University Press.

Bailyn, B. 1992. *The Ideological Origins of the American Revolution*. Cambridge, MA: The Belknap Press.

Bailyn, B. 2003. *To Begin the World Anew: The Genius and Ambiguities of the American Founders*. New York: Vintage Books.

Baker, P. 2000. *The Breach: Inside the Impeachment and Trial of William Jefferson Clinton*. New York: Scribner.

Baldwin, N. 1995. *Edison: Inventing the Century*. New York: Hyperion.

Ball, T. and R. Dagger. 1999. *Political Ideologies and the Democratic Ideal*. New York: Longman.

Balzac, H. 1960. *The Works of Honore de Balzac*. New York: Crowell.

Banfield, E.C. 1961. *Political Influence: A New Theory of Urban Politics*. New York: The Free Press.

Bannister, R.C. 1979. *Social Darwinism: Science and Myth in Anglo-American Social Thought*. Philadelphia, PA: Temple University Press.

Bard, M.G. 2001. *Myths and Facts: A Guide to the Arab-Israeli Conflict*. Chevy Chase, MD: AICE.

Barlett, D.L. and Steele, J.B. 1996. *America: Who Stole the Dream?* Kansas City,MO: Andrews and McMeel.

Barnard, C. 1938. *The Function of the Executive*. Cambridge, MA: Harvard University Press.

Barnes, B. 1988. *The Nature of Power*. Chicago: The University of Illinois Press.

Baron-Cohen, S. 2003. *The Essential Difference: The Truth about the Male and Female Brain*. New York: Basic Books.

Barone, M. 2001. *The New Americans: How the Melting Pot Can Work Again*. Washington, DC: Regnery Publishing.

Barone, M. 2004. *Hard America Soft America*. New York: Crown Forum.

Barraclough, G. 1976. *The Crucible of Europe: The Ninth and Tenth Centuries in European History*. Berkeley: University of California Press.

Barzun, J. 2000. *From Dawn to Decadence: 500 Years of Western Cultural Life*. New York: HarperCollins Publishers.

Becker, H.S. 1963. *The Outsiders: Studies in the Sociology of Deviance*. New York: Free Press of Glencoe.

Becker, H.S. (Ed.) 1964. *The Other Side*. New York: Free Press.

Becker, H.S. 1970. *Sociological Work: Method and Substance*. Chicago, IL: Aldine Publishing Co.

Becker, S.D. 1981. *The Origins of the Equal Right Amendment: American Feminism between the Wars*. Westport, CT: Greenwood Press.

Bell, D. 1978. *The Cultural Contradictions of Capitalism*. New York: Basic Books.

Bellah, R.N., R. Madsen, W.M. Sullivan, A. Swindler, and S.M. Tipton. 1985. *Habits of the Heart: Individualism and Commitment in American Life*. Berkeley, CA: University of California Press.

Bellow, A. 2003. *In Praise of Nepotism: A Natural History*. New York: Doubleday.

Bendix, R. and S.M. Lipset. (Eds.) 1953. *Class, Status, and Power: Social Stratification in Comparative Perspective*. New York: The Free Press.

Benedict, R. 1934. *Patterns of Culture*. Boston, MA: Houghton Mifflin.

Benn, S.I. and R.S. Peters. 1959. *The Principles of Political Thought: Social Foundations of the Democratic State*. New York: The Free Press.

Bennett, W.J. (Ed.) 1993. *The Book of Virtues: A Treasury of Great Moral Stories*. New York: Simon & Schuster.

Bentham, J. 1948. *An Introduction to the Principles of Morals and Legislation*. Oxford, UK: Clarendon Press.

Bergen, D. 1988. *Play as a Medium of Learning and Development: A Handbook of Theory and Practice*. Portsmouth, NH: Heinemann.

Bergmann, B.R. 1996. *In Defense of Affirmative Action*. New York: Basic Books.

Bernier, O. 1984. *Louis the Beloved: The Life of Louis XV*. Garden City, NY: Doubleday & Co.

Bernstein, C. and B. Woodward. 1974. *All the President's Men*. New York: Simon & Schuster.

Bernstein, R. 1994. *Dictatorship of Virtue: Multiculturalism and the Battle for America's Future*. New York: Alfred A. Knopf.

Best, J. 2001. *Damned Lies and Statistics: Untangling Numbers from the Media, Politicians, and Activists*. Berkeley: University of California Press.

Bettleheim, B. 1977. *The Uses of Enchantment*. New York: Vintage Books.

Bettleheim, B. 1987. *A Good Enough Parent; A Book on Child-Rearing*. New York: Alfred A. Knopf.

Betzig, L.L. 1986. *Despotism and Differential Reproduction: A Darwinian View of History*. New York: Aldine.

Biazine, E. 1992. *Liberty, Retrenchment, and Reform: Popular Liberalism in the Age of Gladstone 1860-1880*. New York: Cambridge University Press.

Biddle, B. 1979. *Role Theory: Expectations, Identities and Behaviors*. New York: Academic Press.

Bierce, A. 1911. *The Devil's Dictionary*. New York: Thomas Cromwell Publishers.

Bierstadt, R. 1950. An Analysis of Social Power. *American Sociological Review*, December 15.

Bindoff, S.T. 1950. *Tudor England*. Baltimore, MD: Penguin Books.

Blankenhorn, D. 1995. *Fatherless America: Confronting Our Most Urgent Social Problem*. New York: Basic Books.

Blanquet, Y. 1995. *The Impressionists*. New York: Chelsea House.

Blassingame, J.W. 1979. *The Slave Community: Plantation Life in the Antebellum South*. New York: Oxford University Press.

Blau, P. 1963. *The Dynamics of Bureaucracy*. Chicago, IL: University of Chicago Press.

Blauner, R. 1969. "Internal Colonialism and Ghetto Revolt." *Social Problems* 16:393-408.

Blauner, R. 1972. *Racial Oppression in America*. New York: Harper & Row.

Bloom. A. 1987. *The Closing of the American Mind*. New York: Simon & Schuster.

Blumin, S.M. 1989. *The Emergence of the Middle Class: Social Experience in the American City 1760-1900.* New York: Cambridge University Press.

Blyth, M. 2004. *Spin Sisters: How the Women of the Media Sell Unhappiness and Liberalism to the Women of America.* New York: St. Martin's Press.

Boas, F. 1928. *Anthropology and Modern Life.* New York: Dover Publishers.

Boehm, C. 1999. *Hierarchy in the Forest: The Evolution of Egalitarian Behavior.* Cambridge, MA: Harvard University Press.

Boone, J. 1992. "Competition, Conflicts and the Development of Social Hierarchies." In: E. Smith and B. Winterhalter (Eds.) *Evolutionary Ecology and Human Behavior.* New York: Aldine de Gruyter.

Boone, J.L. 2000. "Status Signaling. Social Power, and Lineage Survival." In: Diehl, M.W. *Hierarchies in Action: Cui Bono?* Carbondale, IL: Center For Archaeological Investigations.

Boorstin, D.J. 1983. *The Discoverers: A History of Man's Search to Know His World and Himself.* New York: Vintage Books.

Boorstin, D.J. 1987. *Hidden History: Exploring Our Secret Past.* New York: Harper & Row.

Boot, M. 1998. *Out of Order: Arrogance, Corruption, and Incompetence on the Bench.* New York: Basic Books.

Bork, R. 1996. *Slouching Toward Gomorrah: Modern Liberalism and American Decline.* New York: Regan Books.

Boswell, R.B. 1988. *The Kindness of Strangers.* New York: Pantheon Books.

de Botton, A. 2004 *Status Anxiety.* New York: Pantheon Books.

Bourdieu, P. 1990. *The Logic of Practice.* Stanford, CA: Stanford University Press owlby, J. 1969. *Attachment.* New York: Basic Books.

Bowlby, J. 1973. *Separation: Anxiety and Anger.* New York: Basic Books.

Bowlby, J. 1980. *Loss: Sadness and Depression.* New York: Basic Books.

Bowlby, J. 1990. *Charles Darwin: A New Life.* New York: W.W. Norton & Co.

Bowles, S. and H. Gintis. 1976. *Schooling in Capitalist America: Educational Reform and the Contradictions of Capitalist Life.* New York: Basic Books.

Bozell, L.B. 2004. *Weapons of Mass Distortion: The Coming Meltdown of the Liberal Media.* New York: Crown Forum.

Bradford, S. 1982. *Disraeli.* New York: Stein & Day.

Braudel, F. 1972. *The Mediterranean and the Mediterranean World in the Age of Philip II, Vols. I & II.* New York: Harper & Row.

Braudel, F. 1979a. *The Structures of Everyday Life: Civilization & Capitalism 15th-18th Century Volume 1.* New York: Harper & Row.

Braudel, F. 1979b. *The Wheels of Commerce: Civilization & Capitalism 15th-18th Century Volume 2.* New York: Harper & Row.

Braudel, F. 1979c. *The Perspective of the World: Civilization & Capitalism 15th-18th Century Volume 3.* New York: Harper & Row.

Bridenbaugh, C. 1964. *Cities in the Wilderness: Urban Life in America 1625-1742.* New York: Capricorn Books.

Briggs, R. 1977. *Early Modern France 1550-1715.* Oxford,UK: Oxford University Press.

Brimelow, P. 2003. *The Worm in the Apple: How the Teacher Unions Are Destroying American Education.* New York: HarperCollins Publishers.

Brooke, C. 1965. *Europe in the Central Middle Ages 962-1154.* New York: Holt, Rinehart and Winston.

Brookhiser, R. 1996. *Founding Father: Rediscovering George Washington.* New York: The Free Press.

Brookhiser, R. 1999. *Alexander Hamilton: American.* New York: Simon & Schuster.

Brooks, D. 2000. *Bobos in Paradise: The New Upper Class and How They Got There.* New York: Simon & Schuster.

Brooks, D. 2004. *On Paradise Drive.* New York: Simon & Schuster.

Brownmiller, S. 1975. *Against Our Will: Men, Women and Rape.* New York: Bantam.

Brownstein, H.H. 2000. *The Social Reality of Violence and Violent Crime.* Needham Heights, MA: Allyn and Bacon.

Bruce, T. 2001. *The New Thought Police: Inside the Left's Assault on Free Speech and Free Minds.* Roseville, CA: Prima Publishing.

Bruhn, J. 2001. *Trust and the Health of Organizations.* New York: Kluwer/Plenum.

Buckley, K.W. 1989. *Mechanical Man: John Broadus Watson and the Beginnings of Behaviorism.* New York: The Guilford Press.

Bugliosi, V. 1975. *Helter Skelter: The True Story of the Manson Murders.*
New York: Bantam Books.

Burns, E. 2004. *The Spirits of America: A Social History of Alcohol.*
Philadelphia, PA: Temple University Press.

Caesar, J. [1967] *The Civil War,* translated by Jane Gardner. New York:
Dorset Press.

Caesar, J. [1980] *The Battle for Gaul.* Boston, MA: David R. Godine,
Publisher.

Campos, P.F. 1998. *Jurismania: The Madness of American Law.* New
York: Oxford University Press.

Cannadine, D. 1999. *The Rise and Fall of Class in Britain.* New York:
Columbia University Press.

Cantor, N.F. 1997. *Imagining the Law: Common Law and the Foundations
of the American Legal System.* New York: HarperCollins Publishers.

Caplow, T., H.B. Howard, B.A. Chadwick, R. Hill, and M.H.
Williamson. 1982. *Middletown Families: Fifty Years of Change and
Continuity.* Minneapolis: University of Minnesota Press.

Caplow, T., L. Hicks, and B.J. Wattenberg. 2001. *The First Measured
Century: An Illustrated Guide to Trends in America, 1900-2000.*
Washington, DC: AEI Press.

Carcopino, J. 1940. *Daily Life in Ancient Rome.* New Haven: Yale
University Press.

Carter, S.L. 1991. *Reflections of an Affirmative Action Baby.* New York:
Basic Books.

Carter, S.L. 1997. *The Culture of Disbelief: How American Law and
Politics Trivialize Religious Devotion.* New York: Basic Books.

Carter, S.L. 1998. *Civility: Manners, Morals and the Etiquette of
Democracy.* New York: Basic Books.

Cashman, S.D. 1981. *Prohibition: The Lie of the Land.* New York: Free
Press.

Cassel, J.F. 1993. *Critical Thinking: An Annotated Bibliography.*
Metuchen, NJ: The Scarecrow Press.

Cassidy, C. 1991. *Off the Road: My Years with Cassidy, Kerouac, and
Ginsberg.* New York: Penguin Books.

Cavalli-Sforza, L. and M.F. Feldman. 1981. *Cultural Transmission and
Evolution.* Princeton, NJ: Princeton University Press.

Cavalli-Sforza, L. and F. Cavalli-Sforza. 1993. *The Great Human Diasporas: The History of Diversity and Evolution.* Reading, MA: Perseus Books.

Cavalli-Sforza, L., P. Menozzi, and A. Piazza. 1994. *The History and Geography of Human Genes.* Princeton, NJ: University of Princeton Press.

Chamberlain, E.R. 1993. *The Bad Popes.* New York: Barnes & Noble Press.

Charen, M. 2003. *Useful Idiots: How Liberals Got It Wrong in the Cold War and Still Blame America First.* Washington, DC: Regnery Publishing.

Charen, M. 2004. *Do-Gooders: How Liberals Hurt Those They Claim to Help.* New York: Sentinel.

Chatfield, C. 1992. *The American Peace Movement: Ideals and Activism.* New York: Twayne Publishers.

Cheney, L. 1995. *Telling the Truth.* New York: Simon & Schuster.

Cherlin, A.J. 1992. *Marriage, Divorce, and Remarriage.* Cambridge, MA: Harvard University Press.

Chirot, D. 1986. *Social Change in the Modern Era.* New York: Harcourt, Brace, Jovanovich.

Chirot, D. 1994a. *How Societies Change.* Thousand Oaks: Pine Forge Press.

Chirot, D. 1994b. *Modern Tyrants.* Princeton, NJ: Princeton University Press.

Chong, D. 2000. *Rational Lives: Norms and Values in Politics and Society.* Chicago: University of Chicago Press.

Chuck, D. with Yusef Jah. 1998. *Fight the Power: Rap, Race, and Reality.* New York: Delta Trade Books.

Churchill, R. S. 1966. *Winston S. Churchill.* Boston: Houghton, Mifflin.

Churchill, W. 1958. *A History of the English-Speaking Peoples.* New York: Dorset Press.

Clausen, J. (Ed.) 1968. *Socialization and Society.* Boston, MA: Little Brown.

Clausewitz, C. 1908. *On War.* New York: Penguin Books.

Cleaver, E. 1967. *Soul on Ice.* New York: McGraw-Hill.

Clements, K.A. 1987. *Woodrow Wilson: World Statesman.* Boston: Twayne.

Colby, G. 1984. *DuPont Dynasty: Behind the Nylon Curtain*. Secaucus, NJ: Lyle Stuart Inc.

Cole, S. (Ed.) 2001. *What's Wrong with Sociology?* New Brunswick, NJ: Transaction Publishers.

Coleman, J.S., E.Q. Campbell, C.J. Hobson, J. McPartland, A.M. Mood, F.D. Weinfeld, and R.L. York. 1966. *Equality of Educational Opportunity*. Washington, DC: U.S. Government Printing Office.

Coleman, J.S. 1990. *Foundations of Social Theory*. Cambridge, MA: Harvard University Press.

Collier, P. and D. Horowitz. 1976. *The Rockefellers: An American Dynasty*. New York: Holt, Rinehart & Winston.

Collier, P. and D. Horowitz. 1984. *The Kennedys: An American Drama*. New York: Summit Books.

Collier, P. and D. Horowitz. 1987. *The Fords: An American Epic*. New York: Summit Books.

Collier, P. and D. Horowitz. 1989. *Destructive Generation: Second Thoughts about the '60s*. New York: The Free Press.

Collins, R. and Makowsky, M. 1993. *The Discovery of Society, Fifth Ed*. New York: McGraw-Hill.

Collins, R. 1998. *The Sociology of Philosophies: A Global Theory of Intellectual Change*. Cambridge, MA: Harvard University Press.

Coltrane, S. 1996. *Family Man: Fatherhood, Housework, and Gender Equity*. New York: Oxford University Press.

Colville, J. 1985. *The Fringes of Power: 10 Downing Street Diaries 1939-1955*. New York: W.W. Norton & Co.

Connerly, W. 2000. *Creating Equal: My Fight Against Race Preferences*. San Francisco, CA: Encounter Books.

Cook, A.E., T.G. Jelen, C. Wilcox. 1992. *Between Two Absolutes: Public Opinion and the Politics of Abortion*. Boulder, CO: Westview Press.

Cooley, C.H. 1956. *Human Nature and the Social Order*. Glencoe, IL: The Free Press.

Coontz, S. 1992. *The Way We Never Were: American Families and the Nostalgia Trap*. New York: Basic Books.

Corey, L. 1935. *The Crisis of the Middle Class*. New York: Columbia University Press.

Coulter, A. 2002. *Slander: Liberal Lies about the American Right*. New York: Crown Forum.

Coulter, A. 2003. *Treason: Liberal Treachery from the Cold War to the War on Terrorism*. New York: Crown Forum.

Courtois, S., N. Werth, J.-L. Panne, A. Paczkowski, Bartosek, and J.-L. Margolin. 1999. *The Black Book of Communism: Crimes, Terror, Repression*. Cambridge, MA. Harvard University Press.

Cowell, F.R. 1961. *Life in Ancient Rome*. New York: G.P. Putnam's Sons.

Cranston, M. 1982. *Jean-Jacques*. New York: W.W. Norton & Co.

Crawford, J. 1989. *Bilingual Education: History, Politics, Theory, and Practice*. Trenton, NJ: Crane Publishing Co.

Crier, C. 2002. *The Case Against Lawyers*. New York: Broadway Books.

Cronk, L. 1999. *That Complex Whole: Culture and the Evolution of Human Behavior*. Boulder, CO: Westview Press

Cronk, L., N. Chanon, and W. Irons. (Eds) 2000. *Adaptation and Human Behavior: An Anthropological Perspective*. New York: Aldine de Gruyter.

Cronkite, W. 1996. *A Reporter's Life*. New York: Alfred A. Knopf.

Crosby, A.W. 1997. *The Measure of Reality: Quantification and Western Society 1250-1600*. Cambridge, UK: Cambridge University Press.

Crossman, R.H. (Ed.) *The God That Failed*. 1963. New York: Harper& Row.

Crozier, M. 1964. *The Bureaucratic Phenomenon*. Chicago: University of Chicago Press.

Cumston, C.C. 1987. *The History of Medicine: From the Time of the Pharaohs to the End of the XVIII Century*. New York: Dorset Press.

Dahrendorf, R. 1959. *Class and Class Conflict in Industrial Society*. Stanford, CA: Stanford University Press.

Dalrymple, T. 2001. *Life at the Bottom: The Worldview That Makes the Underclass*. Chicago, IL: Ivan R. Dee.

Darwin, C. 1974. *The Descent of Man, and Selection in Relation to Sex*. Detroit: Gale Research.

Darwin, C. 1979. *The Origin of Species*. New York: Avnel Books.

Davies, H. 1968. *The Beatles*. New York: Dell Books.

Davies, T. 1997. *Humanism*. New York: Routledge.

Dawes, R.M. 2000. *Everyday Irrationality: How Pseudo-Scientists, Lunatics, and the Rest of Us Systematically Fail to Think Rationally*. Boulder, CO: Westview.

Day, D. 1962. *Will Rogers: A Biography*. New York: D. McKay Co.

De Beauvoir, S. 1978. *The Second Sex*. New York: Alfred A. Knopf.

Demott, B. 1990. *The Imperial Middle: Why American Can't Think Straight About Class*. New Haven: Yale University Press.

Derrida, J. 1997. *Deconstruction in a Nutshell*, edited by D. Caputo. New York: Fordham University Press.

Deveaux, M. 2000. *Cultural Pluralism and Dilemmas of Justice*. Ithaca, NY: Cornell University Press.

Dewey, J. 1943. *The School and Society*. Chicago: University of Chicago Press.

Diamond, J. 1997. *Guns, Germs, and Steel: The Fates of Human Societies*. New York: W.W. Norton and Co.

Dickens, C. 1884. *Barnaby Rudge: Hard Times*. Boston, MA: Perry Mason & Co.

Diehl, M.W. (Ed) 2000. *Hierarchies in Action: Cui Bono?* Carbondale IL: Center for Archeological Investigations.

Diel, C. 1969. *The History of the Byzantine Empire*, translated by George B. Ives. New York: AMS Press.

Dockes, P. 1979. *Medieval Slavery and Liberation*, translated by Arthur Goldhammer. Chicago, IL: University of Chicago Press.

Dollard, J. 1937. *Caste and Class in a Southern Town*. New Haven: Yale University Press.

Doty, C.S. (Ed.) 1969. *The Industrial Revolution*. New York: Holt, Rinehart and Winston.

Douthat, R. 2005. *Privilege: Harvard and the Education of the Ruling Class*. New York: Hyperion.

D'Souza, D. 1991. *Illiberal Education: The Politics of Race and Sex on Campus*. New York: The Free Press.

D'Souza, D. 1995. *The End of Racism: Principles for a Multiracial Society*. New York: The Free Press.

D'Souza, D. 2000. *The Virtue of Prosperity: Finding Values in an Age of Techno-Affluence*. New York: The Free Press.

Duby, G. 1973. *The Early Growth of the European Economy*. Ithaca, NY: Cornell University Press.

Duby, G. 1980. *The Three Orders: Feudal Society Imagined*. Chicago: University of Chicago Press.

Duby, G. 1983. *The Knight, The Lady, and the Priest: The Making of Modern Marriage in Medieval France.* New York: Pantheon Books.

Dulles, F.R. 1966. *Labor in America: A History.* Arlington Heights, IL: Harlan Davidson.

Dumanont, L. 1980. [1966] *Homo Hierarchicus: The Caste System and Its Implications.* Chicago,IL: University of Chicago Press.

Dunbar, R., C. Knight, and C. Power. 1999. (Eds.) *The Evolution of Culture.* New Brunswick, NJ: Rutgers University Press.

Duncan, O.D. 1965. The Trend of Occupational Mobility in the United States. *American Sociological Review*, 30: 491-498.

Durant, A. and W. Durant. 1963. *The Age of Louis XIV.* New York: MJF Books.

Durant, A. and W. Durant. 1967. *Rousseau and the Revolution.* New York: MJF Books.

Durkheim, E. 1915. *The Elementary Forms of Religious Life.* New York: The Free Press.

Durkheim, E.   1933. *The Division of Labor in Society.* New York: The Free Press.

Durkheim, E.   1961. *Moral Education.* New York: The Free Press.

Dvornik, F. 1962. *The Slavs in European History and Civilization.* New Brunswick, NJ: Rutgers University Press.

Dye, T.R. 1975. *Power and Society: An Introduction to the Social Sciences.* Belmont, CA: Wadsworth Publishing.

Eaton, R.M. (Ed.) *Descartes Selections.* New York: Scribner's Sons.

Ebenstein, A. 2001. *Friedrich Hayek: A Biography.* New York: Palgrave.

Eberhard, W. 1977. *A History of China.* London: Routledge & Kegan Paul.

Eberstadt, M. 2004. *Home-Alone America: The Hidden Toll of Day Care, Behavioral Drugs, and Other Parent Substitutes.* New York: Sentinel,

Eckstein, H and T.R. Gurr. 1975. *Patterns of Authority: A Structural Basis for Political Inquiry.* New York: John Wiley & Sons.

Edman, I. (Ed.) 1928. *The Works of Plato.* New York: The Modern Library.

Eisenstadt, S.N. 1971. *Social Differentiation and Stratification.* Glencoe, IL: Scott, Foresman.

Elias, N. 1982. *Power and Civility.* New York: Pantheon Books.

Elias, N. 1983. *The Court Society*. New York: Pantheon Books.

Elias, N. 1998. *On Civilization, Power, and Knowledge*, edited by Stephen Mennell and Johan Goudsblom. Chicago: University of Chicago Press.

Elliott, J.H. 1968. *Europe Divided 1559-1598*. London: Fontana Press.

Ellis, J.J. 1979. *After the Revolution: Profiles of Early American Culture*. New York: W.W. Norton.

Ellis, J.J. 1993. *Passionate Sage: The Character and Legacy of John Adams*. New York: W.W. Norton.

Ellis, J.J. 1996. *American Sphinx: The Character of Thomas Jefferson*. New York: Alfred A. Knopf.

Ellis, J.J. 2000. *Founding Brothers: The Revolutionary Generation*. New York: Alfred A. Knopf.

Ellis, J.M. 1997. *Literature Lost: Social Agendas and the Corruption of the Humanities*. New Haven: Yale University Press.

Ellis, R.J. 1998. *The Dark Side of the Left: Illiberal Egalitarianism in America*. Lawrence: University of Kansas Press.

Elshtain, J.B. 1995. *Democracy on Trial*. New York: Basic Books.

Engels, F. 1972. *The Origin of the Family, Private Property, and the State*. New York: International Publishers.

Entine, J. 2000. *Taboo: Why Black Athletes Dominate Sports and Why We're Afraid to Talk About It*. New York: Public Affairs.

Entwisle, D.R., K.L. Alexander, and L.S. Olson. 1997. *Children, Schools & Inequality*. Boulder, CO: Westview Press.

Epstein, C.F. 1970. *Woman's Place: Options and Limits in Professional Careers*. Berkeley: University of California Press.

Epstein, J. 2002. *Snobbery: The American Version*. Boston: Houghton Mifflin Co.

Epstein, J. 2003. *Envy: The Seven Deadly Sins*. New York: Oxford University Press.

Erickson, C. 1983. *The First Elizabeth*. New York: Summit Books.

Erikson, E. 1958. *Young Man Luther*. New York: W.W. Norton.

Erikson, E. 1968. *Identity: Youth and Crisis*. New York: W.W. Norton.

Erikson, E. 1969. *Gandhi's Truth: On the Origins of Militant Nonviolence*. W.W. Norton.

Etzioni, A. 1993. *The Spirit of Community: Reinvention of American Society*. New York: Simon & Schuster.

Faludi, S. 1991. *Backlash: The Undeclared War Against American Women.* New York: Crown Publishers.

Farber, D.A. and S. Sherry. 1997. *Beyond All Reason: The Radical Assault on Truth in American Law.* New York: Oxford University Press.

Farley, R. 1996. *The New American Reality: Who We Are, How We Got Here, Where We Are Going.* New York: Russell Sage Foundation.

Farrell, W. 2005. *Why Men Earn More.* New York: Amacom.

Feagin, J.R. and M.P. Sikes. 1994. *Living with Racism: The Black Middle-Class Experience.* Boston, MA: Beacon Press.

Fein, M. 1990. *Role Change: A Resocialization Perspective.* New York: Praeger.

Fein, M. 1992. *Analyzing Psychotherapy: A Social Role Interpretation.* New York: Praeger.

Fein, M. 1993. *I.A.M.*: A Common Sense Guide to Coping with Anger.* Westport, CT: Praeger.

Fein, M. 1997. *Hardball Without an Umpire: The Sociology of Morality.* Westport, CT: Praeger.

Fein, M. 1999. *The Limits of Idealism: When Good Intentions Go Bad.* New York: Kluwer/Plenum.

Ferguson, N. 2001. *The Cash Nexus: Money and Power in the Modern World, 1700 – 2000.* New York: Basic Books.

Festinger, L. 1957. *A Theory of Cognitive Dissonance.* Evanston, IL: Row, Peterson.

Festinger, L., H.W. Rieken, and S. Schacter. 1964. *When Prophesy Fails.* New York: Harper & Row.

Finley, M.I. 1973. *The Ancient Economy.* Berkeley: University of California Press.

Fischer, L. 1964. *The Life of Lenin.* New York: Harper & Row.

Fish, S. 1989. *Doing What Comes Naturally: Change, Rhetoric, and the Practice of Theory in Literary and Legal Studies.* NC: Duke University Press.

Fisher, H. 1982. *The Sex Contract: The Evolution of Human Behavior.* New York: William Morrow and Co.

Fisher, H.E. 1992. *Anatomy of Love: The Natural History of Monogamy, Adultery and Divorce.* New York: W.W. Norton.

Fishman, R. 1987. *Bourgeois Utopias: The Rise and Fall of Suburbia.* New York: Basic Books.

Flaubert, G. 1959. *Madame Bovary*. New York: Bantam.

Flynn, D.J. 2004a. *Why the Left Hates America: Exposing the Lies That Have Obscured Our Nation's Greatness*. New York: Three Rivers Press.

Flynn, D.J. 2004b. *Intellectual Morons: How Ideology Makes Smart People Fall for Stupid Ideas*. New York: Crown Forum.

Forbes, J.D. 1981. *J.P. Morgan, Jr.* Charlottesville, VA: University of Virginia Press.

Ford, G.R. 1979. *A Time to Heal: The Autobiography of Gerald R. Ford*. New York: Harper & Row.

Fornara, C. 1991. *Athens from Cleisthenes to Pericles*. Berkeley: University of California Press.

Forrest, W.G. 1968. *A History of Sparta 950-192 B.C.* New York: & Co.

Foucault, M. 1965. *Madness and Civilization: A History of Insanity in the Age of Reason*. New York: Pantheon Books.

Foucault, M. 1979. *Discipline and Punish: The Birth of the Prison*. New York: Random House.

Fox-Genovese, E. 1996. *Feminism is Not the Story of My Life: How Today's Feminist Elite Has Lost Touch with the Real Concerns of Women*. New York: Doubleday.

Frank, S.A. 1998. *Foundations of Social Evolution*. Princeton: University of Princeton Press.

Frankel, N. and N.S. Dye. (Eds.) 1991. *Gender, Class, Race and Reform in the Progressive Era*. Lexington, KY: University of Kentucky Press.

Franklin, D. L. 1997. *Ensuring Inequality: The Structural Transformation of the African-American Family*. New York: Oxford University Press.

Fraser, A. 1979. *King Charles II*. London: Weidenfeld and Nicolson.

Freeman, D. 1983. *Margaret Mead and Samoa: The Making and Unmaking of an Anthropological Myth*. Cambridge, MA: Harvard University Press.

Freidel, F.B. 1973. *Franklin Roosevelt: Launching the New Deal*. Boston, MA: Little, Brown.

French, M. 1992. *The War Against Women*. New York: Summit Books.

Friedan, B. 1963. *The Feminine Mystique*. New York: W.W. Norton.

Friedman, M. 1962. *Capitalism and Freedom.* Chicago, IL: University of Chicago Press.

Friedman, R.E. 1987. *Who Wrote the Bible?* New York: Summit Books.

Freud, A. 1966. *The Ego and the Mechanisms of Defense.* New York: International Universities Press.

Freud, S. 1953-1974. *The Standard Edition of the Complete Psychological Works of Sigmund Freud,* edited by J. Strachey. London: Hogarth Press and Institute for Psychoanalysis.

Fromm, E. 1941. *Escape From Freedom.* New York: Holt, Rinehart and Winston.

Fukuyama, F. 1995. *Trust: The Social Virtues and the Creation of Prosperity.* New York: Free Press.

Fukuyama, F. 1999. *The Great Disruption: Human Nature and The Reconstitution of Social Order.* New York: Free Press.

Fussell, P. 1983. *Class: A Guide Through the American Status System.* New York: Simon & Schuster.

Gabler, N. 1988. *An Empire of Their Own: How the Jews Invented Hollywood.* New York: Random House.

Galbraith, J.K. 1958. *The Affluent Society.* Boston: Houghton Mifflin.

Galileo. 1997. *Galileo on the World Systems.* Berkeley: University of California Press.

Gambino, R. 1975. *Blood of My Blood: The Dilemma of the Italian Americans.* Garden City, NY: Doubleday.

Gans, H.J. 1962. *The Urban Villagers: Group and Class in the Life of Italian-Americans.* New York: The Free Press,

Gans, H.J. 1967. *The Levittowners: Way of Life and Politics in a New Suburban Community.* New York: Alfred A. Knopf.

Gans, H.J. 1988. *Middle American Individualism: Political Participation and Liberal Democracy.* New York: Oxford University Press.

Garbarino, J., C.J. Schellenbach, and J. Sebes. 1986. *Troubled Youth, Troubled Families.* New York: Aldine De Gruyter.

Garder, R.D. 1978. *Horatio Alger: or the American Hero Era.* New York: Arco Publishers.

Gardiner, M. 2000. *Did Adam and Eve Have Navels?: Debunking Pseudoscience.* New York: W.W. Norton.

Gardiner, M. 2003. *Are Universes Thicker Than Blackberries?* New York: W.W. Norton & Co.

Garfinkel, H. 1967. *Studies in Ethnomethodology.* Englewood, NJ: Prentice-Hall.

Garreau, J. 1991. *Edge City: Life on the New Frontier.* New York: Random House.

Gatrell, P. 1986. *The Tsarist Economy 1850-1917.* London: B.T. Batsford.

Gay, P. 1988. *Freud: A Life for Our Time.* New York: W.W. Norton.

Gay, P. 2002. *Schnitzler's Century: The Making of Middle-Class Culture 1815-1914.* New York: W.W. Norton.

Gelles, R.J. 1997. *Intimate Violence in Families (3rd Edition).* Beverly Hills, CA: Sage Publications.

Gelles, R.J and M.A. Straus. 1989. *Intimate Violence: The Causes and Consequences of Abuse in the American Family.* New York: Touchstone Books.

Gerson, M. (Ed.) 1996. *The Essential Neo-Conservative Reader.* Reading, MA: Addison-Wesley Publishing.

Gerth, H. and C.W. Mills. (Eds.) 1946. *From Max Weber: Essays in Sociology.* New York: Oxford University Press.

Gibbon, E. [1963] *The Decline and Fall of the Roman Empire.* New York: Dell Publishing.

Gibbs, J. 1989. *Control: Sociology's Central Notion.* Chicago: University of Illinois Press.

Giddens, A. 1973. *The Class Structure of the Advanced Societies.* New York: Harper & Row.

Gies, F. and J. Gies. 1987. *Marriage and the Family in the Middle Ages.* New York: Harper & Row.

Gilbert, D. and J.A. Kahl. 1993. *The American Class Structure.* Fourth Edition. Belmont, CA: Wadsworth Publishing.

Gilligan, C. 1982. *In a Different Voice.* Cambridge, MA: Harvard University Press.

Ginsberg, A. 1972. *The Gates of Wrath: Rhymed Poems.* Bolinas, CA: Grey Fox Press.

Giuliani, R.W. 2002. *Leadership.* New York: Miramax Books.

Gladwell, M. 2000. *The Tipping Point: How Little Things Can Make a Big Difference.* Boston: Little, Brown and Co.

Glass, I.B. (Ed.) 1991. *The International Handbook of Addiction.* New York: Tavistock/Routledge.

Glazer, N. 1997. *We Are All Multiculturalists Now.* Cambridge, MA: Harvard University Press.

Gleick, J. 2003. *Isaac Newton.* New York: Pantheon Books.

Glendon, M.A. 1991. *Rights Talk: The Impoverishment of Political Discourse.* New York: Free Press.

Glendon, M.A. and D. Blankenhorn. (Eds.) 1995. *Seedbeds of Virtue: Sources of Competence, Character, and Citizenship in American Society.* Lanham, MD: Madison Books.

Glenn, N. 1997. *Closed Hearts, Closed Minds: The Textbook Story of Marriage.* New York: Institute for American Values.

Glubb, J.B. 1963. *The Great Arab Conquests.* London: Quartet Books.

Goffen, R. 2002. *Renaissance Rivals: Michelangelo, Leonardo, Raphael, Titian.* New Haven: University Press.

Goffman, E. 1959. *The Presentation of Self in Everyday Life.* Garden City: Doubleday and Co.

Gohau, G. 1990. *A History of Geology,* translated by Albert Carozzi and Marguerite Carozzi. New Brunswick, NJ: Rutgers University Press.

Goldberg, B. 2002. *Bias: A CBS Insider Exposes How the Media Distort the News.* Washington, DC: Regnery Publishing.

Goldberg, B. 2003. *Arrogance: Rescuing America from the Media Elite.* New York: Warner Books.

Goldwater, B.M. 1964. *Conscience of a Conservative.* New York: MacFadden-Bartell.

Goleman, D. 1995. *Emotional Intelligence: Why It Can Matter More Than IQ.* New York: Bantam Books.

Good, T.L. and J.S. Braden. 2000. *The Great School Debate: Choice, Vouchers, and Charters.* Mahwah, NJ. Lawrence Erlbaum Associates.

Goodwin, D.K. 1995. *No Ordinary Time: Franklin and Eleanor Roosevelt.* New York: Simon & Schuster.

Gottfredson, M.R. and T. Hirschi. 1990. *A General Theory of Crime.* Stanford, CA: Stanford University Press.

Goubert, P. 1966. *Louis XIV and Twenty Million Frenchmen.* New York: Vintage Books.

Gould, S.J. 1996. *Full House: The Spread of Excellence from Plato to Darwin.* New York: Three Rivers Press.

Gouldner, A.W. 1970. *The Coming Crisis of Western Sociology*. New York: Basic Books.

Gordon, M. M. 1964. *Assimilation in American Life: The Role of Race, Religion, and National Origins*. New York: Oxford University Press.

Graglia, F.C. 1998. *Domestic Tranquility: A Brief Against Feminism*. Dallas, TX: Spence Publishing Co.

Graham, T. 1996. *Patterns of Deception: The Media's Role in the Clinton Presidency*. Alexandria, VA: Media Research Center.

Gramsci, A. 1977. *Antonio Gramsci: Selections from Political Writings*. New York: International Publications.

Gray, T. 1976. *Champion of Peace: The Story of Alfred Nobel, the Peace Prize, and the Laureates*. New York: Paddington Press.

Green, D.P. and I. Shapiro. 1994. *Pathologies of Rational Choice Theory: A Critique of Applications in Political Science*. New Haven: Yale University Press.

Greenwood, E. 1957. "Attributes of a Profession." *Social Work*, II, 3, July.

Greer, C. and H. Kohl. 1995. *A Call to Character*. New York: HarperCollins.

Gregorovius, F. 1971. *Rome and Medieval Culture*. Chicago, IL: University of Chicago Press.

Griswold, W. 1994. *Cultures and Societies in a Changing World*. Thousand Oaks: Pine Forge Press.

Grousett, R. 1970. *The Empire of the Steppes: A History of Central Asia*, translated by Naomi Walford. New Brunswick: Rutgers University Press.

Grun, B. 1979. *The Timetables of History: A Horizontal Linkage of People and Events*. New York: Simon & Schuster.

Grusky, O. and G.A. Miller. (Eds.) 1970. *The Sociology of Organizations: Basic Studies* (Second Edition). New York: The Free Press.

Gutmann, S. 2000. *The Kinder, Gentler Military: Can America's Gender-Neutral Fighting Force Still Win Wars?* New York: Scribner.

Guy, M.E. 1997. "Counterpoint: By Thine Own Voice, Shall Thou Be Known." *Public Productivity and Managment Review*, Vol. 20, No. 3, March, pp.237-242.

Halberstam, D. 1969. *The Best and the Brightest*. New York: Random House.

Halberstam, D. 1986. *The Reckoning.* New York: William Morrow Co.

Hall, C. 1997. *Steel Phoenix: The Fall and Rise of the U.S. Steel Industry.* New York: St. Martin's Press.

Hall, R.H. 1975. *Occupations and the Social Structure.* Englewood Cliffs, NJ: Prentice-Hall, Inc.

Hall, R.H. 1999. *Organizations: Structures, Processes, and Outcomes.* Upper Saddle River, NJ: Prentice-Hall.

Hamilton, E. 1958. *The Greek Way.* New York: W.W. Norton.

Hamilton, R.F. 1996. *The Social Misconstruction of Reality: Validity and Verification in the Scholarly Community.* New Haven, CT: Yale University Press.

Handel, G. [Ed.] 1967. *The Psychosocial Interior of the Family: A Sourcebook for the Study of Whole Families.* Chicago, IL: Aldine-Atherton.

Handlin, O. 1951. *The Uprooted.* Boston, MA: Little, Brown and Co.

Handlin, O. 1959. *The Newcomers: Negroes and Puerto Ricans in a Changing Metropolis.* New York: Doubleday and Co.

Hanson, V.D. 2001. *Carnage and Culture: Landmark Battles in the Rise of Western Power.* New York: Doubleday.

Hanson, V.D. 2003a. *Ripples of Battle: How Wars of the Past Still Determine How We Fight, How We Live, And How We Think.* New York: Doubleday.

Hanson, V.D. 2003b. *Mexifornia: A State of Being.* San Francisco: Encounter Books.

Harre, R. 1964. *Matter and Method.* London: MacMillan and Co.

Harris, M. 1977. *Cannibals and Kings: The Origins of Cultures.* New York: Random House.

Harrison, L.E. and S.P. Huntington. (Eds.) 2000. *Culture Matters: How Values Shape Human Progress.* New York: Basic Books.

Hatab, L.J. 1990. *Myth and Philosophy: A Contest of Truths.* La Salle, IL: Open Court.

Hayek, F.A. 1944. *The Road to Serfdom.* London: Routledge.

Hayek, F.A. 1988. *The Fatal Conceit: The Errors of Socialism.* Chicago, IL: The University of Chicago Press.

Haynes, J.E. and H. Klehr. 2003. *In Denial: Historians, Communism and Espionage.* San Francisco, CA: Encounter Books.

Hearn, F. 1997. *Moral Order and Social Disorder: The American Search for Civil Society.* New York: Aldine de Gruyter.

Heilbroner, R.L. 1980. *The Worldly Philosophers.* New York: Simon & Schuster.

Henry, J. 1963. *Culture Against Man.* New York: Vintage Books.

Herodotus 1954. *The Histories,* translated by Aubery de Selincourt. Harmondworth, UK: Penguin Books.

Herrnstein, R.J. & C. Murray. 1994. *The Bell Curve: The Reshaping of American Life by Differences in Intelligence.* New York: Basic Books.

Hersey, J. 1946. *Hiroshima.* New York: Bantam Books.

Hersh, S.M. 1983. *Kissinger: The Price of Power.* London: Faber and Faber.

Hewitt, J.P. 1998. *The Myth of Self-Esteem: Finding Happiness and Solving Problems in America.* New York: St. Martins.

Himmelfarb, G. 1995. *The De-Moralization of Society: From Victorian Virtues to Modern Values.* New York: Alfred A. Knopf.

Himmelfarb, G. 1999. *One Nation, Two Cultures.* New York: Alfred A. Knopf.

Hitler, A. 1972, *Mein Kampf,* translated by Ralph Manheim. Boston: Houghton Mifflin Company.

Hobbes, T. 1956. *Leviathan; Part I.* Chicago: Henry Regnery Co.

Hochschild, A.R. 1983. *The Managed Heart: Commercialization of Human Feeling.* Berkeley: University of California Press.

Hochschild, J. 1995. *Facing Up to the American Dream.* Princeton, NJ: Princeton University Press.

Hoffer, E. 1951. *The True Believer: Thoughts on the Nature of Mass Movements.* New York: Harper & Row.

Hoffer, P.C. 2004. *Past Imperfect: Facts, Fictions, Fraud—American History from Bancroft and Parkman to Ambrose, Bellesiles, Ellis and Goodwin.* New York: Public Affairs.

Hoffman, A. 2001. *The Autobiography of Abbie Hoffman.* New York: Four Walls Eight Windows.

Hollander, P. 1992. *Anti-Americanism: Critiques at Home and Abroad 1965-1990.* New York: Oxford University Press.

Hollingshead, A. and F. Redlich. 1958. *Social Class and Mental Health.* New York: John Wiley.

Hollis, F. 1964. *Casework: A Psychosocial Therapy*. New York: Random House.

Holmes, S.J. 1961. *Louis Pasteur*. New York: Dover.

Hoogenboom, A.A. 1968. *Outlawing the Spoils: A History of the Civil Service reform Movement 1865-1883*. Urbana: University of Illinois Press.

Horowitz, D. 1998. *Betty Friedan and the Making of the Feminine Mystique*. Amherst: University of Massachusetts Press.

Horowitz. D. 1997. *Radical Son: A Generational Odyssey*. New York: The Free Press.

Horowitz, D. 2003. *Left Illusions: An Intellectual Odyssey*. Dallas, TX: Spence Publishing Co.

Horowitz, I.L (Ed.) 1971. *Power, Politics, and People: The Collected Essays of C. Wright Mills*. London: Oxford University Press.

Hospers, J. 1953. *An Introduction to Philosophical Analysis*. Englewood Cliffs, NJ: Prentice-Hall Inc.

Hospers, J. 1961. *Human Conduct: An Introduction to the Problem of Ethics*. New York: Harcourt, Brace, World.

Howard, P.K. 1995. *The Death of Common Sense: How Law Is Suffocating America*. New York: Random House.

Howard, P.K. 2001. *The Lost Art of Drawing the Line: How Fairness Went Too Far*. New York: Random House.

Howe, I. 1976. *The World of Our Fathers*. New York: Harcourt, Brace, Jovanovich, Publishers.

Howell, J.T. 1973. *Hard Living on Clay Street: Portraits of Blue Collar Families*. Prospect Heights, IL: Waveland Press, Inc.

Howell, R. 1977. *Cromwell*. Boston, MA: Little, Brown & Co.

Hughes, E.C. 1958. *Men and Their Work*. New York: Free Press of Glencoe.

Hughes, R. 1993. *Culture of Complaint: The Fraying of America*. New York: Oxford University Press.

Hugo, V. 1887. *Les Miserables*. Boston, MA: Little, Brown and Co.

Hume, D. 1739. *A Treatise on Human Nature*. London.

Humphrey, H.H. 1964. *War on Poverty*. New York: McGraw-Hill.

Hunt, A. 1999. *Governing Morals: A Social History of Moral Regulation*. New York: Cambridge University Press.

Hunter, F. 1953. *Community Power Structure: A Study of Decision Makers.* Chapel Hill: University of North Carolina Press.

Hunter, J.D. 1991. *Culture Wars: The Struggle to Define America.* New York: Basic Books.

Hunter, J.D. 2000. *The Death of Character: Moral Education in an Age Without Good and Evil.* New York: Basic Books.

Huntington, S.P. 1996. *The Clash of Civilizations and the Remaking of World Order.* New York: Simon & Schuster.

Huntington, S.P. 2004. *Who Are We?: The Challenges to America's National Identity.* New York: Simon & Schuster.

Hurst, C.E. 1995. *Social Inequality: Forms, Causes, and Consequences.* Second Edition. Boston: Allyn and Bacon.

Hutchinson, H.F. 1967. *King Henry V: A Biography.* New York: Dorset Press.

Ignatiev, N. 1995. *How the Irish Became White.* New York: Routledge.

Isaacson, W. 2003. *Benjamin Franklin: An American Life.* New York: Simon & Schuster.

Jackson, K.T. 1985. *Crabgrass Frontier: The Suburbanization of the United States.* New York: Oxford University Press.

Jacobs, R. 1997. *The Way the Wind Blew: A History of the Weather Underground.* New York: Verso.

Jagger, A.M. 1988. *Feminist Politics and Human Nature.* Totowa, NJ: Rowman & Littlefield.

Jakle, J.A. and K.A. Sculle. 1999. *Fast Food: Roadside Restaurants in the Automobile Age.* Baltimore: Johns Hopkins University Press.

James, H. 1909. *The Portrait of a Lady.* New York: Modern Library.

James, P. and N. Thorpe. 1994. *Ancient Inventions.* New York: Ballantine Books.

Jardine, L. 1999. *Ingenious Pursuits: Building the Scientific Revolution.* New York: Doubleday.

Jencks, C. 1972. *Inequality: A Reassessment of the Effect of Family and Schooling in America.* New York: Basic Books.

Jencks, C. 1992. *Rethinking Social Policy: Race, Poverty and the Underclass.* Cambridge, MA: Harvard University Press.

Jencks, C. 1994. *The Homeless: Rethinking Social Policy.* Cambridge, MA: Harvard University Press.

Joes, A.J. 1989. *The War for South Viet Nam 1954-1975.* New York: Praeger.

Johnson, A.G. 2001. *Privilege, Power, and Difference.* Mountain View, CA: Mayfield Publishing.

Johnson, P. 1997. *A History of the American People.* New York: HarperCollins Publishers.

Johnson, P.E. 1978. *A Shopkeeper's Millennium: Society and Revivals in Rochester New York 1815-1837.* New York: Hill and Wang.

Johnson, V.E. 2002. *Grade Inflation: A Crisis in College Education.* New York: Springer.

Jones, J.H. 1997. *Alfred C. Kinsey: A Life.* New York: W.W. Norton & Co.

Kagan, D. 2003. *The Peloponnesian War.* New York: Penguin Books.

Kahl, J.A. 1967. *The American Class Structure.* New York: Holt, Rinehart and Winston.

Katz, L.D. (Ed.) 2000. *Evolutionary Origins of Morality: Cross-Disciplinary Perspectives.* Bowling Green, OH: Imprint Academic.

Keen, M. 1969. *The Pelican History of Medieval Europe.* Baltimore: Penguin Books.

Kelly, A. 1950. *Eleanor of Acquitaine and the Four Kings.* Cambridge, MA: Harvard University Press.

Kelly, C. 1974. *Conspiring Against God and Man.* Boston, MA: Western Lands.

Kendall, P.M. 1971. *Louis XI: The Universal Spider.* New York: W.W. Norton & Co.

Kennedy, P. 1987. *The Rise and Fall of the Great Powers: Economic Change and Military Conflict From 1500 to 2000.* New York: Random House.

Kennedy, R. 2003. *Nigger: The Strange Career of a Troublesome Word.* New York: Vintage Books.

Kerbo, H.R. 1996. *Social Stratification and Inequality.* Third Edition. New York: McGraw-Hill.

Kimball, R. 1990. *Tenured Radicals: How Politics Has Corrupted Our Higher Education.* Chicago: Ivan R. Dee.

Kinder, R.R. and L.M. Sanders. 1996. *Divided by Color: Racial Politics and Democratic Ideals.* Chicago, IL: University of Chicago Press.

Kinross, L. 1977. *The Ottoman Centuries: The Rise and Fall of the Ottoman Empire.* New York: Morrow.

Kirk, R. 1993. *The Politics of Prudence.* Wilmington, DE: ISI Books.

Kirk, R. 1997. *Edmund Burke: A Genius Reconsidered.* Wilmington, DE: Intercollegiate Studies Institute.

Klein, M. 2003. *The Change Makers; From Carnegie to Gates.* New York: Times Books.

Klein, R.G and B. Elgar. 2002. *The Dawn of Human Culture: A Bold New Theory on What Sparked the "Big Bang" of Human Consciousness.* New York: John Wiley and Sons.

Knight, R.H. 1998. *The Age of Consent: The Rise of Relativism and the Corruption of Popular Culture.* Dallas, TX: Spence Publishing.

Knox, T.W. 1886. *The Life of Robert Fulton.* New York: G.P. Putnam.

Kobler, J. 1971. *Capone: The Life and World of Al Capone.* New York: Putnam.

Kohn, B. 2003. *Journalistic Fraud: How The New York Times Distorts the News and Why It Can No Longer Be Trusted.* Nashville, TN: WND Books.

Kohn, M.L. 1969. *Class and Conformity: A Study in Values.* Homewood, IL: The Dorsey Press.

Kohn, M.L. and C. Schooler. 1983. *Work and Personality: An Inquiry Into the Impact of Social Stratification.* Norwood, NJ: Ablex Publishing.

Kors, A.C. and H.A. Silverglate. 1998. *The Shadow University: The Betrayal of Liberty on America's Campuses.* New York: The Free Press.

Kramer, H. and R. Kimball. 1999. *The Betrayal of Liberalism: How the Disciples of Freedom and Equality Helped Foster the Illiberal Politics of Coercion and Control.* Chicago, IL: Ivan R. Dee.

Kramer, R. 1991. *Ed School Follies: The Miseducation of America's Teachers.* New York: The Free Press.

Krimmerman, L.I. (Ed.) 1969. *The Nature and Scope of Social Science: A Critical Anthology.* New York: Appleton-Century-Crofts.

Kubler-Ross, E. 1969. *On Death and Dying.* New York: MacMillan.

Kuhn, T.S. 1970. *The Structure of Scientific Revolutions; Second Edition.* Chicago, IL: University of Chicago Press.

Kurtines, W.M. and J.L. Gewirtz. (Eds.) 1987. *Moral Development Through Social Interaction.* New York: John Wiley & Sons.

Kurtz, P. 2000. *Humanist Manifesto 2000: A Call for a New Planetary Humanism*. Amherst, NY: Prometheus Books.

Lacey, R. 1986. *Ford: The Men and the Machine*. Boston, MA: Little, Brown and Co.

Ladd, E.C. 1999. *The Ladd Report*. New York: The Free Press.

Laing, R.D. 1960. *The Divided Self*. London: Tavistock.

Lamont, M. 1992. *Money, Morals, and Manners: The Culture of the French and the American Upper-Middle Class*. Chicago, IL: University of Chicago Press.

Lanczos, C. 1965. *Albert Einstein and the Cosmic World Order*. New York: Interscience Publishers.

Landry, B. 1987. *The New Black Middle Class*. Berkeley, CA: University of California Press.

Lantham, R. (Ed.) 1983. *The Illustrated Pepys: Extracts from the Diary*. Berkeley: University of California Press.

Larson, M.S. 1977. *The Rise of Professionalism: A Sociological Analysis*. Berkeley: University of California Press.

Lasch, C. 1979. *The Culture of Narcissism: American Life in an Age of Diminishing Expectations*. New York: Warner Books.

Lattimore, R. (Trans.) 1951. *The Iliad of Homer*. Chicago, IL: University of Chicago Press.

Laudan, L. 1977. *Progress and Its Problems: Towards a Theory of Scientific Growth*. Berkeley: University of California Press.

Leaky, R. 1981. *The Making of Mankind*. London: Michael Joseph Ltd.

Leary, T. 1983. *Flashbacks: An Autobiography*. Boston, MA: Houghton, Mifflin Co.

Le Goff, J. 1980. *Time, Work, & Culture in the Middle Ages*. Chicago, IL: University of Chicago Press.

Lemert, E.M. 1967. *Human Deviance: Social Problems and Social Control*. Englewood Cliffs, NJ: Prentice-Hall.

Lenski, G. 1966. *Power and Privilege: A Theory of Social Stratification*. New York: McGraw-Hill.

Leo, J. 1994. *Two Steps Ahead of the Thought Police*. New York: Simon & Schuster.

Leo, J. 2001. *Incorrect Thought: Notes on Our Wayward Culture*. New Brunswick, NJ: Transaction Publishers.

Levine, D.N. (Ed.) 1971. *Georg Simmel on Individuality and Social Forms.* Chicago, IL: University of Chicago Press.

LeVine, R. 1973. *Culture, Behavior and Personality.* Chicago,IL: Aldine Publishing.

Lewis, B. 2002. *What Went Wrong: Western Impact and Middle Eastern Response.* New York: Oxford University Press.

Lewis, M. and C. Saarni. (Eds.) 1985. *The Socialization of Emotions.* New York: Plenum Press.

Lewis, O. 1966. *La Vida: A Puerto Rican Family in the Culture of Poverty.* New York: Random House.

Lewis, S. 1922. *Babbitt.* New York: Harcourt. Brace & Co.

Lichter, S.R., L.S. Lichter, and S. Rothman. 1994. *Prime Time: How TV Portrays American Culture.* Washington, DC: Regnery Publishing.

Lindsey, B.B. and W. Evans. 1927. *Companionate Marriage.* New York: Boni and Liveright.

Lindzey, G. and E. Aronson. (Eds.) 1985. *Handbook of Social Psychology; Third Edition.* New York: Random House.

Link, A.S. 1954. *Woodrow Wilson and the Progressive Era 1910-1917.* New York: Harper.

Lipset, S.M. 1996. *American Exceptionalism: A Double-Edged Sword.* New York: W.W. Norton.

Lipset, S.M. and R. Bendix. 1959. *Social Mobility in Industrial Society.* Berkeley: University of California Press.

Liszt, F. 1963. *Frederic Chopin,* translated by Edward N. Waters. New York: Free Press of Glencoe.

Locke, J. 1959. (1765) *An Essay Concerning Human Understanding.* New York: Dover Publications.

Loewen, J.W. 1995. *Lies My Teacher Told Me: Everything Your American History Textbook Got Wrong.* New York: The New Press.

Lofland, L.H. 1973. *A World of Strangers.* New York: Basic Books.

Lomborg, B. 2001. *The Skeptical Environmentalist: Measuring the Real State of the World.* New York: Cambridge University Press.

Lopreato, J. and T. Crippen. 1999. *Crisis in Sociology: The Need For Darwin.* New Brunswick, NJ: Transaction Publishers.

Lorber, J. 1994. *Paradoxes of Gender.* New Haven: Yale University Press.

Lorenz, K. 1966. *On Aggression.* London: Metheun.

Lortie, D.C. 1975. *Schoolteacher: A Sociological Study.* Chicago, IL: University of Chicago Press.

Loseke, D.R. 1999. *Thinking About Social Problems: An Introduction to Constructivist Perspectives.* New York: Aldine de Gruyter.

Lott, J.R. 1998. *More Guns, Less Crime: Understanding Crime and Gun Control Laws.* Chicago: University of Chicago Press.

Lowe, D. 1967. *Ku Klux Klan: The Invisible Empire.* New York: W.W. Norton.

Lowery, R. 2003. *Legacy: Paying the Price for the Clinton Years.* Washington, DC: Regnery Publishing.

Ludwig, A.M. 2002. *King of the Mountain: The Nature of Political Leadership.* Lexington: University of Kentucky Press.

Lynch, F.R. 1997. *The Diversity Machine.* New York: The Free Press.

Lynd, R. and H. Lynd. 1929. *Middletown.* New York: Harcourt, Brace, Jovanovich.

Lynd, R. and H. Lynd. 1937. *Middletown in Transition.* New York: Harcourt, Brace, Jovanovich.

Lynn, D.B. 1974. *The Father: His Role in Child Development.* Monterey, CA: Brooks/Cole.

Lyons, M. 1994. *Napoleon Bonaparte and the Legacy of the French Revolution.* New York: St. Martin's Press.

Machiavelli, N. 1966. *The Prince*, translated by Daniel Donnos. New York: Bantam Books.

MacDonald, H. 2000. *The Burden of Bad Ideas: How Modern Intellectuals Misshape Our Society.* Chicago, IL: Ivan R. Dee.

MacDonald, H. 2003. *Are Cops Racist?: How the War Against the Police Harms Black Americans.* Chicago, IL: Ivan R. Dee.

MacKinnon, C.A. 1987. *Feminism Unmodified: Discourses on Life and Law.* Cambridge, MA: Harvard University Press.

MacMillan, M. 2001. *Paris 1919: Six Months that Changed the World.* New York: Random House.

McBride, J. 1996. *The Color of Water: A Black Man's Tribute to His White Mother.* New York: Riverhead Books.

McClelland, D. 1975. *Power: The Inner Experience.* New York: Irvington Publishers.

McCullough, D. 1992. *Truman.* New York: Simon & Schuster.

McCullough, D. 2001. *John Adams.* New York: Simon & Schuster.

McCullough, E. 2000. *Good Old Coney Island.* New York: Fordham University Press.

McElvaine, R.S. 1984. *The Great Depression: America 1929-1941.* New York: Times Books.

McFeely, W.S. 1981. *Grant: A Biography.* New York: W.W. Norton & Co.

McFeely, W.S. 1991. *Frederick Douglass.* New York: W.W. Norton Co.

McGowan, W. 2001. *Coloring the News: How Crusading for Diversity Has Corrupted American Journalism.* San Francisco, CA: Encounter Books.

McNeil, A. 1996. *Total Television: The Comprehensive Guide to Programming from 1948 to the Present.* New York: Penguin Books.

McNeill, W.H. 1963. *The Rise of the West: A History of the Human Community.* Chicago: University of Chicago Press.

McNeill, W.H. 1977. *Plagues and Peoples.* New York: Doubleday.

McShane, C. 1994. *Down the Asphalt Path: The Automobile and the American City.* New York: Columbia University Press.

McWhorter, J. 2001. *The Power of Babel: A Natural History of Language.* New York: HarperCollins.

McWhorter, J. 2003. *Authentically Black: Essays for the Black Silent Majority.* New York: Gotham Books.

Madison, J., A. Hamilton, and J. Jay. 2000. *The Federalist Papers.* London: Phoenix Press.

Madsen, A. 2001. *John Jacob Astor: America's First Multimillionaire.* New York: John Wiley & Sons.

Magnet, M. 1993. *The Dream and the Nightmare: The Sixties Legacy to the Underclass.* New York: William Morrow & Co.

Malthus, T.M. 1926. [1798] *First Essay on Population.* New York: St. Martin's Press.

Manchester, W. 1992. *A World Lit Only By Fire: The Medieval Mind and the Renaissance.* Boston, MA: Little, Brown & Co.

Mannheim, K. 1936. *Ideology and Utopia.* New York: Harcourt, Brace, and World, Inc.

Mannheim, K. 1940. *Man and Society.* London: Routledge and Kegan Paul.

Mapp, A.J. 1987. *Thomas Jefferson: A Strange Case of Mistaken Identity.* Lanham, MD: Madison Books.

Maraniss, D. 1995. *First in His Class: The Biography of Bill Clinton.* New York: Simon & Schuster.

Marcuse, H. 1966. *Eros and Civilization: A Philosophical Inquiry into Freud.* Boston, MA: Beacon Press.

Marcuse, H. 1972. *Counterrevolution and Revolt.* Boston, MA: Beacon Press.

Markmann, C.L. 1965. *The Noblest Cry: A History of the American Civil Liberties Union.* New York: St. Martin's Press.

Marshall, P.D. 1977. *Celebrity and Power: Fame in Contemporary Culture.* Minneapolis, Minn.: The University of Minnesota Press.

Marx, K. 1967. *Das Capital,* edited by F. Engels, translated by Samuel Moore and Edward Aveling. New York: International Publishing.

Marx, K. and F. Engels. [1848] 1935. *The Communist Manifesto,* in *Selected Works.* London: Lawrence and Wishart.

Mason, W.A. and S.P. Mendoza. (Eds) 1993. *Primate Social Conflict.* Albany: State University Press of New York.

Matthews, K.D. 1964. *The Early Romans: Farmers to Empire Builders.* New York: McGraw-Hill.

Mathiesen, M.M. 2000. *Global Warming in a Politically Correct Climate.* San Jose, CA: Writers Club Press.

Mayhead, R. 1967. *John Keats.* Cambridge: Cambridge University Press.

Mazer, S. 1998. *Professional Wrestling: Sport and Spectacle.* Jackson: University of Mississippi Press.

Mead, G.H. 1934. *Mind, Self and Society.* Chicago, IL: University of Chicago Press.

Merton, R. 1949. *Social Theory and Social Structure.* New York: Free Press.

Meyer, E.P. 1974. *"Not Charity, But Justice," The Story of Jacob A. Riis.* New York: Vanguard Press.

Meyerson, J. (Ed.) 1982. *Emerson Centenary Essays.* Carbondale, IL: Southern Illinois University Press.

Michael, R.T., J.H. Gagnon, E.O. Laumann, and G. Kolata. 1994. *Sex in America: A Definitive Study.* New York: Warner Books.

Miller, Z. 2003. *A National Party No More: The Conscience of a Conservative Democrat.* Atlanta: Stroud & Hall Publishing.

Mill, J.S. 1857. *Utilitarianism.* Indianapolis: Bobbs-Merrill.

Mill, J.S. 1863. *On Liberty.* London.

Millingham, B.M. 1984. *Wagner.* London: J.M. Dent.

Mills, C.W. 1951. *White Collar; The American Middle Classes.* New York: Oxford University Press.

Mills, C.W. 1956. *The Power Elite.* London: Oxford University Press.

Mills, C.W. 1959. *The Sociological Imagination.* New York: Oxford University Press.

Moir, A. and D. Jessel. 1989. *Brain Sex: The Real Difference Between Men and Women.* New York: Delta.

Moore, M. 2001. *Stupid White Men...and Other Sorry Excuses for the State of the Nation.* New York: ReganBooks.

Moore, S. and J.L. Simon. 2000. *It's Getting Better All the Time: 100 Greatest Trend of the Last 100 Years.* Washington, DC: Cato Institute.

Montefiore, S.S. 2004. *Stalin: The Court of the Red Tsar.* New York: Alfred A. Knopf.

Montesquieu, C. 1977. *The Spirit of the Laws.* Berkeley: University of California Press.

Morgan, H.W. 1981. *Drugs in America 1800-1980.* Syracuse, NY: University of Syracuse Press.

Morin, R. 1969. *Dwight D. Eisenhower: A Gauge of Greatness.* New York: Simon & Schuster.

Morison, S.E. 1978. *The Great Explorers: The European Discovery of America.* New York: Oxford University Press.

Morris, E. 1999. *Dutch: A Memoir of Ronald Reagan.* New York: Random House.

Morris, E. 2001. *Theodore Rex.* New York: Random House.

Morris, H. (Ed.) 1961. *Freedom and Responsibility.* Stanford, CA: Sanford University Press.

Morris, K.E. 1991. *Jimmy Carter, American Moralist.* Athens: University of Georgia Press.

Morris, R.B. 1985. *Witnesses at the Creation: Hamilton, Madison, Jay, and the Constitution.* New York: New American Library.

Mortimer, E. 1982. *Faith and Power: The Politics of Islam.* New York: Random House.

Moynihan, D.P. 1965. *The Negro Family: The Case for National Action.* Washington, DC: U.S. Government.

Moynihan, D.P. 1993. "Defining Deviancy Down." *American Scholar.*

Munz, P. 1969. *Life in the Age of Charlemagne.* New York: G.P. Putnam's Sons.

Murray, C. 1986. *Losing Ground: American Social Policy.* New York: Basic Books.

Murray, D., J. Schwartz, and S.R. Lichter. 2001. *It Ain't Necessarily So: How Media Make and Unmake the Scientific Picture of Reality.* Lanham, MD: Rowman & Littlefield Publishers.

Myrdal, G. 1944. *An American Dilemma: The Negro Problem and American Democracy.* New York: Harper & Row.

Nahm, M.C. (Ed.) 1934. *Selections from Early Greek Philosophy.* New York: Appleton-Century-Crofts.

Nasaw, D. 2000. *The Chief: The Life of William Randolph Hearst.* Boston, MA: Houghton, Mifflin.

National Center for Educational Statistics. 2001. *Digest of Educational Statistics, 2001.* Washington, DC: Government Printing Office

Nauert, C.G. 1995. *Humanism and the Culture of Renaissance Europe.* New York: Cambridge University Press.

Neill, A.S. 1960. *Summerhill: A Radical Approach to Child Rearing.* New York: Hart Publishing Co.

Newnan, H.H. 1969. *Evolution, Genetics, and Eugenics.* New York: Greenwood Press.

Norris, C. 1997. *Against Relativism: Philosophy of Science, Deconstruction and Critical Theory.* Oxford, UK: Blackwell Publishers.

Nye, F.I. 1976. *Role Structure and the Analysis of the Family.* Beverly Hills, CA: Sage Publications.

Nye, F.I. (Ed.) 1982. *Family Relationships: Rewards and Costs.* Beverly Hills, CA: Sage Publications.

Oberschell, A. 1995. *Social Movements: Ideologies, Interests, and Identities.* New Brunswick, NJ: Transaction Press.

Ogbu, J.U. 1974. *The Next Generation: An Ethnography of Education in an Urban School.* New York: Academic Press.

Ogburn, W. 1922. (1966) *Social Change with Respect to Culture and Original Nature.* New York: Heubsch.

Olasky, M. 1992. *The Tragedy of American Compassion.* Washington, DC: Regnery Publishing.

Olson, R.E. 1999. *The Story of Christian Theology: Twenty Centuries of Tradition and Reform.* Dowers Grove, IL: Intervarsity Press.

Olson, S. 2000. *Mapping Human History: Discovering the Past Through Our Genes.* Boston, MA: Houghton Mifflin Co.

Olson, W.K. 1992. *The Litigation Explosion.* New York: Truman Talley Books.

Olson, W.K. 1997. *The Excuse Factory: How Employment Law is Paralyzing the American Workplace.* New York: The Free Press.

Olson, W.K. 2002. *The Rule of Lawyers: How the New Litigation Elite Threatens America's Rule of Law.* New York: St. Martin's Press.

O' Neill, N.O. and G.O. O'Neill. 1972. *Open Marriage: A New Life Style for Couples.* New York: M. Evans.

Orwin, C. and N. Tarcov. (Eds.) 1997. *The Legacy of Rousseau.* Chicago, IL: University of Chicago Press.

Osborne, R.A. 1999. *70 Years of Oscar: The Official History of the Academy Awards.* New York: Abbeville Press.

Owen, F. 1960. *The Germanic People: Their Origin, Expansion and Culture.* New York: Dorset Press.

Packard, V. 1959. *The Status Seekers.* New York: D. McKay Co.

Paine, T. 1953. *Common Sense and Other Political Writings*, edited by Nelson F. Adkins. New York: Liberal Arts Press.

Pareto, V. 1991. *The Rise and Fall of Elites: An Application of Theoretical Sociology.* New Brunswick, NJ: Transaction Publishers.

Park, R. 1950. *Race and Culture.* Glencoe, IL: Free Press.

Parker, G. 1984. *The Thirty Years' War.* New York: Military Heritage Press.

Parsons, T. 1951. *The Social System.* New York: The Free Press.

Parsons, T. and R.F. Bales. 1955. *Family, Socialization and Interaction Process.* New York: Free Press.

Parsons, T. and E. Shils. (Eds.) 1951. *Toward a General Theory of Action.* New York: Harper and Row.

Partridge, W.L. 1973. *The Hippie Ghetto: The Natural History of a Subculture.* New York: Holt, Rinehart and Winston.

Patterson, O. 1982. *Slavery and Social Death: A Comparative Study.* Cambridge, MA: Harvard University Press.

Payne, R. 1965. *The Rise and Fall of Stalin.* New York: Avon Books.

Payne, R. 1978. *Leonardo.* Garden City, NY: Doubleday.

Perrow, C. 1970. *Organizational Analysis: A Sociological View.* Belmont, CA.: Cole/Brooks.

Peyrefitte, A. 1977. *The Chinese: Portrait of a People.* New York: Bobbs-Merrill Co.

Pfeiffer, J.E. 1977. *The Emergence of Society: A Prehistory of the Establishment.* New York: McGraw-Hill.

Pinker, S. 1994. *The Language Instinct: How the Mind Creates Language.* New York: William Morrow & Co.

Pirenne, H. 1936. *Economic and Social History of Medieval Europe.* New York:

Harcourt, Brace & World.

Piven, F.F. and R.A. Cloward. 1977. *Poor People's Movements: Why They Succeed, How They Fail.* New York: Vintage.

Plato 1928. *The Works of Plato*, translated by Jowett. New York: The Modern Library.

Plato 1941. *The Republic*, translated by Jowett. New York: The Modern Library.

Plumb, J.H. 1961. *The Italian Renaissance.* New York: American Heritage.

Plutarch [1959] *Lives of Noble Greeks*, edited by Edmund Fuller. New York: Nelson Doubleday.

Plutarch [1959] *Lives of Noble Romans*, edited by Edmund Fuller. New York: Nelson Doubleday.

Pocock, T. 1988. *Horatio Nelson.* New York: Alfred A Knopf.

Pollock, W. 1999. *Real Boys: Rescuing Our Sons from the Myths of Boyhood.* New York: Henry Holt and Co.

Popenoe, D. 1996. *Life Without Father: Compelling New Evidence that Fatherhood and Marriage Are Indispensable for the Good of Children and Society.* New York: The Free Press.

Popper, K.R. 1959. *The Logic of Scientific Discovery.* London: Hutchinson & Co.

Popper, K.R. 1971. [1945.] *The Open Society and Its Enemies.* (5th Edition) Princeton: Princeton University Press.

Porter, R. 1982. *English Society in the Eighteenth Century.* New York: Penguin Books.

Posner, G.L. 1993. *Case Closed: Lee Harvey Oswald and the Assassination of JFK.* New York: Random House.

Potter, J.M. 2000. "Ritual, Power, and Social Differentiation in Small-Scale Societies." In: Diehl, M.W., *Hierarchies in Action: Cui Bono?* Carbondale, IL: Center For Archaeological Investigations.

Powell, C. with J. E. Persico. 1995. *My American Journey.* New York: Random House.

Powell, J. 2003. *FDR's Folly: How Roosevelt and His New Deal Prolonged the Great Depression.* New York: Crown Forum.

Prawdin, M. 1967. *The Mongol Empire: Its Rise and Legacy.* New York: Free Press.

Price, J.L. 1994. *Holland and the Dutch Republic in the Seventeenth Century: The Politics of Particularism.* New York: Oxford University Press.

Pruitt, D.G. 1981. *Negotiation Behavior.* New York: Academic.

Putnam, R.D. 1993. *Making Democracy Work: Civic Traditions in Modern Italy.* Princeton: Princeton University Press.

Putnam, R.D. 2000. *Bowling Alone: The Collapse and Revival of American Community.* New York: Simon & Schuster.

Pyatt, S.E. 1986. *Martin Luther King, Jr.: An Annotated Bibliography.* New York: Greenwood Press.

Radosh, R and Radosh, A. 2005. *Red Star Over Hollywood: The Film Colony's Long Romance with the Left.* San Francisco: Encounter Books.

Ranke-Heinmann, U. 1990. *Eunuchs for the Kingdom of Heaven.* New York: Doubleday.

Rand, A. 1966. *Capitalism: The Unknown Ideal.* New York: New American Library.

Rand, A 1992. *Atlas Shrugged.* New York: Dutton.

Raskin, J. 2004. *American Scream: Allen Ginsberg's Howl and the Making of the Beat Generation.* Berkeley: University of California Press.

Ravitch, D. 1974. *The Great School Wars: A History of the New York C*? *Public Schools.* New York: Basic Books.

Ravitch, D. 2000. *Left Back: A Century of Failed School Reforms.* N York: Simon & Schuster.

Ravitch, D. 2003. *The Language Police: How Pressure Groups Re Students Learn.* New York: Alfred A. Knopf.

Rawlinson, G. 1993. *Ancient History: The Great Civilization B.C. to the Fall of Rome.* New York: Barnes & Nobl.

Rawls, J. 1971. *A Theory of Justice.* Cambridge, MA: The Belknap Press.

Rebach, H.M. and J.G. Bruhn. (Eds.) 1991. *Handbook of Clinical Sociology.* New York: Plenum Press.

Redstone, L.G. and R.R. Redstone. 1981. *Public Art: New Directions.* New York: McGraw-Hill.

Rice, E. 1990. *Captain Sir Richard Francis Burton.* New York: Scribner's Sons.

Rice, E. 1997. *The O.J. Simpson Trial.* San Diego, CA: Lucent Books

Rice, L. and L. Greenberg. (Eds.) 1984. *Patterns of Change.* New York: Guilford Press.

Richards, M. 1974. *The Integration of a Child into a Social World.* London: Cambridge University Press.

Richardson, J. 1977. *Victoria and Albert.* New York: The New York Times Book Co.

Ridely, J. 1982. *Statesman and Saint: Cardinal Wolsey, Sir Thomas More and the Politics of Henry VIII.* New York: The Viking Press.

Riech, C.A. 1971. *The Greening of America.* New York: Bantam.

Rieder, J. 1985. *Canarsie: The Jews and Italians of Brooklyn Against Liberalism.* Cambridge, MA: Harvard University Press.

de Riencourt, A. 1974. *Sex and Power in History.* New York: Delta Books.

Riesman, D. 1950. *The Lonely Crowd.* New Haven: Yale University Press.

Ritzer, G. 2000. *The McDonaldization of Society.* Thousand Oaks, CA: Pine Forge Press.

Robinson, R. 2000. *The Debt: What America Owes to Blacks.* New York: Dutton.

Rochester, J.M. 2002. *Class Warfare: Besieged Schools, Bewildered Parents, Betrayed Kids and the Attack on Excellence.* San Francisco, CA: Encounter Books.

Rochon, T.R. 1998. *Culture Moves: Idea, Activism, and Changing Values.* Princeton: Princeton University Press.

Rogers, C. 1951. *Client Centered Therapy.* Boston, MA: Houghton Mifflin.

Rogers, C. 1961. *On Becoming a Person.* Boston, MA: Houghton Mifflin.

Roiphe, K. 1993. *The Morning After: Sex, Fear, and Feminism On Campus.* Boston: Little, Brown, & Co.

Rose, P.I. 1997. *Tempest-Tost: Race, Immigration, and the Dilemmas of Diversity.* New York: Oxford University Press.

Rossi, A.S. (Ed.) 1973. *The Feminist Papers: From Adams to de Beauvoir.* New York: Bantam Books.

Roth, C. 1961. *A History of the Jews: From Earliest Times Through the Six Day War.* New York: Schocken Books.

Rothwax, H.J. 1995. *Guilty: The Collapse of Criminal Justice.* New York: Random House.

Rousseau, J.J. 1968. (1762) *The Social Contract*, translated by Maurice Cranston. New York: Penguin Books.

Rousseau, J.J. [1762] 1979. *Emile*, translated by A. Bloom. New York: Basic Books.

Rousseau, J.J. 1992. *The Discourse on the Origins of Inequality*, edited by Roger D. Masters and Christopher Kelly. Hanover, NH: University Press of New England.

Rubin L. B. 1972. *Busing & Backlash: White Against White in an Urban School District.* Berkeley: University of California Press.

Rude, G. 1964. *Revolutionary Europe 1783-1815.* London: Fontana Press.

Rudolph, F. 1990. *The American College and University: A History.* Athens: University of Georgia Press.

Rule, J.B. 1997. *Theory and Progress in Social Science.* Cambridge, UK: Cambridge University Press.

Russell, B. 1929. *Marriage and Morals.* New York: H. Liveright.

Sale, K. 1973. *SDS.* New York: Random House.

Salvatore, N. 1982. *Eugene V. Debs: Citizen and Socialist.* Urbana: University of Illinois Press.

Samuelson, R. 1996. *The Good Life and Its Discontents: The American Dream in the Age of Entitlement 1945-1995.* New York: Times Books.

Sandeen, E.R. 1970. *The Roots of Fundamentalism: British and American Millenarianism* 1800-1930. Chicago, IL: University of Chicago Press.

Sanderson, S.K. 1995. *Social Transformations: A General Theory of Historical Development.* Oxford, UK: Blackwell.

Sanderson, S.K and A.S. Alderson. 2005. *World Societies: The Evolution of Human Social Life.* Boston, MA: Pearson/Allyn & Bacon.

Sarbin, T. and V. Allen. 1968. "Role Theory," in G. Lindzey and E. Aronson, (Eds.), *Handbook of Social Psychology.* Boston, MA: Addison, Wesley.

Sarton, G. 1962. *The History of Science and the New Humanism.* Bloomington: Indiana University Press.

Satel, S. 2000. *PC, M.D.: How Political Correctness is Corrupting Medicine.* New York: Basic Books.

Scarf, M. 1987. *Intimate Partners: Patterns in Love and Marriage.* New York: Random House.

Schaffer, H. 1971. *The Growth of Sociability.* Baltimore: Penguin Books.

Schama, S. 1989. *Citizens: A Chronicle of the French Revolution.* New York: Alfred A. Knopf.

Scheff, T. 1990. *Microsociology: Discourse, Emotion, and Social Structure.* Chicago, IL: University of Chicago Press.

Schippers, A. 2000. *Sellout: The Inside Story of President Clinton's Impeachment.* Washington, DC: Regnery Publishing.

Schlafly, P. and C. Ward. 1968. *The Betrayers.* Alton, IL: Pere Marquette Press.

Schlesinger, A.M. 1992. *The Disuniting of America.* New York: W.W. Norton & Co.

Schmalleger, F. 2002. *Criminology Today: An Integrative Introduction.* Upper Saddle River, NJ: Prentice-Hall.

Schumpeter, J.A. 1942. *Capitalism, Socialism and Democracy.* New York: Harper & Brothers.

Scott, M. 1964. *Medieval Europe.* New York: Dorset Press.

Sears, D.O. and J.B. McConahay. 1973. *The Politics of Violence: The New Urban Black and the Watts Riot.* Boston, MA: Houghton Mifflin.

Seigel, J.E. 1999. *Bohemian Paris: Culture, Politics, and the Boundaries of Bourgeois Life, 1830-1930.* Baltimore: Johns Hopkins Press.

Seligman, A.B. 1992. *The Idea of Civil Society.* Princeton, NJ: Princeton University Press.

Sennett, R. and J. Cobb. 1966. *The Hidden Injuries of Class.* New York: The Free Press.

Setton, K.M. (Ed.) 1969. *The History of the Crusades.* Madison: University of Wisconsin Press.

Seward, K. 1978. *The American Family: A Demographic History.* Beverly Hills, CA: Sage Publications.

Shapiro, B. 2004. *Brainwashed: How Universities Indoctrinate America's Youth.* Nashville TN: WND Books.

Sheed, W. 1975. *Muhammad Ali: A Portrait in Words and Photographs.* New York: Crowell.

Sheehy, G. 1999. *Hillary's Choice.* New York: Random House.

Sherrow, V. 1995. *The Triangle Factory Fire.* Brookfield, CT: Millbrook Press.

Shilts, R. 1988. *And the Band Played On: Politics, People and the AIDS Epidemic.* New York: Penguin Books.

Shirer, W.L. 1960. *The Rise and Fall of the Third Reich.* New York: Simon & Schuster.

Shogan, R. 2001. *Bad News: Where the Press Goes Wrong in the Making of the President.* Chicago, IL: Ivan R. Dee.

Shone, R. 1979. *The Post Impressionists.* London: Octopus Books.

Sidanius, J and F. Pratto. 1999. *Social Dominance: An Intergroup Theory of Social Hierarchy and Oppression.* Cambridge: Cambridge University Press.

Silberman, C.E. (Ed.) 1973. *The Open Classroom Reader.* New York: Random House.

Simon, H.A. 1947. *Administrative Behavior.* New York: MacMillan.

Sinclair, U. 1988. *The Jungle.* Urbana: University of Illinois Press

Skocpol, T. 2000. *The Missing Middle: Working Families and the Future of American Social Policy.* New York: W.W. Norton & Co.

Skrentny, J.L. 1996. *The Ironies of Affirmative Action: Politics, Culture, and Justice in America.* Chicago: University of Chicago Press.

Sleeper, J. 1997. *Liberal Racism.* New York: Viking.

Smaje, C. 2000. *Natural Hierarchies: The Historical Sociology of Race and Caste.* Oxford: Blackwell Publishers.

Smigel, E.O. (Ed.) 1963. *Work and Leisure.* New Haven: College & University Press.

Smith, A. 1776. *An Inquiry into the Nature and Causes of the Wealth of Nations.* London: W. Strahan & T. Cadell.

Smith, H. 1988. *The Power Game: How Washington Works.* New York: Random House.

Sniderman, P.M. and E.G. Carmines. 1998. *Reaching Beyond Race.* Cambridge, MA: Harvard University Press.

Sobel, D. 1995. *Longitude: The True Story of a Lone Genius Who Solved the Greatest Scientific Problem of His Time.* New York: Walker & Co.

Sobel, D. 1999. *Galileo's Daughter: A Historical Memoir of Science, Faith, and Love.* New York: Walker & Co.

Sommers, C.H. 1994. *Who Stole Feminism: How Women Have Betrayed Women.* New York: Simon & Schuster.

Sommers, C.H. 2000. *The War Against Boys: How Misguided Feminism is Harming Our Young Men.* New York: Simon & Schuster.

Sommers, P.M. (Ed.) 1982. *Welfare Reform in America: Perspectives and Prospects.* Boston, MA: Kluwer and Nijhoff.

Sowell, T. 1981. *Ethnic America.* New York: Basic Books.

Sowell, T. 1996. *Migrations and Cultures: A World View.* New York: Basic Books.

Sowell, T. 1999. *The Quest for Cosmic Justice.* New York: The Free Press.

Sowell, T. 2004. *Affirmative Action Around the World: An Empirical Study.* New Haven: Yale University Press.

Speck, W.A. 1977. *Stability and Strife: England, 1714-1760.* Cambridge: Harvard University Press.

Spencer, H. 1891. *The Study of Sociology.* New York: Appleton.

Spencer, H. [1899] 1969. *The Principles of Sociology* (3 Vols.) (S. Andreski, Ed.) New York: MacMillan.

Spencer, R. 2003. *Onward Muslim Soldiers: How Jihad Still Threatens America and the West.* Washington DC: Regnery Publishing.

Sperber, A.M. 1986. *Murrow: His Life and Times.* New York: Freundlich Books.

Spock, B. 1957. *The Common Sense Book of Baby and Child Care.* New York: Duell, Sloan and Pearce.

Stampp, K.M. 1956. *The Peculiar Institution: Slavery in the Ante-Bellum South.* New York: Alfred A. Knopf.

Stampp, K.M. 1965. *The Era of Reconstruction: 1865-1877.* New York: Vintage Books.

Stanford, C.B. 1999. *The Hunting Apes: Meat Eating and the Origins of Human Behavior.* Princeton, NJ: Princeton University Press.

Starr, P. 1982. *The Social Transformation of American Medicine.* New York: Basic Books.

Starr, P. 2004. *The Creation of the Media: Political Origins of Modern Communications.* New York: Basic Books.

Steele, C.M., S.J. Spencer, and M. Lynch. 1993. "Self-Image, Resilience and Dissonance: The Role of Affirmational Resources." *Journal of Personality and Social Psychology,* 66(6): 885-896.

Steele, S. 1990. *The Content of Our Character: A New Vision of Race in America.* New York: St. Martin's Press.

Steele, S. 1998. *A Dream Deferred: The Second Betrayal of Black Freedom in America.* New York: HarperCollins Publishers.

Steffens, L. 1957. *The Shame of the Cities.* New York: Hill and Ward.

Stein, H. 2000. *How I Accidentally Joined the Vast Right-Wing Conspiracy (And Found Inner Peace).* New York: Delacorte Press.

Stein, H. and M. Foss. 1999. *The Illustrated Guide to the American Economy, Third Edition.* Washington, DC: AEI Press.

Steinbeck, J. 1986. *The Grapes of Wrath.* New York: Penguin Books.

Steinem, G. 1992. *Revolution From Within: A Book of Self-Esteem.* Boston, MA: Little, Brown.

Stone, I.F. 1988. *The Trial of Socrates.* Boston, IL: Little, Brown, & Co.

Stone, L.J., H.T. Smith, and L.B. Murphy. (Eds.) 1973. *The Competent Infant: Research and Commentary.* New York: Basic Books.

Stossel, J. 2004. *Give Me a Break: How I Exposed Hucksters, Cheats, and Scam Artists and Became the Scourge of the Liberal Media.* New York: HarperCollins.

Straus, B.R. 1987. *The Catholic Church.* London: David & Charles.

Strauss, A. 1978. *Negotiations: Varieties, Contexts, Processes and Social Order.* San Francisco, CA: Jossey-Bass.

Strayer, J.R. 1970. *On the Medieval Origins of the Modern State.* Princeton, NJ: Princeton University Press.

Strieder, J. 1984. *Jacob Fugger The Rich: Merchant and Banker of Augsburg 1459-1525,* translated by Mildred Hartsough. Westport, CT: Greenwood Press.

Sullivan, H.S. 1953. *The Interpersonal Theory of Psychiatry.* New York: W.W. Norton Co.

Sumner, W.G. 1960. *Folkways.* New York: New American Library.

Sun-tzu 1988. (6th Century BC) *The Art of War*, translated by Thomas Cleary. Boston, MA: Shambala.

Suttles, G.D. 1972. *The Social Construction of Communities*. Chicago, IL: University of Chicago Press.

Swanberg. W.A. 1972. *Luce and His Empire*. New York: Scribner.

Swartz, D. 1997. *Culture and Power: The Sociology of Pierre Bourdieu*. Chicago: University of Chicago Press.

Swift, J. 1948. *The Portable Swift*, edited by Carl Van Doren. New York: Viking Press.

Sykes, B. 2001. *The Seven Daughters of Eve: The Science That Reveals Our Genetic Ancestry*. New York: W.W. Norton.

Szasz, T. 1961. *The Myth of Mental Illness: Foundations of a Theory of Personal Conduct*. New York: Dell.

Szasz, T. 1970. *Ideology and Insanity*. New York: Anchor.

Tacitus [1977] *The Annals of Imperial Rome*. New York: Dorset Press.

Tallentyre, S.G. 1969. *The Life of Voltaire*. New York: Kraus Reprint Co.

Talmon, J.L. 1985. *Political Messianism: The Romantic Phase*. Boulder, CO: Westview Press.

Tanenhaus, S. 1997. *Whittaker Chambers: A Biography*. New York: Random House.

Tannen, D. 1990. *You Just Don't Understand: Women and Men in Conversation*. New York: William Morrow and Co.

Tarbell, I. 1904. *The History of the Standard Oil Co*. New York: McClure, Phillips.

Tattersall, I. and J. Schwartz. 2000. *Extinct Humans*. New York: Westview Press.

Taylor, A.J.P. 1987. *Bismarck: The Man and the Statesman*. New York: Vintage Books.

Taylor, F.W. 1911. *The Principles of Scientific Management*. New York: Harper and Brothers.

Taylor, G.R. 1951. *The Transportation Revolution 1815-1860*. New York: Rinehart.

Terrill, R. 1980. *A Biography: Mao*. New York: Harper & Row.

Tharpa, R. 1966. *A History of India. (Vols. I & II.)* London: Penguin Books.

Thernstrom, S. and A. Thernstrom. 1997. *America in Black and White: One Nation, Indivisible*. New York: Simon & Schuster.

Thernstrom, S. and A. Thernstrom. 2003. *No Excuses: Closing the Racial Gap in Learning.* New York: Simon & Schuster.

Thomas, A. 2001. *Clarence Thomas: A Biography.* San Francisco, CA: Encounter Books.

Thomas, B.P. 1952. *Abraham Lincoln: A Biography.* New York: The Modern Library.

Thomas, H. 1997. *The Slave Trade: The Story of the Atlantic Slave Trade: 1440-1870.* New York: Simon & Schuster.

Thomas, R.M. 1997. *Moral Development Theories—Secular and Religious.* Westport, CT: Greenwood Press.

Thomas, W.I. and D.S. Thomas. 1928. *The Child in America: Behavior, Problems and Progress.* New York: Alfred A. Knopf.

Thomas, W.I. and F. Znaniecki. 1918/1958. *The Polish Peasant in Europe and America.* New York: Dover Publications.

Thucydides. 1998. *The Peloponnesian War,* translated by Walter Blanco. New York: W.W. Norton.

Tiger, L. 1970. *Men in Groups.* New York: Vintage Books.

Tiger, L. and H.T. Fowler. (Eds.) 1978. *Female Hierarchies.* Chicago, IL: Beresford Book Service.

Tilly, C. (Ed.) 1975. *The Formation of National States in Western Europe.* Princeton, NJ: Princeton University Press.

Tilly, C. 1997. *Roads from Past to Future.* Lanham, MD: Rowman & Littlefield Publishers.

Tilly, C. 1998. *Durable Inequality.* Berkeley: University of California Press.

Tipton, S.M. 1982. *Getting Saved from the Sixties.* Berkeley: The University of California Press.

Tittle, C.K. 1981. *Careers and Family: Sex Roles and Adolescent Life Plans.* Beverly Hills, CA: Sage Publications.

de Tocqueville, A. 1966. *Democracy in America,* translated by George Lawrence. New York: Harper & Row.

Toennies, F. 1966. (1887) *Community and Society.* New York: Harper Row.

Toland, J. 1980. *No Man's Land: 1918, The Last Year of the Great War.* New York: Ballantine Books.

Tracy, J.D. 1990. *Holland Under Hapsburg Rule 1506-1566: The Founding of a Body Politic.* Berkeley: University of California Press.

Troyat, H. 1984. *Ivan the Terrible.* New York: E.P. Dutton.

Tuchman, B.W. 1962. *The Guns of August.* New York: MacMillan.

Tuchman, B.W. 1966. *The Proud Tower: A Portrait of the World Before The War: 1890-1914.* New York: MacMillan.

Tuchman, B.W. 1978. *A Distant Mirror: The Calamitous 14ᵗʰ Century.* New York: Ballantine Books.

Tumen, M.M. 1985. *Social Stratification: The Forms and Functions of Inequality.* Upper Saddle River, NJ: Prentice-Hall.

Turner, R.H. 1962. *Role Taking: Process vs. Conformity?* In: Rose, A.M. (Ed.), Human Behavior and Social Processes. Boston, MA: Houghton Mifflin.

Twain, M. 1915. *The Gilded Age.* New York: Harper.

Twain, M. 1989. *The Adventures of Huckleberry Finn.* New York: Tom Doherty Associates, Inc.

U.S. Census Bureau. 1997. *American Housing Survey for the United States: 1997.* Washington, DC: Government Printing Office.

U.S. Dept. of Labor. 1991. "Research Summaries." *Monthly Labor Review, December.* Washington, DC: Government Printing Office.

U.S. Dept. of Labor, Bureau of Labor Statistics. 1980. *Occupational Outlook Handbook, 1980-81 Edition.* Washington, DC: Government Printing Office.

U.S. Dept. of Labor, Bureau of Labor Statistics. 2000. *Dictionary of Occupational Titles.* Washington, DC: Government Printing Office.

U.S. Dept. of Labor, Bureau of Labor Statistics. 2001. *2001 National Occupational Employment and Wage Estimates.* Washington, DC: Government Printing Office.

Valenstein, E.S. 1986. *Great and Desperate Cures: The Rise and Decline of Psychosurgery and Other Radical Treatments for Mental Illness.* New York: Basic Books.

Valentine, C. 1968. *Culture and Poverty.* Chicago, IL: University of Chicago Press.

Van Hoffman, N. 1968. *We Are the People Our Parents Warned Us Against.* Chicago, IL: Quadrangle Books.

Van Tine, W. 1977. *John L. Lewis: A Biography.* New York: Quadrangle/New York Times.

Veblen, T. 1967. (1899) *The Theory of the Leisure Class*. New York: Viking Penguin.

Vidich, A. and J. Bensman. 1958. *Small Town in Mass Society: Class, Power, and Religion in a Rural Community*. Princeton, NJ: Princeton University Press.

Vollmer, H. and D. Mills. (Eds.) 1968. *Professionalization*. Englewood Cliffs, NJ: Prentice-Hall.

de Waal, F. 1982. *Chimpanzee Politics*. New York: Harper & Row.

de Waal, F. 1989. *Peacekeeping Among Primates*. Cambridge, MA: Harvard University Press.

de Waal, F. 1996. *Good Natured: The Origins of Right and Wrong in Humans and Other Animals*. Cambridge, MA: Harvard University Press.

de Waal, F. 2001a. *The Ape and the Sushi Master: Cultural Reflections of a Primatologist*. New York: Basic Books.

de Waal, F. (Ed.) 2001b. *Tree of Origin: What Primate Behavior Can Tell Us About Human Social Evolution*. Cambridge, MA: Harvard University Press.

Waite, C.J. and M. Gallagher. 2000. *The Case for Marriage: Why Married People are Happier, Healthier, and Better Off Financially*. New York: Doubleday.

Wallace, J. 1993. *Hard Drive: Bill Gates and the Making of the Microsoft Empire*. New York: HarperBusiness.

Wallenstein, J.S., J.M. Lewis, and S. Blakesee. 2000. *The Unexpected Legacy of Divorce: A 25 Year Landmark Study*. New York: Hyperion.

Waller, W. 1967. *The Sociology of Teaching*. New York: John Wiley & Sons.

Warner, W.L. et al. 1949. *Democracy in Jonesville*. New York: Harper & Brothers.

Warren, W.L. 1961. *King John*. Berkeley: University of California Press.

Washington, B.T. 1901. (1985) *Up From Slavery*. New York: Oxford University Press.

Watson, D.R. 1972. *The Life and Times of Charles I*. London: Weidenfeld and Nicolson.

Watson, J.B. 1928. *Psychological Care of Infant and Child*. New York: Norton.

Wead, D. 2003. *All The Presidents' Children: Triumph and Tragedy in the Lives of America's First Families.* New York: Atria Books.

Weber, M. 1947. *The Theory of Social and Economic Organization.* New York: Free Press.

Weber, M. 1958a. *The Protestant Ethic and the Spirit of Capitalism.* New York: Scribner's Sons.

Weber, M. 1958b. *The City.* New York: The Free Press.

Weiss, R.S. 1975. *Marital Separation: Coping with the End of Marriage.* New York: Basic Books.

Weiss, R.S. 1990. *Staying the Course: The Emotional and Social Lives of Men Who Do Well at Work.* New York: Free Press.

Wells, S. 2002. *The Journey of Man: A Genetic Odyssey.* Princeton, NJ: Princeton University Press.

Wentworth, W. 1980. *Context and Understanding: An Inquiry into Socialization Theory.* New York: Elsevier.

West, T.G. 1997. *Vindicating the Founders: Race, Sex, Class, and Justice in the Origins of America.* Lanham, MD: Rowman & Littlefield Publishers

Westermarck, E. 1960. *Ethical Relativity.* Paterson, NJ: Littlefield, Adams, and Co.

Whitehead, B.D. 1998. *The Divorce Culture: Rethinking Our Commitments to Marriage and the Family.* New York: Random House.

Whiting, J. and I. Child. 1953. *Child Training and Personality.* New Haven, CT: Yale University Press.

Whittier, N. 1995. *Feminist Generations: The Persistence of the Radical Women's Movement.* Philadelphia, PA: Temple University Press.

Whyte, W.F. 1943. *Street Corner Society.* Chicago, IL: University of Chicago Press.

Whyte, W.H. 1956. *The Organization Man.* New York: Simon & Schuster.

Wicker, T. 1991. *One of Us: Richard Nixon and the American Dream.* New York: Random House.

Wiener, D and M. Berley. 1999. *The Diversity Hoax: Law Students Report from Berkeley.* New York: FAST.

Wild, J. (Ed.) 1958. *Spinoza Selections.* New York: Scribner's Sons.

Williams, J. 1998. *Thurgood Marshall: American Revolutionary.* New York: Times Books.

Williams, T.H. 1952. *Lincoln and His Generals.* New York: Alfred A. Knopf.

Williams, T.I. 1984. *A Short History of Twentieth Century Technology.* New York: Oxford University Press.

Willie, C.V. 1979. *Caste and Class Controversy.* New York: General Hall.

Wilson, J.Q. 1975. *Thinking About Crime.* New York: Basic Books.

Wilson, J.Q. 1993. *The Moral Sense.* New York: The Free Press.

Wilson, J.Q. 1997. *Moral Judgment.* New York: The Free Press.

Wilson, J.Q. 2002. *The Marriage Problem: How Culture Has Weakened Families.* New York: HarperCollins Publishers.

Wittfogel, K.A. 1957. *Oriental Despotism: A Comparative Study of Total Power.* New Haven, CT: Yale University Press.

Wolfe, A. 1989. *Whose Keeper?* Berkeley, CA: University of California Press.

Wolfe, A. 1996. *Marginalized in the Middle.* Chicago, IL: University of Chicago Press.

Wolfe, A. 1998. *One Nation, After All: What Middle-Class Americans Really Think.* New York: Viking.

Wolfe, A. 2001. *Moral Freedom: The Search for Virtue in a World of Choice.* New York: W.W. Norton.

Wolfe, A. 2003. *The Transformation of American Religion: How We Actually Live Our Faith.* New York: The Free Press.

Wolfensberger, W. with Nirje et al. 1972. *The Principle of Normalization in Human Services.* Toronto: National Institute on Mental Retardation.

Wolff, K.H. (Ed.) 1950. *The Sociology of Georg Simmel.* New York: The Free Press.

Wood, G. 1991. *The Radicalization of the American Revolution.* New York: Random House.

Wood, P. 2003. *Diversity: The Invention of a Concept.* San Francisco, CA: Encounter Books.

Woodring, C. 1966. *Virginia Woolf.* New York: Columbia University Press.

Woodward, B. 2002. *Bush at War.* New York: Simon & Schuster.

Wuthnow, R. 1987. *Meaning and Moral Order: Explorations in Cultural Analysis.* Berkeley, CA: University of California Press.

Wuthnow, R. 1996. *Poor Richard's Principle: Recovering the American Dream through the Moral Dimension of Work, Business, & Money.* Princeton, NJ: University of Princeton Press.

Zarefsky, D. 1986. *President Johnson's War on Poverty.* University, AL: University of Alabama Press.

Zartman, I.W. 1978. *The Negotiation Process: Theories and Applications.* Beverly Hills, CA: Sage Publications.

Zeldin, T. 1994. *An Intimate History of Humanity.* New York: HarperCollins Publishers.

Zigler, E. and J. Valentines. (Eds.) 1979. *Head Start: A Legacy of the War on Poverty.* New York: Free Press.

Zinsser. H. 1935. *Rats, Lice and History.* Boston, MA: Little, Brown, Co.

Zurcher, L. 1983. *Social Roles: Conformity, Conflict and Creativity.* Beverly Hills, CA: Sage Publications

CPSIA information can be obtained at www.ICGtesting.com
Printed in the USA
238117LV00001B/12/A